The Zohar

by
Rav Shimon bar Yochai
From The Book of Avraham

with
The Sulam Commentary

by
Rav Yehuda Ashlag

The First Ever Unabridged
English Translation with Commentary

Published by
The Kabbalah Centre International Inc.
Dean Rav S. P. Berg Shlita

Edited and Compiled by
Rabbi Michael Berg

Kabbalah Centre Publishing is a registered DBA of
The Kabbalah Centre International, Inc.

For further information:

The Kabbalah Centre
155 E. 48th St., New York, NY 10017
1062 S. Robertson Blvd., Los Angeles, CA 90035

1.800.Kabbalah www.kabbalah.com

First Printing 2001
Revised Edition 2003
Fifth Printing 2015

Printed in USA

ISBN: 978-157189-239-3

May the Light of the Zohar shine
through the soul of my dearest father

Maer Abravanel Aysoy

APPLYING THE POWER OF THE ZOHAR

The Zohar is a book of great mystical power and wisdom. It is Universally recognized as the definitive work on the Kabbalah – and it is also so Much more.

The Zohar is a wellspring of spiritual energy, a fountainhead of metaphysical power that not only reveals and explains, but literally brings blessing, protection, and well-being into the lives of all those who read or peruse its sacred texts. All that is required is worthy desire, the certainty of a trusting heart, and an open and receptive mind. Unlike other books, including the great spiritual texts of other traditions, The Zohar is written in a kind of code, through which metaphors, parables, and cryptic language at first conceal but ultimately reveal the forces of creation.

As electrical current is concealed in wire and cable before disclosing itself as an illuminated light bulb, the spiritual Light of the Creator is wrapped in allegory and symbolism throughout the Aramaic text of the Zohar. And while many books contain information and knowledge, the Zohar both expresses and embodies spiritual Light. The very letters on its pages have the power to bring spiritual wisdom and positive energy into every area of our lives.

As we visually scan the Aramaic texts and study the accompanying insights that appear in English, spiritual power is summoned from above – and worlds tremble as Light is sent forth in response.

It's primary purpose is not only to help us acquire wisdom, but to draw Light from the Upper Worlds and to bring sanctification into our lives. Indeed, the book itself is the most powerful of all tools for cleansing the soul and connecting to the Light of the Creator. As you open these pages, therefore, do not make understanding in the conventional sense your primary goal.

Although you may not have a knowledge of Aramaic, look first at the Aramaic text before reading the English. Do not be discouraged by difficulties with comprehension. Instead, open your heart to the spiritual transformation the Zohar is offering you.

Ultimately, the Zohar is an instrument for refining the individual soul – for removing darkness from the earth – and for bringing well being and blessing to our fellow man.

Its purpose is not only to make us intellectually wise, but to make us spiritually pure.

Glossary of Hebrew words

Torah

Also known as the Five Books of Moses, the Torah is considered to be the physical body of learning, whereas the Zohar is the internal soul. The literal stories of the Torah conceal countless hidden secrets.` The Zohar is the Light that illuminates all of the Torah's sublime mysteries.

Beresheet	Genesis
Shemot	Exodus
Vayikra	Leviticus
Bemidbar	Numbers
Devarim	Deuteronomy

Prophets

Amos	Amos
Chagai	Haggai
Chavakuk	Habakkuk
Hoshea	Hosea
Malachi	Malachi
Melachim	Kings
Michah	Micah
Nachum	Nahum
Ovadyah	Obadiah
Shmuel	Samuel
Shoftim	Judges
Tzefanyah	Zephaniah
Yechezkel	Ezekiel
Yehoshua	Joshua
Yeshayah	Isaiah
Yirmeyah	Jeremiah
Yoel	Joel
Yonah	Jonah
Zecharyah	Zechariah

Writings

Daniel	Daniel
Divrei Hayamim	Chronicles
Eicha	Lamentations
Ester	Esther
Ezra	Ezra
Nechemiah	Nehemiah
Iyov	Job
Kohelet	Ecclesiastes
Mishlei	Proverbs
Rut	Ruth

Sir Hashirim	Songs of Songs
Tehilim	Psalms

The Ten Sfirot – Emanations

To conceal the blinding *Light* of the Upper World, and thus create a tiny point into which our universe would be born, ten *curtains* were fabricated. These ten *curtains* are called Ten Sfirot. Each successive Sfirah further reduces the emanation of *Light*, gradually dimming its brilliance to a level almost devoid of *Light* – our physical world known as *Malchut*. The only remnant of Light remaining in this darkened universe is a *pilot light* which sustains our existence. This Light is the life force of a human being and the force that gives birth to stars, sustains suns and sets everything from swirling galaxies to busy ant hills in motion. Moreover, the Ten Sfirot act like a prism, refracting the Light into many *colors* giving rise to the diversity of life and matter in our world.

The Ten Sfirot are as follows:

Keter	Crown
Chochmah	Wisdom
Binah	Understanding
Da'at	Knowledge
Zeir Anpin	Small Face,
	(includes the next six Sfirot):
Chesed	Mercy (Chassadim - plural)
Gvurah	Judgment (Gvurot - Plural)
Tiferet	Splendor
Netzach	Victory (Eternity)
Hod	Glory
Yesod	Foundation
Malchut	Kingdom

The Partzufim - Spiritual forms

One complete structure of the Ten Sfirot creates a *Partzuf* or Spiritual Form. Together, these forces are the building blocks of all reality. As water and sand combine to create cement, the Ten Sfirot

combine to produce a Spiritual Form [*Partzuf*]. Each of the Spiritual Forms below are therefore composed of one set of Ten Sfirot.

These Spiritual Forms are called:

Atik	Ancient
Atik Yomin	Ancient of Days
Atika Kadisha	Holy Ancient
Atik of Atikin	Anceint of Ancients
Aba	Father
Arich Anpin	Long Face
Ima	Mother
Nukva	Female
Tevunah	Intelligence
Yisrael Saba	Israel Grandfather
Zachar	Male

These names are not meant to be understood literally. Each represents a unique spiritual force and building block, producing a substructure and foundation for all the worlds make up reality.

The Five Worlds

All of the above Spiritual Forms [*Partzufim*] create one spiritual world. There are Five Worlds in total that compose all reality, therefore, five sets of the above Spiritual Forms are required.

Our physical world corresponds to the world of: Asiyah – Action

Adam Kadmon	Primordial Man
Atzilut	Emanation
Briyah	Creation
Yetzirah	Formation
Asiyah	Action

The Five Levels of the soul

Nefesh	First, Lowest level of Soul
Ruach	Second level of Soul
Neshamah	Third level of Soul
Chayah	Fourth level of Soul
Yechidah	Highest, fifth level of Soul

Names of God

As a single ray of white sunlight contains the seven colors of the spectrum, the one Light of the Creator embodies many diverse spiritual forces. These different forces are called *Names of God*. Each Name denotes a specific attribute and spiritual power. The Hebrew letters that compose these Names are the interface by which these varied Forces act upon our physical world. The most common Name of God is the Tetragrammaton (the four letters, *Yud Hei Vav Hei* יהוה.) Because of the enormous power that the Tetragrammaton transmits, we do not utter it aloud. When speaking of the Tetragrammaton, we use the term *Hashem* which means, *The Name*.

Adonai, El, Elohim, Hashem, Shadai, Eheyeh, Tzevaot, Yud Hei Vav Hei

People

Er	The son of Noach
Rabbi Elazar	The son of Rabbi Shimon bar Yochai
Rabbi Shimon bar Yochai	Author of the Zohar
Shem, Cham, Yefet	Noach's children
Shet	Seth
Ya'akov	Jacob
Yishai	Jesse (King David's father)
Yitzchak	Isaac
Yosef	Joseph
Yitro	Jethro
Yehuda	Judah

Angels

Angels are distinct energy components, part of a vast communication network running through the upper worlds. Each unique Angel is responsible for transmitting various forces of influence into our physical universe.

Adriel, Ahinael, Dumah (name of Angel in charge of the dead), Gabriel, Kadshiel, Kedumiel, Metatron, Michael, Rachmiel,

Raphael, Tahariel, Uriel

Nations

Nations actually represent the inner attributes and character traits of our individual self. The nation of Amalek refers to the doubt and uncertainty that dwells within us when we face hardship and obstacles. Moab represents the dual nature of man. Nefilim refers to the sparks of Light that we have defiled through our impure actions, and to the negative forces that lurk within the human soul as a result of our own wrongful deeds.

Amalek, Moab, Nefilim

General

Aba	Father
	Refers to the male principle and positive force in our universe. Correlates to the proton in an atom.
Arvit	The Evening prayer
Chayot	Animals
Chupah	Canopy (wedding ceremony)
Et	The
Avadon	Hell
Gehenom	Hell
Sheol	Hell
	The place a soul goes for purification upon leaving this world.
Ima	Mother
	The female principle and minus force in our universe. Correlates to the electron in an atom.
Kiddush	Blessing over the wine
Klipah	Shell (negativity)
Klipot	Shells (Plural)
Kriat Sh'ma	The Reading of the Sh'ma
Mashiach	Messiah
Minchah	The Afternoon prayer
Mishnah	Study
Mochin	Brain, Spiritual levels of Light
Moed	A designated time or holiday
Negev	The south of Israel
Nukva	Female

Partzuf	Face
Shacharit	The Morning prayer
Shamayim	Heavens (sky)
Shechinah	The Divine presence, The female aspect of the Creator
Tefilin	Phylacteries
The Dinur river	The river of fire
Tzadik	Righteous person
Zion	Another name for Jerusalem
Yisrael	The land of Israel
	The nation of Israel or an individual Israelite
Zohar	Splendor

The Hebrew vowels

Chirik אָ, Cholam אוֹ אֹ, Kamatz אָ, Patach אַ, Segol אֶ, Sh'va אְ, Shuruk אוּ אֻ, Tzere אֵ.

The Twelve Tribes

Asher, Dan, Ephraim, Gad, Issachar, Judah, Levi, Menasheh, Naphtali, Reuben, Shimon, Zebulun

Jewish Holidays

Rosh Hashanah	The Jewish New Year
Yom Kippur	Day of Atonement
Sukkot	Holiday of the Booths
Shmini Atzeret	The day of Convocation
Simchat Torah	Holiday on which we dance with the Torah
Pesach	Passover
Shavout	Holiday of the Weeks

כרך יב

פרשת תצוה, כי תשא, ויקהל

Vol. XII

Tetzaveh, Ki Tisa, Vayak'hel

A Prayer from The Ari

To be recited before the study of the Zohar

Ruler of the universe, and Master of all masters, The Father of mercy and forgiveness, we thank You, our God and the God of our fathers, by bowing down and kneeling, that You brought us closer to Your Torah and Your holy work, and You enable us to take part in the secrets of Your holy Torah. How worthy are we that You grant us with such big favor, that is the reason we plead before You, that You will forgive and acquit all our sins, and that they should not bring separation between You and us.

And may it be your will before You, our God and the God of our fathers, that You will awaken and prepare our hearts to love and revere You, and may You listen to our utterances, and open our closed heart to the hidden studies of Your Torah, and may our study be pleasant before Your Place of Honor, as the aroma of sweet incense, and may You emanate to us Light from the source of our soul to all of our being. And, may the sparks of your holy servants, through which you revealed Your wisdom to the world, shine.

May their merit and the merit of their fathers, and the merit of their Torah, and holiness, support us so we shall not stumble through our study. And by their merit enlighten our eyes in our learning as it is stated by King David, The Sweet Singer of Israel: "Open my eyes, so that I will see wonders from Your Torah" (Tehilim 119:18). Because from His mouth God gives wisdom and understanding.

"May the utterances of my mouth and the thoughts of my heart find favor before You, God, my Strength and my Redeemer" (Tehilim 19:15).

TETZAVEH

Names of the articles

1. "And you shall command"

A Synopsis

This passage tells about the Shechinah, Zeir Anpin and the Nukva in the context of building the Tabernacle. In the title verse, Rabbi Shimon finds that "And you" is written to be inclusive of the Shechinah. Rabbi Yitzchak believes that the Upper Light, Zeir Anpin, and the Lower Light, the Nukva, are included in that phrase. He says that the sun, Zeir Anpin, dwelled in the moon, the Nukva, and they came together to dwell upon the work of the tabernacle. Rabbi Shimon talks about the Shechinah that is called 'heart' and the Nukva that is called 'heart', so that when the sun dwells in the moon everything is replete with everything. We are also told that the unity of the name "And you" includes male and female, and therefore all that are wise-hearted. Those who built the tabernacle were able to do so only after the Holy Spirit secretly whispered to them how it should be done, since the Holy Spirit is alluded to in the name "And you." Rabbi Shimon prays that the Supernal Light will not move away from the Lower Light, because when it does, light is not present in the world; it was because of this that the Temple was destroyed in the days of Jeremiah. And although the Temple was later rebuilt, the light did not return properly even then. The name Isaiah brings redemption and the return of the Supernal Light, and the final rebuilding of the Temple. Rabbi Shimon explains that vast significance of the two names Jeremiah and Isaiah, one meaning 'shall rise' and the other meaning 'salvation', and tells us that it is the combination of the letters in names that brings about action according to their meaning, both good and evil. The letters of the Holy Names cause supernal secrets to appear according to the meaning of the name, for the letters themselves cause holy, supernal secrets to appear in them.

1. וְאַתָּה תְּצַוֶּה אֶת בְּנֵי יִשְׂרָאֵל וגו'. וְאַתָּה הַקְרֵב אֵלֶיךָ אֶת אַהֲרֹן אָחִיךָ וגו'. אָמַר רְבִּי חִיָּיא, מַאי שְׁנָא הָכָא מִבְכָל אֲתָר, דִּכְתִּיב וְאַתָּה הַקְרֵב אֵלֶיךָ וְאַתָּה תְּדַבֵּר אֶל כָּל חַכְמֵי לֵב. וְאַתָּה תְּצַוֶּה אֶת בְּנֵי יִשְׂרָאֵל. וְאַתָּה קַח לְךָ בְּשָׂמִים רֹאשׁ מָר דְּרוֹר. אֶלָּא כֹּלָּא בְּרָזָא עִלָּאָה אִיהוּ, לְאַכְלְלָא שְׁכִינְתָּא בַּהֲדֵיהּ.

1. "And you shall command the children of Yisrael..." (Shemot 27:20), "And take you to you Aaron your brother..." (Shemot 28:1). Rabbi Chiya said: Why is this different than all other places? For it is written: "And take

you to you"; "And you shall speak to all that are wise hearted" (Ibid. 3); "And you shall command the children of Yisrael"; "Take you also to you the best spices, of pure myrrh" (Shemot 30:23). IT IS NOT WRITTEN, AS IN ALL OTHER PLACES: 'AND OFFER', 'AND SPEAK', 'AND COMMAND', 'AND TAKE'. HE ANSWERS, but everything is done with a supernal secret, in order to include the Shechinah with Him. BECAUSE THE SHECHINAH IS CALLED 'YOU'; AND WHEN IT IS WRITTEN, "AND YOU," IT IS DONE TO INCLUDE THE SHECHINAH WITH HIM IN COMMANDING, SPEAKING, ETC.

2. אָמַר רִבִּי יִצְחָק, נְהוֹרָא עִלָּאָה, וּנְהוֹרָא תַּתָּאָה כָּלִיל כַּחֲדָא, אִקְרֵי וְאַתָּה. כְּמָה דְאַתְּ אָמַר וְאַתָּה מְחַיֶּה אֶת כֻּלָּם. וְעַל דָּא לָא כְּתִיב, וְהִקְרַבְתָּ אֶת אַהֲרֹן אָחִיךָ. וְצִוִּיתָ אֶת בְּנֵי יִשְׂרָאֵל. וְדִבַּרְתָּ אֶל כָּל חַכְמֵי לֵב. בְּגִין דְּהַהוּא זִמְנָא שַׁרְיָא שִׁמְשָׁא בְּסִיהֲרָא, וְאִשְׁתַּתַּף כֹּלָּא כַּחֲדָא, לְשַׁרְיָא עַל אוּמָנוּתָא דְּעוֹבָדָא. אָמַר רִבִּי אֶלְעָזָר, מֵהָכָא, אֲשֶׁר נָתַן יְיָ׳ חָכְמָה וּתְבוּנָה בָּהֵמָּה.

2. Rabbi Yitzchak said: The Upper Light, WHICH IS ZEIR ANPIN, and the Lower Light, WHICH IS THE NUKVA, are included together IN, "AND YOU," BECAUSE "YOU" IS THE NAME OF THE NUKVA, AS MENTIONED BEFORE, AND THE EXTRA *VAV* (= AND) IS ZEIR ANPIN. As you say, "And You do preserve them all" (Nechemyah 9:6) THAT ALLUDES TO ZEIR ANPIN AND THE NUKVA. Therefore, it is not written: 'And take to you Aaron your brother'; 'And command the children of Yisrael'; 'And speak to all that are wise hearted,' because at that time the sun, WHICH IS ZEIR ANPIN, dwelt in the moon, WHICH IS THE NUKVA, and they came together, NAMELY ZEIR ANPIN AND THE NUKVA, to dwell upon the craftsmanship of this work. THEREFORE, IT IS WRITTEN OF THEM, "AND YOU," WHICH DENOTES ZEIR ANPIN AND THE NUKVA. Rabbi Elazar said: From here, IT IS IMPLIED THAT THE HOLY ONE, BLESSED BE HE, DWELT UPON THE CRAFT OF THE WORK OF THE TABERNACLE, AS WRITTEN: "In whom Hashem put wisdom and understanding" (Shemot 36:1).

3. רִבִּי שִׁמְעוֹן אָמַר מֵהָכָא, וְאַתָּה תְּדַבֵּר אֶל כָּל חַכְמֵי לֵב אֲשֶׁר מִלֵּאתִיו רוּחַ חָכְמָה. אֲשֶׁר מִלֵּאתִים מִבָּעֵי לֵיהּ. אֶלָּא אֲשֶׁר מִלֵּאתִיו, לְהַהוּא לִבָּא, מִלֵּאתִיו רוּחַ חָכְמָה. כד״א וַתִּנָּחָה עָלָיו רוּחַ יְיָ׳ רוּחַ חָכְמָה

וְגוֹ' וְעַל דָּא אִצְטְרִיךְ אֲשֶׁר מִלֵּאתִיו רוּחַ חָכְמָה, דְּשַׁרְיָא שִׁמְשָׁא בְּסִיהֲרָא בְּאַשְׁלְמוּתָא דְכֹלָּא, וְעַל דָּא אִתְרְשִׁים כֹּלָּא בְּכָל אֲתָר. אָמַר רִבִּי אֶלְעָזָר, אִי הָכִי הָנֵי וְאַתָּה וְאַתָּה, הֵיאַךְ מִתְיַישְׁבָן בִּקְרָאֵי.

3. Rabbi Shimon said: From this IT IS IMPLIED THAT ZEIR ANPIN AND THE NUKVA DWELT UPON THE CRAFT OF THE WORK OF THE TABERNACLE, AS IT IS WRITTEN: "And you shall speak to all that are wise hearted, whom I have filled with the spirit of wisdom" (Shemot 28:3). 'Whom (sing.) I have filled' should have been IN PLURAL, IF IT REFERS TO THE WISE HEARTED. But, "whom I have filled," IS IN SINGULAR, REFERING TO that heart, THE SHECHINAH THAT IS CALLED 'HEART', AS IS WRITTEN: "And the spirit of Hashem shall rest upon him, the spirit of wisdom..." (Yeshayah 11:2). Therefore, it should SAY, "whom (sing.) I have filled with the spirit of wisdom," TO TEACH that the sun, WHICH IS ZEIR ANPIN, dwells in the moon, WHICH IS THE NUKVA THAT IS CALLED 'HEART', replete with everything. Therefore, they are all recorded, NAMELY ZEIR ANPIN AND THE NUKVA, throughout the texts OF THE WORK OF THE TABERNACLE, THAT IT IS WRITTEN OF THEM, "AND YOU," WHICH ALLUDES TO ZEIR ANPIN AND THE NUKVA. Rabbi Elazar said to him: If so, how are all these instances of "and you," explained in the course of the passages, IF WE EXPLAIN THAT THEY PERTAIN TO ZEIR ANPIN AND THE NUKVA?

4. אָמַר לֵיהּ, כֻּלְּהוּ מִתְיַישְׁבָן נִינְהוּ. וְאַתָּה הַקְרֵב אֵלֶיךָ: לְיַחֲדָא בַּהֲדֵיהּ, וּלְקָרְבָא בַּהֲדֵיהּ, רָזָא דִשְׁמָא קַדִּישָׁא כַּדְקָא יֵאוֹת. וְאַתָּה תְּדַבֵּר אֶל כָּל חַכְמֵי לֵב: בְּגִין דְּכֻלְּהוּ לָא אַתְיָין לְמֶעְבַּד עֲבִידְתָּא, עַד דְּרוּחַ קֻדְשָׁא מְמַלְּלָא בְּגַוַוייְהוּ, וְלָחַשׁ לוֹן בִּלְחִישׁוּ, וּכְדֵין עַבְדֵי עֲבִידְתָּא. וְאַתָּה תְּצַוֶּה אֶת בְּנֵי יִשְׂרָאֵל: רוּחַ קֻדְשָׁא פַּקְדָּא עֲלַייְהוּ, וְאַנְהִיר עֲלַייְהוּ, לְמֶעְבַּד עוֹבָדָא בִּרְעוּתָא שְׁלִים. וְאַתָּה קַח לְךָ: כְּמָה דְּאוֹקִימְנָא. וְאַתָּה הַקְרֵב אֵלֶיךָ, וְהָנֵי כֻּלְּהוּ, הָכָא בְּעוֹבָדָא דְמַשְׁכְּנָא. דְּכֹלָּא אִתְעֲבֵיד בְּרָזָא דָא.

4. Rabbi Shimon said to him: They are all satisfactorily defined: "And take you to you," MEANS THAT HE SAID TO MOSES TO TAKE "AND YOU," WHICH IS ZEIR ANPIN AND THE NUKVA, TO AARON – NAMELY, to properly unite in him and take to him the secret of the Holy Name, "AND

YOU." SIMILARLY, "And you shall speak to all that are wise hearted," MEANS THAT HE SHOULD SPEAK AND BRING NEAR AND DECLARE THE UNITY OF THE NAME "AND YOU," WHICH IS MALE AND FEMALE, TO ALL THAT ARE WISE HEARTED. For they all came to do the work of the Tabernacle only after the Holy Spirit spoke to them and secretly whispered to them HOW TO DO IT. Only then did they do the work. IN THE SAME MANNER: "And you shall command the children of Yisrael," MEANING the Holy Spirit, WHICH IS ALLUDED TO IN THE NAME, "AND YOU" shall command the children of Yisrael and shine on them so they do the work with complete willingness. So we have established what, "(And) Take you also to you" (Shemot 30:23), MEANS. And so, "And take you to you," and all of these occurrnces OF "AND YOU," THAT ARE WRITTEN here are by the work of the Tabernacle. For it was all done by means OF THE NAME "AND YOU."

5. פָּתַח ר״ש וְאָמַר וְאַתָּה יְיָ׳ אַל תִּרְחָק אֱיָלוּתִי לְעֶזְרָתִי חוּשָׁה. וְאַתָּה יְיָ׳ כֹּלָּא חַד. אַל תִּרְחָק: לְאִסְתַּלְּקָא מִינָן, לְמֶהֱוֵי סָלִיק נְהוֹרָא עִלָּאָה מִתַּתָּאָה. דְּהָא כַּד אִסְתָּלַּק נְהוֹרָא עִלָּאָה מִתַּתָּאָה, כְּדֵין אִתְחַשַּׁךְ כָּל נְהוֹרָא, וְלָא אִשְׁתְּכַח כְּלַל בְּעָלְמָא.

5. Rabbi Shimon opened the discussion, saying: "But (And) you, Hashem, be not far from me. O, my strength, haste You to help me" (Tehilim 22:20). In, "And You, Hashem," "YOU" IS THE NUKVA AND THE NAME YUD HEI VAV HEI (HASHEM) IS ZEIR ANPIN. He PRAYS that it all SHALL BECOME one, THAT THEY SHALL BE UNITED TOGETHER. "Be not far," MEANS He shall not distance Himself and leave him; that the Supernal Light, ZEIR ANPIN, shall not move away from the Lower Light, THE NUKVA, because when the Supernal Light moves away from the Lower Light, every light is darkened and is not present in the world. BECAUSE THE WORLD RECEIVES ONLY FROM MALCHUT, WHICH IS THE LOWER LIGHT, IF THE SUPERNAL LIGHT, WHICH IS ZEIR ANPIN, DOES NOT ILLUMINATE IN HER, SHE HAS NOTHING TO SHINE TO THIS WORLD.

6. וְעַל דָּא אִתְחֲרַב בֵּי מַקְדְּשָׁא בְּיוֹמוֹי דְּיִרְמְיָהוּ. וְאע״ג דְּאִתְבְּנֵי לְבָתַר, לָא אַהֲדַר נְהוֹרָא לְאַתְרֵיהּ כַּדְקָא יָאוֹת. וְעַל רָזָא דָּא, שְׁמָא דְּהַהוּא נְבִיאָה דְּאִתְנַבֵּי עַל דָּא, יִרְמְיָהוּ. אִסְתַּלְּקוּתָא דִּנְהוֹרָא עִלָּאָה, דְּאִסְתָּלַּק לְעֵילָא לְעֵילָא, וְלָא אַהֲדַר לְאַנְהָרָא לְבָתַר כַּדְקָא יָאוֹת.

יִרְמְיָהוּ: אִסְתַּלַּק וְלָא אַהְדָּר לְאַתְרֵיהּ, וְאִתְחָרַב בֵּי מַקְדְּשָׁא וְאִתְחַשָּׁכוּ נְהוֹרִין.

6. Because of this, the Temple was destroyed in the days of Jeremia, MEANING BECAUSE ZEIR ANPIN WAS REMOVED FROM MALCHUT. Although it was later rebuilt, NAMELY THE SECOND TEMPLE, nonetheless, the light did not properly return to its place. Therefore, the name of the prophet who predicted this is Jeremia, WHICH IS COMPOSED OF THE LETTERS *YARUM* (ENG. 'SHALL RISE') YUD HEI VAV, WHICH MEANS the rising of the Supernal Light high up FROM MALCHUT. And it did not again afterwards illuminate properly DURING THE SECOND TEMPLE. THE NAME Jeremia SIGNIFIES THAT THE SUPERNAL LIGHT was gone up FROM MALCHUT, and did not return to its place, the Temple was destroyed and the luminaries were darkened.

7. אֲבָל יְשַׁעְיָהוּ, שְׁמָא גָּרִים לְפוּרְקָנָא, וּלְאַהְדָּרָא נְהוֹרָא עִלָּאָה לְאַתְרֵיהּ, וּלְמִבְנֵי בֵּי מַקְדְּשָׁא, וְכָל טָבִין וְכָל נְהוֹרִין, יָהַדְרוּן כִּדְבְקַדְמֵיתָא. וְעַל דָּא, שְׁמָהָן דִּתְרֵין נְבִיאִין אִלֵּין, קַיְימִין דָּא לָקֳבֵל דָּא, בְּגִין דִּשְׁמָא גָּרִים, וְצֵרוּפָא דְּאַתְוָון דָּא בְּדָא, גַּרְמִין עוֹבָדָא, הֵן לְטָב וְהֵן לְבִיש. וְעַל רָזָא דָּא, צֵרוּפָא דְּאַתְוָון דִּשְׁמָהָן קַדִּישִׁין, וְכֵן אַתְוָון בִּגְרַמַיְיהוּ, גַּרְמִין לְאִתְחֲזָאָה רָזִין עִלָּאִין, כְּגַוְונָא דִּשְׁמָא קַדִּישָׁא, דְּאַתְוָון בִּגְרַמַיְיהוּ, גַּרְמִין רָזִין עִלָּאִין קַדִּישִׁין לְאִתְחֲזָאָה בְּהוּ.

7. But the name Isaiah, WHICH IS COMPOSED OF THE LETTERS *YESHA* (ENG. 'SALVATION') YUD HEI VAV, brings redemption and the return of the Supernal Light to its place, TO MALCHUT, the rebuilding of the Temple, and ensures that every goodness and every light will return as before. Therefore, the names of these two prophets are in opposition to each other. FOR THE NAME OF ONE MEANS 'YUD HEI VAV WILL RISE' AND THE NAME OF THE OTHER IS THE OPPOSITE, 'YUD HEI VAV WILL SAVE'. The name causes, and the combination of the letters with each other brings about action, ACCORDING TO THEIR MEANING, both good and evil. And based on this secret is the combination of the letters of the Holy Names and also the letters on their own. They cause supernal secrets to appear according to the meaning of the name, for the letters themselves cause holy, supernal secrets to appear in them.

2. The secret of the letters of the Holy Name

A Synopsis

In this section, Rabbi Shimon expounds upon the shapes of letters and vowels. He tells us that the Sfirot of Chochmah are called 'dots', corresponding to the vowels. The purpose of all permutations of the Holy Name Ayin-Bet is to reveal the wisdom in thought. Rabbi Shimon then talks at length about the Holy Name, and says that the entire secret of the Holy Name is based on the letter Yud, while the first Hei is the secret of the sanctuary. We learn that there are large letters above and small letters below. There are holy supernal letters above in Binah that are drawn only by a willing of the spirit and heart, without any speech at all. And there are lower Holy Names in Malchut that are drawn by speech, and by directing thought and will towards them. There are also other names below, of the Other Side. The Vav in Yud Hei Vav Hei is the secret of the form of man, and the last Hei is Malchut. The Vav between the two Hei's, therefore, unites the Upper World, Binah with the Lower World, Malchut, and they become one.

8. רָזָא קַדְמָאָה, יוּ״ד, נְקוּדָה קַדְמָאָה דְּקַיְּימָא עַל תֵּשַׁע סַמְכִין דְּסַמְכִין לָהּ. וְאִינּוּן קַיְּימִין לְאַרְבַּע סִטְרֵי עָלְמָא. כְּמָה דְּסוֹפָא דְּמַחֲשָׁבָה, נְקוּדָה בַּתְרָאָה, קַיְּימָא לְאַרְבַּע סִטְרֵי עָלְמָא. בַּר דְּהַאי דְּכַר, וְאִיהִי נוּקְבָּא.

8. The first secret is *Yud* OF YUD HEI VAV HEI, WHICH IS the first point, NAMELY CHOCHMAH, which stands upon nine pillars that support it. They are stationed to the four directions of the world: SOUTH, NORTH, EAST AND WEST, WHICH ARE THE THREE COLUMNS AND MALCHUT. Similarly, the end of thought, the last point, WHICH IS MALCHUT, stands to the four directions of the world, WHICH ARE SOUTH, NORTH, EAST AND WEST, THE THREE COLUMNS AND MALCHUT THAT RECEIVES THEM. THEY ARE ALL EQUAL, ONE TO THE OTHER, except THAT THE UPPER POINT, WHICH IS *YUD* OF YUD HEI VAV HEI, is male, and THE LAST POINT, WHICH IS MALCHUT, is female.

9. וְהַאי קַיְּימָא בְּלָא גּוּפָא, וְכַד קַיְּימָא בִּלְבוּשָׁא, דְּאִתְלָבַּשׁ בְּהוּ, אִיהִי קַיְּימָא עַל תֵּשַׁע סַמְכִין, בְּרָזָא דְּאָת מ בְּלָא עֲגוּלָא. וְאע״ג דְּאָת ס׳

אִיהִי בְּעֲגוּלָא, וְקַיְּימָא בְּעֲגוּלָא. אֲבָל בְּרָזָא דְּאַתְוָון חֲקִיקָן, גּוֹ נְקוּדֵי, טְהִירִין לְעֵילָא, אִינּוּן בְּרִבּוּעָא, דִּלְתַּתָּא אִיהוּ בְּעֲגוּלָא.

9. This *YUD*, WHICH IS CHOCHMAH, has no body. When it is clothed by them, it stands on nine pillars, WHICH ARE CHOCHMAH, BINAH, DA'AT, CHESED, GVURAH, TIFERET, NETZACH, HOD AND YESOD, according to the secret of the letter final *Mem*, without a circle. Even though the letter *Samech* is round and shaped like a circle, *YUD* IS THE SECRET OF *SAMECH*, AND FIRST *HEI* IS THE SECRET OF FINAL *MEM*. According to the secret of the letters that are engraved with dots, MEANING THOSE LETTERS THAT ALLUDE TO THE ASPECT OF CHOCHMAH THAT IS CALLED 'DOTS', IT IS CONSIDERED that the supernal lights are a quadrangle and those of below are circular.

10. הַאי בְּרִבּוּעַ אִיהוּ קַיְּימָא בְּשִׁיעוּרָא דְּתֵשַׁע נְקוּדִין, תְּלַת תְּלַת לְכָל סְטַר. וְאִינּוּן בְּשִׁיעוּרָא דְּחוּשְׁבָּנָא תְּמַנְיָא נְקוּדִין, וְאִינּוּן תֵּשַׁע. וְאִלֵּין אִינּוּן דְּקַיְּימִין מֵרָזָא דִּבוּצִינָא בְּרִיבּוּעָא בְּסַמְכִין תִּשְׁעָה לְאָת יוֹ"ד, נְקוּדָה חֲדָא. אִינּוּן תִּשְׁעָה. אִינּוּן תְּמַנְיָא בְּרָזָא דְּאָת ם בְּרִבּוּעָא, כְּגַוְונָא דָּא תְּלַת תְּלַת לְכָל סְטַר.

10. This square has the amount of three points, three to each side. They amount to the number of eight points, which are nine POINTS. AND HE ELABORATES: And these exist by AND COME FROM the secret of the luminary quadrupled, NAMELY FINAL *MEM* with nine pillars for the letter *Yud*, WHICH IS one OF THEIR points – NAMELY CHESED, GVURAH AND TIFERET, NETZACH, HOD AND YESOD are nine. Yet they are eight by means of the quadrupled letter final *Mem*, three to each side WHEN YOU DO NOT COUNT THE *YUD* ITSELF, MEANING BINAH, DA'AT, CHESED, GVURAH, TIFERET, NETZACH, HOD AND YESOD.

11. וְדָא אִיהוּ רָזָא. דְּאָת יוֹ"ד נְקוּדָה חֲדָא, וְאַף עַל גַּב דְּאִיהִי נְקוּדָה חֲדָא, דְּיוּקְנָא דִּילָהּ, רֵישָׁא לְעֵילָא, וְקוֹצָא לְתַתָּא, וְשִׁיעוּרָא דִּילָהּ תְּלַת נְקוּדִין כְּגַוְונָא דָּא וְעַל דָּא אִתְפַּשְׁטוּתָא לְאַרְבַּע סִטְרִין, תְּלַת תְּלַת לְכָל סְטַר, אִיהִי תֵּשַׁע, וְאִיהִי תְּמַנְיָא.

11. HE EXPLAINS FURTHER SAYING: And this is the secret. The letter *Yud* is one point (dot) and even though it is one point, its shape has a head above, WHICH IS THE UPPER TIP OF THE *YUD*, a tip below, AND THE DOT ITSELF. THEREFORE, it amounts to three points like the Hebrew dot *Segol*, IN THE SECRET OF RIGHT, LEFT AND CENTRAL, WHICH IS THE INNER MEANING OF THE THREE COLUMNS. Therefore, the expansion to four sides, three on each side, equals nine TOGETHER WITH THE *YUD*, and eight WITHOUT THE *YUD* ITSELF, AS EXPLAINED.

12. וְאִלֵּין אִינּוּן סַמְכִין דְּנָפְקִין מֵרָזָא דְּבוּצִינָא, לְמֶהֱוֵי סַמְכִין לְאָת יוֹ"ד, וְאִלֵּין אִקְרוּן רְתִיכָא דִּילָהּ. וְלָא קַיְימִין בִּשְׁמָא, בַּר בְּרָזָא דְּתֵשַׁע נְקוּדִין דְּאוֹרַיְיתָא.

12. These EIGHT POINTS are pillars that stem from the secret of the luminary to support the letter *Yud*, and they are considered its Chariot. They are not called by name, just by the secret of the nine vowels in the Torah, WHICH ARE *KAMATZ*, *PATACH*, *TZEREI*, THE FIRST THREE SFIROT. *SEGOL*, *SHVA* AND *CHOLAM* ARE CHESED, GVURAH AND TIFERET. *CHIRIK*, *KUBUTZ*, *SHURUK* THAT ARE ALSO CALLED *CHIRIK*, *SHURUK*, *MELAFUM*, ARE NETZACH, HOD AND YESOD, BECAUSE THE SFIROT OF CHOCHMAH ARE CALLED 'DOTS.'

13. וּבְרָזָא דְּסִפְרָא דְּאָדָם, אִתְפְּלָגוּ אִלֵּין תֵּשַׁע דְּאִינּוּן תְּמַנְיָא, בְּצֵרוּפָא דְּאַתְוָון דִּשְׁמָא קַדִּישָׁא, לְצָרְפָא לוֹן וּלְיַחֲדָא לוֹן בְּכָל אִינּוּן גַּוְונִין, כַּד נַטְלִין אִלֵּין תְּמַנְיָא דְּאִינּוּן תֵּשַׁע, נַהֲרִין בִּנְהִירוּ דְּאָת ם בְּרִבּוּעָא, וְאַפִּיק נְהוֹרִין תְּמַנְיָא, אִתְחֲזֵן וְאַתְוָון תִּשְׁעָה. וְאִתְפַּלְּגָן לְתַתָּא לְנַטְלָא כָּל מַשְׁכְּנָא.

13. In the secret of the Book of Adam, these nine that are eight divided into permutations of letters of the Holy Name. This is in order to combine and unite them in all these manners, because when these eight, which are nine, travel – MEANING WHEN THEY SHINE BY MEANS OF THE THREE COLUMNS, ONE AFTER THE OTHER – they shine with the illumination of the letter final *Mem* quadrupled, and extract eight lights that appear like nine. They divide below to carry the Tabernacle.

14. וְאִינּוּן צֵרוּפָא דִּשְׁמָא קַדִּישָׁא, בְּרָזָא דְּשַׁבְעִין וּתְרֵין אַתְוָון מְחַקְּקָן, דְּנָפְקֵי מֵרָזָא דִּתְלַת גַּוְונִין, יְמִינָא וּשְׂמָאלָא וְאֶמְצָעִיתָא. וְכֹלָּא מֵרָזָא דִּתְלַת נְקוּדִין, שִׁעוּרָא דְּאָת יוֹ"ד, דְּאִיהִי לְד' סִטְרִין, וְאִינּוּן תְּמַנְיָא נְקוּדִין, וְאִינּוּן תֵּשַׁע נְקוּדִין, וְאִינּוּן תְּרֵיסַר נְקוּדִין עִלָּאִין. ג' ג' לְכָל סְטָר וּסְטָר, וּמֵהָכָא נַחְתִּין לְתַתָּא בִּתְרֵיסַר לְשִׁית סִטְרִין. וְכַד אִתְחַקְּקָן תְּרֵיסַר אִלֵּין בְּשִׁית סִטְרִין, אִינּוּן שַׁבְעִין וּתְרֵין שְׁמָהָן, רָזָא דִּשְׁמָא קַדִּישָׁא דְּשַׁבְעִין וּתְרֵין דְּאִינּוּן שְׁמָא דָּא קַדִּישָׁא.

14. They are the permutation of the Holy Name by means of 72 engraved letters that stem from the secret of the three colors – right, left and central – WHICH ARE CHESED, GVURAH AND TIFERET OF ZEIR ANPIN. And they all come from the secret of the three points, which are the dimension of the letter *Yud,* NAMELY ITS TOP, MIDDLE AND END, AS MENTIONED, and it ILLUMINATES to four directions. They are eight points BESIDES CHOCHMAH and nine points INCLUDING CHOCHMAH, AS MENTIONED, FOR EACH OF THE THREE POINTS OF THE TOP, MIDDLE AND END OF THE *YUD* INCLUDES THE THREE. THEY ARE NINE, WHICH ARE CHOCHMAH, BINAH, DA'AT, CHESED, GVURAH, TIFERET, NETZACH, HOD AND YESOD. And they are twelve supernal points, three to every side. From here, they descend as twelve to the six extremities. When these twelve are engraved on the six extremities OF ZEIR ANPIN, they are 72 Names, BECAUSE SIX TIMES TWELVE EQUALS 72, for they are the secret of the Holy Name of *Ayin-Bet* (72). They are the Holy Name THAT EMANATES FROM THE TWELVE POINTS OF *YUD* OF YUD HEI VAV HEI.

15. וְכֹלָּא אִיהוּ סָלִיק בִּרְעוּתָא, דְּסָמִיכוּ דְּמַחֲשָׁבָה בְּאִינּוּן סַמְכִין דְּאָת יוֹ"ד, וְעַל דָּא אַתְוָון בְּצֵרוּפַיְיהוּ, תְּלַת תְּלַת בְּכָל צֵרוּפָא דִּילֵיהּ, בְּגִין לְסַלְּקָא בִּרְעוּתָא דְּאָת י', דִּתְלַת נְקוּדִין, כְּמָה דְּאִתְּמַר, וְעַל דָּא לָא אִסְתְּלִיק בִּסְלִיקוּ דְּצֵרוּפָא, אֶלָּא מֵעִקָּרָא וְשָׁרְשָׁא דְּרָזָא דְּאִלֵּין סַמְכִין, דְּסַמְכִין לְאָת י' רָזָא דְּאָת מ' בְּרִבּוּעָא, ט' נְקוּדִין, תְּמַנְיָא נְקוּדִין, תְּרֵיסַר נְקוּדִין, שַׁבְעִין וּתְרֵין נְקוּדִין. אִשְׁתְּכַח, דְּכָל רָזָא דִּשְׁמָא קַדִּישָׁא, קַיְימָא בְּאָת י', וְכֹלָּא רָזָא בְּרָזָא חֲדָא, וְקַיְימָא בְּרָזָא דְּבוֹצִינָא, כְּמָה דְּאִתְּמַר לְמֶעְבַּד סְמִיכוּ לְכָל אָת וְאָת. וְאִינּוּן סַמְכִין אִינּוּן רְתִיכָא

דִּלְהוֹן, דְּכָל אָת וְאָת, כְּמָה דְּאִתְּמַר.

15. And the wish comes to support thought, WHICH IS CHOCHMAH, with the supports of the letter *Yud,* MEANING THAT THE PURPOSE OF ALL THE PERMUTATIONS OF THE NAME OF *AYIN-BET* (72) IS TO REVEAL THE CHOCHMAH THAT IS IN THE *YUD* OF YUD HEI VAV HEI, THAT IS CALLED 'THOUGHT'. Therefore, the letters come permuted IN THE NAME OF *AYIN-BET* (72), three letters to each permutation, in order to gain favor with the letter *Yud* OF YUD HEI VAV HEI THAT CONTAINS three points – TOP, MIDDLE, AND END, as we have said. Therefore the permutation comes up only from the essence and root of the secret of the supports of the letter *Yud,* according to the secret of the letter final *Mem* quadrupled, AS MENTIONED. FOR THEY ARE THE THREE POINTS: TOP, MIDDLE AND END, WHICH ARE THE ESSENCE AND ROOT OF ALL THE SUPPORTS THAT EVOLVE FROM IT, WHICH ARE nine points, eight points, twelve points, 72 points. Thus the entire secret of the Holy Name is based on the letter *Yud*. It all pertains to the same secret, MEANING THE SECRET OF DRAWING CHOCHMAH, and exists by means of the luminary – WHICH IS BINAH OF ARICH ANPIN, THE KETER OF THIS *YUD,* WHICH IS ABA AND IMA, as we have said – to support every letter OF THE NAME YUD HEI VAV HEI. And the supports, THE NINE, THE EIGHT, THE TWELVE AND THE 72, MENTIONED ABOVE, are a Chariot to every letter OF THE NAME YUD HEI VAV HEI, as we have said.

16. רָזָא תִּנְיָינָא, אָת ה', דְּקַיְּימָא עַל חֲמִשָׁה סַמְכִין, דְּסַמְכִין לָהּ, דְּנַפְקִין מֵרָזָא דְּבוּצִינָא, כַּד אִתְכְּנַשׁ לְאִסְתַּלְּקָא לְעֵילָא, מֵרָזָא דִּמְשָׁחָתָא.

16. The second secret is the letter *Hei* OF YUD HEI VAV HEI that stands upon five pillars that support it, that emerge from the secret of luminary, WHICH IS BINAH OF ARICH ANPIN after it was gathered in and ascended above the secret of the curtain.

17. אָת דָּא הֵיכְלָא קַדִּישָׁא אִקְרֵי, לְגוֹ, נְקוּדָה דְּקָאמְרָן. וְכֹלָּא אִיהוּ בְּרָזָא דְּקָאמְרָן דְּאָת ם בְּרִבּוּעָא. אֲבָל הָכָא לָא אִתְרְשִׁים בַּר אָת ה', וּרְתִיכָא דִּילָהּ חֲמִשָׁה סַמְכִין דְּקָאמְרָן.

17. This letter is called 'the Holy Sanctuary' for the point that we mentioned, NAMELY THE *YUD* OF YUD HEI VAV HEI. For everything is based on the secret we spoke of, that of the letter final *Mem* quadrupled. Here, THE LETTER FINAL *MEM* is not imprinted, but rather the letter *Hei*, BECAUSE HERE STARTS THE REVELATION, and its Chariot is the five pillars we mentioned.

18. דְּכַד בָּטַשׁ נְהִירוּ דְּבוּצִינָא בְּאָת י', אִתְנְהִיר, וּמֵהַהוּא בְּטִישׁוּתָא, אִתְעֲבִידוּ אִינּוּן תֵּשַׁע סַמְכִין דְּקָאמְרָן. וּמִגּוֹ נְהִירוּ דְּאִתְנְהָר אָת י', אִתְפְּשָׁטוּ תְּלַת נְקוּדִין דִּי'. תְּרֵין לְעֵילָּא, דְּאִינּוּן רֵישָׁא. וְחַד לְתַתָּא, דְּאִיהוּ קוֹצָא דִּי', כְּגַוְונָא דָא דְּקָאמְרָן. כַּד אִתְפְּשָׁטוּ תְּרֵין, אִתְעֲבִידוּ תְּלַת. חַד אִתְעֲבִיד תְּרֵין. וְאִתְפְּשָׁטוּ, וְאִתְעֲבֵיד חַד הֵיכָלָא. דָּא הֵיכָלָא, לְבָתַר דְּאִתְעֲבֵיד הֵיכָלָא לְחַד נְקוּדָה קַדְמָאָה, אִתְעֲבֵיד בִּגְנִיזוּ טָמִיר רָזָא דְּאָת דָּא, וְקַיְּימָא עַל חָמֵשׁ אַחֲרָנִין.

18. HE EXPLAINS WHAT THE FIVE SUPPORTS ARE, SAYING when the light of the luminary illuminates the letter *Yud,* it is lit up. For from that illumination the luminary projected, these nine pillars that we said were made – WHICH ARE THE SECRET OF CHOCHMAH, BINAH, DA'AT, CHESED, GVURAH, TIFERET, NETZACH, HOD AND YESOD, THAT SPREAD FROM THE TOP, MIDDLE, AND END OF *YUD,* AS MENTIONED. AND THEN, from the illumination that lit the letter *Yud,* the three points of the *Yud* spread, two points up, which are at the top OF *YUD,* NAMELY, THE UPPER TIP AND THE BODY OF THE *YUD,* and one point down, which is the LOWER tip of the *Yud,* like THE HEBREW DOT SEGOL, as we explained. When two points expanded IN THE SECRET OF CHIRIK and they became three, the one, WHICH IS THE CENTRAL COLUMN, became two, and became one sanctuary. After the sanctuary became the first point, the secret of the letter *Hei* became concealed and hidden, and stands on other five.

19. אַרְבְּעָה גְּנִיזִין אִינּוּן, בְּחַד נְקוּדָה דְּקַיְּימָא לְגוֹ בְּאֶמְצָעִיתָא, אִינּוּן חָמֵשׁ. וְאִיהִי ה'. כְּמָה דְהֵ"א דִּלְתַתָּא, קַיְּימָא עַל אַרְבַּע, וְאִיהִי נְקוּדָה עַל אַרְבַּע, דְּקַיְּימָא בְּגוֹ אֶמְצָעִיתָא. אוּף הָכָא נָמֵי הַאי. וּמַה דְּקַיְּימָא עַל ה' סַמְכִין, הָכִי הוּא וַדַּאי, בְּגִין דְּהַאי נְקוּדָה עִלָּאָה, אִיהִי עַל תְּרֵין

גְּווֹנִין, חַד בְּלְחוֹדוֹי, וְחַד בְּטְמִירוּ.

19. There are four concealed together with one point between them in the middle. They are five, which is *Hei*. Just as the lower *Hei*, NAMELY MALCHUT, stands on four, NAMELY, ON THREE COLUMNS AND MALCHUT THAT RECEIVES THEM, and is a point over four – MEANING THAT MALCHUT HERSELF, WHICH IS A POINT, standing in their midst – here it is also like that. And as for its standing on five OTHER supports, NAMELY ON THE *Hei* OF YUD HEI VAV HEI, it is certainly so, because this supernal point, THE *YUD* OF YUD HEI VAV HEI, is of two aspects, one on its own and one concealed. THEREFORE, THERE ARE TWO *HEI'S*.

20. וּבְסִפְרָא דְּרָזִין דְּחֲנוֹךְ, ה' וַדַּאי קַיְימָא עַל חֲמֵשׁ סַמְכִין דְּנָפְקִין מִגּוֹ בּוּצִינָא. וּכְדֵין אַפִּיק חֲמֵשׁ קַיְימִין אַחֲרָנִין, וְאִשְׁתְּכַח הַאי ה' בְּרָזָא דַּעֲשָׂרָה. וְכַד אִתְפָּרְשַׁת, קַיְימָא ה' דָּא, עַל סַמְכִין, וְאִינּוּן הֲווֹ תְּלֵיסַר מְכִילָן דְּרַחֲמֵי, בְּחַד דַּרְגָּא דְּאִתּוֹסָף עֲלַיְיהוּ.

20. In the Book of Secrets of Enoch, HE SAYS, *Hei* certainly stands on five supports that stem from the luminary, WHICH IS BINAH OF ARICH ANPIN. Then THIS *Hei* produces five other pillars, WHICH ARE THE FIRST *Hei* OF YUD HEI VAV HEI. So this *Hei* is of the secret of ten, NAMELY ITS OWN FIVE SUPPORTS AND FIVE SUPPORTS OF THE *Hei* OF YUD HEI VAV HEI, WHICH TOGETHER ARE IN PLACE OF THE *YUD*. When *Hei* OF YUD HEI VAV HEI separates FROM THE *HEI*, AND RETURNS TO ITS PLACE, this *Hei* stands on FIVE supports; THE FOUR SUPPORTS ARE THE THREE COLUMNS AND MALCHUT THAT RECEIVES THEM, AND THE FIFTH IS THE SECRET OF THE POINT IN THEIR CENTER. AND THE FOUR SUPPORTS ARE INCLUDED WITHIN EACH OTHER IN SUCH A WAY THAT THERE ARE THREE COLUMNS IN EACH OF THE FOUR SUPPORTS, WHICH ARE TWELVE. They are the thirteen Attributes of Mercy together with one level added to them, NAMELY, THE POINT IN THE CENTER OF THE FOUR SUPPORTS.

21. וְאִלֵּין אִינּוּן תְּרֵיסַר דְּקַיְימִין בְּשִׁית. זִמְנִין אִינּוּן אַרְבְּעִין וּתְרֵין. זִמְנִין שַׁבְעִין וּתְרֵין הֲווֹ, אֲבָל נַחְתִּין לְתַתָּא. וְהָכָא אִתְפָּרְשׁוּ שְׁבִילִין לְכָל סְטַר, דְּאִינּוּן תְּלָתִין וּתְרֵין, אִשְׁתְּאַר אַרְבְּעִין. וּתְרֵין אוֹדְנִין יְמִינָא

-14-

וּשְׂמָאלָא, הָא אַרְבְּעִין וּתְרֵין, אִלֵּין מ״ב אַתְוָון עִלָּאִין, דְּאִינּוּן אַתְוָון
רַבְרְבָן דְּאוֹרַיְיתָא.

21. These twelve pillars are in the six. Sometimes they are considered AS THE NAME OF *Mem Bet* (42), and sometimes *Ayin Bet* (72), but THIS IS when they go down - here, FROM THE 72, paths extend in all directions, namely 32 PATHS OF CHOCHMAH. WHEN YOU SUBTRACT 32 FROM 72, 40 remains, which together with the two ears to the right and left equal 42, WHICH IS THE SECRET OF THE NAME OF *MEM BET*. These are the 42 supernal large letters in the Torah.

22. בְּגִין דְּאִית אַתְוָון רַבְרְבָן, וְאִית אַתְוָון זְעֵירִין. אַתְוָון רַבְרְבִין אִינּוּן
לְעֵילָּא, אַתְוָון זְעֵירִין לְתַתָּא. וְכֹלָּא לְתַתָּא כְּגַוְונָא דִּלְעֵילָּא. בְּגִין
דְּאִית שְׁמָהָן קַדִּישִׁין עִלָּאִין, דְּקַיְימִין בִּרְעוּ דְּרוּחָא וְלִבָּא בְּלָא מִלּוּלָא
כְּלַל. וְאִית שְׁמָהָן קַדִּישִׁין תַּתָּאִין, דְּקַיְימִין בְּמִלָּה, וּבִמְשִׁיכוּ דְּמַחֲשָׁבָה
וּרְעוּ עֲלַיְיהוּ.

22. There are large letters and small letters. Large letters are above IN BINAH, and small letters are below IN MALCHUT. Everything below, IN MALCHUT, is in the likeness of above, IN BINAH, because there are holy, supernal names IN BINAH that are drawn only by a willing of the spirit and heart, without any speech at all. And there are lower Holy Names IN MALCHUT that are drawn by speech, and with directing thought and will towards them.

23. וְאִית שְׁמָהָן אַחֲרָנִין לְתַתָּא, דְּאִינּוּן מֵהַהוּא סִטְרָא אַחֲרָא, דְּאִיהוּ
מִסִּטְרָא דִּמְסָאֲבָא, וְאִלֵּין לָא קַיְימִין, אֶלָּא בִּרְעוּ דְּעוֹבָדָא לְתַתָּא,
לְסַלְּקָא רְעוּ דְּהַהוּא עוֹבָדָא דִּלְתַתָּא לְגַבֵּיהּ. בְּגִין דְּאִיהוּ סִטְרָא אַחֲרָא
לָאו אִיהוּ, אֶלָּא בְּעוֹבָדִין דְּהַאי עָלְמָא, לְאִסְתָּאֲבָא בְּהוֹן. כְּגַוְונָא
דְּבִלְעָם, וְאִינּוּן בְּנֵי קֶדֶם, וְכָל אִינּוּן דְּמִתְעַסְּקֵי בְּהַהוּא סִטְרָא אַחֲרָא.

23. There are other names below, which are of the Other Side, which is the Side of Impurity. These are drawn only by the willingness in an action below to raise to them that wish contained in the action below. For the

Impure Side AWAKENS only through actions in this world, to be defiled through them, such as Bilaam and the people of the east countries and all those who are occupied with that Other Side, WHO AWAKENED IT BY PERFORMING ACTIONS BELOW TO AWAKEN IT.

24. וְאִלֵּין, לָא קַיְּימֵי בְּאַתְוָון רְשִׁימִין מִן כ"ב דְּאוֹרַיְיתָא, בַּר תְּרֵין, וְאִלֵּין ח' וק', וְסַמְכִין לוֹן בִּסְמִיכוּ אַתְוָון דְּשֶׁקֶר. אֲבָל אִלֵּין אִינוּן אִשְׁתְּמוֹדְעָאן לְגַבַּיְיהוּ יַתִּיר. וְע"ד בִּתְּהָלָה לְדָוִד, בְּכֻלְּהוּ כְּתִיב ו' בְּכָל אָת וְאָת, בַּר מֵאִלֵּין תְּרֵין, דְּלָא כְּתִיב ו', דְּהָא ו' שְׁמָא דְּקוּדְשָׁא בְּרִיךְ הוּא אִיהוּ.

24. Those THAT ARE OF THE OTHER SIDE are not based on any of the imprinted letters of the 22 letters of the Torah except for two, which are *Chet* and *Kuf.* FOR THE KLIPAH OF YESOD IS CALLED 'CHET', WHICH IS THE SECRET OF THE CHILDREN OF CHET WHO NEGOTIATED WITH ABRAHAM ABOUT THE CAVE OF MACHPELAH, AND THE KLIPAH OF MALCHUT IS CALLED 'KUF'. They support THE OTHER SIDE with the support of THE THREE letters – *Shin, Kuf, Resh* (Heb. *sheker*, Eng. 'lie') – THAT ARE ATTACHED TO THEM, but CHET AND KUF frequent them even more. Therefore, in "A praise of David" (Tehilim 145), a *Vav* is written in THE MIDDLE OF EVERY SENTENCE of every letter AFTER THE CANTILLATION MARK *ETNACHTA*, FOR EACH SENTENCE BEGINS WITH A DIFFERENT LETTER OF THE ALPHABET, except for these two letters, CHET AND KUF. NAMELY, "HASHEM IS GRACIOUS (HEB. *CHANUN*), AND FULL OF COMPASSION; SLOW TO ANGER, AND OF ABUNDANT LOVE" (TEHILIM 145:8), which has no *Vav*, FOR IT IS NOT WRITTEN, 'AND SLOW TO ANGER AND OF ABUNDANT LOVE...' AND ALSO, "HASHEM IS NEAR (HEB. *KAROV*) TO ALL WHO CALL UPON HIM, TO ALL WHO CALL UPON HIM IN TRUTH" (IBID. 18), WHERE IT IS WRITTEN: 'AND TO ALL WHO CALL UPON HIM IN TRUTH.' The reason is that Vav (lit. 'and') is the Name of the Holy One, blessed be He, MEANING THE CENTRAL COLUMN THAT UNITES RIGHT AND LEFT, AND THE OTHER SIDE HAS NO DESIRE FOR THE CENTRAL COLUMN. THEREFORE, SINCE THOSE LETTERS HAVE AN ATTACHMENT TO THE OTHER SIDE, THERE IS NO VAV (ENG. 'AND') IN THE MIDDLE OF THE SENTENCE IN ORDER TO SHOW THAT THEY HAVE AN ASSOCIATION WITH THE OTHER SIDE.

25. וּבג״כ אִינוּן אַרְבְּעִין וּתְרֵין אַתְוָון, דְּעָלְמָא דָּא אִתְבְּרֵי בְּהוּ, אִשְׁתְּכַח הַאי ה׳ עִלָּאָה, לְסַלְּקָא לְתִשְׁעִין וּתְרֵין, תִּשְׁעִין הֲווֹ, בַּר תְּרֵין אוּדְנִין יְמִינָא וּשְׂמָאלָא. וְרָזָא דָּא וְאִם שָׂרָה הֲבַת תִּשְׁעִים שָׁנָה תֵּלֵד. אֲבָל אִיהוּ בְּחֻשְׁבָּנָא תִּשְׁעִין וּתְרֵין, וְכַד אִתּוֹסַף דַּרְגָּא דְּרָזָא דִּבְרִית, דְּאִיהוּ רְקִיעָא תְּמִינָאָה, וְקַיְּימָא לִתְמַנְיָא יוֹמִין, הָא מֵאָה. וְאִלֵּין וַדַּאי מֵאָה בִּרְכָּאן בְּכָל יוֹמָא דְּאִצְטְרִיכָא כְּנֶסֶת יִשְׂרָאֵל לְאִתְעַטְּרָא בְּהוּ. וְכֹלָּא בְּרָזָא דְּה׳.

25. HE RETURNS TO THE FIRST SUBJECT AND SAYS: Therefore, those 42 letters by which this world was created, together with this supernal *Hei* OF YUD HEI VAV HEI equal 92. THEY ARE THE FORTY REMAINING FROM ITS 72, WHICH, TOGETHER WITH THE TWO EARS, RIGHT AND LEFT, AS MENTIONED, ARE 42; EACH OF ITS FIVE SUPPORTS COMPRISED TEN, WHICH AMOUNT TO FIFTY. FIFTY PLUS 42 IS 92. They are ninety besides the two ears, right and left. This is the secret of: "And shall Sarah, that is ninety years old, give birth?" (Beresheet 17:17) BECAUSE SARAH ALLUDES TO IMA, THE UPPER *HEI* OF YUD HEI VAV HEI. But it amounts to 92, THAT IS, WITH THE TWO EARS. When the grade of Covenant is added to them, WHICH IS YESOD, which is the eighth firmament, and rests on the eighth day – MEANING THAT CIRCUMCISION IS AT THE EIGHTH DAY – 92 AND EIGHT OF YESOD EQUAL one hundred. They are certainly the hundred blessings that the Congregation of Yisrael, WHICH IS MALCHUT, needs to be daily adorned with. This is all by means of *Hei*.

26. הַאי ה׳, אִיהִי דְּיוּקְנָא דִּילָהּ בִּתְרֵין נוּנִין, רָזָא דְּמֵאָה, וְאִינוּן חָמֵשׁ סַמְכִין רְתִיכִין, דְּנַפְקֵי מִגּוֹ בּוּצִינָא, וְאִינוּן חָמֵשׁ אַחֲרָנִין דְּנַפְקִין מִינָהּ. וע״ד דְּיוּקְנָהָא כְּגַוְונָא דָּא ז-ן, תְּרֵין נוּנִין, וּנְקוּדָה דְּקַיְּימָא בְּאֶמְצָעִיתָא. וע״ד ו׳ קַיְּימָא בֵּינַיְיהוּ תָּדִיר, כְּגַוְונָא דָּא נוּן, בְּגִין דְּהָכָא אִיהוּ אַתְרֵיהּ לְאִתְעַטְּרָא, וְאע״ג דְּרָזִין אַחֲרָנִין אִינוּן בְּרָזָא דְּה׳, אֲבָל דָּא אִיהוּ בְּרָזִין דְּסִפְרָא דַּחֲנוֹךְ, וְהָכִי הוּא וַדַּאי.

26. This *Hei* is shaped like two *Nun's*, which is the secret meaning of one hundred, MEANING THAT THE TWO *HEI'S*, EACH OF WHICH HAS TEN

SUPPORTS, EACH COMPRISED OF TEN, AMOUNT TO ONE HUNDRED. ONE *HEI* IS five supports and Chariots that emerge from the luminary. THE SECOND *HEI* IS the other five supports that emerge from it, FROM THE FIRST *HEI* OF YUD HEI VAV HEI. AND THE TEN SUPPORTS OF THE TWO *HEI'S* ARE THE TWO *NUN'S*. Therefore, their shapes are like two final *Nun's* with a dot in the middle. Therefore, there is always a *Vav* between them, thus: *Nun Vav Nun*, because here is where ZEIR ANPIN, WHICH IS *VAV* is crowned, MEANING IT RECEIVES THE MOCHIN OF THE THREE FIRST SFIROT. Even though there are other secrets to the *Hei*, they are among the secrets of the Book of Enoch, and it is certainly so.

27. וְכַד אִתְתַּקְנָא בְּאִינּוּן חַמְשִׁין בִּלְחוֹדַיְיהוּ, אִיהוּ נְקוּדָה חֲדָא דְּקַיְימָא בְּרָזָא דְּנֹ', כְּגַוְונָא דָא נוּ"ן, וְחַד נְקוּדָה בְּאֶמְצָעִיתָא דְּאִיהִי שַׁלְטָא עָלַיְיהוּ, וְכֹלָּא רָזָא חֲדָא. זַכָּאִין אִינּוּן דְּיַדְעֵי אָרְחוֹי דְּאוֹרַיְיתָא, לְמֵהַךְ בְּאָרְחֵי קְשׁוֹט. זַכָּאִין אִינּוּן בְּהַאי עָלְמָא, וְזַכָּאִין אִינּוּן בְּעָלְמָא דְּאָתֵי.

27. When it is fixed only with fifty, it is in one dot that is based on the secret of the *Nun*, thus: *Nun Vav Nun* – MEANING IT IS SO HEARD ON PRONUNCIATION. FOR THE *VAV* IS a dot between them which dominates them, and it all pertains to one secret, AS MENTIONED. Blessed are they who know the ways of Torah, to go in the way of Truth. Blessed are they in this world and blessed are they in the World to Come.

28. רָזָא תְּלִיתָאָה אָת ו', הַאי אָת הַיּוּקְנָא דְּרָזָא דְּאָדָם, כְּמָה דְּאִתְּמַר. וְהָא אוּקִימְנָא, דְּהַאי אָת, קַיְימָא עַל י"ב רְתִיכִין. וְכַד מִתְפָּרְשָׁאן, אִינּוּן כ"ד רְתִיכִין, דִּכְלִילָן בְּהַאי אָת פְּשִׁיטוּ דְּיוּקְנָא דְּבַר נָשׁ, לָקֳבֵל דְּרוֹעִין וְיַרְכִּין וְגוּפָא שַׁיְיפִין דִּלְהוֹן כ"ד אִינּוּן דִּדְרוֹעִין, וְיַרְכִּין, וְגוּפָא, הָא אִתְּמַר, אֲבָל כֻּלְּהוּ סְתִימִין בְּגוּפָא, וְגוּפָא קַיְימָא בְּכֻלְּהוּ כ"ד, וְכֻלְּהוּ רְתִיכִין כְּלִילָן בֵּיהּ בְּגוּפָא, וּבְגִין דִּכְלִילָן כֻּלְּהוּ בֵּיהּ, קַיְימָא, ו' פְּשִׁיטוּ חַד.

28. The third secret is the letter *Vav* OF YUD HEI VAV HEI. This letter is the secret of the form of man, MEANING ZEIR ANPIN, FOR WITHIN HIM IS YUD

HEI VAV HEI FULLY SPELLED WITH ALEPHS, WHICH AMOUNTS TO THE NUMERICAL VALUE OF ADAM (MAN), NAMELY 45, as we have learned. We have established that this letter, WHICH IS *VAV* THAT ALLUDES TO ITS THREE EXTREMITIES, stands on twelve Chariots, THE TWELVE OF WHICH SHINE ON EVERY EXTREMITY IN THE *VAV*, AND TWELVE TIMES SIX EQUALS 72. When divided BY THREE, there are 24 Chariots, BECAUSE THREE TIMES 24 EQUALS 72. In this letter is included the expansion of the form of man, corresponding to the arms, WHICH ARE CHESED AND GVURAH, the legs, WHICH ARE NETZACH AND HOD, and the torso, WHICH IS TIFERET AND YESOD. There are 24 limbs in the arms, 24 in the legs, AND 24 in the torso, as we have already learned, but they are all concealed in the torso, WHICH IS TIFERET, and the body stands in all THREE 24's. All 72 Chariots are included in the body and, because they are all included in it, the *Vav* expands once, MEANING ONE LINE THAT INCLUDES THEM ALL.

29. גּוּפָא חַד כָּלִיל בְּכ"ד רְתִיכִין, וְאִלֵּין אִינּוּן: רֵישָׁא בְּשִׁית. גּוּפָא בְּי"ח, וְאע"ג דְּכָל רְתִיכִין אִינּוּן י"ב לְכָל סְטָר, בְּכֹלָּא קַיְּימָא גּוּפָא. אֲבָל עֶשְׂרִים וְאַרְבַּע אִינּוּן שִׁית דְּרֵישָׁא, דְּאִינּוּן שַׁיְּיפִין לְאַעֲלָאָה רֵישָׁא. תְּמַנֵי סְרֵי חוּלְיָין דְּקַיְּימָא רֵישָׁא, וְסַמְכָא גּוּפָא עֲלַיְיהוּ.

29. AND HE EXPLAINS: a body includes 24 Chariots. They are the head OF THE *VAV* with six CHARIOTS and the body OF THE *VAV* with eighteen CHARIOTS, AND SIX AND EIGHTEEN EQUALS 24. Even though in all there are twelve Chariots at each end OF THE SIX EXTREMITIES, AND SIX TIMES TWELVE IS 72 AND NOT 24, ASSUREDLY the body is in them all, but FROM THE ASPECT OF 24, MEANING WHEN WE CONSIDER THE BODY AS ONLY A THIRD OF 72, AS MENTIONED ABOVE, they are DEFINED AS six in the head, NAMELY CHESED, GVURAH, TIFERET, NETZACH, HOD AND YESOD, THAT ARE IN THE HEAD. They are limbs by which to carry the head – NAMELY, THE THREE FIRST SFIROT THAT ARE CALLED 'HEAD', AND 18 ARE the 18 vertebrae OF THE SPINAL CORD, upon which the head stands and by which the body is supported.

30. וְכֻלְּהוּ פְּשִׁיטוּ חַד, בְּרֵישָׁא וְגוּפָא, וְאִינּוּן שִׁיתִּין כֻּלְּהוּ כָּלִיל לוֹן, דְּאִיהוּ רָזָא דְּשִׁית. וְעַל דָּא שִׁיעוּרָא דְּאָת ו', רֵישָׁא שִׁיעוּרָא בְּשִׁית נְקוּדִין מַמָּשׁ, גּוּפָא בְּתַמְנֵי סְרֵי. כְּגַוְונָא דָּא כָּל אִלֵּין רָזִין מִתְפָּרְשָׁן,

לְאַכְלְלָא לוֹן בְּגוּפָא, בְּגִין דִּדְרוֹעִין וְיַרְכִין כֻּלְהוּ בְּגְנִיזוּ, וְעַ״ד כֹּלָּא אִתְכְּלִיל בְּרָזָא דְאַת ו' וּדְיוּקְנָא דִּילָה.

30. All ABOVE-MENTIONED 24 CHARIOTS expand in one in the head and body OF THE VAV. The sixty SFIROT are all included IN THE VAV, which is the secret of six SFIROT, CHESED, GVURAH, TIFERET, NETZACH, HOD AND YESOD, EACH INCLUDING TEN. Therefore, the measure of the letter *Vav*, the head OF THE VAV is actually six points, NAMELY CHESED, GVURAH, TIFERET, NETZACH, HOD AND YESOD AND the body is eighteen. Similarly, all the secrets are explained as included in the torso, because the arms and legs, THAT ARE CHESED, GVURAH, NETZACH AND HOD, are hidden. Therefore, everything is included in the letter *Vav* and its form.

31. וְכַד שְׁלִימוּ דְּאַת דָּא אִתְחֲזֵי, כְּדֵין כָּל סְטְרִין בִּישִׁין אִסְתָּתְמוּ, וְאִתְפָּרְשָׁן מִסִּיהֲרָא, וְלָא אִתְחַפְיָין, בְּגִין דְּאִיהוּ מַבְקַע כָּל מַשְׁקוֹפִין דִּרְקִיעִין, וְאַנְהִיר לָהּ, וְלָא יַכְלָא מְקַטְרְגָא לְאַבְאָשָׁא כְּלַל. וְכַד הַאי אִסְתַּלָּק, כְּדֵין סָלִיק וְאַסְטֵי וּמְפַתֵּי, וְיָכִיל לְקַטְרְגָא עַל כָּל בְּנֵי עָלְמָא, בְּגִין דְּאִיהוּ מֶלֶךְ זָקֵן וּכְסִיל, וְהָא אוֹקִימְנָא.

31. When the letter appears to perfection, NAMELY THE VAV, WHICH IS THE CENTRAL COLUMN, AS MENTIONED, all the Evil Sides are blocked and depart from the moon, WHICH IS MALCHUT, and do not cover it. Because THE CENTRAL COLUMN cleaves through all the lintels in the firmament and illuminates on it, ON MALCHUT, the Inciter is unable to cause any harm. When it departs, NAMELY THE VAV THAT IS THE CENTRAL COLUMN, the Inciter rises, incites and accuses and seduces, and can denounce all the people of the world because he is an old and foolish king, as we have already established.

32. ו' אִיהוּ נְהוֹרָא דְּנָהִיר לְסִיהֲרָא, וְאע״ג דְּנְהִירִין סַגִּיאִין אִתְכְּלִילָן בֵּיהּ, נְהוֹרָא דְּנָהִיר לְסִיהֲרָא אִיהוּ חַד פְּשִׁיטוּ לְמַלְיָא לָהּ. וְאִיהוּ רָזָא דְּאָלֶף, רְשִׁימוּ בְּכָל אִינּוּן רָזִין. וְכַד נָהִיר לְסִיהֲרָא בְּרָזָא דְּו' נָהִיר לָהּ.

32. The *Vav* OF YUD HEI VAV HEI is the light that illuminates the moon, WHICH IS MALCHUT. Even though many lights are included IN THE VAV,

WHICH IS ZEIR ANPIN, the light that illuminates the moon is just one expansion that fills it. He, ZEIR ANPIN, is the secret of the *Aleph*, WHICH IS SHAPED AS A *VAV* IN BETWEEN TWO *YUD'S* TO ITS RIGHT AND LEFT, NAMELY ZEIR ANPIN THAT IS THE CENTRAL COLUMN THAT RECONCILES AND UNITES THE RIGHT AND LEFT. AND HE IS imprinted with all those secrets THAT ARE IN THE *ALEPH*. When he illuminates the moon, WHICH IS MALCHUT, he shines on it with the secret of the *Vav*, THE SHAPE OF WHICH IS ONE LINE, WHICH IS THE EXPANSION OF THE CENTRAL COLUMN ALONE.

33. וּבְסִפְרָא דְּאָדָם קַדְמָאָה, בְּדִיּוּקְנִין דְּאַתְוָון, ו' חַד נְקוּדָה לְעֵילָא, וְחָמֵשׁ נְקוּדִין לְתַתָּא, וְכֵן שִׁעוּרָא דִּילָהּ כְּגַוְונָא דָּא, וְכָל נְקוּדָה קַיְימָא בְּרָזָא דְעֶשֶׂר, בְּגִין דְּלֵית לָךְ נְקוּדָה דְּלָא אַשְׁלִים לְעֶשֶׂר, דְּכָל נְקוּדָה אִית בֵּיהּ תֵּשַׁע סַמְכִין רְתִיכִין, וְהַהִיא נְקוּדָה אַשְׁלִים לְעֶשֶׂר. נְקוּדָה דִּימִינָא תֵּשַׁע סַמְכִין רְתִיכִין לָהּ, וְאִיהִי עֲשָׂרָה. וְכֵן לִשְׂמָאלָא. וְכֵן לְכָל סְטְרִין. וְע״ד, כֻּלְּהוּ נְקוּדִין אִינּוּן כָּל חַד וְחַד כְּלָלָא דְעֶשֶׂר, אִיהִי וּרְתִיכוֹי. וְכֻלְּהוּ כְּלִילָן בְּהַהוּא פְּשִׁיטוּ דְּאָת ו', בג״כ כֹּלָּא אִיהוּ בְּדִיּוּקְנָא בְּרָזָא דְּאָת ו'.

33. In the Book of Adam, regarding the shape of the letters HE SAYS THAT THE SHAPE OF THE *Vav* is one point on top, WHICH ALLUDES TO THE *YUD* OF YUD HEI VAV HEI, and five points below, WHICH ARE THE FIRST *HEI* OF YUD HEI VAV HEI, THE SECRET OF FIVE POINTS, WHICH ARE FIVE SUPPORTS. Also the measure OF THE *VAV* OF YUD HEI VAV HEI, WHICH IS ZEIR ANPIN, is such, NAMELY, IT INCLUDES IN IT *YUD-HEI* OF YUD HEI VAV HEI, WHICH IS THE SECRET OF THE SON OF *YUD-HEI*. Every point OF THE SIX POINTS THAT ARE IN IT is based on the secret of ten, for there is no point that is not completed to ten, for every point has nine supports and Chariots, WHICH ARE ITS TOP, MIDDLE, AND END, EACH COMPRISING THREE COLUMNS. THEY ARE THE THREE POINTS OF *SEGOL*. With the point itself it completes ten, for the point on the right has nine supports and Chariots and, with itself, it is ten. And so it is with the point on the left and so on all sides. Therefore, all the points comprise ten each, it and its Chariots. They are part of the expansion of the letter *Vav*. Therefore, everything has the shape of the letter *Vav*, NAMELY, IT HAS THE FORM OF ONE POINT ABOVE AND FIVE POINTS.

34. וְכַד עָיֵיל שִׁמְשָׁא בְּסִיהֲרָא, נָפַק מֵהַאי ו' חַד פְּשִׁיטוּ רָזָא דִּבְרִית,
בְּגַוְונָא דָא ג', וְדָא אִיהוּ לְאָעֲלָא בְּנוּקְבָּא. וְכַד אִתְכְּלִיל כֹּלָּא בְּהַאי
פְּשִׁיטוּ דְּאָת ו', כְּדֵין קַיְימָא לְשַׁמְּשָׁא בְּנוּקְבָּא. וְרָזָא דָא דִּכְתִּיב, וְאַתָּה
הַקְרֵב אֵלֶיךָ אֶת אַהֲרֹן אָחִיךָ, לְאִתְכַּלְּלָא דְּרוֹעָא בְּגוּפָא, וְאֶת בָּנָיו
אִתּוֹ, אִלֵּין כָּל אִינּוּן רְתִיכִין וְסַמְכִין דִּילֵיהּ. דְּרוֹעָא שְׂמָאלָא לְגַבֵּיהּ,
דִּכְתִּיב קַח אֶת הַלְוִיִּם, לְאִשְׁתַּכְּחָא ו' דְּכָלִיל כֹּלָּא. בְּחַד פְּשִׁיטוּ, לְמֶהֱוֵי
חַד.

34. When the sun, WHICH IS ZEIR ANPIN, entered the moon, WHICH IS MALCHUT, an expansion emerges from this *Vav*, which is the secret of the Covenant, NAMELY YESOD, which is in the likeness of *Gimel*. Its purpose is to come into the Nukva, WHICH IS MALCHUT, and when all this is included in this expansion of the letter *Vav*, WHICH IS ZEIR ANPIN, then it is ready to mate with the Nukva. This is the secret of the scripture: "And take you to you Aaron your brother" (Shemot 28:1), who came to include the RIGHT arm, WHICH IS CHESED THAT IS CALLED 'AARON', with the torso, WHICH IS MOSES. "And his sons with him" (Ibid.), refers to his Chariots and supports. The left arm is included IN MOSES, WHO IS A CHARIOT TO ZEIR ANPIN, WHICH IS *VAV*, as it is written: "Take the Levites" (Bemidbar 3:45), THE LEVITES BEING THE LEFT ARM, WHICH IS GVURAH. So the *Vav* THAT IS MOSES includes everything in one expansion so as to be one.

35. וְע"ד אִשְׁתְּכַח יְחוּדָא בְּהַאי, יְמִינָא וּשְׂמָאלָא וְאֶמְצָעִיתָא, כֹּלָּא
אִיהוּ חַד. וְע"ד אִתְעֲבֵיד חַד פְּשִׁיטוּ, וְאִקְרֵי אֶחָד, וְלָא תִּשְׁכַּח בַּר
פְּשִׁיטוּ חַד בִּלְחוֹדוֹי, וְדָא הוּא חַד.

35. Therefore, there is unity in this *VAV* – in the right, left and center – FOR THE CENTER IS MOSES AND THE RIGHT IS AARON AND THE LEFT ARE THE LEVITES, and it is all one. Therefore, a single expansion is formed, which is called 'one' and there is only one expansion IN THE *VAV*, NAMELY, ONE LINE. This is THE SECRET MEANING OF one.

36. ה' בַּתְרָאָה, אִתְעֲבֵיד חַד גּוּפָא, בְּהַאי נְקוּדָה דְּאֶמְצָעִיתָא. וְאָעִיל
בָּהּ ו', וְאִשְׁתְּכַח ו' בֵּין ב' נְקוּדִין, חַד לְעֵילָּא, וְחַד לְתַתָּא. וּכְדֵין,

אִתְאֲחִיד עָלְמָא עִלָּאָה, בְּעָלְמָא תַּתָּאָה, וְאִיהוּ חַד. וְאוֹקִימְנָא. אָתָא רִבִּי אֶלְעָזָר וְרִבִּי אַבָּא וְנָשְׁקוּ יְדוֹי. בָּכָה רִבִּי אַבָּא וְאָמַר, וַוי לְעָלְמָא כַּד יִתְכְּנִישׁ שִׁמְשָׁא וְיִתְחֲשָׁךְ עָלְמָא.

36. The last *Hei* OF YUD HEI VAV HEI, WHICH IS MALCHUT, becomes a body in the central point. The *Vav* OF YUD HEI VAV HEI, WHICH IS ZEIR ANPIN, enters it so the *Vav* is located between two points, one above, WHICH IS IMA, and one below, WHICH IS MALCHUT. Then the Upper World, WHICH IS BINAH, unites with the Lower World, WHICH IS MALCHUT, and they become one, as we have established. Rabbi Elazar and Rabbi Aba came and kissed the hands OF RABBI SHIMON. Rabbi Aba wept and said: Woe to the world when the sun will set, THAT IS, RABBI SHIMON, and the world will become dark.

37. אָמַר ר' אֶלְעָזָר, יַרְכִּין לְתַתָּא, בְּרָזָא דְּאַת ו', מְנָ"ל דְּאִתְכְּלִילוּ בְּהַאי אָת. אָמַר לֵיהּ, דִּכְתִּיב זִכְרוּ תּוֹרַת מֹשֶׁה עַבְדִּי, וְלָא כְּתִיב נְבִיאַי, לְאִתְחֲזָאָה דְּכֹלָּא אִתְכְּלִיל בְּרָזָא דְּו', וְאָת ו' אִקְרֵי חַד, וְאִיהוּ חַד בִּלְחוֹדָהָא, וּפְשִׁיטוּ חַד וְהָא אִתְּמַר.

37. Rabbi Elazar said: How do we know that the legs below, WHICH ARE NETZACH AND HOD, that pertain to the secret of the letter *Vav*, WHICH IS TIFERET, are included in the letter *Vav*? He said to him: It is written: "Remember the Torah of Moses my servant" (Malachi 3:22). It is not written, 'my prophet' to show that everything is included in the *Vav*, WHICH IS TIFERET, AND PROPHETS, THE SECRET OF NETZACH AND HOD, ARE INCLUDED IN MOSES, WHO IS TIFERET. THEREFORE, IT IS NOT NECESSARY TO WRITE 'MOSES MY PROPHET'. The letter *VAV* is considered 'one'; it is but one and one expansion, as explained.

3. "And take you to you"

A Synopsis

Rabbi Shimon says that Moses, the sun, did not unite with the moon, Malchut, until he comprised all aspects including right and left. When the offering is proper, the shining countenance of God is present in the world in the Temple, and the Other Side is subdued and hides, and the side of Holiness rules with light and joy. But when the offering is not done properly, or the unison is not performed correctly, then the moon is concealed and the Other Side rules in the world. Lastly we hear that God did not test Job, but instead aroused the Inciter against him, as the Inciter is constantly coming around to denounce people.

38. וְאַתָּה הַקְרֵב אֵלֶיךָ וְגוֹ'. אָמַר רִבִּי שִׁמְעוֹן, לָא שִׁמֵּשׁ מֹשֶׁה דְּאִיהוּ שִׁמְשָׁא בְּסִיהֲרָא, עַד דְּאִתְכְּלִיל בְּכָל סִטְרִין בְּרָזָא דְו', כְּמָה דְּאוּקִימְנָא. תָּא חֲזֵי, מַה כְּתִיב, מִתּוֹךְ בְּנֵי יִשְׂרָאֵל לְכַהֲנוֹ לִי. לְכַהֵן לִי לָא כְּתִיב, אֶלָּא לְכַהֲנוֹ לִי, לְשִׁמּוּשָׁא דִּילֵיהּ, לְשִׁמּוּשָׁא דְּאַת דָּא, לְשִׁמּוּשָׁא דִּילֵיהּ וַדַּאי. לִי דָּא אָת ה', לְאַעֲלָא וּלְשַׁמְּשָׁא ו' בָּהּ, לְמֶהֱוֵי כֹּלָּא חַד. זַכָּאִין אִינּוּן יִשְׂרָאֵל, דְּעָאלוּ וְנַפְקוּ, וְיַדְעֵי בְּרָזָא דְּאָרְחוֹי דְּאוֹרַיְיתָא, לְמֵהַךְ בְּאֹרַח קְשׁוֹט.

38. "And take you to you" (Shemot 28:1). Rabbi Shimon said: Moses, who is the sun, did not unite with the moon, WHICH IS MALCHUT, until he comprised all aspects in accordance with the secret meaning of the letter *Vav*, as we have established, NAMELY, HE INCLUDED AARON AND THE LEVITES, WHO ARE RIGHT AND LEFT. Come and behold: it is written, "From among the children of Yisrael that he may minister to Me" (Ibid.). 'To minister to Me' is spelled with an extra *Vav*, WHICH LITERALLY MEANS 'for its service' – for the service of the letter *Vav*, assuredly for its service. IT IS AS IF IT WERE WRITTEN, 'TO SERVE *VAV*', WHICH IS TIFERET, 'TO Me' which is the letter *Hei*, NAMELY MALCHUT, to bring in the *Vav* to unite with the *Hei*, so everything will become one. Blessed are the children of Yisrael who entered IN THE SECRETS OF TORAH and came out. They know the secrets of the ways of the Torah so as to walk the true path.

39. מִתּוֹךְ בְּנֵי יִשְׂרָאֵל אֲמַאי מִתּוֹךְ בְּנֵי יִשְׂרָאֵל. אֶלָּא כֹּלָּא לָא אִתְקְרֵי

לְמֶהֱוֵי חַד כַּדְקָא יֵאוֹת, אֶלָּא מִתּוֹךְ בְּנֵי יִשְׂרָאֵל. דְּהָא בְּנֵי יִשְׂרָאֵל
קַיְימֵי לְתַתָּא, לְאִתְפַּתְּחָא אָרְחִין, וּלְאַנְהָרָא שְׁבִילִין, וּלְאַדְלְקָא
בּוּצִינִין, וּלְקָרְבָא כֹּלָּא מִתַּתָּא לְעֵילָּא, לְמֶהֱוֵי כֹּלָּא חַד, וּבְגִינֵי כַּךְ
כְּתִיב וְאַתֶּם הַדְּבֵקִים בַּיְיָ' וְגוֹ'.

39. HE ASKS: Why "from among the children of Yisrael"? HE ANSWERS:
nothing is called 'one' or is properly one, except from among the children of
Yisrael. For the children of Yisrael stand below to open ways and to
illuminate paths and to kindle the candles, WHICH ARE THE SUPERNAL
SFIROT, and to take everything from below upwards, so that everything
shall be one. Therefore, it is written: "But you who did cleave to Hashem
your Elohim..." (Devarim 4:4).

40. וְאַתָּה הַקְרֵב אֵלֶיךָ וְגוֹ' אר״ש, כֹּלָּא אִיהוּ קְרִיבָה, לְמַאן דְּיָדַע
לְיַחֲדָא יִחוּדָא, וּלְמִפְלַח לְמָארֵיהּ, דְּהָא בְּזִמְנָא דְּאִשְׁתְּכַח קׇרְבָּנָא
כַּדְקָא יֵאוֹת, כְּדֵין אִתְקְרִיב כֹּלָּא כַּחֲדָא, וּנְהִירוּ דְּאַנְפִּין, אִשְׁתְּכַח,
בְּעָלְמָא בְּבֵי מַקְדְּשָׁא, וְאִתְכַּפְיָא וְאִתְכַּסְיָא סִטְרָא אַחֲרָא, וְשָׁלִיט סִטְרָא
דִּקְדוּשָׁא בִּנְהִירוּ וְחֵידוּ. וְכַד קׇרְבָּנָא לָא אִשְׁתְּכַח כַּדְקָא יֵאוֹת, אוֹ
יִחוּדָא לָא הֲוֵי כַּדְקָא יֵאוֹת, כְּדֵין אַנְפִּין עֲצִיבוּ. וּנְהִירוּ לָא אִשְׁתְּכַח,
וְאִתְכַּסְיָא סִיהֲרָא, וְשַׁלְטָא סִטְרָא אַחֲרָא בְּעָלְמָא, בְּגִין דְּלָא אִית מַאן
דְּיָדַע לְיַחֲדָא שְׁמָא קַדִּישָׁא, כַּדְקָא יֵאוֹת.

40. "And take you to you...": Rabbi Shimon said: Everything is taken near
by one who knows how to affect unity and to serve his Master, for when the
offering is found to be proper, everything is brought together, MEANING THE
RIGHT AND LEFT SIDES. The shining countenance OF THE HOLY ONE,
BLESSED BE HE, is present in the world in the Temple, and the Other Side
is subdued and hides, and the side of Holiness rules with light and joy. But
when the offering is not found to be proper, or the unity was not properly
affected, then the face is sad and light is not prevalent. And the moon,
WHICH IS MALCHUT, is concealed and the Other Side rules in the world,
because there is no one who knows how to unite the Holy Name properly.

41. אר״ש, קוּדְשָׁא בְּרִיךְ הוּא לָא נַסֵּי לְאִיּוֹב, וְלָא אָתָא עִמֵּיהּ

בְּנִסְיוֹנָא, כְּנִסְיוֹנָא דִּשְׁאָר צַדִּיקַיָּא, דְּהָא לָא כְּתִיב בֵּיהּ וְהָאֱלֹהִים נִסָּה
אֶת אִיּוֹב, כְּמָה דִכְתִיב בְּאַבְרָהָם וְהָאֱלֹהִים נִסָּה אֶת אַבְרָהָם. דְּאִיהוּ
בִּידֵיהּ אַקְרִיב לִבְרֵיהּ יְחִידָאי לְגַבֵּיהּ. וְאִיּוֹב לָא יָהִיב לֵיהּ וְלָא מָסַר
לֵיהּ כְּלוּם. וְלָא אִתְּמַר לֵיהּ, אֲבָל אִתְמְסַר בִּידָא דִּמְקַטְרְגָא, בְּדִינָא
דְקוּדְשָׁא בְּרִיךְ הוּא. דְּאִיהוּ אִתְּעַר לְהַהוּא מְקַטְרְגָא לְגַבֵּיהּ, מַה דְּאִיהוּ
לָא בָּעָא. דְּהָא בְּכָל זִמְנָא אָתָא הַהוּא מְקַטְרְגָא לְאִתְעָרָא עַל בְּנֵי
נָשָׁא, וְהָכָא קוּדְשָׁא בְּרִיךְ הוּא אִתְּעַר לְגַבֵּיהּ, דִּכְתִיב הֲשַׂמְתָּ לִבְּךָ עַל
עַבְדִּי אִיּוֹב. אֲבָל רָזָא עֲמִיקָא אִיהוּ.

41. Rabbi Shimon said: The Holy One, blessed be He, did not test Job and did not bring him to a test like the tests of other righteous people. For is it not written of him: 'Elohim tested Job', as is written about Abraham: "Elohim did test Abraham" (Beresheet 22:1), who offered his only son to Him with his own hand. Job did not give Him or hand Him anything. It is not said to him THAT HE SHOULD GIVE, but he was given over to the Inciter through the Judgment of the Holy One, blessed be He, as He aroused the Inciter against him, which he did not request. The Inciter is constantly coming to denounce people. Here, the Holy One, blessed be He, aroused the Inciter against him, as is written: "Have you considered My servant Job" (Iyov 1:8), but this is a deep secret.

4. "And it came to pass at the end of days"

A Synopsis

Rabbi Shimon tells us that "the end of days" means impurity, while "the end of right" is holiness. He says that Cain's offering was not accepted because it "came to pass" "at the end of days," so it came from the Other Side. Abel included a small portion for the Other Side in his offering with the largest portion for God, while Cain included the largest portion for the Other Side. We are also told that Job did not properly arrange his offering either.

42. פָּתַח וְאָמַר וַיְהִי מִקֵּץ יָמִים וַיָּבֵא קַיִן מִפְּרִי הָאֲדָמָה מִנְחָה לַיְיָ'. וַיְהִי מִקֵּץ יָמִים, רָזָא אִיהוּ, מִקֵּץ יָמִים, וְלָא מִקֵּץ יָמִין, דָּחָה לְקֵץ יָמִין, וְקָרִיב לְקֵץ יָמִים. וְהָא אוֹקִימְנָא, דִּכְתִיב וְאַתָּה לֵךְ לַקֵּץ. אָמַר קוּדְשָׁא בְּרִיךְ הוּא לְדָנִיֵּאל וְאַתָּה לֵךְ לַקֵּץ. אָמַר לֵיה, לְאָן קֵץ, לְקֵץ הַיָּמִים אוֹ לְקֵץ הַיָּמִין, עַד דְּאָמַר לֵיה לְקֵץ הַיָּמִין.

42. He opened the discussion, saying: "And in process of time (lit. 'at the end of days') it came to pass, that Cain brought of the fruit of the ground an offering to Hashem" (Beresheet 4:3). "At the end of days," has a secret meaning; it is "the end of days (Heb. *yamim*)," WHICH IS IMPURITY, rather than 'the end of right (Heb. *yamin*; also 'days')', WHICH IS HOLINESS. He rejected the 'end of right (Heb. *yamin*)' and sought to bring near the "end of days (Heb. *yomin*)." We have established that it is written: "But go you your way till the end be" (Daniel 12:13). The Holy One, blessed be He, said to Daniel: "But go you your way till the end be." He kept asking Him: 'which end? the end of days or end of right?', until He said to him: 'The end of the right.'

43. וְעַ"ד דָּחִיל דָּוִד, דִּכְתִיב הוֹדִיעֵנִי יְיָ' קִצִּי. אוֹ לְקֵץ הַיָּמִים, אוֹ לְקֵץ הַיָּמִין. וְהָכָא מַה כְּתִיב, וַיְהִי מִקֵּץ יָמִים וְלָא מִקֵּץ יָמִין. וּבְגִינֵי כַּךְ לָא אִתְקַבַּל קָרְבָּנֵיה דְּהָא מִסִּטְרָא אַחֲרָא הֲוָה כֹּלָּא.

43. This is what David feared, as it is written: "Let me know, Hashem, my end" (Tehilim 39:5), whether the end of the days or the end of the right. And here, BY CAIN, it is written: "And it came to pass" "at the end of days," rather than 'at the end of the right'. Therefore, his offering was not

accepted, because it all came from the Other Side.

44. ת״ח מָה כְּתִיב, וְהֶבֶל הֵבִיא גַם הוּא. מַאי גַם הוּא. לְאַסְגָּאָה כֹּלָּא דָּא בְּדָא. קָרְבְּנָא כֹּלָּא וְעִקָּרָא דִּילֵיהּ הֲוָה לְקוּדְשָׁא בְּרִיךְ הוּא, וְיָהִיב חוּלָקֵיהּ לְסִטְרָא אַחֲרָא, כד״א וּמֵחֶלְבֵיהֶן. וְקַיִן, עִקָּרָא עָבֵד מִקֵּץ יָמִים, וְיָהַב חוּלָקָא לְקוּדְשָׁא בְּרִיךְ הוּא, וְעַל דָּא אִתְדְּחָא אִיהוּ וְקָרְבָּנֵיהּ.

44. Come and behold: it is written, "And Abel, he also brought" (Beresheet 4:4). What is the meaning of "he also"? Its purpose is to add everything, one within the other – MEANING THAT IN THE OFFERING OF ABEL THERE WAS ALSO A PORTION FOR THE OTHER SIDE, AND IN THE OFFERING OF CAIN THERE WAS ALSO A PORTION FOR HOLINESS. HOWEVER, WITH ABEL, the whole and main part of his offering was to the Holy One, blessed be He, and he gave a portion for the Other Side, as is written: "And of the fat parts thereof" (Ibid.); THE FATTEST AND BEST WAS FOR THE HOLY ONE, BLESSED BE HE. But with Cain, the main was for "the end of days," WHICH IS THE OTHER SIDE, and he gave only a small portion to the Holy One, blessed be He. Therefore, he and his offering were rejected.

45. בְּאִיּוֹב מַה כְּתִיב, וְהָלְכוּ בָנָיו וְעָשׂוּ מִשְׁתֶּה וְגו'. וּכְתִיב וַיְהִי כִּי הִקִּיפוּ יְמֵי הַמִּשְׁתֶּה. וּכְתִיב וְשָׁלְחוּ וְקָרְאוּ לִשְׁלֹשֶׁת אַחְיוֹתֵיהֶם לֶאֱכֹל וְלִשְׁתּוֹת עִמָּהֶם, דְּדָא אִיהוּ עִקָּרָא לְסִטְרָא אַחֲרָא. וּלְבָתַר אַקְרִיב עוֹלוֹת, וְעוֹלָה אִיהוּ דְּכַר, וְלָא נוּקְבָּא, וְסַלְקָא לְעֵילָא, וְקָרְבָּנָא לָא קָרִיב לְאַכְלְלָא לֵיהּ כִּדְקָא יָאוּת.

45. About Job, it is written: "And his sons used to go and feast… And when the days of their feasting were gone about" (Iyov 1:4-5), and also, "And they used to send and call for their three sisters to eat and drink with them" (Ibid.). This was the main portion HE GAVE to the Other Side, and only afterwards did he offer burnt offerings. Now, a burnt offering (Heb. *olah*) is male rather than female, and wholly rises (Heb. *olah*) up, but he did not offer a sacrifice that would properly include it as well, MEANING TO ALSO GIVE A PORTION TO THE OTHER SIDE.

5. Giving a portion to the Other Side

A Synopsis

We read that if Job had given a portion to everyone then the 'Inciter' or negative force would not have been able to approach him later. Rabbi Shimon says that when the Other Side is given a proper portion, it removes itself from the Sanctuary; therefore the side of Holiness rises higher and higher. God aroused the Inciter against Job because of his incorrect offering. We are told that God united with Yisrael in Egypt at Pascal while the Other Side was occupied with Job. Regarding the unleavened bread, Rabbi Shimon says that the Evil Inclination in a person is like yeast in a dough: it enters the belly of a person slowly and then multiples there until the whole body is mixed with it. This is idolatry.

46. וְתָ"ח, אִלְמָלֵא חוּלָקָא יָהַב לְכֹלָּא, מְקַטְרְגָא לָא יָכִיל לֵיהּ לְבָתַר, וְאִי תֵּימָא אֲמַאי אַבְאִישׁ לֵיהּ קוּדְשָׁא בְּרִיךְ הוּא. אֶלָּא, בְּגִין דְּגָרִים לְכַסְיָא נְהוֹרָא וּלְאִתְחַפְיָא, וְאִיהוּ לָא קָרִיב קָרְבְּנָא אַחֲרָא, לְאַתְזָנָא בֵּיהּ אַחֲרָנִין, אֶלָּא עוֹלָה, דְּסַלְקָא לְעֵילָּא, וְעַל דָּא כְּתִיב, כָּכָה יַעֲשֶׂה אִיּוֹב כָּל הַיָּמִים, דְּאִלְמָלֵא סִטְרָא אַחֲרָא אִתְזָנַת בְּחוּלָקָא, אִתְעֲבַר מֵעַל מַקְדְּשָׁא וְאִסְתַּלָּק מִנֵּיהּ, וְסִטְרָא דִּקְדוּשָׁה הֲוָה סָלִיק לְעֵילָּא לְעֵילָּא.

46. Come and behold: had he given a portion to everyone, MEANING ALSO TO THE OTHER SIDE, then the Inciter could not have approached him later. One may ask why the Holy One, blessed be He, did him evil FOR NOT GIVING A PORTION TO THE OTHER SIDE? WHAT IS THE SIN HERE? HE ANSWERS: It was because he caused the light to be covered and concealed, for he did not properly offer another offering to sustain others, MEANING THE OTHER SIDE, AS IT HAS A PORTION IN THE OFFERINGS, but rather offered ONLY a burnt offering (Heb. *olah*), that ascends (Heb. *olah*) above, AND THE OTHER SIDE HAS NO PART IN IT. Therefore, it is written: "Thus Job did all the days" (Iyov 1:5); HE DID NOT GIVE A PORTION TO THE OTHER SIDE, for if the Other Side had been nourished with a proper portion, it would have been removed from the Sanctuary and would have departed from it, and the side of Holiness would have risen higher and higher.

47. אֲבָל אִיהוּ לָא בָּעָא דְּאִתְהֲנֵי אַחֲרָא מִקָּרְבְּנֵיהּ, וְאַעֲדֵי גַּרְמֵיהּ מִנֵּיהּ. מְנָא לָן. דִּכְתִּיב, וְסָר מֵרָע. וְעַל דָּא קָרִיב תָּדִיר עוֹלָה, דְּהָא

עוֹלָה לָא אִתְהֲנֵי מִנֵּיה סִטְרָא אַחֲרָא לְעָלְמִין. וּבְגִין כַּךְ, כָּל מַה דְּנָטִיל לְבָתַר, מִדִּידֵיהּ נָטִיל. וְעַל דָּא אִיּוֹב גָּרִים לְחַפְיָא עָרְלָה עַל בְּרִית קַיָּימָא, דְּלָא הֲוָה אַעֲדֵי מִנֵּיה. וּבְגִין כַּךְ קוּדְשָׁא בְּרִיךְ הוּא אִתְעַר לְהַהוּא מְקַטְרְגָא, דִּכְתִיב הֲשַׂמְתָּ לִבְּךָ עַל עַבְדִּי אִיּוֹב.

47. But he did not want another, MEANING THE OTHER SIDE, to gain any benefit from his offering, so he removed himself from it. Whence do we know this from? From the verse: "And turns away from evil" (Iyov 1:8); HE REMOVED HIMSELF FROM EVIL, SO AS NOT TO GIVE IT ANY PORTION. Therefore, he always offered a burnt offering, because the Other Side never receives any pleasure from it. Thus, whatever the Other Side took afterwards FROM JOB, it took from its own. In this way, Job caused a foreskin to cover the Holy Covenant, and it did not move from it, FROM THE HOLY COVENANT. Therefore, the Holy One, blessed be He, aroused against him the Inciter, as it is written: "Have you considered My servant Job?"

48. ת״ח, כַּד בָּעָא קוּדְשָׁא בְּרִיךְ הוּא לְאִתְאַחֲדָא בְּהוּ בְּיִשְׂרָאֵל בְּמִצְרַיִם, לָא קַיְימָא שַׁעֲתָא. בְּגִין דְּעָרְלָה חַפְיָא נְהוֹרָא, עַד זִמְנָא דְּהַהוּא מְקַטְרְגָא הֲוָה נָטִיל דִּילֵיה מֵאִיּוֹב, וְעַל דָּא פָּקִיד לֵיה קוּדְשָׁא בְּרִיךְ הוּא לְמֵיכְלֵיה לְהַהוּא פֶּסַח בִּבְהִילוּ, עַד דְּהַהוּא סִטְרָא אַחֲרָא אִשְׁתָּדַּל בֵּיה בְּאִיּוֹב, וּפָקִיד לְאִתְעַבְּרָא עָרְלָה מִנַּיְיהוּ, וּכְדֵין אִתְאֲחַד קוּדְשָׁא בְּרִיךְ הוּא בְּיִשְׂרָאֵל, וְהַהוּא סִטְרָא אַחֲרָא אִתְפְּרַשׁ מִן קַדְשָׁא, וְאִשְׁתָּדַּל בֵּיה בְּאִיּוֹב, וְנָטִיל מִדִּילֵיה. וּכְדֵין פֶּסַח הוּא לַיְיָ׳ וַדַּאי. דְּעַד הַשְׁתָּא לָא הֲוָה פֶּסַח לַיְיָ׳. זַכָּאִין אִינּוּן דְּיַדְעֵי וּמְיַחֲדֵי יְחוּדָא דְּמָארֵיהוֹן כַּדְקָא יֵאוֹת.

48. Come and behold: when the Holy One, blessed be He, wished to unite with Yisrael in Egypt, the time was not propitious because the foreskin, MEANING THE OTHER SIDE, covered the light, until the time came and the Inciter took that which belonged to him from Job. Then the Holy One, blessed be He, commanded to eat the Pascal sacrifice in haste, MEANING while the Other Side was occupied with Job, and commanded the removal of the foreskin from them. The Holy One, blessed be He, united with

Yisrael, and the Other Side separated from Holiness and was occupied with Job and took what was its own. Then "it is Hashem's passover" (Shemot 12:11), for until now, the passover was not Hashem's. Blessed are they who know how to properly affect the unity of their Master.

49. כְּתִיב אֱלֹהֵי מַסֵּכָה לֹא תַעֲשֶׂה לָךְ, וּכְתִיב בַּתְרֵיהּ אֶת חַג הַמַּצוֹת תִּשְׁמֹר. מַאי הַאי לְגַבֵּי הַאי. אֶלָּא הָכִי אוּקְמוּהָ, מַאן דְּאָכִיל חָמֵץ בְּפֶסַח כְּמַאן דְּפָלַח לכו"ם אִיהוּ.

49. It is written: "You shall make you no molten Elohim" (Shemot 34:17), followed by, "The feast of unleavened bread (Heb. *matzot*) shall you keep" (Ibid. 18). HE ASKS: why is one adjacent to the other? HE ANSWERS: This is what has been explained, that whoever eats leaven (Heb. *chametz*) on Pesach (Passover), it is as if he worships idols.

50. ת"ח, כַּד נָפְקוּ יִשְׂרָאֵל מִמִּצְרַיִם נָפְקוּ מֵרְשׁוּ דִּלְהוֹן, מֵרְשׁוּ אַחֲרָא, מֵהַהוּא רְשׁוּ דְּאִקְרֵי חָמֵץ, נַהֲמָא בִּישָׁא. וְעַ"ד אִקְרֵי כו"ם הָכִי, וְדָא אִיהוּ רָזָא דְּיֵצֶר הָרָע, פּוּלְחָנָא נוּכְרָאָה, דְּאִקְרֵי אוּף הָכִי שְׂאוֹר. וְדָא אִיהוּ יֵצֶר הָרָע, דְּהָכִי אִיהוּ יֵצֶר הָרָע בְּבַר נָשׁ, כְּחָמִיר בְּעִיסָה, עָאל בִּמְעוֹי דְּבַר נָשׁ זְעֵיר, וּלְבָתַר אַסְגֵּי בֵּיהּ, עַד דְּכָל גּוּפָא אִתְעֲרַב בַּהֲדֵיהּ. וְדָא אִיהוּ כו"ם. וְעַל דָּא כְּתִיב, לֹא יִהְיֶה בְךָ אֵל זָר. אֵל זָר וַדַּאי.

50. Come and behold: when Yisrael left Egypt, they left their jurisdiction, namely the rule of the other SIDE, the rule that is called 'leaven', evil bread. Therefore, idol worship is called by that name, *CHAMETZ* (ENG. 'LEAVEN'). This is the secret of the Evil Inclination that is idol worship, which is also called 'leaven' (lit. 'yeast'). This is the Evil Inclination, because the Evil Inclination in the person is like yeast in a dough. It enters the belly of the person slowly and then multiplies there until the whole body is mixed with it. This is idolatry. Therefore, it is written: "There shall be no strange El among you" (Tehilim 81:10), a strange El assuredly.

6. "Cease from man, though his breath be in his nostrils"

A Synopsis

Rabbi Yehuda wonders if the title verse means that people should avoid one another, but Rabbi Shimon answers that God has cautioned people to guard themselves from those who have turned to evil. We learn that the Holy Spirit in man consists of three – Nefesh, Ruach and Neshamah, Neshamah being the highest of all, since it is a supernal force with which to know and keep the commandments of God. The only thing that can significantly damage the Neshamah and lead to idolatry is anger, which Rabbi Shimon warns us about strongly. He says that one must not even look at the face of an angry man, and should certainly not associate with him.

51. אֶת חַג הַמַּצוֹת תִּשְׁמֹר, רַבִּי יְהוּדָה פָּתַח, חִדְלוּ לָכֶם מִן הָאָדָם אֲשֶׁר נְשָׁמָה בְּאַפּוֹ כִּי בַּמֶּה נֶחְשָׁב הוּא. הַאי קְרָא אוּקְמוּהָ. אֲבָל מַאי חִדְלוּ לָכֶם מִן הָאָדָם, וְכִי אַזְהַר לֵיהּ לְבַר נָשׁ לְאִתְמַנְּעָא מִשְּׁאַר בְּנֵי נָשָׁא. אוּף אִינּוּן נָמֵי לְגַבֵּיהּ, יִשְׁתַּכְחוּן בְּנֵי נָשָׁא דְּלָא יִקְרְבוּן אִלֵּין בְּאִלֵּין לְעָלְמִין. אֶלָּא הָא אוּקְמוּהָ בְּמַאן דְּאַשְׁכִּים לְפִתְחָא דְּחַבְרֵיהּ לְמֵיהַב לֵיהּ שְׁלָם.

51. "The festival of unleavened bread (Heb. *matzot*) shall you keep" (Shemot 34:18). Rabbi Yehuda opened the discussion, saying: "Cease from man, though his breath be in his nostrils, for in what is he to be accounted of" (Yeshayah 2:22). They have established this passage, yet what is the meaning of "Cease from man"? Is THE PROPHET warning to avoid other people and that likewise, other PEOPLE should avoid him? It would then come to pass that people would never come near each other. HE ANSWERS: They have established this passage as referring to one who arrives early at the door of his friend to greet him, BEFORE HE HAS BLESSED THE HOLY ONE, BLESSED BE HE. AND THEREFORE IT IS SAID, "CEASE..."

52. וַאֲנָא אוּקִימְנָא לֵיהּ בִּקְרָא אַחֲרָא, דִּכְתִּיב, מְבָרֵךְ רֵעֵהוּ בְּקוֹל גָּדוֹל בַּבֹּקֶר הַשְׁכֵּם קְלָלָה תֵּחָשֶׁב לוֹ. וְאַף עַל גַּב דְּכֹלָּא שַׁפִּיר. אֲבָל מַאי חִדְלוּ לָכֶם מִן הָאָדָם אֲשֶׁר נְשָׁמָה בְּאַפּוֹ. הָכָא פָּקִיד קוּדְשָׁא בְּרִיךְ הוּא לְבַר נָשׁ, וְאַזְהִיר לֵיהּ לְאִסְתַּמְּרָא מֵאִינּוּן בְּנֵי נָשָׁא, דְּסָטוּ אָרְחַיְיהוּ

-32-

מֵאֹרַח טָב לְאֹרַח בִּישׁ, וּמְסָאֲבֵי נַפְשַׁיְיהוּ בְּהַהוּא מְסָאֲבוּ אַחֲרָא.

52. I have explained the passage: "CEASE…" together with another passage that says: "He that blesses his friend with a loud voice, rising early in the morning, it shall be counted a curse to him" (Mishlei 27:14). Even though it is all well, MEANING EVEN THOUGH HE HAS ALREADY BLESSED THE HOLY ONE, BLESSED BE HE, AND IT IS NOT NECESSARY TO CAUTION ABOUT IT "CEASE…", what is "Cease from man, though his breath be in his nostrils"? Here, the Holy One, blessed be He, has commanded the man and cautioned him to guard himself from those people who have turned from a good way to an evil way, and defile themselves with the impurity of the Other Side.

53. דְּהָא כַּד בָּרָא קוּדְשָׁא בְּרִיךְ הוּא לְבַר נָשׁ, עָבֵד לֵיהּ בְּדִיּוּקְנָא עִלָּאָה, וְנָפַח בֵּיהּ רוּחָא קַדִּישָׁא, דְּכָלִיל בִּתְלַת כְּמָה דְּאוּקִימְנָא, דְּאִית בֵּיהּ נֶפֶשׁ רוּחַ וּנְשָׁמָה, וְעֵילָּא מִכֹּלָּא נְשָׁמָה, דְּאִיהִי חֵילָא עִלָּאָה לְמִנְדַּע, וּלְמֶטַר פִּקּוּדוֹי דְּקוּדְשָׁא בְּרִיךְ הוּא. וְאִי הַהִיא נִשְׁמָתָא קַדִּישָׁא אָעִיל לָהּ בְּפוּלְחָנָא אַחֲרָא, הַאי אִיהוּ מַסְאִיב לָהּ, וְנָפִיק מִפּוּלְחָנָא דְּמָארֵיהּ. בְּגִין דִּתְלַת חֵילִין אִלֵּין, כֻּלְּהוּ חַד, נֶפֶשׁ רוּחַ וּנְשָׁמָה מִשְׁתַּתְּפֵי כַּחֲדָא, וַהֲווֹ חַד, וְכֹלָּא כְּגַוְונָא דְּרָזָא עִלָּאָה.

53. When the Holy One, blessed be He, created man, He made him in the supernal image and blew into him a Holy Spirit combined of three, as we have established, so that he would contain Nefesh, Ruach, Neshamah. And Neshamah is the highest of all of them, for it is a supernal force with which to know and to keep the commandments of the Holy One, blessed be He. If one brings the sacred Neshamah into another worship, he defiles it and leaves the service of his Master. For these three forces are all one, Nefesh, Ruach and Neshamah, together in partnership. And they are one, as in the supernal secret THAT BINAH AND ZEIR ANPIN AND MALCHUT ARE ONE, SO TO NEFESH, RUACH AND NESHAMAH ARE ONE, BECAUSE THEY STEM FROM THEM.

54. וְאִי חֲזֵינָן לְהַאי בַּר נָשׁ, דַּהֲווֹ בֵּיהּ אִלֵּין דַּרְגִּין כֻּלְּהוּ. עַד לָא קַיְימָא בְּקִיּוּמֵיהּ לְמִנְדַּע מַאן אִיהוּ, בְּמַאי אִתְיְדַע לְקָרְבָא בַּר נָשׁ

בַּהֲדֵיהּ, אוֹ לְאִתְמַנְעָא מִנֵּיהּ. בְּרוּגְזֵיהּ מַמָּשׁ, יָדַע לֵיהּ בַּר נָשׁ, וְיִשְׁתְּמוֹדַע מַאן אִיהוּ. אִי הַהִיא נִשְׁמְתָא קַדִּישָׁא נָטַר בְּשַׁעֲתָא דְּרוּגְזוֹי, דְּלָא יֶעֱקַר לָהּ מֵאַתְרָהָא, בְּגִין לְמִשְׁרֵי תְּחוֹתָהּ הַהוּא אֵל זָר, דָּא אִיהוּ בַּר נָשׁ כַּדְקָא יֵאוֹת. דָּא אִיהוּ עַבְדָּא דְּמָארֵיהּ, דָּא אִיהוּ גְּבַר שְׁלִים.

54. If we see a man that has all these levels, WHICH ARE NEFESH, RUACH AND NESHAMAH, and still not know clearly what he is, how can we determine whether to approach that man or avoid him? Here then, in his real anger, one could know and recognize him for what he is. If he guards the holy Neshamah in his anger, so as not to uproot it from its place and bring a foreign El to replace it, then he is a proper man. Such is a servant of his Master; such is a whole man.

55. וְאִי הַהוּא בַּר נָשׁ לָא נָטִיר לָהּ, וְאִיהוּ עָקַר קְדוּשָׁה דָּא עִלָּאָה מֵאַתְרֵיהּ, לְמִשְׁרֵי בְּאַתְרֵיהּ סִטְרָא אַחֲרָא. וַדַּאי דָּא אִיהוּ בַּר נָשׁ דְּמָרִיד בְּמָארֵיהּ, וְאָסִיר לְקָרְבָא בַּהֲדֵיהּ וּלְאִתְחַבְּרָא עִמֵּיהּ, וְדָא אִיהוּ טוֹרֵף נַפְשׁוֹ בְּאַפּוֹ. אִיהוּ טָרִיף וְעָקַר נַפְשֵׁיהּ, בְּגִין רוּגְזֵיהּ, וְאַשְׁרֵי בְּגַוֵּיהּ אֵל זָר. וְעַל דָּא כְּתִיב חִדְלוּ לָכֶם מִן הָאָדָם אֲשֶׁר נְשָׁמָה בְּאַפּוֹ, דְּהַהִיא נִשְׁמְתָא קַדִּישָׁא טָרִיף לָהּ, וְסָאִיב לָהּ, בְּגִין אַפּוֹ, אֲשֶׁר נְשָׁמָה אַחְלַף בְּאַפּוֹ. כִּי בַמֶּה נֶחְשָׁב הוּא. כו"ם אִתְחֲשִׁיב הַהוּא בַּר נָשׁ.

55. If that man does not guard it but uproots this supernal Holiness BY BECOMING ANGRY, and causes the Other Side to dwell in its place, assuredly such a man has rebelled against his Master. It is forbidden to come near him or join him. Such a one "tears himself in his anger" (Iyov 18:4). He tears and uproots his soul because of his anger and causes a foreign El to dwell within him. In reference to him, it is written: "Cease from man, though his breath be in his nostrils" (Yeshayah 2:22), meaning that he tears his holy Neshamah and defiles it in his anger, MEANING BECAUSE HE BECAME ANGRY, exchanging his Neshamah in his anger. "For in what (Heb. *bameh*) is he to be accounted of" (Ibid.), means that man is considered A STAGE (HEB. *BAMAH*), ON WHICH idols ARE WORSHIPPED.

56. וּמַאן דְּאִתְחַבָּר עִמֵּיהּ, וּמַאן דְּאִשְׁתְּעֵי בַּהֲדֵיהּ, כְּמַאן דְּאִתְחַבָּר

בְּכוּ״ם מַמָּשׁ. מ״ט. בְּגִין דכו״ם מַמָּשׁ שָׁארֵי בְּגַוֵּיהּ. וְלָא עוֹד, אֶלָּא דְּעִקָּר קְדוּשָׁה עִלָּאָה מֵאַתְרֵיהּ, וְשָׁארֵי בְּאַתְרֵיהּ כו״ם אֵל זָר. מַה אֵל זָר כְּתִיב בֵּיהּ אַל תִּפְנוּ אֶל הָאֱלִילִים, כְּגַוְונָא דָא, אָסִיר לְאִסְתַּכְּלָא בְּאַנְפּוֹי.

56. Whoever joins him and whoever speaks with him, is as though he actually joins with idolatry. What is the reason? Because actual idolatry dwells within him, MEANING A STRANGE EL. Moreover, he has uprooted the supernal Holiness from its place and caused idolatry to dwell instead, a strange El. As it is written of a strange El: "Turn not to idols" (Vayikra 19:4), it is similarly forbidden to look at the face OF THE ANGRY MAN.

57. וְאִי תֵּימָא הָא רוּגְזָא דְּרַבָּנָן. רוּגְזָא דְּרַבָּנָן טָב אִיהוּ לְכָל סִטְרִין, דְּהָא תָּנֵינָן דְּאוֹרַיְיתָא אֶשָּׁא אִיהִי, וְאוֹרַיְיתָא קָא מַרְתְּחָא לֵיהּ, דִּכְתִיב הֲלֹא כֹה דְּבָרַי כָּאֵשׁ נְאֻם יְיָ׳. רוּגְזָא דְּרַבָּנָן בְּמִלֵּי דְּאוֹרַיְיתָא. רוּגְזָא דְּרַבָּנָן לְמֵיהַב יְקָרָא לְאוֹרַיְיתָא, וְכֹלָּא לְפוּלְחָנָא דְּקוּדְשָׁא בְּרִיךְ הוּא הֲוֵי, לְכַךְ נֶאֱמַר כִּי יְיָ׳ אֱלֹהֶיךָ אֵשׁ אוֹכְלָה הוּא אֵל קַנָּא.

57. You may ask: But what about the anger of sages? HE ANSWERS: The anger of sages is good from every aspect, for we have learned that the Torah is fire and the Torah causes him to seethe, as it is written: "'Is not My word like a fire,' says Hashem" (Yirmeyah 23:29). The anger of sages is in the words of Torah. The anger of sages is to give honor to the Torah, and it is all in the service of Hashem. Therefore, it says, "Hashem your Elohim is a consuming fire, a jealous El" (Devarim 4:24).

58. אֲבָל אִי בְּמִלִּין אַחֲרָנִין, לָאו פּוּלְחָנָא דְּקוּדְשָׁא בְּרִיךְ הוּא הַאי, בְּגִין דִּבְכָל חַטָּאִים דְּקָא עָבִיד בַּר נָשׁ, לָאו אִיהוּ כו״ם מַמָּשׁ כְּהַאי, וְאָסִיר לְקָרְבָא בַּהֲדֵיהּ, דְּהַאי. וְאִי תֵּימָא הָא לְשַׁעֲתָא הֲוָה, דְּעָבַר וְהָדַר אַהְדָּר. לָאו הָכִי, דְּכֵיוָן דְּאֶעֱקַר קְדוּשָׁא דְּנַפְשֵׁיהּ מִנֵּיהּ וּמֵאַתְרֵיהּ, וְהַהוּא אֵל זָר, מַקְפַּח הַהוּא אֲתָר, אִתְתַּקַּף בֵּיהּ, וְלָא שָׁבִיק לֵיהּ. בַּר כַּד אִתְדְּכֵי בַּר נָשׁ מִכֹּל וְכֹל, וְעָקַר לֵיהּ לְעָלְמִין, וּלְבָתַר

אִשְׁתַּדַּל לְאִתְקַדְּשָׁא וּלְאַמְשָׁכָא קְדוּשָׁה עָלֵיה. כְּדֵין וּלְוַאי דְּאִתְקַדַּשׁ. אָ״ל רִ׳ יוֹסֵי, אִתְקַדַּשׁ מַמָּשׁ.

58. But if THE ANGER is for other matters, AND NOT FOR WORDS OF TORAH, then it is not the service of the Holy One, blessed be He. Of all the sins that a person commits, none are actual idol worship like one WHO IS ANGRY. It is forbidden to approach him. If you say that he only temporarily transgressed AND BECAME ANGRY but afterwards repented, it is not so! Since once he has uprooted the Holiness of his soul from himself and from its place and that strange El appropriated that place, he strengthens himself there and does not leave him. The only exception is when that person becomes entirely purified and has uprooted from himself THE STRANGE EL forever, and afterwards endeavors to become holy and to draw Holiness upon himself, THEN hopefully he will become holy. Rabbi Yosi said to him: He actually becomes holy.

59. אָ״ל ת״ח, בְּשַׁעֲתָא דְּאִיהוּ עָקַר קְדוּשָׁה דְּנַפְשֵׁיה, וְשַׁרְיָא בְּאַתְרֵיהּ הַהוּא אֵל זָר דְּאִקְרֵי טָמֵא, אִסְתְּאַב בַּר נָשׁ, וְסָאִיב לְמַאן דְּקָרִיב בַּהֲדֵיה, וְהַהִיא קְדוּשָׁה עָקְרַת מִנֵּיה, וְכֵיוָן דְּעָקְרַת מִנֵּיה זִמְנָא חֲדָא, כַּמָה דִּיעֲבִיד בַּר נָשׁ עוֹד, לָא תֵּיתוּב לְאַתְרָהָא.

59. He said to him: Come and behold. At the moment he uproots the Holiness of his soul and in its place dwells that strange El that is called 'impure', the person becomes defiled and he defiles whoever approaches him. That Holiness is uprooted from him, and when it has been uprooted once, in relation to what he did, it will never return to its place.

60. אָ״ל אִי הָכִי, כַּמָה מְסָאֲבִין אִינּוּן דְּמִתְדַּכְּאָן. אָ״ל שָׁאנֵי מְסָאֲבוּ אַחֲרָא, דְּלָא יָכִיל לְמֶעְבַּד יַתִּיר. אֲבָל דָּא שַׁנְיָא מִכֹּלָּא, דְּכָל גּוּפָא סָאִיב מִגּוֹ וּמִבַּר, וְנַפְשָׁא, וְכֹלָּא מַסְאִיב. וּשְׁאַר מְסָאֲבוּ דְּעָלְמָא, לָאו אִיהוּ אֶלָּא גּוּפָא לְבַר בִּלְחוֹדוֹי, וּבְג״כ כְּתִיב חִדְלוּ לָכֶם מִן הָאָדָם אֲשֶׁר נְשָׁמָה בְּאַפּוֹ, דְּאַחְלַף קְדוּשָׁה דְּמָארֵיה בְּגִין אַפּוֹ, דְּדָא אִיהוּ מְסָאֲבוּ דְּמַסְאִיב כֹּלָּא. כִּי בַּמֶּה נֶחְשָׁב הוּא. בַּמֶּה כּו״ם וַדַּאי נֶחְשָׁב אִיהוּ.

60. He said to him: Yet there are many defiled people who are purified. He said to him: Other impurities are different, for they cannot do more THAN DEFILE HIM ON THE OUTSIDE, but one WHO GETS ANGRY is different from them all, for his whole body becomes defiled inside and out, and he contaminates the soul and everything else. Other impurities in the world only defile the body on the outside. Therefore, it is written: "Cease from man, though his breath be in his nostrils (or: 'anger')"; MEANING that he exchanged the Holiness of his Master for his anger. Such an impurity defiles everything, "For in what (Heb. *bameh*) is he to be accounted of," he is certainly considered an altar (Heb. *bamah*) for idol worship.

7. Matzot and the counting of the Omer

A Synopsis

We read that in order to raise Malchut to be connected with the supernal days above, men must stand on their feet to count the Omer. The counting of the Omer is the secret of the male, being connected to the Holy Covenant, so women are exempted from this counting. Rabbi Shimon says that throughout the seven supernal days of Zeir Anpin, one of the lower days of Malchut becomes holy, and this lower day is called a week. When the seven Sfirot of Malchut are sanctified through the 49 supernal Sfirot, the House is prepared so that Malchut can join with Zeir Anpin; then it is called Shavuot. Then the fiftieth day, Binah, rules over the 49 days and, by way of awakening the lower beings, produces the Torah.

61. ת״ח, הַאי אִיהוּ רוּגְזָא דְּאִיהוּ כו״ם, סְטְרָא אַחֲרָא, כְּמָה דְּאֲמָרָן, דְּבָעֵי בַּר נָשׁ לְאִסְתַּמְּרָא מִנֵּיהּ וּלְאִתְפָּרְשָׁא מֵעֲלוֹי, וְע״ד כְּתִיב אֱלֹהֵי מַסֵּכָה לֹא תַעֲשֶׂה לָךְ. לָךְ: בְּגִין לְאַבְאָשָׁא גַרְמָךְ. וּכְתִיב בַּתְרֵיהּ אֶת חַג הַמַּצּוֹת תִּשְׁמֹר. תִּשְׁמֹר: דָּא סִטְרָא דִּקְדוּשָׁה, דְּבָעֵי בַּר נָשׁ לְנַטְרָא לֵיהּ, וְלָא יָחֲלָף לֵיהּ בְּגִין סִטְרָא אַחֲרָא. וְאִי יָחֲלָף לֵיהּ הָא אִיהוּ מַסְאִיב, וְסָאִיב לְכָל מַאן דְּקָרִיב בַּהֲדֵיהּ.

61. Come and behold: this anger is idolatry, the Other Side, as we have said. Thus, a person must guard himself against it and separate from it. Therefore, it is written: "You shall make you no molten Elohim" (Shemot 34:17). "Make you" MEANS you shall NOT harm yourself. And immediately following, it is written: "The feast of unleavened bread shall you keep" (Ibid. 18). "Keep" refers to the side of Holiness that a person should keep and not exchange it for the Other Side. If he exchanges it FOR THE OTHER SIDE, he becomes defiled and defiles whoever comes near him.

62. אֶת חַג הַמַּצּוֹת תִּשְׁמֹר, הַאי אִיהוּ אֲתָר דְּאִקְרֵי שָׁמוֹר. וּבְג״כ כְּתִיב, אֶת חַג הַמַּצּוֹת תִּשְׁמֹר שִׁבְעַת יָמִים תֹּאכַל מַצּוֹת כַּאֲשֶׁר צִוִּיתִיךָ. שִׁבְעַת יָמִים אִלֵּין, לָאו אִינּוּן כְּשִׁבְעַת הַיָּמִים דְּסֻכּוֹת, דְּאִינּוּן עִלָּאִין וְאִלֵּין תַּתָּאִין. וְעַל דָּא, בְּאִינּוּן הַלֵּל גָּמוּר, וּבְהָנֵי לָאו הַלֵּל גָּמוּר, וְעַל

דְּאִינּוּן לְתַתָּא, שִׁבְעַת יָמִים תֹּאכַל מַצּוֹת. מַצֹּת כְּתִיב חָסֵר בְּלָא ו׳,
דְּעַד לָא שָׁרָאן אִינּוּן יוֹמִין עִלָּאִין, רָזָא דְו׳.

62. This is a place called "Shmor" ('observe', 'be careful with', 'guard')
NAMELY MALCHUT THAT IS CALLED "SHMOR": therefore it is written, "The
Festival of Matzot shall you observe, seven days shall you eat matzot as I
have commanded you" (Shemot 34:18). These seven days OF THE FESTIVAL
OF MATZOT, are not like the seven days of Sukkot (holiday of the booths),
BECAUSE THOSE OF SUKKOT are supernal, NAMELY THE SEVEN SFIROT
CHESED, GVURAH, TIFERET, NETZACH, HOD AND MALCHUT OF BINAH
THAT ZACHAR AND NUKVAH ASCENDED AND CLOTHED. BUT THOSE OF
THE FESTIVAL OF MATZOT are of below, NAMELY THE SEVEN SFIROT
CHESED, GVURAH, TIFERET, NETZACH, HOD AND MALCHUT OF
MALCHUT. Therefore DURING THOSE OF SUKKOT we say whole Hallel
AND DURING THOSE OF THE FESTIVAL OF MATZOT, we do not say whole
Hallel. And because they are SEVEN DAYS of below, OF MALCHUT, it is
written "seven days shall you eat Matzot." The word "Matz-t" is found
wanting, namely, missing the letter Vav, TO SHOW, that it was still (the
interval) prior to the dwelling upon them of the supernal days (that
incorporated) the secret of the letter Vav, WHICH IS ZEIR ANPIN.

63. וְאִי תֵּימָא, כֵּיוָן דְּהַאי רָזָא דְּחַג הַמַּצוֹת אִתְקַדָּשׁ, אַמַּאי נַחְתָּא,
דְּהָא תָּנֵינָן מַעֲלִין בַּקֹּדֶשׁ וְלָא מוֹרִידִין, אַמַּאי נַחְתָּא לְתַתָּא בְּאִינּוּן
יוֹמִין תַּתָּאִין.

63. If you ask: if the secret meaning of the feast of unleavened bread has
been sanctified, SINCE ON THE FIRST NIGHT OF PESACH, MALE AND
FEMALE WERE SANCTIFIED AND RECEIVED THE MOCHIN OF SUPERNAL
ABA AND IMA, THAT IS, THEY ROSE TO BE A GARMENT TO THEM, why did
MALCHUT AGAIN go down from Her place? Have we not learned that 'One
should enhance (raise), and not lessen (Lower), (the importance of) holy
matters'? Why did She go FROM ABA AND IMA down to the lower seven
days?

64. ת״ח, כְּתִיב וְכִפֶּר בַּעֲדוֹ וּבְעַד בֵּיתוֹ וְגו׳, מַאן דְּיִכַפֵּר, אִצְטְרִיךְ
לְכַפְּרָא עֲלֵיהּ בְּקַדְמֵיתָא, וּבָתַר עַל בֵּיתֵיהּ. כְּגַוְונָא דָּא, הַאי דַּרְגָּא,

שָׁארֵי לְאִתְקַדְּשָׁא וּלְנָפְקָא בְּקְדוּשָׁה, לְכַפְּרָא עָלֵיהּ, וְכֵיוָן דְּאִיהוּ
אִתְקַדָּשׁ, בָּעֵי לְכַפְּרָא עַל בֵּיתֵיהּ, וּלְקַדְּשָׁא לוֹן, וְעַל דָּא נַחְתָּא לְתַתָּא
לְקַדְּשָׁא בֵּיתֵיהּ. וּבַמֶּה מְקַדֵּשׁ לוֹן, בְּיִשְׂרָאֵל דִּלְתַתָּא. וְכֵיוָן דְּאִלֵּין
מִתְקַדְּשָׁאן, בָּעֵינָן לְסַלְּקָא לָהּ לְעֵילָּא, דְּהָא כַּד בֵּיתָא דְּמַטְרוֹנִיתָא
אִתְקַדָּשַׁת, כְּדֵין סַלְּקַת לְעֵילָּא, לְאִתְקַשְּׁרָא בְּאִינוּן יוֹמִין עִלָּאִין
לְעֵילָּא.

64. Come and behold: it is written, "And make atonement for himself, and for his house" (Vayikra 16:6), TO TEACH that one who atones has to atone for himself first, and afterward for his household. Similarly this grade, NAMELY MALCHUT, started to be sanctified and to emerge into Holiness DURING THE FIRST NIGHT OF PESACH, in order to atone for Herself. As soon as She was sanctified, She had to atone for Her household and sanctify them. Therefore, She came down to sanctify Her house. How are they sanctified? It is through Yisrael below. Once they were sanctified, they need to raise Her up, because when the house of the Queen, WHICH IS MALCHUT, is sanctified, She then rises to be connected with the supernal days above.

65. וְעַל דָּא אֲנָן עַבְדִּין חוּשְׁבָּנָא, בְּקִיּוּמָא עַל קַיְימִין, בְּגִין דְּאִינוּן
יוֹמִין יוֹמִין עִלָּאִין אִינוּן, וְכֵן בְּכָל זִמְנָא דְּעָאל בַּר נָשׁ לְאִינוּן יוֹמִין
עִלָּאִין, בֵּין בִּצְלוֹתָא, בֵּין בְּשַׁבְחָא, אִצְטְרִיךְ לְקַיְימָא עַל רַגְלוֹי, יַרְכִין
וְגוּפָא כַּחֲדָא תַּמָּן. יַרְכִין וְגוּפָא לְקַיְימָא, כִּדְכוּרָא דְּקַיְימָא בְּחֵילֵיהּ,
וְלָא כְּנוּקְבָּא דְּאָרְחָהָא לְמֵיתַב. וְעוֹד בְּגִין שַׁבְחָא דְּעָלְמָא עִלָּאָה.

65. For this purpose, we make a reckoning, MEANING THAT WE COUNT THE OMER, standing on our feet, because the days that we count are supernal days, NAMELY THE SFIROT OF ZEIR ANPIN, WHICH IS MALE. Likewise, every time a person enters the supernal days OF ZEIR ANPIN, both in prayer and in praise, that person must stand on his legs so that the legs and body SERVE there, IN ZEIR ANPIN, EQUALLY together. The legs and body MUST stand like a man who stands with power, and not like a woman who customarily sits. Also, for the praise of the Upper World, ONE SHOULD STAND.

66. וּבְגִין דְּאִיהוּ רָזָא דִּדְכוּרָא, נָשִׁים פְּטוּרוֹת מֵחוּשְׁבָּנָא דָּא, וְלָא מִתְחַיְּיבָן לְמִימְנֵי בַּר דְּכוּרִין, לְאִתְקַשְּׁרָא כָּל חַד כַּדְקָא יָאוֹת. כְּגַוְונָא דָא, יֵרָאֶה כָּל זְכוּרְךָ, דְּכוּרִין, וְלָא נָשִׁין. בְּגִין דְּרָזָא דִּבְרִית בִּדְכוּרָא אִיהוּ, וְלָא בְּנוּקְבָּא, וּבְגִין דְּקַיְּימָא רָזָא לְעֵילָּא, נָשִׁין לָא מִתְחַיְּיבָן.

66. Since THE COUNTING OF THE OMER is the secret of the Male, FOR WE DRAW THE SUPERNAL SFIROT OF ZEIR ANPIN, women are exempted from this counting. Only the men are obligated to count, in order to bind each one properly. Thus, "All you males shall appear" (Shemot 23:17), for the males are obligated to appear, but not the women. This is because the secret of the Covenant is in the Male but not in the Female. Since the secret is above IN THE MALE, IN ZEIR ANPIN, women are not obligated.

67. וְרָזָא אוֹלִיפְנָא הָכָא, דִּבְכָל שִׁבְעַת יוֹמִין מֵאִלֵּין יוֹמִין עִלָּאִין, נַטְלָא קְדוּשָׁא יוֹמָא חַד דְּאִלֵּין תַּתָּאֵי, וְהַאי תַּתָּאָה אִקְרֵי שָׁבוּעַ, דְּאִתְקַדָּשׁ בְּשִׁבְעָה יוֹמִין עִלָּאִין. וְכֵן בְּכָל שִׁבְעָה וְשִׁבְעָה מֵאִינּוּן חַמְשִׁין יוֹמִין, עַד וְלָא עַד בִּכְלַל, וְכַד אִשְׁתְּכָחוּ אַרְבְּעִין וּתְשַׁע יוֹמִין עִלָּאִין, אִשְׁתְּכָחוּ לְתַתָּא שֶׁבַע יוֹמִין, דְּאִתְקַדָּשׁוּ בְּהוּ וְכָל חַד אִקְרֵי שָׁבוּעַ, דְּעָאל בְּאִינּוּן שֶׁבַע. וְעַל דָּא כְּתִיב, שֶׁבַע שַׁבָּתוֹת תְּמִימוֹת תִּהְיֶינָה. בְּגִין דְּאִינּוּן נוּקְבִין, נָקַט קְרָא לִישָׁנָא דְּנוּקְבִין.

67. Here, we have learned a secret: throughout the seven supernal days OF ZEIR ANPIN, one of the lower days OF MALCHUT becomes holy. This lower day OF MALCHUT is called a week, because it is sanctified from the seven supernal days. Similarly, it is so for each and every seven of these fifty supernal days, until (but not including) THE FIFTIETH DAY, MEANING THAT THE FIFTIETH DAY IS NOT INCLUDED AMONG THOSE WHICH AMEND THE LOWER DAYS. When there are 49 supernal days present, then below, IN MALCHUT, HER seven days are sanctified, BECAUSE EACH DAY IS AMENDED BY SEVEN SUPERNAL DAYS. FOR THROUGH CHESED, GVURAH, TIFERET, NETZACH, HOD, YESOD AND MALCHUT OF CHESED OF ZEIR ANPIN, CHESED OF MALCHUT IS AMENDED AND THROUGH CHESED, GVURAH, TIFERET, NETZACH, HOD, YESOD AND MALCHUT OF GVURAH OF ZEIR ANPIN, GVURAH OF MALCHUT IS AMENDED, AND

SO ON IN THIS MANNER. Each one THAT IS AMENDED IN MALCHUT is called a week, because it enters into those seven SUPERNAL DAYS. Therefore, it is written: "Seven complete Shabbatot shall there be," (Vayikra 23:15), WHICH INDICATES THE SEVEN LOWER DAYS, WHICH ARE CHESED, GVURAH, TIFERET, NETZACH, HOD, YESOD AND MALCHUT OF MALCHUT, AS EACH ONE IS CALLED A 'WEEK'. Because they are female, BEING THE SEVEN SFIROT OF MALCHUT, the Torah uses the feminine suffix FOR THEM, AS IS WRITTEN: "SEVEN COMPLETE SHABBATOT SHALL THERE BE" (FEM.).

68. וְכַד אִתְקַדְּשׁוּ בְּהוּ, וּבֵיתָא, מִתַּתְקְנָא לְאִתְחַבְּרָא אִתְּתָא בְּבַעְלָה, כְּדֵין אִקְרֵי חַג שָׁבוּעוֹת, מֵאִינוּן נוּקְבֵי דְּשָׁארוּ עֲלַיְיהוּ אִינוּן יוֹמִין עִלָּאִין, דְּאִתְקַדָּשׁוּ בְּהוּ. וּבג"כ כְּתִיב בְּשָׁבוּעוֹתֵיכֶם, אִינוּן דִּלְכוֹן, וְלָא כְּתִיב בְּשָׁבוּעוֹת, בְּגִין דְּהָכִי נָמֵי מִתְקַדְּשִׁין יִשְׂרָאֵל לְתַתָּא עִמְּהוֹן.

68. When THE SEVEN SFIROT OF MALCHUT are sanctified through them, THE 49 SUPERNAL SFIROT, the House, WHICH IS THE SEVEN SFIROT OF MALCHUT THAT WERE NOT CORRECTED DURING THE FIRST NIGHT OF PESACH, is prepared so a wife would unite with her husband, NAMELY, SO MALCHUT WOULD JOIN WITH ZEIR ANPIN. Then it is called Shavuot (holiday of weeks',) after the females, MEANING THE SEVEN SFIROT OF MALCHUT THAT ARE CALLED 'SEVEN WEEKS', AS MENTIONED ABOVE, over which the supernal days dwell, WHICH ARE THE 49 DAYS OF ZEIR ANPIN, through which they are sanctified. Therefore, it is written "in your (feast of) weeks" (Bemidbar 28:26), WHICH MEANS that they are yours. It is not written 'in the feast of weeks', BECAUSE JUST AS THE SEVEN SFIROT OF MALCHUT WERE SANCTIFIED, WHICH ARE CALLED 'WEEKS', Yisrael below were also sanctified with them, BECAUSE YISRAEL BELOW DEPEND UPON THE SANCTIFICATION OF MALCHUT, FROM WHOM THEY RECEIVE; THEREFORE, IT SAYS: "IN YOUR WEEKS."

69. וְעַל דָּא כַּד מָטוֹן לְתֵשַׁע וְאַרְבְּעִין יוֹמִין, הַהוּא יוֹמָא עִלָּאָה דְּעֲלַיְיהוּ, דְּאִיהוּ יוֹמָא דְּחַמְשִׁין, דְּשַׁלִּיט עַל תִּשְׁעָה וְאַרְבְּעִין יוֹמִין, רָזָא דִּכְלָלָא דְּאוֹרַיְיתָא, בְּתִשְׁעָה וְאַרְבְּעִין אַנְפִּין, וּכְדֵין הַהוּא יוֹמָא עִלָּאָה, יוֹמָא דְּחַמְשִׁין, בְּאִתְעָרוּתָא דִּלְתַתָּא, אַפִּיק אוֹרַיְיתָא כְּלָלָא בְּתִשְׁעָה וְאַרְבְּעִין אַנְפִּין.

69. When we reach 49 days, that supernal day which is above them, the fiftieth day, WHICH IS BINAH, rules over the 49 days – NAMELY THE 49 SFIROT OF ZEIR ANPIN, which are the secret of the entirety of the Torah, MEANING ZEIR ANPIN THAT IS CALLED 'TORAH', that has 49 aspects. Then the supernal day, WHICH IS the fiftieth day, BINAH, by means of the awakening of the lower beings, produces the Torah – WHICH IS ZEIR ANPIN, MEANING THE MOCHIN OF HIS THREE FIRST SFIROT, which is the entirety of the 49 aspects CORRECTED THROUGH THE COUNTING OF THE 49 DAYS.

8. "Even the sparrow has found a home"

A Synopsis

Rabbi Elazar continues the theme of Binah, the fiftieth day, and the creation of the Torah. The sparrows alluded to in the title verse are the birds of the sky, the ultimate meaning of which is 'freedom'. 'Freedom' alludes to Binah and 'sparrow' to Malchut. Since freedom emerges from the fiftieth year, Binah, the Torah that emerges from Binah is called 'freedom'. We are told that Upper freedom is Binah or Jubilee, and Lower freedom is Malchut or the Sabbatical Year – but both are as one.

70. ר' אֶלְעָזָר פָּתַח וְאָמַר, גַּם צִפּוֹר מָצְאָה בַיִת וּדְרוֹר קֵן לָהּ אֲשֶׁר שָׁתָה אֶפְרוֹחֶיהָ אֶת מִזְבְּחוֹתֶיךָ וְגוֹ'. גַּם צִפּוֹר מָצְאָה בַיִת, אִלֵּין צִפֳּרֵי שְׁמַיָא, דְּמִנְהוֹן שַׁוְיָין מָדוֹרֵיהוֹן לְבַר, וּמִנְהוֹן שַׁוְיָין מָדוֹרַיְיהוּ בְּבֵיתָא, כְּגוֹן דְּרוֹר, דְּאִיהוּ עוֹפָא דְּשַׁוֵּי דִּיוּרֵיהּ בְּבֵיתָא דְּכָל בַּר נָשׁ, וְלָא דָּחִיל. אֲמַאי. בְּגִין דְּכֹלָּא קַרְאָן לֵיהּ דְּרוֹר. מַאי דְּרוֹר. חֵירוּ, כד"א, וּקְרָאתֶם דְּרוֹר, וְתַרְגּוּמוֹ חֵירוּ. וְדָא אִיהוּ צִפּוֹר דְּרוֹר. דְּהָא מִיּוֹמָא דְּעָבֵיד קַנָּא בְּבֵיתָא אַפִּיק בְּנִין, מָדוֹרֵיהּ בְּבֵיתָא חַמְשִׁין יוֹמִין, וּלְבָתַר מִתְפַּרְשָׁן אִלֵּין מֵאִלֵּין, וְדָא הוּא עוֹפָא דְּאִקְרֵי דְּרוֹר: חֵירוּ.

70. Rabbi Elazar opened the discussion, saying: "Even the sparrow has found a home, and the swallow (Heb. *dror*) a nest for herself, where she may lay her young. Your altars..." (Tehilim 84:4). "Even the sparrow has found a home": these are the birds of the sky. Some of them nest outside and some of them nest in an abode, THE DWELLING PLACE OF A MAN, like the swallow (Heb. *dror*) that is a bird that places its nest in the home of any man and has no fear. Why? Because everyone calls it '*dror*'. What is *dror*? It is freedom, as it is written: "And proclaim liberty (Heb. *dror*)" (Vayikra 25:10) in its Aramaic translation, freedom. Such is the swallow, from the day it nests in the house and has young, it lives (Heb. *dar*) in the house fifty days, and then they separate from each other. This is the bird that is called '*dror*', WHICH MEANS freedom, WHICH ALLUDES TO BINAH AND MALCHUT IS CALLED SPARROW.

71. תָּא חֲזֵי מַה כְּתִיב, וְקִדַּשְׁתֶּם אֵת שְׁנַת הַחֲמִשִּׁים שָׁנָה וּקְרָאתֶם

דְּרוֹר בָּאָרֶץ. מֵהָכָא נָפְקָא חֵירוּ לְכֹלָּא, וּבְגִין דְּנָפְקָא מִנֵּיהּ חֵירוּ,
אוֹרַיְיתָא דְּנַפְקַת מִנֵּיהּ אִקְרֵי חֵירוּ. וְעַל דָּא כְּתִיב, חָרוּת עַל הַלֻּחֹת,
אַל תִּקְרֵי חָרוּת, אֶלָּא חֵירוּת, וְדָא אוֹרַיְיתָא דְּאִתְקְרֵי חֵירוּת דְּהָא מַה
דְּאַפִּיק יוֹמָא דָּא עִלָּאָה, אִקְרֵי חֵירוּ, וְאִיהוּ חֵירוּ דְּכֹלָּא. וְהַאי יוֹמָא
אִיהוּ חֵירוּ עִלָּאָה, בְּגִין דְּאִית חֵירוּ תַּתָּאָה, וְחֵירוּ עִלָּאָה. ה"א עִלָּאָה,
ה"א תַּתָּאָה. חֵירוּ עִלָּאָה. חֵירוּ תַּתָּאָה שְׁמִטָּה וְיוֹבֵל כַּחֲדָא אִינּוּן.

71. Come and behold: it is written, "And you shall hallow the fiftieth year, and proclaim liberty throughout all the land" (Vayikra 25:10). THE FIFTIETH YEAR IS BINAH, for from here freedom emerges to everyone. Because freedom emerges from it, the Torah that emerges FROM BINAH is called 'freedom' (Heb. *cherut*). Therefore, it is written: "engraved (Heb. *charut*) on the tablets" (Shemot 32:16). Do not pronounce it '*charut*', but rather "*cherut,*" for this is the Torah that is called 'freedom', because whatever this supernal day, WHICH IS BINAH, brings forth is called 'freedom' and it is freedom for all. That day is supernal freedom, because there is upper freedom and lower freedom, MEANING upper *Hei*, WHICH IS BINAH, and lower *Hei*, WHICH IS MALCHUT. Upper freedom and lower freedom, which are Sabbatical year, WHICH IS MALCHUT, and Jubilee, WHICH IS BINAH, are as one, MEANING THAT THEY CLOTHE EACH OTHER. AND THEN BINAH IS CALLED 'UPPER FREEDOM' AND MALCHUT 'LOWER FREEDOM'.

9. The bread of the first fruits

A Synopsis

We learn that two types of bread were eaten by Yisrael: when they left Egypt they ate matzah, the bread from Malchut; when they were in the wilderness they ate manna, the bread from heaven, Zeir Anpin. The question is asked why, now that Yisrael merited the higher bread, was leavened bread not abolished entirely? Why was the offering of the first fruits leavened bread? Rabbi Shimon explains that as soon as Yisrael had eaten matzah, leavened bread could no longer harm them. The chametz is burned on the altar and can have no power over Yisrael. When God gave the Torah to Yisrael He had them taste the supernal bread, manna, through which they knew and observed the teachings of the Torah. After these explanations Rabbi Shimon and his companions meet an old man holding a boy by the hand.

72. תְּרֵין נַהֲמֵי אָכְלוּ יִשְׂרָאֵל, חַד, כַּד נָפְקוּ מִמִּצְרַיִם, אָכְלוּ מַצָּה, לֶחֶם עוֹנִי. וְחַד בְּמַדְבְּרָא, לֶחֶם מִן הַשָּׁמַיִם. דִּכְתִיב הִנְנִי מַמְטִיר לָכֶם לֶחֶם מִן הַשָּׁמַיִם וְעַל דָּא קָרְבָּנָא דְּיוֹמָא דָּא נַהֲמָא אִיהוּ. וְעַל נַהֲמָא, אִתְקְרִיבוּ כָּל שְׁאַר קָרְבָּנִין. דְּנַהֲמָא אִיהוּ עִקָּר, דִּכְתִיב וְהִקְרַבְתֶּם עַל הַלֶּחֶם שִׁבְעַת כְּבָשִׂים וְגוֹ', מִמּוֹשְׁבוֹתֵיכֶם תָּבִיאוּ לֶחֶם תְּנוּפָה וְגוֹ', דְּדָא אִיהוּ נַהֲמָא דְּאִתְחַכְּמוּ בֵּיהּ יִשְׂרָאֵל, חָכְמְתָא עִלָּאָה דְּאוֹרַיְיתָא, וְעָאלוּ בְּאָרְחָהָא.

72. Two types of bread were eaten by Yisrael: when they left Egypt, they ate *matzah*, the bread of affliction, WHICH IS BREAD FROM MALCHUT. And in the wilderness they ate bread from heaven, WHICH IS THE BREAD OF ZEIR ANPIN, THAT IS CALLED 'HEAVEN', as it is written: "Behold, I will rain bread from heaven for you" (Shemot 16:4). Therefore, the offering of this day OF THE FEAST OF WEEKS is bread, and all the other offerings were offered with the bread. The bread is the main part, as is written: "And you shall offer with the bread seven lambs..." (Vayikra 23:18), "You shall bring out of your habitations two wave loaves" (Ibid. 17). For this is the bread with which Yisrael became wise with the supernal Wisdom of the Torah, and entered its ways.

73. הַשְׁתָּא אִית לָן לְאִסְתַּכְּלָא, בַּפֶּסַח נָפְקוּ יִשְׂרָאֵל מִנַּהֲמָא דְּאִתְקְרֵי

חָמֵץ, כְּתִיב, וְלֹא יֵרָאֶה לְךָ חָמֵץ, וּכְתִיב כִּי כָּל אוֹכֵל מַחֲמֶצֶת מַאי
טַעֲמָא. בְּגִין יְקָרָא דְּהַהוּא נַהֲמָא דְּאִתְקְרֵי מַצָּה. הַשְׁתָּא דְּזָכוּ יִשְׂרָאֵל
לְנַהֲמָא עִלָּאָה יַתִּיר לָא יֵאוֹת הֲוָה לְאִתְבַּטְּלָא חָמֵץ, וְלָא אִתְחֲזְיָא
כְּלָל. וְאַמַּאי קָרְבָּנָא דָּא, חָמֵץ הֲוָה, דִּכְתִיב סֹלֶת תִּהְיֶינָה חָמֵץ
תֵּאָפֶינָה. וְתוּ, דְּהַשְׁתָּא בְּיוֹמָא דָּא אִתְבַּטַּל יֵצֶר הָרָע, וְאוֹרַיְיתָא
דְּאִתְקְרֵי חֵירוּ אִשְׁתְּכַחַת.

73. We should now observe that during Pesach, Yisrael came away from the bread that is called 'chametz', as it is written: "And there shall no leavened bread (Heb. *chametz*) be seen" (Shemot 13:7), and: "For whoever eats that which is leavened" (Shemot 12:19). What is the reason THAT THEY ABANDONED CHAMETZ? It is because of the honor of the bread that is called 'matzah'. HE ASKS: Now that Yisrael merited a higher bread, THE BREAD OF ZEIR ANPIN, would it not have been proper for the *chametz* to be abolished and not be seen at all? Why was the offering OF THE FIRST FRUITS BREAD *chametz*, as it is written: "they shall be of fine flour; they shall be baked with leaven" (Vayikra 23:17). Also on this day, the Evil Inclination was negated, WHICH IS THE SECRET OF CHAMETZ, as the Torah, that is called 'freedom', was available. WHY THEN DID THEY BRING CHAMETZ?

74. אֶלָּא, לְמַלְכָּא דַּהֲוָה לֵיהּ בַּר יְחִידָאי, וְחָלַשׁ. יוֹמָא חַד הֲוָה תָּאיב
לְמֵיכַל, אָמְרוּ יֵיכוּל בְּרֵיהּ דְּמַלְכָּא אַסְוָותָא דָּא, וְעַד דְּיֵיכוּל לֵיהּ, לָא
יִשְׁתְּכַח מֵיכְלָא וּמְזוֹנָא אַחֲרָא בְּבֵיתָא. עָבְדוּ הָכִי. כֵּיוָן דְּאָכַל הַהוּא
אַסְוָותָא, אָמַר מִכָּאן וּלְהָלְאָה יֵיכוּל כָּל מַה דְּאִיהוּ תָּאיב, וְלָא יָכִיל
לְנִזְקָא לֵיהּ.

74. HE ANSWERS: THIS IS SIMILAR to a king who had an only son who became ill. One day he wished to eat. They said: Let the king's son take this medicine, but before he eats it, no food whatsoever should be in the house. They did so. After he had taken the medicine, they said: From now on he may eat whatever he desires and it will do him no harm.

75. כָּךְ כַּד נָפְקוּ יִשְׂרָאֵל מִמִּצְרַיִם, לָא הֲוֵי יַדְעֵי עִקָּרָא וְרָזָא

דִּמְהֵימְנוּתָא, אָמַר קוּדְשָׁא בְּרִיךְ הוּא, יִטְעֲמוּן יִשְׂרָאֵל אַסְוָותָא, וְעַד דְּיֵיכְלוּן אַסְוָותָא דָּא, לָא אִתְחֲזֵי לְהוֹן מֵיכְלָא אַחֲרָא. כֵּיוָן דְּאָכְלוּ מַצָּה, דְּאִיהִי אַסְוָותָא לְמֵיעַל וּלְמִנְדַּע בְּרָזָא דִּמְהֵימְנוּתָא. אָמַר קוּדְשָׁא בְּרִיךְ הוּא, מִכָּאן וּלְהָלְאָה אִתְחֲזֵי לוֹן חָמֵץ, וְיֵיכְלוּן לֵיהּ, דְּהָא לָא יָכִיל לְנַזְקָא לוֹן. וְכ"שׁ דְּבְיוֹמָא דְּשָׁבוּעוֹת, אִזְדַּמַן נַהֲמָא עִלָּאָה, דְּאִיהוּ אַסְוָותָא בְּכֹלָּא.

75. Similarly, when Yisrael left Egypt, they did not know the essence and secret of Faith. The Holy One, blessed be He, let Yisrael taste medicine, but while they take this medicine, no other food should be visible to them, NAMELY CHAMETZ. As soon as they had eaten *matzah*, which is a curative to aid in coming into and knowing the secret of Faith, WHICH IS MALCHUT, the Holy One, blessed be He, said: 'From now on, *chametz* is suitable for them and they may eat it, because it can no longer harm them'. And more so on the day of Shavuot, when the supernal bread OF ZEIR ANPIN is present, which is a complete cure!

76. וְע"ד מְקָרְבִין חָמֵץ, לְאִתּוֹקְדָא עַל מַדְבְּחָא. וּמְקָרְבִין תְּרֵין נַהֲמִין אַחֲרָנִין כַּחֲדָא. וְחָמֵץ, אִתּוֹקְדָא בְּנוּרָא דְּמַדְבְּחָא וְלָא יָכִיל לְשַׁלְטָאָה, וּלְנַזְקָא לוֹן לְיִשְׂרָאֵל. וּבְגִינֵי כָּךְ, יִשְׂרָאֵל קַדִּישִׁין אִתְדַּבְּקוּ בֵּיהּ בְּקוּדְשָׁא בְּרִיךְ הוּא, בְּאַסְוָותָא דְּאוֹרַיְיתָא בְּיוֹמָא דָּא. וְאִלְמָלֵי הֲווֹ נַטְרֵי יִשְׂרָאֵל תְּרֵין סִטְרִין דְּנַהֲמֵי אִלֵּין, לָא הֲווֹ עַיְילִין בְּדִינָא לְעָלְמִין.

76. Therefore, we offer *chametz*, WHICH IS THE EVIL INCLINATION, to be burnt on the altar, MEANING THROUGH THE OFFERINGS THAT ARE OFFERED ON THE ALTAR. Two other loaves of bread are offered BY WAVING THEM together. 'OTHERS' MEANS IN ADDITION TO THE OFFERINGS. The *chametz*, WHICH IS THE EVIL INCLINATION, is burned in the fire on the altar, THROUGH THE OFFERINGS, and cannot have power over nor harm Yisrael. Therefore, Yisrael cleave to the Holy One, blessed be He, on this day through the remedy of Torah. If Yisrael observed those two types of bread, NAMELY MATZAH AND THE HOLY SUPERNAL BREAD OF ZEIR ANPIN, they would never be punished.

77. בְּיוֹמָא דְּרֹאשׁ הַשָּׁנָה, דְּאִיהוּ יוֹמָא דְּדִינָא, דְּלָאו אִיהוּ, אֶלָּא

לְאִינוּן דְּלָא נַטְלוּ מֵיכְלָא דְּאַסְוָותָא, וְשָׁבְקוּ לְאַסְוָותָא דְּאוֹרַיְיתָא, בְּגִין מֵיכְלָא אַחֲרָא דְּאִיהוּ חָמֵץ. דְּהָא בְּיוֹמָא דָּא דר״ה, הַהוּא חָמֵץ סַלְקָא, וּמְקַטְרְגָא עֲלֵיהּ דְּבַר נָשׁ, וְאַלְשִׁין עֲלֵיהּ, וְאִיהוּ קַיְּימָא בְּיוֹמָא דָא מְקַטְרְגָא עַל עָלְמָא. וְקוּדְשָׁא בְּרִיךְ הוּא יָתִיב בְּדִינָא עַל כֹּלָא וְדָאִין עָלְמָא.

77. The day of Rosh Hashanah (the Jewish New Year), which is the Day of Judgment, is only for those who did not take the medicine, WHICH IS MATZOT, and abandoned the remedy of Torah. FOR THROUGH THESE TWO REMEDIES the other food IS FIXED, which is *chametz*. On this day of Rosh Hashanah, that *chametz* ascends and accuses the person and slanders him, and is on this day an Accuser of the world. The Holy One, blessed be He, sits in Judgment over everything and judges the world.

78. וּבְגִינֵי כַּךְ כַּד יָהַב קוּדְשָׁא בְּרִיךְ הוּא אוֹרַיְיתָא לְיִשְׂרָאֵל, אַטְעִים לְהוּ מֵהַהוּא נַהֲמָא עִלָּאָה, דְּהַהוּא אֲתָר, וּמִגּוֹ הַהוּא נַהֲמָא, הֲווֹ יַדְעִין וּמִסְתַּכְּלִין בְּרָזֵי דְּאוֹרַיְיתָא, לְמֵהַךְ בְּאֹרַח מֵישָׁר, וְהָא אוּקְמוּהָ מִלָּה אִינוּן חַבְרַיָּיא בְּרָזִין אִלֵּין כִּדְקָאמְרָן.

78. Because of this, when the Holy One, blessed be He, gave the Torah to Yisrael, He had them taste that supernal bread from that place, MALCHUT. Through that bread, they knew and observed the secrets of the Torah so as to walk the right way, and the friends have already explained these matters through these secrets, as we have said.

79. ר׳ שִׁמְעוֹן וְרִבִּי אֶלְעָזָר בְּרֵיהּ, הֲווֹ אַזְלֵי בְּאָרְחָא, וַהֲווֹ אַזְלִין עִמְּהוֹן, רִבִּי אַבָּא וְרִבִּי יוֹסֵי, עַד דַּהֲווֹ אַזְלֵי אִעָרְעוּ בְּחַד סָבָא, וַהֲוָה אָחִיד בִּידֵיהּ חַד יַנּוּקָא, זָקַף עֵינוֹי רִבִּי שִׁמְעוֹן וְחָמָא לֵיהּ, אָמַר לֵיהּ לְרִבִּי אַבָּא וַדַּאי מִלִּין חַדְתִּין אִית גַּבָּן בְּהַאי סָבָא.

79. Rabbi Shimon and Rabbi Elazar, his son, were traveling on the road accompanied by Rabbi Aba and Rabbi Yosi. While they were walking, they met an old man who was holding a young boy by the hand. Rabbi Shimon raised his eyes and saw him. He said to Rabbi Aba: assuredly this old man has new ideas for us.

80. כַּד מָטוּ לְגַבֵּיהּ, אָמַר רִבִּי שִׁמְעוֹן, בְּמָטוּל דְּקוּפְטְרָךְ בְּגַבָּךְ קָא אָתֵית, מַאן אַנְתְּ. אָמַר לֵיהּ, יוּדָאי אֲנָא. אָמַר, מִלִּין חַדְתִּין וַדַּאי יוֹמָא דָּא לְגַבָּךְ, אָמַר לֵיהּ לְאָן הוּא אַרְעָךְ. אָמַר לֵיהּ, דִּיּוּרִי הֲוָה בְּאִינּוּן פְּרִישֵׁי מַדְבְּרָא, דַּהֲוֵינָא, מִשְׁתַּדַּל בְּאוֹרַיְיתָא, וְהַשְׁתָּא אַתֵינָא לְיִשׁוּבָא, לְמֵיתַב בְּצִלָּא דְּקוּדְשָׁא בְּרִיךְ הוּא, בְּאִלֵּין יוֹמֵי דְּיַרְחָא שְׁבִיעָאָה דָּא.

80. When they reached him, Rabbi Shimon said to him: Why do you come with a load tied to your back — MEANING, DO YOU NOT HAVE A DONKEY TO CARRY YOUR LOAD? Who are you? He said to him: I am a Jew. RABBI SHIMON said to him: You must definitely have certain new matters with you today. RABBI SHIMON said to him: Where is your country? He said to him: I used to live among those who retired to the wilderness, for I was endeavoring there in the Torah. Now, I have come to civilization to sit in the shadow of the Holy One, blessed be He, during the days of this seventh month.

81. חַדֵּי ר' שִׁמְעוֹן, אָמַר, נָתִיב דְּוַדַּאי קוּדְשָׁא בְּרִיךְ הוּא שַׁדְרָךְ לְגַבָּן. אָמַר לֵיהּ, חַיֶּיךָ דְּנִשְׁמַע מִלָּה מִפּוּמָךְ, מֵאִינּוּן מִלִּין חַדְתִּין עַתִּיקִין, דִּנְטַעְתּוּן תַּמָּן בְּמַדְבְּרָא, מֵהַאי יַרְחָא שְׁבִיעָאָה. וְאַמַּאי אִתְפְּרַשְׁתּוּן הַשְׁתָּא מִמַּדְבְּרָא, לְמֵיתֵי לְיִשׁוּבָא. אָמַר לֵיהּ הַהוּא סָבָא, בִּשְׁאֶלְתָּא דָּא, יְדַעְנָא דְּחָכְמְתָא גַּבָּךְ, וּמִילָּךְ מָטוּ לִרְקִיעֵי דְּחָכְמְתָא.

81. Rabbi Shimon rejoiced and said: Let us sit, because certainly the Holy One, blessed be He, has sent you to us. He said to him: upon your life, we shall hear a word from your mouth of those new yet old matters that you planted there, in the wilderness, concerning this seventh month. Why did you leave the wilderness to come to civilization? The old sage said to him: From this question I know that you possess wisdom and your words reach the firmament of Wisdom.

10. "And in the wilderness, where you have seen"

A Synopsis

The old sage speaks about the reason that God led Yisrael into the powerful wilderness, the domain of Samael, when they left Egypt. Had they not sinned, God would have crushed Samael so he would have had no power, but because they sinned they spent forty years in the wilderness to fulfill the verse, "And you shall bruise his heel." We are told that the only light is that light which comes out of the darkness. There is no service of God except from out of darkness, and no good except from out of evil. Overall perfection is good and evil together that rise to the good afterward.

82. פָּתַח הַהוּא סָבָא וְאָמַר, וּבַמִּדְבָּר אֲשֶׁר רָאִיתָ אֲשֶׁר נְשָׂאֲךָ יְיָ׳ אֱלֹהֶיךָ כַּאֲשֶׁר יִשָּׂא אִישׁ אֶת בְּנוֹ וְגוֹ׳. הַאי קְרָא הָכִי מִבָּעֵי לֵיהּ, וּבַמִּדְבָּר אֲשֶׁר נְשָׂאֲךָ, מַהוּ רָאִיתָ. אֶלָּא קוּדְשָׁא בְּרִיךְ הוּא דָּבַר לוֹן לְיִשְׂרָאֵל בְּמַדְבְּרָא, מַדְבְּרָא תַקִּיפָא, כְּמָה דִכְתִּיב, נָחָשׁ שָׂרָף וְעַקְרָב וְגוֹ׳. וּמַדְבְּרָא דְּאִיהוּ תַּקִּיף מִשְּׁאָר מַדְבְּרִין בְּעָלְמָא. מַאי טַעְמָא.

82. The old sage opened the discussion, saying: "And in the wilderness, where you have seen how that Hashem your Elohim bore you, as a man bears his son..." (Devarim 1:31). This passage should have said, 'And in the wilderness, where He bore you'. Why does it say, "where you have seen"? HE ANSWERS: The Holy One, blessed be He, spoke to Yisrael in the wilderness, a potent wilderness, as is written: "venomous serpents, and scorpions..." (Devarim 8:15). This wilderness is more potent than any wilderness in the world. What is the reason THAT HE LED YISRAEL THERE?

83. בְּגִין דְּהַהוּא שַׁעֲתָא דְּנָפְקוּ יִשְׂרָאֵל מִמִּצְרַיִם וְאִשְׁתְּלִימוּ לְשִׁתִּין רִבְבָּן, אִתְתַּקַּף מַלְכוּתָא קַדִּישָׁא, וְאִסְתַּלַּק עַל כֹּלָּא, וְסִיהֲרָא אִתְנְהִירַת וּכְדֵין אִתְכַּפְיָא מַלְכוּ חַיָּיבָא סְטְרָא אַחֲרָא. וְאַפִּיק לוֹן קוּדְשָׁא בְּרִיךְ הוּא לְמֵיהַךְ בְּמַדְבְּרָא תַקִּיפָא. דְּאִיהוּ אֲתָר וְשַׁלְטָנוּ דְּסָמָאֵ״ל חַיָּיבָא, דְּאִיהוּ דִילֵיהּ מַמָּשׁ, בְּגִין לְתַבְּרָא תוּקְפֵּיהּ וְחֵילֵיהּ, וּלְכַתְּתָא רֵישֵׁיהּ וּלְאַכְפְיָא לֵיהּ, דְּלָא יִשְׁלוֹט. וְאִלְמָלֵא דְּחָאבוּ יִשְׂרָאֵל, בָּעָא קוּדְשָׁא בְּרִיךְ הוּא לְאַעְבְּרָא לֵיהּ מֵעָלְמָא, וְעַ״ד אַעְבַּר לוֹן בְּאַחֲסַנְתֵּיהּ וְעַדְבֵיהּ וְחוּלְקֵיהּ מַמָּשׁ.

83. HE ANSWERS: When the children of Yisrael left Egypt and reached the number of 600,000, the Holy Malchut was strengthened and rose above everything, and the moon, THAT IS MALCHUT, shone. Then the Evil Malchut, the Other Side, was subdued and the Holy One, blessed be He, took YISRAEL into the powerful wilderness, which is the place and the domain of evil Samael, his very own, in order to break his power and strength, crush his head and subdue him, so he will have no power. If the children of Yisrael had not sinned, the Holy One, blessed be He, planned to remove him from the world. Therefore, He caused YISRAEL to actually pass through his inheritance, lot, and portion.

84. כֵּיוָן דְּחָאבוּ בְּכַמָּה זִמְנִין, נָשִׁיךְ לוֹן חִוְיָא, וּכְדֵין אִתְקַיַּים הוּא יְשׁוּפָךְ רֹאשׁ וְגוֹ'. יִשְׂרָאֵל מָחוּ רֵישֵׁיהּ בְּקַדְמֵיתָא, וְלָא יַדְעֵי לְאִסְתַּמְּרָא מִינֵּיהּ, וּלְבָתַר אִיהוּ מָחָא בְּבַתְרַיְיתָא, וְנָפְלוּ כֻּלְּהוּ בְּמַדְבְּרָא, וְאִתְקַיַּים וְאַתָּה תְּשׁוּפֶנּוּ עָקֵב. וְאַרְבְּעִין שְׁנִין לָקוּ מִנֵּיהּ, לָקֳבֵל מ' מַלְקוּת דְּבֵי דִּינָא.

84. Since they sinned many times, the snake bit them, and then was fulfilled: "He will bruise your head" (Beresheet 3:15). That is, the children of Yisrael hit his head first, but did not know how to guard themselves from him. Afterward, the snake bit them, and they all fell in the wilderness, and, "And you shall bruise his heel" (Ibid.), was fulfilled. For forty years were they smitten by him, corresponding to the forty lashes decreed by court of law.

85. וְעַ"ד כְּתִיב אֲשֶׁר רָאִיתָ, בְּעֵינַיְיהוּ הֲוֵי חֲמָאן לְהַהוּא מָארֵי דְּמַדְבְּרָא, אָזִיל כָּפִית קַמַּיְיהוּ, וְנָטְלֵי אַחֲסַנְתֵּיהּ וְעַדְבֵיהּ. מְנָלָן. מִדִּכְתִיב אָז נִבְהֲלוּ אַלּוּפֵי אֱדוֹם, וְאִלֵּין אִינּוּן נָחָשׁ שָׂרָף וְעַקְרָב. וַאֲנַן אוּף הָכִי אִתְפְּרַשְׁנָא מִישׁוּבָא לְמַדְבְּרָא תַּקִּיפָא, וּלְעַיְינָא תַּמָּן בְּאוֹרַיְיתָא, בְּגִין לְאַכְפְּיָא לְהַהוּא סִטְרָא.

85. Therefore, it is written: "where you have seen," because they saw with their own eyes the landlord of the wilderness walking, bound, before them, and they took his possession and lot. Whence do we know this? From the verse: "Then the chiefs of Edom shall be amazed" (Shemot 15:15), who are

the venomous serpents and scorpions. We too retired from civilization to go into the potent wilderness to be occupied there with Torah, in order to subdue that side.

86. וְתוּ דְּלָא מִתְיַשְּׁבָן מִלֵּי דְּאוֹרַיְיתָא, אֶלָּא תַּמָּן. דְּלֵית נְהוֹרָא אֶלָּא הַהוּא דְּנָפִיק מִגּוֹ חֲשׁוֹכָא, דְּכַד אִתְכַּפְיָא סִטְרָא דָּא, אִסְתַּלָּק קוּדְשָׁא בְּרִיךְ הוּא לְעֵילָּא, וְאִתְיָיקַר בִּיקְרֵיהּ. וְלֵית פּוּלְחָנָא דְּקוּדְשָׁא בְּרִיךְ הוּא, אֶלָּא מִגּוֹ חֲשׁוֹכָא, וְלֵית טוּבָא אֶלָּא מִגּוֹ בִּישָׁא. וְכַד עָאל בַּר נָשׁ בְּאוֹרַח בִּישָׁא, וְשָׁבִיק לֵיהּ, כְּדֵין אִסְתַּלָּק קוּדְשָׁא בְּרִיךְ הוּא בִּיקְרֵיהּ, וְעַל דָּא שְׁלִימוּ דְּכֹלָּא טוֹב וָרַע כַּחֲדָא, וּלְאִסְתַּלָּקָא לְבָתַר בְּטוֹב, וְלֵית טוֹב אֶלָּא הַהוּא דְּנָפַק מִגּוֹ בִּישָׁא. וּבְהַאי טוֹב, אִסְתַּלָּק יְקָרֵיהּ, וְדָא אִיהוּ פּוּלְחָנָא שְׁלִים.

86. The words of Torah become clear only there and the only light is that which comes out of the darkness. When this side is subdued, the Holy One, blessed be He, rises, and His glory becomes greater. There is no service of the Holy One, blessed be He, except from out of darkness and no good except from out of evil. When a person enters the evil way and then leaves it, the Holy One, blessed be He, rises in His glory. Therefore, overall perfection is good and evil together and rising to the good afterward. The only good is good that emerges from evil, and through this good the glory OF THE HOLY ONE, BLESSED BE HE, is elevated. This is perfect service.

87. וַאֲנָן, עַד הַשְׁתָּא יָתִיבְנָא תַּמָּן, כָּל יוֹמֵי שַׁתָּא, בְּגִין לְאַכְפְּיָא בְּמַדְבְּרָא לְהַהוּא סִטְרָא. הַשְׁתָּא דְּמָטָא זִמְנָא דְּפוּלְחָנָא קַדִּישָׁא, דְּסִטְרָא דְּקְדוּשָׁא, אַהֲדַרְנָא לְיִשׁוּבָא דְּתַמָּן אִיהוּ פּוּלְחָנָא דִּילֵיהּ. וְתוּ, דְּהַשְׁתָּא בָּרְ"ה מָטָא זִמְנָא דְּהַהוּא חִוְיָא, לְמִתְבַּע דִּינָא מִקַּמֵי קוּדְשָׁא בְּרִיךְ הוּא, וְתַמָּן אִיהוּ שַׁלִּיט. וּבְגִין כָּךְ נָפַקְנָא מִתַּמָּן וַאֲתֵינָא לְיִשׁוּבָא.

87. We have dwelt there throughout the year until now in order to subdue that Side in the wilderness. Now that the time for the holy service of the side of Holiness has come, we return to civilization, for the service OF THE HOLY ONE, BLESSED BE HE, is there. And also, now, during Rosh

Hashanah, the time has arrived for that serpent to request Judgment before the Holy One, blessed be He. He rules there in the wilderness. Therefore, we left it and came to civilization.

11. "Blow a Shofar at the new moon"

A Synopsis

The old sage continues by saying that at the new moon, on the feast day, Harsh Judgment awakens and strengthens the Other Side; then the whole world is under Judgment, as the moon, Malchut, radiates no light. All the acts of correction that preserve the worlds arise from the lower beings if their deeds are correct; if they are not, Malchut remains without illumination until the wicked are separated from the righteous, and then Judgment awakens. We learn that God gave the Shofar to Yisrael in order to break the covering on the moon that prevents it from shining; the sound of the Shofar arouses Mercy below and Binah above. The upper world, Binah, always gives to the lower world, Malchut, according to its present state, so human gladness below draws supernal gladness. The old sage says that on Yom Kippur Malchut lights up with a supernal illumination from the light of the World to Come, Binah.

88. פָּתַח הַהוּא סָבָא וְאָמַר, תִּקְעוּ בַחֹדֶשׁ שׁוֹפָר בַּכֶּסֶה לְיוֹם חַגֵּנוּ, הַשְׁתָּא אִיהוּ זִמְנָא, לְאִתְעָרָא דִּינָא עִלָּאָה תַּקִּיפָא, וְכַד אִיהוּ אִתְּעַר סִטְרָא אַחֲרָא אִתְתַּקַּף בַּהֲדֵיהּ, וְכֵיוָן דְּאִיהוּ אִתְתַּקַּף, סָלִיק וְחַפְיָא לְסִיהֲרָא, דְּלָא נָהִיר נְהוֹרָא, וְאִתְמַלְיָא מִסִּטְרָא דְּדִינָא. כְּדֵין כָּל עָלְמָא אִיהוּ בְּדִינָא, עִלָּאִין וְתַתָּאִין, וְכָרוֹזָא כָּרִיז בְּכֻלְּהוּ רְקִיעִין, אַתְקִינוּ כֻּרְסְיָא דְּדִינָא, לְמָארֵיהּ דְּכֹלָּא, דְּאִיהוּ בָּעֵי לְמֵידָן.

88. The old sage opened the discussion, saying: "Blow a Shofar at the new moon, at the full moon (lit. 'the covering') on our feast day" (Tehilim 81:4). Now is the time for the supernal Harsh Judgment to awaken. When it awakens, the Other Side is strengthened by it. Once the Other Side grows strong, it rises and covers the moon, WHICH IS MALCHUT, so it does not radiate any light but is filled from the aspect of Judgment. Then the whole world is under Judgment, both higher and lower beings, and a proclamation is issued throughout all the firmaments: "Prepare the Throne of Judgment for the Master over everything, for He wishes to Judge."

89. וְרָזָא הָכָא, וְאִתְנְהִיר לוֹן בְּמַדְבְּרָא, אֲמַאי אִתְּעַר דִּינָא עִלָּאָה בְּיוֹמָא דָּא. אֶלָּא כָּל רָזִין וְכָל קְדוּשִׁין יַקִּירִין, כֻּלְּהוּ תַּלְיִין בִּשְׁבִיעָאָה.

וְהַהוּא שְׁבִיעָאָה עִלָּאָה, עָלְמָא עִלָּאָה, דְּאִקְרֵי עָלְמָא דְּאָתֵי. מִנֵּיהּ
נַהֲרִין כָּל בּוֹצִינִין, וְכָל קְדוּשִׁין, וְכָל בִּרְכָּאן. וְכַד מָטֵי זִמְנָא, לְחַדְתּוּתֵי
בִּרְכָּאן וְקִדּוּשִׁין לְאַנְהֲרָא, בָּעֵא לְאַשְׁגָּחָא בְּכָל תִּקּוּנָא דְּעָלְמִין כֻּלְּהוּ,
וְכָל אִינּוּן תִּקּוּנִים לְאִתְקַיְּימָא כֻּלְּהוֹן, סַלְקִין מִגּוֹ תַּתָּאֵי, אִי אִינּוּן
כַּשְׁרָאן. וְאִי לָא כַּשְׁרָאן, כְּדֵין קַיְּימָא דְּלָא נָהִיר, עַד דְּאִתְפָּרְשָׁן חַיָּיבִין
מִגּוֹ זַכָּאִין, כְּדֵין אִתְּעַר דִּינָא.

89. There is a secret here, which shone upon us in the wilderness. Why did supernal Judgment awaken on this day? HE ANSWERS: All the precious secrets and holy acts stem from the seventh, WHICH IS MALCHUT, and that supernal seventh, which is the supernal world that is called 'the World to Come', NAMELY BINAH. All the candles, sanctifications and blessings shine ON MALCHUT from there. When the time arrives to renew the blessings and holy acts so they will shine, one should observe the corrections of all the worlds, IN ORDER TO RENEW THE BLESSINGS AND SANCTIFICATIONS. All the acts of correction that preserve the worlds rise from the lower beings if their deeds are suitable. If they are not right, MALCHUT remains without illumination until the wicked are separated from the righteous, and then Judgment awakens.

90. וּמֵהַהוּא דִּינָא, אִתְתָּקַף סְטְרָא אַחֲרָא, וְאִשְׁתְּכַח מְקַטְרְגָא, בְּגִין
דְּיִנָּתְנוּן לֵיהּ אִינּוּן, חַיָּיבַיָּא. בְּגִין דְּעָלֵיהּ כְּתִיב, וּלְכָל תַּכְלִית הוּא
חוֹקֵר. וְחַפְיָא לְסִיהֲרָא, אֲמַאי לָא מָסְרָא לוֹן בִּידָא דִּמְקַטְרְגָא. בְּגִין
דְּלֵית תִּיאוּבְתֵּיהּ דְּקוּדְשָׁא בְּרִיךְ הוּא, לְאוֹבָדָא לְעוֹבָדֵי יְדוֹי.

90. From that Judgment, the Other Side is strengthened, and the Accuser is present so that the wicked be given over to him, for it is written of him: "And searches out all perfection" (Iyov 28:3), and covers the moon so it will not shine. Why does He not give over THE WICKED to the Accuser? Because the Holy One, blessed be He, does not wish to destroy the works of His hands.

91. וְהַהוּא סְטְרָא אַחֲרָא, קַיְּימָא קְלִיפָא תַּקִּיפָא, דְּלָא יָכִיל לְאִתְבְּרָא,
בַּר בְּהַהוּא עֵיטָא דְּקוּדְשָׁא בְּרִיךְ הוּא יָהִיב לְיִשְׂרָאֵל, דִּכְתִּיב תִּקְעוּ

בַּחֹדֶשׁ שׁוֹפָר בַּכֶּסֶה לְיוֹם חַגֵּנוּ. בְּגִין לְתַבְרָא הַהוּא כֶּסֶה דְּאִתְחַפְיָא סִיהֲרָא, וְלָא נָהִיר.

91. In the Other Side there is a hard Klipah that is impossible to break, except with the counsel the Holy One, blessed be He, gave the children of Yisrael, as written: "Blow a Shofar at the new moon, at the full moon (lit. 'the covering') on our feast day" (Tehilim 81:4) in order to break that cover with which the moon is covered, WHICH IS MALCHUT, so it does not shine.

92. וְכַד מִתְעֲרֵי יִשְׂרָאֵל לְתַתָּא בְּשׁוֹפָר, הַהוּא קָלָא דְּנָפְיק מִשּׁוֹפָר, בָּטַשׁ בַּאֲוִירָא, וּבָקַע רְקִיעִין, עַד דְּסַלְקָא לְגַבֵּי הַהוּא טִנָרָא תַּקִּיפָא, דְּחָפֵי לְסִיהֲרָא, אַשְׁגַּח, וְאַשְׁכַּח אִתְעֲרוּתָא דְרַחֲמֵי, כְּדֵין הַהוּא דְּסַלִיק וְקַיְּימָא לְעֵילָא, אִתְעַרְבָּב. כְּדֵין הַהוּא קָלָא קַיְּימָא, וְאַעֲבַר הַהוּא דִּינָא, וְכֵיוָן דִּלְתַתָּא אִתְעָרוּ רַחֲמֵי, הָכִי נָמֵי לְעֵילָא, אִתְּעַר שׁוֹפְרָא אַחֲרָא עִלָּאָה, וְאַפִּיק קָלָא דְּאִיהוּ רַחֲמֵי, וְאִתְעָרְעוּ קָלָא בְּקָלָא, רַחֲמֵי בְּרַחֲמֵי, וּבְאִתְעֲרוּתָא דִּלְתַתָּא, אִתְּעַר הָכִי נָמֵי לְעֵילָא.

92. When the children of Yisrael awaken below by the blow of the Shofar, the sound that emanates from the Shofar blasts the air and splits firmaments until it rises to that hard rock, NAMELY THE OTHER SIDE, that covers the moon. It observes and brings forth an awakening of Mercy. Then THE OTHER SIDE that rises and remains above COVERING THE MOON is confounded. That sound stands and removes that Judgment FROM MALCHUT. Since Mercy has awakened below, IN MALCHUT, another supernal shofar also awakens above, WHICH IS BINAH, and produces a sound, NAMELY THE MOCHIN OF ZEIR ANPIN THAT IS CALLED 'SOUND', which is Mercy. Sound meets sound, mercy meets mercy, because by the lower awakening there is also an awakening above.

93. וְאִי תֵּימָא, הֵיךְ יָכִיל קָלָא דִּלְתַתָּא, אוֹ אִתְעֲרוּתָא דִּלְתַתָּא לְאִתְעֲרָא, הָכִי נָמֵי. תָּא חֲזֵי, עָלְמָא תַּתָּאָה, קַיְּימָא לְקַבְּלָא תָּדִיר, וְהוּא אִקְרֵי אֶבֶן טָבָא. וְעָלְמָא עִלָּאָה לָא יָהִיב לֵיהּ, אֶלָּא כְּגַוְונָא דְּאִיהוּ קַיְּימָא. אִי אִיהוּ קַיְּימָא בִּנְהִירוּ דְּאַנְפִּין מִתַּתָּא, כְּדֵין הָכִי

-57-

נַהֲרִין לֵיהּ מִלְּעֵילָא. וְאִי אִיהוּ קַיְּימָא בַּעֲצִיבוּ, יַהֲבִין לֵיהּ דִּינָא בְּקַבְלֵיהּ.

93. You may ask how a sound below or an awakening below awaken THAT WHICH CORRESPONDS TO IT ABOVE. Come and behold: the Lower World, WHICH IS MALCHUT, is always ready to receive and is called a 'precious stone'. The Upper World, WHICH IS BINAH, gives it according to its state. If its state is of a shiny countenance from below, in the same manner it is shone upon from above, but if it is in sadness, it is correspondingly given Judgment.

94. כְּגַוְונָא דָא, עִבְדוּ אֶת יְיָ' בְּשִׂמְחָה. חֶדְוָה דב"נ, מָשִׁיךְ לְגַבֵּיהּ חֶדְוָה אַחֲרָא עִלָּאָה. הָכִי נָמֵי הַאי עָלְמָא תַּתָּאָה, כְּגַוְונָא דְּאִיהִי אִתְעַטְּרַת, הָכִי אַמְשִׁיךְ מִלְּעֵילָא. בג"כ מְקַדְּמֵי יִשְׂרָאֵל, וְאִתְּעָרֵי בַּשׁוֹפָר קָלָא דְּאִיהוּ כָּלִיל בְּאֶשָּׁא וּמַיָּא וְרוּחָא, וְאִתְעָבֵיד חַד, וְסַלְקָא לְעֵילָא, וּבָטַשׁ בְּהַאי אֶבֶן טָבָא, וְאִצְטְבַע בְּאִינּוּן גַּוְונִין דְּהַאי קָלָא, וּכְדֵין כְּמָה דְּאִתְחֲזִיאַת, הָכִי מָשִׁיךְ מִלְּעֵילָא.

94. Similarly, "Serve Hashem with gladness" (Tehilim 100:2), because human gladness draws another, supernal gladness. Thus, just as the Lower World, NAMELY MALCHUT, is crowned, so it draws from above. Therefore, the children of Yisrael are early to rouse with the shofar a sound, which is combined of fire, water and air – NAMELY, THE CENTRAL COLUMN, WHICH IS COMBINED OF THREE COLUMNS. They become one, which rises and strikes that precious stone that is colored with these three colors – WHICH ARE WHITE, RED AND GREEN, WHICH ARE THREE COLUMNS COMBINED in this sound – and then it draws from above as it deserves.

95. וְכֵיוָן דְּאִתַּקְּנַת בְּהַאי קָלָא. רַחֲמֵי נַפְקֵי מִלְּעֵילָא, וְשַׁרְיָין עֲלָה, וְאִתְכְּלִילָא בְּרַחֲמֵי, מִתַּתָּא וּמִלְּעֵילָא. וּכְדֵין אִתְעַרְבַּב סִטְרָא אַחֲרָא. וְאִתְחַלָּשׁ תֻּקְפֵּיהּ, וְלָא יָכִיל לְקַטְרְגָא. וְהַאי אֶבֶן טָבָא, קַיְּימָא בִּנְהִירוּ דְּאַנְפִּין, מִכָּל סִטְרִין, בִּנְהִירוּ דִּלְתַתָּא, וּבִנְהִירוּ דִּלְעֵילָא.

95. Once MALCHUT has been perfected with this sound FROM BELOW,

Mercy emerges from above and dwells upon Her, and She becomes included in Mercy from below and above. Then the Other Side is confounded, and its power is weakened and it cannot accuse. This precious stone, WHICH IS MALCHUT, remains with radiant countenance in every direction, with illumination from below and illumination from above.

96. אֵימָתַי קַיְימָא בִּנְהִירוּ דִּלְעֵילָא, הֲוֵי אוֹמֵר בְּיוֹמָא דְּכִפּוּרֵי. וּבְיוֹמָא דְּכִפּוּרֵי אִתְנְהִיר הַהוּא אֶבֶן טָבָא, בִּנְהִירוּ דִּלְעֵילָא, מִגּוֹ נְהִירוּ דְּעָלְמָא דְּאָתֵי, וּכְדֵין מְתַקְּנִין יִשְׂרָאֵל לְתַתָּא חַד שָׂעִיר, וּמְשַׁדְּרִין לְהַאי מַדְבְּרָא תַּקִּיפָא, דְּאִיהוּ שַׁלְטָא עֲלֵיהּ.

96. When does She remain with the illumination from above? On Yom Kippur (Day of Atonement), for on Yom Kippur that precious stone is lit up, NAMELY MALCHUT, with a supernal illumination from the light of the world to come, WHICH IS BINAH. Then the children of Yisrael prepare a goat and send it to this potent wilderness, which rules over it.

12. The Kingdom of Heaven is divided by two points

A Synopsis

We are told that the central point of the desolate world is the Other Side, and the central point of the inhabited world is the holy side, where Jerusalem is found. The Kingdom of Heaven stands on two points: one is Jerusalem, and the other is the terrestrial Garden of Eden. In the middle of that Garden is a hidden point into which a pillar is inserted from below; from there water flows that separates to the four directions of the world.

97. וְהַהוּא סְטְרָא אַחֲרָא, אִיהוּ נְקוּדָה אֶמְצָעִיתָא דְּחָרִיבוּ דְּעָלְמָא, בְּגִין דְּכָל חָרִיבוּ וְשָׁמְמוֹן מִנֵּיהּ, הַהוּא סְטְרָא אַחֲרָא שַׁלִּיט עֲלֵיהּ. וּנְקוּדָה אֶמְצָעִיתָא דְּכָל יְשׁוּבָא, סְטְרָא דִּקְדוּשָׁה אִיהוּ, וְעַל דָּא, קַיְּימָא יְרוּשָׁלַם בְּאֶמְצָעִיתָא דְּכָל יְשׁוּבָא דְּעָלְמָא.

97. That Other Side is the central point of the portion of the desolate world, because the Other Side has power over all destruction and desolation THAT IS IN THE WORLD. The central point of that portion of the inhabited world is the holy side, WHICH IS MALCHUT. Therefore, Jerusalem is in the center of the inhabited world, WHICH IS THE SECRET OF MALCHUT.

98. בִּתְרֵין נְקוּדִין אִתְפְּרָשַׁת מַלְכוּ שְׁמַיָּא, סְטְרָא דִּקְדוּשָׁא, חַד דִּילָהּ, וְחַד דְּעָלְמָא דְּאָתֵי, נְקוּדָה עִלָּאָה טְמִירָאָה, וְעַ"ד קַיְּימָא בִּתְרֵין נְקוּדִין: נְקוּדָה דִּילָהּ קַיְּימָא תְּחוֹתָהּ, יְרוּשָׁלַם, אֶמְצָעִיתָא דְּכָל יְשׁוּבָא. נְקוּדָא דְּנַטְלָא מֵאִימָּא עִלָּאָה טְמִירָא, אִיהוּ ג"ע דְּאַרְעָא, דְּקַיְּימָא בְּאֶמְצָעִיתָא דְּכָל עָלְמָא, לְכָל סְטְרִין, דְּחָרִיבוּ וְיִשּׁוּבָא, וְכָל סְטְרִין דְּעָלְמָא.

98. The Kingdom of Heaven, the side of Holiness, is divided by two points: one of its own, and another that it received from the world to come, WHICH IS BINAH, WHICH IS a supernal, hidden point. Therefore, the kingdom stands on two points. Its own point is under it, which is Jerusalem, which is the center of the whole civilization. The hidden point that it received from supernal Ima, the World to Come, is the terrestrial Garden of Eden that is

located in the center of the world in all its aspects, those of desolation and habitation, and all the aspects of the world.

99. וְע״ד, בְּאֶמְצָעִיתָא דְּגַן עֵדֶן, קַיְּימָא נְקוּדָה חֲדָא עִלָּאָה טְמִירָא וּגְנִיזָא, דְּלָא יְדִיעַ. וְחַד עַמּוּדָא, נָעִיץ מִתַּתָּא לְעֵילָא, גּוֹ הַהִיא נְקוּדָה, וּמִתַּמָּן נַבְעֵי מַיָּא, דְּאִתְפְּרִישׁוּ לְאַרְבַּע סִטְרֵי עָלְמָא. אִשְׁתְּכָחוּ תְּלַת נְקוּדִין בְּעָלְמָא, דְּקַיְּימָאן דָּא עַל דָּא, כְּגַוְונָא דִּתְלַת נְקוּדִין דְּאוֹרַיְיתָא.

99. Therefore, in the middle of the Garden of Eden there is a supernal point, covered and concealed, since it is unknown. A pillar is inserted from below up within that point, and from there gushes water that separates to the four directions of the world. So we find that there are three points in the world one on top of the other, like the three points in the Torah!

13. Two goats

A Synopsis

The old sage wonders why Yisrael sent two goats for sacrifice: one for Azazel in the wilderness, and one to God. Rabbi Shimon explains that the Slanderer will think he ate from His meal and will not know of the other joyous meal prepared for God and those He loved. Even when Yisrael are in exile, when they pray Malchut ascends before God on Yom Kippur and asks mercy for her children; then God declares all His vengeance against Edom, and the Slanderer is removed from the world. Because of this, the children of Yisrael are free and joyful. Rabbi Shimon tells why a young goat is sacrificed rather than a grown one. He speaks about 'atonement' (Kippur) and says that it is so called because it cleanses all impurity from a person so that God forgives him. We read that there are five deprivations on Yom Kippur – eating and drinking, washing, anointing, wearing shoes, and having marital relations. These deprivations are so that the person may be helped by the five supernal aspects – Chesed, Gvurah, Tiferet, Netzach and Hod.

100. תָּא חֲזֵי, הַהוּא שָׂעִיר דִּמְשַׁדְּרִין יִשְׂרָאֵל לַעֲזָאזֵל, לְהַהוּא מַדְבְּרָא, בְּגִין לְמֵיהַב חוּלָקָא לְהַהוּא סִטְרָא אַחֲרָא, לְאִתְעַסְּקָא בַּהֲדֵיהּ. וְאִי תֵּימָא, תְּרֵין שְׂעִירִין אֲמַאי הָכָא, חַד לַיְיָ׳ וְחַד לְהַהוּא סִטְרָא אַחֲרָא. תֵּינַח הַהוּא שָׂעִיר דְּסִטְרָא אַחֲרָא. לַיְיָ׳ אֲמַאי.

100. Come and behold: Yisrael sent the goat to Azazel, to the wilderness, so as to give a portion to the Other Side with which to be occupied. You may ask why there are two goats here, one for Hashem and one for the Other Side. It is understandable TO SEND the goat of the Other Side TO AZAZEL, but why the goat to Hashem?

101. אֶלָּא לְמַלְכָּא דַּהֲוָה אַרְגִּיז עַל בְּרֵיהּ, קָרָא לְסַנְטִירָא, הַהוּא דְּעָבֵיד דִּינָא בִּבְנֵי נָשָׁא תָּדִיר, בְּגִין דִּיזְדַּמַּן לְמֶעְבַּד דִּינָא בִּבְרֵיהּ. הַהוּא סַנְטִירָא חֲדֵי, וְעָאל בְּבֵי מַלְכָּא לְמֵיכַל תַּמָּן, כֵּיוָן דְּאַשְׁגַּח בֵּיהּ בְּרֵיהּ, אָמַר, וַדַּאי לָא עָאל סַנְטִירָא דָּא בְּבֵי אַבָּא, אֶלָּא בְּגִין דְּאַרְגִּיז מַלְכָּא עָלַי. מָה עָבַד, אָזַל וְאִתְפַּיַּיס בַּהֲדֵיהּ. כֵּיוָן דְּאִתְפַּיַּיס בַּהֲדֵיהּ, פָּקִיד מַלְכָּא לְמֶעְבַּד סְעוּדָתָא עִלָּאָה לֵיהּ וְלִבְרֵיהּ, וּפָקִיד דְּלָא יָדַע

בֵּיהּ הַהוּא סַנְטִירָא. לְבָתַר עָאל הַהוּא סַנְטִירָא. אָמַר מַלְכָּא הַשְׁתָּא אִי יִנְדַּע דָּא, מִסְּעוּדָתָא עִלָּאָה דְּאַתְקִינִית לִי וְלִבְרִי, יִתְעַרְבַּב פָּתוֹרָא. מָה עֲבַד. קָרָא לַמְמֻנָּא עַל סְעוּדָתָא, אָמַר לֵיהּ, אַתְקִין מִדִּי, וּתְשַׁוֵּי קַמָּאי, וּתְשַׁוֵּי קַמֵּיהּ דְּהַהוּא סַנְטִירָא, בְּגִין דְּיַחֲשִׁיב דְּסָעִיד קַמָּאי מִדִּילִי, וְלָא יִנְדַּע בְּהַהִיא סְעוּדָתָא יַקִּירָא דְּחֶדְוָה דִּילִי וְדִבְרִי, וְיִטּוֹל הַהוּא חוּלָקָא וְיֵזִיל לֵיהּ, וְיִתְפְּרַשׁ מֵחֶדְוָה דִּסְעוּדָתָא דִּילָן. וְאִי לָאו דְּמַלְכָּא עָבִיד הָכִי, לָא יִתְפְּרַשׁ הַהוּא סַנְטִירָא מִבֵּי מַלְכָּא.

101. HE ANSWERS: IT IS SIMILAR to a king who was angry with his son. He summoned a bailiff, who regularly meted out justice to people, in order to come and punish his son. The bailiff rejoiced and entered the king's palace to eat there. As soon as the son saw him, he thought: Certainly, the only reason this bailiff has come to my father's palace is because the king is angry with me. What did he do? He tried to please him. Once he pleased him, the king ordered a magnificent feast for himself and his son, and commanded that the bailiff would not know of it. Afterward, the bailiff came. The king thought: Now if he knows of the grand feast that I prepared for my son and myself, there will be confusion at the table. What did he do? He called the butler in charge over the feast and told him, 'prepare something to put before me and the bailiff, so that the bailiff would think that he dined with me, and would not know about that other precious feast for me and my son. He would then take that portion and leave, and disengage from our joyous feast.' If the king had not done this, that bailiff would not have left the king's palace.

102. כָּךְ אָמַר קוּדְשָׁא בְּרִיךְ הוּא לְיִשְׂרָאֵל, אַזְמִינוּ תְּרֵין שְׂעִירִין, חַד לִי וְחַד לְהַהוּא דִּלְטוֹרָא, בְּגִין דְּיַחֲשִׁיב דְּמִסְּעוּדָתָא דִּילִי קָאֲכִיל, וְלָא יִנְדַּע בִּסְעוּדָתָא דְּחֶדְוָה אַחֲרָא דִּילָן, וְיִסַּב הַהוּא חוּלָקָא, וְיֵזִיל לְאָרְחֵיהּ, וְיִתְפְּרַשׁ מִבֵּיתִי. כֵּיוָן דְּאִמָּא עִלָּאָה, עָלְמָא דְּאָתֵי, אָתֵי לְמִשְׁרֵי גּוֹ הֵיכְלָא דְּעָלְמָא תַּתָּאָה, לְאַשְׁגָּחָא עָלָהּ בִּנְהִירוּ דְּאַנְפִּין, דִּין הוּא דְּלָא יִשְׁתְּכַח הַהוּא דִּלְטוֹרָא, וְלָא מָארֵי דְּדִינִין לְקַמֵּיהּ, כַּד אַפִּיק כָּל בִּרְכָאן, וְאַנְהִיר לְכֹלָּא. וְכָל הַהוּא חִירוּ יִשְׁתְּכַח, וְיִשְׂרָאֵל נַטְלֵי מֵאִינּוּן בִּרְכָאן.

102. So did the Holy One, blessed be He, say to Yisrael: 'Prepare two goats, one for Me and one for that Slanderer', NAMELY THE OTHER SIDE, 'so that he will think that he ate from My meal and will not know of the other, our own joyous meal. Let him take that portion and go his way and depart from My house.' Since supernal Ima, which is the World to Come, NAMELY BINAH, came to dwell in the sanctuary of the Lower World, to observe it with a radiant face, it is only right that the slanderer would not be present, nor the plaintiffs, when He takes out all the blessings and illuminates everything. And all manner of freedom is available IN MALCHUT, and Yisrael receive those blessings.

103. דְּהָא כַּד עָלְמָא דְּאָתֵי, עָאל לְהֵיכָלָא דְּעָלְמָא תַּתָּאָה, וְאַשְׁכַּח דְּחֶדֵי עָלְמָא תַּתָּאָה עִם בְּנוֹי בְּהַהִיא סְעוּדָתָא עִלָּאָה, כְּדֵין אִיהוּ בָּרִיךְ פָּתוֹרָא, וְעָלְמִין כֻּלְּהוּ מִתְבָּרְכִין, וְכָל חֵידוּ וְכָל נְהִירוּ דְּאַנְפִּין אִשְׁתְּכָחוּ תַּמָּן. הה״ד לִפְנֵי יְיָ׳ תִּטְהָרוּ.

103. When the world to come, WHICH IS BINAH, enters the sanctuary of the Lower World, WHICH IS MALCHUT, and the Lower World rejoices in its children in that magnificent feast THAT IS DRAWN FROM BINAH, then BINAH blesses the table. All the worlds are blessed and every kind of joy and shining face are present there. This is what is written: "that you may be clean...before Hashem" (Vayikra 16:30).

104. כְּתִיב וְנָתַן אַהֲרֹן עַל שְׁנֵי הַשְּׂעִירִים גּוֹרָלוֹת גּוֹרָל אֶחָד לַיְיָ׳ וְגוֹרָל אֶחָד לַעֲזָאזֵל. דָּא אִיהוּ הַהוּא חֶדְוָה דְּהַהוּא דִלְטוֹרָא, בְּגִין דְּקוּדְשָׁא בְּרִיךְ הוּא יָטִיל עִמֵּיה גּוֹרָל, וְזַמִּין לֵיה, וְלָא יָדַע דְּנוּר דָּלִיק אַטִיל עַל רֵישֵׁיה, וְעַל עַמָּא דִילֵיה, כד״א כִּי גֶחָלִים אַתָּה חוֹתֶה עַל רֹאשׁוֹ.

104. It is written: "And Aaron shall cast lots on the two goats; one lot for Hashem and the other lot for Azazel" (Ibid. 8). This is the joy of the Slanderer, that the Holy One, blessed be He, casts lots with him and invites him TO TAKE THE SCAPEGOAT. But he does not realize that He pours a flaming fire on his head and on his people, as is written: "For You will heap coals of fire upon his head" (Mishlei 25:22).

105. וְסִימָנָךְ, אַף לֹא הֵבִיאָה אֶסְתֵּר הַמַּלְכָּה עִם הַמֶּלֶךְ אֶל הַמִּשְׁתֶּה

אֲשֶׁר עָשְׂתָה כִּי אִם אוֹתִי. וּכְתִיב, וַיֵּצֵא הָמָן בַּיּוֹם הַהוּא שָׂמֵחַ וְטוֹב
לֵב. בְּהַהוּא חוּלָקָא דְּנָטִיל, וְאָזִיל לֵיהּ. וּלְבָתַר כַּד אָתֵי מַלְכָּא עִלָּאָה,
לְבֵי מַטְרוֹנִיתָא, מַטְרוֹנִיתָא תַּבְעַת עֲלָהָא, וְעַל בְּנָהָא, וְעַל עַמָּא מִן
מַלְכָּא.

105. You may derive this FROM THE PASSAGE: "Even Ester the queen let no one come in with the king to the banquet that she prepared but myself" (Esther 5:12), and: "Then Haman went out that day joyful and with a glad heart" (Ibid. 9) with that portion that he received, and went his way. Afterward, when the Supernal King came to the Queen's palace, the Queen asked for Herself, for Her children and for the people of the King.

106. וַאֲפִילוּ בְּזִמְנָא דְּיִשְׂרָאֵל בְּגָלוּתָא, וְצַלּוֹ צְלוֹתִין בְּכָל יוֹמָא, אִיהִי
סַלְקַת בְּיוֹמָא דָא, לְקָמֵי מַלְכָּא עִלָּאָה, וְתַבְעַת עַל בְּנָהָא. וּכְדֵין
אִתְגְּזָרוּ, כָּל אִינּוּן נוּקְמִין, דְּזַמִּין קוּדְשָׁא בְּרִיךְ הוּא לְמֶעְבַּד עִם אֱדוֹם,
וְאִתְגְּזַר הֵיךְ זַמִּין דַּלְטוֹרָא דָא לְאִתְעַבְּרָא מֵעָלְמָא, כד"א בִּלַּע הַמָּוֶת
לָנֶצַח.

106. Even when the children of Yisrael are in exile and pray daily, MALCHUT ascends on this day, YOM KIPPUR, before the King and asks for Her children. Then all vengeance that the Holy One, blessed be He, is going to bring against Edom are decreed, and it is decreed how this Slanderer will be removed from this world, as is written: "He will destroy death forever" (Yeshayah 25:8).

107. וְסִימָנָךְ, בְּזִמְנָא דְּגָלוּתָא כִּי נִמְכַּרְנוּ אֲנִי וְגו'. כִּי אֵין הַצַּר שׁוֶֹה
בְּנֵזֶק הַמֶּלֶךְ. מַאי בְּנֵזֶק הַמֶּלֶךְ. כד"א, וְהִכְרִיתוּ אֶת שְׁמֵנוּ מִן הָאָרֶץ
וּמַה תַּעֲשֵׂה לְשִׁמְךָ הַגָּדוֹל. דְּהָא שְׁמָא עִלָּאָה, לָא אִתְקַיַּים בְּקִיּוּמֵיהּ,
וְדָא אִיהוּ בְּנֵזֶק הַמֶּלֶךְ.

107. Bear in mind that it is written about the time of exile: "For we are sold, I and my people...since the affliction would not have equaled the king's damage" (Esther 7:4). What is "the king's damage?" It is as you say, "And

cut off our name from the earth, and what will You do for Your Great Name?" (Yehoshua 7:9) because the Great Name will no longer be maintained, and this is the king's damage!

108. וּכְדֵין וְהָמָן נִבְעַת מִלִּפְנֵי הַמֶּלֶךְ וְהַמַּלְכָּה כְּדֵין, נְהִירוּ דְּאַנְפִּין, וְכָל חֵידוּ אִשְׁתְּכַח, וְיִשְׂרָאֵל נַפְקֵי לְחֵירוּ, בְּהַהוּא יוֹמָא. כְּדֵין מֵהַהוּא יוֹמָא וּלְהָלְאָה, חֵירוּ וְחֶדְוָה בְּאִתְגַּלְיָא, לְשַׁלְטָאָה עֲלַיְיהוּ, כְּדֵין בָּעֵי לְמֶחֱדֵי עִמְּהוֹן, מִכָּאן וּלְהָלְאָה, כְּמָה דְּיָהֲבוּ לֵיהּ חוּלָקָא לְאִתְפָּרְשָׁא מִנְּהוֹן, הָכִי נָמֵי יַהֲבִין לִשְׁאָר עַמִּין, לְאִתְפָּרְשָׁא מִנְּהוֹן לְתַתָּא.

108. "Then Haman – WHO IS THE OTHER SIDE – was struck with terror before the king and the queen" (Esther 7:6). Then every shining face and every joy is present, and the children of Yisrael go out free on that day – YOM KIPPUR. From that day and onward, freedom and joy openly rule over them and He wishes to rejoice with them. From here on, just as a portion is given TO THE OTHER SIDE, so that he shall depart FROM YISRAEL, a portion is also given to the other nations, so that they depart FROM YISRAEL below.

109. תָּא חֲזֵי, מַה הוּא רָזָא דְּקָרְבְּנָא, לְקָרְבָא שָׂעִיר, וְלָא מִלָּה אַחֲרָא. וְאַמַּאי שָׂעִיר בְּרֹאשׁ חֹדֶשׁ, וְהָכָא נָמֵי שָׂעִיר. אֶלָּא אִי תֵּימָא בְּגִין דְּאִיהוּ סִטְרָא דִּילֵיהּ יָאוֹת. אַמַּאי לָא הֲוֵי עֵז.

109. Come and behold: what is the secret meaning of offering a goat rather than something else? Why is it that on the first day of the month we offer a goat, and also here ON YOM KIPPUR? If you say that it is because the goat is of its aspect, it is well, but why not an adult goat (Heb. *ez*), BUT A YOUNG GOAT (HEB. *SEIR*), WHICH IS SMALL?

110. אֶלָּא מִלָּה דָּא אִצְטְרִיךְ, וְאִיהִי אִשְׁתְּכַחַת לְמָארֵיהוֹן דְּחָרָשִׁין, דְּכָל עוֹבָדַיְיהוּ בְּמָה דְּלָא אִתְחַבַּר בְּנוּקְבָּא. וְעַ״ד שָׂעִיר לָא אִתְחַבַּר בְּנוּקְבָּא, בְּסִטְרִין דִּילֵיהּ כֻּלְּהוּ. עֵז כַּד אִתְחַבַּר בְּנוּקְבָּא. וּבְגִין דְּאִיהוּ מַלְכָּא, יַהֲבִין לֵיהּ בְּגִין יְקָרָא דִּילֵיהּ, הַאי דְּלָא אִתְחַבַּר בְּנוּקְבָּא, וְלָא

יָהִיב חֵילֵיהּ לְאַחֲרָא. וְדָא אִשְׁתְּמוֹדַע לְאִינּוּן חָרָשִׁין, דִּמְשְׁתַּמְּשִׁין בְּהָנֵי עוֹבָדֵי. וּבְגִינֵי כַּךְ, שַׁרְיָין עַל הַהוּא שָׂעִיר, כָּל אִינּוּן חֲטָאֵיהוֹן.

110. HE ANSWERS: This is needed, NAMELY JUST A GOAT, and it is known to all those who perform witchcraft, who perform it only with that which has not yet mated with a female. Therefore, all the young goats, which have not yet mated with a female, are among its species OF THE OTHER SIDE. AND THE REASON IS THAT A STRANGE EL IS STERILE AND PRODUCES NO FRUIT. But a grown goat has already mated with a female AND PRODUCED FRUIT. THEREFORE, IT IS NOT IN THE PORTION OF THE OTHER SIDE. Since THE OTHER SIDE is a king, AS IS WRITTEN, "AN OLD AND FOOLISH KING" (KOHELET 4:13), in its honor, A YOUNG GOAT is given, one that never mated with a female, and did not give of his strength to another, OF HIS OWN KIND, AS MENTIONED. And each sorcerer who performs these functions knows this. Therefore, they lay all their sins on that young goat.

111. וְת״ח, אע״ג דְּאִיהוּ חוּלָקָא לְהַהוּא סִטְרָא אַחֲרָא, רָזָא הָכָא, כָּל הָנֵי סִטְרִין אַחֲרָנִין דִּלְתַתָּא, כֻּלְּהוּ מְסָאֲבִין יַתִּיר. וְכָל מַה דְּנַחְתִּין דַּרְגִּין תַּתָּאִין, הָכִי מְסָאֲבוּ דִּלְהוֹן יַתִּיר. וּבְגִין כַּךְ, בְּעֵז יַתִּיר חוּלָקְהוֹן, בְּגִין דְּשַׂעֲרָא דִּילֵיהּ תַּלְיָא יַתִּיר מִבְּעִירָא אַחֲרָא, כְּמָה דְּדִינָא דִּלְהוֹן תַּלֵי לְתַתָּא בִּמְסָאֲבוּ. אֲבָל הַאי מַלְכוּ חַיָּיבְתָּא אַחֲרָא, מַלְכָּא דְּכֹלָּא בְּהַהוּא סִטְרָא, בָּרוּר אִיהוּ יַתִּיר מְסָאֲבוּ דִּילֵיהּ, וְלָא מְסָאֲבוּ שְׁלִים כְּהָנֵי תַּתָּאֵי. וְעַל דָּא שָׂעִיר, דְּשַׂעֲר דִּילֵיהּ לָא תַּלְיָא, וְלָא שְׁעִיעַ. לָא שְׁעִיעַ, בְּגִין דְּהַהוּא מְסָאֲבוּ דִּילֵיהּ. וְלָא תַּלְיָא, בְּגִין דְּלָא יִתְתְּקַף בֵּיהּ מְסָאֲבוּ כְּהָנֵי תַּתָּאֵי, וְעַל דָּא וַדַּאי שָׂעִיר וְלָא אַחֲרָא.

111. Come and behold: even though the young goat is the portion of the Other Side, there is a secret here, FOR IN THE SIDE OF IMPURITY the lower the aspects, the greater their impurity, and the more the lower grades descend, the greater is their impurity. Therefore, the portion OF THE OTHER SIDE is greater in a grown goat, because its hairs hang DOWN more than any other animal, just as their Judgments stem below in impurity. The impurity of this evil kingdom, which is the king of the entire Other Side is clearer AND MORE REFINED, and is not as completely impure as the lower ones. Therefore, it is given a young goat (Heb. *seir*, lit. 'hairy') whose hair does

not hang DOWN, and is not smooth. It is not smooth because of its impurity, but the hair does not hang downward, so that the impurity shall not grow strong, like these lower GRADES OF THE OTHER SIDE. Therefore, it is surely a young goat, and nothing else.

112. כְּפוּר, אֲמַאי אִקְרֵי כְּפוּר, אֶלָּא בְּגִין דְּנָקֵי כָּל מְסָאֲבוּ, וְאַעְבָּר לֵיהּ מִקַּמֵּיהּ, בְּהַהוּא יוֹמָא. וְעַל דָּא, יוֹם כְּפוּר: יוֹמָא דְּנַקְיוּתָא, וְהָכִי קָרֵינָא לֵיהּ. כְּתִיב כִּי בַיּוֹם הַזֶּה יְכַפֵּר עֲלֵיכֶם לְטַהֵר אֶתְכֶם, כִּי הַיּוֹם הַזֶּה מִבָּעֵי לֵיהּ, מַאי כִּי בַיּוֹם הַזֶּה. אֶלָּא בְּגִין דְּאִתְדְּכֵי מַקְדְּשָׁא לְעֵילָּא, וְאִתְנְהִיר, כְּתִיב כִּי בַיּוֹם הַזֶּה יְכַפֵּר עֲלֵיכֶם, יְכַפֵּר וִינַקֵּי בְּקַדְמֵיתָא בַּיּוֹם הַזֶּה, בְּגִין דְּיִתְדְּכֵי, וּלְבָתַר עֲלֵיכֶם.

112. HE ASKS: Why is it called 'atonement' (Heb. *kippur*)? HE ANSWERS: Because it cleanses all impurity and removes it from before Him on this day. Therefore, it is called 'Yom Kippur', WHICH MEANS a day of cleansing. Thus we call it. It is written: "For on that day will He forgive you, to cleanse you" (Vayikra 16:30). HE ASKS: Why does it say, "for on that day"? It should have said, 'for this day'. HE ANSWERS: Because the celestial Temple, WHICH IS MALCHUT, was purified and lit up. Therefore, it is written: "For on that day will He forgive you," WHICH MEANS He shall forgive and cleanse first this day, NAMELY MALCHUT, so that He may purify and forgive you afterwards.

113. תּוּ, יְכַפֵּר בַּיּוֹם הַזֶּה, וִינַקֵּי לֵיהּ בְּקַדְמֵיתָא, וְכָל דָּא עֲלֵיכֶם, בְּגִינֵיכוֹן אִצְטְרִיךְ לְנַקָּאָה לֵיהּ, וּלְדַכְּאָה לֵיהּ בְּקַדְמֵיתָא. יְכַפֵּר, מַאן יְכַפֵּר. אֶלָּא דָּא הוּא עָלְמָא עִלָּאָה, דְּנָהִיר וְנָקֵי לְכֹלָּא. וְע"ד כֻּלְּהוּ סִטְרִין בִּישִׁין, דְּאִקְרוֹן מְצוּלוֹת יָם, אִתְעֲבָרוּ. וּכְמָה דְּאִינּוּן מְצוּלוֹת יָם תַּלְיָין, הָכִי נָמֵי תַּלְיָיא שַׂעֲרָא דִּילֵיהּ, דְּהוּא סִטְרָא דִּלְהוֹן, וְשַׂעֲרָא דְּהַהוּא סִטְרָא לָא שְׁעִיעַ.

113. Another EXPLANATION: He shall forgive on that day, WHICH IS MALCHUT, and cleanse it first. The only reason it needs to be cleansed is "you", that is, for your sake it needs to be cleansed and purified first. "He shall forgive", HE ASKS: Who shall forgive. AND HE ANSWERS: it is the Upper World, WHICH IS BINAH that illuminates and cleanses everything.

Therefore, all the evil aspects, which are called 'the depths of the sea', are removed. As these depths of the sea are drooping down, so are the hairs OF THE YOUNG GOAT, which pertains to its side, NAMELY THE OTHER SIDE. The hairs of that Side are not smooth, BUT ARE COARSE, WHICH ALLUDES TO JUDGMENTS.

114. כְּגַוְונָא דָא כְּתִיב, וְכִפֶּר עַל הַקֹּדֶשׁ מִטֻּמְאֹת בְּנֵי יִשְׂרָאֵל וּמִפִּשְׁעֵיהֶם לְכָל חַטֹּאתָם. דְּלָא יָכִיל מְקַטְרְגָא לְשַׁלְטָאָה עָלַיְיהוּ וְעַל דָּא בְּיוֹמָא דְּכִפּוּר, דְּאִיהוּ קְנוּחָא דְּכָל חוֹבִין, וְנַקְיוּ דִּלְהוֹן. בָּעָאן יִשְׂרָאֵל לְנַקָּאָה גַּרְמַיְיהוּ, וּלְמֵהַךְ יְחֵפֵי רַגְלִין, כְּמַלְאֲכֵי עִלָּאִין. חָמֵשׁ עִנּוּיִין, בְּגִין לְאִסְתַּיְיעָא בְּחָמֵשׁ סִטְרִין עִלָּאִין, דְּיוֹמָא דְּכִפּוּרֵי אַפִּיק לוֹן, וְאִינּוּן תַּרְעִין דִּילֵיהּ.

114. Similarly, it is written: "And he shall make atonement for the holy place, because of the uncleanness of the children of Yisrael, and because of their transgression in all their sins" (Vayikra 16:16), meaning that the Accuser will not have power over them. Therefore, on Yom Kippur, which is the wiping away of all the sins and their cleansing, Yisrael should purify themselves and walk barefoot like the lofty angels. THERE ARE five deprivations ON YOM KIPPUR, WHICH ARE EATING AND DRINKING, WASHING, ANOINTING, WEARING SHOES AND MARITAL RELATIONS, in order to be helped by five supernal aspects, WHICH ARE CHESED, GVURAH, TIFERET, NETZACH, AND HOD, which Yom Kippur, WHICH IS BINAH, brought forth, and which are its gates.

115. וְאִי שְׁתִיָּה קָא חָשִׁיב, דְּאִיהוּ מִסִּטְרָא דְּיִצְחָק, הָא שִׁית, וְאע"ג דִּבְכְלָל אֲכִילָה אִיהוּ, וּכְדֵין אִינּוּן שִׁית, וְעִנּוּיָא בַּתְרָאָה תַּשְׁמִישׁ הַמִּטָּה אִיהוּ, וּבְדַרְגָּא שְׁתִיתָאָה שְׁכִיחַ, וְלָקָבְלֵיהּ אֲנַן עָבְדִין עִנּוּיָא דָא.

115. If drinking is considered as a separate deprivation, then there are six deprivations, because drinking is from the side of Isaac, WHICH IS GVURAH, AND EATING IS FROM THE SIDE OF ABRAHAM, WHICH IS CHESED. THIS IS WHY THEY ARE TWO, even though drinking is included in eating, so then they are six. The last deprivation is marital relations and is located in the sixth level, WHICH IS YESOD, and corresponding to it we perform the deprivation.

14. "On the tenth day of this seventh month"

A Synopsis

The old sage explains why the Yom Kippur is on the tenth day. We learn of the seventy years that apply to everyone. We learn that on Yom Kippur one must not reveal his sins to another, because the accusers may use it against him, and besides, it is shameless to reveal one's sins – it is a desecration of God's Holy Name. The seventh month is God's, but He gave it to Yisrael as a revelation. This entire month is from the Upper World, Binah; therefore it is covered because the Upper World is in concealment. On the fifteenth day of the month, it is revealed, since everything becomes revealed with the fullness of the moon. From this day the Sfirot descend to the secret of the Lower World, Malchut. The old sage and Rabbi Shimon discuss the question of who passed Judgment on the world on Rosh Hashanah, and why Malchut judges only those who are twenty years of age or older.

116. כְּתִיב וּבֶעָשׂוֹר לַחֹדֶשׁ הַשְּׁבִיעִי הַזֶּה, וּכְתִיב אַף בֶּעָשׂוֹר לַחֹדֶשׁ. בֶּעָשׂוֹר בַּעֲשִׂירִי מִבָּעֵי לֵיהּ, מַאי בֶּעָשׂוֹר. אֶלָּא, בְּגִין דְּהַשְׁתָּא בְּיוֹמָא דָּא, כָּל דַּרְגִּין עִלָּאִין, אַתְיָין אִלֵּין עַל אִלֵּין, לְמִשְׁרֵי עַל סִיהֲרָא, וּלְאַנְהָרָא לָהּ. וְכֻלְּהוּ בְּרָזָא דְּעֶשֶׂר, עַד דְּסַלְקָא לְמֵאָה. וְכַד קַיְּימָא בְּרָזָא דְּמֵאָה, כְּדֵין כֹּלָּא חַד, וְאִקְרֵי יוֹם הַכִּפּוּרִים. וְעַל דָּא בֶּעָשׂוֹר, כְּמָה דְּאַתְּ אָמַר זָכוֹר שָׁמוֹר דְּכֻלְּהוּ אַתְיָין בְּגִין לְעַשְׂרָא וּלְאַנְהָרָא בְּרָזָא דְּעֶשֶׂר.

116. It is written: "On the tenth day (Heb. *be'asor*) of this seventh month" (Bemidbar 29:7), and: "Also on the tenth day of this month" (Vayikra 23:27). HE ASKS WHY IT IS WRITTEN *"be'asor"* (lit. 'on day ten') when it should say 'tenth'. Why "ten?" HE ANSWERS: It is because now, on this day, all the high grades come upon each other, MEANING THAT THE TEN SFIROT THAT HAVE THREE FIRST SFIROT ARE DRAWN FROM IMA to rest upon the moon, WHICH IS MALCHUT, to shine on it. And they all pertain to the secret of ten so they add up to a hundred, BECAUSE TEN TIMES TEN EQUALS A HUNDRED. When it is based on the secret of a hundred, MEANING THAT IT HAS FIRST THREE SFIROT, then it is all one, FOR MALCHUT IS ONE WITH IMA. And BOTH are called 'the Day of Atonement'. Therefore, it is written, "on day ten (Heb. *asor*)", WHICH IS

DERIVED FROM THE WORD 'SOURCE', as written, "Remember" (Shemot 20:8) and "Keep" (Devarim 5:12). THIS IS BECAUSE 'TENTH' (HEB. *ASIRI*) MEANS AN ALLUSION TO MALCHUT ONLY, WHICH IS THE TENTH SFIRAH, BUT "TEN", WHICH IS DERIVED FROM 'SOURCE', INDICATES ALL TEN SFIROT TOGETHER. For they all come FROM IMA in order to multiply by ten EVERY SFIRAH and shine by means of ten – NAMELY, ALSO INCLUDING THE THREE FIRST SFIROT.

117. אַהֲדָּר הַאי סָבָא רֵישֵׁיה לְקַבְלֵיה דְּר״ש, וְאָמַר לֵיה, הָא יָדַעְנָא דִּשְׁאֶלְתָּא תִּבְעֵי בְּהַאי, בְּעֶשּׂוֹר לַחֹדֶשׁ הַשְּׁבִיעִי. א״ל ר״ש וַדַּאי, בְּעֶשּׂוֹר יָאוֹת הוּא. אִי הָכִי הוּא, אֲמַאי סָלִיק לְמֵאָה, וְהָא מִקְרָא לָא אִתְחֲזֵי, אֶלָּא דְּסָלִיק לְשַׁבְעִין, מַשְׁמַע דִּכְתִיב בְּעֶשּׂוֹר לַחֹדֶשׁ הַשְּׁבִיעִי, וְכַד מְעַשְׂרֵי לְשַׁבְעָאָה עֲשַׂר זִמְנִין, הָא וַדַּאי סָלִיק לְשַׁבְעִין. א״ל, עַל דָּא אַהֲדַרְנָא רֵישָׁא לְגַבָּךְ, דְּהָא יָדַעְנָא דְּחַכִּימָא אַנְתְּ.

117. The old sage turned towards Rabbi Shimon and said to him: I know that you have a question about this passage, "On the tenth day of this month". Rabbi Shimon said to him: Certainly, "on day ten," WHAT YOU SAID, THAT IT POINTS TO TEN is fitting. But if it is so, why does it add up to a hundred? From the passage, it seems that it all adds up only to seventy, for it is written: "On day ten of this seventh month…" And when you multiply seven by ten, it equals seventy. He said to him: For this did I turn to you, because I know you are a wise man.

118. ת״ח, תְּרֵין רָזִין הָכָא, חַד דְּהָא סִיהֲרָא חֹדֶשׁ הַשְּׁבִיעִי אִקְרֵי, וּבג״כ אִקְרֵי חֹדֶשׁ הַשְּׁבִיעִי עָשׂוֹר, בְּגִין דְּקָא מְנַהֲרִין לָה עֶשֶׂר זִמְנִין, הָא מֵאָה. וְתוּ, הַאי מִלָּה דְּקָאָמְרַת, וַדַּאי לְשַׁבְעִין סָלִיקָא בְּהַאי יוֹמָא, וּבְדַרְגָּא דְּשַׁבְעִין אִיהוּ, וּבְדַרְגָּא דְּמֵאָה אִיהוּ. לְדַרְגָּא דְּמֵאָה לְאַשְׁלְמָא וּלְאַנְהֲרָא. וּבְהַאי דַּרְגָּא דְּשַׁבְעִין, דְּהָא בְּיוֹמָא דָּא נָטִיל לְכָל עַמָּא דְיִשְׂרָאֵל לְמֵידָן, וְכֻלְּהוּ קַיְימִין בְּנִשְׁמָתָא יַתִּיר מִגּוּפָא, דְּהָא בְּיוֹמָא דָּא עִנּוּיָא דְּנַפְשָׁא אִיהוּ, וְלָא מִגּוּפָא, כְּמָה דְאַתְּ אָמַר וְעִנִּיתֶם אֶת נַפְשֹׁתֵיכֶם כִּי כָל הַנֶּפֶשׁ אֲשֶׁר לֹא תְעֻנֶּה. וְהַאי יוֹמָא נָטִיל לְכָל נַפְשָׁאן וַהֲווֹ בִּרְשׁוּתֵיה, וְאִי לָא קַיְימָא בְּרָזָא דְּשַׁבְעִין, לֵית לֵיה רְשׁוּ

בְּנַפְשָׁאן, דְּקִיּוּמָא דְּנַפְשָׁאן בְּרָזָא דְּשַׁבְעִין, כד״א יְמֵי שְׁנוֹתֵינוּ בָהֶם שִׁבְעִים שָׁנָה וְגוֹ'.

118. Come and behold: there are two secrets here. The first is that the moon, WHICH IS MALCHUT, is called 'the seventh month' and therefore the seventh month is called 'ten', AS IT SAYS, "ON DAY TEN OF THIS SEVENTH MONTH." This is because they shine on it tenfold, MEANING TEN SFIROT, AND TEN TIMES TEN equals a hundred. THERE IS another SECRET HERE, because what you said, THAT "TEN" INDICATES MULTIPLYING SEVEN BY TEN, assuredly amounts to seventy on that day, IN SUCH A MANNER, that it is both in the level of seventy and in the level of a hundred. IT IS in the level of a hundred in order to make it whole WITH THE THREE FIRST SFIROT and shine on it; AND IT IS in the level of seventy because on this day MALCHUT receives all Yisrael in order to judge them. They are all in the soul rather than in the body, because on this day the soul is afflicted but not the body, as is written: "And you shall afflict your souls" (Vayikra 23:27), and, "for whatever person (lit. 'soul') shall not be afflicted" (Ibid. 29). For that day takes all the souls, and they are under its authority. Had it not been of the secret of seventy, it would not have authority over the souls, because souls are maintained by means of seventy, as it is written: "The days of our years are seventy" (Tehilim 90:10).

119. וְאִי תֵּימָא נַפְשָׁאן דְּרַבְיֵי דְּלָא אַשְׁלִימוּ לְשַׁבְעִין שְׁנִין לָא שַׁלְטָא בְּהוּ. וַדַּאי שַׁלְטָא בְּהוּ, אֲבָל לָא בִּשְׁלִימוּ, כְּמַאן דְּזָכֵי יוֹמִין סַגִּיאִין לְפִקּוּדֵי אוֹרַיְיתָא, וְעכ״ד בְּכֻלְּהוּ שַׁבְעִין שְׁנִין אַזְלָא. וְעַל דָּא תָּנֵינָן אֶחָד הַמַּרְבֶּה וְאֶחָד הַמַּמְעִיט. מַאן אֶחָד. בְּיִחוּדָא דְּשַׁבְעִין שְׁנִין, מַאן דְּאַסְגֵּי, וּמַאן דְּאַמְעִיט.

119. You may argue that the souls of the children have not completed seventy years, AND SAY that MALCHUT has no power over them. HE ANSWERS: Certainly, She has power over them, but not completely, as over one who merited for many days the commandments of the Torah. Even so, the seventy years apply to everyone, BOTH CHILDREN AND OLD PEOPLE. Of this we learned of 'Both the one who increases and the one who decreases'. What is 'one'? It is the unification of seventy years, of he who increases, NAMELY THE OLD, and he who decreases, NAMELY THE CHILD.

120. וְעַל דָּא, בְּיוֹמָא דְּכִפּוּרֵי אַעֲבַר בְּכֻלְּהוּ שַׁבְעִין, וְאִשְׁתְּלִים הַאי דַּרְגָּא בְּכֻלְּהוּ, וְכָל נִשְׁמָתִין סַלְקִין קַמֵּיהּ, וְדָאִין לְהוֹן בְּדִינָא, וְקוּדְשָׁא בְּרִיךְ הוּא חַיִּיס עֲלַיְיהוּ דְּיִשְׂרָאֵל בְּיוֹמָא דָא, מַאן דְּלָא אַעֲבַר טִינָא מְרוּחֵיהּ לְכַפְּרָא עֲלֵיהּ, כַּד סָלִיק צְלוֹתֵיהּ בְּהַאי יוֹמָא, טָבַע בְּהַהוּא אֲתָר דְּאִקְרֵי רֶפֶשׁ וָטִיט, וְאִיהוּ מְצוּלוֹת יָם וְלָא סָלִיק לְאִתְעַטְּרָא בְּרֵישָׁא דְּמַלְכָּא.

120. Therefore, on Yom Kippur, MALCHUT passes through all these seventy, and this level is completed with all THE SFIROT, FOR EACH SFIRAH OF THE SEVEN SFIROT ACQUIRED THE ASPECT OF FIRST THREE SFIROT AND THEY BECOME TEN SFIROT. HOWEVER, THERE ARE NO INCLUSIVE THREE FIRST SFIROT AND THEREFORE THEY ARE SEVENTY. All the souls ascend before Him and He judges them with Judgment. The Holy One, blessed be He, has mercy on the children of Yisrael on that day. Whoever has not removed the filth from his soul to cleanse it, when his prayer ascends on that day it sinks into that place that is called 'mud' and 'clay', WHICH ARE SAMAEL AND LILIT, and the depths of the sea. HIS PRAYER does not ascend to adorn the head of the King.

121. בְּיוֹמָא דָא לָא אִצְטְרִיךְ בַּר נָשׁ לְפָרְשָׁא חֲטָאוֹי קַמֵּי אַחֲרָא, בְּגִין דְּכַמָּה אִינּוּן דְּנַטְלֵי הַהִיא מִלָּה, וְסַלְקֵי לָהּ לְעֵילָּא, וְאִית סָהֲדִין בְּהַהִיא מִלָּה. וּמַה מְשׁוֹכֶבֶת חֵיקֶךָ שְׁמוֹר פִּתְחֵי פִיךָ, כָּל שֶׁכֵּן אִינּוּן דְּאַזְלֵי וְעַיְינֵי לְקַטְרְגָא לוֹן, וְסָהֲדֵי עֲלֵיהּ. וְכָל שֶׁכֵּן דְּחָצִיפוּ אִיהוּ לְקַמֵּי כֹּלָּא, וְחִלּוּל שְׁמָא דְּקוּדְשָׁא בְּרִיךְ הוּא. וְעַ"ד כְּתִיב, אַל תִּתֵּן אֶת פִּיךָ לַחֲטִיא אֶת בְּשָׂרֶךָ.

121. On this day, a person should not reveal his sins before another, because there are many ACCUSERS who take this word, which he has revealed and bring it up and testify against that word. As THE VERSE SAYS, "From her that lies in your bosom, guard the doors of your mouth" (Michah 7:5), surely these ACCUSERS go AFTER HIM and study HOW to accuse him and testify against him. BUT IN ADDITION TO THIS, he is shameless towards everyone, WHO IS NOT ABASHED TO REVEAL HIS SINS, which is a desecration of the Name of the Holy One, blessed be He. Therefore, it is written: "Do not let your mouth cause your flesh to sin" (Kohelet 5:5).

122. פָּתַח וְאָמַר, הַחֹדֶשׁ הַזֶּה לָכֶם רֹאשׁ חֳדָשִׁים וְגוֹ', וְכִי כֻּלְּהוּ זִמְנִין וְחַדְשִׁין לָאו אִינוּן דְּקוּדְשָׁא בְּרִיךְ הוּא. אֶלָּא הַחֹדֶשׁ הַזֶּה לָכֶם, דִּילִי אִיהוּ, אֲבָל אֲנָא מָסְרִית לֵיהּ לְכוֹן, דִּלְכוֹן אִיהוּ בְּאִתְגַּלְיָא, אֲבָל שְׁבִיעָאָה דִּילִי אִיהוּ, וְע"ד אִיהוּ בַּכֶּסֶה, וְלָא בְּאִתְגַּלְיָא. יַרְחָא דִּלְכוֹן, אִיהוּ בְּסִדּוּרָא, כְּסֶדֶר דְּאַתְוָון אָבִיב, דְּאִיהוּ אב"ג. י"ב אִיהוּ רָזָא דְג'. אֲבָל יַרְחָא שְׁבִיעָאָה דִּילִי אִיהוּ מְסוֹפָא דְּאַתְוָון. מַאי טַעֲמָא. אַתּוּן מִתַּתָּא לְעֵילָא, וַאֲנָא מֵעֵילָא לְתַתָּא.

122. He opened the discussion, saying: "This month shall be to you the beginning of months..." (Shemot 12:2). HE ASKS: Do not all the holidays and months belong to the Holy One, blessed be He? WHY DOES IT SAY, "THIS MONTH SHALL BE TO YOU"? HE ANSWERS: "This month shall be to you," MEANS it is Mine, but I gave it over to you. "To you," MEANS that it is revealed, MEANING THAT THE LIGHTS ARE REVEALED IN IT FOR YISRAEL, but the seventh month is Mine. Therefore, it is covered and not revealed, AS IS WRITTEN: "AT THE FULL MOON (LIT. 'COVERED') OF OUR FEAST DAY" (TEHILIM 81:4). Your month is according to the sequence OF THE ALPHABET, in the order of *Aviv* (lit. 'Spring'), BECAUSE *NISAN* IS CALLED 'THE MONTH OF *AVIV* (ALEPH BET YUD BET)'. This is *Aleph-Bet-Gimel*, because *Yud-Bet* OF *AVIV* IS THE secret of *Gimel*, BECAUSE THE REDUCED NUMERICAL VALUE OF YUD IS ONE. THUS THE LETTERS OF *AVIV* (ALEPH BET YUD BET) NUMERICALLY EQUAL *ALEPH BET GIMEL*. But the seventh month is Mine; therefore ITS NAME STARTS with the last letters OF THE ALPHABET, NAMELY *TISHREI* (*TAV-SHIN-RESH-YUD*). What is the reason? You are IN FORWARD SEQUENCE *ALEPH BET GIMEL*, WHICH IS from below up, NAMELY, THE LETTERS INCREASE IN NUMERICAL VALUE, FIRST *ALEPH* (= 1) THEN *BET* (= 2), ETC. But I am IN BACKWARD ORDER *TAV-SHIN-RESH-YUD* - WHICH IS from above down, BECAUSE THE LETTERS DECREASE IN VALUE, FIRST TAV (= 400), SHIN (= 300), AND THEN RESH (= 200).

123. הַאי דִּילִי. בְּרֵישָׁא דְיַרְחָא, אֲנָא אִיהוּ בְּאִתְכַּסְיָיא. בַּעֲשָׂרָה דְּיַרְחָא, אֲנָא אִיהוּ, בְּגִין דַּאֲנָא בְּחַמֵשׁ קַדְמָאֵי, וּבְחַמֵשׁ אַחֲרָנִין, וּבְחַמֵשׁ תְּלִיתָאֵי. בְּקַדְמֵיתָא דְיַרְחָא אֲנָא אִיהוּ, בְּגִין חֲמִשָׁא יוֹמִין.

בַּעֲשָׂרָה דִּירַחָא אֲנָא אִיהוּ, בְּגִין חֲמֵשׁ יוֹמִין אַחֲרָנִין. בט״ו דְּיַרְחָא אֲנָא אִיהוּ, בְּגִין חֲמֵשׁ תְּלִיתָאֵי.

123. This SEVENTH MONTH is Mine. At the beginning of the month, I am covered. On the tenth of the month, I am COVERED because I am so during the first five days OF THE MONTH, during the other five days, and during the third set of five days. At the beginning of the month, I am so, because it is of the five first days. During the tenth day of the month, I am so, because it is part of the other five days. During the fifteenth day of the month, I am so, because it is part of the third five days.

124. מ״ט כּוּלֵי הַאי. בְּגִין דְּכָל יַרְחָא דָּא מֵעָלְמָא עִלָּאָה אִיהוּ, וְעָלְמָא עִלָּאָה בְּרָזָא דַּחֲמֵשׁ אִיהוּ, בְּכָל זִמְנָא וְזִמְנָא, וּבְגִינֵי כַּךְ יַרְחָא דָּא אִיהוּ בְּכֶסֶה, וְלָא בְּאִתְגַּלְיָא, בְּגִין דְּעָלְמָא עִלָּאָה בַּכֶּסֶה אִיהוּ, וְכָל מִלּוֹי בְּאִתְכַּסְּיָא. וְיַרְחָא דָּא דְּקוּדְשָׁא בְּרִיךְ הוּא אִיהוּ בִּלְחוֹדוֹי. כֵּיוָן דְּמָטָא יוֹמָא דַּחֲמֵיסַר, כְּדֵין גַּלְיָיא. כֹּלָּא אִיהוּ מָטָא בְּחַדְתּוּתָא דְּסִיהֲרָא, וְסִיהֲרָא אִשְׁתְּלִימַת, וְאִתְנְהִירַת מֵאִימָא עִלָּאָה, וְקַיְימָא לְאַנְהָרָא לְתַתָּאֵי מִגּוֹ נְהוֹרָא דִּלְעֵילָּא, וְעַ״ד אִקְרֵי רִאשׁוֹן, כד״א וּלְקַחְתֶּם לָכֶם בַּיּוֹם הָרִאשׁוֹן. עַד הַשְׁתָּא קַיְימֵי כֻּלְּהוּ יוֹמִין בְּרָזָא עִלָּאָה, מִכָּאן נַחְתִּין לְרָזָא תַּתָּאָה.

124. HE ASKS: What is the reason it is so COVERED, THAT IS, UNTIL THE FIFTEENTH DAY OF THE MONTH? HE ANSWERS: Because this entire month is from the Upper World, MEANING FROM BINAH, and the Upper World is under the secret of five at any time. Therefore, this month is covered rather than revealed, because the Upper World is in concealment and all its aspects are covered. This month is for the Holy One, blessed be He, alone AND IS NOT TO YOU. Upon the fifteenth day OF THE MONTH, it is revealed. Everything reaches the renewal of the moon. THEREFORE, the moon is full and shines from supernal Ima, WHICH IS BINAH, and is ready to illuminate downwards from the lights above. Therefore, THE FIFTEENTH DAY OF THE MONTH is called BY THE NAME first, as is written: "And you shall take for yourselves on the first day" (Vayikra 23:40). Until now, MEANING UNTIL THE FIFTEENTH DAY, all THE SFIROT were based on the

secret of the Upper WORLD, WHICH IS BINAH. From THE FIFTEENTH DAY, the Sfirot descend to the secret of the Lower WORLD, WHICH IS MALCHUT.

125. ת״ח, מִיּוֹמָא עִלָּאָה הֲווֹ אִלֵּין יוֹמִין קַדְמָאִין, רָזָא דְּעָלְמָא עִלָּאָה, מַאן דָּאִין דִּינָא דְּעָלְמָא, דְּהָא דִּינָא לָא אִשְׁתְּכַח בְּהַאי עָלְמָא, אֶלָּא מְדִינָא תַּתָּאָה, דְּדָא אֱלֹהֵי כָל הָאָרֶץ יִקָּרֵא. דְּאִי תֵּימָא דִּינָא דְּעָלְמָא דָּאִין לְעֵילָּא, א״ה לָא אִתְקְרֵי עָלְמָא דְּחֵירוּ, עָלְמָא דִּנְהִירוּ דְּכָל עָלְמִין. עָלְמָא דְּכָל חַיִּין, עָלְמָא דְּכָל חֵירוּ. וְאִי תֵּימָא מְדִינָא דְּיִצְחָק. אִי אִיהוּ אִתְּעַר דִּינָא לְגַבֵּי הַאי עָלְמָא, לָא יַכְלִין כָּל עָלְמָא לְמִסְבַּל, דְּהַהוּא אֶשָׁא תַּקִּיפָא עִלָּאָה, לָא אִית מַאן דְּסָבִיל לֵיהּ, אֶלָּא אֶשָׁא דִּלְתַתָּא, דְּאִיהוּ אֶשָׁא דְּסָבִיל אֶשָׁא.

125. Come and behold. The first days BEFORE THE FIFTEENTH OF THE MONTH came from the supernal day, NAMELY BINAH, as it is the secret of the Upper World, BINAH. HE ASKS: IF SO, who passed Judgment on the world ON ROSH HASHANAH? Who, since there is no Judgment in this world, except the Judgment of the Lower WORLD, which "Elohim of the whole earth shall He be called" (Yeshayah 54:5). If you say that the Judgment of the world is passed above, IN BINAH, then BINAH would not be called 'the World of Freedom', 'a world IN WHICH the lights of all the worlds exist', 'the world THAT CONTAINS all life', 'the world of all liberty'. SINCE BINAH IS CALLED BY ALL THESE NAMES, HOW CAN YOU SAY THAT IT CONTAINS THE JUDGMENT TO JUDGE THE WHOLE WORLD? If you say it is derived from the Judgment of Isaac, NAMELY THE LEFT COLUMN OF BINAH, THIS IS IMPOSSIBLE, because if it aroused Judgment for this world, then the whole world could not bear it. For no one can bear this strong, supernal fire OF THE LEFT COLUMN OF BINAH except for the lower fire, WHICH IS MALCHUT, which is a fire that bears fire.

126. אֶלָּא, כְּמָה דְּעָלְמָא דָּא עָלְמָא תַּתָּאָה דְּכֻלְּהוּ עָלְמִין. הָכִי נָמֵי כָּל דִּינוֹי מֵעָלְמָא תַּתָּאָה, דֶּאֱלֹהִים שׁוֹפֵט. וְדָא אִקְרֵי דִּינָא עִלָּאָה עַל הַאי עָלְמָא, וּבְגִין דְּאִיהוּ דַּרְגָּא שְׁבִיעָאָה, לָא גָּזִיר גְּזֵרָה עַל בַּר נָשׁ, אֶלָּא מֵעֶשְׂרִין שְׁנִין וּלְעֵילָּא.

126. HE ANSWERS: Just as this world OF OURS is the lowest of all worlds, so are all its Judgments from the lowest world IN ATZILUT, WHICH IS MALCHUT, that is CALLED 'Elohim the Judge'. AND HER JUDGMENTS are considered supernal Judgment in relation to this LOWER World of OURS. THEREFORE, THEY ARE CONSIDERED IN RELATION TO US LIKE THE JUDGMENTS OF BINAH, and because She is the seventh level OF ZEIR ANPIN, a decree is only issued against a man who is twenty years and older.

127. אַשְׁגַּח הַאי סָבָא בַּר' שִׁמְעוֹן, וְחָמָא לֵיה דְּזַלְגִּין עֵינוֹי דִּמְעִין. אָמַר רִבִּי שִׁמְעוֹן, אִי הִיא שְׁבִיעָאָה, אֲמַאי מֵעֶשְׂרִין שְׁנִין וּלְעֵילָּא. אֲמַר לֵיה, זַכָּאָה מַאן דִּמַלִּיל עַל אוּדְנִין דְּשַׁמְעִין.

127. That sage looked at Rabbi Shimon and saw that his eyes were shedding tears. Rabbi Shimon said: If She is seventh, WHY DOES SHE JUDGE THE PERSON of twenty years of age and older? He said to him: Blessed is he who speaks to ears that hear.

128. ת"ח, בֵּי דִּינָא דִּלְתַתָּא בְּאַרְעָא, לָא גַּזְרִין דִּינָא עַל בַּר נָשׁ, עַד תְּלֵיסַר שְׁנִין. מַאי טַעֲמָא. בְּגִין דְּשַׁבְקִין שֶׁבַע שְׁנִין לִשְׁבִיעָאָה, אֱלֹהֵי כָּל הָאָרֶץ יִקָּרֵא. וְלֵית רְשׁוּ לְבַר נָשׁ בְּאִינּוּן שֶׁבַע. וְאִינּוּן שֶׁבַע, לָא שַׁרְיָין אֶלָּא עַל תְּלֵיסַר דִּלְתַתָּא, דְּאִינּוּן כּוּרְסְיָיא לְגַבֵּיה, וּבְגִין כַּךְ, כָּל גְּזֵרִין, וְכָל דִּינִין דִּלְתַתָּא, מֵאִינּוּן שֶׁבַע שְׁנִין דִּלְתַתָּא, כְּלָלָא דְּעֶשְׂרִין שְׁנִין אִיהוּ.

128. Come and behold: the lower, terrestrial court of law does not pass judgment against a person until he is thirteen years of age. What is the reason? It is because they leave seven years for the seventh, "Elohim of the whole earth shall He be called" (Yeshayah 54:5). A person has no authority over the seven, and the seven rest upon the thirteen below, which are a throne for it. Therefore, all the decrees and all the Judgments of below come from the lower seven, which sum it to twenty years.

129. וְדִינָא דְּעָלְמָא בַּר"ה, עַל יְדָא דְּהַאי דַּרְגָּא אִיהוּ, דְּאִיהוּ מַמָּשׁ קַיְימָא בְּדִינָא עַל בְּנוֹי בְּהַאי עָלְמָא, בְּגִין לְאִתְדַּכְּאָה לְגַבֵּי עָלְמָא עִלָּאָה, בְּגִין דְּלֵית לֵיה סִיּוּעַ לְסַלְּקָא וּלְאִתְדַּכְּאָה אֶלָּא מִגּוֹ תַּתָּאֵי.

129. The Judgment of the world on Rosh Hashanah is carried through this level that actually stands in Judgment over Her children in this world in order to be purified for the Higher World. She has no assistance to rise and be purified except from the lower beings, NAMELY THAT THEY SHOULD REPENT AND RAISE MAYIM NUKVIN ('FEMALE WATERS').

15. Four kinds

A Synopsis

Rabbi Shimon and the old sage discuss the verse, "And you shall take for yourselves on the first day the fruit of the tree hadar," saying that "hadar" is the Righteous, namely Yesod, and that Malchut is the "fruit of the tree hadar." They speak about the palm trees, the boughs of thick leaved trees, and the two willows of the brook. They conclude that we are commanded to take these four kinds since we need to awaken below in the likeness of above. There is nothing in the world that has no counterpart above, and the reverse is also true.

130. וְכַד יִשְׂרָאֵל אִינּוּן בַּחֲמֵיסָר יוֹמִין, כְּדֵין נָטִיל לִבְנוֹי, לְפָרְשָׂא גַּדְפוֹי עָלַיְיהוּ, וּלְמֶחֱדֵי עִמְּהוֹן. וְעַ״ד כְּתִיב וּלְקַחְתֶּם לָכֶם בַּיּוֹם הָרִאשׁוֹן, פְּרִי דָא, אִיהוּ אִילָנָא דְּאִקְרֵי עֵץ פְּרִי, וְאִשְׁתְּכַח בֵּיהּ פְּרִי. עֵץ הָדָר: כד״א הוֹד וְהָדָר לְפָנָיו. מ״ט אִקְרֵי הָדָר, וּמַאן אִיהוּ הָדָר. אֶלָּא דָּא צַדִּיק.

130. When Yisrael are in the fifteenth day OF THE SEVENTH MONTH, the Holy One, blessed be He, takes His children and spreads His wings over them to rejoice with them. Therefore, it is written: "And you shall take for yourselves on the first day THE FRUIT OF THE TREE HADAR" (Vayikra 23:40). This fruit is the tree that is called 'fruit tree', NAMELY MALCHUT, and bears fruit. "Tree Hadar," as is written, "Honor and majesty (Heb. *hadar*) are before Him" (Tehilim 96:6). Why is it called '*hadar*' and who is *hadar*? It is the Righteous, NAMELY YESOD. AND MALCHUT IS CALLED 'THE FRUIT OF THE TREE HADAR', MEANING MALCHUT THAT RECEIVES FROM YESOD THAT IS CALLED HADAR.

131. אֲמַאי אִקְרֵי הָדָר, וְהָא אֲתָר טְמִירָא אִיהוּ דְּלֵית לֵיהּ גְּלוּיָא, וּצְרִיכָא לְאִתְכַּסְּיָיא תָּדִיר, וְלֵית הָדָר אֶלָּא מַאן דְּאִתְגַּלְיָיא וְאִתְחֲזֵי. אֶלָּא, אע״ג דְּאִיהוּ דַּרְגָּא טְמִירָא, הַדּוּרָא אִיהוּ דְּכָל גּוּפָא, וְלָא אִשְׁתְּכַח הַדּוּרָא לְגוּפָא, אֶלָּא בֵּיהּ. מַאי טַעֲמָא. מַאן דְּלֵית עִמֵּיהּ הַאי דַּרְגָּא, לֵית בֵּיהּ הַדּוּרָא, לְמֵיעַל בִּבְנֵי נָשָׁא. קָלָא לָאו עִמֵּיהּ בְּדִבּוּרָא, וְהַדּוּרָא דְּקָלָא אִתְפְּסַק מִנֵּיהּ. דִּיקְנָא, וְהַדּוּרָא דְּדִיקְנָא לָאו עִמֵּיהּ,

וְאע״ג דְּאִתְכַּסְיָיא הַהוּא דַּרְגָּא, כָּל הַדּוּרָא דְּגוּפָא בֵּיה תַּלְיָא. וְאִתְכַּסֵּי
וְאִתְגַּלְיָיא. וּבג״כ עֵץ הָדָר אִיהוּ, עֵץ דְּכָל הַדּוּרָא דְּגוּפָא בֵּיה תַּלְיָא,
וְדָא אִיהוּ עֵץ עוֹשֶׂה פְּרִי.

131. HE ASKS: Why is YESOD called 'hadar'? It is a covered place, which is not revealed but should always be covered, yet majesty is only upon someone that is revealed and seen. HE ANSWERS: Even though it is a covered level, it is the majesty of the whole body, and there is no majesty to the body but in it. What is the reason? IT IS because one who does not have that grade has no majesty to come among people; he has no voice when he speaks, because the majesty of the voice is cut from him. He has no beard or the majesty of a beard. SO even though that grade is covered, NEVERTHELESS all the majesty of the body originates in it, and is covered and revealed THROUGH THE MAJESTY OF THE BODY. Therefore, it is the tree hadar (majesty), MEANING a tree from which all the majesty of the body comes. This is a fruit tree yielding fruit. BUT MALCHUT IS CALLED 'FRUIT TREE'.

132. כַּפֹת תְּמָרִים, הָכָא אִתְכְּלִילַת אִתְּתָא בְּבַעְלָה בְּלָא פְּרוּדָא, כַּפוֹת
תְּמָרִים כַּחֲדָא. וַעֲנַף עֵץ עָבוֹת, תְּלָתָא. וְעָלִין דִּילֵיה, דָּא בְּסִטְרָא דָּא,
וְדָא בְּסִטְרָא דָּא, וְחַד דְּשַׁלִּיט עָלַיְיהוּ. וְעַרְבֵי נַחַל, תְּרֵין. דְּלֵית לְהוּ
רֵיחָא וְטַעְמָא, כְּשׁוּקִין בִּבְנֵי נָשָׁא. לוּלָב נָטִיל כֻּלְּהוּ, כְּחוּטָא דְּשִׁדְרָה
קַיְימָא דְּגוּפָא. וּמַה דְּנָפִיק לְבַר טֶפַח, הָכִי הוּא, בְּגִין לְאַשְׁלְמָא
וּלְאַפָּקָא כֹּלָּא, וּלְשַׁמְּשָׁא כַּדְקָא חֲזֵי.

132. "Branches of palm trees" (Vayikra 23:40) IS YESOD, THE RIGHTEOUS, AS IT IS WRITTEN: "THE RIGHTEOUS MAN FLOURISHES LIKE THE PALM TREE" (TEHILIM 92:13). Here, a wife is comprehended in her husband without separation, BECAUSE IT IS WRITTEN, "Branches of palm trees" INSTEAD OF 'AND BRANCHES OF PALM TREES'. FOR THE VAV (LIT. 'AND') WOULD DIVIDE BETWEEN FRUIT OF THE TREE HADAR AND THE BRANCHES OF PALM TREES. THIS SHOWS THAT THEY ARE TIED together, FOR YESOD AND MALCHUT ARE TOGETHER. "And the boughs of thick leaved trees" (Vayikra 23:40): they are three, MEANING THE THREE COLUMNS – CHESED, GVURAH AND TIFERET – because it has THREE

leaves, one on THE RIGHT side, one on the LEFT side and the one IN THE CENTER that dominates them, BECAUSE THE CENTRAL COLUMN UNITES THE RIGHT AND LEFT INTO ONE. "There are two willows of the brook" (Ibid.), NAMELY, NETZACH AND HOD, which have neither scent nor taste, BEING the aspect of legs in people. *Lulav* (lit. 'palm leaf'), WHICH IS YESOD, receives AND COMBINES them all, like the spinal cord that is in the body. It protrudes outside THE OTHER KINDS by a hand's breadth UPWARDS, and so it needs to be in order to perfect and bring forth all THE LEVELS for proper union.

133. בְּהָנֵי זִינִין, בָּעֵי בַּר נָשׁ לְאִתְחֲזָאָה קָמֵי קוּדְשָׁא בְּרִיךְ הוּא. עָלִין וְטַרְפִּין דְּהָנֵי דְּהַנֵי לְתַתָּא כְּגַוְונָא דִּלְעֵילָא, דְּלֵית לָךְ מִלָּה בְּעָלְמָא, דְּלָא אִית לָה דּוּגְמָא לְעֵילָא, כְּגַוְונָא דִּלְעֵילָא הָכִי אִית לְתַתָּא, וּבְעוּ יִשְׂרָאֵל לְאִתְאַחֲדָא בְּרָזָא דָּא דִּמְהֵימְנוּתָא, קָמֵי קוּדְשָׁא בְּרִיךְ הוּא.

133. With these kinds one must show himself before the Holy One, blessed be He, FOR THEY CORRESPOND TO CHESED, GVURAH, TIFERET, NETZACH, HOD, YESOD AND MALCHUT. The leaves of these palm trees ALLUDE TO ALL THE OTHER HOSTS THAT UNITE UNDER ALL THE OTHER APPELLATIONS BY WHICH THE HOLY ONE, BLESSED BE HE, IS CALLED. THEREFORE, WE ARE COMMANDED TO TAKE THESE FOUR KINDS since we need TO AWAKEN below in the likeness of above, for there is nothing in the world that does not have a counterpart above. AND IN REVERSE, as it is above, so is it below, BECAUSE THE WORLDS ARE IMPRINTED BY ONE ANOTHER, AND THE ROOTS ARE ABOVE, FOR THERE IS NOTHING IN THE LOWER WORLDS WHOSE ROOT CANNOT BE FOUND IN THE UPPER WORLDS. THEREFORE, THE ROOTS OF THE FOUR KINDS ARE CHESED, GVURAH, TIFERET, NETZACH, HOD, YESOD AND MALCHUT IN ATZILUT, for Yisrael must unite by means of this secret of Faith before the Holy One, blessed be He.

16. "You shall dwell in booths"

A Synopsis

We read that the title verse refers to the supernal world, Binah, and that this verse was said when the world was created. We read about the supernal Tabernacle formed as supernal Chochmah emerged from the unknown and unseen place, and of the lower Tabernacle, Malchut, that is like a lantern displaying light. Yisrael should sit under the shade of the Tabernacle of Peace in the secret of Faith. During Sukkot Malchut takes the souls of Yisrael and elevates them to Zeir Anpin, as she descends and holds all the blessings that Yisrael draw down during the whole seven days through the actions and sacrifices offered to her. Then on the eighth day she descends to be close to her children and make them happy; this is Shmini Atzeret, the Eighth Day of Convocation.

134. כְּתִיב בַּסֻּכֹּת תֵּשְׁבוּ שִׁבְעַת יָמִים, דָּא הוּא רָזָא דִּמְהֵימְנוּתָא, וְהַאי קְרָא עַל עָלְמָא עִלָּאָה אִתְּמַר, וְהָכִי תָּנֵינָן, כַּד אִתְבְּרֵי עָלְמָא, אִתְּמַר הַאי קְרָא.

134. It is written: "You shall dwell in booths (Heb. *sukkot*) seven days" (Vayikra 23:42). This is the secret of Faith, WHICH IS MALCHUT, WHO RECEIVES ALL HER MOCHIN BY THE SECRET OF THIS PASSAGE. This verse refers to the supernal world, WHICH IS BINAH, as we have learned. When the world was created, this verse was said.

135. כַּד שָׁרָא חָכְמָה לְנָפְקָא, מֵאֲתָר דְּלָא יְדִיעַ וְלָא אִתְחֲזֵי, כְּדֵין נָפִיק חַד מְשַׁחֲתָא, וּבָטַשׁ, וְהַהִיא חָכְמְתָא עִלָּאָה, נָצִיץ וְאִתְפַּשַּׁט לְכָל סִטְרִין, בְּרָזָא דְּמַשְׁכְּנָא עִלָּאָה. וְהַהוּא מַשְׁכְּנָא עִלָּאָה, אַפִּיק שִׁית סִטְרִין, וּכְדֵין הַהוּא נְצִיצוּ דִּמְשַׁחֲתָא נָהִיר לְכֹלָּא, וְאָמַר בַּסֻּכֹּת תֵּשְׁבוּ שִׁבְעַת יָמִים.

135. When Chochmah – NAMELY, SUPERNAL ABA AND IMA THAT ARE CALLED 'ABA' AND 'CHOCHMAH' – commenced to emerge from the unknown and unseen place, NAMELY, FROM THE HEAD OF ARICH ANPIN, then a curtain emerged and struck. That supernal Chochmah sparkled and spread in all directions in the secret of the supernal Tabernacle, WHICH IS YISRAEL-SABA AND TEVUNAH, THAT IS CALLED 'BINAH' AND 'IMA'. That

supernal Tabernacle brought forth six extremities, WHICH ARE ZEIR ANPIN, and then the sparkling of the curtain illuminated everything, and is written, "You shall dwell in booths seven days".

136. מַאן סְכַּת חָסֵר ו'. דָּא מַשְׁכְּנָא תַּתָּאָה, דְּאִיהוּ כַּעֲשָׁשִׁיתָא, לְאַחֲזָאָה לְכָל נְהוֹרִין, וּכְדֵין אָמַר, בַּסֻּכַּת תֵּשְׁבוּ שִׁבְעַת יָמִים. מַאן שִׁבְעַת יָמִים. מֵעָלְמָא עִלָּאָה לְתַתָּאָה, דְּכֻלְּהוּ קַיְימֵי בְּקִיּוּמָא, לְאַנְהָרָא לְהַאי סֻכַּת. וּמַאן אִיהִי. דָּא סֻכַּת דָּוִד הַנּוֹפֶלֶת. סֻכַּת שָׁלוֹם. וּבָעֵי עַמָּא קַדִּישָׁא לְמֵיתַב תְּחוֹת צְלָהָא, בְּרָזָא דִּמְהֵימְנוּתָא, וּמַאן דְּיָתִיב בְּצִלָּא דָּא, יָתִיב בְּאִינּוּן יוֹמִין עִלָּאִין.

136. Why is "Sukkot" spelled without the Vav? This is the lower Tabernacle, NAMELY MALCHUT, that is like a lantern, WHICH IS A GLASS UTENSIL INTO WHICH A CANDLE IS PLACED TO LIGHT, to show all lights. Then THE GLITTERING OF THE CURTAIN said: "You shall dwell in booths (Heb. sukkot) seven days". Who are the seven days? They are from the Supernal World, WHICH IS BINAH, to the Lower WORLD, WHICH IS MALCHUT, for all THE SEVEN DAYS, WHICH ARE CHESED, GVURAH, TIFERET, NETZACH, HOD, YESOD AND MALCHUT OF BINAH, maintain their existence to shine on this tabernacle (Heb. sukkah). What is it? It is "the Tabernacle of David that is fallen" (Amos 9:11), the Tabernacle of Peace, NAMELY MALCHUT, and the Holy Nation should sit under its shade in the secret of Faith, WHICH IS MALCHUT. One who sits in this shadow, sits among these supernal days OF BINAH.

137. וְע"ד כֻּלְּהוּ בְּסֻכַּת וְחַד בְּסוּכּוֹת שְׁלִים, חַד שְׁלִים, לְאַחֲזָאָה דְּמַאן דְּיָתִיב בְּצִלָּא דָּא, יָתִיב בְּאִינּוּן יוֹמִין עִלָּאִין לְעֵילָּא, דְּקַיְימִין עַל הַאי תַּתָּאָה, לְאַנְהָרָא לֵיהּ, לְחַפְיָא עָלֵיהּ, וּלְאַגָּנָא לֵיהּ, בְּשַׁעֲתָא דְּאִצְטְרִיךְ.

137. Therefore, "Sukkot" IS ALWAYS SPELLED WITHOUT A VAV, WHICH ALLUDES TO MALCHUT, AS MENTIONED. BUT IN one PLACE, it is spelled, "sukkot," plane. It shows that whoever sits in the shadow OF THE GLITTERING OF THE CURTAIN, MENTIONED ABOVE, sits among these supernal days of above – NAMELY CHESED, GVURAH, TIFERET,

NETZACH, HOD, YESOD AND MALCHUT OF BINAH, that are over the lower, WHICH IS MALCHUT, to illuminate Her, cover Her and protect Her when necessary.

138. וְתוּ, כֻּלְּהוּ אִקְרוּן סֻכּוֹת בִּשְׁלִימוּ, וּכְתִיב סֻכַּת חָסֵר, דָּא עָלְמָא תַּתָּאָה, דְּבָעָא בְּהָנֵי ז׳ יוֹמִין קַדִּישִׁין, לְמֵיזָן לִשְׁאַר מְמָנָן רַבְרְבָן דְּעַמִּין, בְּעוֹד דְּאִיהִי נָטְלָא חֶדְוָה בְּבַעְלָהּ, וְלָא יְקַטְרְגוּן חֶדְוָותָא, בְּגִין דְּיִתְעָדְּנוּן בְּהַהוּא מְזוֹנָא, קָרְבָּנִין דִּלְהוֹן סַגִּיאִין יַתִּיר מִשְּׁאַר יוֹמִין, בְּגִין דְּיִתְעַסְּקוּן בְּהוּ, וְלָא יִתְעָרְבוּן לְבָתַר בְּחֶדְוָה דְּיִשְׂרָאֵל. וּמַאן חֶדְוָה דְּיִשְׂרָאֵל, דָּא יוֹמָא תְּמִינָאָה דַּעֲצֶרֶת.

138. AND IT CAN also BE SAID that they are all read "Sukkot," in full, and that which is written "Sukkot," without the Vav, refers to the Lower World, WHICH IS MALCHUT. She has to feed the other appointed Ministers of the world during these holy seven days, WHICH IS THE SECRET OF THE SEVENTY OXEN THAT ARE OFFERED DURING THE SEVEN DAYS OF SUKKOT, while She still receives joy from Her husband. THIS IS NECESSARY FOR HER in order that they do not incite during the joy, AND SHE ALLOWS THEM to delight themselves with that food. Their offerings are more plentiful than usual so that they are occupied with them and do not mingle in the joy of the children of Yisrael. THIS IS SIMILAR TO GIVING A PORTION OF THE GOAT OF THE FIRST DAY OF THE MONTH, AND THE GOAT TO AZAZEL. What is the joy of the children of Yisrael? This is on *Shmini Atzeret* (the eighth day of Sukkot, day of Convocation).

139. וְת״ח, בְּעוֹד דְּאִינּוּן שְׁאַר מְמָנָן חַדָּאן, וְאַכְלִין בְּהַהוּא מְזוֹנָא דִּמְתַקְנֵי לוֹן יִשְׂרָאֵל. אִינּוּן מְתַקְנֵי כֻּורְסְיָיא לְקוּדְשָׁא בְּרִיךְ הוּא מִתַּתָּא, וּלְסַלְּקָא לֵיהּ לְעֵילָּא, בְּאִינּוּן זִינִין, וּבְחֶדְוָה, וּבְהִלּוּלָא, וּלְאַקְפָא מַדְבְּחָא. כְּדֵין אִיהִי סַלְּקָא, וְנַטְלָא בִּרְכָּאן וְחֶדְוָה בְּבַעְלָהּ.

139. Come and behold: while the other appointed princes are rejoicing and eating that food that the children of Yisrael prepare for them, NAMELY THE SEVENTY OXEN, they prepare a throne for the Holy One, blessed be He, from below AT THE SAME TIME – MEANING THAT THEY ARE PREPARING MALCHUT TO BE A THRONE FOR THE HOLY ONE, BLESSED BE HE, to

elevate Her up with these FOUR kinds, with the joy OF SUKKOT AND THE RECITATION OF Hallel, and by circling the altar. She, MALCHUT, ascends and receives blessings and joy in Her husband, IN ZEIR ANPIN.

140. וּשְׁאַר חֵיוָון רַבְרְבָן מִמָנָן דְּעַמִין, אָכְלָן וּמַדְקָן וְרַפְסָן וְאִתְּזָנוּ. וְאִיהִי נַקְטָא נַפְשָׁאן בְּעִנּוּגִין לְעֵילָא, כְּמָה דְאִתְּמַר. כֵּיוָן דְּנַחְתָּא, וְהָא נַקְטָא כָּל בִּרְכָּאן וְכָל קְדוּשִׁין וְכָל עִנּוּגִין, וְיִשְׂרָאֵל כָּל הָנֵי שִׁבְעָה יוֹמִין הֲווֹ מַשְׁכִין לָהּ בְּאִינּוּן עוֹבָדִין דְּקָא עַבְדִין וּמְקָרְבִין בַּהֲדָה, כְּדֵין נַחְתָּא לְקָרְבָא בִּבְנָהָא, וּלְמֶחֱדֵי לוֹן יוֹמָא חַד, וְהַהוּא יוֹמָא אִיהוּ יוֹמָא תְּמִינָאָה, בְּגִין דְּכָל ז' יוֹמִין אַחֲרָנִין בַּהֲדָה. וְע"ד אִיהוּ תְּמִינָאָה, וּתְמַנְיָא יוֹמִין כַּחֲדָא. וּבְגִין כַּךְ אִקְרֵי עֲצֶרֶת: כְּנִישִׁין. כְּנִישִׁין כֻּלְּהוּ בְּהַאי יוֹמָא. וְאִקְרֵי שְׁמִינִי, וְלֵית שְׁמִינִי אֶלָּא מִגּוֹ שִׁבְעָה.

140. The other living creatures, WHICH ARE THE SEVENTY appointed princes of the nations, eat and chew well, AND THE RESIDUE OF THEIR EATING they trample with their feet, and they are sustained, THAT IS, BY THE SEVENTY OXEN, AS MENTIONED. She, MALCHUT, takes the souls and elevates them to the supernal delight, TO ZEIR ANPIN, as we have said, as She descended and holds all the blessings and Holiness and delights that the children of Yisrael draw down during all these seven days, through these actions and offered sacrifices to Her. Then She descends to be close to Her children and to make them happy for one day. That day is the eighth day, because all the other seven days are with Her, as explained. Therefore, it is the eighth, and it is eight days united. Therefore, it is called 'Atzeret', MEANING gathered, because all THE SEVEN DAYS gather together on that EIGHTH day (Heb. Shmini Atzeret), and it is called 'eighth', NAMELY THE 'EIGHTH DAY OF CONVOCATION'. It is eighth only because of the inclusion of the seven. THEREFORE, IT IS CALLED BY TWO NAMES: IT IS CALLED 'EIGHTH' BECAUSE IT IS EIGHTH OF THE SEVEN DAYS, AND IT IS CALLED 'CONVOCATION' BECAUSE IT INCLUDES WITHIN ITSELF ALL THE SEVEN DAYS TOGETHER.

17. "May the name of Hashem be blessed"

A Synopsis

We learn that the secret of the title verse was revealed to Rabbi Yitzchak Kaftora in a dream. It means that the word "blessed," *mevorach*, begins hard but ends soft; this is like on Rosh Hashanah where it is hard with harsh Judgment, and on Shmini Atzeret where it is soft with joy. We read of the difference between the Upper Judgment that is Male, and the Lower Judgment that is Female; the latter begins hard but softens until it is joyful on the Eighth Day of Convocation. The Upper Judgment awakened on the day of the flood, but since then it has not dwelt upon the world because the world can not bear it even for a moment. It was the mercy of Hashem that saved the entire world from being destroyed. After this explanation the old sage reveals his identity – he is Nehorai Saba, and we learn that Nehorai means 'light'.

141. כְּתִיב יְהִי שֵׁם יְיָ' מְבוֹרָךְ. מַאי מְבוֹרָךְ. אֲבָל רָזָא חֲדָא יָדַע חַד מֵחַבְרָנָא, בְּמַדְבְּרָא אַחֲזִיאוּ לֵיהּ בְּחֶלְמָא, וְרִבִּי יִצְחָק כַּפְתּוֹרָא שְׁמֵיהּ. מַאי מְבוֹרָךְ. שֵׁירוּתָא קַשְׁיָא, וְסוֹפֵיהּ רַךְ. מ"ב קַשֶׁה, וְדִינָא אִיהוּ וַדַּאי. כְּגַוְונָא דָא, יוֹמָא דר"ה מ"ב, דְּהָא בְּמ"ב אַתְווָן אִתְבְּרֵי עָלְמָא, וְע"ד אִתְבְּרֵי בְּדִינָא. לְבָתַר רַךְ, וְעַל דָּא תָּנֵינָן, כָּל שֵׁירוּתִין קַשְׁיִין, וְסוֹפָא דִּלְהוֹן רָכִין. בְּיוֹמָא דְּראשׁ הַשָּׁנָה מ"ב קַשֶׁה בְּדִינָא. בְּיוֹמָא דַּעֲצֶרֶת רַךְ בְּחֶדְוָה.

141. It is written: "blessed be the Name of Hashem" (Iyov 1:21). What is meant by "blessed"? There is one secret that one of our friends knew that was shown to him in a dream, and his name is Rabbi Yitzchak Kaftora. HE SAID: What is meant by "blessed (Heb. *mevorach*)"? IT MEANS that its beginning is hard and its end soft, BECAUSE *MEVORACH* IS SPELLED WITH THE LETTERS *MEM – BET-VAV-RESH-CAF*. *Mem Bet* is hard and is definitely Judgement, like the day of Rosh Hashanah is *Mem Bet*, because the world was created with *Mem Bet* (42) letters, NAMELY 32 TIMES ELOHIM AND THE TEN SAYINGS, WHICH EQUAL 42. SIMILARLY, THERE ARE 42 LETTERS FROM THE *BET* OF *BERESHEET* (LIT. 'IN THE BEGINNING'), UNTIL THE *BET* OF THE WORD *VOHU* (ENG. 'VOID'). Therefore, it was created with Judgment; but afterwards it is *Rach* (*Resh Caf*, lit. 'soft'). Therefore, we have learned that all beginnings are hard but

their endings are easy, because on the day of Rosh Hashanah, it is *Mem Bet* with harsh Judgment, and on *Shmini Atzeret,* it is soft with joy.

142. ת״ח, מָה בֵּין דִּינָא עִלָּאָה, לְהַאי דִּינָא. דִּינָא עִלָּאָה שֵׁירוּתָא וְסוֹפָא קַשְׁיָא, וְלֵית מַאן דִּיְקוּם בֵּיהּ, וְכָל מָה דְּאָזִיל אִתְתַּקַּף, וּבָתַר דְּשָׁארֵי, לָא סָלִיק מִנֵּיהּ, עַד דְּאָכִיל וְשֵׁצֵי כֹּלָּא, דְּלָא אִשְׁתְּאַר כְּלוּם. אֲבָל דִּינָא אַחֲרָא דִּתַתָּא, שֵׁירוּתָא קַשְׁיָא, וְכָל מָה דְּאָזִיל אִתְחַלָּשׁ, עַד דְּנָהִיר אַנְפִּין, כְּגַוְּונָא דְּנוּקְבָּא דְּחַלָּשׁ חֵילָהָא.

142. Come and behold: what is the difference between the Upper Judgment – NAMELY, THE LEFT COLUMN OF BINAH WHICH IS THE SECRET OF ISAAC, THAT IT IS THE MALE LIGHT – and this Judgment OF THE FEMALE? In the supernal Judgment IN THE MALE THAT ILLUMINATES FROM ABOVE DOWNWARDS, both the beginning and the end are hard, and no one can withstand THOSE JUDGMENTS. The more it goes ON, the stronger it grows. Once it begins, it does not leave one until it consumes and destroys everything and nothing is left. But in the other lower Judgment – NAMELY IN MALCHUT, WHICH IS THE LIGHT OF THE FEMALE THAT ILLUMINATES FROM BELOW UPWARDS – the beginning is hard, NAMELY ON ROSH HASHANAH, and as it proceeds AND EXPANDS, it weakens until THE MOCHIN OF the face shines ON THE EIGHTH DAY OF CONVOCATION. This is like the female, whose strength is weak.

143. אֵימָתַי אִתְעַר דִּינָא דִּלְעֵילָּא לְמִשְׁרֵי עַל עָלְמָא. בְּיוֹמָא דְּטוֹפָנָא. וְעַל דָּא לָא אִשְׁתְּאַר כְּלוּם בְּעָלְמָא, בַּר הַהוּא תֵּיבוּתָא דְּנֹחַ, דְּאִיהִי כְּגַוְּונָא עִלָּאָה, דְּסָבִיל לְהַהוּא תּוּקְפָּא. וְאִי לָאו דְּזַמִּין קוּדְשָׁא בְּרִיךְ הוּא, וְאִשְׁתְּכַח בְּרַחֲמֵי עַל עָלְמָא, כָּל עָלְמָא אִתְאֲבִיד, דִּכְתִיב יְיָ׳ לַמַּבּוּל יָשָׁב, וְעַ״ד לָא שַׁרְיָא דִּינָא דִּלְעֵילָּא עַל עָלְמָא, דְּלָא יָכִיל עָלְמָא לְמִסְבַּל לֵיהּ, אֲפִילוּ רִגְעָא חֲדָא.

143. HE ASKS: When does the Upper Judgment OF THE MALE awaken to dwell on the world? HE ANSWERS: On the day of the flood. Therefore, nothing was left in the world except for Noah's ark, which is similar to the supernal ARK, WHICH IS MALCHUT, which bears that harshness OF

JUDGMENT, BEING A FIRE THAT BEARS FIRE. If the Holy One, blessed be He, had not prepared THE ARK FOR HIM, and if there has been no Mercy in the world, the whole world would have been destroyed, as it is written: "Hashem (Yud Hei Vav Hei) sat enthroned at the flood" (Tehilim 29:10). FOR THE NAME OF YUD HEI VAV HEI IS MERCY. Therefore, FROM THEN AND ONWARDS, the Upper Judgment does not dwell upon the world, because the world can not bear it even for one moment.

144. אַדְהָכִי הֲוָה ר' שִׁמְעוֹן בָּכֵי וְחַדֵּי. זָקְפוּ עַיְינִין, וְחָמוּ חֲמִשָּׁה מֵאִינוּן פְּרוּשִׁים, דְּהַהוּ אַזְלֵי אֲבַתְרֵיהּ, לְמִתְבַּע לֵיהּ. קָמוּ. אָמַר ר' שִׁמְעוֹן, מִכָּאן וּלְהָלְאָה מָה שְׁמָךְ. אָמַר, נְהוֹרַאי סָבָא, בְּגִין דִּנְהוֹרַאי אַחֲרָא אִית גַּבָּן. אַזְלוּ ר' שִׁמְעוֹן וְאִינּוּן חַבְרַיָּיא עִמֵּיהּ תְּלַת מִילִין, אָמַר רַבִּי שִׁמְעוֹן, לְאִינּוּן אַחֲרָנִין, מַה אָרְחָא דָּא גַּבַּיְיכוּ. אָמְרוּ, לְמִתְבַּע לֵיהּ לְהַאי סָבָא, דְּמֵימוֹי אֲנָן שָׁתָאן בְּמַדְבְּרָא. אָתָא ר' שִׁמְעוֹן וּנְשָׁקֵיהּ, אָמַר לֵיהּ, נְהוֹרַאי שְׁמָךְ, וּנְהוֹרָא אַנְתְּ, וּנְהוֹרָא עִמָּךְ שָׁרֵי.

144. In the meantime, Rabbi Shimon was weeping and rejoicing. They raised their eyes and saw five people of those who retired TO THE WILDERNESS, who went after THE OLD SAGE to seek him TO SPEAK TO THEM OF THE TORAH. They rose. Rabbi Shimon said: From now on, what is your name? He said: Nehorai Saba. Since there is another Nehorai among us THEY CALL ME NEHORAI SABA. They walked with him, Rabbi Shimon and his company, for three miles. Rabbi Shimon said to these OTHER people: Why are you making this trip? They said: We came to seek this sage TO TEACH US TORAH, because we drink his water in the wilderness. THAT IS, THEY ARE HIS STUDENTS IN THE WILDERNESS. Rabbi Shimon approached and kissed THAT SAGE. He said to him: Your name is Nehorai and you are a light, and the light dwells with you, BECAUSE NEHORAI MEANS LIGHT.

18. "He knows what is in the darkness"

A Synopsis

Rabbi Shimon explains that the title verse means that God revealed profound and concealed things, for were it not for the darkness of the Left, the depths and the concealed things would not be revealed. He says that "the light dwells with Him" refers to the light that has been revealed from within the darkness, and this light was revealed to all of us from the darkness that was in the wilderness.

145. פָּתַח ר׳ שִׁמְעוֹן וְאָמַר, הוּא גָּלֵא עֲמִיקָתָא וּמְסַתְּרָתָא יָדַע מָה בַּחֲשׁוֹכָא וּנְהוֹרָא עִמֵּהּ שָׁרֵא. הוּא גָּלֵה עֲמִיקָתָא וּמְסַתְּרָתָא, קוּדְשָׁא בְּרִיךְ הוּא גָּלֵי עֲמִיקָתָא וּמְסַתְּרָתָא, דְּכָל עֲמִיקִין סְתִימִין עִלָּאִין אִיהוּ גָּלֵי לוֹן. וּמַאי טַעֲמָא גָּלֵי לוֹן. בְּגִין דְּיָדַע מָה בַּחֲשׁוֹכָא. דְּאִלְמָלֵא חֲשׁוֹכָא לָא אִתְיְדַע נְהוֹרָא. וְאִיהוּ יָדַע מָה בַּחֲשׁוֹכָא. וּבְגִין כָּךְ גָּלֵי עֲמִיקָתָא וּמְסַתְּרָתָא, דְּאִי לָאו חֲשׁוֹכָא לָא יִתְגַּלְיָין עֲמִיקִין וּמְסַתְּרָאן. וּנְהוֹרָא עִמֵּהּ שָׁרֵא. מַאן נְהוֹרָא דָּא. נְהוֹרָא דְּאִתְגַּלְיָיא מִגּוֹ חֲשׁוֹכָא.

145. Rabbi Shimon opened the discussion, saying: "He reveals the deep and secret things. He knows what is in the darkness and the light dwells with Him" (Daniel 2:22). "He reveals the deep and secret things", means that the Holy One, blessed be He, reveals the deep and secret things. He reveals all the supernal, concealed depths, NAMELY, THE CENTRAL COLUMN THAT REVEALS THE DEPTHS OF THE TWO COLUMNS OF BINAH. Why did He reveal them? It is because "He knows what is in the darkness," NAMELY IN THE DARKNESS OF THE LEFT WHERE THE LIGHT OF CHOCHMAH SINKS BECAUSE OF THE LACK OF CHASSADIM. If there was not darkness, the light would not LATER be revealed THROUGH THE CENTRAL COLUMN. "He knows what is in the darkness," MEANING THAT HE INCLUDED IT IN THE RIGHT COLUMN. Therefore, He revealed deep and concealed things, for were it not for the darkness OF THE LEFT, the depths and the concealed would not be revealed. Then "The light dwells with Him". What is this light? It is the light that has been revealed from within the darkness, WHICH IS CHOCHMAH.

146. וַאֲנָן מִגּוֹ חֲשׁוֹכָא דַּהֲוָה בְּמַדְבְּרָא, אִתְגְּלֵי לָן נְהוֹרָא דָּא. רַחֲמָנָא

יַשְׁרֵי עִמָּךְ נְהוֹרָא, בְּעָלְמָא דֵין, וּבְעָלְמָא דְּאָתֵי. אָזְלֵי ר"ש וְחַבְרַיָּיא,
אִלֵּין תְּלַת מִילִין אֲבַתְרֵיה, אָמַר לֵיה, אֲמַאי לָא אָזְלֵי אִלֵּין עִמָּךְ
בְּקַדְמִיתָא. א"ל, לָא בְּעֵינָא לְאַטְרָחָא לְבַר נָשׁ עִמִּי, הַשְׁתָּא דְּאָתוּ נֵזִיל
כַּחֲדָא. אָזְלוּ, ור"ש אָזַל לְאָרְחֵיה. א"ר אַבָּא, הָא אֲנָן יַדְעֲנָא שְׁמֵיה,
וְאִיהוּ לָא יָדַע שְׁמֵיה דְּמָר, אָמַר לֵיה, מִנֵּיה יַדְעֲנָא דְּלָא לְאִתְחֲזָאָה.

146. And from within the darkness that was in the wilderness, this light was revealed to us. May the Merciful One cause light to dwell with you in this world and in the World to Come. Rabbi Shimon and the friends followed him for three miles. RABBI SHIMON said to him: Why did they not go with you, YOUR FIVE PEOPLE, in the beginning, BUT RATHER THEY CAME JUST NOW? THE SAGE said to him: I did not want to bother anyone TO ACCOMPANY ME. But now that they have come, we will travel together. They left and Rabbi Shimon went on his way. Rabbi Aba said to him: We know the name OF THE SAGE, but he does not know the name of my master. He said to him: From him I learnt not to reveal myself, FOR HE DID NOT TELL ME HIS NAME BEFORE I ASKED HIM.

KI TISA

Names of the articles

1. "Then shall they give every man a ransom for his soul"

A Synopsis

We are reminded that heavenly blessings do not accrue to anything that has been counted or numbered, and yet the children of Yisrael were subjected to a census. Yisrael were blessed nonetheless because they were ransomed.

וַיְדַבֵּר יְיָ' אֶל מֹשֶׁה לֵּאמֹר. כִּי תִשָּׂא אֶת רֹאשׁ בְּנֵי יִשְׂרָאֵל לִפְקוּדֵיהֶם וְגוֹ', ר' אַבָּא וְר' אָחָא וְר' יוֹסֵי הֲווֹ אַזְלֵי מִטְּבֶרְיָה לְצִפֹּרִי. עַד דַּהֲווֹ אַזְלֵי, חָמוּ לֵיהּ לְר' אֶלְעָזָר דַּהֲוָה אָתֵי, וְר' חִיָּיא עִמֵּיהּ. א"ר אַבָּא, וַדַּאי נִשְׁתַּתֵּף בַּהֲדֵי שְׁכִינְתָּא. אוֹרִיכוּ לְהוּ, עַד דְּמָטוּ לְגַבַּיְיהוּ. כֵּיוָן דְּמָטוּ גַבַּיְיהוּ, א"ר אֶלְעָזָר, וַדַּאי כְּתִיב, עֵינֵי יְיָ' אֶל צַדִּיקִים וְאָזְנָיו אֶל שַׁוְעָתָם. הַאי קְרָא קַשְׁיָא וְכוּ'.

1. "And Hashem spoke to Moses, saying, 'When you do take the sum of the children of Yisrael after their number" (Shemot 30:11-13). Rabbi Aba, Rabbi Acha and Rabbi Yosi were traveling from Tiberias to Tzipori. While they were traveling, they saw Rabbi Elazar coming with Rabbi Chiya. Rabbi Aba said: we shall surely join the Shechinah. They waited until they reached them. As soon as they came to them, Rabbi Elazar said: it is most certainly written: "The eyes of Hashem are towards the righteous, and His ears are open to their cry" (Tehilim 34:16). This passage is difficult; (THE END OF THE SUBJECT IS IN THE PORTION OF PEKUDEI, PARA. 68F).

ת"ח, הָא אוּקְמוּהָ, לֵית בִּרְכָתָא דִּלְעֵילָּא שַׁרְיָיא עַל מִלָּה דְּאִתְמְנֵי. וְאִי תֵּימָא, יִשְׂרָאֵל הֵיךְ אִתְמְנוּן. אֶלָּא כּוּפְרָא נָטִיל מִנַּיְיהוּ, וְהָא אוּקְמוּהָ, וְחוּשְׁבְּנָא לָא הֲוֵי עַד דְּאִתְכְּנִישׁ כָּל הַהוּא כּוּפְרָא, וְסָלִיק לְחוּשְׁבְּנָא. וּבְקַדְמֵיתָא מְבָרְכִין לְהוּ לְיִשְׂרָאֵל, וּלְבָתַר מִנְיַן הַהוּא כּוּפְרָא, וּלְבָתַר אָהַדְרָן וּמְבָרְכִין לוֹן לְיִשְׂרָאֵל. אִשְׁתְּכָחוּ יִשְׂרָאֵל מִתְבָּרְכָאן בְּקַדְמֵיתָא וּבְסוֹפָא, וְלָא סָלִיק בְּהוֹן מוֹתָנָא.

2. Come and behold: it has been established that celestial blessing does not dwell on something that is numbered. And if you ask how Yisrael were counted, he took from them a ransom for themselves. And they did not

count until all the ransom that was gathered was counted. THUS at first Yisrael are blessed WHEN THE RANSOM IS RECEIVED, afterwards, once they counted the ransom, Yisrael are blessed again. So we find that Yisrael is blessed at the beginning and at the end, and they did not suffer a plague.

3. מוֹתָנָא אֲמַאי סָלִיק בְּמִנְיָינָא. אֶלָּא בְּגִין דְּבִרְכָתָא לָא שַׁרְיָא בְּמִנְיָינָא, כֵּיוָן דְּאִסְתַּלַּק בִּרְכָתָא, סִטְרָא אַחֲרָא שַׁרְיָא עֲלֵיהּ, וְיָכִיל לְאַנְזְקָא, בְּגִין כַּךְ נַטְלִין כּוּפְרָא וּפִדְיוֹנָא לְסַלְּקָא עֲלֵיהּ מִנְיָינָא, וְהָא אוּקְמוּהָ, וְאִתְּמַר.

3. HE ASKS: Why is a plague caused by counting? HE ANSWERS: Because the blessing does not dwell on anything numbered, and since the blessing has departed, the Other Side dwells on it and can harm. Therefore, we receive ransom and redeem it in order to do the counting. And we have already discussed and learned this.

2. Half a Shekel

A Synopsis

Rabbi Shimon begins by speaking about the commandment to give half a shekel, and says it is like the Vav placed between the two Heis. The Faithful Shepherd, Moses, then follows with a discussion of the commandment to sanctify the month. He says that the holy moon, Malchut, is the bride that becomes hallowed by Gvurah of Zeir Anpin, in which are the Levites, who shall also be hallowed. Then when the moon becomes visible we bless it with Tiferet.

רעיא מהימנא

4. פְּקוּדָא לִיתֵּן מַחֲצִית הַשֶּׁקֶל בְּשֶׁקֶל הַקֹּדֶשׁ. מַאן מַחֲצִית הַשֶּׁקֶל אִיהוּ כְּגוֹן חֲצִי הַהִין, וְדָא ו׳, מְמוּצָע בֵּין שְׁנֵי הֵהִי״ן. אַבְנָא לְמִשְׁקַל בָּה, דָּא י׳, עֶשְׂרִים גֵּרָה הַשֶּׁקֶל: דָּא יו״ד. הֶעָשִׁיר לָא יַרְבֶּה, דָּא עַמוּדָא דְּאֶמְצָעִיתָא, לָא יַרְבֶּה עַל י׳. וְהָכִי אִתְּמַר בְּס״י, עֶשֶׂר סְפִירוֹת בְּלִימָה, עֶשֶׂר וְלָא אֶחָד עָשָׂר. וְהַדַּל לָא יַמְעִיט, דָּא צַדִּיק, לָא יַמְעִיט מֵעֶשֶׂר, כְּד״א עֶשֶׂר וְלָא תֵּשַׁע. מִמַּחֲצִית הַשֶּׁקֶל, דְּאִיהוּ י׳.

Ra'aya Meheimna (the Faithful Shepherd)

4. There is a commandment to give half a shekel after the shekel of the sanctuary. HE ASKS: What is the half-shekel? HE ANSWERS: It is like a half-*hin*, which is *Vav*, WHICH IS placed between the two *Heis*. The stone with which to weigh is *Yud*, "A shekel is Twenty *gera*" (Shemot 30:13), refers to *Yud-Vav-Dalet*. "The rich shall not give more" (Ibid. 15), refers to the Central Column, ZEIR ANPIN that should not give more than ten. And so have we learned in the Book of Formation, 'Ten Sfirot of nothingness – ten, not eleven.' "And the poor shall not give less" (Ibid.) refers to the Righteous, THAT IS, YESOD. He must "not give less" than ten, as is said IN THE BOOK OF FORMATION, 'ten and not nine,' then half a shekel, which is ten.

5. א״ל רַעְיָא מְהֵימָנָא, אַנְתְּ בַּשָּׁמַיִם, רָחִים אַנְתְּ מִמָּארֵיךָ, לֵית תַּוָּוהָא בְּכָל אִינּוּן מִלִּין יַקִּירִין דְּיִפְקוּן מִפּוּמָךְ, דְּהָא מַאן דְּאִיהוּ מַלְכָּא, אוֹ

בְּרָא דְמַלְכָּא, לֵית תַּוְוהָא, דִּיפְּקוּן מַרְגְּלָאִין בְּפָתוֹרֵיה, מַלְיָין סְגוּלוֹת, מַלְיָין נְהוֹרִין. לְבַר נָשׁ אַחֲרָא, אִיהוּ תַּוְוהָא. א"ל בְּרִיךְ אַנְתְּ רַעְיָא מְהֵימָנָא. מִתַּמָּן וְאֵילָךְ אֵימָא אַנְתְּ, דְּעֶלָּאִין וְתַתָּאִין נַחְתוּ לְמִשְׁמַע מִינָךְ. אָמַר לֵיה, אַשְׁלִים מִלּוּלָךְ, אָמַר לֵיה, לָא אִית כְּעַן לְמֵימַר יַתִּיר, אֵימָא אַנְתְּ עַד זִמְנָא אַחֲרָא.

5. IT SEEMS THAT THE AUTHOR OF THE PREVIOUS PARAGRAPH WAS RABBI SHIMON. And the Faithful Shepherd said to him: You are in heaven; you are loved by your Master, therefore it is no wonder that all these precious words come from your mouth. For if one is a king or a prince, there is no wonder his table is full of gems and treasures, and full of lights. For anyone else this would be a wonder. He said to him: Blessed are you, faithful shepherd; from now on you speak, for those above and below have come to hear. He said to him: finish your words. He said to him: I have nothing more to say for the time being. You speak.

6. פָּתַח רַעְיָא מְהֵימָנָא, פִּקּוּדָא בָּתַר דָּא, לְקַדֵּשׁ אֶת הַחֹדֶשׁ. בְּגִין דְּסִיהֲרָא קַדִּישָׁא אִיהִי כַּלָּה, דְּמִתְקַדֶּשֶׁת ע"פ ב"ד, דְּאִיהוּ גְבוּרָה, בְּגִין דְּתַמָּן לֵיוָאֵי, דְּאִתְּמַר בְּהוּ וְקִדַּשְׁתָּ אֶת הַלְוִיִם. וּלְבָתַר דְּאִתְחֲזֵי סִיהֲרָא דְּיֵיאוֹתוּ לְאוֹרָה, מְבָרֵךְ עֲלֵיהּ בָּרוּךְ אַתָּה יְיָ' אֱלֹהֵינוּ מֶלֶךְ הָעוֹלָם, אֲשֶׁר בְּמַאֲמָרוֹ בָּרָא שְׁחָקִים, וּבְרוּחַ פִּיו כָּל צְבָאָם. וּבְמִי מִתְקַדֶּשֶׁת וּמִתְבָּרֶכֶת, בְּתִפְאֶרֶת בְּגִין דְּאִיהוּ עֲטֶרֶת תִּפְאֶרֶת לַעֲמוּסֵי בָטֶן.

ע"כ רעיא מהימנא

6. The Faithful Shepherd opened the discussion with: The following commandment is to sanctify the month. The holy moon, NAMELY MALCHUT, is the bride that becomes hallowed by the Court of Law, which is Gvurah OF ZEIR ANPIN – BECAUSE MALCHUT IS BUILT FROM THE LEFT SIDE, WHICH IS GVURAH, as therein, GVURAH OF ZEIR ANPIN, are the Levites. For it is said of them, 'And you shall hallow the Levites.' ALSO MALCHUT, WHICH IS OF THE GVURAH OF ZEIR ANPIN, NEEDS SANCTIFICATION. And afterwards, when the moon is visible and we can enjoy its light, MEANING AFTER IT RECEIVED MOCHIN, we bless it,

'Blessed are You, Hashem our Elohim, King of the Universe, With His utterance He created the heavens, and with the breath of His mouth, all their hosts.' And with what is it hallowed and blessed? It is with Tiferet (glory), because it is glory to those born by Him from birth.

End of Ra'aya Meheimna (the Faithful Shepherd)

3. Sun worship

A Synopsis

At dawn Rabbi Chiya remarks how all the inhabitants of the East are at that moment worshipping the rising sun. He says that from ancient days it was known that before the sun emerges the prince appointed over it goes forth with the holy letters of the Supernal Name written on his head, and with the power of those letters he opens the windows of heaven and passes through. Then he remains there until the sun emerges. Rabbi Chiya adds that that prince is in charge over gold and red jewels. He says that the sun worshippers know the spots of the sun. Rabbi Yosi asks how long it will be that idols are still in the world, and says that falsehood can not endure.

7. רִבִּי יוֹסֵי וְר׳ חִיָּיא הֲווֹ אַזְלֵי בְּאָרְחָא, עַד דַּהֲווֹ אַזְלִין רָמַשׁ לֵילְיָא, יָתְבוּ. אַדְהֲווֹ יַתְבִין, שְׁרִיאַת צַפְרָא לְאַנְהֲרָא, קָמוּ וְאָזְלוּ. א״ר חִיָּיא, חָמֵי אַנְפּוֹי דְּמִזְרָח דְּקָא מְנַהֲרִין, הַשְׁתָּא כָּל אִינּוּן בְּנֵי מְדִינְחָא דְּטוּרֵי נְהוֹרָא, סַגְדִּין לְגַבֵּי הַאי נְהוֹרָא, דְּנָהִיר בַּאֲתָר דְּשִׁמְשָׁא, עַד לָא יִפּוֹק, וּפַלְחִין לֵיהּ, דְּהָא כֵּיוָן דְּנָפִיק שִׁמְשָׁא, כַּמָה אִינּוּן דְּפַלְחִין לְשִׁמְשָׁא. וְאִלֵּין אִינּוּן דְּקָא פַּלְחִין לִנְהוֹרָא דָּא, וְקַרָאן לְהַאי נְהוֹרָא, אֱלָהָא דְּמַרְגְּלָא דְּנָהִיר. וְאוֹמָאָה דִּלְהוֹן בֵּאֱל״ה דְּמַרְגְּלָא דְּנָהִיר.

7. Rabbi Yosi and Rabbi Chiya were traveling. While they were still walking, it became dark and they sat down. While they were still sitting dawn began to light up. They got up and went on. Said Rabbi Chiya: See, the East has lit up. Now all those inhabitants of the East, of the mountains of light, are bowing to this light that illuminates in the place of the sun, before it emerges OVER THE FACE OF THE EARTH, and worship it. Many worship the sun after it comes out. They worship this light OF THE BREAKING DAWN, and call this light 'the Deity of the Illuminating Jewels'. And they swear by the Deity of the Illuminating Jewels.

8. וְאִי תֵּימָא פּוּלְחָנָא דָּא לְמַגָּנָא הוּא. מִיּוֹמִין עַתִּיקִין קַדְמָאֵי, חָכְמְתָא יָדְעוּ בֵּיהּ. בְּזִמְנָא דְּשִׁמְשָׁא נָהִיר, עַד לָא יִפּוֹק, הַהוּא מְמָנָא דְּפָקִיד עַל שִׁמְשָׁא, נָפִיק, וְאַתְוָון קַדִּישִׁין דִּשְׁמָא עִלָּאָה קַדִּישָׁא רְשִׁימָן עַל רֵישֵׁיהּ, וּבְחֵילָא דְּאִינּוּן אַתְוָון, פָּתַח לְכָל כַּוֵּי שְׁמַיָא וּבָטַשׁ בְּהוּ,

-98-

וְעָבַר. וְהַהוּא מְמָנָא עָאל גּוֹ הַהוּא זֹהֲרָא דְּנָהִיר סָחֲרָנֵיהּ דְּשִׁמְשָׁא,
וְתַמָּן שְׁכִיחַ, עַד דְּנָפַק שִׁמְשָׁא, וְאִתְפָּשַׁט בְּעָלְמָא.

8. And you may ask if this worship is not in vain. From the early, ancient days the wisdom was known that when the sun shines, before it emerges OVER THE FACE OF THE EARTH, the prince appointed over the sun goes forth, with the holy letters of the Supernal Name written on his head. With the power of these letters, he opens all the windows of heaven, smites them, and passes through. And that prince enters into the glow that shines around the sun, BEFORE IT EMERGES, and remains there until the sun emerges and spreads over the world.

9. וְהַהוּא מְמָנָא, אִיהוּ פְּקִידָא, עַל דַּהֲבָא, וְעַל מַרְגְּלָן סוּמָקָן. וְאִינּוּן
פָּלְחִין לְהַהוּא דִּיּוּקְנָא דְּתַמָּן, וּבְנְקוּדִין וְסִימָנִין דְּיָרְתוּ מִקַּדְמָאֵי מִיּוֹמִין
עַתִּיקִין, אַזְלֵי וְיַדְעֵי נְקוּדִין דְּשִׁמְשָׁא, לְמִשְׁכַּח אַתְרִין דְּדַהֲבָא וּמַרְגְּלָן,
א"ר יוֹסֵי, עַד כַּמָּה יְהוֹן פּוּלְחָנִין סַגִּיאִין אִלֵּין בְּעָלְמָא, דְּהָא שְׁקְרָא
לֵית לֵיהּ קַיָּימִין לְקַיָּימָא.

9. And that prince is in charge over gold and red jewels. They worship that form that is there IN THE LIGHT OF THE SUN, WHICH IS THE PRINCE, with the spots and signs that they inherited from the ancient in olden days. They then know the spots of the sun, and they go and find the places of gold and jewels. Said Rabbi Yosi: How long will the many idols be in the world? Falsehood has no pillars TO SUPPORT IT in order to exist.

4. "The lip of truth shall be established forever"

A Synopsis

We read that the light and radiation from the sun is true, and the stars in the firmament are true; just because in their lack of wisdom people call them 'Elohim', God does not have to destroy the sun and stars. They will not perish, but eventually those that worship them will perish. Yisrael are the lip of Truth, and they will still exist in the time to come. The story is recounted of a General who tells Rabbi Elazar that since the kingdom of Yisrael was removed from them, it is Yisrael who are the "lying tongue." But Rabbi Elazar explains to him that the verse says "The lip of truth shall be established forever" in the future, not now – for now the lip of falsehood endures. We are told that the General converted after this encounter.

10. פְּתַח אִידָךְ וְאָמַר, שְׂפַת אֱמֶת תִּכּוֹן לָעַד וְעַד אַרְגִּיעָה לְשׁוֹן שָׁקֶר. תַּ״ח, אִלּוּ כָּל בְּנֵי עָלְמָא הֲווֹ פַּלְחִין לְשִׁקְרָא, הֲוָה הָכִי, אֲבָל הַאי נְהוֹרָא וְזָהֲרָא דְּנָהִיר, וַדַּאי קְשׁוֹט אִיהוּ. כֹּכְבֵי רוּמָא דִּרְקִיעָא קְשׁוֹט אִינּוּן. אִי בְּטִפְּשׁוּ וְחֶסְרוֹנָא דְּדַעְתָּא דִּלְהוֹן, אִינּוּן אַמְרֵי וְקָרָאן לְהוּ אֱלָהָא, לָא בָּעֵי קוּדְשָׁא בְּרִיךְ הוּא לְשֵׁיצָאָה עוֹבָדוֹי מֵעָלְמָא. אֲבָל לִזְמְנָא דְּאָתֵי לָא יִשְׁתְּצוּן כֹּכְבַיָּא וּנְהוֹרִין דְּעָלְמָא. אֲבָל מַאן יִשְׁתְּצֵי. אִינּוּן דְּפָלְחוּ לוֹן.

10. The other opened the discussion, and said, "The lip of truth shall be established forever; but a lying tongue is but for a moment" (Mishlei 12:19). Come and behold: if all the inhabitants of the world always worshiped falsehood, then it would be so, THEY WOULD CEASE TO EXIST. But this light and radiation THAT SHINES FROM THE SUN is certainly true, and the stars that are in the heights of the firmament are also true. And if in their foolishness and lack of understanding, they say and call them 'Elohim', the Holy One, blessed be He, does not have to destroy His creations from the world BECAUSE OF THIS. And also, in the time to come, the stars and luminaries will not perish from the universe. But who will perish? Those that worship them WILL PERISH.

11. וּקְרָא דָּא הָכִי הוּא. שְׂפַת אֱמֶת תִּכּוֹן לָעַד, אִלֵּין יִשְׂרָאֵל, דְּאִינּוּן

-100-

שְׂפַת אֱמֶת. יְיָ׳ אֱלֹהֵינוּ יְיָ׳ אֶחָד. וְכֹלָּא אִיהוּ אֱמֶת, וְרָזָא דֶּאֱמֶת,
וּמְסַיְּימֵי יְיָ׳ אֱלֹהֵיכֶם אֱמֶת. וְדָא אִיהוּ שְׂפַת אֱמֶת תִּכּוֹן לָעַד.

11. And this verse: "The lip of truth shall be established forever," refers to the children of Yisrael, who are the lip of Truth, FOR THEY SAY, "Hashem our Elohim, Hashem is One" (Devarim 6:4). And it is all true and the secret of Truth. And they end THE READING OF SH'MA WITH, 'Hashem your Elohim is true.' And hence "the lip of truth shall be established forever."

12. וְעַד אַרְגִּיעָה, וְעַד רֶגַע מִבָּעֵי לֵיהּ, מַאי אַרְגִּיעָה. אֶלָּא, עַד כַּמָּה
יְהֵא קִיּוּמָא דִּלְהוֹן בְּעָלְמָא, עַד זִמְנָא דְּיֵיתֵי, וְיְהֵא לִי נַיְיחָא מִפּוּלְחָנָא
קַשְׁיָא דְעָלוֹי. וּבְזִמְנָא דְּאַרְגִּיעָה, יִשְׁתְּצֵי לִשׁוֹן שָׁקֶר, אִינוּן דְּקַרְאָן
אֱלָהָא, לְמַאן דְּלָאו הוּא אֱלָהָא. אֲבָל יִשְׂרָאֵל דְּאִינוּן שְׂפַת אֱמֶת,
כְּתִיב בְּהוּ, עַם זוּ יָצַרְתִּי לִי תְּהִלָּתִי יְסַפֵּרוּ.

12. "But for a moment (lit. 'I will calm down')." HE ASKS: It should say 'for a moment', but it says "calm down". HE ANSWERS: They will long exist in the world, until the future to come. Then I will have respite from their difficult worship, BECAUSE "CALM DOWN" MEANS 'I SHALL HAVE REST.' And at the time that I will calm, the false tongue will perish – meaning those who call 'Elohim' that which is not Elohim. But of the children of Yisrael, who are the lip of truth, it is written: "This people which I have formed for Myself, that they might say My praise" (Yeshayah 43:21).

13. אַדְכַּרְנָא חֲדָא זִמְנָא דַּהֲוֵינָא אָזִיל בַּהֲדֵי ר׳ אֶלְעָזָר, פָּגַע בֵּיהּ
הֶגְמוֹנָא, אָ״ל לְר׳ אֶלְעָזָר, אַנְתְּ יַדְעַת מֵאוֹרַיְתָא דִּיהוּדָאֵי. אָ״ל יַדְעֲנָא.
אָ״ל, לֵית אַתּוּן אַמְרִין דִּמְהֵימְנוּתָא דִּלְכוֹן קְשׁוֹט, וְאוֹרַיְיתְכוֹן קְשׁוֹט,
וַאֲנָן דִּמְהֵימְנוּתָא דִּילָן שָׁקֶר, וְאוֹרַיְיתָא דִּילָן שָׁקֶר. וְהָא כְּתִיב שְׂפַת
אֱמֶת תִּכּוֹן לָעַד וְעַד אַרְגִּיעָה לִשׁוֹן שָׁקֶר. אֲנָן מִיּוֹמִין דְּעָלְמָא, קַיְימִין
בְּמַלְכוּתָא, וְלָא אַעֲדֵי מִינָן לְעָלְמִין, דָּרָא בָּתַר דָּרָא, תִּכּוֹן לָעַד וַדַּאי.
וְאַתּוּן, זְעֵיר הֲוָה לְכוּ מַלְכוּתָא, וּמִיַּד אַעֲדֵי מִנְּכוֹן, וּקְרָא אִתְקַיִּים בְּכוּ
דִּכְתִיב וְעַד אַרְגִּיעָה לִשׁוֹן שָׁקֶר.

13. I remember one time when I was traveling with Rabbi Elazar, he met a general. He said to Rabbi Elazar: Do you know the Torah of the Jews? He said to him: I know. He said to him: Do you not say that your faith is true and your Torah is true but our faith is false and our bible is false? But it is written, "The lip of truth shall be established forever, and a lying tongue is but for a moment" (Mishlei 12:19). We have existed from time immemorial, and our kingdom has never left us, generation after generation. Hence, assuredly it is "established forever." But as for you, for a short period you had a kingdom and immediately it was removed from you. Thus, the passage has been fulfilled by you that says: "And a lying tongue is but for a moment."

14. א״ל, חֲמֵינָא בָּךְ דְּאַנְתְּ חַכִּים בְּאוֹרַיְיתָא. תִּפַּח רוּחֵיהּ דְּהַהוּא גַּבְרָא. אִלּוּ אָמַר קְרָא, שְׂפַת אֱמֶת כּוֹנַנְתָּ לָעַד, הֲוָה כִּדְקָאמְרָן, אֲבָל לָא כְּתִיב אֶלָּא תִּכּוֹן, זְמִינָא שְׂפַת אֱמֶת דְּתִתְכּוֹן, מַה דְּלָאו הָכִי הַשְׁתָּא, דְּהַשְׁתָּא שְׂפַת שֶׁקֶר קַיָּימָא, וּשְׂפַת אֱמֶת שְׁכִיבָא לְעַפְרָא, וּבְהַהוּא זִמְנָא דֶּאֱמֶת יָקוּם עַל קִיּוּמֵיהּ, וּמִגּוֹ אֶרֶץ תִּצְמַח, כְּדֵין שְׂפַת אֱמֶת תִּכּוֹן לָעַד וְגוֹ׳.

14. He said to him: I see that you are a scholar in Torah. May that man breathe his last. Had it said, "The lip of truth was established forever," then it would be as you said. But it is written, 'shall be established forever', MEANING that the true lip will be established in the future, but not now. For now the lip of falsehood endures, and the lip of truth lies in the dust. And when Truth will stand firm and sprout from the ground then, "the lip of truth shall be established forever."

15. א״ל הַהוּא הֶגְמוֹן, זַכָּאָה אַנְתְּ. וְזַכָּאָה עַמָּא דְּאוֹרַיְיתָא דִּקְשׁוֹט יָרְתִין. בָּתַר יוֹמִין שְׁמַעְנָא דְּאִתְגַּיַּיר. אֲזְלוּ, מָטוּ חַד בֵּי חַקְל, וְצַלּוּ צְלוֹתְהוֹן. כֵּיוָן דְּצַלּוּ צְלוֹתְהוֹן, אָמְרוּ מִכָּאן וּלְהָלְאָה נִתְחַבַּר בִּשְׁכִינְתָּא, וְנֵזִיל וְנִתְעַסֵּק בְּאוֹרַיְיתָא.

15. The General said to him: You are right. Blessed are the people of the Torah, who inherited the Truth. After some time we heard that he converted.

They went on, reached a certain field, and recited their prayer. After they prayed, they said: From now on let us join the Shechinah, and walk and be occupied with Torah.

5. "Behold, all who were incensed against you shall be ashamed and confounded"

A Synopsis

Rabbi Yosi says that the children of Yisrael suffered many evils when they were in exile, and they were only able to bear it because of the promise of good that God told them was to be theirs in the future. Other nations have scorned and reviled Yisrael, saying, Where is your God? Where is this good you have been promised? We are told that there are no people that revile Yisrael like the children of Edom, yet in the future they "shall be ashamed and confounded" from all the goodness they will see in the children of Yisrael.

16. פָּתַח ר' יוֹסֵי וְאָמַר, הֵן יֵבוֹשׁוּ וְיִכָּלְמוּ כֹּל הַנֶּחֱרִים בָּךְ וְגוֹ'. זַמִּין קוּדְשָׁא בְּרִיךְ הוּא לְמֶעְבַּד לְיִשְׂרָאֵל, כָּל אִינּוּן טָבָאן, דְּקָאָמַר עַל יְדֵי נְבִיאֵי קְשׁוֹט, וְיִשְׂרָאֵל סָבְלוּ עֲלֵיהוֹן, כְּמָה בִּישִׁין בְּגָלוּתְהוֹן. וְאִלְמָלֵא כָּל אִינּוּן טָבָאן דְּקָא מְחַכָּאן וְחָמָאן כְּתִיבִין בְּאוֹרַיְיתָא, לָא הֲווֹ יַכְלִין לְמֵיקָם וּלְמִסְבַּל גָּלוּתָא.

16. Rabbi Yosi opened the discussion, saying: "Behold, all who were incensed against you shall be ashamed and confounded" (Yeshayah 41:11). The Holy One, blessed be He, shall do all this good that He said through the true prophets for Yisrael. Yisrael suffered much evil in exile, and were it not for all this good written in the Torah that they were waiting to see, they would not have been able to withstand and tolerate the exile.

17. אֲבָל אַזְלִין לְבֵי מִדְרָשׁוֹת, פַּתְחִין סִפְרִין, וְחָמָאן כָּל אִינּוּן טָבָאן, דְּקָא מְחַכָּן, וְחָמָאן כְּתִיבִין בְּאוֹרַיְיתָא, דְּאַבְטַח לוֹן קוּדְשָׁא בְּרִיךְ הוּא עֲלַיְיהוּ, וּמִתְנַחֲמִין בְּגָלוּתְהוֹן, וּשְׁאָר עַמִּין מְחָרְפִין וּמְגַדְּפִין לוֹן, וְאַמְרֵי אָן הוּא אֱלָהֲכוֹן, אָן אִינּוּן טָבָאן דְּאַתּוּן אַמְרִין דִּזְמִינִין לְכוֹן, וְכִי כָּל עַמִּין דְּעָלְמָא יִכְסְפוּן מִנַּיְיכוּ.

17. But they go to the study hall, open books, and read all the hoped for good. And they see written in the Torah what the Holy One, blessed be He,

promised them, and they are comforted in exile. But the other nations scorn and revile them, and say, "Where is your Elohim? Where is the good you say shall be yours, when all the other nations shall be shamed before you?"

18. הה״ד שָׁמְעוּ דְּבַר יְיָ׳ הַחֲרֵדִים אֶל דְּבָרוֹ אָמְרוּ אֲחֵיכֶם שׂוֹנְאֵיכֶם וְגו׳. מַאי הַחֲרֵדִים אֶל דְּבָרוֹ, אִינוּן דְּסַבְלוּ כַּמָה בִּישִׁין, כַּמָה שְׁמוּעוֹת שְׁמַעֵי, אִלֵּין עַל אִלֵּין, וְאִלֵּין בָּתַר אִלֵּין, וְחֲרִידָן עֲלֵיהוֹן, כד״א כִּי וְגו׳ קוֹל חֲרָדָה שָׁמָעְנוּ פַּחַד וְאֵין שָׁלוֹם וְגו׳. אִינוּן חֲרֵדִים תָּדִיר אֶל דְּבָרוֹ כַּד אִתְעֲבֵיד דִּינָא.

18. This is the meaning of: "Hear the word of Hashem, you that tremble at His word. Your brethren that hated you, who cast you out for My Name's sake…" (Yeshayah 66:5). Who are they "that tremble at His word?" It is those who have suffered many evils, many EVIL tidings, one upon another and one after another, THEY HEARD AND trembled because of them, as it is written, "For thus says Hashem, we have heard a voice of trembling, of fear, and not of peace" (Yirmeyah 30:5). They tremble constantly over His word when Judgment is executed.

19. אָמְרוּ אֲחֵיכֶם שׂוֹנְאֵיכֶם, אִלֵּין אִינוּן אֲחוּכוֹן בְּנֵי עֵשָׂו. מְנַדֵּיכֶם, כד״א סוּרוּ טָמֵא קָרְאוּ לָמוֹ. דְּלֵית עַמָּא דְּקָא מְבַזִין לוֹן בְּאַנְפֵּי, וּמְרַקְּקִין בְּאַנְפַּיְיהוּ לְיִשְׂרָאֵל כִּבְנֵי אֱדוֹם. וְאָמְרֵי כֻּלְּהוּ מְסָאֲבִין כַּנִּדָּה, וְדָא אִיהוּ מְנַדֵּיכֶם. לְמַעַן שְׁמִי יִכְבַּד יְיָ׳, אֲנָן בְּנוֹי דְּאֵל חַי. דִּי בֵּן יִתְיַיקַּר שְׁמֵיה. אֲנָן שַׁלְטָנִין עַל עָלְמָא בְּגִין הַהוּא דְּאִקְרֵי גָּדוֹל. עֵשָׂו בְּנוֹ הַגָּדוֹל. וּבִשְׁמָא דָּא אִקְרֵי קוּדְשָׁא בְּרִיךְ הוּא גָּדוֹל, גָּדוֹל יְיָ׳ וּמְהוּלָּל מְאֹד. אֲנָן בְּנֵי הַגָּדוֹל, וְאִיהוּ גָּדוֹל. וַדַּאי לְמַעַן שְׁמִי יִכְבַּד יְיָ׳.

19. "Your brethren that hated you". They are your brethren, the children of Esau "who cast you out," as it is written: "'Away! Unclean!', they cried at them" (Eichah 4:15). There are no people that shame Yisrael to their faces and spit in their faces like the children of Edom. And they say ABOUT YISRAEL that they are all impure like the impurity of a menstruating woman. This is "…who cast you out for My Name's sake, have said: Let Hashem be glorified." FOR THEY SAY: We are the children of the living El

and by us will His name be glorified. We rule over the world, because of him who is called 'big,' as it is written, "Esau the bigger (lit. 'elder') son" (Beresheet 27:15). With this name, 'big', is the Holy One, blessed be He, called, AS IT IS WRITTEN: "Great is Hashem and highly to be praised" (Tehilim 145:3). We are His big (lit. 'elder') son and He is great; most certainly, IT IS SAID OF US, "for My Name's sake…let Hashem be glorified."

20. אֲבָל אַתּוּן זְעֵירִין מִכֹּלָּא, יַעֲקֹב בְּנָהּ הַקָּטָן כְּתִיב, אָן הוּא אֱלָהֲכוֹן. אָן הוּא אִינּוּן טָבָאן, דְּיִכְסְפוּן כָּל עַמְמַיָּא מֵחֶדְוָה דִּלְכוֹן. מַאן יִתֵּן וְנִרְאֶה בְשִׂמְחַתְכֶם כְּמָה דְּאַתּוּן אַמְרִין. וְהֵם יֵבוֹשׁוּ כְּמַאן דְּתָלֵי קְלָלָתָא בְּאַחֲרָא, בְּגִין דְּאַתּוּן אַמְרִין דִּכְדֵין יֵבוֹשׁוּ וְיִכָּלְמוּ, וּבג"ד רוּחַ קֻדְשָׁא הֲוָה אָמַר מִלָּה הָכִי, וְעַל דָּא, הֵן יֵבוֹשׁוּ וְיִכָּלְמוּ כֹּל הַנֶּחֱרִים בָּךְ. מַאי כֹּל הַנֶּחֱרִים בָּךְ. דְּאִתְקְפוּ נְחִירֵיהוֹן בְּרוּגְזָא עֲלָךְ בְּגָלוּתָא דָּא. בְּהַהוּא זִמְנָא, יֵבוֹשׁוּ וְיִכָּלְמוּ מִכָּל טָבִין דְּיֶחֱמוּן לְהוֹן לְיִשְׂרָאֵל.

20. AND THEY SAY TO THE CHILDREN OF YISRAEL: But you are the smallest of all, AS IT IS WRITTEN, "Jacob her small (lit. 'younger') son" (Beresheet 27:15). Where is your Elohim? Where is your goodness that all the nations shall be shamed before your joy? Who will grant it so that we see your joy, as you say? "They…shall be ashamed" (Yeshayah 41:11)? THEY SHOULD HAVE SAID, 'YOU WILL BE ASHAMED', BUT they spoke as if referring to someone else, saying, then YISRAEL "shall be ashamed and confounded." YET THEY SAID, "THEY…SHALL BE ASHAMED," AS CURSING ANOTHER. Therefore, the Holy Spirit said the phrase SO THAT IN TRUTH THEY WILL BE SHAMED. And of this IT IS WRITTEN: "Behold, all they that were incensed against you shall be ashamed and confounded." What is "all they that were incensed (Heb. *necherim*) against you?" Their nostrils (Heb. *nechiraim*) became hardened in their anger against you, in this exile, BECAUSE at that time, IN THE FUTURE, they "shall be ashamed and confounded" from all the goodness they shall see in Yisrael.

6. The Exile goes on

A Synopsis

Rabbi Chiya says that the exile has gone on for a long time, but still the son of David has not come. Rabbi Chiya answers that the pledge that God has guaranteed them enables them to bear their exile; otherwise they would never be able to tolerate it. Although everything depends on repentance, still there are many people who will not repent. We read a story about the mother of a wayward son, who weeps for her child who has been exiled by the father, and thereby persuades the father to take him back. After the son sins again, the father exiles both the boy and his mother. The story shows why God exiled the children of Yisrael to Egypt. We read that God wants the children of Yisrael to be as a reflection of above, perfect lilies like the supernal lily; therefore he sowed seventy couples that were seventy souls and put them among the thorns that were the Egyptians. Then the thorns grew branches and ruled over the world, with the lily blooming among them. When God wished to retrieve his lilies the dead thorns were cast aside and destroyed. During the exile in Babylon the children of Yisrael sinned greatly, and Malchut pleaded with Zeir Anpin on their behalf. When they sinned again God exiled them together with Malchut, their guarantor. We are told that if people repent, even one pain that they have undergone will be considered as though they have suffered all the pains of exile; if they do not repent, they must wait until all the generations that precede the end appear.

21. א״ר חִיָּיא הָכִי הוּא וַדַּאי, אֲבָל חֲמֵינָן וְהָכִי חָמוּ תַּקִּיפֵי עָלְמָא, דְּהָא גָּלוּתָא אִתְמְשַׁךְ וַעֲדַיִין בְּרֵיהּ דְּדָוִד לָא אָתֵי. א״ר יוֹסֵי, וְכָל דָּא הָכִי הוּא, אֲבָל מַאן עָבִיד דְּיִסְבְּלוּן יִשְׂרָאֵל גָּלוּתָא דָּא, כָּל אִינּוּן הַבְטָחוֹת דְּאַבְטַח לוֹן קוּדְשָׁא בְּרִיךְ הוּא. וְהָא אִתְּמַר, דְּעָאלִין לְבָתֵּי כְּנֵסִיּוֹת וּלְבָתֵּי מִדְרָשׁוֹת, וְחָמָאן כָּל אִינּוּן נֶחָמוֹת, וְחָדָאן בְּלִבַּיְיהוּ לְמִסְבַּל כָּל מַה דְּיֵיתֵי עֲלַיְיהוּ, וְאִלְמָלֵא דָּא לָא יַכְלִין לְמִסְבַּל.

21. Said Rabbi Chiya: It is certainly so, but we see, as well as the mighty ones of the world, MEANING THE NATIONS, that the exile grows long yet the son of David has still not come. Said Rabbi Yosi: All this is so. But all these pledges that the Holy One, blessed be He, has guaranteed them to enable Yisrael to bear this exile. And we have learned that they enter synagogues and study halls and see all these consolations IN THE HOLY BOOKS, and

rejoice in their hearts to suffer whatever comes upon them. And were it not for that they would not be able to tolerate it.

22. א״ר חִיָּיא וַדַּאי הָכִי אִיהוּ, וְכֹלָּא בִּתְשׁוּבָה תַּלְיָא. וְאִי תֵּימָא דְּיָכְלוּן הַשְׁתָּא לְאִתְעָרָא תְּשׁוּבָה כֻּלְּהוּ כַּחֲדָא. לָא יַכְלִין. מ״ט לָא יַכְלִין. בְּגִין דִּכְתִּיב, וְהָיָה כִּי יָבֹאוּ עָלֶיךָ כָּל הַדְּבָרִים הָאֵלֶּה. וּכְתִיב וַהֲשֵׁבֹת אֶל לְבָבֶךָ בְּכָל הַגּוֹיִם אֲשֶׁר הִדִּיחֲךָ וְגו׳. וּכְתִיב וְשַׁבְתָּ עַד יְיָ׳ אֱלֹהֶיךָ וְגו׳. וּכְדֵין אִם יִהְיֶה נִדַּחֲךָ בִּקְצֵה הַשָּׁמַיִם מִשָּׁם יְקַבֶּצְךָ וְגו׳. וְעַד דְּכָל אִינּוּן מִלִּין לָא יִתְקַיְּימוּן, לָא יַכְלִין לְאִתְעָרָא תְּשׁוּבָה מִנַּיְיהוּ.

22. Rabbi Chiya said: Certainly, it is so. And everything depends upon repentance. If you believe that everyone together can be aroused to repent, even now, it is not so. What is the reason that they can not? Because it is written: "And it shall come to pass, when all these things are come upon you...and you shall call them to mind among all the nations, into which Hashem your Elohim has driven you, and shall return to Hashem your Elohim" (Devarim 1:2). And then, "If your outcasts be at the utmost parts of heaven, from there will Hashem your Elohim gather you" (Ibid. 4). And before all these things are fulfilled they can not be aroused to repentance.

23. א״ר יוֹסֵי, כַּמָה סַתָּמְתְּ כָּל אָרְחִין וּשְׁבִילִין מִכָּל בְּנֵי גָלוּתָא, וְלָא שַׁבְקַת לוֹן פִּתְחוֹן פֶּה. אִי הָכִי, לְהֱווֹ כְּמָה דַּהֲווֹ בְּכָל דָּרָא וְדָרָא, דְּלָא יִסְבְּלוּן גָּלוּתָא וְלָא אַגְרָא, וְיִפְקוּן מְדִינָא דְּאוֹרַיְיתָא, וְיִתְעָרְבוּן בִּשְׁאַר עַמִּין.

23. Rabbi Yosi said: How concealed you have made the ways and paths for all those in exile, and have not left them any excuse. For otherwise they will remain as they are, MEANING THAT THEY WILL NOT STRIVE FOR REPENTANCE in every generation, and will not bear the exile, and will not REQUEST reward, but will depart from the laws of the Torah, and will intermingle with the other nations.

24. פָּתַח וְאָמַר, כְּמוֹ הָרָה תַּקְרִיב לָלֶדֶת תָּחִיל תִּזְעַק בַּחֲבָלֶיהָ וְגו׳.

מַאי כְּמוֹ הָרָה, אָרַח אִיהוּ לְעוּבַּרְתָּא, לְאַעְבְּרָא עָלָה תֵּשַׁע יַרְחִין
שְׁלֵמִין. וְאִית בְּעָלְמָא כַּמָה וְכַמָה, דְּלָא עָבַר עָלָה אֶלָּא יוֹמָא חַד אוֹ
תְּרֵין יוֹמִין מִתְּשִׁיעָאָה, וְכָל צִירִין וַחֲבָלִין דְּעוּבַּרְתָּא בִּתְשִׁיעָאָה אִינּוּן.
וְאע״ג דְּלָא אַעְבַּר עָלָה אֶלָּא יוֹמָא חֲדָא, אִתְחֲשִׁיב עָלָה כְּאִילוּ
אִתְעֲבָרוּ כָּל תְּשִׁיעָאָה שְׁלִים. אוּף הָכִי יִשְׂרָאֵל, כֵּיוָן דְּאִטְעֲמֵי טַעַם
גָּלוּתָא, אִי יָהַדְרוּן בִּתְשׁוּבָה, יִתְחֲשַׁב עָלַיְיהוּ כְּאִלוּ אַעְבָּרוּ עָלַיְיהוּ כָּל
אִינּוּן מִלִּין דִּכְתִיבִין בְּאוֹרַיְיתָא. כ״ש וְכ״ש דְּכַמָה וְכַמָה יִסוּרִין אַעְבָּרוּ
עָלַיְיהוּ מִן יוֹמָא דְּגָלוּתָא שָׁרֵי.

24. He opened the discussion, saying: "Like a woman with child, that draws near the time of her delivery, is in pain, and cries out in her pangs..." (Yeshayah 26:17). What is "Like a woman with child?" It is the way of a pregnant woman to undergo nine complete months. There are many in the world for whom only one or two days of the ninth MONTH pass, when all labor and birth pangs are. Nevertheless, it is considered for her as though she has undergone the entire ninth MONTH. This is also the case with Yisrael: since they had the taste of exile, if they repent it is considered by them as though all THE TROUBLES that are written in the Torah befell them, especially since so many troubles have befallen them.

25. אֲבָל מַאי דִּכְתִיב, בַּצַּר לְךָ וּמְצָאוּךָ כֹּל הַדְּבָרִים הָאֵלֶּה בְּאַחֲרִית
הַיָּמִים. ת״ח, כַּמָה רַחֲמָנוּתָא רָחִים קוּדְשָׁא בְּרִיךְ הוּא לְיִשְׂרָאֵל בְּמִלָּה
דָא. לְמַלְכָּא דַּהֲוָה לֵיה בְּרָא יְחִידָאָה, וְרָחִים לֵיה רְחִימוּ דְנַפְשָׁא, וּמִגּוֹ
רְחִימוּ דִּילֵיה, יָהַב לֵיה לְאִמֵּיה מַטְרוֹנִיתָא דִּתְרַבֵּי לֵיה, וְתוֹלִיף לֵיה
אָרְחֵי מִתַּתְקְנָן. זִמְנָא חֲדָא חָב לְגַבֵּי אֲבוּה, אָתָא אֲבוֹהִי וְאַלְקֵי לֵיה,
וּלְבָתַר אַעְבָּר עַל חוֹבֵיה. תָּב כְּמִלְּקַדְמִין וְחָב לַאֲבוּה, וְאַפְקֵיה אֲבוּה
מִבֵּיתֵיה, וְאַרְגִּיז עָלֵיה, נָפַק הַהוּא בְּרָא מִבֵּיתֵיה.

25. But what of the words: "When you are in distress, and all these things are come upon you, in the latter days" (Devarim 4:30)? Come and behold: how much Mercy has the Holy One, blessed be He, shown on Yisrael in this matter. It is like a king who had an only son whom he loved with his whole soul. In his great love for him he gave him over to his mother, the queen, to

raise him and teach him the right ways. Once the son sinned against his father. His father came and beat him, and afterwards forgave him. When he sinned against his father again, his father put him out of his house, and was angry with him; the son left his house.

26. וּבְאֲתָר דְּיָהַךְ בְּאֹרַח קְשׁוֹט, וִיהֵא זַכָּאָה כַּדְקָא יֵאוֹת, בְּגִין דְּיִשְׁמַע מַלְכָּא אֲבוּהַ, וִיהֵא תִּיאוּבְתֵּיה עֲלֵיהּ. מָה עֲבַד. אָמַר הוֹאִיל וְנָפְקֲנָא מֵהֵיכְלָא דְּאַבָּא, אֶעְבִּיד מִכָּאן וּלְהָלְאָה כָּל מָה דַּאֲנָא בָּעֵי. מָה עֲבַד. אֲזַל וְאִתְחַבַּר בְּזוֹנוֹת, וְאִתְלַכְלֵךְ בְּלִכְלוּכָא דְּטִנּוּפָא בַּהֲדַיְיהוּ, וְלָא הֲוָה מִשְׁתְּכַח אֶלָּא בַּהֲדַיְיהוּ, בְּחַבּוּרָא דִּלְהוֹן. דְּמַטְרוֹנִיתָא אֲמֵיהּ פַּקְדַת בְּכָל יוֹמָא עַל הַהוּא בְּרָא, וְיָדְעַת דִּבְרָהּ בַּהֲדֵי זוֹנוֹת אִתְחַבַּר, וְכָל חַבְרוּתָא דִּידֵיהּ בַּהֲדַיְיהוּ הֲוָות. שָׁרִיאַת לְמִבְכֵּי, וּלְאִתְמָרְרָא עַל בְּרָהּ.

26. Instead of going in the right path to be meritorious, as is proper, so that his father, the king, should hear about it and long for him, what did he do? He thought: after having left my father's palace, from now on I will do whatever I please. Then he associated with prostitutes and was besmirched and soiled with them, and remained only in their company. His mother, the queen, visited her son daily and knew that her son had joined with prostitutes and associated only with them. She started to weep and grieve for her son.

27. יוֹמָא חַד עָאל מַלְכָּא לְגַבָּהּ, חָמָא לָהּ דְּאִיהִי מְבַכָּה. שָׁאִיל לָהּ עַל מָה אַתְּ בָּכָאת. אָמְרָה וְלָא אֶבְכֶּה, דְּהָא בְּרָנָא לְבַר מֵהֵיכְלָא דְּמַלְכָּא. וְלָא דִּי דְּהוּא לָא יָתִיב בְּהֵיכְלָא דְּמַלְכָּא, אֶלָּא דְּהוּא יָתִיב בַּהֲדֵי זוֹנוֹת. מַה יֵימְרוּן כָּל בְּנֵי עָלְמָא, בְּרֵיה דְּמַלְכָּא אִיהוּ דְּיָתִיב בְּבֵי זוֹנוֹת. שָׁרִיאַת לְמִבְכֵּי, וּלְאִתְחַנְּנָא לְמַלְכָּא. אָמַר מַלְכָּא, בְּגִינָךְ אַהְדָּר לֵיהּ, וְאַנְתְּ עַרְבָא דִּילֵיהּ. אֲמָרַת הָא וַדַּאי.

27. One day, the king came to her and saw her weeping. He asked her why she was weeping. She said to him: How can I not weep? Our son is outside the king's palace, and not only does he no longer live in the king's palace, he lives in a brothel. What will people say of the king's son who lives in a brothel? She started to weep and beseech the king. The king said: for your

sake I will return him, but you must be his surety THAT HE DOES NOT SIN. She said: I WILL surely BE HIS GUARANTOR.

28. אָמַר מַלְכָּא הוֹאִיל וְכַךְ הוּא, לָא אִצְטְרִיךְ לְאַהֲדְרָא לֵיהּ בִּימָמָא בְּאִתְגַּלְיָא. דְּכְסוּפָא דִּילָן אִיהוּ לְמֵהַךְ בְּגִינֵיהּ לְבֵי זוֹנוֹת. וְאִי לָא הֲוֵי בְּגַוְונָא דָא, דְּטַנֵּף גַּרְמֵיהּ הָכִי וְחַלֵּל יְקָרִי. הֲוֵינָא אֲנָא, וְכָל חַיָּילִין דִּילִי, אַזְלִין בְּגִינֵיהּ בְּכַמָּה יְקָר, בְּכַמָּה בּוֹקִינָס קַמֵּיהּ, בְּכַמָּה מָאנֵי קְרָבָא, מִימִינֵיהּ וּמִשְׂמָאלֵיהּ, עַד דְּכָל בְּנֵי עָלְמָא יִזְדַּעְזְעוּן, וְיִנְדְּעוּן כֹּלָא, דִּבְרָא דְמַלְכָּא אִיהוּ. הַשְׁתָּא כֵּיוָן דְּאִיהוּ טַנֵּף גַּרְמֵיהּ, וְחַלֵּל יְקָרִי, אִיהוּ יֶהֱדַר בִּטְמִירוּ, דְּלָא יִנְדְּעוּן בֵּיהּ. אַהֲדָר לְגַבֵּי מַלְכָּא, יָהֲבֵיהּ לְגַבֵּי אִמֵּיהּ.

28. The king said: Since it is so, then it is not advisable to return him during the day, publicly, for it is an embarrassment for us to follow him to the brothel. Had it not been so, that he soiled himself so and desecrated my honor, I and all my hosts would go after him with much glory, with many trumpeters before him, with many weapons on his right and left, so all the inhabitants of the world would tremble and everyone would know that he is the king's son. But now, since he has soiled himself and desecrated my honor, he must return stealthily, so he will not be recognized. The son returned to the king, who gave him over to his mother.

29. לְיוֹמִין סָרַח כְּמִלְּקַדְמִין. מָה עֲבַד מַלְכָּא. אַפִּיק לֵיהּ וּלְאִמֵּיהּ בַּהֲדֵיהּ מִגּוֹ הֵיכָלָא, אָמַר תַּרְוַוְיְיכוּ תֵּהֲכוּן, וְתַרְוַוְיְיכוּ תְּסַבְּלוּן גָּלוּתָא, וּמַלְקִיּוּתָא תַּמָּן. כֵּיוָן דְּתַרְוַוְיְיכוּ תְּסַבְּלוּן כַּחֲדָא, כְּדֵין יָדַעְנָא דִּבְרִי יְתוּב כַּדְקָא חֲזֵי.

29. After some time, he sinned again. What did the king do? He exiled him and his mother with him out of his palace. He said: Both of you go, and both of you suffer exile and blows there. Since both of you will suffer together, then I know that my son will repent properly.

30. כַּךְ יִשְׂרָאֵל בְּנוֹי דְמַלְכָּא קַדִּישָׁא אִינּוּן. אָחִית לוֹן לְמִצְרַיִם. וְאִי

תֵּימָא בְּהַהוּא זִמְנָא לָא חָאבוּ, גְזֵרָה דִּגְזַר קוּדְשָׁא בְּרִיךְ הוּא בֵּין הַבְּתָרִים הֲוָה אִתְחֲזֵי לְמֶהֱוֵי קַיָּים, וְקוּדְשָׁא בְּרִיךְ הוּא אַשְׁגַּח לִתְרֵין מִלִּין, חַד בְּגִין הַהוּא מִלָּה דְּאָמַר אַבְרָהָם, בַּמָּה אֵדַע כִּי אִירָשֶׁנָּה, דָּא הוּא סִבָּה וְעִילָה. אֲבָל עַד דְּנַפְקוּ מִמִּצְרַיִם, לָא הֲוֵי גּוֹי, וְלָא אִתְחֲזוּ כַּדְקָא יֵאוּת.

30. Thus, He brought Yisrael, the children of the Holy King, down to Egypt. And you may argue that at that time they had not sinned AND HE DID NOT BRING THEM DOWN BECAUSE OF SIN, but rather it was a decree that the Holy One, blessed be He, decreed between the parts that had to be fulfilled. SO IT WAS, for the Holy One, blessed be He, looked at two things. One was because of that which Abraham said, "by what shall I know that I shall inherit it" (Beresheet 15:8), which was the cause and grounds FOR THE EGYPTIAN EXILE. AND ONE WAS that before they left Egypt, they were not a nation and were not worthy TO BE A NATION.

31. פָּתַח וְאָמַר, כְּשׁוֹשַׁנָּה בֵּין הַחוֹחִים כֵּן רַעֲיָתִי בֵּין הַבָּנוֹת. בָּעָא קוּדְשָׁא בְּרִיךְ הוּא לְמֶעְבַּד לוֹן לְיִשְׂרָאֵל כְּגַוְונָא דִלְעֵילָא וּלְמֶהֱוֵי שׁוֹשַׁנָּה חֲדָא בְּאַרְעָא, כְּגַוְונָא עִלָּאָה. וְשׁוֹשַׁנָּה דְּסַלְקָא רֵיחָא, וְאִתְבְּרִיר מִכָּל שְׁאָר וְורְדִין דְּעָלְמָא, לָא הֲוֵי אֶלָּא הַהִיא דְסַלְקָא בֵּין הַחוֹחִים. וְדָא אָרְחָא כַּדְקָא יֵאוּת. וְע״ד זָרַע שַׁבְעִין זוּגִין, דְּהֲווֹ שִׁבְעִין נֶפֶשׁ, וְאָעֵיל לוֹן בֵּין הַחוֹחִים, וְאִינּוּן חוֹחִים, מִיַּד דְּהֲווֹ אִינּוּן זוּגִין תַּמָּן, סְלִיקוּ עַנְפִין וְטַרְפִין וְשָׁלִיטוּ עַל עָלְמָא, וּכְדֵין פַּרְחַת שׁוֹשַׁנָה בֵּינַיְיהוּ.

31. He opened the discussion and said: "Like the lily among thorns, so is my love among the daughters" (Shir Hashirim 2:2). The Holy One, blessed be He, wanted to make the children of Yisrael as a reflection of the above, so that they would be one lily on the earth like the supernal lily, WHICH IS MALCHUT. And the lily that exudes fragrance and is the choicest of all the other lilies in the world is the one that grows among thorns. This one gives off fragrance properly. Therefore, he sowed seventy couples, which were seventy souls, and brought them among thorns, WHO WERE THE EGYPTIANS. Now as soon as the couples came among them, these thorns grew branches and leaves and ruled over the world. Then the lily bloomed among them.

‏32. כֵּיוָן דְּבָעָא קוּדְשָׁא בְּרִיךְ הוּא לְאַפָּקָא שׁוֹשַׁנָה וְלָקִיט לָהּ מִבֵּינַיְיהוּ, כְּדֵין יָבְשׁוּ חוֹחִים, וְאִזְדְּרִיקוּ, וְאִשְׁתְּצִיאוּ, וְלָא אִתְחַשְׁבוּ לִכְלוּם. בְּשַׁעֲתָא דְּאָזִיל לְמִלְקְטָא שׁוֹשַׁנָה דָּא, לְאַפָּקָא בְּרֵיהּ בּוּכְרֵיהּ, בְּהַהוּא זִמְנָא אָזַל מַלְכָּא גּוֹ כַּמָּה חַיָּילִין רַבְרְבָנִין וְשַׁלִּיטִין, עִם דְּגָלִין פְּרִישָׁן, וְאָפִיק לִבְרֵיהּ בּוּכְרֵיהּ בְּכַמָּה גִּבּוֹרִין, וְאַיְיתֵי לֵיהּ לְהֵיכָלֵיהּ, וְיָתִיב סַגִּי בְּבֵי מַלְכָּא.

32. As soon as the Holy One, blessed be He, wanted to take out the lily and pick her out from among them, the thorns dried up and were cast aside, destroyed, and were regarded as worthless. At the time that He went to pluck this lily, meaning to take out His firstborn son, the king went among many hosts, princes and ministers, with banners spread, and brought out his firstborn with many warriors, brought him to this palace, and he sat properly in the king's house.

‏33. כֵּיוָן דְּחָב לְגַבֵּי אֲבוּהָ, אוֹכַח לֵיהּ, וְאַלְקֵי לֵיהּ, דִּכְתִּיב, וַיִּחַר אַף יְיָ' בְּיִשְׂרָאֵל וַיִּתְּנֵם בְּיַד שׁוֹסִים וְגוֹ', סָרַח כְּמִלְּקַדְמִין, וּמָרַד בְּאֲבוּהָ, אַפְקֵיהּ מִבֵּיתֵיהּ. מַה עַבְדוּ יִשְׂרָאֵל, חָמוּ דְּהָא אִתְבַּדְרוּ לְבָבֶל, אִתְעָרְבוּ בְּעַמְמַיָּא, נָסִיבוּ נָשִׁין נָכְרִיּוֹת, וְאוֹלִידוּ בְּנִין מִנְּהוֹן. עכ"ד, אִימָּא קַדִּישָׁא הֲוַת אַפְטְרוֹפּוֹסָא עֲלַיְיהוּ.

33. When he sinned against his father, he admonished him and beat him, as it is written: "And the anger of Hashem burned against Yisrael, and He delivered them into the hands of spoilers..." (Shoftim 2:14). When he sinned as before and rebelled against his father, he put him out of his house. What did the children of Yisrael do? They saw that they were dispersed in Babylon, they mingled with the nations, married foreign women, and begot children by them. With all this, the Holy Mother, NAMELY MALCHUT, was their guardian. SHE PLEADED ON THEIR BEHALF BEFORE THE KING, ZEIR ANPIN.

‏34. וְעַל דְּעָבֵד הָכִי, קוּדְשָׁא בְּרִיךְ הוּא אָמַר, הוֹאִיל וְכִסּוּפָא אִיהוּ, לֵיתֵי בְּרִי אִיהוּ מִגַּרְמֵיהּ, הוֹאִיל וְחִלֵּל יְקָרִי, לָא אִתְחֲזֵי דְּאֲנָא אֵיזִיל תַּמָּן לְאַפָּקָא לֵיהּ, וּלְמֶעְבַּד לֵיהּ נִסִּין וּגְבוּרָן כְּמִלְּקַדְמִין. תָּבוּ אִינּוּן,

בְּלָא סִיוּעָא דְּאִתְחֲזוּ לוֹן, בְּלָא פְּלִיאָן וְנִסִין, אֶלָּא כֻּלְּהוּ מִתְבַּדְּרָן, כֻּלְּהוּ לְאָן בְּמִסְכְּנוּ, וְתָבוּ לְהֵיכָלָא דְּמַלְכָּא בְכִסּוּפָא, וְאֵימָא קַדִּישָׁא עֲרָבַת לוֹן.

34. Because they did this, the Holy One, blessed be He, said: 'Since this is an embarrassment for Me, let My son come by himself. Since he desecrated My honor, he is not worthy that I should go there to take him out and perform miracles and mighty deeds as before, IN EGYPT'. They returned without the help that they should have had, without wonders and miracles. Rather, they were dejected, weary in poverty, and returned to the King's palace in shame, and the Holy Mother, WHO IS MALCHUT, was a guarantor for them.

35. חָאבוּ כְּמִלְּקַדְמִין. מַה עֲבַד קוּדְשָׁא בְּרִיךְ הוּא. אַפִּיק לְהַאי בְּרָא כְּמִלְּקַדְמִין מֵהֵיכָלֵיהּ, וְאִמֵּיהּ בַּהֲדֵיהּ. אָמַר, מִכָּאן וּלְהָלְאָה, אִימָּא וּבְרָהּ יִסְבְּלוּן כַּמָּה בִּישִׁין כַּחֲדָא, הה"ד וּבְפִשְׁעֵיכֶם שֻׁלְּחָה אִמְּכֶם. וְעַל דָּא כְּתִיב, בַּצַּר לְךָ וּמְצָאוּךָ כֹּל הַדְּבָרִים הָאֵלֶּה בְּאַחֲרִית הַיָּמִים. מַאי בְּאַחֲרִית הַיָּמִים. אֶלָּא דָּא הִיא אִימָּא קַדִּישָׁא, דְּהִיא אַחֲרִית הַיָּמִים, וְעִמָּהּ סָבְלוּ כָּל מָה דְּסַבְלוּ בְּגָלוּתָא.

35. They sinned as before. What did the Holy One, blessed be He, do? He took His son out of His palace again, and his Mother with him. He said: 'From now on, the mother and her son are together. Let them suffer many evils.' This is the meaning of, "And for your transgressions was your mother put away" (Yeshayah 50:1). Of this is it written, "When you are in distress, and all these things are come upon you, in the latter days" (Devarim 4:30). What is "the latter days?" This is the Holy Mother, NAMELY MALCHUT, WHICH IS THE LAST OF THE TEN SFIROT, and together with Her they suffered whatever they suffered in exile.

36. וְאִילוּ יְהַדְרוּן בְּתִיוּבְתָּא, אֲפִילוּ חַד בִּיש, אוֹ חַד צַעֲרָא, דִּיעֲבַר עֲלַיְיהוּ, אִתְחֲשַׁב עֲלַיְיהוּ, כְּאִילוּ סַבְלוּ כֹּלָּא וְאִי לָא. כַּד יִסְתַּיֵּים קִיצָא, וְכָל דָּרִין דִּילֵיהּ. כְּמָה דְּאָמַר בּוּצִינָא קַדִּישָׁא, דִּכְתִיב לִצְמִיתוּת לַקּוֹנֶה

אוֹתוֹ לְדוֹרוֹתָיו. וְכָל דָּא, בְּתִיוּבְתָּא תַּלְיָא מִילְתָא. א"ר חִיָּיא, וַדַּאי הָכִי הוּא. וְע"ד גָּלוּתָא אִתְמְשָׁךְ.

36. But if they repent, then even one pain or one evil they underwent would be considered for them as though they suffered all the troubles of exile; but if not, IF THEY DO NOT REPENT, THEY MUST WAIT until the end with all its generations. As the holy luminary said, the words, "for ever" (Vayikra 25:23), refer to the purchaser for generations – THAT IS, UNTIL ALL THE GENERATIONS THAT PRECEDE THE END APPEAR. And with all this, it depends upon repentance. Rabbi Chiya said: It is certainly so. Therefore, the exile goes on.

7. "And it shall come to pass in the last days"

A Synopsis

We learn that in the "last days," God will perform both miracles and vengeance for the children of Yisrael. The discussion moves to the Cup of Blessing, that must be raised high; this is alluded to in "And shall be exalted above the hills", and means that the good that will befall Yisrael will be in the last days. We are told that God told Moses that even though Yisrael sin in every generation, He still does not want anyone else to slander them. He has given them many blessings in order that they may repent and return to their Father in heaven.

37. אֲבָל קוּדְשָׁא בְּרִיךְ הוּא, כָּל מָה דְּחָמֵי לוֹן לְיִשְׂרָאֵל, בְּהַאי אַחֲרִית הַיָּמִים, וּבְהַאי אַחֲרִית הַיָּמִים יַעֲבִיד לוֹן נִסִּין וְנוּקְמִין, דִּכְתִיב וְהָיָה בְּאַחֲרִית הַיָּמִים נָכוֹן יִהְיֶה הַר בֵּית יְיָ' בְּרֹאשׁ הֶהָרִים. מַאן רֹאשׁ הֶהָרִים. דָּא אַבְרָהָם סָבָא, כַּהֲנָא רַבָּא, רֹאשׁ דְּכֹלָּא. וּבְגִין דְּאִיהוּ רֹאשׁ, כּוֹס דִּבְרָכָה, יִהְיֶה נָכוֹן בְּרֹאשׁ הֶהָרִים, דָּא אַבְרָהָם סָבָא, קַדְמָאָה לִשְׁאַר הֶהָרִים. כּוֹס דִּבְרָכָה, אִצְטְרִיךְ לְמֶהֱוֵי מְתַקְנָא בִּימִינָא.

37. However, all that the Holy One, blessed be He, saw pertaining to the children of Yisrael is at this end of days, MEANING MALCHUT. And in this "last days," He will perform for them miracles and vengeance, as is written: "And it shall come to pass in the last days, that the mountain of Hashem's house shall be established on the top of the mountains" (Yeshayah 2:2). What is "the top of the mountains?" This is Abraham the patriarch, WHO IS CHESED, CALLED 'High Priest', MEANING CHESED THAT ASCENDED TO CHOCHMAH, which is the top of them all, BECAUSE CHESED IS THE TOP OF THE SEVEN LOWER SFIROT. And because he is the top of the Cup of Blessing, WHICH IS MALCHUT, he will be established at the top of the mountains. This is Abraham the patriarch, the first of the other mountains, BECAUSE CHESED, GVURAH, AND TIFERET ARE CALLED 'MOUNTAINS', AND CHESED IS THE FIRST OF THEM. Thus, the Cup of Blessing, WHICH IS MALCHUT, has to be prepared on the right, WHICH IS CHESED.

38. וְנִשָּׂא מִגְּבָעוֹת. אִצְטְרִיךְ לְמֶהֱוֵי זָקִיף מִן פַּתוֹרָא, שִׁיעוּרָא דְּאַקְרֵי זֶרֶת, לְבָרְכָא לְקוּדְשָׁא בְּרִיךְ הוּא, וְדָא הוּא וְנִשָּׂא מִגְּבָעוֹת. מִגְּבָעוֹת

מַאי הוּא. אֶלָּא בֵּינָה, וּבֵין בְּתוּלוֹת אַחֲרֶיהָ רְעוֹתֶיהָ, שִׁעוּרָא דְזֶרֶת אִיהוּ. נָשָׂא כּוֹס דִּבְרָכָה מִגְּבָעוֹת וַדַּאי, וְע"ד טָבָא דִּיהֵא לֵיהּ לְהַאי בְּרָא בּוּכְרָא, בְּאַחֲרִית הַיָּמִים אִיהוּ.

38. "And shall be exalted above the hills" (Ibid.). THIS ALLUDES TO THE CUP OF BLESSING that should be raised above the table to the measure called a 'span', to bless the Holy One, blessed be He. This is the meaning of, "exalted above the hills." What is "above the hills?" HE ANSWERS: Binah, and between, "the virgins, her companions that follow her" (Tehilim 45:15), there is the measurement of a span. Therefore, the cup of blessing is definitely raised above the hills. Therefore, the good that will befall the firstborn son, NAMELY YISRAEL, will be in the last days.

39. א"ל שַׁפִּיר קָאמַרְתְּ, הַאי קְרָא וַדַּאי הָכִי הוּא. בְּרֹאשׁ הֶהָרִים, דָּא יְמִינָא, אַבְרָהָם סָבָא, דְּאִיהוּ רֹאשׁ הֶהָרִים וַדַּאי. וְנִשָּׂא מִגְּבָעוֹת, מִשִּׁעוּרָא דִּגְבָעוֹת, דְּאִינּוּן רְעוֹתֶיהָ. וְשַׁפִּיר קָאמֶרֶת. וְנָהֲרוּ אֵלָיו כָּל הַגּוֹיִם. מַאי הוּא. א"ל, וַאֲפִילוּ נָשִׁים וּקְטַנִּים וְשַׁמָּשׁ דְּפָלַח עַל פָּתוֹרָא, אע"ג דְּאִיהוּ לָא אָכַל, אִצְטְרִיךְ לְמִשְׁמַע, וּלְמֵימַר אָמֵן. דְּלָא יֵימָא בַּר נָשׁ, אֲנָא לָא אֲכָלִית, וְהוֹאִיל דְּלָא אִצְטְרִיפְנָא לְזִמּוּן, לָא אֶשְׁמַע וְלָא אֵימָא אָמֵן. הַכֹּל חַיָּיבִין בֵּיהּ.

39. He said to him: You have spoken well. This verse is certainly so. "On the top of the mountains," is right, which is Abraham the patriarch, who is certainly the top of the mountains, THE TOP OF CHESED, GVURAH, AND TIFERET, THAT ARE CALLED 'MOUNTAINS'. "And exalted above the hills," MEANING the measure of hills, which are her companions. And you spoke well. "And all the nations shall flow to it" (Yeshayah 2:2): what is its meaning, ACCORDING TO YOUR WORDS THAT THE PASSAGE REFERS TO THE CUP OF BLESSING? He said to him: IT MEANS even women and children and the waiter who serves at the table. Even if one does not eat, one must listen TO THE BLESSINGS and answer: Amen, so that no one would say: if I do not eat, since I am not included in a quorum, I will not listen nor say Amen. THEREFORE IT SAYS, "AND ALL THE NATIONS SHALL FLOW TO IT," since everyone is obligated in it.

40. ד"א וְנָהֲרוּ אֵלָיו כָּל הַגּוֹיִם, אע"ג דְּנָשִׁים וּקְטַנִּים פְּטוּרִין מִן הַמִּצְוֹת, בְּכוֹס דִּבְרָכָה הַכֹּל חַיָּיבִין, בִּלְבַד דְּיִנְדְּעוּן לְמַאן מְבָרְכִין, וְדָא הִיא וְנָהֲרוּ אֵלָיו כָּל הַגּוֹיִם. אָתָא רְבִּי יוֹסֵי וּנְשָׁקֵיהּ, אָמַר כַּמָּה שַׁפִּיר מִלָּה דָא, וּמְתִיקָא לְחִכָּא.

40. Another explanation of: "And all the nations will flow to it." Although women and children are exempted from commandments, everyone is obligated to the cup of blessing, only they have to know whom they are blessing. And this is the meaning of, "And all the nations shall flow to it." Rabbi Yosi came and kissed him. He said: How beautiful are these words, and how sweet to the palate!

41. הַשְׁתָּא אִית לְדַיְּיקָא, אִי הַאי אַחֲרִית הַיָּמִים, אִיהוּ כּוֹס דִּבְרָכָה מַמָּשׁ, מַהוּ הַר בֵּית יְיָ', הֲוָה לֵיהּ לְמִכְתַּב הָכִי, וְהָיָה אַחֲרִית הַיָּמִים נָכוֹן יִהְיֶה בְּרֹאשׁ הֶהָרִים. מַהוּ בְּאַחֲרִית הַיָּמִים נָכוֹן יִהְיֶה הַר בֵּית יְיָ'. א"ל, אַחֲרִית הַיָּמִים אִיהוּ אִילָנָא כֹּלָא, מֵרֵישֵׁיהּ וְעַד סֵיפֵיהּ, דְּהוּא אִילָנָא דְּטוֹב וָרָע. וְאָתָא קְרָא לְבָרְרָא בְּאַחֲרִית הַיָּמִים, וְאַפִּיק הַר בֵּית יְיָ', דָּא טוֹב בְּלָא רָע. הַר בֵּית יְיָ' וַדַּאי דְּלֵית תַּמָּן חוּלָקָא לְסִטְרָא אַחֲרָא, דְּהָא אִתְבְּרִיר הַר בֵּית יְיָ', מִגּוֹ אִילָנָא דְּאִיהוּ אַחֲרִית הַיָּמִים. וְדָא אִיהוּ כּוֹס דִּבְרָכָה, דְּאִיהוּ נָכוֹן בְּרֹאשׁ הֶהָרִים.

41. Here we must point out that if "the last days" is the actual Cup of Blessing, MEANING MALCHUT, what is "the mountain of Hashem's house?" It should have been written thus: 'And it shall come to pass in the last days, that it will be established on the top of the mountains.' What is the meaning of "in the last days, that the mountain of Hashem's house shall be established?" THIS IS A REPETITION, BECAUSE "THE LAST DAYS" IS MALCHUT, AND "THE MOUNTAINS OF HASHEM'S HOUSE," IS ALSO MALCHUT. He replies: "the last days," refers to the whole Tree, MEANING THE ENTIRE MALCHUT from top to end, which is the Tree of Knowledge of Good and Evil – ACCORDING TO THE SECRET OF 'IF HE MERITS, IT IS GOOD, BUT IF HE DOES NOT MERIT, IT IS EVIL'. And the passage came to refine "the last days," and extracted, "the mountain of Hashem's house," which is the good OF MALCHUT, without evil. This is surely "The mountain

of Hashem's house," where the Other Side has no part, because the mountain of Hashem's house has been extracted from the Tree, which is "the last days." And this is the Cup of Blessing, which is established on the top of the mountains.

42. א״ר יוֹסֵי, זַכָּאָה אָרְחָא דָא, דְּזָכֵינָא לְהַאי מִלָּה. א״ל מִמָּאן שַׁמְעַת לָהּ. א״ל, יוֹמָא חֲדָא הֲוֵינָא אָזִיל בְּאָרְחָא, וּשְׁמַעְנָא וַחֲמֵינָא לֵיהּ לְרַב הַמְנוּנָא סָבָא, דַּהֲוָה דָּרִישׁ לְהַאי קְרָא לְרַבִּי אַחָא, וְכֵיוָן דְּשַׁמַעְנָא חַדֵּינָא בֵּיהּ, וּנְטִירְנָא לֵיהּ צָרִיר בְּכַנְפָא דִּלְבוּשַׁאי, דְּלָא יִתְעֲדֵי מִנַּאי לְעָלְמִין. א״ל, וַדַּאי מִלָּה קַדִּישָׁא דָא, מִנְּהִירוּ דְּבוּצִינָא קַדִּישָׁא אִתְנְהִיר. זַכָּאָה דָּרָא, דְּקַיְימֵי עָלְמָא וְסַמְכוֹי, שַׁרְיָין בְּגַוֵּיהּ. וְאִי אַנְתְּ צָרִירַת לְהַאי מִלָּה בְּקִשְׁרָא חֲדָא דְּלָא יִתְעֲדֵי מִנָּךְ. אֲנָא אֶצְרוֹר לָהּ בִּתְלָתִין, אוֹ בְּאַרְבְּעִין קִשְׁרִין בְּכִיסַאי, דְּלָא יִתְעֲדֵי מִינַּאי לְעָלְמִין.

42. Rabbi Yosi said: Blessed is this path that we merited that interpretation. He said to him: From whom did you hear it? He said to him: One day, I was walking on the road and I heard and saw Rav Hamnuna Saba expounding upon this passage for Rabbi Acha. When I heard it, I rejoiced over it and kept it bound in the corner of my garment so that it should never leave me. He said: Certainly, this holy subject was illuminated by the holy luminary. Blessed is the generation that preserves the world, which pillars dwell in it. And if you tie this interpretation with a knot, so that it shall not leave you, I will tie it with thirty or forty knots in my pocket, so that it shall never leave me.

43. עַל הַהִיא מִלָּה דְּאַחֲמֵי קוּדְשָׁא בְּרִיךְ הוּא לְמֹשֶׁה, בְּגִין דְּאע״ג דְּיִשְׂרָאֵל חָבִין קַמֵּיהּ בְּכָל דָּרָא וְדָרָא, לָא בָּעֵי דְּיֵימָא עֲלַיְיהוּ דְּלָטוֹרִין. מְנָלָן. מֵהוֹשֵׁעַ. דִּכְתִיב תְּחִלַּת דִּבֶּר יְיָ' בְּהוֹשֵׁעַ, הָא אוּקְמוּהָ מִלָּה. וע״ד וְהָיָה מִסְפַּר בְּנֵי יִשְׂרָאֵל כְּחוֹל הַיָּם וְגוֹ'. ובג״ד בָּרִיךְ לוֹן בְּכַמָּה בִּרְכָאן, לְאַהֲדָרָא בִּתְיוּבְתָּא, וּלְאָתָבָא לוֹן לְגַבֵּי אֲבוּהוֹן דְּבִשְׁמַיָּא, וְלָא אַעְדֵּי מִתַּמָּן, עַד דְּקוּדְשָׁא בְּרִיךְ הוּא מָחַל עַל חוֹבַיְיהוּ, וְאִתְנְקִיאוּ קַמֵּיהּ.

43. (THE BEGINNING OF THIS ESSAY IS MISSING). In this subject, the Holy

One, blessed be He, showed Moses that even though the children of Yisrael sin before Him in every generation, He does not wish anyone to slander them. How do we know this? From Hosea, as it is written: "When Hashem spoke at first with Hosea" (Hoshea 1:2). And we have established the matter, THAT HE ANSWERED THE HOLY ONE, BLESSED BE HE, TO PASS THEM TO ANOTHER NATION, AS WRITTEN THERE. And hence: "And the number of the children of Yisrael shall be like the sand of the sea" (Hoshea 2:1). For because of this, He blessed them with many blessings to cause them to repent and return to their Father in heaven. And he did not move from there until the Holy One, blessed be He, forgave their sins and they were purified before Him.

8. "What are you doing here, Elijah"

A Synopsis

This section tells how God questioned Elijah as to why, after having been so zealous in His service, he was now in hiding. He reminds him that He had, through Moses, given him His Covenant of peace, since Elijah is Pinchas in reincarnation.

44. אֵלִיָּהוּ מָה כְּתִיב בֵּיהּ, וַיָּבֹא וַיֵּשֶׁב תַּחַת רֹתֶם אֶחָד וְגוֹ', אָמַר מָארֵיהּ דְּעָלְמָא, אִתְּתָא חֲדָא שַׁדַּרַת לוֹן לְיִשְׂרָאֵל, וּדְבוֹרָה שְׁמָהּ, דִּכְתִּיב וְהִיא יוֹשֶׁבֶת תַּחַת תֹּמֶר דְּבוֹרָה. דָּא הוּא רֹתֶם, וְאַהֲדַרַת לוֹן לְמוּטָב, דִּכְתִּיב עַד שַׁקַּמְתִּי דְּבוֹרָה. וְאֲנָא עָאלִית בֵּינַיְיהוּ, וְאַכְרָזִית קַמַּיְיהוּ וְלָא יָכִילְנָא.

44. Of Elijah, it is written: "and came and sat down under a broom tree" (I Melachim 19:4). He said: Master of the universe, you sent a woman to Yisrael, Deborah by name, as it is written, "and she dwelt under the palm tree of Deborah" (Shoftim 4:5). This is the broom tree ELIJAH SAT UNDER. And she returned them to good conduct, as it is written, "Until I Deborah arose" (Shoftim 5:7). And I have come among them and have spoken loud before them, yet I cannot MAKE THEM REPENT.

45. עַד דַּהֲוָה יָתִיב, אִתְגְּלֵי עָלֵיהּ קוּדְשָׁא בְּרִיךְ הוּא, א"ל מַה לְּךָ פֹה אֵלִיָּהוּ, בְּקַדְמֵיתָא קָא הֲוֵית מְקַטְרְגָא וּמְקַנֵּי עַל בְּרִית, וּמִדְּחָמֵינָא בָּךְ דְּקַנִית עָלַי בְּהַהוּא בְּרִית, נַטְלִית לֵיהּ בִּרְעוּ דְּמֹשֶׁה, וְיָהֵיבְנָא לָךְ, עַד דְּמֹשֶׁה הֲוָה אָמַר הִנְנִי נוֹתֵן לוֹ אֶת בְּרִיתִי שָׁלוֹם. הַשְׁתָּא דְּאִיהוּ דִילָךְ, לָא אִתְחֲזֵי לָךְ לְקַטְרְגָא עֲלוֹי, הֲוָה לָךְ לְמִשְׁבַּק קְנוּיָירְ לִי, כְּמָה בְּקַדְמֵיתָא דַּהֲוָה דִילִי, שְׁבַקְנָא לֵיהּ לִידָא אָחֳרָא, וְלָא קַטְרִיגְנָא עֲלוֹי.

45. While he was still sitting, the Holy One, blessed be He, appeared to him. He said to him, "'What are you doing here, Elijah?" (I Melachim 19:9). At first you were accusing and zealous for the Covenant, MEANING DURING THE DAYS OF MOSES. And when I saw that you were zealous for Me through that Covenant, I took it, with the agreement of Moses, and gave it to you, so Moses said, "Behold I give to him My Covenant of peace,"

(Bemidbar 25:12), AS PINCHAS IS ELIJAH. And now that it is yours, it is not proper for you to denounce it. You should have left your zealousness to Me, as before when THE COVENANT was Mine; and I gave it to another, but did not speak against it'.

46. מַה לְךָ פֹה. מַאי פֹה. בְּרִית קַיָּימָא, פֶּה יְיָ׳ אִיהוּ. כֵּיוָן דְּלָא בָּעָאת לְשַׁבְקָא לִי פּוּמָךְ, יֵתוּב בַּאֲתָר דְּהַהוּא פּוּמָא. תְּנָן, בְּהַהִיא שַׁעֲתָא, אִתְעֲבַר מִנֵּיהּ הַהוּא נְבִזְבְּזָא דְּיָהַב לֵיהּ מֹשֶׁה. דִּתְנָן, מַאי דִּכְתִיב וַיֵּלֶךְ בְּכֹחַ הָאֲכִילָה הַהִיא וְגוֹ׳. עַד הַר הָאֱלֹהִים חוֹרֵבָה. לְמִתְבַּע מִתַּמָּן, וְכִי מִתַּמָּן הֲוָה בָּעֵי. אֶלָּא לְמִתְבַּע כְּמִלְּקַדְמִין, מֵהַהוּא דְּיָרִית בְּהַר הָאֱלֹהִים, בְּרִית דָּא. פִּנְחָס הוּא אֵלִיָּהוּ, וַדַּאי בְּדַרְגָּא חֲדָא. א״ל מֹשֶׁה, לֵית אַנְתְּ יָכִיל לְקַבְּלָא מִנַּאי, אֶלָּא זִיל לְיַנּוּקַיְיהוּ דְּיִשְׂרָאֵל, וּמֵאִינּוּן תִּרְוַוח, וְאִינּוּן יַהֲבֵי לָךְ, וְכַךְ הוּא עָבִיד.

46. "What are you doing here (Heb. *poh*)?" HE ASKS: What is *poh*? HE ANSWERS: The Holy Covenant is the mouth (Heb. *peh*) of Hashem. REFERRING TO IT, IT IS WRITTEN: "BEHOLD I GIVE TO HIM MY COVENANT OF PEACE." AND THE HOLY ONE, BLESSED BE HE, SAID TO HIM: 'Since you did not want to let go of your mouth, NAMELY THE MOUTH THAT IS ZEALOUS FOR THE COVENANT, let the mouth THAT I GAVE YOU, NAMELY THE COVENANT OF PEACE, return to the place of that EARLIER mouth', NAMELY TO HASHEM. We have learned that at that moment the present that Moses gave him, NAMELY THE COVENANT OF PEACE, was taken from him. This we have learned from the words: "And went in the strength of that meal...to Horeb the Mountain of Elohim" (I Melachim 19:8), meaning, to ask it from there. HE ASKS: did he ask it from there? ONE ASKS FROM HASHEM. HE ANSWERS: But it was to ask for what he had before from him who inherited this Covenant on the Mountain of Elohim, THAT IS, MOSES. Pinchas is Elijah. Certainly, they are on the same level. Moses said to him: You cannot receive the Covenant of peace from me, but go to the male children of Yisrael, MEANING THE COVENANT OF CIRCUMCISION OF THE MALE CHILDREN OF YISRAEL and from them you will earn THE SECRET OF THE COVENANT, and they will give it to you. And so he did.

9. Moses, Aaron and Miriam

A Synopsis

We learn that God sent Moses, Aaron and Miriam to Yisrael to bring them manna, leadership, the law, glory and a well to drink from. Yet even then the children of Yisrael scorned and reviled them.

47. כַּמָּה טִיבוּ עָבֵיד קוּדְשָׁא בְּרִיךְ הוּא בְּכָל דָּרָא וְדָרָא לְיִשְׂרָאֵל. תָּא חֲזֵי, מָה כְּתִיב, וָאֶשְׁלַח לְפָנֶיךָ אֶת מֹשֶׁה אַהֲרֹן וּמִרְיָם. וְהָא כַּמָּה נְבִיאֵי הֲווֹ לְבָתַר מֹשֶׁה, וָאֶשְׁלַח לְפָנֶיךָ אֶת מֹשֶׁה אַהֲרֹן וְאֶלְעָזָר וּפִנְחָס יְהוֹשֻׁעַ וְאֵלִיָּהוּ וֶאֱלִישָׁע, וְכַמָּה שְׁאַר צַדִּיקֵי וַחֲסִידֵי מִבְּעֵי לֵיהּ. אִלֵּין תְּלָתָא אֲמַאי. אֶלָּא אָמַר קוּדְשָׁא בְּרִיךְ הוּא , עַמִּי, בָּנַי, אֲמַאי לָא תִּדְכְּרוּן לְכָל טָבִין דַּעֲבָדִית לְכוּ, דְּשַׁדָּרִית לְכוּ לְמֹשֶׁה אַהֲרֹן וּמִרְיָם.

47. How much good did the Holy One, blessed be He, do with Yisrael in every single generation. Come and behold: it is written, "And I sent before you Moses, Aaron and Miriam" (Michah 6:4). HE ASKS: There were many prophets after Moses, thus it should have said, 'And I sent before you Moses, Aaron, Elazar, Pinchas, Joshua, Elijah and Elisha and many other righteous and pious people.' Why these three ALONE? HE ANSWERS: the Holy One, blessed be He, said, 'My people, My children, why do not you remember all the good that I have done for you, in sending you Moses, Aaron and Miriam?'

48. לְמֶלֶךְ בָּשָׂר וָדָם, דְּאִית לֵיהּ מְדִינְתָּא, וְשָׁדַר לְגַבָּהּ, גּוּבְרִין, אַפַּרְכִין רַבְרְבָנִין, דִּיהוֹן מְנַהֲלֵי עַמָּא, וּמְעַיְּינִין בְּהוּ, וּבְדִינַיְיהוּ. מָאן אִצְטְרִיךְ לְמֶהֱוֵי זָקוּק בִּמְזוֹנַיְיהוּ, בְּמִלִּין דְּיִצְטָרְכוּן. לָאו עַמָּא דִּמְדִינְתָּא, בַּעֲל כָּרְחַיְיהוּ יִצְטָרְכוּ לְעַיְּינָא בְּהוּ, וּלְמֵיהַב לְהוּ יְקָרָא.

48. This is similar to a king of flesh and blood, who has a country. Once he sent rulers and princes to the people, to be the leaders of the people and observe them and their customs. Then, who is responsible and obligated to provide for their (the leaders) food and necessities, if not the people of that country? They are obligated to provide for them, SO THEY SHALL LACK FOR NOTHING, and to honor them!

49. שַׁדָּרִית לְמֹשֶׁה, אִיהוּ אַיְיתֵי קַמַיְיכוּ מָן לְמֵיכַל, וְנָהִיל לְכוּ
וְלִבְנַיְיכוּ וְלִבְעִירַיְיכוּ, וְאִשְׁתְּדַל בְּדִינַיְיכוּ, וּבְכָל מָה דְּאִצְטְרִיךְ לְכוּ.
שַׁדָּרִית לְאַהֲרֹן, אַיְיתֵי הֵיכָלִין יְקָר דַּעֲנָנֵי לְחַפָּאָה עָלַיְיכוּ, כְּמַלְכִין.
אַסְחֵי לְכוּ בְּטַלֵּי יְקָר, דְּלָא אִתְרַקְבוּ לְבוּשֵׁיכוֹן וּמְנָעֲלֵיכוֹן, וַהֲווֹ
מִתְחַדְּשֵׁי בְּכָל יוֹמָא. שַׁדָּרִית לְמִרְיָם, אַיְיתִיאַת בֵּירָא לְאַשְׁקָאָה לְכוּ,
וְשָׁתִיתוּן אַתּוּן וּבְעִירַיְכוֹן. אִינּוּן יָהֲבוּ לְכוּ, וּמִדִּלְהוֹן אֲכַלְתּוּן וְשָׁתִיתוּן,
וְיָתִיבְתּוּן בְּחוּפָּאָה דִּיקַר דִּלְהוֹן. וּמִדִּלְכוֹן לָא יָהַבְתּוּן לוֹן. וְלָא עוֹד,
אֶלָּא דְּאִשְׁתַּדַּלוּ עֲלֵיכוֹן, וְנַטְלוּ עַל צַוָּארֵיהוֹן מְטוּלְכוֹן, וַהֲוֵיתוּן
מְחָרְפִין וּמְגַדְּפִין לוֹן.

49. I sent Moses, and he brought you manna to eat, led you and your children and your animals, and strove in your laws and in everything you needed. I sent Aaron. He brought sanctuaries of clouds of glory to cover you like kings. He moistened you with the dew of glory so that your clothes and shoes would not decay, but would be renewed daily. I sent Miriam. She brought a well to give you drink, so you and your animals drank water. They gave to you, and it is of their own that you ate and drank and dwelt under the cloud of glory. But, from your own, you gave nothing. Moreover, they strove for your sakes and took your burden on their necks, yet you scorned and reviled them.

10. "Now therefore let Me alone"

A Synopsis

Rabbi Yosi tells us that God is the most merciful Father of all, for He has never failed one word of all His good promises. Even though God threatened judgment, the Mother, Malchut, held His arm and averted that judgment. We are told that Moses did the same thing for Yisrael as she did, and Rabbi Yosi wonders where Malchut was at the time. When approached with this question, Rabbi Shimon says that all the friends who study Torah together must love one another, otherwise they cause a blemish in their counterparts above – Abraham, Isaac and Jacob, who are the secret of Chesed, Gvurah and Tiferet. He says that he can reveal a secret he learned from the dean of the Yeshivah in the Garden of Eden, that when Yisrael joined in the sins of the heathen nation, they committed a sin against the Mother, Malchut. Thus they caused the Shechinah to be exiled with them, and exchanged their glory for the likeness of an ox. Rabbi Shimon tells us the secret of the likeness of the ox, and what it means that the ox "eats grass." The conclusion to be drawn is that the Mother was blemished, and was thus absent when Moses stayed the hand of God from judging Yisrael. Rabbi Shimon says, though, that both the one who raises the lash and the one who restrains it are both of the same mind.

50. אָמַר רִבִּי יוֹסֵי, לָאו הֲוָה אַבָּא רַחֲמָן עַל בְּנוֹי כְּקוּדְשָׁא בְּרִיךְ הוּא, וּקְרָא הוּא דִּכְתִּיב, לֹא נָפַל דָּבָר אֶחָד מִכֹּל דְּבָרוֹ הַטּוֹב וְגוֹ'. ת"ח רַחֲמָנוּ דִּילֵיהּ, אִלּוּ אָמַר לֹא נָפַל דָּבָר אֶחָד מִכֹּל דְּבָרוֹ וְלָא יַתִּיר, נֹחַ לְעָלְמָא דְּלָא אִתְבְּרֵי. אֲבָל מִדְּאָמַר מִכֹּל דְּבָרוֹ הַטּוֹב, וְאַפִּיק בִּישׁ לַאֲחוֹרָא, דְּהָא מִלָּה דְּבִישׁ לָא בָּעֵי לְמֶעְבַּד.

50. Rabbi Yosi said: There is no father more merciful to his children than the Holy One, Blessed Be He. For it is written: "there has not failed one word of all His good promise..." (I Melachim 8:56). Come and behold His mercy. If it had said, 'there has not failed one word of all His promise,' and no more, THIS WOULD HAVE INCLUDED HIS HARSH WORDS ALSO. Then it would be better for the world not to have been created, BECAUSE IT WOULD BE IMPOSSIBLE TO BEAR IT. But since it said, "of all His good promise," and left His harshness, it implies that THAT HE LEFT OFF THE HARSH WORDS HE SPOKE OF YISRAEL, AND THEY DID NOT COME TRUE. FROM HERE WE SEE HIS MERCY, because He does not want to do an evil thing.

51. וְאע״ג דְּאַגְזִים, וְאָרִים רְצוּעָה, אָתַאת אִמָּא וְאִתְקְפַת בִּדְרוֹעֵיהּ
יְמִינָא, וְקָם רְצוּעָה בְּקִיוּמֵיהּ, וְלָא נָחִית לְתַתָּא, וְלָא אִתְעֲבִיד, בְּגִין
דְּבַעֲיטָא חֲדָא הֲווֹ תַּרְוַוייהוּ, אִיהוּ דְּאַגְזִים, וְאִיהוּ דַּאֲחִידַת בִּימִינֵיהּ.

51. And even though He threatened and raised the lash, his Mother came
and held His right arm, and the lash remained in its place, and did not
descend AND JUDGMENT was not executed, because they were really of one
mind, the one who threatened and the one who held His arm!

52. וְאִי תֵּימָא מְנָלָן. מִמִּלָּה דְּאִיהִי בְּאִתְגַּלְיָא, דִּכְתִיב לֶךְ רֵד כִּי שִׁחֵת
עַמְּךָ, שָׁרֵי לְאָרָמָא רְצוּעָה, וּמֹשֶׁה דְּלָא הֲוָה יָדַע אָרְחָא דְּאִמָּא, שָׁתִיק.
כֵּיוָן דְּחָמָא קוּדְשָׁא בְּרִיךְ הוּא כַּךְ, אַנְקִיד לֵיהּ, וּבָטַשׁ בֵּיהּ וְאָמַר וְעַתָּה
הַנִּיחָה לִי, מִיָּד אַרְגִּישׁ מֹשֶׁה, וְאָחִיד בִּדְרוֹעֵיהּ דְּקוּדְשָׁא בְּרִיךְ הוּא,
דִּכְתִיב זְכוֹר לְאַבְרָהָם, דָּא דְּרוֹעֵיהּ יְמִינָא, וּבג״כ לָא נָחִית רְצוּעָה.

52. And you may ask whence we derive this. This is well known, as it is
written, "Go, get you down; for your people...have become corrupt"
(Shemot 32:7). THE HOLY ONE, BLESSED BE HE, started to raise the lash,
but Moses did not know the way of the Mother, NAMELY TO HOLD HIS
RIGHT HAND AND DETAIN HIM, and remained silent. When the Holy One,
blessed be He, saw this, He hinted to him and pressed him and said, "now
therefore let Me alone" (Ibid. 10). Immediately, Moses realized and grasped
the arm of the Holy One, blessed be He, as it is written: "Remember
Abraham" (Ibid. 3). For this is the right arm, WHICH IS CHESED. Therefore,
He did not bring down the lash.

53. וְאִי תֵּימָא, אִמָּא דְּאִיהִי רְגִילָה לְאַחֲדָא בִּרְצוּעָה דְּמַלְכָּא, אָן הֲוַת,
דְּשַׁבְקַת מִלָּה לְמֹשֶׁה. שְׁאִילְנָא וַאֲמֵינָא וְהָא לָא יְדַעְנָא בְּרִירָא דְּמִלָּה,
עַד דְּנֶהֱוֵי קָמֵיהּ דְּבוּצִינָא קַדִּישָׁא. כַּד אָתוּ לְקָמֵיהּ דר״ש, חָמָא
בְּאַנְפּוֹייהוּ סִימָן. אָמַר עוּלוּ בְּנֵי קַדִּישִׁין, עוּלוּ רְחִימִין דְּמַלְכָּא, עוּלוּ
רְחִימִין דִּילִי, עוּלוּ רְחִימִין אִלֵּין בְּאִלֵּין.

53. You may wonder where was the Mother, WHO IS MALCHUT, who is
accustomed to hold the King's lash, AS MENTIONED, and who left the

matter to Moses? I have asked and I still do not know the explanation of the matter, until we are before the holy luminary, MEANING RABBI SHIMON. When they came before Rabbi Shimon, he saw a sign on their faces. HE RECOGNIZED WHAT THEY HAD COME TO INQUIRE OF HIM. He said: Come, holy children, come, King's beloved, come my beloved, come, those that are beloved by each other.

54. דְּאָמַר רִבִּי אַבָּא, כָּל אִלֵּין חַבְרַיָּיא, דְּלָא רְחִימִין אִלֵּין לְאִלֵּין, אִסְתַּלָּקוּ מֵעָלְמָא עַד לָא מָטָא זִמְנַיְיהוּ, כֹּל חַבְרַיָּיא בְּיוֹמוֹי דר״ש, רְחִימוּ דְנַפְשָׁא וְרוּחָא הֲוָה בֵּינַיְיהוּ, ובג״כ בְּדָרָא דִר׳ שִׁמְעוֹן בְּאִתְגַּלְיָיא הֲוָה, דַּהֲוָה אָמַר רִבִּי שִׁמְעוֹן, כָּל חַבְרַיָּיא דְּלָא רַחֲמִין אִלֵּין לְאִלֵּין, גַּרְמִין דְּלָא לִיהַךְ בְּאֹרַח מֵישָׁר. וְעוֹד דְּעַבְדִין פְּגִימוּ בָּהּ, דְּהָא אוֹרַיְיתָא רְחִימוּ וְאַחֲוָה וּקְשׁוֹט אִית בָּהּ. אַבְרָהָם רָחִים לְיִצְחָק, יִצְחָק לְאַבְרָהָם, מִתְחַבְּקָן דָּא בְּדָא, יַעֲקֹב תַּרְוַוייְהוּ אֲחִידָן בֵּיהּ, בִּרְחִימוּ, וּבְאַחֲוָה, יָהֲבִין רוּחַיְיהוּ דָּא בְּדָא. חַבְרַיָּיא כְּהַהוּא דּוּגְמָא אִצְטְרִיכוּ, וְלָא לְמֶעְבַּד פְּגִימוּ.

54. For Rabbi Aba said: All the friends who do not love each other die before their time. All the friends during the days of Rabbi Shimon loved each other, soul and spirit. Therefore, in the generation of Rabbi Shimon THE SECRETS OF THE TORAH WERE unveiled, for Rabbi Shimon used to say: All the friends that do not love each other cause THEMSELVES to deviate from the straight path. Also, they blemish it, THE TORAH, because the Torah has in it love, friendship and truth. Abraham loved Isaac and Isaac loved Abraham, so they embraced each other. Both were attached to Jacob with love and friendship, and gave their spirit to each other. The friends must be like them, and not cause a blemish in them. FOR IF THEY LACK LOVE, THEY CAUSE A BLEMISH IN THEIR COUNTERPART ABOVE, IN ABRAHAM, ISAAC AND JACOB, WHICH ARE THE SECRET OF CHESED, GVURAH, AND TIFERET.

55. כֵּיוָן דְּחָמָא סִימָן בְּאַנְפַּיְיהוּ, וְאָמַר לוֹן הָכִי. אָמְרוּ לֵיהּ וַדַּאי רוּחַ נְבוּאָה שָׁרָא עַל בּוּצִינָא קַדִּישָׁא, וְהָכִי אִצְטְרִיךְ לָן לְמִנְדַּע. בָּכָה רִבִּי שִׁמְעוֹן וְאָמַר, חַד מִלָּה מֵאִינּוּן מִלִּין דִּלְחִישׁוּ לִי מִגּוֹ רֵישׁ מְתִיבְתָּא

דְּגִּנְתָּא דְּעֵדֶן, דְּלָא אָמְרוּ בְּאִתְגַּלְיָא מִלָּה דָּא סִתְרָא אִיהִי, וְאֵימָא לְכוּ בָּנַי רְחִימָאי, בְּנֵי רְחִימִין דְּנַפְשָׁאי, מָה אַעֲבִיד, אָמְרוּ לִי בִּלְחִישָׁא, וַאֲנָא אֵימָא בְּאִתְגַּלְיָיא. וּלְזִמְנָא דְּנֶחֱמֵי אַנְפִּין בְּאַנְפִּין, כָּל אַנְפִּין יִסְתַּמְכוּן בְּדָא.

55. As soon as RABBI SHIMON saw the sign on their faces, HE RECOGNIZED WHAT THEY CAME TO ASK HIM. He said to them: WELCOME, MY BELOVED. They said to him: Assuredly the Spirit of Prophecy dwells upon the holy luminary, and this is what we need to know, NAMELY, THE QUESTION MENTIONED ABOVE. Rabbi Shimon wept and said: This is one of the subjects I was told in secret by the dean of the Yeshivah in the Garden of Eden. It was not told me openly, this subject is a secret, yet I will tell it to you, my beloved sons, children beloved of my soul. What shall I do? They told it to me secretly, but I will tell it to you openly. And in the future, when we shall see THE SHECHINAH face to face, all the faces will be supported, MEANING THAT THEY WILL ILLUMINATE by this SECRET.

56. בָּנַי. חוֹבָא דְּעָבְדוּ עַמָּא דִּלְבַר. וְאִשְׁתַּתָּפוּ בֵּיהּ עַמָּא קַדִּישָׁא, בְּאִמָּא חָאבוּ, דִּכְתִיב קוּם עֲשֵׂה לָנוּ אֱלֹהִים, אֱלֹהִים וַדַּאי. כְּבוֹד יִשְׂרָאֵל דָּא, אִיהוּ דְּשַׁרְיָא עֲלַיְיהוּ כְּאִמָּא עַל בְּנִין, וְדָא הוּא רָזָא דִּכְתִיב, וַיָּמִירוּ אֶת כְּבוֹדָם בְּתַבְנִית שׁוֹר. דָּא כְּבוֹדָם דְּיִשְׂרָאֵל, אִמָּא דִּלְהוֹן. וְדָא הוּא דִּכְתִיב גָּלָה כָבוֹד. דְּגָרְמוּ לִשְׁכִינְתָּא דְּאִתְגְּלֵי בְּגָלוּתָא עִמְּהוֹן. וְעַל דָּא וַיָּמִירוּ אֶת כְּבוֹדָם, בְּמָה. בְּתַבְנִית שׁוֹר.

56. My children, the sins that the outside people – NAMELY, THE MIXED MULTITUDE – performed, and which the holy people joined in, was a sin against the Mother, WHICH IS MALCHUT, as is written, "Up, make us Elohim" (Shemot 32:1). It is Elohim for sure, MEANING THAT HE SHOULD MAKE THEM A STRANGE ELOHIM, INSTEAD OF MALCHUT, THAT IS CALLED 'ELOHIM', INSTEAD OF the Glory of Yisrael, NAMELY MALCHUT, that hovered over them like a mother over her children. And this is the secret of, "Thus they exchanged their glory for the likeness of an ox" (Tehilim 106:20). This is the Glory of Yisrael, MEANING, their Mother, WHICH IS MALCHUT. This is the meaning of: "Honor is departed" (I Shmuel

4:21), that they caused the Shechinah to be exiled with them. Therefore, "they exchanged their glory"; for what "...for the likeness of an ox."

57. הָכָא אִיהוּ רָזָא דְּמִלָּה, ת״ח, לְתַתָּא גּוֹ שְׁמָרִים דְּחַמְרָא, דּוּרְדְּיָין בִּישִׁין, נָפַק חַד עַרְעוּרָא, מְקַטְרְגָּא, מַזִּיקָא קַדְמָאָה, וְאִיהוּ בְּרָזָא דְּיוּקְנָא דְּאָדָם. כַּד קָרִיב לְגוֹ קֻדְשָׁא. כֵּיוָן דְּאִתְעֲבַר מִתַּמָּן, וּבָעֵי לְנַחְתָּא לְתַתָּא. בָּעֵי לְאִתְלַבְּשָׁא בִּלְבוּשָׁא, לְנַזְקָא עָלְמָא. וְנָחִית הוּא וּרְתִיכוֹי. וּלְבוּשָׁא קַדְמָאָה דְּקָא נָקִיט, תַּבְנִית שׁוֹר, דְּיוּקְנָא דְּשׁוֹר, וְקַדְמָאָה לַנְּזִיקִין מֵאִינּוּן אַרְבַּע, שׁוֹר אִיהוּ. וְאִינּוּן אַרְבַּע אָבוֹת לְנַזְקָא עָלְמָא. וְכֻלְּהוּ תְּלָתָא דְּאָבוֹת נְזִיקִין בַּר שׁוֹר, כֻּלְּהוּ דִּילֵיהּ, וְעַל דָּא כְּתִיב, וַיָּמִירוּ אֶת כְּבוֹדָם בְּתַבְנִית שׁוֹר.

57. Here is the secret of the matter OF "THE LIKENESS OF AN OX." Come and behold: below, in the dregs of the wine, in the evil sediment, a demon emerged, an Accuser, the primordial harmful spirit, in the secret of the likeness of man, and approached Holiness. When he departed from there, FROM HOLINESS, and wanted to descend, he had to be clothed in a garment in order to harm the world. Thus, he and his chariots descended and the first garment he took was the likeness of an ox, NAMELY the image of an ox. The first of the four primary causes of injury is the ox, and THE OTHER three primary causes of injury beside the ox pertain to it, TO THE OX. Therefore, it is written, "Thus they exchanged their glory with the likeness of an ox THAT EATS GRASS."

58. מַהוּ אוֹכֵל עֵשֶׂב. הָא דַּרְשִׁינָן בֵּיהּ. אֲבָל עִקָּרָא דְּמִלָּה, מִתַּמְצִית דְּלֶחֶם וְשִׁבְעָה זִינֵי דָּגָן, לֵית לֵיהּ בְּהוּ חוּלָקָא. וּבְגִינֵי כַּךְ, אִימָּא לָא הֲוַת תַּמָּן, וְלָא יֵאוֹת לָהּ לְמֶהֱוֵי תַּמָּן. וּבְגִין דְּאַבָּא הֲוָה יָדַע רַחֲמָנוּ דְּאִמָּא וְאָרְחָא דִּילָהּ, אָמַר לְמֹשֶׁה, בְּנֵי רְחִימָאי, עֵיטָא בְּתַרְוַויְיהוּ בְּדָא תָּדִיר. וְדָא הוּא דְּלְחִישׁוּ לִי בִּלְחִישׁוּ, דְּלָא חֲזֵי לְגַלָּאָה, דְּבַרָא לָא יִנְדַע, וְיֶחֱמֵי דְּהָא רְצוּעָה אִתְתַּקְּנַת, וְיִדְחַל תָּדִיר. אֲבָל תַּרְוַויְיהוּ בְּעֵיטָא דָּא, וּבְעֵיטָא חֲדָא.

58. What is the meaning of, "that eats grass" IN THE WORDS, "FOR THE

LIKENESS OF AN OX THAT EATS GRASS?" HE ANSWERS: We have already expounded upon it, but the main point is that it does not have any of the essence of bread and seven species of grain BUT EATS ONLY GRASS. And because of this, SINCE THEY BLEMISHED THE MOTHER, WHICH IS MALCHUT, AS MENTIONED, Mother was not present, and it would not be proper for Her to be there, BECAUSE THEY BLEMISHED HER. And since the Father, WHO IS ZEIR ANPIN, knew the Mercy of the Mother and Her ways, He said to Moses: My beloved son, the remedy for this, so THAT THE CHILDREN OF YISRAEL SHALL NOT BE PUNISHED, is always in twosomes. ONE RAISES THE LASH AND THE OTHER HOLDS IT BACK AND RESTRAINS, AS MENTIONED. AND SINCE THE MOTHER IS NOT PRESENT, IT IS INCUMBENT UPON YOU. And this is what they told me secretly, for it is not proper to reveal it so that the son may not know of it, but always see the lash and fear it. Yet both are of this mind, the same mind, MEANING THAT THE ONE WHO RAISES THE LASH AND THE ONE WHO RESTRAINS IT ARE OF THE SAME MIND.

11. The golden Calf

A Synopsis

We read that when Yisrael left Egypt they traveled with the mixed multitude, though it is not said exactly which other nations they were. This section tells us about the magicians and sorcerers of Egypt that went with them. In it, Rabbi Shimon tells why Aaron made the golden calf, and explains the significance of the golden earrings that people gave for the idol. We read of the role of the magicians in the creation of the calf, and the correspondence of this event with the three worlds Briyah, Yetzirah and Asiyah. The only reason that Aaron was able to remedy the problem when the Other Side became stronger was because he made proclamations and said, "Tomorrow is a feast to Hashem"; had he not done this, the world would have ceased to exist. The text returns to the fact that Moses had to restrain the arm of God from judgment. Then we are told that just as Adam was united with the Tree of Life before he sinned, so were the children of Yisrael when they stood before Mount Sinai. And like the sin in the Garden, the sin of the golden calf again caused death for the whole world. Lastly, Rabbi Aba speaks about the Tent of appointed time, that has now been blemished, thereby interrupting the union of Malchut and Zeir Anpin.

59. ת״ח כְּתִיב וַיַּרְא הָעָם כִּי בֹשֵׁשׁ מֹשֶׁה. מַאן הָעָם. אִינּוּן עֵרֶב רַב. מַאן עֵרֶב רַב. וְכִי לוּדִים וְכוּשִׁים וְכַפְתּוֹרִים וְתוּגַרְמִים הֲווֹ, דְּקָרָאן לוֹן עֵרֶב רַב, וַהֲלֹא מִצְרִיִּים הֲווֹ, וּמִמִּצְרַיִם נַטְלוּ, וְאִלּוּ הֲווֹ עִרְבּוּבְיָא דְּעַמִּין סַגִּיאִין, הָכִי הֲוָה לֵיהּ לְמִכְתַּב, עֵרֶב רַב עָלוּ אִתָּם לְפִי עִרְבּוּבְיָא דִּלְהוֹן.

59. Come and behold: it is written, "And when the people saw that Moses delayed" (Shemot 32:1). Who are "the people?" HE ANSWERS: They are the mixed multitude. And who was the mixed multitude? Were they Ludim and Kushim and Kaftorim and Togarmin, who are called mixed multitude? They were Egyptian and traveled from Egypt. And if they were a mixture of many nations, it should have stated so. "And a mixed multitude went up also with them" (Shemot 12:38) – LUDIM, KUSHIM, ETC., according to their mixture.

60. אֶלָּא עֵרֶב רַב עָלוּ אִתָּם. עַמָּא חַד הֲוָה, וְלִישָׁן חַד, אֲבָל כָּל חָרָשֵׁי

מִצְרַיִם, וְכָל חַרְטוּמֵי דִּלְהוֹן הֲווֹ, דִּכְתִיב בְּהוּ, וַיַּעֲשׂוּ גַם הֵם חַרְטוּמֵי מִצְרַיִם. דְּבָעוּ לְמֵיקָם לָקֳבֵל פְּלִיאָן דְּקוּדְשָׁא בְּרִיךְ הוּא, כֵּיוָן דְּחָמוּ נִסִּין וּפְלִיאָן דְּעָבַד מֹשֶׁה בְּמִצְרַיִם, אָהַדְרוּ לְגַבֵּי מֹשֶׁה. א"ל קוּדְשָׁא בְּרִיךְ הוּא לְמֹשֶׁה, לָא תְקַבֵּל לוֹן. אָמַר מֹשֶׁה, מָארֵיהּ דְּעָלְמָא, כֵּיוָן דְּחָמוּ גְּבוּרְתָּא דִּילָךְ, בָּעָאן לְאִתְגַּיְּירָא. יֶחֱמוּן גְּבוּרְתָּךְ בְּכָל יוֹמָא, וְיִנְדְּעוּן דְּלֵית אֱלָהָא בַּר מִנָּךְ. וְקַבֵּל לוֹן מֹשֶׁה.

60. HE ANSWERS: But THE VERSE SAYS, "And a mixed multitude went up also with them," YET DOES NOT MENTION THE NAMES OF THE NATIONS because they were all of one nation and one language. But all the magicians and sorcerers of Egypt were there, as it is written: "And the magicians of Egypt, they also did in like manner..." (Shemot 7:11), because they wanted to stand up against the wonders of the Holy One, blessed be He, AND SHOW THAT THEY ALSO COULD DO AS HE DOES. But when they saw the miracles and wonders that Moses performed in Egypt, they returned to Moses. The Holy One, blessed be He, said to Moses: 'Do not accept them.' Moses said: 'Master of the universe, since they saw Your mighty deeds they want to convert. Let them see Your mighty deeds every day and then they will know that there is no Elohim except You.' And Moses accepted them.

61. אֲמַאי קָרָא לוֹן עֵרֶב רַב. אֶלָּא כָּל חַרְשִׁין דְּמִצְרַיִם הֲווֹ, וּבְרֵישֵׁיהוֹן יוֹנוֹס וְיַמְבְּרוֹס, וּבְשַׁעֲתָא דְּיוֹמָא הֲווֹ עַבְדֵי תָּדִיר חַרְשַׁיְיהוּ. וְכָל אִלֵּין חַרְשִׁין עִלָּאִין, הֲווֹ מִסְתַּכְּלֵי מִכִּי נָטֵי שִׁמְשָׁא, מִשֵּׁירוּתָא דְּשִׁית שָׁעוֹת וּמֶחֱצָה, עַד שֵׁירוּתָא דְּתֵשַׁע וּמֶחֱצָה. דְּהַיְינוּ עֵרֶב רַבְרְבָא. כָּל אִינּוּן חַרְשִׁין זְעִירִין, מִשֵּׁירוּתָא דְּתֵשַׁע וּמֶחֱצָה, עַד פַּלְגוּת לֵילְיָא.

61. HE ASKS: Why did he call them a mixed multitude? HE ANSWERS: Because all the magicians of Egypt were present, and at their head were Yunus and Yambrus. They practiced magic FROM THE SIXTH HOUR after sunrise. The greater magicians would start to perform their magic at six-and-a-half hours after sunrise, when the sun started TO SET, until the beginning of nine-and-a-half hours, namely the full setting of the sun, WHEN IT IS TIME FOR EARLY MINCHAH. But all the minor magicians WOULD PRACTICE MAGIC from nine-and-a-half hours until midnight.

62. אִינּוּן עִלָּאִין דִּבְהוּ, הֲווֹ מִסְתַּכְּלֵי מִכִּי נָטֵי שִׁמְשָׁא. דְּהָא כְּדֵין שַׁרְאָן תְּשַׁע מְאָה וְתִשְׁעִין וַחֲמֵשׁ דַּרְגִּין, לְמִשַׁטְטָא עַל טוּרֵי חָשׁוּךְ. וְרוּחָא דִּלְהוֹן, הֲוָה מְשַׁטְּטָא עַל כָּל אִינּוּן חֲרָשִׁין בְּחַרְשַׁיְיהוּ. וְאִלֵּין הֲווֹ עַבְדֵי, כָּל מַה דְּאִינּוּן בָּעָאן. עַד דְּכָל מִצְרָאֵי רַחֲצָנוּ דִּלְהוֹן בְּאִלֵּין הֲוָה. וְקָרְאָן לוֹן עֵרֶב רַב. בְּגִין דְּאִית עֶרֶב זְעֵירָא, מִתְּשַׁע שָׁעוֹת וּמֶחֱצָה וּלְתַתָּא, דָּא עֶרֶב זְעֵירָא. וּתְרֵי עַרְבֵי אִינּוּן, וְע"ד וְגַם עֶרֶב רַב עָלָה אִתָּם.

62. The greater ones among them practiced from the time the sun started to set, because then nine hundred and ninety-five grades start to float over the Mountains of Darkness, and their spirit hovered over all these magicians in their magic. They were able to do whatever they desired, so much so that all the Egyptians placed their trust in them. They were called a mixed multitude (or: 'a great evening'), because there is also a small evening, which is before nine and a half. And since there are two kinds of evening, it says, "And a mixed multitude ('a great evening') went up also with them."

63. וְחָכְמְתָא דִּלְהוֹן, הֲוָה סַגִּי. וְאִינּוּן אִסְתַּכְּלוּ בְּשַׁעֲתֵי דְיוֹמָא, וְאִסְתַּכְּלוּ בְּדַרְגָּא דְּמֹשֶׁה, וְחָמוּ דְּהָא בְּכָל סִטְרִין בְּשֵׁשׁ מֹשֶׁה: בְּשֵׁשׁ שַׁעֲתֵי קַדְמָאִין דְּיוֹמָא, דְּאִינּוּן לָא יַכְלִין לְשַׁלְטָאָה בְּהוּ, בְּשִׁית דַּרְגִּין עִלָּאִין דְּאָחִיד בְּהוּ. וּבְכָל סִטְרִין בְּשִׁית הֲוָה, וּבְעִטְרִין דְּאִלֵּין שִׁית, הֲוָה זַמִּין לָרֶדֶת מִן הָהָר, דִּכְתִיב כִּי בֹשֵׁשׁ מֹשֶׁה לָרֶדֶת מִן הָהָר.

63. The wisdom OF THE MIXED MULTITUDE was great. They observed the hours of the day, and they observed the level of Moses and saw that on all sides Moses was of six, during the first six hours of daytime. They had no power over the six higher levels to which MOSES was connected. And in every direction he was of six (Heb. *beshesh*), THAT IS, HE WAS COMBINED OF SIX EXTREMITIES, CHESED, GVURAH, TIFERET, NETZACH, HOD AND YESOD. And with these six crowns OF THE SIX HOURS OF THE DAY, WHICH ARE CHESED, GVURAH, TIFERET, NETZACH, HOD, AND YESOD, he was destined to descend from the mountain, as it is written: "Moses delayed (Heb. *boshesh*) to come down from the mountain" (Shemot 32:1).

64. מִיַּד וַיִּקָּהֵל הָעָם עַל אַהֲרֹן, אֲמַאי עַל אַהֲרֹן. בְּגִין לְאִתְכַּלְּלָא

בְּסִטְרָא דִּימִינָא, דְּהָא אִינּוּן שְׂמָאלָא בָּעוּ מִנֵּיהּ, וּבְגִין דְּלֶהֱוֵי כָּלִיל
בִּימִינָא, אִתְכְּנָשׁוּ עַל אַהֲרֹן, וַיֹּאמְרוּ אֵלָיו קוּם עֲשֵׂה לָנוּ אֱלֹהִים.

64. Immediately: "the people gathered themselves together to Aaron" (Ibid.). HE ASKS: Why to Aaron? HE ANSWERS: in order to become included in the Right Side, BECAUSE THE LEFT EMERGES FROM THE RIGHT. But they actually wanted from him the Left, NOT THE RIGHT, in order to become included in the Right Side, MEANING HIS ROOT. Thus, they gathered to Aaron, WHO IS THE RIGHT, CHESED. And they said to him: "Rise up, make for us Elohim" (Ibid.).

65. ת״ח, כָּל זִמְנָא דַּהֲוָה מֹשֶׁה בְּמִצְרַיִם, שְׁמָא דֶּאֱלֹהִים לָא דָּכִיר,
אֶלָּא שְׁמָא דַּיְיָ', וְע״ד קַשְׁיָא לֵיהּ לְפַרְעֹה בְּגִין דְּלָא יְהֵא תּוּקְפָּא
לְהַהוּא סִטְרָא אַחֲרָא, וְלָא יִתְתָּקַף בְּעָלְמָא. הַשְׁתָּא בָּעוּ הַהִיא מִלָּה,
וְהַיְינוּ קוּם עֲשֵׂה לָנוּ אֱלֹהִים. לָנוּ דַּיְיקָא, דַּאֲנָן צְרִיכִין לְהַאי מִלָּה,
לְתַקְפָּא סִטְרָא דִּילָן, דַּהֲוָה אִתְדַּחְיָא עַד הַשְׁתָּא.

65. Come and behold: the entire time Moses was in Egypt, he did not mention the name Elohim, just the Name Yud Hei Vav Hei. Therefore, Pharaoh was angry AND SAID: "I KNOW NOT HASHEM" (SHEMOT 5:2). The reason was not to empower the Other Side in this world, BECAUSE THE OTHER SIDE IS ALSO CALLED OTHER ELOHIM. Now THE MIXED MULTITUDE wanted that, NAMELY THE POWER OF THE LEFT, THAT IS CALLED 'ELOHIM'. And that is the meaning of: "Rise up, make for us Elohim." "Us" is exact, FOR THE MIXED MULTITUDE SAID THAT they needed this in order to strengthen their side that had been thrust aside until now, BECAUSE MOSES DID NOT MENTION THE NAME 'ELOHIM.'

66. אֲשֶׁר יֵלְכוּ לְפָנֵינוּ. מַאי אָמְרוּ. אֶלָּא הָכִי אָמְרוּ, חֲמֵינָן דְּאַתּוּן
יִשְׂרָאֵל, כָּל טוֹב וְכָל יְקָר דְּעָלְמָא לְכוּ, וַאֲנָן דַּחְיָין לְבַר. דִּלְכוּ, וַיְיָ'
הוֹלֵךְ לִפְנֵיהֶם יוֹמָם. אוּף הָכִי אֱלֹהִים אֲשֶׁר יֵלְכוּ לְפָנֵינוּ, כְּמָה דְּאָזִיל
קַמַּייכוּ יְיָ'. דְּהָא רְשׁוּ אִית לְסִטְרָא דִּילָן לְמֶהַךְ אוּף הָכִי לְקַמָּנָא, אִי
נַזְמִין לֵיהּ עוֹבָדָא.

66. "Which shall go before us" (Ibid.). HE ASKS: what did they mean by this? HE ANSWERS: This is what they meant. We saw that you, the children of Yisrael, have all that is good and precious in the world, but we are put aside. For you, "Hashem went before them by day" (Shemot 13:21). We too WANT THAT, Elohim to go before us, the same way Yud Hei Vav Hei goes before you. Our side also has the power to go before us if we summon it by an action, NAMELY, MAKING THE GOLDEN CALF.

67. ת"ח, כָּל עֲנָנֵי יְקָר דְּאָזְלוּ בְּמַדְבְּרָא, לָא הֲווֹ חַפְיָין אֶלָּא לִבְנֵי יִשְׂרָאֵל לְחוֹדַיְיהוּ. וְהַהוּא עֲנָנָא דִּיקָר, דִּכְתִּיב וַיְיָ' הוֹלֵךְ לִפְנֵיהֶם יוֹמָם, אַזְלָא לְקַמַּיְיהוּ. וְאִלֵּין עֵרֶב רַב, וְכָל אִינּוּן בְּעִירֵי עָאנִין וְתוֹרִין, הֲווֹ אַזְלוּ לְבַר מִמַּשְׁרְיָיתָא, לְבַתְרַיְיתָא. וְת"ח, כָּל אִינּוּן אַרְבְּעִין שְׁנִין דְּקָא אָזְלוּ יִשְׂרָאֵל בְּמַדְבְּרָא, שׁוּם לִכְלוּכָא וְטִנּוּפָא לָא הֲוָה גּוֹ עֲנָנֵי לְגוֹ. וְעַ"ד עָאנֵי וְתוֹרֵי דַּהֲווֹ אָכְלֵי עֵשֶׂב לְבַר הֲווֹ, וְכָל אִינּוּן דְּנַטְרֵי לוֹן.

67. Come and behold: all the clouds of glory that traveled in the wilderness covered the children of Yisrael alone. And that precious cloud about which it is written, "And Hashem went before them by day," went before them, but the mixed multitude and cattle and sheep and animals were traveling outside the camp, in the rear. Come and behold: all those forty years that Yisrael traveled in the wilderness, there was no dirt or dust within the place where the clouds were. Therefore, the sheep and cattle that ate grass were outside with all those who guarded them.

68. א"ר אֶלְעָזָר, אַבָּא, אִי הָכִי אִינּוּן עֵרֶב רַב לָא הֲווֹ אַכְלֵי מִן מַנָּא. א"ל וַדַּאי הָכִי הוּא. אֶלָּא מָה דְּיָהֲבִין לוֹן יִשְׂרָאֵל, כְּמַאן דְּיָהִיב לְעַבְדֵּיהּ. וּמִמָּה הֲווֹ אַכְלֵי. מִתַּמְצִית, מָה דְּאִשְׁתְּאַר מִבָּתַר רֵיחַיָּא, פְּסוֹלֶת. וּקְרָא אַכְרִיז וְאָמַר, וּבְנֵי יִשְׂרָאֵל אָכְלוּ אֶת הַמָּן אַרְבָּעִים שָׁנָה. בְּנֵי יִשְׂרָאֵל, וְלָא אַחֲרָא. וַיִּרְאוּ בְּנֵי יִשְׂרָאֵל וַיֹּאמְרוּ מָן הוּא, וְלָא שְׁאַר עֵרֶב רַב, עָאנֵי וְתוֹרֵי, דַּהֲווֹ בֵּינַיְיהוּ.

68. Rabbi Elazar said: Father, if so then the mixed multitude did not eat of the manna. He said to him: Certainly it is so, except what Yisrael gave them as one gives to his servant. And what did they eat? They ate the leftovers,

whatever was left behind the millstones, the inferior quality. The Torah proclaims and says: "And the children of Yisrael did eat the manna (Heb. *mah*) for forty years" (Shemot 16:35), the children of Yisrael and no other. "And when the children of Yisrael saw it, they said... 'What (Heb. *man*) is it?'" (Ibid. 15), but not the mixed multitude, or the sheep and cattle that were among them.

69. עַד הַשְׁתָּא, הֲווֹ אִתְכַּפְיָין אִינּוּן עֵרֶב רַב וְהַשְׁתָּא קָמוּ וּבָעוּ עוֹבָדָא, לְאַתְקְפָא לְסִטְרָא אַחֲרָא. אָמְרוּ, אוֹ נְהֵא כֻּלָּנָא עַמָּא חֲדָא, וְנֶהֱוֵי בִּכְלָלָא עִמְּכוֹן, אוֹ יְהֵא לָן מַאן דְּיֵיהַךְ קָמָנָא, כְּמָה דְּיֵיהַךְ אֱלָהֲכוֹן קַמֵּיכוֹן. אָמַר אַהֲרֹן, ח"ו דְּאִלֵּין יִשְׁתַּתְּפוּן בְּעַמָּא קַדִּישָׁא, לְמֶהֱוֵי כֹּלָּא כְּלָלָא חֲדָא, וְלָא יִתְעָרְבוּן עַמָּא קַדִּישָׁא בְּעַמָּא דָּא, כְּלָלָא חֲדָא, אֶלָּא טָב אִיהוּ לְאַפְרָשָׁא לוֹן מִגּוֹ עַמָּא קַדִּישָׁא, עַד דְּיֵיתֵי מֹשֶׁה.

69. Until this time the mixed multitude was subdued, but now they arose and searched for an action to strengthen the Other Side. They said: Either we are all one nation, and we will be included AMONG YISRAEL with you, or let us have someone to go before us just as your Elohim goes before you. Aaron said: Heaven forbid that they should be part of the holy people, so all would be united into one. The Holy Nation should not mingle with these people into a whole. It is better to separate them from the Holy Nation until Moses comes.

70. וְאַהֲרֹן לְטָב אִתְכְּווֹן, אֶלָּא סַגִּיאִין הֲווֹ מִיִּשְׂרָאֵל דְּאִשְׁתַּתָּפוּ בַּהֲדַיְיהוּ בְּלִבָּא. וּבְגִין כָּךְ, כַּד אָתָא מֹשֶׁה, אִצְטְרִיךְ לְבָרְרָא וּלְלַבְּנָא לְעַמָּא קַדִּישָׁא מֵהַהוּא חוֹבָא, וְאַשְׁקֵי לוֹן שַׁקְיוּ, עַד דְּאִתְבְּרִירוּ כֻּלְּהוּ וְלָא אִשְׁתְּאַר בְּהוּ פְּסוֹלֶת כְּלַל.

70. Aaron's intention was good, but many of Yisrael joined with the mixed multitude in their hearts. Therefore, when Moses came he had to purify and cleanse the Holy Nation of that sin, and he gave them drink until they were all cleansed and no refuse at all remained in them.

71. אָמַר לוֹן אַהֲרֹן, פָּרְקוּ נִזְמֵי הַזָּהָב, וְכִי לָא הֲוָה לוֹן דַּהֲבָא אַחֲרָא.

אֶלָּא אָמַר אַהֲרֹן, בְּעוֹד דְּאִית לוֹן קְטָטָה בִּבְנַיְיהוּ וּבִנְשַׁיְיהוּ, יִתְעַכְּבוּן,
וּבֵין כַּךְ יֵיתֵי מֹשֶׁה. ת"ח, תָּנֵינָן קַשִׁים גֵּרִים לְיִשְׂרָאֵל כְּסַפַּחַת בִּבְשַׂר
הַחַי, כ"ש אִלֵּין, דְּלָא הֲווֹ גֵּרִים כַּדְקָא יָאוֹת. אִינּוּן מָה עָבְדוּ. וַיִּתְפָּרְקוּ
כָּל הָעָם אֶת נִזְמֵי הַזָּהָב אֲשֶׁר בְּאָזְנֵיהֶם. כַּמָּה אַלְפֵי וְרִבְווֹן הֲווֹ
מִנִּזְמֵיהוֹן תַּמָּן.

71. Aaron said to them: "Break off the golden earrings" (Shemot 32:2). HE ASKS: Did they not have any other gold, EXCEPT FOR THE GOLDEN EARRINGS? HE ANSWERS: But Aaron thought, 'While they are quarreling with their children and wives, they will be delayed and in the meantime Moses will arrive.' Come and behold: we have learned that proselytes are as bad to Yisrael as a sore on the skin. And this is especially the case for this mixed multitude who were not proper converts. What did they do? "And all the people broke off the golden earrings that were in their ears" (Ibid. 3). Many thousands and tens of thousands of earrings were there of the earrings OF THE MIXED MULTITUDE!

72. מַה כְּתִיב, וַיִּקַּח מִיָּדָם וַיָּצַר אוֹתוֹ בַּחֶרֶט וְגוֹ'. אַהֲרֹן לָא אִסְתָּמַּר,
מֵאִינּוּן תְּרֵין חַכִּימִין, דַּהֲווֹ בְּרֵישֵׁיהוֹן דְּהַהוּא עֵרֶב רַב. חַד מִנַּיְיהוּ הֲוָה
קַמֵּיה, וְאַחֲרָא הֲוָה עָבֵיד בְּחַרְשׁוֹי. כֵּיוָן דְּתַרְוַויְיהוּ אִתְיָיעֲטוּ כַּחֲדָא,
נַטְלוּ הַהִיא דַּהֲבָא, תְּרֵין שְׁלִישֵׁי בִּידָא דְּחַד, וּשְׁלִישׁ בִּידָא דְּאַחֲרָא.
בְּגִין דְּהָכִי אִצְטְרִיךְ בְּהַהוּא זִינָא דְּחַרְשָׁא.

72. It is written: "And he received the gold at their hands, and fashioned it with a graving tool" (Ibid. 4). Aaron did not protect himself from the two wise men who were at the head of the mixed multitude. One of them was in front of them while the other one was performing his magic. After discussing it together, they took that gold, two thirds in the hand of one and a third in the hand of the other, because that is the way it has to be in this type of magic.

73. בָּכָה ר"ש, אָמַר אִי חֲסִידָא קַדִּישָׁא, אַהֲרֹן מְשִׁיחָא דֶּאֱלָהָא רַבָּא,
בַּחֲסִידוּתָךְ נַפְלוּ כַּמָּה מֵעַמָּא קַדִּישָׁא. וְאַנְתְּ לָא הֲוֵית יָדַע לְאִסְתַּמְּרָא.
מַהוּ עָבְדוּ. כַּד מָטוּ שִׁית שַׁעֲתִין, וְיוֹמָא הֲוָה בְּמַתְקְלָא, נַטְלוּ הַהוּא

דַּהֲבָא דְּפָרִיקוּ מֵאוּדְנֵיהוֹן. מ״ט. בְּגִין דְּמַאן דְּאִצְטְרִיךְ לְמֶעְבַּד חַרְשָׁא, לָא בָּעֵי לְמֵיחַס עֵינוֹי עַל מָמוֹנָא. וְאִינּוּן אַמְרֵי, שַׁעֲתָא קַיְימָא לָן, אִי אֲנָן לָא מְעַכְּבִין. לָאו שַׁעֲתָא לְמֵיחַס עַל דַּהֲבָא, מִיַּד וַיִּתְפָּרְקוּ כָּל הָעָם. מַאי וַיִּתְפָּרְקוּ. כד״א מְפָרֵק הָרִים וּמְשַׁבֵּר סְלָעִים, דְּחַבִּילוּ וְתַבְרוּ אוּדְנַיְיהוּ. בָּכָה כְּמִלְּקַדְמִין וְאָמַר אִי עַמָּא קַדִּישָׁא אִי עַמָּא קַדִּישָׁא, דְּקוּדְשָׁא בְּרִיךְ הוּא.

73. Rabbi Shimon wept. He said: O, holy pious Aaron, the anointed of the holy El! How many of the people of the Holy Nation fell in your piety, and you did not know how to protect yourself. What did they do? When the sixth hour passed, and the day was in balance, NAMELY AT NOON WHEN THE SUN IS IN THE MIDDLE OF THE SKY AND TURNS NEITHER TO THE EAST NOR THE WEST LIKE THE TONGUE OF A SCALE, they took the gold that they broke off from their ears. What is the reason for this? It is because if one wants to practice magic then he should not spare money. They said: The hour is auspicious for us if we do not delay. This is not the time to spare gold. Immediately, "All the people broke off..." What is the meaning of "broke off?" It is the same as in: "rent the mountains, and broke the rocks in pieces" (I Melachim 19:11), because they bruised and tore their ears. He wept as before and said: O Holy Nation, O Holy Nation of the Holy One, blessed be He!

74. פָּתַח ר״ש בִּבְכִיָה, וְאָמַר, וְהִגִּישׁוֹ אֲדֹנָיו אֶל הָאֱלֹהִים וְגוֹ'. הָא אוּקְמוּהָ חַבְרַיָּיא, אֹזֶן דְּשָׁמַע בְּסִינַי, כִּי לִי בְּנֵי יִשְׂרָאֵל עֲבָדִים וְגוֹ'. וְאִיהוּ פָּרִיק עוֹל מַלְכוּת שָׁמַיִם מֵעֲלֵיהּ, וְזַבִּין גַּרְמֵיהּ לְאַחֵר, תִּרְצַע. וְאִלֵּין חַיָּיבַיָּא רְשִׁיעַיִן, גּוּבְרִין בִּישִׁין, בְּתִיאוּבְתָּא דִּלְהוֹן לְמֶהֱדַר לְסִרְחָנַיְיהוּ, לָא בָּעוּ מִנְשֵׁיהוֹן וּבְנֵיהוֹן אֶלָּא חַבִּילוּ אוּדְנַיְיהוּ וְאִתְפָּרְקוּ מֵעוֹל שְׁמַיָּא דְּפָקִיד לְהוּ מֹשֶׁה, וְתַבְרוּ אוּדְנַיְיהוּ, דְּלֵית לוֹן חוּלְקָא בִּשְׁמָא קַדִּישָׁא, וְעַמָּא קַדִּישָׁא.

74. Rabbi Shimon started weeping and said: "Then his master shall bring him to the judges..." (Shemot 21:6). The friends explained that one whose ear heard at Mount Sinai, "For to Me the people of Yisrael are servants..." (Vayikra 25:55), yet threw off himself the yoke of the Kingdom of Heaven

and sold himself to another, his ears should be pierced. And these sinners, wicked, evil people, in their desire to return to their evil ways, did not request the jewelry from their wives and children, but rather tore them from their own ears — MEANING THAT THEY DAMAGED THE EAR THAT HEARD AT MOUNT SINAI, "YOU SHALL HAVE NO OTHER ELOHIM BESIDE ME" (SHEMOT 20:3). THIS IS WORSE THAN HE WHO SELLS HIMSELF TO BE A SLAVE. And then they threw off themselves the yoke of heaven that was ordered by Moses, and tore their ears, THUS REVEALING that they have no portion in the Holy Name and the Holy Nation.

75. מָה עֲבָדוּ, פְּלִיגוּ תַּרְוַוייהוּ הַהוּא דַּהֲבָא, חַד נָטִיל תְּרֵין שְׁלִישִׁין, וְחַד שְׁלִישׁ. קָמוּ לָקֳבֵל שִׁמְשָׁא, בְּשִׁית שַׁעֲתִּין. עֲבָדוּ חַרְשַׁייהוּ, וּבְלִיטוּ בִּלְטֵיהוֹן בְּחַרְשָׁא דְּפוּמָא. כֵּיוָן דְּמָטָא שֵׁירוּתָא דִּשְׁבַע, אֲרִימוּ תַּרְוַוייהוּ יְדַייהוּ עַל יְדוֹי דְּאַהֲרֹן. דִּכְתִיב וַיִּקַּח מִיָּדָם, תַּרְוַוייהוּ הֲווֹ, וְלָא יַתִּיר. כֵּיוָן דְּאִיהוּ קַבִּיל מִיָּדָם, קָלָא נָפַק וְאָמַר, יָד לְיָד לֹא יִנָּקֶה רָע, דִּכְתִיב כִּי בְרַע הוּא. אַייְתֵי רָע לְעָלְמָא.

75. What did they do? They divided that gold between them, YUNUS AND YAMBRUS, AS MENTIONED EARLIER. One took two thirds and the other took one third. They rose with the sun at the sixth hour OF THE DAY, practiced their sorcery and employed their secret arts with verbal magic. Upon the beginning of the seventh hour, they both raised their hands to the hands of Aaron, as the words: "And he received the gold at their hand" (Shemot 32:4), refer to two and not more, NAMELY YUNUS AND YAMBRUS. As soon as he received from their hands, a voice came out and said: "They who join hands for wicked ends shall not go unpunished" (Mishlei 11:21). For it is written: "they are bent on mischief," (Shemot 32:22), MEANING, "AND AARON SAID...YOU KNOW THE PEOPLE, THAT THEY ARE BENT ON MISCHIEF" because he has brought evil into the world.

76. רָזָא דְּמִלָּה. אִינּוּן רְשָׁעִים חַיָּיבִין חַרְשִׁין בְּנוֹי דְּבִלְעָם חַיָּיבָא, בְּנֵי בְּנוֹי דְּלָבָן רְשִׁיעָא, חָמוּ דְּכוֹס שֶׁל בְּרָכָה בְּיָמִין אִיהוּ, וּמָן יְמִינָא אִתָּקַף תָּדִיר. אָמְרוּ, אִי יְהֵא בְּסִטַר דָּא, הַהוּא רֵישָׁא דִּימִינָא, הָא תּוּקְפָּא דִּילָן כַּדְקָא יָאוֹת.

76. The secret of the matter is that these wicked sinners, magicians, were the

sons of the evil Bilaam, the grandsons of the evil Laban. They saw that the Cup of Blessing, NAMELY MALCHUT, is on the right, and is always strengthened by the right, NAMELY FROM CHESED. They said: If the head of the right, NAMELY AARON, will be on this side, NAMELY THE OTHER SIDE, our strength and power will be as they should.

77. כֵּיוָן דְּמָטָא שְׁבַע שַׁעֲתִין דְּיוֹמָא, יָהֲבוּ לֵיהּ לְאַהֲרֹן מִיָּד. אִי אִיהוּ הֲוָה אָמַר לוֹן שַׁווּ לֵיהּ בְּאַרְעָא בְּקַדְמֵיתָא, וַאֲנָא אֶטּוֹל, לָא הֲווֹ יַכְלִין בְּחַרְשַׁיְיהוּ כְּלוּם, אֶלָּא מִיָּדָם נָטַל. וּקְרָא מִתְרָעֵם וְאָמַר, וַיִּקַּח מִיָּדָם, חֲמוּ מָה עֲבַד אַהֲרֹן גְּבַר נְבִיאָה גְּבַר חַכִּים, לָא יָדַע לְאִסְתַּמְּרָא, דְּאִילּוּ נָטִיל מֵאַרְעָא, כָּל חַרְשִׁין דְּעָלְמָא לָא הֲווֹ יַכְלִין לְאַצְלָחָא. אֲבָל בְּמָה אַצְלָחוּ בְּעוֹבָדָא דָא, בְּגִין דְּוַיִּקַּח מִיָּדָם וְלָא מֵאַרְעָא.

77. When the seventh hour of the day arrived, they immediately gave it to Aaron. If he had said to them, 'First put THE GOLD on the ground and I will pick it up FROM THE GROUND', then they would not have been able to accomplish anything with their magic. But he took it from their hands, and the Torah complains, saying: "And he received the gold at their hand." See what Aaron did; a prophet, wise man, yet he did not know how to protect himself. For had he taken it from the ground, then all the magic in the world would not have been successful. But why were they successful here? Because, "he received the gold at their hand," and not from the ground.

78. וַיָּצַר אוֹתוֹ בַּחֶרֶט, לָאו כְּמָה דְּחַשְׁבִין בְּנֵי נָשָׁא, דְּעָבַד צִיּוּרִין בְּמָחוּגָה, אוֹ בְּמִלָּה אַחֲרָא. אֶלָּא אָתָא קְרָא לְאוֹכָחָא מִלָּה, דְּאַהֲרֹן לָא יָדַע לְאִסְתַּמְּרָא. אִילּוּ כַּד נָטַל מִיְּדֵיהוֹן, הֲוָה שַׁדֵּי לְאַרְעָא, וְאַע"ג דְּיִטּוֹל לֵיהּ לְבָתַר, לָא הֲוָה אַצְלַח עוֹבָדָא בִּישָׁא דָא. אֲבָל בְּכֹלָּא סִיּוּעָא בִּישָׁא הֲוָה, דְּנָקִיט דַּהֲבָא, וּטְמָרֵיהּ מֵעֵינָא, בִּישׁ בָּתַר בִּישׁ מַאי וַיָּצַר אוֹתוֹ בַּחֶרֶט. דְּשַׁוֵּי כָּל דַּהֲבָא בְּכִיסָא חֲדָא, וְאִסְתְּמַר מֵעֵינָא. כְּדֵין סָלִיק כֹּלָּא לְעוֹבָדָא.

78. "And fashioned it with a graving tool" (Ibid.). THE MEANING IS not as people think, that he made images with a chisel or something else, but rather the Torah emphasizes that Aaron was not cautious enough, because had he

thrown it to the ground immediately upon receiving the gold from their hand, even if he had later picked it up FROM THE GROUND, this evil action would not have been successful. But throughout there was evil assistance, so that he took the gold and concealed it from the eye. HE INTERPRETS: "AND FASHIONED (HEB. *VAYATZR*) IT WITH A GRAVING TOOL" THAT HE WRAPPED (HEB. *TZRAR*) IT IN A CLOTH. There was evil after evil. THE FIRST WAS THAT HE ACCEPTED IT AT THEIR HAND. THE SECOND WAS THAT HE DID NOT THROW IT ON THE GROUND AFTER ACCEPTING IT AT THEIR HAND. THE THIRD IS THAT HE WRAPPED IT IN A CLOTH AND CONCEALED IT FROM THE EYE. What is "And fashioned it with a graving tool?" It means he put all the gold in a bag, and it was kept from eye SIGHT. Then everything BECAME definite.

79. בְּסִפְרָא דַּחֲנוֹךְ אַשְׁכַּחְנָא, דַּהֲוָה אָמַר הָכִי, בְּרָא יְחִידָאָה יִתְיְילִד לְהַהוּא רֵישָׁא חִוָּורָא, וְכַד יֵיתוּן מִבִּשְׂרָא דַּחֲמָרֵי, יָטְעִין לֵיהּ, בְּהַהוּא דְּעָיֵיל מַרְגְּלָן בְּזַגִּין דְּדַהֲבָא, בְּלָא דַעְתָּא דִּילֵיהּ, וּדְיוּקְנָא יְצַיֵּיר בְּצִיּוּרָא בַּחֶרֶט. מַאי בַּחֶרֶט. בְּחֶרֶט אֱנוֹשׁ. דָּא קֻלְמוֹסָא דֶּאֱנוֹשׁ חַיָּיבָא, דְּאַטְעֵי לִבְנֵי נָשָׁא.

79. In the Book of Enoch I found that he said: An only son will be born to that white head, NAMELY AARON, WHO WAS BORN FROM THE SIDE OF CHESED, WHICH ROOT IS CALLED 'THE WHITE HEAD'. And when those who are of asses' flesh come – NAMELY THE MIXED MULTITUDE OF WHOM IT SAYS, "WHOSE FLESH WERE LIKE THOSE OF DONKEYS" (YECHEZKEL 23:20) – they will deceive him by inserting gems into golden bells without his knowledge, and he will make a form with the engraving tool. What kind of engraving tool. The graving tool of Enosh, the engraving stylus of evil Enosh, who led people astray.

80. וַדַּאי דָּא בְּרִירָא דְּמִלָּה, דֶּאֱנוֹשׁ כַּד אַטְעֵי עָלְמָא, בְּקֻלְמוֹסָא הֲוָה רָשִׁים רְשִׁימִין, דְּכָל דְּיוּקְנִין וּפֻלְחָנִין נִכְרָאִין בְּהַהוּא קֻלְמוֹסָא, וְעַ"ד כְּתִיב בַּחֶרֶט, הַהוּא דְּאִשְׁתְּמוֹדַע לְמֶעְבַּד הָכִי. וְדָא הוּא בְּרִירוּ דְּמִלָּה.

80. This is the elucidation of the matter, for when Enosh led the world astray TO WORSHIP IDOLS with his stylus, he made etchings of all the

images and idols with that implement. Therefore, it is written: "with a graving tool," which indicates that SPECIFIC TOOL that was known to do so. And this is the clarification of the matter.

81. וְכֹלָּא הֲוָה, דְּוַדַּאי בְּכִיסָא אַרְמֵי דַּהֲבָא, וְכַסֵּי לֵיהּ מֵעֵינָא, כְּמָה דְּאָמְרוּ אִינּוּן חַרְשִׁין, וְהָכִי אִצְטְרִיךְ בְּזִינֵי דְּחַרְשִׁין אָלֵין. וְדָא הוּא עוֹבָדָא דְּחַרְשִׁין אָלֵין, מִלָּה דְּאִצְטְרִיךְ בְּאִתְגַּלְיָא, לְאִתְגַּלְּאָה לְבָתַר, אִצְטְרִיךְ טְמִירוּ וְכִסּוּיָא בְּקַדְמֵיתָא, דְּיִתְכַּסֵּי מֵעֵינָא, וּבָתַר יִפּוֹק אוּמָנָא לְאוּמָנוּתֵיהּ. וּמִלָּה דְּאִצְטְרִיךְ בְּכִסּוּיָא לְבָתַר, אִצְטְרִיךְ בְּאִתְגַּלְיָא בְּקַדְמֵיתָא.

81. And it all transpired, MEANING THAT BOTH THE EXPLANATION OF THE WORD GRAVING TOOL IN THE BOOK OF ENOCH AND THAT OF RABBI SHIMON WERE PRESENT, because he certainly placed the gold in a bag and concealed it from view, AS IN THE WORDS OF RABBI SHIMON. As the magicians say, so must it be with this type of magic, that things that need to be revealed must be concealed and hidden first – MEANING that it should be concealed from view FIRST, and afterwards the craftsman uses his craft TO REVEAL IT. And that which must eventually be hidden, must first be revealed.

82. הַשְׁתָּא בְּנֵי רְחִימָאי, רְחִימִין דְּנַפְשָׁאי, מָה אַעֲבִיד, וַדַּאי אִצְטְרִיכְנָא לְגַלָּאָה, אֲצִיתוּ וְאַטְמִירוּ מִלִּין. בְּסִטַר קְדוּשָׁה הַהוּא, אֱלֹהִים דִּקְשׁוֹט, מֶלֶךְ עַל עָלְמָא, בִּתְלַת עָלְמִין אִתְתָּקַף. בִּבְרִיאָה. בִּיצִירָה. בַּעֲשִׂיָּה. וְהָא אִתְּמַר, רָזָא דְּכָל חֲדָא וַחֲדָא הָכָא. לְקָבֵל בְּרִיאָה, וַיִּקַּח מִיָּדָם, מִלָּה דְּלָא הֲוָה בֵּיהּ עַד כְּעַן כְּלוּם. לְקָבֵל יְצִירָה. וַיָּצַר אוֹתוֹ בַּחֶרֶט, לְקָבֵל עֲשִׂיָּה. וַיַּעֲשֵׂהוּ עֵגֶל מַסֵּכָה. מַאן חָמָא חַרְשִׁין בְּכָל עָלְמָא כְּאִלֵּין.

82. Now, my beloved sons, beloved of my soul, what shall I do? I certainly must disclose, so listen closely and then conceal the words. On the side of Holiness the True Elohim, who is King of the World, has become strengthened in three worlds, Briyah, Yetzirah and Asiyah. And we have

already learned the secret OF EACH WORLD. Here THE MIXED MULTITUDE DREW FROM ALL THESE THREE WORLDS. Corresponding to Briyah, IT IS WRITTEN, "he received the gold at their hand," MEANING THAT HE RECEIVED SOMETHING that he did not have until now, MEANING GOLD. THIS INDICATES THE WORLD OF BRIYAH ('CREATION'), BECAUSE CREATION MEANS A NEW THING THAT WAS NOT IN EXISTENCE BEFORE. Corresponding to Yetzirah ('Formation'), IT IS WRITTEN: "he fashioned it with an engraving tool". And corresponding to Asiyah, IT IS WRITTEN: "And made it a molten calf" (Shemot 32:4). Who has ever seen such sorcerers in the entire world?

83. הַשְׁתָּא אִית לְמֵימַר, וְכִי לָא כְּתִיב וָאַשְׁלִיכֵהוּ בָּאֵשׁ, וְלָא יַתִּיר, וּכְדֵין וַיֵּצֵא הָעֵגֶל הַזֶּה. וְהַשְׁתָּא אַתְּ אָמְרַתְּ וַיַּעֲשֵׂהוּ עֵגֶל מַסֵּכָה אֶלָּא ח"ו דְּאַהֲרֹן עֲבַד, וּקְרָא אוֹכַח דִּכְתִיב וַיִּקַּח אֶת הָעֵגֶל אֲשֶׁר עָשׂוּ. אֲבָל מִמַּה דִּכְתִיב וַיִּקַּח מִיָּדָם, וּכְתִיב וַיָּצַר אוֹתוֹ. מֵחֵילָא דִּתְרֵין אִלֵּין, אִתְעֲבֵיד כֹּלָּא. כִּבְיָכוֹל הוּא עָבֵיד לֵיהּ, דְּאִי תְרֵין אִלֵּין לָא הֲווֹ, לָא אִתְעֲבֵיד וְלָא נָפַק לְאוּמָנוּתָא. אֲבָל מַאן גָּרַם דְּאִתְעֲבֵיד. אִינּוּן תְּרֵין. בְּעוֹד דְּאִיהוּ לָקַח מִיָּדָם, אִינְהוּ עַבְדֵי חַרְשַׁיְיהוּ, וּמְלַחֲשֵׁי בְּפוּמַיְיהוּ, וּמָשְׁכֵי רוּחָא לְתַתָּא, מִן סִטְרָא אַחֲרָא.

83. Now it can be asked, is not it written: "then I threw it into the fire" (Shemot 32:24), and DID nothing further, then "and there came out this calf" (Ibid.)? And yet you say that he "made it a golden calf?" HE ANSWERS: But heaven forbid that Aaron made THIS CALF, and the Torah proves it, as it is written: "And he took the calf which they had made" (Ibid. 20), AND IT IS NOT WRITTEN, 'WHICH HE HAD MADE'. It is written, "And he took the gold at their hand, and fashioned it." It means that by the power of these two, YUNUS AND YAMBRUS, everything was made, AND IT WAS as though AARON himself did it. But if these two had not been present THE CALF would not have been made, and would not have come out with skill. But who caused it to be made? These two, because while he was receiving it from their hand, they performed their magic and uttered incantations with their mouths, and drew a spirit from the Other Side.

84. וּמָשְׁכוּ תְּרֵין רוּחִין כַּחֲדָא, חַד מִן דְּכָר, וְחַד מִן נוּקְבָּא. דְּכַר

אִתְלְבַשׁ בְּדִיּוּקְנָא דְּשׁוֹר. נוּקְבָּא בְּדִיּוּקְנָא דַּחֲמוֹר, תַּרְוַוְיְיהוּ הֲווֹ כְּלִילָן כַּחֲדָא. אֲמַאי תְּרֵין אִלֵּין. אֶלָּא שׁוֹר הָא אִתְּמַר. חֲמוֹר אֲמַאי. בְּגִין דְּחָרְשִׁין אִלֵּין דְּמִצְרָאֵי, כְּתִיב בְּהוֹ, אֲשֶׁר בְּשַׂר חֲמוֹרִים בְּשָׂרָם.

84. They drew two spirits together, one from the Male and one from the Female. THE SPIRIT OF the Male was clothed in the form of an ox, and THE SPIRIT OF the Female in the form of an donkey, and they were both combined into one. Why these two? The ox, as we have already learned, BECAUSE THE FIRST PRIMARY CAUSE OF INJURY OF THE OTHER SIDE IS CALLED 'AN OX'. BUT why an donkey? HE ANSWERS: Because it is written of the Egyptian magicians that, "Whose flesh is as the flesh of donkeys" (Yechezkel 23:20).

85. וְעַל דָּא, כָּל אִינּוּן דְּיִשְׂרָאֵל דְּמִיתוּ, אִתְחַבָּרוּ בַּהֲדַיְיהוּ בְּלִבַּהוֹן. וּבְגִין דַּהֲווֹ תְּרֵין דִּיּוּקְנִין, כְּתִיב אֵלֶּה אֱלֹהֶיךָ יִשְׂרָאֵל, וְלָא כְּתִיב זֶה, אֶלָּא אֵלֶּה, תְּרֵין הֲווֹ כַּחֲדָא, אֲשֶׁר הֶעֱלוּךָ מֵאֶרֶץ מִצְרָיִם. הֶעֱלוּךָ וְלָא הֶעֶלְךָ כְּתִיב.

85. Therefore, all those of Yisrael died who joined them, WITH THE MIXED MULTITUDE, in their hearts. And because there were two forms, AN OX AND AN DONKEY, it is written: "These are your Elohim, Yisrael" (Shemot 32:4), instead of 'this', IN THE SINGULAR, because the two were together. SIMILARLY, "that brought you up out of Egypt" (Ibid.), "brought you up OUT OF EGYPT" has a plural form, instead of singular.

86. וַיַּעֲשֵׂהוּ עֵגֶל מַסֵּכָה וַיֹּאמְרוּ. וַיֹּאמֶר לָא כְּתִיב, אֶלָּא וַיֹּאמְרוּ, דְּאַהֲרֹן לָא אָמַר מִדִי. תָּנֵינָן, מֵאָה וְעֶשְׂרִים וְחָמֵשׁ קַנְטְרִין הֲווֹ בֵּיהּ.

86. "...and made it a molten calf, and they said..." It is not written: 'and he said', but rather, "and they said," because Aaron said nothing. We have learned that it weighed 125 Kanterin (a certain measurement.)

87. הֵיךְ כְּתִיב וַיִּקַּח מִיָּדָם, וְכִי בְּיָדָם הֲווֹ כָּל אִלֵּין קַנְטְרִין. אֶלָּא מִכְּלָלָא דְּאִינּוּן קַנְטְרִין נַטְלוּ מְלֵי יְדַיְיהוּ. וְהַהוּא זְעֵיר, אִסְתַּלָק עַל

כְּלָא, כְּאִילוּ הֲוָה כְּלָא בִּידַיְיהוּ.

87. How can it be written that "he received the gold at their hands"? HE ASKS: Is it possible that all 125 centenaria were in their hands? HE ANSWERS: They had their arms full of the 125 centenaria, and that small amount in their hand was considered as the whole amount.

88. ת"ח, מָה כְּתִיב וַיַּרְא אַהֲרֹן וַיִּבֶן מִזְבֵּחַ לְפָנָיו. אִי חֲסִידָא קַדִּישָׁא, כַּמָּה רְעוּתָךְ הֲוָה לְטַב, וְלָא יַדְעַת לְאִסְתַּמְּרָא. כֵּיוָן דְּאַרְמֵי לֵיהּ בְּנוּרָא, אִתְתָּקַּף חֵילָא דְּסִטְרָא אַחֲרָא תַּמָּן בְּנוּרָא, וְנָפַק דְּיוּקְנָא דְּשׁוֹר, כְּמָה דְּאִתְּמַר בִּתְרֵין מְשִׁיכִין דְּסִטְרָא אַחֲרָא. מִיָּד וַיַּרְא אַהֲרֹן. מַהוּ וַיַּרְא אַהֲרֹן. חָמָא דְּסִטְרָא אַחֲרָא אִתְתָּקַּף, מִיָּד וַיִּבֶן מִזְבֵּחַ לְפָנָיו, דְּאִלְמָלֵא דְּאַקְדִּים וּבָנָה מִזְבֵּחַ דָּא, עָלְמָא אִתְהֲדַר לְחָרְבָּנָא.

88. Come and behold: it is written, "And when Aaron saw it he built an altar before it" (Ibid. 5). O holy pious one, how good was your intention, but you did not know how to protect yourself. As soon as he cast it into the fire, the power of the Other Side grew stronger in the fire and the form of the ox emerged, as they have talked about the two drawn from the Other Side, NAMELY AN OX AND AN DONKEY. Immediately, "Aaron saw it," meaning that he saw the Other Side growing strong, immediately, "he built an altar before it." Had he not built this altar before, then the world would have returned to its destroyed state.

89. לְלִסְטִים דַּהֲוָה נָפִיק לְקַפְּחָא וּלְקַטְלָא בְּנֵי נָשָׁא, חָמָא לִגְיוֹנָא דְּמַלְכָּא, דְּהַהוּא לִסְטִים נָפַק בְּחֵילָא תַּקִּיף מָה עֲבַד הַהוּא לִגְיוֹנָא, אִשְׁתַּדַּל בַּהֲדֵי מַלְכָּא לְנָפְקָא בְּאָרְחָא. וּמָשִׁיךְ לֵיהּ הַהוּא לִגְיוֹנָא בְּהַהוּא אָרְחָא, עַד דְּאָזִיל הַהוּא לִסְטִים בְּהַהוּא אָרְחָא, חָמָא דְּיוּקְנָא דְּמַלְכָּא קָאִים קַמֵּיהּ, כֵּיוָן דְּחָמָא לֵיהּ לְמַלְכָּא דַּהֲוָה אָזִיל קַמֵּיהּ בְּאָרְחָא, מִיָּד נִרְתַּע וְאַהֲדַר לַאֲחוֹרָא.

89. THIS IS LIKE a robber who goes out to destroy and kill people. The king's legion saw the robber going out with great strength. What did they

do? They persuaded the king to go out onto the road, and the legion led him to that road WHERE THE ROBBER WAS. While the robber was traveling on the road, he saw the image of the king standing before him. As soon as he saw the king's image, he trembled and retreated.

90. כַּךְ וַיַּרְא אַהֲרֹן דְּסִטְרָא אַחֲרָא אִתְּקַּף, אָחִיד בְּאַסְוָותָא, וְאִתְקִיף בְּסִטְרָא קְדוּשָׁה וְשַׁוֵּי לֵיהּ קָמֵיהּ. כֵּיוָן דְּחָמָא סִטְרָא בִּישָׁא דְּיוּקְנָא דְּמַלְכָּא דְּקָאִים קָמֵיהּ, מִיַּד אַהֲדַר לַאֲחוֹרָא, וְאִתְחֲלָשׁ תֶּקְפֵּיהּ וְחֵילֵיהּ, דְּהָא אִתְתַּקַּף, וּמִזְבַּח דָּא אִתְגַּבָּר, וְאִתְחֲלָשׁ סִטְרָא אַחֲרָא.

90. Similarly, "When Aaron saw" that the Other Side became stronger, he gripped onto a remedy. He strengthened himself with AND DREW the Holy Side and placed it STANDING before it. As soon as the Other Side saw the image of the King standing before it, it immediately retreated, and its strength and power were weakened. SINCE AARON grew strong and the altar, WHICH IS THE SECRET OF MALCHUT, grew strong, the Other Side grew weak.

91. תָּא חֲזֵי מָה כְּתִיב וַיִּקְרָא אַהֲרֹן וַיֹּאמַר חַג לַיְיָ' מָחָר. חַג לַיְיָ', וְלֹא לָעֵגֶל. וְלִסְטַר קְדוּשָׁה עֲבַד, וְלִסְטַר קְדוּשָׁה קָרָא וְאָמַר. וְדָא אַסְוָותָא אַקְדִּים, דְּאִלְמָלֵא דְּעָבַד דָּא, לָא קָאִים עָלְמָא עַל קִיּוּמֵיהּ, וְעִם כָּל דָּא, לָא שָׁכִיךְ רוּגְזֵיהּ מֵאַהֲרֹן, אע"ג דְּלָא אִתְכַּוָּון לְבִישׁ.

91. Come and behold: it is written, "and Aaron made proclamations, and said, 'Tomorrow is a feast to Hashem'" (Ibid.), "a feast to Hashem," not to the calf. It was to the side of Holiness that he made it, and to the side of Holiness did he proclaim. This is the remedy that he hastened to use. Had he not done this, the world would not have remained in existence. Even so, His anger did not abate over Aaron, even though he did not intend any evil.

92. א"ל קוּדְשָׁא בְּרִיךְ הוּא, אַהֲרֹן, תְּרֵין חַרְשִׁין אִלֵּין מַשְׁכוּ לָךְ לְמַה דְּבָעוּ. חַיֶּיךָ, תְּרֵין בְּנָךְ יִפְּלוּן, וְעַל חוֹבָא דָא יִתְפְּסוּן הה"ד וּבְאַהֲרֹן הִתְאַנַּף יְיָ' מְאֹד לְהַשְׁמִידוֹ. מַאי לְהַשְׁמִידוֹ. אִלֵּין בְּנוֹי, כד"א וָאַשְׁמִיד פִּרְיוֹ מִמַּעַל, דְּפִרְיוֹ דְּבַר נָשׁ בְּנוֹי אִינּוּן.

-146-

92. The Holy One, blessed be He, said to him: Aaron, these two magicians drew you toward what they wanted. By your life, two of your sons will fall, and they will be seized for this sin. This is what is written, "And Hashem was very angry with Aaron to have destroyed him" (Devarim 9:20). This refers to his sons, as is written, "Yet I destroyed his fruit from above" (Amos 2:9), because the fruits of a man are his children.

93. ת״ח, אַהֲרֹן שַׁוֵּי לֵיהּ לְהַהוּא מִזְבֵּחַ לְפָנָיו, וְעֶגְלָא תָּב לַאֲחוֹרָא. בְּנוֹי שַׁוּוּ לִסְטַר אַחֲרָא לִפְנַיְיהוּ, וּסְטַר קְדוּשָׁה אַהְדָּר לַאֲחוֹרָא, דִּכְתִיב וַיַּקְרִיבוּ לִפְנֵי יְיָ׳, לִפְנֵי יְיָ׳ שַׁוּוּ. אִתְפָּסוּ בְּחוֹבָה דָּא.

93. Come and behold: Aaron placed that altar, WHICH IS MALCHUT, before him, and put the calf, WHICH IS THE OTHER SIDE, behind him. But his sons placed the Other Side in front and returned the side of the Holiness back LIKE IN THE SIN OF THE CALF, as it is written, "and offered STRANGE FIRE before Hashem" (Vayikra 10:1). They put THE STRANGE FIRE, WHICH IS THE OTHER SIDE, "before Hashem." So we see that HIS SONS were caught for this sin OF THE GOLDEN CALF.

94. אַהֲרֹן חָשַׁב, דְּבֵין כָּךְ יֵיתֵי מֹשֶׁה, וְע״ד הַהוּא מִזְבֵּחַ לָא סָתִיר לֵיהּ מֹשֶׁה, דְּאִילּוּ הֲוָה כְּמָה דְּחַשְׁבִין בְּנֵי נָשָׁא, מִלָּה קַדְמָאָה דְּאִבְעֵי לְמֹשֶׁה, לְנַתְצָא לְהַהוּא מִזְבֵּחַ אִצְטְרִיךְ, כְּמָה דְּנַבֵּי עִדוֹ עַל מִזְבֵּחַ דְּבֵית אֵל, וּנְבוּאָתֵיהּ עַל הַהוּא מִזְבֵּחַ הֲוָה. אֲבָל הָכָא מִלָּה אַחֲרָא הֲוָה כְּמָה דְּאִתְּמַר. וּכְתִיב, וַיִּקַּח אֶת הָעֵגֶל אֲשֶׁר עָשׂוּ, וְלָא כְּתִיב וַיִּנְתֹּץ אֶת הַמִּזְבֵּחַ.

94. Aaron thought that in the meantime Moses would come. THEREFORE HE SAID: "TOMORROW IS A FEAST TO HASHEM." Therefore, Moses did not smash that altar that he made. For if it were, as people think, THAT HE BUILT THE ALTAR BEFORE THE CALF, the first thing that Moses should have DONE WOULD BE to smash that altar, as Ido prophesied regarding the altar of Bet El, and his prophecy was about that altar IN BET EL, AS WRITTEN IN I MELACHIM 13:32. But here, AT THE ALTAR OF AARON, it was a different matter, as we have explained. THEREFORE, it is written, "And he took the calf which they had made" (Shemot 32:20), and it does not

say, 'and smashed the altar.'

95. ת״ח וַיִּקְרָא אַהֲרֹן. אַכְרִיז אִיהוּ בְּקָלָא וְאָמַר. כְּתִיב הָכָא וַיִּקְרָא וַיֹּאמַר, וּכְתִיב בְּיוֹנָה וַיִּקְרָא וַיֹּאמַר, מַה לְהַלָּן כָּרִיז לְדִינָא, אוּף הָכָא כָּרִיז לְדִינָא. חַג לַיְיָ' מָחָר, נָבֵּי נְבוּאָה בְּהַהוּא רוּחַ דְּמִזְבֵּחַ, דְּזַמִּין דִּינָא לְשַׁרְיָא עֲלַיְיהוּ. חַג לַיְיָ', לְמֶעְבַּד בְּכוּ דִּינָא.

95. Come and behold: "and Aaron made proclamation" (Ibid. 5), meaning that he cried aloud, and said, "TOMORROW IS A FEAST TO HASHEM." It is written here, "made proclamation, and said" and by Jonah it is written, "and he cried, and said" (Yonah 3:4). Just as by JONAH it is a call for Judgment, so here also, BY AARON, it is a call for Judgment. "Tomorrow is a feast to Hashem," he prophesied with that spirit of the altar, WHICH IS MALCHUT, that Judgment would dwell upon them. A feast (Heb. *chag*) to Hashem," IS DERIVED FROM BREAKING (ARAMAIC *CHAGA*), THAT IS, to execute Judgment upon you.

96. וּתְלַת דִּינִין הֲווֹ, חַד, וַיִּגּוֹף יְיָ' אֶת הָעָם. וְחַד, בִּבְנֵי לֵוִי. וְחַד, דְּאַשְׁקֵי לִבְנֵי יִשְׂרָאֵל. וְהַיְינוּ חַג דִּבְנֵי לֵוִי. לַיְיָ', דְּוַיִּגּוֹף יְיָ'. מָחָר, דְּאַשְׁקֵי לוֹן מֹשֶׁה. וּבֵיתוּ בְּהַהוּא לֵילְיָא, וּלְמָחָר אִשְׁתְּכָחוּ נְפִיחִין וּמֵתִין. וְאִינּוּן מַיִין הֲווֹ מְכַשְׁכְּשִׁין בִּמְעֵיהוֹן כָּל לֵילְיָא, וּבְצַפְרָא אִשְׁתְּכָחוּ מֵתִין, וְעַ״ד חַג לַיְיָ' מָחָר. וְכָל אַסְוָותָא דְּעָבֵד אַהֲרֹן, בְּגִין דִּכְתִיב וַיִּבֶן מִזְבֵּחַ לְפָנָיו.

96. And there were three types of judgment. One: "And Hashem plagued the people" (Shemot 32:35); second, by the sons of Levi THAT KILLED AMONG THE CHILDREN OF YISRAEL, and third, he gave the children of Yisrael to drink. This is the meaning of, "TOMORROW IS A feast (Heb. *chag*) TO HASHEM," AS 'CHAG' REFERS TO THE KILLING by the sons of Levi; "Hashem," INDICATES THAT "Hashem plagued the people," and "tomorrow" INFORMS US THAT Moses made them drink THE ASHES OF THE CALF. For they lay down that night, and in the morning they were found swollen and dead. Pertaining to this, HE SAID: "tomorrow is a feast to Hashem." And the entire remedy that Aaron administered consists of the words, "he built an altar before it."

תׄ״ח, דִּכְתִיב וַיַּרְא אֶת הָעֵגֶל וּמְחֹלֹת, וְאִלּוּ מִזְבֵּחַ לָא כְּתִיב. .97
דְּהָא אַהֲרֹן מִנְדַּע הֲוָה יָדַע, דִּכְתִיב זֹבֵחַ לָאֱלֹהִים יָחֳרָם בִּלְתִּי לַיְיָ׳
לְבַדּוֹ, וַדַּאי אִשְׁתְּזִיב אַהֲרֹן בְּעֵיטָא טָבָא דְּדָבַר לְנַפְשֵׁיהּ, וְכֹלָּא
בִּרְעוּתָא שְׁלִים טָב, דְּלָא אִתְכַּוָּין לְבִישׁ.

97. Come and behold: it is written, "he saw the calf, and the dancing," (Ibid. 19) but the altar is not mentioned because Aaron knew that verse, "He that sacrifices to any Elohim, save to Hashem alone, shall be utterly destroyed" (Shemot 22:19). Certainly, Aaron was saved by the good advice he gave himself, TO MAKE AN ALTAR TO HASHEM. And everything was done with perfect good will, for he had no evil intent.

א״ל ר׳ אֶלְעָזָר, אַבָּא וַדַּאי הָכִי הוּא, וְיִשְׂרָאֵל לָא הֲווֹ. אֲבָל יָרָבְעָם .98
דְּעָבֵד עֶגְלִין, הָא יִשְׂרָאֵל הֲווֹ, וְעֵגֶל עָבְדוּ. א״ל וַדַּאי, וְאוּקְמוּהָ, אֲבָל
יָרָבְעָם חָטָא וְהֶחֱטִיא, וְלָאו כְּמָה דְּאָמְרוּ. דְּוַדַּאי חוֹבָא בִּישָׁא עָבֵד
וּבְמַלְכוּת חָטָא.

98. Rabbi Elazar said to him: Father, certainly it is so, and Yisrael did not make THE CALF. But as for Jerobaam making the calves, Yisrael were involved and made a calf. He said to him: Certainly IT WAS SO, and they have explained it. But Jerobaam sinned and caused others to sin. And it is not as some say IN THE COMMENTARIES OF THE SCRIPTURE, THAT HE MADE ONLY THE APPEARANCE OF CALVES SO THAT THE CHILDREN OF YISRAEL WOULD NOT GO TO JERUSALEM, BUT THEY WERE NOT REAL, because he certainly committed a grave sin. And he sinned against the divine Kingdom, JUST LIKE THE MIXED MULTITUDE BY THE SIN OF THE CALF.

אָמַר יָרָבְעָם, וַדַּאי יְדַעְנָא דְּהָא סְטַר קְדוּשָׁה לָא שַׁרְיָא, אֶלָּא .99
בְּלִבָּא דְּכָל עָלְמָא, וְדָא יְרוּשָׁלַ͏ם. אֲנָא לָא יָכִילְנָא לְאַמְשָׁכָא לְהַהוּא
סְטַר הָכָא, מָה אַעֲבִיד. מִיַּד וַיִּוָּעַץ הַמֶּלֶךְ וַיַּעַשׂ וְגוֹ׳. נָטַל עֵיטָא בִּישָׁא,
אָמַר הָא סִטְרָא אַחֲרָא, דְּאִתְמַשְּׁכָא מִיַּד לְכָל אֲתָר. וְכ״ש בְּאַרְעָא דָּא,
דְּתִיאוּבְתֵּיהּ לְאַשְׁרָאָה בְּגַוֵּיהּ, אֲבָל לָא יַכְלָא לְאִתְלַבְּשָׁא אֶלָּא
בְּדִיּוּקְנָא דְּשׁוֹר.

99. Jerobaam said: I know that the side of Holiness dwells only in the heart of the world, which is Jerusalem. I can not draw that side OF HOLINESS in here, so what should I do? Immediately, "the king took counsel, and made..." (I Melachim 12:28). He took bad advice. He said: The Other Side is immediately drawn to any place and to this land all the more, for it desires to dwell in it. But it can be clothed only in the form of an ox.

סס1. תְּרֵין עֶגְלִים אֲמַאי. אֶלָּא אָמַר יָרָבְעָם, בְּמַדְבְּרָא הֲוֹו אִינּוּן חָרָשִׁין, דִּכְתִּיב בְּשַׂר חֲמוֹרִים בְּשָׂרָם. הָכָא, אִינּוּן תְּרֵין רוּחִין בִּישִׁין, יִתְלַבְּשׁוּ כַּדְקָא חֲזֵי לוֹן, דְּכַר וְנוּקְבָּא אִינּוּן. דְּכַר הֲוָה בְּבֵית אֵל, וְנוּקְבָּא הֲוַת בְּדָן. וּמִגּוֹ דִּכְתִּיב, נֹפֶת תִּטֹּפְנָה שִׂפְתֵי זָרָה, אִתְמְשָׁכוּ יִשְׂרָאֵל אֲבַתְרֵהּ יַתִּיר, דִּכְתִּיב וַיֵּלְכוּ הָעָם לִפְנֵי הָאֶחָד עַד דָּן. וּבְג״כ תְּרֵין עֶגְלִין הֲוֹו. וּמָשִׁיךְ לוֹן יָרָבְעָם בְּאַרְעָא קַדִּישָׁא, וַהֲוָה חוֹבָא עֲלֵיהּ וְעַל יִשְׂרָאֵל, וּמָנַע בִּרְכָּאן מִן עָלְמָא. וַעֲלֵיהּ כְּתִיב גּוֹזֵל אָבִיו וְאִמּוֹ וְגוֹ'.

100. HE ASKS: Why DID HE MAKE two calves? HE ANSWERS: Jerobaam said, 'In the wilderness were magicians of whom it is written, "whose flesh were like those of donkeys" (Yechezkel 23:20). AND THEREFORE THEY DREW TWO SPIRITS, AN OX AND AN DONKEY, MALE AND FEMALE, BUT THEY FORMED THEM BOTH IN ONLY ONE CALF. Here, those two evil spirits will be clothed, as befits them, INTO TWO CALVES, because they are male and female, the male will be in Bet El and the female in Dan. And since, as it is written: "the lips of a strange woman drip honey" (Mishlei 5:3), the children of Yisrael were powerfully attracted to them, as it is written: "for the people went as far as Dan, to worship before that one" (I Melachim 12:30). Therefore, there were two calves. And Jerobaam drew them in the Holy Land. And the sin was upon him and the children of Yisrael. And he withheld blessings from the world. Of him, it is written, "He who robs his father or his mother..." (Mishlei 28:24) BECAUSE HE BLEMISHED MALE AND FEMALE, WHO ARE HIS FATHER AND MOTHER.

סא1. וְעַ״ד הֲוֹו עֶגְלִין, דְּהָא לְבוּשָׁא קַדְמָאָה דְּמִתְלַבַּשׁ סִטְרָא אַחֲרָא שׁוֹר אִיהוּ, כְּמָה דְּאִתְּמַר. וְאִי תֵּימָא אֲמַאי אִיהוּ עֵגֶל וְלָא שׁוֹר. אֶלָּא וַדַּאי כַּךְ אִתְחֲזֵי, וְכֵן בְּכָל סִטְרִין, שֵׁירוּתָא דִּלְבוּשָׁא זוּטָא אִיהוּ, וְהָא אוּקִימְנָא.

101. Therefore, they were calves, because the first garment which the Other Side dons is the ox, as we have said earlier. And you may question why it is a calf and not an ox? Certainly this is the way it should be in any case, because one first dons something small, NAMELY A CALF, as explained.

102. וְעַל דָּא בָּנַי רְחִימָאי, כֵּיוָן דֶּאֱלֹהִים בָּעוּ, וּבְסִטְרָא דֶּאֱלֹהִים אִתְבְּנֵי עוֹבָדָא, אֱלֹהִים קַדִּישָׁא, אִימָא, דַּאֲחִידַת תָּדִיר בִּדְרוֹעָא דְּמַלְכָּא, וְסַלִּיקַת רְצוּעָה, לָא הֲוַת תַּמָּן, וְאִצְטְרִיךְ לֵיהּ לְמֹשֶׁה לְמֶהֱוֵי תַּמָּן בְּאַתְרָהָא, כֵּיוָן דְּאַנְקִיד לֵיהּ קוּדְשָׁא בְּרִיךְ הוּא , אִסְתָּכַּל.

102. Therefore, my beloved children, they wanted to draw the name Elohim, WHICH IS THE NAME OF MALCHUT. And it is on the side of Elohim that work was built. Therefore holy Elohim, which is Mother, THAT IS, MALCHUT, that constantly holds the arm of the King and holds back the lash, was not there, and so, Moses had to be there in Her place. As soon as the Holy One, blessed be He, hinted to him, he observed AND UNDERSTOOD.

103. תְּלַת זִמְנִין אַנְקִיד לֵיהּ, אִי מֹשֶׁה רַעְיָא מְהֵימָנָא, כַּמָּה חֵילָךְ תַּקִּיף, כַּמָּה גְּבוּרְתָּךְ רַב, תְּלַת זִמְנִין אַנְקִיד לֵיהּ, דִּכְתִיב וְעַתָּה הַנִּיחָה לִי הָא חַד. וַיִּחַר אַפִּי בָהֶם וַאֲכַלֵּם, הָא תְּרֵין. וְאֶעֱשֶׂה אוֹתְךָ לְגוֹי גָּדוֹל, הָא תְּלַת. חָכְמְתָא דְּמֹשֶׁה בִּתְלַת נְקוּדִין אִלֵּין. אָחִיד בִּדְרוֹעֵיהּ יְמִינָא, לְקַבֵּל הַנִּיחָה לִי. אָחִיד בִּדְרוֹעֵיהּ שְׂמָאלָא, לְקַבֵּל וַיִּחַר אַפִּי בָהֶם וַאֲכַלֵּם. אִתְחַבַּק בְּגוּפָא דְּמַלְכָּא, לְקַבֵּל וְאֶעֱשֶׂה אוֹתְךָ לְגוֹי גָּדוֹל. וְכַד אִתְחַבַּק בְּגוּפָא, תְּרֵין דְּרוֹעִין מִסִּטְרָא דָּא וּמִסִּטְרָא דָּא, לָא יָכִיל לְאִתְנַעְנְעָא לִסְטְרָא בְּעָלְמָא. דָּא הֲוֵי חָכְמְתָא דְּמֹשֶׁה, דְּמִינֵי נְקוּדִין דְּמַלְכָּא יָדַע בְּכָל חַד מִנַּיְיהוּ, בְּאָן אֲתָר יִתְתְּקַף, וּבְחָכְמְתָא עֲבַד.

103. He hinted to him three times. O, Moses, faithful shepherd, how strong is your power, how great is your might. Three times He hinted to him, as written: "Let me alone" (Shemot 32:10), is one; "that My wrath may burn against them, and that I may consume them" (Ibid.) is the second; "And I will make you a great nation" (Ibid.), is the third. The wisdom of Moses IN STAYING THE LASH was in these three hints. For he held the right arm, in

correspondence to, "let me alone," WHICH IS THE SECRET OF CHESED. He
held the left arm, in correspondence to, "that My wrath may burn against
them, and that I may consume them," WHICH IS GVURAH. He embraced the
body of the King, WHICH IS TIFERET, corresponding to, "and I will make
you a great nation." And when he had embraced the body and the two arms
from each side, MEANING WITH ALL THREE SFIROT, CHESED, GVURAH,
AND TIFERET, He was not able to move AND AROUSE JUDGMENT in any
direction in the world. This was the wisdom of Moses, who, from the hints
of the King, recognized in each one of them where it would prevail, and he
acted with wisdom.

104. אָתוּ רִבִּי אֶלְעָזָר וְחַבְרַיָּיא, וְנַשְׁקוּ יְדוֹי. הֲוָה תַּמָּן רִבִּי אַבָּא, אָמַר,
אִלְמָלֵי לָא אָתֵינָא לְעָלְמָא אֶלָּא לְמִשְׁמַע דָּא, דַּי לָן. בָּכָה וְאָמַר, וַוי
ר', כַּד תִּסְתָּלַק מֵעָלְמָא, מַאן יַנְהַר וִיגַלֵּי נְהוֹרִין דְּאוֹרַיְיתָא. מִלָּה דָא,
בַּחֲשׁוֹכָא אִתְטְמַר עַד הַשְׁתָּא, דְּנָפַק מִתַּמָּן, וְהָא נָהִיר עַד רוּם רְקִיעָא,
וּבְכֻרְסְיָיא דְּמַלְכָּא רָשִׁים, וְקוּדְשָׁא בְּרִיךְ הוּא חַדֵי הַשְׁתָּא בְּהַאי מִלָּה.
וְכַמָּה חֶדוּ עַל חֶדוּ, אִתּוֹסַף מִקַּמֵּי מַלְכָּא קַדִּישָׁא. מַאן יִתְעַר מִלֵּי
דְּחָכְמְתָא בְּעָלְמָא דֵין כְּוָותָיךְ.

104. Rabbi Elazar and the friends approached and kissed the hands OF
RABBI SHIMON. Rabbi Aba who was there, said: If we had come to this
world just to hear this subject it would suffice for us. He wept and said:
Woe to us, Rabbi, when you will depart from this world! Who will enlighten
and reveal the lights of the Torah? This matter – NAMELY, THE QUESTION
IN VERSE 53 – was concealed in the darkness until now when it emerged
from there. It illuminates the heights of the sky, as it is marked upon the
King's throne, and the Holy One, blessed be He, is now rejoicing with this
matter. How much joy upon joy has been added before the Holy King. Who
will awaken words of wisdom in this world, as you do?

105. תָּא חֲזֵי, עַד לָא חָטָא אָדָם, הֲוָה סָלִיק וְקָאִים בְּחָכְמָה דִּנְהִירוּ
עִלָּאָה, וְלָא הֲוָה מִתְפְּרַשׁ מֵאִילָנָא דְּחַיֵּי. כֵּיוָן דְּאַסְגֵּי תִּיאוּבְתָּא
לְמִנְדַּע, וּלְנַחְתָּא לְתַתָּא, אִתְמְשִׁיךְ אֲבַתְרַיְיהוּ, עַד דְּאִתְפְּרַשׁ מֵאִילָנָא
דְּחַיֵּי, וְיָדַע רַע וְשָׁבַק טוֹב. וְעַ"ד כְּתִיב, כִּי לֹא אֵל חָפֵץ רֶשַׁע אָתָּה לֹא

יְגוּרְךָ רָע, מַאן דְּאִתְמְשַׁךְ בְּרָע, לֵית לֵיהּ דִּיּוּרָא עִם אִילָנָא דְּחַיֵּי. וְעַד
לָא חָטְאוּ, הֲווֹ שַׁמְעִין קַלָּא מִלְעֵילָא, וְיַדְעִין חָכְמְתָא עִלָּאָה, וְלָא
דַּחֲלֵי. כֵּיוָן דְּחָטְאוּ, אֲפִילוּ קַלָּא דִּלְתַתָּא, לָא הֲווֹ יַכְלִין לְמֵיקַם בֵּיהּ.

105. Come and behold: before Adam sinned, he ascended and stood in the Wisdom of the Supernal Light, and was not separated from the Tree of Life. When his desire to know GOOD AND EVIL and to go down became strong, he was attracted TO THE OTHER SIDE, until he separated from the Tree of Life, knew evil and abandoned good. Therefore, it is written: "For you are not an El that has pleasure in wickedness, nor shall evil dwell with You" (Tehilim 5:5). One who is drawn after evil can not reside with the Tree of Life. Before they sinned they heard a voice from above, FROM BINAH, and knew supernal Wisdom, and were not afraid. But after they sinned, they were not able to endure even the lower voice OF MALE AND FEMALE, AS IT IS WRITTEN: "I HEARD YOUR VOICE IN THE GARDEN, AND I WAS AFRAID..." (BERESHEET 3:10).

106. כְּגַוְונָא דָּא, עַד לָא חָאבוּ יִשְׂרָאֵל, בְּשַׁעֲתָא דְּקַיְימוּ יִשְׂרָאֵל עַל
טוּרָא דְּסִינַי, אִתְעֲבַר מִנַּיְיהוּ זוּהֲמָא דְּהַאי חִוְיָא, דְּהָא כְּדֵין בָּטוּל יֵצֶר
הָרָע הֲוָה מֵעָלְמָא, וְדָחוּ לֵיהּ מִנַּיְיהוּ. וּכְדֵין אִתְאֲחִידוּ בְּאִילָנָא דְּחַיֵּי,
וּסְלִיקוּ לְעֵילָא, וְלָא נַחְתּוּ לְתַתָּא. כְּדֵין הֲווֹ יַדְעִין, וַהֲווֹ חֲמָאן,
אַסְפַּקְלַרְיָאן עִלָּאִין, וְאִתְנַהֲרָן עֵינַיְיהוּ, וְחַדָּאן לְמִנְדַּע וּלְמִשְׁמַע. וּכְדֵין
חָגַר לוֹן קוּדְשָׁא בְּרִיךְ הוּא, חַגִּירִין דְּאַתְווָן דִּשְׁמָא קַדִּישָׁא, דְּלָא יָכִיל
לְשַׁלְטָאָה עֲלַיְיהוּ הַאי חִוְיָא, וְלָא יְסָאֵב לוֹן כְּדִבְקַדְמֵיתָא.

106. Similarly, before the children of Yisrael sinned, at the time that they stood at Mount Sinai, the filth of the Serpent was removed from them, because the Evil Inclination was made void in the world. And they pushed it away from them. They then were united with the Tree of Life, rose up to the highest levels, and did not go down. Then they knew and saw supernal visions OF ZEIR ANPIN; their eyes shone, and they rejoiced to know and hear. Then the Holy One, blessed be He, girded them with belts of the letters of the Holy Name, WHICH IS THE SECRET OF "THEIR ORNAMENTS BY THE MOUNT HOREB" (Shemot 33:6), so that the Serpent would not be able to have power over them or defile them again AS IN EGYPT.

107. כֵּיוָן דְּחָטוּ בַּעֶגְלָא, אִתְעֲבָרוּ מִנַּיְיהוּ כָּל אִינוּן דַּרְגִּין, וּנְהוֹרִין עִלָּאִין, וְאִתְעֲבָר מִנַּיְיהוּ חֲגִירוּ מְזַיְינִין, דְּאִתְעַטָּרוּ מִשְׁמָא קַדִּישָׁא עִלָּאָה, וְאַמְשִׁיכוּ עֲלַיְיהוּ חִוְיָא בִּישָׁא כְּמִלְּקַדְמִין, וְגָרִימוּ מוֹתָא לְכָל עָלְמָא. וּלְבָתַר מַה כְּתִיב. וַיַּרְא אַהֲרֹן וְכָל בְּנֵי יִשְׂרָאֵל אֶת מֹשֶׁה וְהִנֵּה קָרַן עוֹר פָּנָיו וַיִּירְאוּ מִגֶּשֶׁת אֵלָיו.

107. When they sinned with the calf, all these supernal levels and lights were removed from them. And the armored belts that were adorned with the supernal Holy Name were removed from them. And they drew upon themselves the Evil Serpent as before, and again caused death for the whole world. Afterwards, it is written: "And when Aaron and all the children of Yisrael saw Moses, behold, the skin of his face shone; and they were afraid to come near him" (Shemot 34:30). THEY EVEN FEARED THE RADIANCE OF MOSES' FACE.

108. ת"ח, מָה כְּתִיב בְּקַדְמֵיתָא, וַיַּרְא יִשְׂרָאֵל אֶת הַיָּד הַגְּדוֹלָה, וְכֻלְּהוּ חֲמָאן זָהֲרִין עִלָּאִין, אִתְנַהֲרִין בְּאַסְפַּקְלַרְיָאה דְּנַהֲרָא, דִּכְתִיב וְכָל הָעָם רוֹאִים אֶת הַקּוֹלוֹת. וְעַל יַמָּא, הֲווֹ חֲמָאן וְלָא דַּחֲלִין, דִּכְתִיב זֶה אֵלִי וְאַנְוֵהוּ, לְבָתַר דְּחָטוּ, פְּנֵי הַסַּרְסוּר לָא הֲווֹ יַכְלֵי לְמֶחֱמֵי. מָה כְּתִיב, וַיִּירְאוּ מִגֶּשֶׁת אֵלָיו.

108. Come and behold: it is written at first, "And Yisrael saw the great hand…" (Shemot 14:31). They all saw the supernal lights which illuminated in the illuminating mirror, WHICH IS ZEIR ANPIN, as it is written: "And all the people perceived the thunderings…" (Shemot 20:15). By the sea they saw yet did not fear, as it is written: "He is my El, and I will praise Him" (Shemot 15:2). But after they sinned, they could not even look at the face of the mediator, as it is written: "And they were afraid to come near him."

109. וְת"ח, מָה כְּתִיב בְּהוּ וַיִּתְנַצְּלוּ בְּנֵי יִשְׂרָאֵל אֶת עֶדְיָם מֵהַר חֹרֵב, דְּאִתְעֲבָרוּ מִנַּיְיהוּ, אִינוּן מְזַיְינִין דְּאִתְחַבָּרוּ בְּהוּ בְּטוּרָא דְּסִינַי, בְּגִין דְּלָא יִשְׁלוֹט בְּהוּ הַהוּא חִוְיָא בִּישָׁא, כֵּיוָן דְּאִתְעֲבָר מִנַּיְיהוּ, מָה כְּתִיב, וּמֹשֶׁה יִקַּח אֶת הָאֹהֶל וְנָטָה לוֹ מִחוּץ לַמַּחֲנֶה הַרְחֵק מִן הַמַּחֲנֶה. אָמַר

רַבִּי אֶלְעָזָר, מַאי הַאי קְרָא לְגַבֵּי הַאי. אֶלָּא, כֵּיוָן דְּיָדַע מֹשֶׁה,
דְּאִתְעֲבָרוּ מִנַּיְיהוּ דְּיִשְׂרָאֵל אִינּוּן זַיְינִין עִלָּאִין, אָמַר, הָא וַדַּאי מִכָּאן
וּלְהָלְאָה, חִוְיָא בִּישָׁא יֵיתֵי לְדַיְירָא בֵּינַיְיהוּ, וְאִי יְקוּם מַקְדְּשָׁא הָכָא
בֵּינַיְיהוּ יִסְתָּאַב, מִיַּד וּמֹשֶׁה יִקַּח אֶת הָאֹהֶל וְנָטָה לוֹ מִחוּץ לַמַּחֲנֶה
הַרְחֵק מִן הַמַּחֲנֶה. בְּגִין דְּחָמָא מֹשֶׁה, דְּהָא כְּדֵין יִשְׁלוֹט חִוְיָא בִּישָׁא,
מַה דְּלָא הֲוָה מִקַּדְמַת דְּנָא.

109. Come and behold: it is written of them, "And the children of Yisrael stripped themselves of their ornaments by the Mount Horeb" (Shemot 33:6). For the armor they received at Mount Horeb was removed from them so that the Evil Serpent could not have power over them. Once it was removed from them, it is written: "And Moses would take the Tent, and pitch it outside the camp, afar off from the camp" (Ibid. 7). Rabbi Elazar said: What has this passage, "AND THE CHILDREN OF YISRAEL STRIPPED..." to do with that passage, "AND MOSES WOULD TAKE..."? HE ANSWERS: When Moses knew that the supernal armor was removed from the children of Yisrael, he said: Surely from now on the Evil Serpent will come to dwell among them, and if the Temple, NAMELY, THE TENT OF MEETING, would stand here among them, it will become defiled. Immediately, "Moses would take the Tent and pitch it outside the camp, afar off from the camp," because Moses foresaw that the Evil Serpent would have power over them, unlike what was before.

110. וְקָרָא לוֹ אֹהֶל מוֹעֵד, וְכִי לָא הֲוָה בְּקַדְמֵיתָא אֹהֶל מוֹעֵד. אֶלָּא,
בְּקַדְמֵיתָא אֹהֶל סְתָם, הַשְׁתָּא אֹהֶל מוֹעֵד. מַאי מוֹעֵד. ר' אֶלְעָזָר אָמַר
לְטָב, רַבִּי אַבָּא אָמַר לְבִישׁ, ר' אֶלְעָזָר אָמַר לְטָב, מָה מוֹעֵד דְּאִיהוּ יוֹם
חֶדְוָה דְּסִיהֲרָא, דְּאִיתּוֹסְפָא בֵּיהּ קְדוּשָׁה, לָא שַׁלְטָא בָּהּ פְּגִימוּתָא, אוּף
הָכָא קָרֵי לֵיהּ בִּשְׁמָא דָּא, לְאַחֲזָאָה דְּהָא אִתְרְחִיק מִבֵּינַיְיהוּ, וְלָא
אִתְפְּגִים, וְע"ד וְקָרָא לוֹ אֹהֶל מוֹעֵד כְּתִיב.

110. "And he called it the Tent of Meeting (also: 'appointed time')" (Ibid.). HE ASKS: was it not a Tent of Meeting from the start? HE ANSWERS: at first it was a plain tent; now HE CALLED IT the 'Tent of Meeting'. What is the meaning of "appointed time?" Rabbi Elazar said: it has good connotations. Rabbi Aba said: it has bad connotations. Rabbi Elazar said: it

has good connotations. Just as an appointed time is a day of joy for the moon, WHICH IS MALCHUT, for Holiness is increased in it and no blemish rules over it, here too he gave it this name, FESTIVE TIME, to show THAT THE TENT, WHICH IS THE SECRET MALCHUT, was distanced from them and not blemished. Therefore, it is written: "And he called it the Tent of appointed time."

111. וְר' אַבָּא אָמַר לְבִישׁ, דְּהָא בְּקַדְמֵיתָא הֲוָה אֹהֶל סְתָם, כד"א אֹהֶל בַּל יִצְעָן בַּל יִסַּע יְתֵדוֹתָיו לָנֶצַח. וְהַשְׁתָּא אֹהֶל מוֹעֵד. בְּקַדְמֵיתָא, לְמֵיהַב חַיִּין אֲרוּכִין לְעָלְמִין, דְּלָא יִשְׁלוֹט בְּהוּ מוֹתָא. מִכָּאן לְהַלְאָה אֹהֶל מוֹעֵד, כד"א וּבֵית מוֹעֵד לְכָל חַי, הַשְׁתָּא, אִתְיְיהִיב בֵּיהּ זִמְנָא וְחַיִּין קְצוּבִין לְעָלְמָא. בְּקַדְמֵיתָא לָא אִתְפְּגִים, וְהַשְׁתָּא אִתְפְּגִים. בְּקַדְמֵיתָא חַבְרוּתָא וְזִווּגָא לְסִהֲרָא בְּשִׁמְשָׁא, דְּלָא יַעְדוּן. הַשְׁתָּא אֹהֶל מוֹעֵד, זִווּגָא דִּלְהוֹן מִזְמַן לִזְמַן, וּבג"כ וְקָרָא לוֹ אֹהֶל מוֹעֵד, מַה דְּלָא הֲוָה קוֹדֶם.

111. Rabbi Aba said: it has bad connotations, because originally it, MALCHUT, was a plain tent, as it is written: "A tent that shall not be taken down; its pegs shall not be removed for ever" (Yeshayah 33:20). But now it is the Tent of appointed time, MEANING ONLY FOR A TIME, BUT NOT FOREVER, FOR AN APPOINTED TIME. Originally the tent, WHICH IS MALCHUT, gave long life to the world, so that death should not rule over them. From then on, it is the Tent of appointed time, as in the verse "And to the house appointed (Heb. mo'ed) for all living" (Iyov 30:23). For now it has been given a set time and life for the world. Before, there was no blemish in it, but now it has been blemished. Before there was a connection and union of the moon, WHICH IS MALCHUT, and the sun, WHICH IS ZEIR ANPIN, that is never interrupted. Now their union is from time to time. Therefore, he called it the 'Tent of appointed time,' which was not the case before.

12. "Ornaments by the Mount Horeb"

A Synopsis

Rabbi Yehuda wonders why Joshua was punished along with the children of Yisrael even though he had not sinned – he had been with Moses at the time of the golden calf. Rabbi Shimon answers that when God judges the world, he judges it according to the majority of people. He explains about the right above and the right below, and about the left above and the left below, and says that death is drawn to all those who become attached to the Serpent and distanced from the Tree of Life. Rabbi Shimon concludes by saying that since the moon, Malchut, was blemished, Joshua alone could not have been spared from the blemish.

112. ר' שִׁמְעוֹן, הֲוָה יָתִיב לֵילְיָא חֲדָא, וְלָעֵי בְּאוֹרַיְיתָא, וַהֲווֹ יַתְבֵי קַמֵּיהּ רַבִּי יְהוּדָה וְרַבִּי יִצְחָק וְר' יוֹסֵי. אָמַר ר' יְהוּדָה, הָא כְּתִיב וַיִּתְנַצְּלוּ בְּנֵי יִשְׂרָאֵל אֶת עֶדְיָם מֵהַר חֹרֵב. וְקָאַמְרֵינָן דְּגַרְמוּ מוֹתָא עֲלַיְיהוּ, מֵהַהוּא זִמְנָא וּלְעֵילָא, וְשַׁלִּיט בְּהוּ הַהוּא חִוְיָא בִּישָׁא, דְּאַעֲדֵי לֵיהּ מִנַּיְיהוּ בְּקַדְמֵיתָא. יִשְׂרָאֵל תֵּינַח. יְהוֹשֻׁעַ דְּלָא חָטָא, אִתְעֲדֵי מִנֵּיהּ הַהוּא זַיְינָא עִלָּאָה דְּקַבִּיל עִמְּהוֹן בְּטוּרָא דְּסִינַי, אוֹ לָא.

112. Rabbi Shimon was sitting one night studying the Torah. Rabbi Yehuda, Rabbi Yitzchak and Rabbi Yosi were sitting in front of him. Said Rabbi Yehuda: It is written: "And the children of Yisrael stripped themselves of their ornaments by the Mount Horeb" (Shemot 33:6). And we said that they brought death upon themselves from that time on, and the Evil Serpent ruled over them, after they had removed him from before. HE ASKS: Yisrael deserved it; but what of Joshua, who did not sin with the calf? HE ASKS: was the supernal armor, that is, the ornament, which he received together with the others at Mount Sinai, removed from him or not?

113. אִי תֵּימָא דְּלָא אִתְעֲדֵי מִנֵּיהּ. אִי הָכִי, אֲמַאי מִית כִּשְׁאַר כָּל בְּנֵי נָשָׁא. וְאִי תֵּימָא דְּאִתְעֲדֵי מִנֵּיהּ, אֲמַאי. וְהָא לָא חָטָא, דְּהָא אִיהוּ עִם מֹשֶׁה הֲוָה בְּשַׁעֲתָא דְּחָבוּ יִשְׂרָאֵל. וְאִי תֵּימָא דְּלָא קַבִּיל הַהוּא עִטְרָא בְּטוּרָא דְּסִינַי, כְּמָה דְּקַבִּילוּ יִשְׂרָאֵל. אֲמַאי.

113. If you say that THE ORNAMENT was not removed from him, then why

did he die like other people? BECAUSE THROUGH THE ORNAMENT THEY ACHIEVED FREEDOM FROM THE ANGEL OF DEATH, AS MENTIONED. And if you say that THE ORNAMENT was removed from him, HE ASKS, why THEN WAS IT REMOVED FROM HIM? For he did not sin, because he was with Moses at the time that Yisrael sinned. And if you say that he did not receive that crown, NAMELY THE ORNAMENT at Mount Sinai, as Yisrael did, HE ASKS why not?

114. פָּתַח ר"ש וְאָמַר, כִּי צַדִּיק יְיָ' צְדָקוֹת אָהֵב יָשָׁר יֶחֱזוּ פָנֵימוֹ, הַאי קְרָא אָמְרוּ בֵּיהּ חַבְרַיָּיא מַה דְּאָמְרוּ, אֲבָל כִּי צַדִּיק יְיָ', צַדִּיק הוּא, וּשְׁמֵיהּ צַדִּיק, וּבג"כ צְדָקוֹת אָהֵב. יָשָׁר. וְאִיהוּ יָשָׁר, כד"א צַדִּיק וְיָשָׁר. וְע"ד יֶחֱזוּ פָנֵימוֹ, כָּל בְּנֵי עָלְמָא, וִיתַקְּנוּן אָרְחַיְיהוּ, לְמֵהַךְ בְּאֹרַח מֵישָׁר כַּדְקָא יֵאוֹת.

114. Rabbi Shimon opened the discussion, and said: "For Hashem is righteous, He loves righteousness; the upright shall behold His face" (Tehilim 11:7). Concerning this passage, the friends said what they had to say. Yet, "For Hashem is righteous," MEANS that He is righteous and His Name is righteous. Consequently, "He loves righteousness," MEANING MALCHUT, WHOSE NAME IS RIGHTEOUSNESS. "The upright"; He is upright, as it is written: "Just and right is He" (Devarim 32:4). Therefore, all the people of the world "shall behold His face...", and mend their ways, and proceed on the straight path as they should.

115. וְת"ח, כַּד דָּאִין קוּדְשָׁא בְּרִיךְ הוּא עָלְמָא, לָא דָן לֵיהּ אֶלָּא לְפוּם רוּבָּן דִּבְנֵי נָשָׁא. וְת"ח, כַּד חָב אָדָם בְּאִילָנָא דְּאָכַל מִנֵּיהּ, גָּרַם לְהַהוּא אִילָנָא, דְּשָׁרֵי בֵּיהּ מוֹתָא לְכָל עָלְמָא, וְגָרַם פְּגִימוּ לְאַפְרְשָׁא אִתְּתָא מִבַּעְלָה, וְקָאִים חוֹבָה דִּפְגִימוּ דָא בְּסִיהֲרָא, עַד דְּקַיְימָן יִשְׂרָאֵל בְּטוּרָא דְּסִינַי, כֵּיוָן דְּקַיְימוּ יִשְׂרָאֵל בְּטוּרָא דְּסִינַי, אִתְעֲבַר הַהוּא פְּגִימוּ דְּסִיהֲרָא, וְקַיְימָא לְאַנְהָרָא תָּדִיר. כֵּיוָן דְּחָבוּ יִשְׂרָאֵל בְּעֶגְלָא, תָּבַת סִיהֲרָא כְּמִלְּקַדְמִין לְאִתְפַּגְּמָא, וְשַׁלְטָא חִוְיָא בִּישָׁא, וְאָחִיד בָּהּ, וּמָשִׁיךְ לָהּ לְגַבֵּיהּ, וְאִתְפְּגִימַת.

115. Come and behold: when the Holy One, blessed be He, judges the world, He judges it according to the majority of people. Come and behold:

when Adam sinned with the tree from which he ate, he caused that tree, WHICH IS MALCHUT, to become the dwelling place of Death for the whole world, and caused a blemish that separates a wife from her husband, NAMELY THE SEPARATION OF MALCHUT FROM ZEIR ANPIN. And this sin remained in the moon, WHICH IS MALCHUT, until the children of Yisrael stood at Mount Sinai. When the children of Yisrael stood at Mount Sinai, that blemish of the moon was removed, MEANING THE BLEMISH OF SEPARATION AND DEATH THROUGH THE TREE OF KNOWLEDGE OF GOOD AND EVIL and it shone constantly, WITHOUT INTERRUPTION. But when the children of Yisrael sinned with the calf, the moon again became blemished as before. The Evil Serpent ruled and held to it and drew it to him, and it became blemished.

116. וְכַד יָדַע מֹשֶׁה דְּחָבוּ יִשְׂרָאֵל, וְאִתְעֲבָרוּ מִנַּיְיהוּ אִינּוּן זַיְינִין קַדִּישִׁין, יָדַע וַדַּאי, דְּהָא חִוְיָא אָחִיד בָּהּ בְּסִיהֲרָא, לְאַמְשָׁכָא לָהּ לְגַבֵּיהּ, וְאִתְפְּגִימַת. כְּדֵין אַפִּיק לֵיהּ לְבַר. וְכֵיוָן דְּקַיְימָא לְאִתְפַּגְּמָא, אע"ג דִּיהוֹשֻׁעַ קָאִים בְּעִטְרָא דְּזַיְינִין דִּילֵהּ, כֵּיוָן דִּפְגִימוּ שַׁרְיָא בָּהּ, וְאִתְהַדְרַת כְּמָה דְּאִתְפְּגִימַת בְּחוֹבָא דְּאָדָם, לָא יָכִיל בַּר נָשׁ לְאִתְקַיְימָא. בַּר מֹשֶׁה, דַּהֲוָה שַׁלִּיט בָּהּ, וּמוֹתֵיהּ הֲוָה בְּסִטַר אַחֲרָא. וע"ד לָא הֲוָה רְשׁוּ בָּהּ, לְקַיְימָא לִיהוֹשֻׁעַ תָּדִיר, וְלָא לְאַחֲרָא. וע"ד אֹהֶל מוֹעֵד קָרֵי לֵיהּ, דְּהָא שַׁרְיָא בֵּיהּ זְמַן קָצִיב, לְכָל עָלְמָא.

116. When Moses learned that the children of Yisrael sinned and that the holy ornaments were removed from them, he knew for certain that the Serpent was attached to the moon to attract it to him. And it became defective, BECAUSE WHEN THE SERPENT WISHES TO NOURISH FROM MALCHUT, THE LIGHT DEPARTS FROM HER SO THAT HE HAS NOTHING TO SUSTAIN HIM. Then he took it outside of the camp. And since it was blemished, even though Joshua retained the crown of his ornament, since a blemish dwelt in it, IN MALCHUT, and it again had the blemish it had through the sin of Adam, no man can survive except Moses, who ruled over MALCHUT. FOR HE WAS IN THE SECRET OF THE HUSBAND OF THE QUEEN, and his death was from a different direction, NAMELY "ACCORDING TO THE WORD OF HASHEM" (DEVARIM 34:5). Therefore, MALCHUT did not have permission to keep Joshua alive forever, SO THAT HE WOULD NOT DIE, nor any other person. Therefore he called it 'the Tent of appointed

time', because a designated time OF LIFE dwells in it for the whole world.

117. וְעַל דָּא, רָזָא דְּמִלָּה, אִית יְמִינָא לְעֵילָא, וְאִית יְמִינָא לְתַתָּא. אִית שְׂמָאלָא לְעֵילָא, וְאִית שְׂמָאלָא לְתַתָּא. אִית יְמִינָא לְעֵילָא, בִּקְדוּשָׁה עִלָּאָה. וְאִית יְמִינָא לְתַתָּא, דְּאִיהוּ בְּסִטְרָא אַחֲרָא. אִית שְׂמָאלָא לְעֵילָא בִּקְדוּשָׁה עִלָּאָה, לְאִתְעֲרָא רְחִימוּתָא, לְאִתְקַשְּׁרָא סִיהֲרָא, בַּאֲתַר קַדִּישָׁא לְעֵילָא, לְאִתְנַהֲרָא.

117. Therefore, the secret of the matter is that there is right above and right below. There is left above and left below. HE EXPLAINS, there is right above, namely in supernal Holiness, and there is right below, which is in the Other Side. There is left above, meaning in supernal Holiness, to awaken love, so that the moon, WHICH IS MALCHUT, shall be connected to the holy place above, IN ZEIR ANPIN, in order to illuminate.

118. וְאִית שְׂמָאלָא לְתַתָּא, דְּאַפְרִישׁ רְחִימוּתָא דִּלְעֵילָא, וְאַפְרִישׁ לָהּ מִלְּאַנְהֲרָא בְּשִׁמְשָׁא, וּלְאִתְקָרְבָא בַּהֲדֵיהּ, וְדָא הוּא סִטְרָא דְּחִוְיָא בִּישָׁא. דְּכַד שְׂמָאלָא דָּא דִּלְתַתָּא אִתְעֲרָא, כְּדֵין מָשִׁיךְ לָהּ לְסִיהֲרָא, וְאַפְרִישׁ לָהּ מִלְּעֵילָא, וְאִתְחֲשַׁךְ נְהוֹרָהָא, וְאִתְדַּבְּקַת בְּחִוְיָא, וּכְדֵין שָׁאִיבַת מוֹתָא לְתַתָּא, לְכֹלָּא דְּאִתְדַּבְּקַת בְּחִוְיָא, וְאִתְרַחֲקַת מֵאִילָנָא דְחַיֵּי, וְעַ"ד גָּרִים מוֹתָא לְכָל עָלְמָא. וְדָא הוּא כַּד אִסְתְּאַב מַקְדְּשָׁא, עַד זִמְנָא קָצִיב, דְּאִתְתַּקֲנַת סִיהֲרָא, וְתָבַת לְאַנְהֲרָא, וְדָא הוּא אֹהֶל מוֹעֵד.

118. And there is left below, that separates the supernal love and separates Her, MALCHUT, from illuminating through the sun and from getting close to it. This is the side of the Evil Serpent, because when the lower left is awakened, it draws the moon to itself, and separates it from above, FROM ZEIR ANPIN, so its light becomes darkened, and it is attached to the Serpent. Then it draws death below, to all those that became attached to the Serpent and became distanced from the Tree of Life. Therefore, he brought death to the whole world, THROUGH THE SIN OF THE TREE OF KNOWLEDGE OF GOOD AND EVIL. And this is what defiled the Temple, WHICH IS

MALCHUT, until the set time when the moon will be mended and shine again. And this is WHY IT IS CALLED 'the Tent of appointed time'.

119. וְעַל דָּא יְהוֹשֻׁעַ לָא מִית, אֶלָּא בְּעֵיטָא דְּנָחָשׁ דָּא, דְּקָרִיב וּפָגִים מַשְׁכְּנָא כְּדְקַדְמֵיתָא. וְדָא הוּא רָזָא דִּכְתִּיב, יְהוֹשֻׁעַ בֶּן נוּן נַעַר. דְּאַע"ג דְּאִיהוּ נַעַר לְתַתָּא, לְקַבְּלָא נְהוֹרָא, לֹא יָמִישׁ מִתּוֹךְ הָאֹהֶל, כְּמָה דְּאִתְפְּגִים דָּא, הָכִי נָמֵי אִתְפְּגִים דָּא אַע"ג דְּזִינָא קַדִּישָׁא הֲוָה לֵיה, כֵּיוָן דְּאִתְפְּגִים סִיהֲרָא, הָכִי הוּא וַדַּאי לָא אִשְׁתְּזִיב בִּלְחוֹדוֹי מִנֵּיה, מֵהַהוּא גַּוְּונָא מַמָּשׁ, וְהָא אִתְּמַר.

119. Therefore Joshua died only because of the scheme of the Serpent who approached and blemished the Tabernacle, WHICH IS MALCHUT, as before. This is the secret of the words, "Joshua the son of Nun, a young man..." (Shemot 33:11). Even though he is a young man below, MEANING HE IS CONSIDERED AS METATRON THAT IS CALLED 'YOUTH', who receives light FROM MALCHUT, he "did not depart out of the Tent" (Ibid.), WHICH MEANS THAT HE IS LIKE THE TENT, WHICH IS MALCHUT. And just as THE TENT was blemished, so was he, JOSHUA, blemished. And although he had the holy ornament FROM MOUNT SINAI, since the moon was blemished, surely he could not have been alone spared from it and from that actual blemish. And we have learned it.

120. זַכָּאִין אִינּוּן צַדִּיקַיָּא, דְּיַדְעִין רָזִין דְּאוֹרַיְיתָא, וּמִתְדַּבְּקִין בָּהּ בְּאוֹרַיְיתָא, וּמְקַיְּימִין קְרָא דִּכְתִּיב, וְהָגִיתָ בּוֹ יוֹמָם וָלַיְלָה וְגו'. וּבְגִינָהּ יִזְכּוּן לְחַיֵּי עָלְמָא דְּאָתֵי, דִּכְתִּיב, כִּי הוּא חַיֶּיךָ וְאוֹרֶךְ יָמֶיךָ וְגו'.

120. Blessed are the righteous, who know the secrets of the Torah, cleave to the Torah, and fulfill the passage which says, "And you shall meditate therein day and night" (Yehoshua 1:8). And for its sake they shall merit the life of the World to Come, as it is written: "for He is your life and the length of your days" (Devarim 30:20).

VAYAK'HEL

Names of the articles

1. "And Moses gathered"

A Synopsis

Rabbi Chiya says that the war that Amalek waged against Yisrael was on all sides, because an evil serpent strengthened up above and down below. He talks about defilement, impurity and nocturnal pollution, and tells how God supplied Bilaam with a place of defilement as he deserved. If it had not been for Moses above and Joshua below Yisrael would not have overcome the evil serpent, who had planned to steal the sign of the covenant. Rabbi Chiya says that wherever there are sinful people the righteous and pious among them are punished for their sins, but because the tabernacle was to be built only for the children of Yisrael, Moses gathered and separated them from the other nations. Rabbi Elazar says that when the people gave a great shout, the sound made the stone tablets fall and break because the letters flew from it, leaving the stones heavy and without spirit. We are told that this loud voice arouses the evil serpent who seizes light. Rabbi Elazar also refers to the four seasons of the year (Chesed, Gvurah, Tiferet and Malchut) and the voice that rises in the four winds of the worlds. Therefore "Joshua heard" means that the voice of evil had seized the light of the moon, that is Malchut that Joshua held on to. Moses, who held on to the sun that is Zeir Anpin, did not hear. And the light of all Yisrael darkened because of that evil, but because God had pardoned their sins, Moses was able to gather them all together.

ו. וַיַּקְהֵל מֹשֶׁה אֶת כָּל עֲדַת בְּנֵי יִשְׂרָאֵל וְגוֹ'. רבִּי חִיָּיא פָּתַח, וַיֹּאמֶר שָׁאוּל אֶל הַקֵּנִי לְכוּ סוּרוּ רְדוּ וְגוֹ'. תָּא חֲזֵי, מַה כְּתִיב בַּעֲמָלֵק, פָּקַדְתִּי אֶת אֲשֶׁר עָשָׂה עֲמָלֵק לְיִשְׂרָאֵל וְגוֹ'. וְקוּדְשָׁא בְּרִיךְ הוּא בְּכֻלְּהוּ קָרְבִּין דְּעַבְדוּ שְׁאָר עַמְמִין לְגַבַּיְיהוּ דְּיִשְׂרָאֵל, מ"ט לָא אַקְשֵׁי קַמֵּיהּ, כְּהַאי קְרָבָא דְּעָבֵד עֲמָלֵק לְגַבַּיְיהוּ. אֶלָּא וַדַּאי, קְרָבָא דְּעֲמָלֵק הֲוָה בְּכָל סְטָרִין, לְעֵילָא וְתַתָּא, דְּהָא בְּהַהוּא זִמְנָא אִתְתַּקַּף חִוְיָא בִּישָׁא לְעֵילָא, וְאִתְתַּקַּף לְתַתָּא.

1. "And Moses gathered all the Congregation of the children of Yisrael..." (Shemot 35:1). Rabbi Chiya opened the discussion with, "and Saul said the Kenite: Go, depart..." (I Shmuel 15:6). Come and see, what is written about Amalek, "I remember that which Amalek did to Yisrael..." (Ibid. 2), but the

Holy One, blessed be He, remembered all the wars that the other nations waged against Yisrael. Why mention this particular war? Because there was not a more difficult war before Him as the one waged by Amalek. HE EXPLAINS, but of course, this war, that Amalek waged, was on all sides; up above and down below, because at that time the evil serpent strengthened up above and strengthened down below IN THIS WORLD!

2. מָה חִוְיָא בִּישָׁא כַּמִין עַל פָּרָשַׁת אָרְחִין, אוּף הָכָא נָמֵי עֲמָלֵק, חִוְיָא בִּישָׁא הֲוָה לְגַבַּיְיהוּ דְיִשְׂרָאֵל, דְּכַמִּין לוֹן עַל פָּרָשַׁת אָרְחִין, דִּכְתִיב אֲשֶׁר שָׂם לוֹ בַּדֶּרֶךְ בַּעֲלוֹתוֹ מִמִּצְרָיִם. כַּמִין הֲוָה לְעֵילָּא, לְסָאֲבָא מַקְדְּשָׁא. וְכַמִּין הֲוָה לְתַתָּא, לְסָאֲבָא לְיִשְׂרָאֵל. מְנָלָן, דִּכְתִיב אֲשֶׁר קָרְךָ בַּדֶּרֶךְ. כְּתִיב הָכָא אֲשֶׁר קָרְךָ, וּכְתִיב הָתָם כִּי יִהְיֶה בְךָ אִישׁ אֲשֶׁר לֹא טָהוֹר מִקְרֵה לָיְלָה.

2. Like an evil serpent that lurks in ambush on the crossroads, so was Amalek an evil serpent before Yisrael, that lurked in wait to ambush them on the crossroads, as written: "how he laid in wait for him in the way, when he came up from Egypt" (I Shmuel 15:2). And he lurked in ambush up above to defile the Temple, WHICH IS MALCHUT, and lurked down below to defile Yisrael. Whence do we know that? From the verse, "met you by the way" (Devarim 25:18). It is written here: "how he met you (Heb. *karcha*) by the way," and there: "If there be among you any man, who is not clean by reason of uncleanness that chances (Heb. *mikre*) by night" (Devarim 23:11). IN BOTH VERSES THE WORDS RELATE TO UNCLEANNESS.

3. וְע"ד בְּבִלְעָם כְּתִיב, וַיִּקָּר אֱלֹהִים אֶל בִּלְעָם. וַיִּקָּר לִישָׁנָא דִּמְסָאֲבָא נָקַט. וְאִי תֵּימָא, הָא כְּתִיב אֱלֹהִים. אֶלָּא קוּדְשָׁא בְּרִיךְ הוּא אַזְמִין לֵיהּ הַהוּא אֲתָר דִּמְסָאֲבָא, לְאִסְתָּאֲבָא בֵּיהּ, בְּהַהוּא דַּרְגָּא דְּאִיהוּ אִתְדַּבָּק לְאִסְתָּאֲבָא בֵּיהּ. מָה עֲבַד בִּלְעָם. אִיהוּ חָשִׁיב בְּאִינּוּן קָרְבָּנִין לְסַלְּקָא לְעֵילָּא, מִיַּד זַמִּין לֵיהּ קוּדְשָׁא בְּרִיךְ הוּא הַהוּא אֲתָר. א"ל הָא מְסָאֲבוּ לְגַבָּךְ, כְּמָה דְּאִתְחֲזֵי לָךְ, וְע"ד וַיִּקָּר אֱלֹהִים אֶל בִּלְעָם.

3. And therefore it is written about Bilaam: "and Elohim met (Heb. *vayikar*) Bilaam" (Bemidbar 23:4). The word 'vayikar' denotes impurity, NAMELY,

-167-

NOCTURNAL POLLUTION AS MENTIONED ABOVE. You may say that Elohim is, WHICH IMPLIES HOLINESS; yet the Holy One, blessed be He, supplied him with that place of defilement, to be defiled in it, so that he (Bilaam) would be defiled by the same grade to which he cleaved. What did Bilaam do? He planned by the offerings he sacrificed to rise TO HOLINESS. Immediately the Holy One, blessed be He, supplied him with that place OF DEFILEMENT. He said to him, 'Here is impurity upon you, as befits you.' Hence it is written: "and Elohim met Bilaam."

4. כְּגַוְונָא דָא אֲשֶׁר קָרְךָ בַּדֶּרֶךְ וְגו'. אַזְמִין לְגַבָּךְ הַהוּא חִוְיָא בִּישָׁא לְעֵילָּא, לְסָאֲבָא לָךְ בְּכָל סִטְרִין. וְאִלְמָלֵא דְּאִתְתַּקַּף מֹשֶׁה לְעֵילָּא, וִיהוֹשֻׁעַ לְתַתָּא, לָא יָכִילוּ יִשְׂרָאֵל לֵיהּ. וּבְגִין כַּךְ, נָטִיר קוּדְשָׁא בְּרִיךְ הוּא הַהוּא דְּבָבוּ, לְדָרֵי דָרִין. מ"ט. בְּגִין דְּחָשִׁיב לְאַעֲקְרָא אָת קַיָּימָא מֵאַתְרֵיהּ. וּבְגִין כַּךְ פָּקַדְתִּי, בִּפְקִידָה, דְּהָא תַּמָּן אִתְרְמִיז רָזָא דְּאָת קַיָּימָא קַדִּישָׁא.

4. In the same manner, "met you (Heb. *karcha*) by the way," REFERS TO that supernal evil serpent that was sent to you to defile you on all sides. And if it had not been for Moses becoming strong up above, and Joshua down below, Yisrael would not have overcome it. Therefore the Holy One, blessed be He, bore a grudge against that one for ages. The reason is that he planned to tear the member of the sign of the covenant from its place. And therefore it is written: "I remember (also: 'visit')" (I Shmuel 15:2), NAMELY, in remembrance (divine visitation), WHICH IS MALCHUT, because the secret of the holy covenant is implied in this word.

5. ת"ח, מָה כְּתִיב, וַיֹּאמֶר שָׁאוּל אֶל הַקֵּנִי. מַאן קֵנִי. דָּא יִתְרוֹ. וְכִי מַאן יָהִיב בְּנֵי יִתְרוֹ הָכָא, לְמֶהֱוֵי דִּיּוּרֵיהוֹן בַּעֲמָלֵק, וְהָא בִּירִיחוֹ הֲווֹ שַׁרְיָין. אֶלָּא הָא הָא כְּתִיב, וּבְנֵי קֵנִי חֹתֵן מֹשֶׁה עָלוּ מֵעִיר הַתְּמָרִים אֶת בְּנֵי יְהוּדָה מִדְבַּר יְהוּדָה וְגו'. וְכַד עָלוּ מִתַּמָּן, שָׁרוּ בִּתְחוּמָא דַעֲמָלֵק, עַד הַהוּא זִמְנָא דְּאָתָא שָׁאוּל מַלְכָּא, דִּכְתִיב וַיָּסַר קֵנִי מִתּוֹךְ עֲמָלֵק.

5. Come and look at the verse, "and Saul said to the Kenite" (I Shmuel 15:6). Who is the Kenite? It is Jethro. HE ASKS: Who placed the children of

Jethro in here, to dwell in Amalek, their abode being in Jericho; AND ANSWERS: it is written "And the children of the Kenite, Moses' father-in-law, went up out of the city of palm trees with the children of Judah into the wilderness of Judah" (Shoftim 1:16). And when they moved from there, they dwelt in the territory of Amalek until that time when King Saul came and removed the Kenite from Amalek.

6. בְּגִין דְּהָא בְּזִמְנָא דְּחַיָּיבַיָּא אִשְׁתְּכָחוּ, אִינּוּן חֲסִידֵי וְזַכָּאֵי דְּמִשְׁתַּכְחִין בֵּינַיְיהוּ, מִתָּפְסָן בְּחוֹבֵיהוֹן, וְהָא אוּקְמוּהָ. כְּגַוְונָא דָּא, אִלְמָלֵא הַהוּא עֵרְבּוּבְיָא דְּאִתְחַבָּרוּ בְּהוּ בְּיִשְׂרָאֵל, לָא אִתְעֲנָשׁוּ יִשְׂרָאֵל, עַל עוֹבָדָא דְּעֶגְלָא.

6. For, when there are evil people, the righteous and pious that are among them are punished for their sins. This was already explained. THAT IS WHY SAUL REMOVED THE KENITE FROM AMONG AMALEK. In the same manner, if not for the mixed multitude who joined Yisrael, Yisrael would not have been punished for the sin of the golden calf.

7. ות״ח מָה כְּתִיב בְּקַדְמֵיתָא, מֵאֵת כָּל אִישׁ אֲשֶׁר יִדְּבֶנּוּ לִבּוֹ, לְאַכְלְלָא כֹּלָּא, בְּגִין דְּבָעָא קוּדְשָׁא בְּרִיךְ הוּא לְמֶעְבַּד עוֹבָדָא דְּמַשְׁכְּנָא מִכָּל סִטְרִין, בְּמוֹחָא וּקְלִיפָה. וּבְגִין דַּהֲווֹ אִינּוּן עֵרֶב רַב בְּגַוְוייהוּ, אִתְּמַר מֵאֵת כָּל אִישׁ אֲשֶׁר יִדְּבֶנּוּ לִבּוֹ, לְאַכְלְלָא לוֹן בֵּינַיְיהוּ דְּיִשְׂרָאֵל, דְּאִינּוּן מוֹחָא. וְכֻלְּהוּ אִתְפְּקָדוּ.

7. Come and see what is written above: "of every man whose heart prompts him" (Shemot 25:2), which includes everyone, EVEN THE MIXED MULTITUDE. This is because the Holy One, blessed be He, wanted to build the tabernacle from all sides, the inner part and the shell. And since there were a mixed multitude among them, it was said, "of every man whose heart prompts him," in order to include them in Yisrael who are the inner part. Thus, everyone was commanded TO TAKE A PART IN THETABERNACLE.

8. לְבָתַר סָטָא זִינָא לְזִינֵיהּ, וְאָתוּ אִינּוּן עֵרֶב רַב וְעָבְדוּ יַת עֶגְלָא, וְסָטוּ אֲבַתְרַייהוּ אִינּוּן דְּמִיתוּ, וְגָרְמוּ לוֹן לְיִשְׂרָאֵל מוֹתָא וְקָטוֹלָא. אָמַר

קוּדְשָׁא בְּרִיךְ הוּא, מִכָּאן וּלְהָלְאָה עוֹבָדָא דְמַשְׁכְּנָא לָא יְהֵא, אֶלָּא
מִסִּטְרָא דְיִשְׂרָאֵל בִּלְחוֹדַיְיהוּ. מִיַּד וַיַּקְהֵל מֹשֶׁה אֶת כָּל עֲדַת בְּנֵי
יִשְׂרָאֵל וְגוֹ'. וּכְתִיב בַּתְרֵיה קְחוּ מֵאִתְּכֶם תְּרוּמָה לַיְיָ'. מֵאִתְּכֶם וַדַּאי,
וְלָא כְּקַדְמִיתָא דִּכְתִיב, מֵאֵת כָּל אִישׁ אֲשֶׁר יִדְּבֶנּוּ לִבּוֹ. וַיַּקְהֵל מֹשֶׁה
וְגוֹ', מֵאָן אֲתַר כָּנִישׁ לוֹן. אֶלָּא בְּגִין דַּהֲווֹ אִינּוּן עֵרֶב רַב בֵּינַיְיהוּ,
אִצְטְרִיךְ מֹשֶׁה לְאַכְנָשָׁא לוֹן, וּלְיַחֲדָא לוֹן מִבֵּינַיְיהוּ.

8. Afterwards, people came together according to their ilk, and the mixed multitude came and created the calf and those from among Yisrael were drawn towards them who eventually died. The mixed multitude brought upon Yisrael death and killings. The Holy One blessed be He, said: from now on the building of the tabernacle would be performed only on the part of Yisrael. At once, "Moses gathered all the Congregation of the children of Yisrael together..." (Shemot 35:1). Afterwards it is written: "Take from among you an offering to Hashem" (Ibid. 5). "From among you" surely, instead of as written before, "of every man whose heart prompts him" (Shemot 25:2). "And Moses gathered..." Where did he gather them from? Because the mixed multitude was among them, Moses had to gather and separate Yisrael from among them.

9. וַיַּקְהֵל מֹשֶׁה. רִבִּי אַבָּא פָּתַח, הַקְהֵל אֶת הָעָם הָאֲנָשִׁים וְהַנָּשִׁים
וְהַטַּף. מַה לְהַלָּן כְּלָלָא דְּכֻלְּהוּ יִשְׂרָאֵל, אוּף הָכָא כְּלָלָא דְּכֻלְּהוּ
יִשְׂרָאֵל, וּמַאן אִינּוּן. שִׁתִּין רִבּוֹא.

9. "And Moses gathered": Rabbi Aba opened the discussion with the scripture, "Gather the people together, men, and women, and children" (Devarim 31:12). What is to be from now on the community of Yisrael, is also here the community of Yisrael, that is six hundred thousand people.

10. רִבִּי אֶלְעָזָר פָּתַח קְרָא בְּיִשְׂרָאֵל, כַּד נָחִית מֹשֶׁה מִן טוּרָא דְסִינַי,
דִּכְתִיב וַיִּשְׁמַע יְהוֹשֻׁעַ אֶת קוֹל הָעָם בְּרֵעֹה וַיֹּאמֶר אֶל מֹשֶׁה קוֹל
מִלְחָמָה בַּמַּחֲנֶה. וַיִּשְׁמַע יְהוֹשֻׁעַ, וְכִי יְהוֹשֻׁעַ שָׁמַע, וּמֹשֶׁה לָא שָׁמַע.
אֶלָּא וַדַּאי, עַד הַשְׁתָּא יְהוֹשֻׁעַ לָא הֲוָה יָדַע, וּמֹשֶׁה הֲוָה יָדַע. אִי הָכִי

מַהוּ בְּרֵעֹה. אֶלָּא בְּרֵעֹה בְּהֵ' כְּתִיב, דְּהַהוּא קָלָא בְּסִטְרָא אַחֲרָא הֲוָה. וִיהוֹשֻׁעַ דַּהֲוָה אַנְפּוֹי דְּסִיהֲרָא, אִסְתָּכַּל בְּהַהוּא קָלָא, דַּהֲוָה דְּסִטְרָא דְּרָעָה, מִיַּד וַיֹּאמֶר אֶל מֹשֶׁה קוֹל מִלְחָמָה בַּמַּחֲנֶה.

10. Rabbi Elazar opened the discussion with Yisrael, when Moses came down from Mount Sinai. It is written: "And when Joshua heard the noise of the people as they shouted (Heb. *bere'oh*), he said to Moses, There is a noise of war in the camp" (Shemot 32:17). HE ASKS: "Joshua heard"-could it be that Joshua heard and Moses did not? AND ANSWERS: until that time Joshua did not know and Moses did know, AND THEREFORE IT WAS WRITTEN: "JOSHUA HEARD." HE ASKS: What then does the word 'bere'oh' mean? AND ANSWERS: 'bere'oh' is spelled with Hei TO INDICATE that that voice was on the Other Side, THAT IS CALLED EVIL (HEB. *RA'AH*). And Joshua was the face of the moon, WHICH IS MALCHUT. He looked at the voice that was from the side of evil, and immediately "said to Moses, There is a noise of war in the camp."

‏11. בְּהַהִיא שַׁעֲתָא אִתְבְּרוּ תְּרֵין לוּחֵי אַבְנָא דַּהֲווֹ בְּקַדְמֵיתָא. וְהָא אוֹקִימְנָא, דְּאִינּוּן אִתְיָיקְרוּ עַל יְדוֹי וְנָפְלוּ וְאִתְבְּרוּ. מ"ט. בְּגִין דְּפָרְחוּ אַתְוָון מִגּוֹ לוּחֵי אַבְנִין.

11. At that time the first stone tablets broke. And we already explained that the stones in the hands of Moses became heavy, fell and broke. What is the reason? the letters have flown from the stone tablets AND THE STONES REMAINED WITHOUT SPIRIT AND THEREFORE GREW HEAVY.

‏12. ת"ח, בְּד' תְּקוּפִין דְּשַׁתָּא, קָלָא אִתְּעַר, בְּד' סִטְרִין דְּעָלְמָא, בְּהַהוּא קָלָא אִתְּעֲרוּתָא דְּסִטְרָא אַחֲרָא אִתְּעַר בֵּיהּ. וְהַהוּא אִתְּעֲרוּתָא דְּסִטְרָא אַחֲרָא עָאל בֵּין קָלָא לְקָלָא, וְאִתְחֲשַׁךְ נְהוֹרָא בְּקָלָא דִּלְתַתָּא. בְּגִין דְּלָא מָטָא נְהוֹרָא דְּקָלָא דִּלְעֵילָּא, לְקָלָא דִּלְתַתָּא, כְּדֵין אַקְדִּים הַהוּא אִתְּעֲרוּתָא, וְעָאל בֵּין דָּא לְדָא נָחַשׁ דִּמְפַתֵּי לְאִתְּתָא, וְנָטִיל נְהוֹרָא. וְהַהוּא קָלָא, הוּא קוֹל מִלְחָמָה, קוֹל רָעָה, וְדָא אִיהוּ בְּרֵעֹה.

12. Come and see, in the four seasons of the year, WHICH ARE CHESED,

GVURAH, TIFERET AND MALCHUT, a voice rises in the four winds of the worlds. THE SEASON OF NISSAN IS SOUTH AND CHESED; THE SEASON OF TISHREI IS NORTH AND GVURAH; THE SEASON OF TAMMUZ IS EAST AND TIFERET AND THE SEASON OF TEVET IS WEST AND MALCHUT. AND EACH SEASON INCORPORATES ALL THE OTHERS. By that voice the Other Side is aroused, and, by that arousal, enters between the voices, NAMELY, BETWEEN THE VOICE OF TIFERET AND THE VOICE OF MALCHUT, so the light in the lower voice darkens, NAMELY IN MALCHUT. This happens because the light of the upper voice-TIFERET-does not reach the lower voice -MALCHUT. Therefore this arousal OF THE OTHER SIDE comes early and the serpent that seduced the woman, EVE, enters between them, THAT IS, BETWEEN TIFERET AND MALCHUT and receives light. And that voice OF THE OTHER SIDE is the voice (noise) of war, the voice of evil (Heb. *ra'ah*). This is the meaning of 'bere'oh' NAMELY, IN THE VERSE: "AND WHEN JOSHUA HEARD THE NOISE OF THE PEOPLE AS THEY SHOUTED (HEB. *BERE'OH*)" (SHEMOT 32:17).

13. וְעַ״ד שָׁמַע יְהוֹשֻׁעַ וְלָא מֹשֶׁה, בְּגִין דְּנָטַל הַהוּא רָעָה נְהוֹרָא דְּסִיהֲרָא דַּהֲוָה אָחִיד בָּהּ יְהוֹשֻׁעַ. וּמֹשֶׁה דַּהֲוָה אָחִיד בְּשִׁמְשָׁא, לָא שָׁמַע. וְיִשְׂרָאֵל כֻּלְּהוּ אִתְחֲשָׁךְ נְהוֹרָא דִּילְהוֹן, בְּגִין הַהוּא רָעָה דְּאִתְדַּבְּקַת בְּהוּ. כֵּיוָן דִּמְחַל קוּדְשָׁא בְּרִיךְ הוּא חוֹבֵיהוֹן, כְּדֵין וַיַּקְהֵל מֹשֶׁה אֶת כָּל עֲדַת בְּנֵי יִשְׂרָאֵל וַיֹּאמֶר אֲלֵיהֶם אֵלֶּה הַדְּבָרִים וְגוֹ', דְּהָא הַהוּא עֵרֶב רַב אִתְעַבָּר מִנַּיְיהוּ.

13. And therefore "Joshua heard" and not Moses, because that evil had seized the light of the moon, WHICH IS MALCHUT that Joshua was attached to. And Moses who was attached to the sun, WHICH IS ZEIR ANPIN, did not hear. And all Yisrael, their light darkened, because of that evil that clung to them. Since the Holy One, blessed be He, had pardoned their iniquity, then "Moses gathered the congregation of the children of Yisrael together and said to them, these are the words..." For the mixed multitude was separated from them.

2. Three night watches

A Synopsis

Rabbi Elazar describes how the night's twelve hours are divided into three, each of which is allotted to a different host of angels. The first is appointed to praise their Master with love. At that time the souls of those on earth leave their bodies to go up: those that are not worthy are rejected and hover about the world, but the worthy ones travel up to see their Master on the holy mountain of Hashem, where their deeds and merits are written down. The second host recites poetry for two hours. These angels of the second watch bewail the destruction of the temple, and weep by the rivers of Babylon. God weeps two tears into the great sea, a flame is awakened and paired with a spirit from the north, and the flame goes to hover about the world. Rabbi Elazar refers to Esther and the secret of judgment of the Left Column, which is at this time. When at midnight God enters the Garden of Eden to commune with the souls of the righteous, all the trees of the Garden and the souls of the righteous open and say "Lift up your heads, O you gates." Then the souls of the righteous return to their bodies, and the angels of the third host encourage them and recite poetry until the light of morning. These last four hours are in the central column.

In the morning all the stars and constellations praise their Master along with the archangels that govern by daytime. All Yisrael sings below and the sweet voice of the wheel of the sun sings above.

14. רִבִּי אֶלְעָזָר וְרִבִּי יוֹסֵי הֲווֹ יַתְבֵי לֵילְיָא חַד, וְקָא מִתְעַסְּקֵי בְּאוֹרַיְיתָא, עַד לָא אִתְפְּלִיג לֵילְיָא. אַדְהָכִי קָרָא גַבְרָא, בְּרִיכוּ בִּרְכָתָא, בָּכָה רִבִּי אֶלְעָזָר וְאָמַר, ת"ח, עַד הַשְׁתָּא קוּדְשָׁא בְּרִיךְ הוּא אִזְדַּעְזַע, תְּלַת מְאָה וְתִשְׁעִין רְקִיעִין, וּבְטַשׁ בְּהוּ, וּבָכָה עַל חָרְבָּן בֵּי מַקְדְּשָׁא, וְאוֹרִיד תְּרֵין דִּמְעִין לְגוֹ יַמָּא רַבָּא, וְאַדְכַּר לִבְנוֹהִי מִגּוֹ בְּכִיָה.

14. Rabbi Elazar and Rabbi Yosi were sitting one night, studying the Torah, before midnight. During that time the rooster crowed, MEANING THAT MIDNIGHT HAD COME. They recited the blessing, "WHO GAVE THE ROOSTER UNDERSTANDING TO DISTINGUISH BETWEEN DAY AND NIGHT." Rabbi Elazar wept and said: come and see, until now the Holy One, blessed be He, has shaken and struck three hundred and ninety firmaments, shed two tears into the great sea, and tearfully remembered His children.

15. בְּגִין דְּלִתְלַת סִטְרִין אִתְפְּלַג לֵילְיָא, בִּתְרֵיסַר שַׁעֲתֵי דַּהֲווֹ רְשִׁימִין בֵּיהּ, וְאִי אִתּוֹסְפָן שַׁעֲתֵי בְּלֵילְיָא, אִינּוּן שַׁעֲתֵי דְּמִתּוֹסְפָאן, דִּימָמָא אִינּוּן, וְלָא אִתְחַשִּׁיבוּ מִלֵּילְיָא, בַּר תְּרֵיסַר דְּאִינּוּן דִּילֵהּ. וְאִינּוּן תְּרֵיסַר, אִתְפְּלָגוּ לִתְלַת סִטְרִין, וּתְלַת מַשִׁרְיָין דְּמַלְאָכִין קַדִּישִׁין, אִתְפְּלָגוּ בְּאִינּוּן תְּלַת סִטְרִין.

15. For the night with its twelve hours is divided into three directions, RIGHT, LEFT AND CENTER. And if there are more THAN TWELVE hours to the night, they are considered to be day and not night, for only twelve hours belong to it, TO MALCHUT CALLED NIGHT. These twelve hours are divided into three directions and three hosts of holy angels are allotted to these three directions.

16. מַשִׁרְיָיא קַדְמָאָה, אִתְמַנָּא בַּד' שַׁעֲתֵי קַמְיָיתָא, דְּשֵׁירוּתָא דְּלֵילְיָא, לְשַׁבְּחָא לְמָארֵיהוֹן, וּמָה קָאַמְרֵי. לַיְיָ' הָאָרֶץ וּמְלֹאָהּ וְגוֹ', כִּי הוּא עַל יַמִּים יְסָדָהּ וְגוֹ', מִי יַעֲלֶה בְהַר יְיָ' וְגוֹ', נְקִי כַפַּיִם וּבַר לֵבָב וְגוֹ'. מ"ט דָּא. בְּגִין דְּכַד לֵילְיָא פָּרִישׂ גַּדְפּוֹי עַל עָלְמָא, כְּדֵין, כָּל בְּנֵי עָלְמָא טַעֲמִין טַעֲמָא דְּמוֹתָא, וְנַפְקֵי נִשְׁמָתַיְיהוּ לְסַלְקָא לְעֵילָּא, וְאִינּוּן מַלְאָכִין קַיְימִין וְקָא אַמְרֵי, מִי יַעֲלֶה בְהַר יְיָ'. הַר יְיָ', דָּא הַר הַבַּיִת. מְקוֹם קָדְשׁוֹ, דָּא עֶזְרַת יִשְׂרָאֵל. כְּגַוְונָא דִּלְעֵילָּא, הָכִי נָמֵי לְתַתָּא.

16. The first host is appointed to the first four hoursof the night to praise their Master, NAMELY, IN THE RIGHT COLUMN, WHICH IS CHESED. What do they say? they say "The earth is Hashem's, and the fullness thereof...for He has founded it upon the seas...who shall ascend the mountain of Hashem?...He that has clean hands, and a pure heart" (Tehilim 24:1-4). What is the reason for saying this? It is because the night spreads its wings over the world, and then all the inhabitants of the world taste death, and their souls leave the body to go up. And these angels stand and say ABOUT THE SOULS, "who shall ascend the mountain of Hashem?" "The mountain of Hashem" refers to the Temple Mount; "His holy place" refers to the men's section. As it is in the celestial TEMPLE, WHICH IS MALCHUT, so it is in the terrestrial TEMPLE .

17. בְּגִין דִּבְכָל רְקִיעָא וּרְקִיעָא, כַּמָּה מְמָנָן, וּכְמָה סַרְכִין קַיְימִין תַּמָּן. וְכַד נִשְׁמָתִין נָפְקִין, בָּעָאן לְסַלְקָא לְעֵילָא, וְאִי לָא זַכְיָין אִינוּן דַּחְיָין לוֹן לְבַר, וְאַזְלִין וְשָׁאטִין בְּעָלְמָא, וְנַטְלִין לוֹן כַּמָּה חֲבִילֵי טְהִירִין, וְאוֹדְעִין לוֹן מִלִּין כְּדִיבָן, וּלְזִמְנִין מִלִּין דִּקְשׁוֹט, מִמַּה דְּאָתֵי לְזְמַן קָרִיב, כְּמָה דְּאוּקְמוּהָ.

17. Because in each firmament there are many chiefs and guards. When the souls leave, they want to go up, but if they are not worthy, they are rejected. Then the souls hover about the world and some troops of spirits take them and tell them some lies and some truths about what is to be in the near future. All this is as was explained.

18. וְאִינוּן נִשְׁמָתִין דְּצַדִּיקַיָּיא, אָזְלִין וְשָׁאטָן לְעֵילָא, וּפַתְחִין לוֹן פִּתְחִין, וְסַלְקִין לוֹן לְגוֹ הַהוּא אֲתָר דְּאִקְרֵי הַר יְיָ', כְּגַוְונָא דְּרָזָא דְּהַר הַבַּיִת לְתַתָּא. וּמִתַּמָּן עָאלִין לְגוֹ הַהוּא אֲתָר דְּאִקְרֵי מָקוֹם קָדְשׁוֹ. דְּתַמָּן אִתְחַזְיָין כָּל נִשְׁמָתִין לְקַמֵּי מָארֵיהוֹן. כְּגַוְונָא דָּא הַהוּא אֲתָר, דְּאִתְחֲזוּן יִשְׂרָאֵל קַמֵּי קוּדְשָׁא בְּרִיךְ הוּא, אֲתָר דְּאִקְרֵי עֶזְרַת יִשְׂרָאֵל. בְּשַׁעֲתָא דְּנִשְׁמָתִין קַיְימִין תַּמָּן, כְּדֵין חֶדְוָה דְּמָארֵיהוֹן, לְאִתְתַּקְנָא בְּהוּ אֲתָר, דְּאִקְרֵי קֹדֶשׁ הַקֳּדָשִׁים. וְתַמָּן רְשִׁימִין כָּל עוֹבְדֵיהוֹן וְזַכְוָון דִּלְהוֹן.

18. And the souls of the righteous travel up and doors are opened before them, and they go up into that place which is called the mountain of Hashem which is like the secret of the terrestrial Temple Mount . Then they go up to that place, which is called His holy place. There all the souls appear before their Master. That place is like that TERRESTRIAL place, where Yisrael appear before the Holy One, blessed be He, in the men's (lit. 'Yisrael's') section. At the time when the souls are standing there, the joy of their master is to construct with them a place that is called Holy of Holies, where all their deeds and merits are recorded.

19. מַשִּׁרְיָיא תִּנְיָינָא, אִתְמַנָּא בְּאַרְבַּע שַׁעֲתֵי אַחֲרָנִין, וְלָא אַמְרֵי שִׁירָתָא, בַּר תְּרֵי שַׁעֲתֵי, עַד דְּאִתְפְּלַג לֵילְיָא, וְעָאל קוּדְשָׁא בְּרִיךְ הוּא בְּגִנְתָּא דְּעֵדֶן.

19. The second host is appointed to recite poetry, in the second four hours. But they recite poetry only for two hours before midnight when the Holy One, blessed be He, THAT IS THE CENTRAL COLUMN, enters the Garden of Eden.

20. וְאִלֵּין אִינּוּן אֲבֵלֵי צִיּוֹן, וְאִינּוּן דְּבָכוּ עַל חָרְבַּן בֵּי מַקְדְּשָׁא. וּבְשֵׁירוּתָא דְּאַרְבַּע שַׁעֲתֵי אֶמְצָעַיָן, פַּתְחֵי וְאָמְרֵי, עַל נַהֲרוֹת בָּבֶל שָׁם יָשַׁבְנוּ גַּם בָּכִינוּ וְגוֹ', וְאִלֵּין אִינּוּן דְּבָכוּ עַל נַהֲרוֹת בָּבֶל, עִמְּהוֹן דְּיִשְׂרָאֵל, מִמַּשְׁמַע דִּכְתִיב גַּם בָּכִינוּ. וּמְנָלָן דְּבָכוּ תַּמָּן. דִּכְתִיב הֵן אֶרְאֶלָּם צָעֲקוּ חוּצָה. מַהוּ חוּצָה. דָּא בָּבֶל, בְּגִין דְּכֻלְּהוּ אוֹזְפוּהָ לִשְׁכִינָה עַד בָּבֶל. וְתַמָּן בָּכוּ עִמְּהוֹן דְּיִשְׂרָאֵל. וְעַ"ד פַּתְחֵי בְּהַאי, וּמְסַיְּימֵי זְכוֹר יְיָ' לִבְנֵי אֱדוֹם וְגוֹ'.

20. And these ANGELS OF THE SECOND WATCH are the mourners of Zion AFTER THE DESTRUCTION OF THE TEMPLE, for they bewail the destruction of the Temple. In the beginning of the second four hours, WHICH ARE THE SECRET OF THE LEFT COLUMN, WHICH THE OTHER SIDE MAINLY HOLDS TO, they open and say "By the rivers of Babylon, there we sat down, and also wept, when we remembered Zion" (Tehilim 137:1). And it is they, who weep by the rivers of Babylon, together with Yisrael. This is the meaning of the verse "and also wept," FOR THE MEANING OF "ALSO" IS THAT WE ALSO WEPT LIKE THE ANGELS. And how do we know that they cried there? It is written: "Behold, the mighty ones shall cry outside" (Yeshayah 33:7). What is outside? It is Babylon, for all the angels escorted the Shechinah to Babylon, sat there and wept with Yisrael, and therefore they opened with this, "BY THE RIVERS OF BABYLON" and concluded with "remember, Hashem, against the children of Edom" (Tehilim 137:7).

21. כְּדֵין אִתְּעַר קוּדְשָׁא בְּרִיךְ הוּא בְּדַרְגּוֹי, וּבָטַשׁ בִּרְקִיעִין כִּדְאַמָּרָן, וְאִזְדַּעְזְעוּ תְּרֵיסַר אַלְפֵי עָלְמִין, וְנָגֵי וּבָכֵי, דִּכְתִיב יְיָ' מִמָּרוֹם יִשְׁאָג וּמִמְּעוֹן קָדְשׁוֹ יִתֵּן קוֹלוֹ שָׁאוֹג יִשְׁאַג עַל נָוֵהוּ, וְאַדְכַּר לוֹן לְיִשְׂרָאֵל, וְאָחִית תְּרֵין דִּמְעִין לְגוֹ יַמָּא רַבָּא. וּכְדֵין אִתְּעַר שַׁלְהוֹבִיתָא חַד דִּבְסְטַר צָפוֹן, וּבָטַשׁ רוּחָא חַד דִּבְסְטַר צָפוֹן בְּהַהוּא שַׁלְהוֹבִיתָא, וְאַזְלָא וְשָׁאֲטָא בְּעָלְמָא, וְהַהִיא שַׁעֲתָא אִתְפְּלַג לֵילְיָא, וְשַׁלְהוֹבִיתָא אַזְלָא

וּבָטַשׁ בְּגַדְפוֹי דְּתַרְנְגוֹלָא, וְקָארֵי, כְּדֵין קוּדְשָׁא בְּרִיךְ הוּא עָאל בְּגִנְתָּא דְּעֵדֶן.

21. Then the Holy One, blessed be He, awakens along with His grades, and strikes the firmaments so that twelve thousand worlds are shaken. He roars and weeps as the verse says, "Hashem shall roar from on high, and utter His voice from His holy habitation; He shall mightily roar because of His habitation" (Yirmeyah 25:30). He remembers Yisrael, THAT THEY ARE IN EXILE, and sheds two tears into the great sea. Then a flame is awakened from the north. One spirit from the north joins that flame, AND THE FLAME goes to hover about the world. Midnight comes then, and the flame goes to beat the wings of the rooster, and he crows. Then the Holy One, blessed be He, enters the Garden of Eden.

22. וְקוּדְשָׁא בְּרִיךְ הוּא לֵית לֵיהּ נַיְיחָא עַד דְּעָאל לְגִנְתָּא דְּעֵדֶן לְאִשְׁתַּעְשְׁעָא בְּנִשְׁמָתֵהוֹן דְּצַדִּיקַיָּיא. וְסִימָן כִּי נִמְכַּרְנוּ אֲנִי וְעַמִּי וְגוֹ'. וַיֹּאמֶר הַמֶּלֶךְ מִי הוּא זֶה וְגוֹ', וְהַמֶּלֶךְ קָם בַּחֲמָתוֹ מִמִּשְׁתֵּה הַיַּיִן אֶל גִּנַּת הַבִּיתָן וְגוֹ'.

22. The Holy One, blessed be He, has no pleasure until He enters the Garden of Eden and enjoys Himself in the souls of the righteous. And the sign TO THIS UNION IS IN THE WORDS OF ESTER – WHO IS MALCHUT-TO THE KING – NAMELY, ZEIR ANPIN, "for we are sold, I and my people, to be destroyed, to be slain, and to be annihilated" (Ester 7:4). THIS IS THE SECRET OF THE DOMINION OF JUDGMENTS OF THE LEFT COLUMN. And the King said: "who is he, and where is he..." (Ibid. 5), AND SHE SAID: "THIS WICKED HAMAN" (IBID. 6), NAMELY, THE KLIPAH THAT IS DRAWN FROM THE LEFT COLUMN. And then "And the king arising from the banquet of wine in his wrath went into the palace garden..." (Ibid. 7), THAT IS, TO THE GARDEN OF EDEN.

23. בְּשַׁעְתָּא דְּקוּדְשָׁא בְּרִיךְ הוּא עָאל בְּגִנְתָּא דְּעֵדֶן, כְּדֵין כָּל אִינּוּן אִילָנִין דְּגִנְתָּא, וְכָל אִינּוּן נִשְׁמָתִין דְּצַדִּיקַיָּיא, פַּתְחֵי וְאַמְרֵי, שְׂאוּ שְׁעָרִים רָאשֵׁיכֶם וְגוֹ'. מִי זֶה מֶלֶךְ הַכָּבוֹד וְגוֹ'. שְׂאוּ שְׁעָרִים רָאשֵׁיכֶם

וְגוֹ'. וּבְשַׁעֲתָא דְּנִשְׁמָתְהוֹן דְּצַדִּיקַיָּיא דִּי בְּאַרְעָא אָהַדְרוּ לְגוּפַיְיהוּ, כְּדֵין אַתְקִיפוּ בְּהוּ כָּל אִינּוּן מַלְאָכִין, וְאַמְרֵי הִנֵּה בָּרְכוּ אֶת יְיָ' כָּל עַבְדֵי יְיָ'. וְאוֹלִיפְנָא דְּדָא מַשְׁרְיָיא תְּלִיתָאָה קָא אַמְרֵי דָא, בְּאַרְבַּע שַׁעֲתֵי בַּתְרַיְיתָא.

23. When the Holy One, blessed be He, enters the Garden of Eden, all the trees of the Garden and all the souls of the righteous open and say "Lift up your heads, O you gates... Who is this king of glory... Lift up your heads, O you gates..." (Tehilim 24:7-8). And when the souls of the righteous that are on earth return to their bodies, then all those angels encourage them and say "Behold, bless Hashem, all you servants of Hashem" (Tehilim 134:1). We learned that the third host says this verse in the last four hours, WHICH ARE THE CENTRAL COLUMN.

24. וְקָאַמְרֵי שִׁירָתָא, עַד דְּסָלִיק נְהוֹרָא דְּצַפְרָא, דִּכְדֵין מְשַׁבְּחִין לְמָרֵיהוֹן כָּל אִינּוּן כֹּכְבַיָּא וּמַזָּלֵי, וְכָל אִינּוּן מַלְאָכִין עִלָּאִין, דִּי שֻׁלְטָנֵיהוֹן בִּימָמָא, כֻּלְּהוּ מְשַׁבְּחָן לְמָארֵיהוֹן, וְאַמְרֵי שִׁירָתָא. הה"ד בְּרָן יַחַד כֹּכְבֵי בֹקֶר וַיָּרִיעוּ כָּל בְּנֵי אֱלֹהִים.

24. And the third host recites poetry until the light of the morning rises and then all those stars and constellations praise their Master and all those archangels that govern by daytime, NAMELY THAT ARE DRAWN FROM ZEIR ANPIN, all praise their Master and recite poetry. This is as said, "when the morning stars sang together, and all the sons of Elohim shouted for joy" (Iyov 38:7). THIS REFERS TO ALL THE ANGELS. BECAUSE AT NIGHT ONLY A PART OF THE ANGELS RECITE POETRY, MEANING THOSE WHO ARE DRAWN FROM MALCHUT. BUT DURING DAYTIME EVERYONE RECITES POETRY, EVEN THE ANGELS WHO ARE DRAWN FROM ZEIR ANPIN.

25. בְּשַׁעֲתָא דְּשִׁמְשָׁא נָפִיק, בִּימָמָא, יִשְׂרָאֵל נַטְלֵי שִׁירָתָא לְתַתָּא, וְשִׁמְשָׁא לְעֵילָא, דִּכְתִיב יִירָאוּךְ עִם שָׁמֶשׁ. בְּשַׁעֲתָא דְּנָטִיל שִׁמְשָׁא בְּגִלְגְּלוֹי, פָּתַח קָל נְעִימוּתָא, וְאָמַר שִׁירָתָא. וּמִי שִׁירָתָא קָאַמְרֵי. הוֹדוּ לַיְיָ' קִרְאוּ בִשְׁמוֹ וְגוֹ'. שִׁירוּ לוֹ זַמְּרוּ לוֹ וְגוֹ'. וְיִשְׂרָאֵל מְשַׁבְּחָן לְקוּדְשָׁא בְּרִיךְ הוּא בִּימָמָא, עִם שִׁמְשָׁא. הה"ד יִירָאוּךְ עִם שָׁמֶשׁ, וְאַף עַל גַּב

דְּהָא אוֹקִימְנָא לְהַאי קְרָא, א״ר אֶלְעָזָר, אִלְמָלֵא דִּבְנֵי עָלְמָא אֲטִימִין
לִבָּא וּסְתִימִין עַיְינִין לָא יַכְלִין לְמֵיקַם מִקָל נְעִימוּתָא דְּגַלְגְּלָא
דְּשִׁמְשָׁא, כַּד נָטִיל וּמְשַׁבַּח קָמֵי קוּדְשָׁא בְּרִיךְ הוּא.

25. When the sun comes out, by day, all Yisrael sing below and the sun above. This is as written: "May they fear You as long as the sun" (Tehilim 72:5). When the sun drives its wheels, a pleasant voice begins to sing. What is it singing? It sings "Oh give thanks to Hashem, call upon His name... Sing to Him, sing psalms to Him..." (Tehilim 105:1-2). And Yisrael praise the Holy One, blessed be He, by day. This is the meaning of the verse "May they fear You as long as the sun." And though we established this scripture, Rabbi Elazar said: if the inhabitants of the world were not hard hearted and blindfolded, they would not have been able to bear the sweet voice of the wheel of the sun, when it drives and praises the Holy One, blessed be He. THIS IS THE MEANING OF "MAY THEY FEAR YOU AS LONG AS THE SUN."

3. The Angel of Death is present among the women

A Synopsis

At daylight the rabbis rise from studying the Torah and go to see Rabbi Shimon. He cautions them not to go outside because the Angel of Death is around, and has permission to destroy whoever he wants. Rabbi Shimon explains that the angel of death can ask for justice before God by repeating someone's offenses; when the person is sentenced, the Angel of Death kills him. When a dead man is taken to the cemetery, the Angel of Death is among the women, so the men must not look at the women. The ancient wise men decreed that a Shofar should be blown when the dead person was taken from his house, in order that the Angel of Death should have no power over the living. Then we hear that when Yisrael made the calf and many died, the angel of death was among the women inside the camp of Yisrael; Moses saw this, so he gathered the men all by themselves. The angel of death did not leave the women until the tabernacle was built. Rabbi Shimon says that if the angel of death is among seven women he seeks justice, but if he is among ten women he blames and seeks to kill. After these admonitions the rabbis study Torah all day. Then Rabbi Shimon discusses the story of the ark, asking why God did not just move Noah to a safe place where the flood waters would not come. He answers saying that since the destroyer came into the world whoever did not protect himself and was found before him in the open forfeits his life because he brings death upon himself. We hear that while the rabbis are hiding at home thirteen people in town died, and Rabbi Shimon says: blessed be the merciful, that the Angel of Death did not behold your images.

26. אַדְהָכִי דְּאִתְעַסְקוּ בְּאוֹרַיְיתָא, נָהַר יְמָמָא. קָמוּ וְאָתוּ לְקַמֵּיהּ דר"ש, כֵּיוָן דְּחָמָא לוֹן, אר"ש, אֶלְעָזָר בְּרִי, אַנְתְּ וְחַבְרַיָּיא אַסְתְּימוּ גַרְמַיְיכוּ אִלֵּין תְּלַת יוֹמִין, דְּלָא תִּפְקוּן לְבַר בְּגִין דְּמַלְאָךְ הַמָּוֶת אִשְׁתְּכַח בְּמָתָא, וְאִית לֵיהּ רְשׁוּ לְחַבְּלָא, וְכֵיוָן דְּאִתְיְיהִיב לֵיהּ רְשׁוּ לְחַבְּלָא, יָכִיל לְחַבְּלָא, לְכָל מַאן דְּאִתְחֲזֵי קַמֵּיהּ.

26. While they were studying the Torah, daylight broke. They stood up and went to be before Rabbi Shimon. When he saw them, Rabbi Shimon said: "Elazar my son, you and the friends, remain hidden for these three days, and

do not go outside, because the Angel of Death is in town and has permission to cause damage. Since permission was given to the Destroyer, he can destroy whomever appears before him.

27. וְתוּ דְּבַר נָשׁ דְּאִתְחֲזֵי קַמֵּיהּ, סָלִיק וְאַסְטֵי עָלֵיהּ, וְאַדְכַּר חוֹבוֹי, וּבָעֵי דִּינָא מִקַּמֵּי קוּדְשָׁא בְּרִיךְ הוּא, וְלָא אִתְעָדֵי מִתַּמָּן, עַד דְּאִתְדָּן הַהוּא בַּר נָשׁ, וְאִתְיְיהִיב לֵיהּ רְשׁוּ וְקָטִיל לֵיהּ.

27. Furthermore, when he, THE ANGEL OF DEATH, wants to destroy a person, he rises to accuse that person and repeats his offenses. He demands justice before the Holy One, blessed be He, and does not leave before that person is sentenced, and permission is given. Then he kills him.

28. אר"ש, הָאֱלֹהִים רוּבָּא דְּעָלְמָא, לָא מִיתוּ, עַד לָא מָטָא זִמְנַיְיהוּ, בַּר דְּלָא יַדְעֵי לְאִסְתַּמְּרָא גַּרְמַיְיהוּ, דְּהָא בְּשַׁעֲתָא דְּמִיתָא אַפְּקֵי לֵיהּ מִבֵּיתֵיהּ לְבֵי קִבְרֵי, מַלְאָךְ הַמָּוֶת אִשְׁתְּכַח בֵּינֵי נָשֵׁי, אֲמַאי בֵּינֵי נָשֵׁי. דְּהָכִי הוּא אוֹרְחוֹי, מִיּוֹמָא דְּפַתֵּי לְחַוָּה, וּבְגִינָהּ גָּרִים מוֹתָא לְכָל עָלְמָא. וע"ד קָטִיל בַּר נָשׁ, וְגוּבְרֵי אִשְׁתְּכָחוּ עִם מִיתָא, עָאל בֵּינֵי נָשֵׁי בְּאָרְחָא.

28. Rabbi Shimon said: 'by Elohim', MEANING THAT HE SWORE IN THE NAME OF ELOHIM, most people do not die before their time, except those who do not know how to protect themselves, because when a dead man is taken from his house to the cemetery, the Angel of Death is among the women. Why is he among the women? BECAUSE this is his way since he seduced Eve and through her he brought death to the whole world. This is why when he kills a man, and the men are with the dead, THE ANGEL OF DEATH comes in among the women, on the way TO THE CEMETERY.

29. וְאִית לֵיהּ רְשׁוּ, לְמִקְטַל בְּנֵי נָשָׁא, וְאִסְתַּכַּל בְּאַנְפַּיְיהוּ בְּאָרְחָא דְּאִתְחֲזִיאוּ קַמֵּיהּ, מִשַּׁעֲתָא דְּמַפְּקֵי לֵיהּ מִבֵּיתֵיהּ לְבֵי קִבְרֵי, עַד דְּאָהַדְרוּ לְבֵיתַיְיהוּ וּבְגִינֵיהוֹן גָּרִים מוֹתָא לְכַמָּה גּוּבְרִין בְּעָלְמָא, עַד לָא מָטָא זִמְנַיְיהוּ. וע"ד כְּתִיב, וְיֵשׁ נִסְפֶּה בְּלֹא מִשְׁפָּט. בְּגִין דְּסָלִיק

וְאַסְטִין, וְאַדְכַּר חוֹבוֹי דְּבַר נָשׁ קַמֵּי קוּדְשָׁא בְּרִיךְ הוּא, וְאִתְדַּן עַל
אִינּוּן חוֹבִין וְאִסְתַּלָּק עַד לָא מָטָא זִמְנֵיהּ.

29. And THEN he has permission to kill people. He looks at the faces of
those seen before him on the way TO THE CEMETERY, from the time when
they take the dead from his house to burial until they get back to their
houses. That is why he causes death for some men in the world before their
time. Of that speaks the verse, "but sometimes ruin comes without
judgment" (Mishlei 13:23). Because he goes up and accuses and repeats the
offenses of that person before the Holy One, blessed be He. That person is
judged for those offenses and passes away before his time.

30. מַאי תַּקְנְתֵיהּ. בְּשַׁעֲתָא דְּנַטְלֵי מֵיתָא לְבֵי קִבְרֵי, יְהַדַּר בַּר נָשׁ
אַנְפּוֹי וְיִשְׁבּוֹק לְנָשֵׁי בָּתַר כַּתְפּוֹי. וְאִי אִינּוּן מְקַדְּמֵי, יְהַךְ לַאֲחוֹרָא, בְּגִין
דְּלָא יִתְחֲזֵי עִמְּהוֹן אַנְפִּין בְּאַנְפִּין. וּלְבָתַר דִּמְהַדְרֵי מִבֵּי קִבְרֵי, לָא
יְהַדַּר בְּהַהוּא אָרְחָא דְּנָשֵׁי קַיְימָן, וְלָא יִסְתַּכַּל בְּהוּ כְּלָל, אֶלָּא יִסְטֵי
בְּאָרְחָא אַחֲרָא. וּבְגִין דִּבְנֵי נָשָׁא לָא יַדְעֵי, וְלָא מִסְתַּכְּלָן דָּא, רוּבָּא
דְּעָלְמָא, אִתְדָּנוּ בְּדִינָא, וְאִסְתַּלָּקוּ עַד לָא מָטָא זִמְנַיְיהוּ.

30. HE ASKS: What his remedy is, HOW TO BEWARE OF THE ANGEL OF
DEATH, AND SAYS that when the dead man is carried to the cemetery, a
man should turn his face away from the women, and let them walk behind
him. And if the women walk first, he should walk behind them, so as not to
see them face to face. And when they come back from the cemetery, he
should not walk on the same way where the women are standing, nor look at
them at all, but go another way. And since most people do not know and do
not care for this, most of them are judged and pass away before their time.

31. א״ר אֶלְעָזָר, אִי הָכִי, טָב לֵיהּ לְבַר נָשׁ דְּלָא יוֹזִיף לְמֵיתָא. א״ל
לָא. דְּהָא בַּר נָשׁ דְּאִסְתָּמַר כְּהַאי גַּוְונָא, אִתְחֲזֵי לְאַרְכָּא דְּיוֹמִין, וְכָל
שֶׁכֵּן לְעָלְמָא דְּאָתֵי.

31. Rabbi Elazar said: if this be so, then it is better for a man not to escort
the dead. Rabbi Shimon said no. For a man who takes care of himself in that
manner is worthy of a long life, and also of the World to Come.

32. ת"ח, לָאו לְמַגָּנָא אַתְקִינוּ קַדְמָאֵי שׁוֹפָר, לְאַמְשָׁכָא מֵיתָא מִן בֵּיתָא לְבֵי קִבְרֵי. אִי תֵּימָא דְּעַל מֵיתָא וִיקָרָא דִּילֵיה לְחוֹד אִיהוּ. לָא. אֶלָּא, בְּגִין לְאַגָּנָא עַל חַיָּיא, דְּלָא יִשְׁלוֹט עֲלַיְיהוּ מַלְאָךְ הַמָּוֶת, לְאַסְטָאָה לְעֵילָא וְיִסְתַּמְרוּן מִנֵּיה.

32. Come and see, not for nothing did the ancient wise men decree that a Shofar was to be blown when the dead was taken from his house. You might say, this is solely to honor the dead. But no. This is to protect the living, so that the Angel of Death would have no power over them to accuse them above, and they might avoid him.

33. פָּתַח וְאָמַר, וְכִי תָבֹאוּ מִלְחָמָה בְּאַרְצְכֶם עַל הַצַּר הַצֹּרֵר אֶתְכֶם וְגוֹ', וְדַיְיקִנָא עַל הַצַּר, דָּא מַלְאָךְ הַמָּוֶת. הַצֹּרֵר אֶתְכֶם תָּדִיר, וְקָטִיל לִבְנֵי נָשָׁא, וּבָעֵי לְקַטְלָא אַחֲרָנִין. מַאי תַּקַנְתֵּיה. וַהֲרֵעֹתֶם. אִם בְּרֹאשׁ הַשָּׁנָה, דְּהוּא יוֹמָא דְּדִינָא לְעֵילָא, הַאי מַלְאָךְ הַמָּוֶת נָחִית לְתַתָּא, בְּגִין לְאַשְׁגָּחָא בְּעוֹבָדִין דִּבְנֵי נָשָׁא, וּלְסַלְקָא לְעֵילָא לְאַסְטָאָה לוֹן. וְיִשְׂרָאֵל דְּיָדְעֵי דְּהָא מַלְאָךְ הַמָּוֶת נָחִית לְתַתָּא וְסָלִיק לְעֵילָא, בְּגִין לְמֶהֱוֵי קַטֵיגוֹרָא עֲלַיְיהוּ. מְקַדְּמֵי בַּשׁוֹפָר לְיַבְּבָא עֲלֵיה, דְּלָא יָכִיל לוֹן וּלְאַגָּנָא עֲלַיְיהוּ.

33. He started by saying, "And if you go to war in your land against the enemy that oppresses you..." (Bemidbar 10:9). I have observed that "the enemy," refers to the Angel of Death, that "oppresses you" forever, killing people and seeking to kill everyone. What is to be done about him? "then you shall blow an alarm" (Bemidbar 10:9). On Rosh Hashanah (the Jewish New Year), which is the day of Judgment above, the Angel of Death comes down to examine people's deeds and then ascends and prosecutes them. And Yisrael, who know that the Angel of Death comes down and then goes up to be their prosecutor, blow the Shofar early and complain against him so he would have no power against them, and in order to protect themselves.

34. וְכָל שֶׁכֵּן בְּשַׁעֲתָא דְּעָבִיד דִּינָא וְקָטִיל בְּנֵי נָשָׁא, וְאִשְׁתְּכַח לְתַתָּא. וְכָל שֶׁכֵּן בְּשַׁעֲתָא דְּאַזְלֵי לְבֵי קִבְרֵי, וְאָהַדְרוּ מִבֵּי קִבְרֵי, דְּהָא בְּשַׁעֲתָא

דְּנָשֵׁי נַטְלֵי רַגְלַיְיהוּ עִם מִיתָא, אִיהוּ נָחִית וְאִשְׁתְּכַח קַמַּיְיהוּ, דִּכְתִּיב רַגְלֶיהָ יוֹרְדוֹת מָוֶת, יוֹרְדוֹת לְמַאן. לְהַהוּא אֲתָר דְּאִקְרֵי מָוֶת. וְעַ"ד חַוָּה גַּרְמַת מוֹתָא לְכָל עָלְמָא, רַחֲמָנָא לְשֵׁזְבִינָן.

34. All the more so when the Angel of Death punishes and takes lives, and also when people go to the cemetery and return from it, because when women walk to the funeral, he comes down and dwells among them, as says the verse "her feet go down to death" (Mishlei 5:5). Where do they go down? NAMELY, to that place which is called death, FOR THE ANGEL OF DEATH COMES BEFORE THEM, WHILE THEY WALK TO ESCORT THE DEAD, because Eve brought death upon the whole world, may the Merciful save us.

35. ת"ח, כְּתִיב כֵּן דֶּרֶךְ אִשָּׁה מְנָאָפֶת וְגוֹ'. וְהָא אוּקִימְנָא. אֲבָל כֵּן דֶּרֶךְ אִשָּׁה מְנָאָפֶת, דָּא הוּא מַלְאָךְ הַמָּוֶת, וְהָכִי הוּא, וְהָכִי אִקְרֵי. אָכְלָה וּמָחֲתָה פִיהָ, אוֹקִידַת עָלְמָא בְּשַׁלְהוֹבוֹי, וְקַטְלַת בְּנֵי נָשָׁא עַד לָא מָטָא זִמְנַיְיהוּ, וְאָמְרָה לֹא פָעַלְתִּי אָוֶן, דְּהָא דִּינָא בָּעָא עֲלַיְיהוּ, וְאִשְׁתְּכָחוּ בְּחוֹבִין, וּבְדִינָא קְשׁוֹט מִיתוּ.

35. Come and see, it is written: "Likewise the way of an adulterous woman" (Mishlei 30:20), which we already interpreted . But "Likewise the way of an adulterous woman" alludes to the Angel of Death. This is him and that is his name. "She eats and wipes her mouth" (Ibid.), for he burns the world with his flames and kills people before their time. "and says I have done nothing wrong" (Ibid.), for he asked for justice and they were found guilty, and died according to true law.

36. בְּשַׁעֲתָא דְּעָבְדוּ יִשְׂרָאֵל יַת עֶגְלָא, וּמִיתוּ כָּל אִינּוּן אוּכְלוֹסִין, הֲוָה מַלְאָךְ הַמָּוֶת אִשְׁתְּכַח בֵּינֵי נָשֵׁי, בְּגוֹ מַשִׁרְיָיתָא דְּיִשְׂרָאֵל. כֵּיוָן דְּאִסְתָּכַּל מֹשֶׁה, דְּהָא מַלְאָךְ הַמָּוֶת אִשְׁתְּכַח בֵּינֵי נָשֵׁי, וּמַשִׁרְיָיתָא דְּיִשְׂרָאֵל בֵּינַיְיהוּ, מִיַּד כָּנִישׁ לְכָל גּוּבְרִין לְחוֹדַיְיהוּ, הה"ד וַיַּקְהֵל מֹשֶׁה אֶת כָּל עֲדַת בְּנֵי יִשְׂרָאֵל. אִלֵּין גּוּבְרִין, דְּכָנִישׁ לוֹן וְאַפְרִישׁ לוֹן לְחוֹדַיְיהוּ.

36. When Yisrael made the calf and many died, the Angel of Death was among the women inside the camp of Yisrael. When Moses saw the Angel of Death among the women, and the camp of Yisrael between them, he immediately gathered all the men by themselves. This is the meaning of the verse "And Moses gathered all the Congregation of the children of Yisrael together" (Shemot 35;10. These were the men alone, who were gathered and separated.

37. וּמַלְאַךְ הַמָּוֶת לָא הֲוָה מִתְפְּרַשׁ מִגּוֹ נָשִׁין, עַד דְּאִתּוֹקַם מַשְׁכְּנָא, דִּכְתִיב וַיָּקֶם מֹשֶׁה אֶת הַמִּשְׁכָּן. וַאֲפִילוּ בְּשַׁעֲתָא דְּנָשִׁין הֲווֹ מַיְיתִין נִדְבָה לְמַשְׁכְּנָא, לָא הֲוָה מִתְעֲדֵי מִבֵּינַיְיהוּ, עַד דְּחָמָא מֹשֶׁה, וְיָהַב לְגוּבְרִין עֵיטָא, דְּלָא יֵיתוּן בְּחִבּוּרָא חֲדָא עִמְּהוֹן, וְלָא יִתְחֲזוּן אַנְפִּין בְּאַנְפִּין, אֶלָּא לְבָתַר כִּתְפַּיְיהוּ. הֲדָא הוּא דִּכְתִיב וַיָּבֹאוּ הָאֲנָשִׁים עַל הַנָּשִׁים וַיָּבִיאוּ לָא כְּתִיב, אֶלָּא וַיָּבֹאוּ בְּאָרְחָא חֲדָא לָא הֲווֹ אַזְלִין, אֶלָּא לְבָתַר כִּתְפַּיְיהוּ. בְּגִין דִּמַלְאַךְ הַמָּוֶת לָא אִתְפְּרַשׁ מִבֵּינַיְיהוּ עַד דְּאִתּוֹקַם מַשְׁכְּנָא.

37. And the Angel of Death did not leave the women until the tabernacle was built, as was written: "and Moses erected the tabernacle" (Shemot 40:18). And even when the women brought offerings to the tabernacle, the Angel of Death did not move away from them, until Moses saw that, and advised the men not to have contact with them and not to look at them face to face, but to walk behind them. This is the meaning of the verse "And they came (Heb. *vayavo'u*), both men and women" (Shemot 35:22). It does not say 'and they brought (Heb. *vayavi'u*)' but - "and they came." THIS TEACHES US THAT THE MEN did not walk with THE WOMEN together but behind them. All this is because the Angel of Death did not leave them until the tabernacle was built.

38. תָּא חֲזֵי, לָא אִשְׁתְּכַח בֵּינֵי נְשֵׁי, פָּחוּת מִשְׁבַע נָשִׁים, וְלָא פָּחוּת מֵעֲשַׂר. וּבְאָרְחָא בְּאִתְגַּלְיָא, בְּשֶׁבַע אִשְׁתְּכַח, וּבָעֵי דִּינָא. בְּעֶשֶׂר, אַסְטֵי לְקַטְלָא. וּבְגִין דְּאִשְׁתְּכַח בֵּינַיְיהוּ בְּאָרְחָא בְּאִתְגַּלְיָא, כְּתִיב וַיָּבֹאוּ הָאֲנָשִׁים עַל הַנָּשִׁים. וְאִסְתְּמָרוּ כָּל הַהוּא יוֹמָא כֻּלְּהוּ חַבְרַיָּיא, וְאִשְׁתַּדָּלוּ בְּאוֹרַיְיתָא.

38. Come and see: THE ANGEL OF DEATH is not among the women when they are less than seven together or less than ten together. HE EXPLAINS: in public he is among seven women and seeks to punish. And if there are ten women he prosecutes in order to kill. And since he is among them openly, it is written: "And they came, both men and women." VIZ. BEHIND THEIR BACKS AS MENTIONED ABOVE. And all the friends were watchful that day and studied Torah.

39. פָּתַח ר"ש וְאָמַר, וַיֹּאמֶר יְיָ' אֶל נֹחַ בֹּא אַתָּה וְכָל בֵּיתְךָ אֶל הַתֵּבָה. הַאי קְרָא אוֹקִימְנָא, אֲבָל ת"ח, וְכִי לָא יָכִיל קוּדְשָׁא בְּרִיךְ הוּא לְנַטְרָא לֵיה לְנֹחַ, בְּאַתָּר חַד בְּעָלְמָא. דְּיֶהֱא מַבּוּל בְּכָל עָלְמָא, וְלָא יְהֵא בְּהַהוּא אֲתָר, כְּמָה דִּכְתִיב בְּגִדְעוֹן, וַיְהִי חוֹרֶב אֶל הַגִּזָּה לְבַדָּהּ. אוֹ לְנַטְרָא לֵיה בְּאַרְעָא דְיִשְׂרָאֵל, דִּכְתִיב בָּהּ, לָא גֻשְׁמָהּ בְּיוֹם זָעַם, דְּלָא נַחְתוּ עָלָהּ מֵי טוֹפָנָא.

39. Rabbi Shimon opened the discussion and said, "And Hashem said to Noah, come you and all your house into the ark" (Beresheet 7:1). We already explained this verse. But come and see, could not the Holy One, blessed be He, keep Noah in one place in the world, so that when there would be flood, it would not reach that particular place? This is as was said concerning Gidon "let it be now only dry upon the fleece" (Shoftim 6:40). Or could He not keep him in the land of Yisrael, of which it is written: "nor rained upon in the day of indignation" (Yechezkel 22:24) meaning that the flood did not come upon it?

40. אֶלָּא, כֵּיוָן דִּמְחַבְּלָא נָחַת לְעָלְמָא, מַאן דְּלָא סָגִיר גַּרְמֵיה, וְאִשְׁתְּכַח קַמֵיה בְּאִתְגַּלְיָיא, אִתְחַיָּיב בְּנַפְשֵׁיה, דְּאִיהוּ קָטִיל גַּרְמֵיה. מְנָא לָן. מִלּוֹט, דִּכְתִיב הִמָּלֵט עַל נַפְשֶׁךָ אַל תַּבִּיט אַחֲרֶיךָ. מַאי טַעֲמָא אַל תַּבִּיט אַחֲרֶיךָ. בְּגִין דִּמְחַבְּלָא אָזִיל בָּתַר כִּתְפוֹי, וְאִי אַהֲדָר רֵישֵׁיה, וְאִסְתְּכַּל בֵּיה אַנְפִּין בְּאַנְפִּין, יָכִיל לְנַזְקָא לֵיה.

40. AND ANSWERS: since the Destroyer came in the world, whoever did not hide himself, and was present before him in openly, forfeits his life, because he brings death on himself. How do we know that? from Lot, as states the verse "Escape for your life, look not behind you" (Beresheet. 19:17). What

is the sense of "look not behind you?" It is because the Destroyer walked behind his back and if Lot had turned his head and looked him face to face, the angel might have done him harm.

41. וְע"ד כְּתִיב, וַיִּסְגֹּר יְיָ' בַּעֲדוֹ. דְּלָא יִתְחֲזֵי קַמֵּי מְחַבְּלָא, וְלָא יִשְׁלוֹט עָלֵיהּ מַלְאַךְ הַמָּוֶת. וְעַד דַּהֲווֹ טְמִירִין, מִיתוּ תְּלֵיסַר גּוּבְרִין בְּמָתָא. אָמַר רִבִּי שִׁמְעוֹן, בְּרִיךְ רַחֲמָנָא, דְּלָא אִסְתַּכַּל בְּדִיּוּקְנַיְיכוּ מַלְאַךְ הַמָּוֶת.

41. And therefore it is written OF NOAH: "and Hashem shut him in" (Beresheet 7:16), so he would not be seen by the destroyer and the Angel of Death would have no power over him . And while the friends were hiding AT HOME, thirteen men in town died. Rabbi Shimon said: blessed be the Merciful, that the Angel of Death did not behold your images.

42. וַיַּקְהֵל מֹשֶׁה וְגוֹ'. אָהֲדַר לוֹן כְּמִלְּקַדְמִין, עוֹבָדָא דְּמַשְׁכְּנָא. אָמַר רִבִּי חִיָּיא, כֹּלָּא כְּמָה דְּאִתְּמַר. וְעוֹבָדָא דְּמַשְׁכְּנָא לָא אִתְעֲבֵיד אֶלָּא מִיִּשְׂרָאֵל בִּלְחוֹדַיְיהוּ, וְלָא מֵאִינּוּן עֵרֶב רַב, בְּגִין דְּאִינּוּן עֵרֶב רַב אַמְשִׁיכוּ לֵיהּ לְמַלְאַךְ הַמָּוֶת לְנַחְתָּא לְעָלְמָא. כֵּיוָן דְּאִסְתַּכַּל מֹשֶׁה בֵּיהּ, אַשְׁדֵּי לְאִינּוּן עֵרֶב רַב, לְבַר, וְכָנִישׁ לוֹן לְיִשְׂרָאֵל בִּלְחוֹדַיְיהוּ, הֲדָא הוּא דִּכְתִיב וַיַּקְהֵל מֹשֶׁה וְגוֹ'.

42. "And Moses gathered." He repeats the building of the tabernacle a second time, as before IN THE PORTION OF TRUMAH. Rabbi Chiya said: everything is as we learned that the building of the tabernacle was done solely by Yisrael and not by the mixed multitude. For the mixed multitude drew AGAIN the Angel of Death and he descended into the world. Since Moses saw that, he threw the riff-raff out and gathered Yisrael only. It is written in the verse: "And Moses gathered," AND NOT LIKE IN TRUMAH, WHERE IT WAS SAID, "OF EVERY MAN WHOSE HEART PROMPTS HIM..." (SHEMOT 25:2), FOR THE MIXED MULTITUDE WAS PART OF THE CONGREGATION. AND THEREFORE THERE WAS NEED TO SAY THE BUILDING OF THE TABERNACLE A SECOND TIME.

4. "Who has ascended up into heaven, and come down"

A Synopsis

We read a lengthy discussion of the verse, "Who has ascended up into heaven, and come down again? Who has gathered the wind in his fists? Who has bound the waters in a garment? Who has established all the ends of the earth? What is His name, and what is His son's name, if you can tell?" Rabbi Shimon explains that this is said about God, Yud Hei Vav Hei, and that the name of his son is Yisrael. "who has ascended up into heaven" refers to Moses. Another explanation for "who has ascended up into heaven" refers to Elijah. Rabbi Shimon says that Elijah left the world in his body, left that body in the storm of wind and donned a new light body to rise above. Then he descended again, regained his body in the storm of wind, and returned to earth. Another explanation is that "who ascended up into heaven" refers to Elijah, and "came down" refers to Jonah, whom the fish brought down deep into the ocean. Rabbi Shimon explains how all the pieces of the opening verse refer to Elijah, but then offers us yet another interpretation, where "who has ascended up into heaven" refers to God, where heaven, that is Zeir Anpin, lifts Binah; this is the secret of the upper Chariot, composed of the four spirits of the world: Chesed, Gvurah, Tiferet and Malchut, that are the primordial elements.

43. רַבִּי שִׁמְעוֹן פָּתַח, מִי עָלָה שָׁמַיִם וַיֵּרַד מִי אָסַף רוּחַ בְּחָפְנָיו מִי צָרַר מַיִם בַּשִּׂמְלָה מִי הֵקִים כָּל אַפְסֵי אָרֶץ מַה שְׁמוֹ וּמַה שֶׁם בְּנוֹ כִּי תֵדָע. הַאי קְרָא הָא אוּקִימְנָא, וְכַמָּה סַמְכִין אִית בֵּיהּ. וְכֹלָּא בְּקוּדְשָׁא בְּרִיךְ הוּא אִתְּמַר, דְּאִיהוּ כֹלָּא. וְאִתְּמַר, מָה שְׁמוֹ וּמַה שֶׁם בְּנוֹ כִּי תֵדַע, דָּא קוּדְשָׁא בְּרִיךְ הוּא . מָה שְׁמוֹ יְדֹנָ"ד. וּמַה שֶׁם בְּנוֹ, יִשְׂרָאֵל דִּכְתִּיב, בְּנִי בְּכֹרִי יִשְׂרָאֵל, וְהָא אוּקִימְנָא. מִי עָלָה שָׁמַיִם. הָא אוּקְמוּהָ, דָּא מֹשֶׁה, דִּכְתִּיב וְאֶל מֹשֶׁה אָמַר עֲלֵה אֶל יְיָ'.

43. Rabbi Shimon opened the discussion with "Who has ascended up into heaven, and come down again? who has gathered the wind in His fists? who has bound the waters in a garment? who has established all the ends of the earth? what is His name, and what is His son's name, if you can tell?" (Mishlei 30:4). We explained this verse, together with its many interpretations. It is all said about the Holy One, blessed be He, which is all! And we learned, "what is His name, and what is His son's name, if you can

tell?" This is the Holy One, blessed be He, What is His name? Yud Hei Vav Hei, and the name of His son-Yisrael. As is written: "Yisrael is My son, My firstborn" (Shemot 4:22), and we already talked about it. And we explained that "who has ascended up into heaven" refers to Moses, as is written: "And He said to Moses, Come up to Hashem" (Shemot 24:1).

44. ד"א מִי עָלָה שָׁמַיִם, דָּא אֵלִיָּהוּ, דִּכְתִיב בֵּיהּ וַיַּעַל אֵלִיָּהוּ בַּסְעָרָה הַשָּׁמָיִם. וְכִי הֵיךְ יָכִיל אֵלִיָּהוּ לְסַלְּקָא לַשָּׁמַיִם. וְהָא כֻּלְּהוּ שָׁמַיִם, לָא יַכְלִין לְמִסְבַּל, אֲפִילוּ גַּרְעִינָא כְּחַרְדָּל מִגּוּפָא דְּהַאי עָלְמָא, וְאַתְּ אַמְרַת וַיַּעַל אֵלִיָּהוּ בַּסְעָרָה הַשָּׁמָיִם.

44. Another explanation for "Who has ascended up into the heaven" (Mishlei 30:4): it speaks about Elijah, of whom it is written: "And Elijah went up by a storm of wind" (II Melachim 2:11). HE ASKS: 'And how could Elijah go up to the sky, for the sky cannot bear a body of this world, even the size of a mustard seed', yet you say "And Elijah went up by a storm of wind."

45. אֶלָּא כְּמָה דְּאַתְּ אָמַר, וַיֵּרֶד יְיָ' עַל הַר סִינַי. וּכְתִיב וַיָּבֹא מֹשֶׁה בְּתוֹךְ הֶעָנָן וַיַּעַל אֶל הָהָר. וְכִי קוּדְשָׁא בְּרִיךְ הוּא דַּהֲוָה בְּטוּרָא דְּסִינַי, וּכְתִיב וּמַרְאֵה כְּבוֹד יְיָ' כְּאֵשׁ אוֹכֶלֶת בְּרֹאשׁ הָהָר, אֵיךְ יָכִיל מֹשֶׁה לְסַלְּקָא לְגַבֵּיהּ. אֶלָּא בְּמֹשֶׁה כְּתִיב, וַיָּבֹא מֹשֶׁה בְּתוֹךְ הֶעָנָן וַיַּעַל אֶל הָהָר. דְּעָאל גּוֹ עֲנָנָא, כְּמַאן דְּאִתְלַבַּשׁ בִּלְבוּשָׁא. הָכִי נָמֵי אִתְלָבַּשׁ בַּעֲנָנָא, וְעָאל בְּגַוֵּיהּ. וּבַעֲנָנָא אִתְקְרִיב לְגַבֵּי אֶשָּׁא, וְיָכִיל לְמִקְרָב. אוּף הָכִי אֵלִיָּהוּ, דִּכְתִיב וַיַּעַל אֵלִיָּהוּ בַּסְעָרָה הַשָּׁמַיִם, דְּעָאל בְּהַהִיא סְעָרָה, וְאִתְלָבַּשׁ בֵּיהּ בְּהַהִיא סְעָרָה, וְסָלִיק לְעֵילָא.

45. AND HE ANSWERS: 'But this is as you say "And Hashem came down upon Mount Sinai" (Shemot 19:20), and "And Moses went into the midst of the cloud, and went up into the mountain." Yet the Holy One, blessed be He, was on mount Sinai, and it is written: "And the sight of the glory of Hashem was like a devouring fire on the top of the mountain" (Shemot 24:17). How could Moses climb it? But it is written about Moses: "And Moses went into the midst of the cloud, and went up into the mountain" (Ibid. 18), meaning that he entered the cloud as if he were donning a

garment. And here, IN THE SCRIPTURE "AND HE SAID TO MOSES, COME UP TO HASHEM" he also donned a cloud and entered it. And in the cloud he approached the fire, and could come nearer. So it was with Elijah, as was written: "And Elijah went up by a storm of wind," meaning that he was clothed with the storm of wind and went up'.

46. וְרָזָא אַשְׁכַּחְנָא, בְּסִפְרָא דְּאָדָם קַדְמָאָה, דְּאָמַר בְּאִינּוּן תּוֹלְדוֹת דְּעָלְמָא, רוּחָא חֲדָא יְהֵא דְּיֵיחוֹת לְעָלְמָא בְּאַרְעָא, וְיִתְלַבַּשׁ בְּגוּפָא, וְאֵלִיָּהוּ שְׁמֵיהּ. וּבְהַהוּא גּוּפָא יִסְתַּלַּק, וְאִשְׁתְּלִיל מִגּוּפֵיהּ, וְיִשְׁתְּאַר בַּסְּעָרָה. וְגוּפָא דִּנְהוֹרָא אַחֲרָא יִזְדַּמַּן לֵיהּ, לְמֶהֱוֵי גּוֹ מַלְאֲכֵי. וְכַד יֵיחוּת, יִתְלַבַּשׁ בְּהַהוּא גּוּפָא, דְּיִשְׁתְּאַר בְּהַהוּא עָלְמָא, וּבְהַהוּא גּוּפָא יִתְחֲזֵי לְתַתָּא, וּבְגוּפָא אַחֲרָא יִתְחֲזֵי לְעֵילָּא. וְדָא אִיהוּ רָזָא, דְּמִי עָלָה שָׁמַיִם וַיֵּרַד. לָא הֲוָה בַּר נָשׁ דְּסָלִיק לִשְׁמַיָּא רוּחָא דִּילֵיהּ, וְנָחִית לְבָתַר לְתַתָּא, בַּר אֵלִיָּהוּ, דְּאִיהוּ סָלִיק לְעֵילָּא וְנָחִית לְתַתָּא.

46. And I found a secret in the book of Adam, which talked about the offspring THAT WOULD COME into the world: that there would be a spirit that would go down to the world to earth, and don a body and which name is Elijah. In that body he would quit the world and then remove the body and remain in the storm of wind. And another body of light would present itself before him, that he may go with it among the angels. And when he descends INTO THIS WORLD, he would don that body that was left in the other world, NAMELY IN THE STORM OF WIND. In this body he shall be seen down below, and in that other body OF LIGHT he would be seen above. And this is the secret of "Who has ascended up into heaven, and come down again? (Mishlei 30:4), for there was no man whose spirit would ascend to heaven AFTER THE BODY IS GONE, and come down again later, like Elijah, who went up and came down.

47. ד"א מִי עָלָה שָׁמַיִם, דָּא אֵלִיָּהוּ. וַיֵּרַד, דָּא יוֹנָה, דְּנָחַת לֵיהּ גּוֹ נוּנָא גּוֹ תְּהוֹמֵי, לְעִמְקֵי יַמָּא. יוֹנָה מֵחֵילָא דְּאֵלִיָּהוּ קָא אָתָא, אֵלִיָּהוּ סָלִיק, יוֹנָה נָחִית, דָּא שָׁאִיל נַפְשֵׁיהּ לְמֵימַת, וְדָא שָׁאִיל נַפְשֵׁיהּ לְמֵימַת, וּבְגִין כַּךְ אִקְרֵי בֶּן אֲמִתַּי. וּכְתִיב, וּדְבַר יְיָ' בְּפִיךְ אֱמֶת.

47. Another explanation: "Who ascended up into heaven" refers to Elijah, and "came down" refers to Jonah, whom the fish brought down deep into the ocean. Jonah draws from the strength of Elijah, FOR HE HAD ELIJAH'S SPIRIT, Elijah ascended and Jonah descended. The one wanted to die and the other wanted to die. That is why Jonah is called "son of Amitai " (Yonah 1:1), as says the verse "and that the word of Hashem in your mouth is truth (Heb. *emet*)" (I Melachim 17:24).

‎48. מִי צָרַר מַיִם, דָּא אֵלִיָּהוּ, דְּצָרִיר צְרוֹרָא דְּמַיָּא בְּעָלְמָא, וְלָא נַחְתּוּ טַלָּא וּמִטְרָא דִּשְׁמַיָּא. בַּשִּׂמְלָה, דָּא אֵלִיָּהוּ, דַּהֲוָה מַיְיתֵי אַדַּרְתֵּיהּ לְמֶעְבַּד נִסִּין. מִי אָסַף רוּחַ בְּחָפְנָיו, דָּא אֵלִיָּהוּ, דְּאַהֲדַר רוּחָא דְּבַר נָשׁ לְגוֹ מְעוֹי.

48. "Who has bound the waters" (Mishlei 30:4) alludes to Elijah, who knotted the knot of water in the world, and there was no dew nor rain from the sky. "In a garment" (Mishlei 30:4) also refers to Elijah, who brought his mantle when he committed miracles. FOR HE DIVIDED, TOGETHER WITH ELISHA, THE JORDAN BY USING HIS MANTLE (II MELACHIM 2:7-8). "who has gathered the wind (or: 'spirit') in his fists?" (Mishlei 30:4) refers to Elijah, who brought a spirit of a man back into his body AFTER HE DIED (I MELACHIM 17:22-24).

‎49. מִי הֵקִים כָּל אַפְסֵי אָרֶץ. דָּא אֵלִיָּהוּ, דִּלְבָתַר דְּצָרַר מַיִם, וְאוֹמֵי עַל מִטְרָא, לְבָתַר אָהֲדַר בִּצְלוֹתֵיהּ, וְאוֹקִים כָּל עָלְמָא, וְנָחִית מִטְרָא, וְאִתְיְהִיב מְזוֹנָא לְכֹלָּא. מַה שְּׁמוֹ, דָּא אֵלִיָּהוּ. וּמַה שֵּׁם בְּנוֹ, דָּא אֵלִיָּהוּ. מַה שְּׁמוֹ, כַּד סָלִיק לְעֵילָא, אֵלִיָּהוּ. וּמַה שֵּׁם בְּנוֹ, כַּד נָחִית לְתַתָּא, וְאִתְעֲבֵיד שְׁלִיחָא לְמֶעְבַּד נִסִּין, אֵלִיָּהוּ שְׁמֵיהּ.

49. "Who has established all the ends of the earth?" refers to Elijah who after bagging the water in the world, and restrained the rain by oath, prayed again, thus reviving the world, so rain and food would be given to everyone. "What is his name"-Elijah, "and what is his son's name?" also Elijah. AND HE EXPLAINS, what is his name?-when he ascended up-it is Elijah. "And what is his son's name" refers to the time he came down, and became a messenger to perform miracles, and his name is Elijah.

‏50. דָּבָר אַחֵר מִי עָלָה שָׁמַיִם, דָּא קוּדְשָׁא בְּרִיךְ הוּא, כְּמָה דְּאוֹקִימְנָא. וְרָזָא דְמִלָּה, מִ"י, וְהָא אוֹקִימְנָא. וְהָכָא אִיהוּ רָזָא דִּרְתִיכָא עִלָּאָה, אַרְבַּע סְטְרִין דְעָלְמָא, דְּאִינוּן יְסוֹדֵי קַדְמָאֵי דְכֹלָּא, וְכֻלְּהוּ תַּלְיָין בְּהַהוּא אֲתָר עִלָּאָה דְּאִקְרֵי מִ"י, כְּמָה דְּאִתְּמַר.

50. Another interpretation: "who (Heb. *mi*) has ascended up into heaven" refers to the Holy One, blessed be He, as we already learned. The secret of it is that the word "Mi" is used. We already said THAT THIS WORD IS THE NAME OF BINAH. AND THE EXPLANATION IS THAT HEAVEN, WHICH IS ZEIR ANPIN, LIFTS BINAH, WHICH IS CALLED "MI," and this is the secret of the upper Chariot, composed of the four directions of the world, NAMELY, THE FOUR SFIROT CHESED, GVURAH, TIFERET AND MALCHUT, FROM THE CHEST UPWARD OF ZEIR ANPIN, THAT FORM A CHARIOT TO BINAH THAT IS CALLED "MI." They are the primordial elements that come all from that place which is called Mi, NAMELY, THEY ARE ITS CHARIOT, as we learned.

5. "whoever is of a willing heart"

A Synopsis

Rabbi Shimon speaks first of the raising of Malchut to be united with Zeir Anpin, the uniting of the supernal Chariot and the lower Chariot. We hear of the upper ministers and the patriarchs who have the honor to bear the holy chair, Malchut. "Whoever is of a willing heart" refers to the four hosts of high angels in which are included the twelve hosts. The four hosts are called the holy animals and the twelve hosts are the offerings. All these Chariots are called "whoever is of a willing heart." Rabbi Yehuda speaks of how a man is blessed with happiness when a poor man comes to him; he is as honored as if he created his soul. Rabbi Aba then talks about the verse: "Since the day that I brought forth my people Yisrael out of Egypt, I chose no city out of all the tribes of Yisrael to build a house…that my name might be there, but I chose David," saying that God does not choose a city until he has a good leader for the people. We hear a discussion on "Happy is he who has the El of Jacob for his help, whose hope is in Hashem his Elohim." The righteous put their trust in God, and are content to break themselves for His sake, therefore they merit miracles and many signs. "Whoever is of a willing heart" refers to he whose heart is willing to draw the Shechinah into himself.

51. ת"ח, כַּד קַיְימָא שַׁעֲתָא דִּרְעוּתָא קַמֵּי קוּדְשָׁא בְּרִיךְ הוּא, לְיַחֲדָא רְתִיכָא עִלָּאָה בִּרְתִיכָא תַּתָּאָה, לְמֶהֱוֵי כֹּלָּא חַד. כְּדֵין קָלָא נָפִיק, מֵהַהוּא אֲתַר עִלָּאָה קַדִּישָׁא, דְּאִקְרֵי שָׁמַיִם, וְכָנִישׁ כָּל אִלֵּין קַדִּישִׁין דִּלְתַתָּא, וְכָל אִינּוּן רַבְרְבָן קַדִּישִׁין, וּמַשִׁרְיָין עִלָּאִין, לְמֶהֱוֵי כֻּלְּהוּ זְמִינִין כַּחֲדָא, הה"ד, וַיַּקְהֵל מֹשֶׁה, דָּא רָזָא דִּשְׁמַיָּא. אֶת כָּל עֲדַת בְּנֵי יִשְׂרָאֵל, אִלֵּין אִינּוּן תְּרֵיסַר מַשִׁרְיָין עִלָּאִין קַדִּישִׁין.

51. Come and see: when it is a time of goodwill before the Holy One, blessed be He, to unite the supernal Chariot with the lower Chariot so that they would become one, a voice issues from the uppermost holy place, which is called heaven, ZEIR ANPIN, and gathers all those who are holy down below, NAMELY, THE RIGHTEOUS IN THIS WORLD, all the holy ministers, MICHAEL, GABRIEL, URIEL AND RAPHAEL, and all the upper hosts, THE ANGELS, so that all would be ready together. This is the meaning of "And Moses gathered"-Moses is the secret of heaven, ZEIR ANPIN, "all

the Congregation of the children of Yisrael" - these are the twelve upper holy hosts, WHICH ARE THE LOWER CHARIOT, UPON WHICH MALCHUT RIDES, AND THEY LIFT MALCHUT TO BE UNITED WITH ZEIR ANPIN.

52. וַיֹּאמֶר אֲלֵיהֶם. וּמַאי קָאָמַר זֶה הַדָּבָר וְגוֹ', קְחוּ מֵאִתְּכֶם תְּרוּמָה, אִתְתָּקָנוּ כֻּלְּכוּן, לְסַלְּקָא עֲלַיְיכוּ, וּלְמֵיטַל עֲלַיְיכוּ, יְקָרָא דְּכֻרְסַיָּיא קַדִּישָׁא, לְסַלְּקָא לְעֵילָא.

52. "And he said to them." What did he say? "This is the thing... Take from among you an offering" (Shemot 35:4-5), which means, prepare yourself, all of you, to bear and carry upon you the honor of the holy throne, WHICH IS MALCHUT, to raise it, TO ZEIR ANPIN.

53. אַפְרִישׁוּ מִנַּיְיכוּ אִינּוּן יַקִּירִין, אִינּוּן רַבְרְבִין עִלָּאִין, לְסַלְּקָא לְהַהִיא תְּרוּמָה, רָזָא דְּכֻרְסַיָּיא קַדִּישָׁא, לְאִתְחַבְּרָא בַּאֲבָהָן, דְּהָא מַטְרוֹנִיתָא לָא אִתְחֲזֵי לְמֵיתֵי לְבַעְלָהּ, אֶלָּא בְּאִינּוּן בְּתוּלְתָן עוּלֶמְתָהָא, דְּיַיתוּן עִמָּהּ, וּמְדַבְּרָן לָהּ, עַד דְּמָטַת לְבַעְלָהּ, כְּמָה דְּאַתְּ אָמַר, בְּתוּלוֹת אַחֲרֶיהָ רֵעוֹתֶיהָ וְגוֹ', וְכָל כַּךְ לָמָּה, לְמֵיתֵי לְאִתְחַבְּרָא בְּבַעְלָהּ.

53. Allocate from among you the honored, the elevated ministers, MICHAEL, GABRIEL, URIEL AND RAPHAEL, to raise this offering, which is the secret of the holy throne, MALCHUT, to be united with the patriarchs, WHO ARE CHESED, GVURAH AND TIFERET OF ZEIR ANPIN. And it is not meet that the Matron, MALCHUT, come to her husband, unescorted by virgin maidens who come with her and conduct her to her husband, ZEIR ANPIN, as is said, "the virgins, her companions that follow her" (Tehilim 45:15). Wherefore all that? To bring her to join her husband, ZEIR ANPIN.

54. כָּל נְדִיב לִבּוֹ, אֶלֵּין אִינּוּן אַרְבַּע מַשְׁרִיָּין עִלָּאִין, דְּבִכְלָלָא דִּלְהוֹן כְּלִילָן, כָּל אִינּוּן שְׁאַר מַשְׁרִיָּין, וְאִלֵּין אִינּוּן דְּנַפְקָן בַּאֲבָהָן עִלָּאִין, דְּאִקְרוּן נְדִיבִים. כְּמָה דְּאוּקְמוּהָ, דִּכְתִיב כָּרוּהָ נְדִיבֵי הָעָם, אִלֵּין אֲבָהָן.

54. "Whoever is of a willing (Heb. *nediv*) heart" (Shemot 35:5) refers to the four hosts of high angels THAT COME FROM NETZACH, HOD, YESOD AND MALCHUT OF MALCHUT; in them are included all the other hosts, NAMELY THE TWELVE HOSTS. SINCE EACH OF THE FOUR HOSTS CONSISTS OF THREE HOSTS, THEY ARE ALTOGETHER TWELVE. And those who come out of the high patriarchs, CHESED, GVURAH AND TIFERET, are called nobles. As we stated, that it is written about the well, "that the nobles of (Heb. *nedivei*) the people delved" (Bemidbar 21:18). 'Nobles' refers to the fathers.

55. יְבִיאֶהָ, יְבִיאוּהָ לָא כְּתִיב, אֶלָּא יְבִיאֶהָ, לְיַחֲדָא כֹּלָּא כַּחֲדָא. וְכֵן יָבִיא לָא כְּתִיב, אֶלָּא יְבִיאֶהָ, לְסַלְקָא לָה לְגַבֵּי בַּעְלָהּ בִּיקָרָא, כְּמָה דְּאִצְטְרִיךְ. אֶת תְּרוּמַת יְיָ', אֶת לְאַסְגָּאָה, כָּל אִינּוּן מַשִׁרְיָין עִלָּאִין אַחֲרָנִין, לְאִתְחַבְּרָא כֹּלָּא כַּחֲדָא, וְאִינּוּן תְּרֵיסַר בִּכְלָלָא חֲדָא. זָהָב. וָכֶסֶף. וּנְחוֹשֶׁת. תְּכֵלֶת. וְאַרְגָּמָן. וְתוֹלַעַת שָׁנִי. וְשֵׁשׁ וְעִזִּים. וְעֹרֹת אֵילִם מְאָדָּמִים. וְעֹרֹת תְּחָשִׁים. וַעֲצֵי שִׁטִּים. וְשֶׁמֶן לַמָּאוֹר. וּבְשָׂמִים לְשֶׁמֶן הַמִּשְׁחָה. וְלִקְטֹרֶת הַסַּמִּים. אִלֵּין אִינּוּן תְּרֵיסַר מַשִׁרְיָין עִלָּאִין, דִּכְלִילָן כֻּלְּהוּ כַּחֲדָא בִּכְלָלָא דְּאַרְבַּע דְּאִקְרוּן חֵיוֹת הַקֹּדֶשׁ כְּמָה דְּאִתְּמַר.

55. HE ASKS: It is written "he will bring it (Heb. *yevi'eha*)" (Shemot 35:5) and not "they will bring it"; AND SAYS, "he will bring it" WHICH IS IN THE SINGULAR, INDICATES the unifying of everything into one, THAT IS TO SAY THE MALE AND FEMALE PRINCIPLES. Also, it does not say 'he will bring (Heb. *yavi*)' but "he will bring it (Heb. *yevie'ha*)," TO INDICATE MALCHUT WHICH IS CALLED AN OFFERING, to be given to her husband honorably as is proper. "an offering to Hashem," the particle 'Et', before "an offering," comes to add all the other hosts of angels, so that everything should be united into one, to make twelve HOSTS into one, WHICH ARE "gold, and silver, and brass, and blue, and purple, and scarlet, and fine linen, and goats' hair, and rams' skins dyed red, and badgers' skins, and acacia wood, and oil for the light, and spices for anointing oil, and for the sweet incense" (Ibid. 5-8) WHICH ARE THE TWELVE KINDS. These are the highest twelve hosts, that are included in these four, which are called the holy living creatures. FOR EACH LIVING CREATURE CONSISTS OF THREE, SO TOGETHER THERE ARE TWELVE.

56. וְכֻלְּהוּ אִלֵּין סַלְקִין לְכֻרְסְיָיא קַדִּישָׁא, לְאַעֲלָא לָהּ לְעֵילָא, לְאִתְחַבְּרָא בְּבַעֲלָהּ, בְּגִין לְמֶהֱוֵי כֹּלָּא חַד, בְּגִין דְּיִשְׁתְּכַח עִמָּהּ בִּיקָרָא עִלָּאָה. כְּדֵין יָתִיב מַלְכָּא עִלָּאָה עַל כֻּרְסְיָיא קַדִּישָׁא, וְאִתְחַבְּרָא אִתְּתָא בְּבַעֲלָהּ, לְמֶהֱוֵי כֹּלָּא חַד. וּכְדֵין, אִיהוּ חֶדְוָותָא דְכֹלָּא.

56. And all of them ascend to the holy throne, WHICH IS MALCHUT, to lift her up to be united with her husband, ZEIR ANPIN, so that all becomes one, and that he be with her in high glory. Then the supreme King sits on the holy throne, and wife is united with her husband, MALCHUT WITH ZEIR ANPIN, so that everything would be one. Then everyone rejoices.

57. ת״ח, הָכָא שָׁארֵי לְמִמְנֵי זָהָב בְּקַדְמֵיתָא, וְכֶסֶף לְבָתַר, בְּגִין דְּהַאי חֻשְׁבָּנָא מִתַּתָּא. אֲבָל כַּד אָתֵי לְמִמְנֵי מַחוּשְׁבָּנָא דִּרְתִיכָא דִּלְעֵילָא, שָׁארֵי לְמִמְנֵי מִיְמִינָא בְּקַדְמֵיתָא, וּלְבָתַר מִן שְׂמָאלָא. מְנָלָן. דִּכְתִּיב, לִי הַכֶּסֶף וְלִי הַזָּהָב. כֶּסֶף בְּקַדְמֵיתָא, וּלְבָתַר הַזָּהָב. וּבִרְתִיכָא דִּלְתַתָּא, שָׁארוּ מִשְּׂמָאלָא וּלְבָתַר מִיְמִינָא, דִּכְתִּיב זָהָב וָכֶסֶף וּנְחֹשֶׁת. זָהָב בְּקַדְמֵיתָא, וּלְבָתַר כֶּסֶף.

57. Come and see, here the count starts with gold, and then silver, because that reckoning is from below UPWARD, FOR GVURAH, THAT IS GOLD, PRECEDE SILVER THAT IS CHESED. But when counting by the reckoning of the supernal Chariot, the counting starts from the right side first, WHICH IS SILVER, and then left, WHICH IS GOLD. Whence do we derive this? It is written: "The silver is Mine, and the gold is Mine" (Chagai 2:8); first silver and then gold, BECAUSE IT RELATES TO THE HIGHER. With the lower Chariot, WHICH IS MALCHUT, it starts with left and then the right, as is written: "gold, and silver, and brass," first gold and then silver.

58. וְכָל אִינּוּן רְתִיכִין אִקְרוּן נְדִיב לֵב. כֹּל: לְאַכְלְלָא כָּל שְׁאָר רְתִיכִין. לֵב. מַאי לֵב. הַיְינוּ רָזָא דִּכְתִּיב, וְטוֹב לֵב מִשְׁתֶּה תָמִיד. וְדָא אִיהוּ לִבָּא דְכֹלָּא, וְדָא כֻּרְסְיָיא קַדִּישָׁא. וְעַל דָּא אִקְרוּן לֵב. כָּל נְדִיב לֵב, כְּמָה דְאוֹקִימְנָא, דְּאַרְבַּע מַשִׁרְיָין אִלֵּין, כֻּלְּהוּ דְּכֻלְּהוּ אִקְרוּן בְּרָזָא

חֲדָא, נְדִיב לֵב. תְּרוּמַת יְיָ', דָּא כֻּרְסְיָיא קַדִּישָׁא. וּבְגִין דְּאָרִימוּ לָהּ לְעֵילָא, וְסַלְּקִין לָהּ לְעֵילָא, אִקְרֵי תְּרוּמַת יְיָ'.

58. And all these Chariots are called "whoever (lit. 'all who') is of a willing heart" (Shemot 35:5). "All," IN THE VERSE "ALL WHO IS OF A WILLING HEART" includes all the other Chariots, WHICH ARE TWELVE. What is heart? It is the secret of the verse "but he that is of a merry heart has a continual feast" (Mishlei 15:15), which refers to the heart of all, and is the holy throne, MALCHUT. Therefore they are called heart. "All who is of a willing heart" is as we stated that the four legions include everything, FOR EACH CONSISTS OF THREE, AND TOGETHER THEY ARE TWELVE, and all are named after the meaning of "all who is of a willing heart." "A heave-offering to Hashem" (Shemot 35:5) is the holy throne. And since they heaved it up and raised itTO ZEIR ANPIN, it is called "an offering to Hashem."

59. וְעַל דָּא, כַּד חָמָא יְחֶזְקֵאל רָזָא דְּחַיּוֹת, דַּהֲווֹ סַלְּקִין, לָא חָמָא מַהוּ דְּסַלְּקִין, בְּגִין דְּאִיהִי סַלְּקָא לְגַבֵּי מַלְכָּא עִלָּאָה בִּגְנִיזוּ בִּטְמִירוּ בִּיקָרָא עִלָּאָה.

59. For that reason, when Ezekiel saw the secret of the living creatures, that were raising MALCHUT TO UNION, he did not see what they were raising, THAT IS-MALCHUT THAT IS RIDING UPON THEM, because she went to the highest King, ZEIR ANPIN, hidden and secretly, within the supreme glory.

60. וְכָל חֲכַם לֵב בָּכֶם, אִלֵּין אִינּוּן שִׁתִּין מְקוֹרִין, דְּאַשְׁקְיָא עָלְמָא, וּמִנְּהוֹן אִתְשְׁקֵי. יָבֹאוּ, אֲמַאי יָבֹאוּ. אֶלָּא דְּיֵיתוּן לְמִנְקַט מֵעִם גִּנְזָא דְּחַיִּין, יָבֹאוּ, וּלְבָתַר וַיַּעֲשׂוּ מַה דְּקוּדְשָׁא בְּרִיךְ הוּא פָּקִיד לוֹן לְאַהֲנָאָה עָלְמָא.

60. "And every wise hearted man among you" (Shemot 35:10) refers to the sixty sources, CHESED, GVURAH, TIFERET, NETZACH, HOD AND YESOD WITHIN ZEIR ANPIN, EACH CONTAINING TEN, that water the world, WHICH IS MALCHUT. From them it is watered. "shall come" (Ibid.) – why is it

written? AND HE ANSWERS: For they shall come to receive from the treasury of life, WHICH IS BINAH. Afterwards they will do what the Holy One, blessed be He, BINAH, commands them – to cause enjoyment to the world.

61. קְחוּ מֵאִתְּכֶם תְּרוּמָה לַיְיָ'. רִבִּי יְהוּדָה פָּתַח, הֲלֹא פָרוֹס לָרָעֵב לַחְמֶךְ וְגוֹ'. ת"ח, זַכָּאָה חוּלָקֵיהּ דְּבַר נָשׁ, כַּד מִסְכְּנָא אִעְרַע לְגַבֵּיהּ. דְּהַהוּא מִסְכְּנָא דּוֹרוֹנָא דְּקוּדְשָׁא בְּרִיךְ הוּא הֲוֵי, דְּשָׁדַר לֵיהּ. מַאן דִּמְקַבֵּל לֵיהּ לְהַהוּא דּוֹרוֹנָא בְּסֵבֶר אַנְפִּין, זַכָּאָה חוּלָקֵיהּ.

61. "Take from among you an offering to Hashem." Rabbi Yehuda opened the discussion with the verse "Is it not to share your bread with the hungry..." (Yeshayah 58:7). Come and see, blessed is a man's portion when a poor man approaches him. Since he is a poor man, he is a gift that the Holy One, blessed be He, sent him. Blessed is the portion of he who welcomes this gift cordially.

62. תָּא חֲזֵי, מַאן דְּחָיֵיס לְמִסְכְּנָא, וְאָתִיב לֵיהּ נַפְשֵׁיהּ, קוּדְשָׁא בְּרִיךְ הוּא סָלִיק עֲלֵיהּ, כְּאִילּוּ הוּא בָּרָא לְנַפְשֵׁיהּ. וְעַ"ד אַבְרָהָם דַּהֲוָה חָיֵיס לְכָל בְּנֵי עָלְמָא, סָלִיק עֲלֵיהּ קוּדְשָׁא בְּרִיךְ הוּא, כְּאִילּוּ הוּא בָּרָא לוֹן, דִּכְתִּיב וְאֶת הַנֶּפֶשׁ אֲשֶׁר עָשׂוּ בְחָרָן.

62. Come and see, whoever pities the poor man and refreshes him, the Holy One, blessed be He, honors him as if he created him. This is why Abraham, who pitied all the inhabitants of the world, the Holy One, blessed be He, treated him as if he created them. Such is the meaning of the verse "and all the souls that they had acquired in Charan" (Beresheet 12:5).

63. וְאע"ג דְּהָא אוֹקִימְנָא הֲלֹא פָרוֹס, מַאי פָרוֹס, לְמִפְרַס לֵיהּ מִפָּה בְּנַהֲמָא וּמְזוֹנָא לְמֵיכַל. ד"א הֲלֹא פָרוֹס, כד"א פָּרֵיס פְּרִיסַת וְגוֹ'. דְּבָעֵי לְמִפְרַס פְּרִיסִין דְּנַהֲמָא קַמֵּיהּ, בְּגִין דְּלָא לְכַסֵּיף. וְיִפְרוֹס קַמֵּיהּ בְּעֵינָא טָבָא. לַחְמֶךָ, לֶחֶם לָא כְּתִיב, אֶלָּא לַחְמֶךָ. הַהוּא דִּילָךְ מִמָּמוֹנָךְ, וְלָא דִּגְזֵילוּ, וְלָא דַעֲשָׁק, וְלָא דִּגְנֵבָה. דְּאִי הָכִי, לָאו זְכוּתָא הוּא, אֶלָּא

וַוי לֵיהּ, דְּאָתֵי לְאַדְכְּרָא חוֹבוֹי. כְּגַוְונָא דָּא קְחוּ מֵאִתְּכֶם תְּרוּמָה, לְאַרְמָא מִמָּה דִלְכוֹן, וְלָא מֵעֹשֶׁק, וְלָא מִגֶּזֶל, וְלָא מִגְּנֵבָה, וְהָא אוּקְמוּהָ.

63. Although we talked about THE VERSE "Is it not to share (Heb. *paros*)" (Yeshayah 58:7), yet what does it mean? It means to spread over a tablecloth bread and food to eat. There is another interpretation for this verse. The word "paros" also means "to break," and so pieces of bread should be broken before him, that he would not feel ashamed. And one should break it before him generously. The word "your bread" (Ibid.) is used and not just "bread," for "your bread" TEACHES US THAT THE BREAD SHOULD BE yours, from your own money and not by theft, oppression or robbery. Otherwise, it is no merit; on the contrary, woe to him, when his sin is brought up. Similarly "Take from among you an offering" means to take and give from your own, not from theft, plunder or robbery, as was already explained.

64. רִבִּי חִיָּיא וְרִבִּי יִצְחָק וְרִבִּי יוֹסֵי, הֲווֹ אַזְלֵי בְּאָרְחָא, עַד דַּהֲווֹ אַזְלֵי, פָּגַע בְּהוּ רִבִּי אַבָּא. אָמַר רִבִּי חִיָּיא, וַדַּאי שְׁכִינְתָּא בַּהֲדָן. כַּד מָטָא לְגַבַּיְיהוּ, אָמַר רִבִּי אַבָּא, כְּתִיב, מִן הַיּוֹם אֲשֶׁר הוֹצֵאתִי אֶת עַמִּי אֶת יִשְׂרָאֵל מִמִּצְרַיִם לֹא בָחַרְתִּי בְעִיר מִכֹּל שִׁבְטֵי יִשְׂרָאֵל וָאֶבְחַר בְּדָוִד וְגוֹ' לִבְנוֹת בַּיִת לִהְיוֹת שְׁמִי שָׁם. הַאי קְרָא, לָאו רֵישֵׁיהּ סֵיפֵיהּ, וְלָאו סֵיפֵיהּ רֵישֵׁיהּ, דִּכְתִיב לֹא בָחַרְתִּי בְעִיר, וָאֶבְחַר בְּדָוִד, מַאי הַאי עִם הַאי. וָאֶבְחַר בִּירוּשָׁלַם מִבָּעֵי לֵיהּ.

64. Rabbi Chiya, Rabbi Yitzchak and Rabbi Yosi were walking on the way. While they were walking, they were met by Rabbi Aba. Rabbi Chiya said: assuredly the Shechinah is with us. When he reached them, Rabbi Aba said, it is written: "Since the day that I brought forth My people Yisrael out of Egypt, I chose no city out of all the tribes of Yisrael to build a house...that My name might be there, but I chose David..." (I Melachim, 8:16). There is a contradiction between the beginning and end of this verse, for it is written: "I chose no city...I chose David." (Ibid.) They do not agree with each other, for it should have been said 'I chose Jerusalem.'

65. אֶלָּא כַּד קוּדְשָׁא בְּרִיךְ הוּא אִית רְעוּתָא קַמֵּיהּ לְמִבְנֵי קַרְתָּא,

אִסְתָּכַּל בְּקַדְמֵיתָא, בְּהַהוּא רֵישָׁא דְּנָהִיג עַמָּא דְקַרְתָּא, וּלְבָתַר בְּנֵי קַרְתָּא, וְאַיְיתֵי לְעַמָּא בֵּיהּ. הה"ד לֹא בָחַרְתִּי בְעִיר, עַד דְּאִסְתַּכַּלְנָא בְּדָוִד, לְמֶהֱוֵי רַעְיָא עַל יִשְׂרָאֵל. בְּגִין דְּמָתָא וְכָל בְּנֵי מָתָא, כֻּלְּהוּ קַיְימִין בְּרַעְיָא דְּנָהִיג לְעַמָּא, אִי רַעְיָא אִיהוּ טָבָא, טַב לֵיהּ, טַב לְמָתָא, טַב לְעַמָּא. וְאִי רַעְיָא אִיהוּ בִּישָׁא, וַוי לֵיהּ, וַוי לְמָתָא וַוי לְעַמָּא. וְהַשְׁתָּא אִסְתָּכַּל קוּדְשָׁא בְּרִיךְ הוּא בְּעָלְמָא, וְסָלִיק בִּרְעוּתֵיהּ לְמִבְנֵי לֵיהּ, וְאוֹקִים בְּרֵישָׁא לְדָוִד, הה"ד וָאֶבְחַר בְּדָוִד עַבְדִּי.

65. But when it pleases the Holy One, blessed be He, to build a city, He looks first at the leader who heads the people of the city, and then builds the city and brings the people thither. This is to say, "I chose no city," until I saw that David will be a good shepherd for Yisrael. For the city and its citizens all depend on the shepherd, the leader of the city. If the shepherd is good, then it is well for him, well for the city, well for the people, but if the shepherd is bad, woe to him, woe to the city, woe to the people. And now the Holy One, blessed be He, looked at the world and it occurred to Him to build it, He first raised David. This was said in, "And I chose David My servant."

66. מִלְתָא חַדְתָּא שְׁמַעְנָא. פָּתַח וְאָמַר, אַשְׁרֵי שֶׁאֵל יַעֲקֹב בְּעֶזְרוֹ שִׂבְרוֹ עַל יְיָ' אֱלֹהָיו. וְכִי אֶל יַעֲקֹב, וְלָא אֶל אַבְרָהָם, וְלָא אֶל יִצְחָק, אֶלָּא אֶל יַעֲקֹב. בְּגִין דְּיַעֲקֹב לָא אִתְרְחִיץ בַּאֲבוֹהִי, וְלָא בְּאִמֵּיהּ, כַּד עָרַק קַמֵּי אֲחוּי, וְאָזַל יְחִידָאי, בְּלָא מָמוֹנָא, כד"א כִּי בְמַקְלִי עָבַרְתִּי אֶת הַיַּרְדֵּן הַזֶּה, וְאִיהוּ אִתְרְחִיץ בֵּיהּ בְּקוּדְשָׁא בְּרִיךְ הוּא, דִּכְתִיב אִם יִהְיֶה אֱלֹהִים עִמָּדִי וּשְׁמָרַנִי וְגוֹ'. וְכֹלָּא שָׁאִיל מִקַּמֵּיהּ דְּקוּדְשָׁא בְּרִיךְ הוּא, וְיָהַב לֵיהּ.

66. I heard a new idea. He opened the discussion and said, "Happy is he who has the El of Jacob for his help, whose hope is in Hashem his Elohim" (Tehilim 146:5). HE ASKS: Why say "El of Jacob" and not "El of Abraham" or "El of Isaac," AND ANSWERS: Because Jacob did not put his trust in his father, nor in his mother, when he fled his brother, and walked alone without money, as was written: "for with my staff I passed over this Jordan"

(Beresheet 32:11). And he put his trust in the Holy One, blessed be He, as is written: "If Elohim will be with me, and will keep me..." (Beresheet 28:20), and everything he asked from the Holy One, blessed be He, was given him.

67. שִׁבְרוֹ עַל יְיָ' אֱלֹהָיו. שִׁבְרוֹ, וְלָא אָמַר תִּקְוָתוֹ, וְלָא בִּטְחוֹנוֹ, אֶלָּא שִׁבְרוֹ. אַל תִּקְרֵי שִׂבְרוֹ, אֶלָּא שִׁבְרוֹ. דְּנִיחָא לְהוּ לְצַדִּיקַיָּיא, לְתַּבְרָא גַּרְמַיְיהוּ, וּלְאִתְבְּרָא תְּבִירוּ עַל תְּבִירוּ, וְכֹלָּא עַל יְיָ' אֱלֹהָיו. כד"א, כִּי עָלֶיךָ הוֹרַגְנוּ כָל הַיּוֹם. כִּי עָלֶיךָ נָשָׂאנוּ חֶרְפָּה.

67. "Whose hope (Heb. *sivro*) is in Hashem his Elohim" (Tehilim 146:5). HE ASKS: IT IS WRITTEN, his hope, not his Faith nor his trust, AND ANSWERS: Do not pronounce it "sivro" with the letter Sin but "shivro" with the letter Shin, which implies breaking. For the righteous are content to break themselves, and to be broken to pieces, and all for the sake of Hashem his Elohim. As much was written: "But for Your sake are we killed all the day long" (Tehilim 44:23), and "Because for Your sake we have borne insult" (Tehilim 69:8).

68. כְּגַוְונָא דְּיַעֲקֹב, דִּכְתִּיב וַיַּרְא יַעֲקֹב כִּי יֶשׁ שֶׁבֶר בְּמִצְרָיִם, דְּהָא תְּבִירוּ דְּגָלוּתָא, חָמָא דַּהֲוָה לֵיהּ בְּמִצְרָיִם, וְשַׁוֵּי תּוּקְפֵּיהּ בְּקוּדְשָׁא בְּרִיךְ הוּא. וּבְנוֹי דְּיַעֲקֹב סָבְלוּ תְּבִירוּ דְּגָלוּתָא, וְלָא אִשְׁתָּנוּ מִגּוֹ רָזָא דִּמְהֵימְנוּתָא דְּאֲבָהַתְהוֹ, וּשְׁמָא דְּקוּדְשָׁא בְּרִיךְ הוּא הֲוָה בְּגָלוּתָא רְגִילָא בְּפוּמַיְיהוּ.

68. The same happened to Jacob, as is written: "Now when Jacob saw that there was corn (Heb. *shever*, also: 'trouble') in Egypt" (Beresheet 42:1). For Jacob saw the calamity of exile awaiting him in Egypt and put his trust in the Holy One, blessed be He. And the children of Jacob also suffered the trouble of exile, yet they did not waver from the Faith of their fathers, and the name of the Holy One, blessed be He, was constantly on their lips.

69. וְע"ד כְּתִיב בְּמֹשֶׁה, וְאָמְרוּ לִי' מַה' שְׁמוֹ' מַה'. בְּגִין דַּהֲווֹ יַדְעֵי לֵיהּ, וְלָא אַנְשׁוּ לֵיהּ לְעָלְמִין, וְסָבְלוּ תְּבִירוּ דְּגָלוּתָא עַל קוּדְשָׁא בְּרִיךְ הוּא, וּבְגִין כַּךְ זָכֵי לְפוּרְקָנִין וּלְנִסִּין וּלְאַתְוָון סַגִּיאִין.

69. That is why it is written about Moses, "And they shall say to me, what is His name?" (Shemot 3:13), FOR THE LAST LETTERS OF THE WORDS OF THE VERSE FORM YUD HEI VAV HEI, A NAME THAT WAS CONSTANTLY ON THEIR LIPS. Since they have known it, they never forgot it, and suffered the trouble of exile for the sake of the Holy One, blessed be He. Therefore they merited many miracles and signs.

סֹ. וְאַתּוּן קַדִּישִׁין עֶלְיוֹנִין, דְּסָבְלִין תְּבִירוּ דְּגוּפָא מֵאֲתָר לְאֲתָר עַל קוּדְשָׁא בְּרִיךְ הוּא, עאכ״ו דְּזַכָּאִין אַתּוּן לְמֶעְבַּד לְכוּ נִסִּין וּפוּרְקָנִין, וְתִזְכּוּן לְחַיֵּי עָלְמָא דְּאָתֵי. אָזְלוּ כֻּלְּהוּ כַּחֲדָא.

70. And you, lofty saints, who suffer the breaking of the body in wandering from place to place for the sake of the Holy One, blessed be He, you are doubly worthy of miracles and redemption, and deserve life in the World to Come. They walked together.

סא. פָּתַח וְאָמַר קְחוּ מֵאִתְּכֶם תְּרוּמָה לַיְיָ' כֹּל נְדִיב לִבּוֹ יְבִיאֶהָ וְגוֹ'. תָּא חֲזֵי, בְּשַׁעֲתָא דְּבַר נָשׁ שַׁוֵּי רְעוּתֵיהּ, לְגַבֵּי פוּלְחָנָא דְּמָארֵיהּ, הַהוּא רְעוּתָא סָלִיק בְּקַדְמֵיתָא עַל לִבָּא, דְּאִיהוּ קְיוּמָא וִיסוֹדָא דְּכָל גּוּפָא. לְבָתַר סָלִיק הַהוּא רְעוּתָא טָבָא, עַל כָּל שַׁיְיפֵי גוּפָא. וּרְעוּתָא דְּכָל שַׁיְיפֵי גוּפָא, וּרְעוּתָא דְּלִבָּא, מִתְחַבְּרָאן כַּחֲדָא, וְאִינּוּן מַשְׁכִין עֲלַיְיהוּ זִיהֲרָא דִּשְׁכִינְתָּא לְדַיְירָא עִמְּהוֹן, וְהַהוּא בַּר נָשׁ אִיהוּ חוּלָקָא דְּקוּדְשָׁא בְּרִיךְ הוּא הֲוֵי, הה״ד קְחוּ מֵאִתְּכֶם תְּרוּמָה. מֵאִתְּכֶם הֲוָה אַמְשְׁכוּתָא, לְקַבְּלָא עֲלַיְיכוּ הַהִיא תְּרוּמָה, לְמֶהֱוֵי חוּלָקָא לַיְיָ'.

71. He opened and said "Take from among you an offering to Hashem: whoever is of a willing heart, let him bring it..." (Shemot 35:5). Come and see, when a man wills himself to worship his Master, the will first reaches the heart, which is the basis and foundation of the entire body. Then that goodwill is diffused in all the members of the body; and the will of the members of the body and the will of the heart combine, and draw to themselves the splendor of the Shechinah to rest on them. Such a man becomes the portion of the Holy One, blessed be He. This is implied in "Take from among you an offering," that is, drawing to receive upon you

that offering, WHICH IS THE SHECHINAH, so that THIS MAN would be a portion to Hashem.

72. וְאִי תֵּימָא דְּלָאו בִּרְשׁוּתֵיהּ דְּב"נ קַיְּימָא מִלָּה. ת"ח, מַה כְּתִיב כָּל נָדִיב לִבּוֹ יְבִיאֶהָ אֶת תְּרוּמַת יְיָ'. כָּל נְדִיב לִבּוֹ וַדַּאי, מַאן דְּיִתְרְעֵי לְבֵיהּ, יַמְשִׁיךְ לָהּ לִשְׁכִינְתָּא לְגַבֵּיהּ. הה"ד יְבִיאֶהָ, אע"ג דְּאִיהִי בְּאִסְתַּלְּקוּתָא לְעֵילָא, יְבִיאֶהָ מֵאֲתַר עִלָּאָה, לְאַמְשָׁכָא לְדַיְּירָא עִמֵּיהּ.

72. And if you say that this is beyond man's power, come and see what is written: "whoever is of a willing heart, let him bring it (her), an offering of Hashem" (Ibid.). "Whoever is of a willing heart," assuredly refers to he whose heart is willing to draw the Shechinah to himself. This is the meaning of "bring her," for though She is highly elevated, he will "bring her," draw Her to reside with him!

73. וְכַד תֵּיתֵי לְאַשְׁרָאָה עִמֵּיהּ, כַּמָּה בִּרְכָּאן וְכַמָּה עָתְרֵי תֵּיתֵי עִמֵּהּ. הה"ד זָהָב וָכֶסֶף וּנְחֹשֶׁת. לָא יֶחְסַר לֵיהּ כָּל עָתְרָא דְּעָלְמָא. דָּא לִשְׁאָר בְּנֵי עָלְמָא. אֲבָל אַתּוּן קַדִּישִׁין עֶלְיוֹנִין, קְחוּ מֵאִתְּכֶם תְּרוּמָה לַיְיָ'. אָמַר רִבִּי חִיָּיא, מַאן דְּשָׁרֵי לְאַרָמָא, הוּא יָרִים.

73. And when She comes to reside with him, how many blessings and how much wealth does She bring with Her, that is, "gold, and silver, and brass (Shemot 35:5)." He would not need any of the wealth of the world, which is for other people. But you, exalted saints, "Take from among you an offering to Hashem," MEANING THAT THEY WILL GIVE NEW INTERPRETATIONS OF THE TORAH TO RAISE THE SHECHINAH. Rabbi Chiya said, whoever started to raise Her, let him continue.

6. In the works of Creation, He set conditions for everything

A Synopsis

Rabbi Aba says that when God created the world He foresaw events and created conditions for everything. When He created the fish he stipulated that a certain fish in the future would swallow Jonah. When He created the heavens He stipulated that they would raise Elijah by a storm of wind. When He created the firmament to divide water from water He stipulated that the waters would divide between defilement and purity so that Yisrael might purify in them. When He divided the land from the sea He stipulated that it would let Yisrael pass on dry land but drown the Egyptians. Also He stipulated that the dry land would open its mouth and swallow Korach and all his community. When He created the sun and moon He stipulated that the sun would stand still in the days of Joshua, and that the stars would fight Sisera. When He created the fish of the sea and the birds of the sky He stipulated that the ravens would feed Elijah and a fish would swallow Jonah and vomit him out again. When He created man He stipulated that a widow woman would descend from him and sustain Elijah. So He saw all these things on the six days of Creation.

74. פָּתַח רִבִּי אַבָּא וְאָמַר, וַיֹּאמֶר יְיָ' לַדָּג וְגוֹ', וְכִי בְּאָן אֲתָר אָמַר לֵיהּ. אֶלָּא בְּשַׁעֲתָא דְּבָרָא קוּדְשָׁא בְּרִיךְ הוּא עָלְמָא בְּעוֹבָדָא דִּבְרֵאשִׁית, בְּיוֹמָא חֲמִישָׁאָה בָּרָא נוּנֵי יַמָּא. כְּדֵין פָּקִיד וְאָמַר, דִּיהֵא זַמִּין חַד נוּנָא לְמִבְלַע לְיוֹנָה, וִיהֵא בִּמְעוֹי תְּלָתָא יוֹמִין וּתְלַת לֵילָוָון, וּלְבָתַר דְּיִרְמֵי לֵיהּ לְבַר.

74. Rabbi Aba opened the discussion and said "and Hashem spoke to the fish" (Yonah 2:11). HE ASKS: And where did He speak to the fish? AND ANSWERS: When the Holy One blessed be He, created the world, He created on the fifth day the fish of the sea. Then He commanded and said that in the future there will be a fish that would swallow Jonah, keep him in its bowels for three days and three nights and than vomit him out.

75. וְלָא דָא בִּלְחוֹדוֹי, אֶלָּא כָּל מַה דְּעָבַד קוּדְשָׁא בְּרִיךְ הוּא בְּעוֹבָדָא דִּבְרֵאשִׁית, בְּכֹלָּא אַתְנֵי עִמֵּיהּ. בְּיוֹמָא קַדְמָאָה בָּרָא שְׁמַיָּא, אַתְנֵי עִמְּהוֹן דְּיִסַּלִּיק לְאֵלִיָּהוּ הַשָּׁמַיְמָה בְּגוֹ סְעָרָה, וְכֵן הֲוָה, דִּכְתִיב וַיַּעַל

אֵלִיָּהוּ בַּסְּעָרָה הַשָּׁמָיִם. בְּהַהוּא יוֹמָא בָּרָא נְהוֹרָא, וְאַתְנֵי עֲמֵיהּ דְּיַחְשִׁיךְ לְשִׁמְשָׁא בְּמִצְרַיִם תְּלָתָא יוֹמִין, דִּכְתִיב וַיְהִי חֹשֶׁךְ אֲפֵלָה בְּכָל אֶרֶץ מִצְרַיִם שְׁלֹשֶׁת יָמִים.

75. And not only that, but to everything that the Holy One blessed be He, created at the time of the Creation, He added certain stipulations. On the first day He created the heavens and stipulated that they would raise Elijah up by a storm of wind. And so it happened, as written: "and Elijah went up by a storm of wind into heaven" (II Melachim 2:12). On that day He created the light, and stipulated that the sun will darken in Egypt for three days, as is written: "and there was a thick darkness in all the land of Egypt three days" (Shemot 10:22).

76. בְּיוֹמָא תִּנְיָינָא בָּרָא רְקִיעָא, דְּיֶהֱא מַפְרִישׁ בֵּין מַיָּא לְמַיָּא, כִּדְכְתִיב וַיֹּאמֶר אֱלֹהִים יְהִי רָקִיעַ בְּתוֹךְ הַמַּיִם וַיְהִי מַבְדִּיל בֵּין מַיִם לָמָיִם. וְאַתְנֵי עִמְּהוֹן קוּדְשָׁא בְּרִיךְ הוּא, דְּמַיָּא יְהוֹן מַפְרִישִׁין לְיִשְׂרָאֵל בֵּין טוּמְאָה לְטָהֲרָה, לְאִתְדַּכְּאָה בְּהוּ, וְכַךְ הֲוָה.

76. On the second day He created the firmament to divide water from water. It was written: "And Elohim said, Let there be a firmament in the midst of the waters, and let it divide water from water" (Beresheet 1:6). The Holy One, blessed be He, stipulated that the water will divide between defilement and purity so that Yisrael might be purified by them. And so it was.

77. בְּיוֹמָא תְּלִיתָאָה אַפִּיק אַרְעָא מִגּוֹ מַיָּא, וְאַכְנִישׁ לְמַיָּא, וַעֲבַד מֵהַהוּא כְּנִישׁוּ דְּאִתְכְּנָשׁוּ לְאֲתַר חַד, יַמָּא. וְאַתְנֵי בְּיַמָּא לְמֶעְבַּר לְיִשְׂרָאֵל בְּגַוֵּיהּ בְּיַבֶּשְׁתָּא, וּלְמִטְבַּע לְמִצְרָאֵי, וְכַךְ הֲוָה, דִּכְתִיב וַיָּשָׁב הַיָּם לִפְנוֹת בֹּקֶר לְאֵיתָנוֹ. אַל תִּקְרֵי לְאֵיתָנוֹ, אֶלָּא לְתְנָאוֹ, לְמַה דְּאַתְנֵי עֲמֵיהּ קוּדְשָׁא בְּרִיךְ הוּא, בְּעוֹבָדָא דִּבְרֵאשִׁית. תּוּ אַתְנֵי בְּאַרְעָא, דְּתִפְתַּח יָת פּוּמָהָא בְּמַחְלְקוּתָא דְּקֹרַח, וְתִבְלַע לְקֹרַח וּלְכָל כְּנִישְׁתֵּיהּ, וְכַךְ הֲוָה, דִּכְתִיב וַתִּפְתַּח הָאָרֶץ אֶת פִּיהָ וַתִּבְלַע אוֹתָם וְאֶת קֹרַח.

77. On the third day He brought out earth out of the water, and collected the water into one place, to wit, the sea. He stipulated with the sea that it would

let Yisrael pass in it on dry land, and drown the Egyptians. And so it was, as is written: "and the sea returned to its strength (Heb. *le'eitano*)" (Shemot 14:27). The word "le'eitano" by transposition of letters becomes "litna'o" (lit. 'to its condition'), viz. to what the Holy One blessed be He, stipulated with it at the time of the Creation. He also stipulated that the dry land would open its mouth at the time of the rebellion of Korah and swallow Korah and his entire community. And so it was, as is written: "and the earth opened her mouth, and swallowed them up, and...Korah" (Bemidbar 16:32).

78. בְּיוֹמָא רְבִיעָאָה, בָּרָא שִׁמְשָׁא וְסִיהֲרָא, דִּכְתִּיב יְהִי מְאֹרֹת בִּרְקִיעַ הַשָּׁמַיִם, וְאַתְנֵי עִם שִׁמְשָׁא, לְמֶהֱוֵי קָאִים בְּפַלְגּוּ שְׁמַיָּא בְּיוֹמֵי דִיהוֹשֻׁעַ, דִּכְתִּיב וַיַּעֲמוֹד הַשֶּׁמֶשׁ בַּחֲצִי הַשָּׁמַיִם. אַתְנֵי בְּכֹכְבַיָּא לְמֶעְבַּד קְרָבָא בְּסִיסְרָא, דִּכְתִּיב הַכֹּכָבִים מִמְּסִלּוֹתָם נִלְחֲמוּ עִם סִיסְרָא.

78. On the fourth day He created the sun and moon, as is written: "let there be lights in the firmaments of heaven" (Beresheet 1:14), and stipulated that with the sun, that it will stand on the zenith in the days of Joshua, as is written: "so the sun stood still in the middle of the sky" (Hoshea 10:13). He stipulated with the stars that they would fight Sisra, as is written: "the stars in their courses fought against Sisra" (Shoftim 5:20).

79. בְּיוֹמָא חֲמִישָׁאָה בָּרָא נוּנֵי יַמָּא, וְעוֹפֵי דִשְׁמַיָּא, אַתְנֵי בְּעוֹפֵי לְמֵיזָן עוֹרְבִים לְאֵלִיָּהוּ, בְּזִמְנָא דְּעָצַר לִשְׁמַיָּא, דִּכְתִּיב וְאֶת הָעוֹרְבִים צִוִּיתִי לְכַלְכֶּלְךָ שָׁם. צִוִּיתִי דַּיְיקָא. וְאַתְנֵי בְּנוּנֵי יַמָּא לְאִזְדַּמְּנָא נוּנָא חַד, לְמִבְלַע לֵיהּ לְיוֹנָה, וּלְאַשְׁדָּאָה לֵיהּ לְבַר.

79. On the fifth day, He created the fish of the sea and the birds in the sky. He stipulated with the birds that the ravens would feed Elijah as is written: "and I have commanded the ravens to feed you there" (I Melachim 17:4); "commanded" precisely, AT THE WORKS OF CREATION. Also He stipulated with the fish that one fish would come and swallow Jonah, and then vomit him out.

80. בְּיוֹמָא שְׁתִיתָאָה בָּרָא לְאָדָם, וְאַתְנֵי עִמֵּיהּ, דְּתִפּוֹק מִנֵּיהּ אִתְּתָא, דְּתֵיזוּן לְאֵלִיָּהוּ, דִּכְתִּיב הִנֵּה צִוִּיתִי שָׁם אִשָּׁה אַלְמָנָה לְכַלְכְּלֶךָ. הִנֵּה

צַוֵּיתִי, מִיּוֹמָא דְּאִתְבְּרֵי עָלְמָא. וְכֵן בְּכָל עוֹבָדָא וְעוֹבָדָא דְּאִתְחַדֵּשׁ בְּעָלְמָא, קוּדְשָׁא בְּרִיךְ הוּא פָּקִיד הַהוּא עוֹבָדָא מִיּוֹמָא דְּאִתְבְּרֵי עָלְמָא. אוּף הָכָא, וַיֹּאמֶר יְיָ' לַדָּג. וַיֹּאמֶר, מִשִּׁית יוֹמִין דִּבְרֵאשִׁית קָאֲמַר לֵיהּ.

80. On the sixth day He created Adam, and stipulated with him that a certain woman would descend from him and sustain Elijah, as is written: "behold, I have commanded a widow woman there to sustain you" (I Melachim 17:9). I have commanded, namely, at the time of the Creation of the World. In the same manner, "Hashem spoke to the fish," spoke on the six days of Creation.

7. Jonah descended into the ship

A Synopsis

In this section Rabbi Aba draws an extended parallel between the story of Jonah who went down into the ship, and the soul of man that descends into this world to dwell in the body of man. The soul is called Jonah (deceived) because after it enters the body it is deceived by the world. Because man in this world is a sinner, God rouses a mighty tempest, that is his prosecution. The soul must use his good inclination and repent of his offenses. The tempest that is the prosecution asks the king to sentence the prisoners; the counselors come forth to defend and accuse, and the prosecution asks for judgment. If the man is not found innocent those who pleaded his cause can not bring him back into this world, and the tempest grows stronger. Then three appointed messengers descend upon him: one to write down his merits and misdeeds, one to do the reckoning of the days, and one who was with him still in his mother's womb. The prosecution does not subside until the man is taken to the cemetery. If he is righteous they proclaim him homage, but if he is wicked they proclaim woe to him. Rabbi Aba says that the grave is the fish that swallowed Jonah. He describes what happens as the body decays and the man is judged and the Nefesh and the body are chastised. When the Nefesh ascends after thirty days the body rots until God rises to resurrect the dead. At that time the angel of death will depart from the world, God will destroy death forever, and there will be no more tears. Some of those in the cemetery will resurrect and some will not. Yisrael will be the first to awaken. Rabbi Aba then lists the seven ordeals that await man when he dies, and says that when King David looked at all these judgments waiting for man he hastened to bless the Holy Name while there was still time.

81. הָכָא אִית לָן סְמֶךְ עָלְמָא, עַל עוֹבָדִין דִּבְנֵי נָשָׁא בְּהַאי עָלְמָא. יוֹנָה דְּנָחַת לַסְּפִינָה, דָּא אִיהִי נִשְׁמָתָא דְּבַר נָשׁ, דְּנַחְתָּא לְהַאי עָלְמָא לְמֶהֱוֵי בְּגוּפָא דְּב״נ. אֲמַאי אִתְקְרֵי יוֹנָה. בְּגִין דְּכֵיוָן דְּאִשְׁתְּתָּפַת בְּגוּפָא, כְּדֵין אִיהִי יוֹנָה בְּהַאי עָלְמָא. כְּמָה דְּאִתְּמַר, וְלָא תוֹנוּ אִישׁ אֶת עֲמִיתוֹ. וּכְדֵין בַּר נָשׁ אָזִיל בְּהַאי עָלְמָא, כַּסְּפִינָה בְּגוֹ יַמָּא רַבָּא, דַּחֲשִׁיבַת לְאִתְּבְּרָא, כד״א וְהָאֳנִיָּה חִשְּׁבָה לְהִשָּׁבֵר.

81. At all events, we find support here, BECAUSE A VERSE ALWAYS RETAINS ITS LITTERAL MEANING, concerning people's actions in this world. The story of Jonah, who went down into the ship, is analogous to the human

soul, that descends into this world to dwell in a human body. Why is it called Jonah (deceived)? Because after it joins the body, it is deceived in this world, THAT IS, BY THE BODY, WHICH DEFRAUDS IT, as was said "You shall not therefore defraud (Heb. *tonu*) one another" (Vayikra. 25:17). And then a man walks about this world like a ship in a great ocean about to break, as written: "and the ship seemed likely to be wrecked" (Yonah 1:4).

82. וּבַר נָשׁ כַּד אִיהוּ בְּהַאי עָלְמָא חַטֵּי, וְחָשִׁיב דְּעָרַק מִקַּמֵּי מָארֵיהּ. וְלָא אַשְׁגַּח בְּהַהוּא עָלְמָא. וּכְדֵין אַטִּיל קוּדְשָׁא בְּרִיךְ הוּא רוּחַ סְעָרָה תַּקִּיפָא. דָּא אִיהִי גְּזֵרַת דִּינָא, דְּקַיְימָא תָּדִיר קַמֵּי קוּדְשָׁא בְּרִיךְ הוּא. וּבַעְאַת דִּינָא דְּבַר נָשׁ מִקַּמֵּיהּ, וְדָא אִיהוּ דְּקָא מָטֵי לַסְּפִינָה, וְאַדְכַּר חוֹבוֹי דְּבַר נָשׁ לְאִתְפְּסָא לֵיהּ.

82. And when man in this world is a sinner and thinks he has fled from his Master, because HIS MASTER does not pay attention to this world, the Holy One, blessed be He, rouses a windstorm, which is the prosecution that always stands before Him and demands to punish that man. And this WINDSTORM came to the ship, and mentioned the sins of the man it wishes to take.

83. כֵּיוָן דְּאִתְפַּס בַּר נָשׁ עַל יְדָא דְּהַהִיא סְעָרָה בְּבֵי מַרְעֵיהּ, מַה כְּתִיב וְיוֹנָה יָרַד אֶל יַרְכְּתֵי הַסְּפִינָה וַיִּשְׁכַּב וַיֵּרָדַם. אע"ג דְּבַר נָשׁ בְּבֵי מַרְעֵיהּ, נִשְׁמְתָא לָא אִתְעָרַת לְאָתָבָא קַמֵּי מָארֵיהּ, לְמִפְרַק חוֹבוֹי. מַה כְּתִיב, וַיִּקְרַב אֵלָיו רַב הַחוֹבֵל. מַאן רַב הַחוֹבֵל. דָּא יֵצֶר טוֹב, דְּאִיהוּ מַנְהִיג כֹּלָּא. וַיֹּאמֶר לוֹ מַה לְךָ נִרְדָּם קוּם קְרָא אֶל אֱלֹהֶיךָ וְגוֹ'. לָאו שַׁעְתָא הוּא לְמִדְמַךְ, דְּהָא סַלְּקִין לָךְ לְדִינָא, עַל כָּל מַה דְּעַבְדַת בְּהַאי עָלְמָא, תּוּב מֵחוֹבָךְ.

83. And since man is seized by that windstorm, he lies in his sickbed, as is written "but Jonah was gone down into the recesses of the ship; and he lay down and was fast asleep" (Yonah 1:5). Though man is lying down sick, the soul does not waken to repent before its Master to redeem his sins. It is written: "so the shipmaster came to him" (Ibid. 6); who is the shipmaster? the Good Inclination that guides everyone? "And said to him, What do you

mean, O sleeper? arise, call upon your Elohim..." (Ibid.). This is not the time to sleep, because you are being brought to judgment for all you have done in this world. Repent your offenses.

84. אִסְתָּכַּל בְּמִלִּין אִלֵּין, וְתוּב לְמָארָךְ. מָה מְלַאכְתֶּךָ דְּאַתְּ עֲסַקְתְּ בָּהּ בְּהַאי עָלְמָא, וְאוֹדֵי עֲלָהּ קַמֵּי מָארָךְ. וּמֵאַיִן תָּבֹא, אִסְתָּכַּל מֵאַיִן בָּאת, מִטִפָּה סְרוּחָה, וְלָא תִּתְגָּאֵי קַמֵּיהּ. מָה אַרְצֶךָ, אִסְתָּכַּל דְּהָא מֵאַרְעָא אִתְבְּרִיאַת, וּלְאַרְעָא תֵּיתוּב. וְאֵי מִזֶּה עַם אָתָּה, אִסְתָּכַּל אִי אִית לָךְ זְכוּ דַּאֲבָהָן, דְּיָגִין עֲלָךְ.

84. Consider these things and repent before your master. "What is your occupation?" with which you have been occupied in this world, confess it before your Master. "And where do you come from?" consider whence you came: "a putrid drop," and you shall not be arrogant before Him. "What is your country?" see that you were created from earth, and to earth you shall return. "And of what people are you?" look for ancestral merits to protect you.

85. כֵּיוָן דְּסַלְקִין לֵיהּ לְדִינָא, בְּבֵי דִּינָא דִּלְעֵילָּא, הַהִיא סְעָרָה, דְּאִיהִי גְּזֵרַת דִּינָא, דְּסָעִיר עָלֵיהּ דְּבַר נָשׁ, תַּבְעַת מִן מַלְכָּא לְמֵידָן אִינּוּן תְּפִיסִין דְּמַלְכָּא, וְכֻלְּהוּ אַתְיָין חַד חַד קָמֵּיהּ. בֵּיהּ שַׁעֲתָא אִתְקְרִיבוּ בֵּי דִּינָא. אִית מִנְּהוֹן דְּפַתְחֵי בִּזְכוּת, וְאִית מִנְּהוֹן דְּפַתְחֵי בְּחוֹבָה. וּגְזֵרַת דִּינָא תַּבְעַת דִּינָא.

85. Once he is brought up to the supernal court, the windstorm, which is the Prosecution that storms against him, demands from the King to sentence the King's prisoners, and they all approach HIM one by one. At that time the court opens. Some defend him, and others accuse him. And the Prosecution asks for punishment.

86. וְאֵי הַהוּא ב"נ לָא זָכֵי בְּדִינָא, מַה כְּתִיב. וַיַּחְתְּרוּ הָאֲנָשִׁים לְהָשִׁיב אֶל הַיַּבָּשָׁה וְלֹא יָכֹלוּ. מִשְׁתַּדְּלִין אִינּוּן דְּאוֹרוּ זְכוּתֵיהּ לְאָתָבָא לֵיהּ לְהַאי עָלְמָא, וְלָא יָכֹלוּ. מַאי טַעֲמָא. כִּי הַיָּם הוֹלֵךְ וְסוֹעֵר עֲלֵיהֶם, גְּזֵרָה דְּדִינָא, אָזִיל וְסָעִיר בְּחוֹבוֹי דְּב"נ, וְאִתְגַּבַּר עֲלַיְיהוּ.

86. And if that man was not found innocent, it is written, "the men rowed hard to bring the ship back to land; but they could not" (Ibid. 13). Those who pleaded his cause try to bring him back into this world but cannot. Why is that? "for the sea grew more and more tempestuous against them," the Prosecution storms with his sins and grows stronger because of them.

87. כְּדֵין נַחְתִּין עֲלֵיהּ תְּלַת שְׁלִיחָן מְמָנָן, חַד, דִּכְתִיב כָּל זַכְוָון, וְכָל חוֹבִין, דְּעָבַד בַּר נָשׁ בְּהַאי עָלְמָא. וְחַד דְּעָבִיד חוּשְׁבָּן יוֹמוֹי. וְחַד דַּהֲוָה אָזִיל עִמֵּיהּ, כַּד הֲוָה בִּמְעֵי אִמֵּיהּ. וְהָא אוּקִימְנָא דִּגְזֵרַת דִּינָא לָא שָׁכִיךְ, עַד הַהוּא זִמְנָא דִּכְתִיב, וַיִּשְׂאוּ אֶת יוֹנָה. וַיִּשָּׂאוּ: כַּד נַטְלֵי לֵיהּ מִבֵּיתֵיהּ, לְבֵי קִבְרֵי.

87. Then three appointed messengers descend upon him; the one writes down all his merits and misdeeds. THESE ARE LIKE TWO COLUMNS, RIGHT AND LEFT; THE MERITS ARE ON THE RIGHT AND THE MISDEEDS ON THE LEFT. Another does the reckoning of the days, LIKE THE RECONCILING CENTRAL COLUMN THAT WEIGHS THEM. Yet another was with him in his mother's womb. THIS IS THE SECRET OF MALCHUT, THE SECRET OF THE VERSE "WHEN HIS CANDLE SHONE UPON MY HEAD" (IYOV 29:2), THAT REFERS TO THE MONTHS OF PREGNANCY. And we explained that the Prosecution does not subside until, as is written: "they took up Jonah" (Yonah 1:15). "They took up" THAT IS, when they take him from his home to the cemetery.

88. כְּדֵין מַכְרְזֵי עֲלוֹי. אִי אִיהוּ זַכָּאָה, מַכְרְזֵי עֲלֵיהּ וְאַמְרֵי, הָבוּ יְקָר לְדִיוּקְנָא דְּמַלְכָּא, יָבֹא שָׁלוֹם יָנוּחוּ עַל מִשְׁכְּבוֹתָם הֹלֵךְ נְכֹחוֹ. מנ"ל. דִּכְתִיב וְהָלַךְ לְפָנֶיךָ צִדְקֶךָ כְּבוֹד יְיָ' יַאַסְפֶךָ. וְאִי חַיָּיבָא אִיהִי, מַכְרִיזֵי עֲלֵיהּ וְאַמְרוּ, וַוי לֵיהּ לִפְלַנְיָא. טַב לֵיהּ דְּלָא יִתְבְּרֵי. כְּדֵין מַה כְּתִיב, וַיִּטִלֻהוּ אֶל הַיָּם וַיַּעֲמֹד הַיָּם מִזַּעְפּוֹ. כַּד עָאלִין לֵיהּ לְבֵי קִבְרֵי דְּאִיהוּ אֲתָר דְּדִינָא. כְּדֵין גְּזֵרַת דִּינָא דַּהֲוָה סָעִיר, שָׁכִיךְ מִזַּעְפֵּיהּ. וְנוּנָא דְּבָלַע לֵיהּ, דָּא אִיהוּ קַבְרָא.

88. Then proclamation is made concerning him. If he is righteous, it is thus proclaimed: render homage to the image of the King. "He that walks in his

uprightness shall enter in peace to them that rest in their graves" (Yeshayah 57:2). Whence do we know this? from the words: "and your righteousness shall go before you, the glory of Hashem shall be your rearguard" (Yeshayah 58:8). But if he be wicked, it is thus proclaimed: woe to that man, for it would be better for him not to be born. And then it is written: "and cast him into the sea; and the sea ceased from its raging," meaning that they put him in his grave, which is the place of punishment. Then the Prosecution, which was storming AND SOUGHT PUNISHMENT, is NOW soothed from its wrath, SINCE WHAT IT WANTED CAME TO PASS. And the fish that swallowed him is his grave.

‏89. מַה כְּתִיב, וַיְהִי יוֹנָה בִּמְעֵי הַדָּג. דָּא אִיהוּ בֶּטֶן שְׁאוֹל. מְנָלָן. דִּכְתִיב מִבֶּטֶן שְׁאוֹל שִׁוַּעְתִּי. וְאִיהוּ בִּמְעֵי דְנוּנָא הֲוָה, וְקָאֲרֵי לֵיהּ בֶּטֶן שְׁאוֹל, שְׁלֹשָׁה יָמִים וּשְׁלֹשָׁה לֵילוֹת, אִלֵּין תְּלַת יוֹמִין, דְּבַר נָשׁ בְּקִבְרָא, וְאִתְבְּקָעוּ מֵעוֹי.

89. It is written: "And Jonah was in the belly of the fish" (Yonah 2:1). The belly of the fish is the belly of Sheol. We know that from the verse "out of the belly of Sheol I cried" (Ibid. 3) for Jonah was in the belly of the fish and called it the belly of Sheol. "three days and three nights" (Ibid. 1) resembles the three days that man is in the grave before his bowels split open.

‏90. לְבָתַר תְּלָתָא יוֹמִין, הַהוּא טִנוּפָא אִתְהַפַּךְ עַל אַנְפּוֹי, וְאוֹמֵר לוֹ טוֹל מַה דִּיְהָבַת בִּי. אֲכַלְתְּ וְשָׁתִית כָּל יוֹמָא, וְלָא יָהַבְתְּ לְמִסְכְּנֵי, וְכָל יוֹמָךְ הֲווֹ כְּחַגִּין וּכְמוֹעֲדִין, וּמִסְכְּנֵי הֲווֹ כַּפְנִין, דְּלָא אָכְלוּ בַּהֲדָךְ, טוֹל מַה דִּיְהָבַת בִּי. הֲדָא הוּא דִּכְתִיב וְזֵרִיתִי פֶרֶשׁ עַל פְּנֵיכֶם וְגוֹ', וְהָא אוֹקִימְנָא.

90. After three days, the filth IN HIS BOWELS is spilt on his face, and says to him: take what you put in me. You ate and drank all day and gave not to the poor; all your days were like feasts and holidays, while the poor were hungry because they did not eat with you. Take what you put in me. This is implied by the verse "and I will spread dung upon your faces" (Malachi 2:3). We already explained that.

91. לְבָתַר דָּא, מִתְּלָתָא יוֹמִין וּלְהָלְאָה, כְּדֵין אִתְדָּן בַּר נָשׁ מֵעֵינוֹי, מִידוֹי, וּמֵרַגְלוֹי, וְאוּקְמוּהָ עַד תְּלָתִין יוֹמִין. כָּל אִינּוּן תְּלָתִין יוֹמִין, אִתְדָנוּ נַפְשָׁא וְגוּפָא כַּחֲדָא. וּבְגִינֵי כַּךְ אִשְׁתְּכַח נִשְׁמָתָא לְתַתָּא בְּאַרְעָא, דְּלָא סַלְּקָת לְאַתְרָהּ. כְּאִתְּתָא דְּיָתְבַת לְבַר, כָּל יוֹמֵי מְסַאֲבוּתָא. לְבָתַר, נִשְׁמָתָא סַלְּקָא, וְגוּפָא אִתְבְּלֵי בְּאַרְעָא. עַד הַהוּא זִמְנָא דְּיִתְּעַר קוּדְשָׁא בְּרִיךְ הוּא לְמֵיתַיָּיא.

91. After three days, man is judged for his eyes FOR LOOKING AT WHAT IS FORBIDDEN, for his hands FOR DOING WHAT IS FORBIDDEN, for his legs FOR GOING TO COMMIT SIN. And it was said that IT LASTS up to thirty days. During those thirty days the Nefesh and body are chastised together. For that reason the soul remains down on earth and does not rise to its place, like a woman who sits apart all the days of her impurity. Afterwards the Soul ascends and the body rots in the dust, until the time comes, when the Holy One, blessed be He, awakens to RESURRECT the dead.

92. וּזְמִינָא קָלָא חֲדָא לְאִתְּעָרָא בְּבֵי קִבְרֵי, וְיֵימָא, הָקִיצוּ וְרַנְּנוּ שׁוֹכְנֵי עָפָר כִּי טַל אוֹרוֹת טַלֶּךָ וָאָרֶץ רְפָאִים תַּפִּיל. אֵימָתַי יְהֵא דָא. בְּזִמְנָא דְּיִתְעֲבַר מַלְאָךְ הַמָּוֶת מֵעָלְמָא, דִּכְתִּיב בִּלַּע הַמָּוֶת לָנֶצַח וְגוֹ'. כֵּיוָן דְּבִלַּע הַמָּוֶת לָנֶצַח, לְבָתַר, וּמָחָה יְיָ' אֱלֹהִים דִּמְעָה מֵעַל כָּל פָּנִים וְחֶרְפַּת עַמּוֹ יָסִיר מֵעַל כָּל הָאָרֶץ. כְּדֵין כְּתִיב, וַיֹּאמֶר יְיָ' לַדָּג וַיָּקֵא אֶת יוֹנָה אֶל הַיַּבָּשָׁה.

92. And a voice will rise in the cemetery and say, "Awake and sing, you that dwell in dust, for your dew is as the dew on herbs, and the earth shall cast out the shades of the dead" (Yeshayah 26:19). When will that be? when the Angel of Death departs from the world, as said in the verse "He will destroy death for ever..." (Yeshayah 25:8) Since He will destroy death for ever then "and Hashem Elohim will wipe away tears from off all faces, and the insult of His people shall He take away from off all the earth" (Ibid.). Then it is written: "And Hashem spoke to the fish, and it vomited out Jonah upon the dry land" (Yonah. 2:11).

93. כֵּיוָן דְּאִתְּעַר הַהוּא קָלָא בֵּינֵי קִבְרֵי, כְּדֵין כָּל קַבְרַיָּיא יָקִיאוּ לְאִינּוּן

מַתְיָיא דִּבְהוֹן לְבַר. הֲדָא הוּא דִכְתִיב וָאָרֶץ רְפָאִים תַּפִּיל. מַאי תַּפִּיל. דְּיָקִיא לוֹן
לְבַר. רְפָאִים, מַהוּ רְפָאִים. דְּקַבִּילוּ. אַסְוָותָא כְּמִלְּקַדְמִין, וְאִתְסִיאוּ
גַרְמִין בְּגַרְמִין. וְאִלֵּין אִקְרוּן רְפָאִים.

93. Since that voice has risen from among the graves, all the graves vomited out the dead that were in them. This is the meaning of "and cast out the shades of the dead (Heb. *refaim* also 'healed')." What is meant by "cast out"? IT MEANS THAT it will vomit them out. What are refaim? They are those who received healing, WERE HEALED AND BECAME like they were before their, and the bones were healed together. These are called refaim.

94. וְאִי תֵּימָא, הָא כְּתִיב רְפָאִים בַּל יָקוּמוּ. אֶלָּא וַדַּאי כָּל עָלְמָא
יִתְּסוּן גַרְמִין בְּבֵי קִבְרֵי, אֲבָל מִנְהוֹן יְקוּמוּן, וּמִנְהוֹן לָא יְקוּמוּן. וְעַל
דָּא כְּתִיב רְפָאִים בַּל יָקוּמוּ. זַכָּאָה חוּלָקֵהוֹן דְּיִשְׂרָאֵל, דִּכְתִיב בְּהוּ
נְבֵלָתִי יְקוּמוּן. וּבְהַאי נוּנָא, אַשְׁכַּחְנָא מִלִּין לְאַסְוָותָא, דְּכָל עָלְמָא.

94. And if you ask why it is written: "the shades of the dead shall not rise" (Yeshayah 26:14), HE ANSWERS: surely all the inhabitants of the world will heal by themselves in the cemetery, but some will resurrect and some will not, NAMELY, THOSE WHO DID NOT BELIEVE IN RESURRECTION. Concerning this the verse says, "the shades of the dead shall not rise." Happy is the portion of Yisrael, about whom is written: "my dead body shall arise" (Ibid. 19). And in that fish, WHO SWALLOWED JONAH, I found IMPLIED words that may heal the whole world, TO WIT, RESURRECT THE DEAD, AS WAS EXPLAINED.

95. הַאי נוּנָא כֵּיוָן דְּבָלַע לְיוֹנָה מִית. וּבֵיהּ הֲוָה יוֹנָה תְּלָתָא יוֹמִין,
לְבָתַר אִתְקַיַּים כְּמִלְּקַדְמִין, וְאָקֵי לְיוֹנָה לְבַר, וְהָא אוּקְמוּהָ, דִּכְתִיב
וַיִּתְפַּלֵּל יוֹנָה אֶל יְיָ׳ אֱלֹהָיו מִמְּעֵי הַדָּגָה. כְּתִיב הָכָא הַדָּגָה, וּכְתִיב
הָתָם וְהַדָּגָה אֲשֶׁר בַּיְאוֹר מֵתָה, וְהָא אוּקְמוּהָ. כְּגַוְונָא דָא, זְמִינַת
אַרְעָא דְּיִשְׂרָאֵל לְאִתְעֲרָא בְּקַדְמֵיתָא, וּלְבָתַר וָאָרֶץ רְפָאִים תַּפִּיל.

95. This fish, when he swallowed Jonah, died, and Jonah was in it for three days. Afterwards it was restored to life and vomited Jonah out. And we

talked about the verse, "Then Jonah prayed to Hashem his Elohim out of the fish's belly" (Yonah 1:2) The word 'fish' also appears in the verse "And the fish that is in the river died" (Shemot 7:21); ALSO HERE THE FISH DIED. And we explained that in a similar way, the land of Yisrael will be the first to awaken, MEANING THAT IT WILL BE PURIFIED OF ALL THE WICKED PEOPLE; AND LIKE THE FISH OF JONAH IT WILL RESURRECT. Afterwards, "and the earth shall cast out the shades of the dead" (Yeshayah 26:19), BY LATER VOMITTING THE DEAD AND THEY WILL REVIVE, AS WAS MENTIONED.

96. וְהָא אוֹקִימְנָא, דְּשִׁבְעָה דִּינִין יַחְלְפוּן עֲלֵיהּ דְּבַר נָשׁ, כַּד נָפִיק מֵהַאי עָלְמָא. חַד, הַהוּא דִּינָא עִלָּאָה, כַּד נָפִיק רוּחָא מִן גּוּפָא. ב', כַּד עוֹבָדוֹי וּמִלּוֹי אַזְלִין קַמֵּיהּ וּמַכְרְזֵי עֲלוֹי. ג', כַּד עָיֵיל לְקִבְרָא. ד', דִּינָא דְּקִבְרָא. ה', דִּינָא דְּתוֹלַעְתָּא. ו', דִּינָא דְּגֵיהִנָּם. ז', דִּינָא דְּרוּחָא דְּאָזְלָא וְשָׁאטַת בְּעָלְמָא, וְלָא אַשְׁכַּחַת אֲתָר נַיְיחָא, עַד דְּיִשְׁתְּלִים עוֹבָדוֹי. בְּגִ"ד, בָּעֵי בַּר נָשׁ לְאִסְתַּכְּלָא תָּדִיר בְּעוֹבָדוֹי, וְיֵתוּב קַמֵּי מָרֵיהּ.

96. As we said, seven ordeals await man, when he departs AND PASSES AWAY from the world. The first is the high ordeal when the Spirit leaves the body, WHICH IS THE ORDEAL OF DEATH. The second is when his deeds and words march before him and proclaim his worth. The third one is when he enters the grave. The fourth one is the ordeal of the grave. The fifth one is the ordeal of the worms THAT EAT HIM. The sixth is the ordeal of Gehenom. The seventh is the ordeal of the Spirit, that roams about the world without a resting place, until his deeds are perfected AND PURIFIED. For that reason a man should always examine his deeds, and repent before his Master.

97. וְכַד אִסְתָּכַּל דָּוִד מַלְכָּא בְּדִינִין אִלֵּין דְּבַר נָשׁ, אַקְדִּים וְאָמַר בָּרְכִי נַפְשִׁי אֶת יְיָ', עַד לָא תִפּוּק מִן עָלְמָא, בְּעוֹד דְּאַנְתְּ אִשְׁתְּכַחַת עִם גּוּפָא. וְכָל קָרְבַי אֶת שֵׁם קָדְשׁוֹ, אִינּוּן שַׁיְיפָא גוּפָא, דְּמִשְׁתַּתְּפֵי כַּחֲדָא בְּרוּחָא. הַשְׁתָּא דְּתִשְׁתַּבְּחוּן עִמָּהּ, אַקְדִּימוּ לְבָרְכָא שְׁמָא קַדִּישָׁא, עַד לָא יִמְטֵי זִמְנָא דְּלָא תֵּיכְלוּן לְבָרְכָא, וּלְאַתָבָא בְּתִיּוּבְתָּא, וְעַל דָּא אָמַר בָּרְכִי נַפְשִׁי אֶת יְיָ' הַלְלוּיָהּ. אָתוּ אִינּוּן חַבְרַיָּיא וְנָשְׁקוּ רֵישֵׁיהּ.

97. When King David looked at those punishments waiting for man, he hastened to say, "bless Hashem, my soul" (Tehilim 104:35), before you leave this world, while you are still with the body. "And all that is within me bless His Holy Name" (Ibid.), the members of the body that are companions to the Ruach. Now that you are with THE NEFESH, hasten to bless the Holy Name, before the time arrives when you will no longer be able to bless and repent. Therefore he repeated "Bless Hashem, my soul, Haleluyah" (Ibid.). The friends came and kissed his head.

8. The book above and the book below

A Synopsis

Rabbi Chiya explains in this section the written and hidden Torah above and the Oral Torah below. He says that when God created the world, He did so solely for Yisrael so they would come and receive the Torah; by the Torah the world was created and upon the Torah it perseveres. The man who studies Torah is saved from the ordeal of this world, the ordeal of the angel of death who cannot have power over him, and the ordeal of Gehenom. The Torah above, that is Chochmah, is referred to as a book of remembrance, the sign of the holy covenant. The Torah below, that is Malchut, is referred to as a book of reckoning. The supernal wisdom is hidden in the palace of the Torah above, but wisdom is revealed in the lower Torah when one deciphers it.

98. רִבִּי חִיָּיא פָּתַח וְאָמַר, קְחוּ מֵאִתְּכֶם תְּרוּמָה לַייָ׳. ת״ח קוּדְשָׁא בְּרִיךְ הוּא כַּד בָּרָא עָלְמָא, לָא בָּרָא לֵיהּ, אֶלָּא בְּגִין דְּיֵיתוּן יִשְׂרָאֵל, וִיקַבְּלוּן אוֹרַיְיתָא. בְּאוֹרַיְיתָא אִתְבְּרֵי עָלְמָא, וְעַל אוֹרַיְיתָא קַיְּימָא. הֲדָא הוּא דִכְתִיב, אִם לֹא בְרִיתִי יוֹמָם וָלָיְלָה חֻקּוֹת שָׁמַיִם וָאָרֶץ לֹא שָׂמְתִּי. אוֹרַיְיתָא אִיהִי אַרְכָּא דְּחַיֵּי בְּהַאי עָלְמָא, וְאַרְכָּא דְּחַיֵּי בְּעָלְמָא דְּאָתֵי.

98. Rabbi Chiya opened the discussion with the text, "Take from among you an offering to Hashem" (Shemot 35:5). Come and see, when the Holy One, blessed be He, created the world, He did so solely so that Yisrael would come and receive the Torah. By the Torah the world was created and upon the Torah it perseveres. This is the meaning of "Were it not for my covenant that endures day and night, the ordinances of heaven and earth I would not have appointed" (Yirmeyah 33:25). The Torah is length of life in this world and length of life in the World to Come.

99. וְכָל מַאן דְּאִשְׁתַּדַּל בְּאוֹרַיְיתָא, כְּאִלּוּ אִשְׁתַּדַּל בְּהֵיכָלֵיהּ דְּקוּדְשָׁא בְּרִיךְ הוּא. דְּהֵיכְלָא עִלָּאָה דְּקוּדְשָׁא בְּרִיךְ הוּא, אוֹרַיְיתָא אִיהִי וְכַד בַּר נָשׁ עָסִיק בְּאוֹרַיְיתָא, קוּדְשָׁא בְּרִיךְ הוּא קָאִים תַּמָּן, וְאָצִית לְקָלֵיהּ, כְּמָה דִכְתִיב, וַיַּקְשֵׁב יְיָ׳ וַיִּשְׁמָע וְגוֹ׳. וְאִשְׁתְּזִיב ב״נ מִתְּלַת דִּינִין: מִדִּינָא דְּהַאי עָלְמָא. וּמִדִּינָא דְּמַלְאָךְ הַמָּוֶת, דְּלָא יָכִיל לְשַׁלְּטָאָה

עֲלֵיהּ. וּמִדִּינָא דְגֵיהִנָּם.

99. And whoever studies the Torah, it is as if he labors in the palace of the Holy One, blessed be He; for the palace of the Holy One, blessed be He, WHICH IS MALCHUT, is the Torah. NAMELY, THE ORAL LAW IS THE SECRET OF MALCHUT. And when a man studies the Torah, the Holy One, blessed be He, stands and listens to his voice, as says "and Hashem hearkened, and heard it..." (Malachi 3:16). This saves man from three ordeals; the ordeal of this world, and the ordeal of the Angel of Death who cannot have power over him, and the ordeal of Gehenom.

100. וַיִּכָּתֵב סֵפֶר זִכָּרוֹן. מַאי אִיהוּ. אֶלָּא אִית סֵפֶר לְעֵילָּא, וְאִית סֵפֶר לְתַתָּא. זִכָּרוֹן אֶת קַיְימָא קַדִּישָׁא, דְּנָטִיל וְכָנִישׁ לְגַבֵּיהּ, כָּל חַיִּין דִּלְעֵילָּא. סֵפֶר זִכָּרוֹן תְּרֵין דַּרְגִּין דְּאִינּוּן חַד, וְרָזָא דָא שֵׁם הֲוָיָ"ה שֵׁם חַד. יְהֹוָ"ה חַד. וְכֹלָּא מִלָּה חֲדָא.

100. "And a book of remembrance was written" (Ibid.): HE ASKS: What is a book of remembrance? AND REPLIES THAT there is a book above, WHICH IS CHOCHMAH, and a book below, WHICH IS MALCHUT. 'Remembrance' is the sign of the holy covenant, WHICH IS YESOD, that receives and gathers to itself all life from above, ALL THE SUPERNAL MOCHIN. The book of remembrance consists of two grades that are one. This is the secret of the name of Yud Hei Vav Hei: name is one, NAMELY MALCHUT, Yud Hei Vav Hei is one, NAMELY ZEIR ANPIN. Together they are one word; IN THE SAME MANNER THE BOOK OF REMEMBRANCE IS ONE WORD, THOUGH IT INCLUDES TWO GRADES: MALCHUT AND YESOD.

101. בְּגִין דְּאִית שֵׁם, וְאִית שֵׁם, שֵׁם לְעֵילָּא, דְּאִיהוּ אִתְרְשִׁים מִמַּה דְּלָא יְדִיעַ, וְלָא אִתְרְמִיז בִּידִיעָה כְּלַל. וְדָא אִקְרֵי נְקוּדָה עִלָּאָה. שֵׁם לְתַתָּא, דְּאִקְרֵי שֵׁם, מִקְצֵה הַשָּׁמַיִם וְעַד קְצֵה הַשָּׁמַיִם, בְּגִין דִּקְצֵה הַשָּׁמַיִם אִקְרֵי זִכָּרוֹן. וְהַאי שֵׁם, אִיהוּ נְקוּדָה דִּלְתַתָּא, דְּאִיהוּ שֵׁם מֵהַהוּא זִכָּרוֹן, דְּאִיהוּ קְצֵה הַשָּׁמַיִם, דְּנָטִיל כָּל חַיִּין דִּלְעֵילָּא. וְדָא אִיהוּ קְצֵה הַשָּׁמַיִם דִּלְתַתָּא. וְשֵׁם דִּילֵיהּ אִיהִי נְקוּדָה דִּלְתַתָּא. נְקוּדָה דָא, אִיהוּ סֵפֶר דְּקַיְימָא בְּחוּשְׁבָּנָא, וְדָא הוּא וּלְחוֹשְׁבֵי שְׁמוֹ. סֵפֶר

-218-

דְּקָאֲמַרָן, וְשֵׁם, חַד מִלָּה הוּא, בְּכָל סִטְרִין.

101. For there is a name and there is a name. HE EXPLAINS, THERE IS a name above, that is implied by that which is unknown and not alluded to by any information, NAMELY BY KETER, called the upper point, WHICH IS CHOCHMAH. AND THERE IS a name below, MALCHUT, that is called 'name', AS WRITTEN: "and from the one end of the heaven to the other" (Devarim 4:32). The end of the heaven, THAT IS YESOD, is called remembrance, and that name is the point below YESOD, NAMELY MALCHUT, which is the name of that remembrance, which is the end of the heaven that draws all supernal vitality, THAT IS THE MOCHIN. And there is the lower end of heaven, YESOD, whose name is the lower point, MALCHUT. This point is a book that can be numbered, MEANING THE MOCHIN OF COUNTING, which is the meaning of: "for those who...took heed of (lit. 'counted') His name," AS WRITTEN: "AND A BOOK OF REMEMBRANCE WAS WRITTEN BEFORE HIM FOR THOSE WHO FEARED HASHEM, AND TOOK HEED OF HIS NAME" (MALACHI 3:16). AND THIS BOOK OF REMEMBRANCE IS FOR THOSE WHO "COUNTED HIS NAME," WHICH BESTOWS MOCHIN OF RECKONING AND COUNTING. The book that we mentioned and the name are the same in all respects, NAMELY MALCHUT.

102. נְקוּדָה דָא בְּגִין דְּקַיְּימָא בְּאֶמְצָעִיתָא, אִיהִי עִלָּאָה עַל כָּל דְּאִתְאַחֲדָן בָּהּ. שִׁית סִטְרִין, אִתְאַחֲדָן בְּסֵפֶר עִלָּאָה, וְאִיהוּ עִלָּאָה עֲלַיְיהוּ. שִׁית סִטְרִין אִתְאַחֲדָן בְּסֵפֶר תַּתָּאָה, וְאִיהוּ עִלָּאָה עֲלַיְיהוּ. וְעַל דָּא, סֵפֶר עִלָּאָה, סֵפֶר תַּתָּאָה, וְכֹלָּא אִקְרֵי תּוֹרָה.

102. This point is superior to all that were united in it, since it is situated in the center. HE EXPLAINS THAT six ends, YISRAEL-SABA AND TEVUNAH, were united in the upper book, WHICH IS CHOCHMAH, and it is above them. Six ends, THE SIX CHAMBERS OF BRIYAH, were united in the lower book, WHICH IS MALCHUT, which is above them. Therefore there are a higher book and a lower book, and everything is considered Torah.

103. מַה בֵּין הַאי לְהַאי. אֶלָּא, סֵפֶר עִלָּאָה אִיהוּ תּוֹרָה שֶׁבִּכְתָב. בְּגִין דְּאִיהִי סְתִימָא, וְלָא קַיְּימָא אֶלָּא בִּכְתָב, דְּתַמָּן אִיהוּ אֲתָר לְאִתְגַּלְאָה לְתַתָּא. וּמַאן אִיהוּ עָלְמָא דְּאָתֵי. סֵפֶר תַּתָּאָה, דָא תּוֹרָה דְּאִקְרֵי תּוֹרָה

שֶׁבְּעַל פֶּה, וּמַאן אִיהוּ עַל פֶּה, אִלֵּין רְתִיכִין דִּלְתַתָּא, דְּאִיהִי קַיְימָא עֲלַיְיהוּ. וּבְגִין דְּלָאו אִינּוּן בִּכְלָלָא דִּכְתִיבָה דִּלְעֵילָּא, אִקְרוּן עַל פֶּה.

103. HE ASKS: What is THE DIFFERENCE between them, THE HIGHER BOOK AND THE LOWER BOOK, AND ANSWERS: the higher book is the Written Law, WHICH IS SUPERNAL CHOCHMAH, for it is concealed and available only in writing, NAMELY, IT IS WORTHY OF BEING REVEALED. For there is a place there, YISRAEL-SABA AND TEVUNAH, where Chochmah may be revealed down below, IN MALCHUT, and that place is the World to Come, YISRAEL-SABA AND TEVUNAH. The lower book is the Torah which is called the Oral Law; by 'oral' are meant the lower Chariots, THE SEVEN CHAMBERS OF BRIYAH, upon which MALCHUT stands, AS WAS MENTIONED BEFORE, and since they are not part of the supernal writing, they are considered oral. THAT IS, THEY ARE NOT IN THE REALM OF THE HIDDEN AS IS SUPERNAL CHOCHMAH IN YISRAEL-SABA AND TEVUNAH, THAT IS CALLED WRITING, AND HENCE they are called oral, WHICH IS THE REVELATION OF ALL THAT IS CONTAINED IN WRITING.

104. וְתוֹרָה דָּא קַיְימָא עַל פֶּה, בְּגִין דִּכְתִיב וּמִשָּׁם יִפָּרֵד וְהָיָה לְאַרְבָּעָה רָאשִׁים וְתוֹרָה עִלָּאָה, אע"ג דְּאִיהִי קַיְימָא לְעֵילָּא, לָא אִקְרֵי עַל הַכְּתָב, אֶלָּא שֶׁבִּכְתָב, דְּקַיְימָא בִּכְתָב, וְהַהוּא כְּתָב אִתְעָבֵיד הֵיכָלָא לְגַבֵּיה, וְאִיהִי קַיְימָא גּוֹ הַהוּא הֵיכָלָא, וְאִתְטַמְרַת תַּמָּן. וּבְגִין כַּךְ אִקְרֵי תּוֹרָה שֶׁבִּכְתָב, וְלָא עַל כְּתָב.

104. And this Torah is established orally, THAT IS, ON SEVEN CHAMBERS THAT ARE ITS MOUTH, BY WHICH CHOCHMAH MAY BE REVEALED. For it is written: "and from thence it was parted, and branched into four streams" (Beresheet 2:10), TO WIT, FROM THE GARDEN (MALCHUT) DOWNWARD BEGINS THE WORLD OF SEPARATION, THEN THE SEVEN CHAMBERS OF BRIYAH ARE ALREADY IN THE WORLD OF SEPARATION. THEREFORE MALCHUT STANDS ON THEM, NAMELY 'ORAL' (LIT. 'ABOVE THE MOUTH'). And the supernal Torah, WHICH IS SUPERNAL CHOCHMAH, though it too stands upon ITS CHARIOT, YISRAEL-SABA AND TEVUNAH, NEVERTHELESS is not called 'TORAH above writing' but only 'Torah in writ' for it is in the midst of the writing. And that writ, YISRAEL-SABA AND TEVUNAH, becomes a chamber ABOVE THE SUPERNAL CHOCHMAH,

WHICH stands in that chamber, and is hidden there. THAT IS, THE WRITING, THAT IS YISRAEL–SABA AND TEVUNAH, IS ALSO THE WORLD OF ATZILUT LIKE SUPERNAL CHOCHMAH, AND HENCE THE SCRIPT IS CONSIDERED ITS CHAMBER, and it is therefore called (lit.) the Torah in writing and not Torah above the writing.

105. אֲבָל תּוֹרָה דִלְתַתָּא, אִיהִי קַיְימָא עַל רְתִיכָהָא, וְאִקְרֵי עַל פֶּה, דְּקַיְימָא עָלַיְיהוּ. וּבְגִין דְּלָא אִתְחַשִּׁיבַת מִלְגוֹ, מִכְּלָלָא דִכְתִיבָה, לָא אִתְעֲבֵידוּ הֵיכָלָא לְהַאי נְקוּדָה, כְּהַהִיא נְקוּדָה עִלָּאָה. וּבְגִין דְּקַיְימָא עָלַיְיהוּ אִקְרֵי תְּרוּמָה.

105. But the lower Torah, MALCHUT, is situated on its Chariot and is literally called 'on mouth', because it stands upon them. It is not considered the inner part of the writing. THAT IS, CHOCHMAH WITHIN IT DOES NOT DISAPPEAR BECAUSE OF THE CHAMBERS, AS IS THE WRITTEN TORAH, SINCE WRITING INDICATES THE HIDDEN, UNTIL SOMEONE COMES, READS THE WRITING AND EXHIBITS IT, AND CHOCHMAH THEREIN IS REVEALED IN THE CHAMBERS AND IS NO LONGER A MYSTERY. THEREFORE THE SEVEN CHAMBERS did not become a chamber to that point, MALCHUT AS YISRAEL-SABA AND TEVUNAH BECAME A CHAMBER to the higher point, SINCE A CHAMBER MEANS A COVER, AND THESE DO NOT COVER. HOWEVER, BY THEMSELVES THEY ARE ALSO CONSIDERED CHAMBERS. And since MALCHUT stands upon them, she is called a heave-offering.

9. Two out of a hundred

A Synopsis
Here Rabbi Chiya explains the meaning of "heave-offering," that is the tithing of two parts out of one hundred. Each of the ten Sfirot includes ten Sfirot, so this makes one hundred. To lift Malchut, she must be raised with her husband Yesod, so these two Sfirot are called a heave-offering.

106. תּוּ שְׁמַעְנָא מִבּוּצִינָא קַדִּישָׁא. תְּרוּמָה. מַהוּ תְּרוּמָה. כְּמָה דְּאוּקִימְנָא, תְּרֵי מִמֵּאָה. ת"ח, כָּל אִינּוּן דַּרְגִּין קַדִּישִׁין, דִּי בְּרָזָא דִּמְהֵימְנוּתָא, דְּקוּדְשָׁא בְּרִיךְ הוּא אִתְגְּלֵי בְּהוֹן, אִינּוּן עֶשֶׂר דַּרְגִּין, וְאִינּוּן עֶשֶׂר אֲמִירָן, כְּמָה דְּאוּקְמוּהָ. וְאִלֵּין עֶשֶׂר סַלְקִין לַמְּאָה, וְכַד אִצְטְרִיךְ לָן לְהַאי נְקוּדָה תַּתָּאָה לְאַרְמָא לָה, אָסִיר לָן לְנַטְלָא לָה בִּלְחוֹדָהָא. אֶלָּא לָה וּלְבַעְלָהּ. וְאִינּוּן תְּרֵי מֵאִינּוּן מֵאָה דְּקָאמְרָן, בְּגִין דְּלָא אִצְטְרִיךְ לְאַפְרְשָׁא לוֹן כְּלָל, אֶלָּא לְיַחֲדָא לָהּ וּלְבַעְלָהּ. וְעַל דָּא אִתְקְרֵי תְּרוּמָה בִּכְלָלָא חֲדָא.

106. I also heard from the holy luminary: what is heave-offering (Heb. *trumah*)? It is like we explained ABOUT SETTING ASIDE THE CONTRIBUTION TO THE PRIEST, TO WIT, two (Aramaic *tri*) PARTS out of hundred (Aramaic *me'ah*) PARTS. Come and see, all those sacred grades that are part of the Faith, in which the Holy One, blessed be He, is revealed, are ten grades, which are ten sayings, NAMELY, THE TEN SFIROT, like we said. And these ten amount to a hundred, BECAUSE EACH SFIRAH INCLUDES TEN SFIROT. And when we have to lift this lower point, MALCHUT, we must not take her by herself, but with her husband YESOD; and these are two SFIROT, YESOD AND MALCHUT, out of the said hundred. For she must never be separated, but united with her husband. Therefore she is called a heave-offering, an inclusive term, A COMBINATION OF YESOD AND MALCHUT.

10. The intent of prayer

A Synopsis

Rabbi Shimon is speaking about the secret of prayer, that when a man devotes his heart and will to prayer, he amends the supernal amendment. We hear of the parts of the prayer, the benedictions, the sitting and the standing. Then we are told that when the High Holy King, Zeir Anpin, reaches for Malchut and they embrace in a kiss, one may ask for any request. During the last three benedictions a man should wish with all his heart and will that the people on earth will be blessed from those three benedictions of the secret bliss of union. If a man prays properly, he is bundled in the bundle of life in this world and in the. Then God calls him "peace." Later when he passes away from this world his soul goes up and cleaves all the firmaments, he enters in, and thirteen mountains of pure balm are opened before his soul. Rabbi Shimon says this is why a man is happy who puts his heart and will into prayer. Rabbi Yosi says that understanding is superior to wisdom because wisdom is contained in the heart, that is found in Malchut, but a man of understanding exists both above and below, and understands himself and others.

107. וְתָא חֲזֵי, בְּכָל יוֹמָא כָּרוֹזָא קָארֵי, כָּל בְּנֵי עָלְמָא, בְּכוּ קַיְּימָא מִלָּה דָא, וְדָא הוּא קְחוּ מֵאִתְּכֶם תְּרוּמָה לַיְיָ׳. וְאִי תֵּימָא דְּקַשְׁיָא מִלָּה עֲלַיְיכוּ. כֹּל נְדִיב לִבּוֹ יְבִיאֶהָ.

107. Come and see, each day the crier calls to all the people of the world, 'this depends upon you'. This is the meaning of, "Take from among you an offering to Hashem" (Shemot 35:5). And if you find this difficult then "whoever is of a willing heart, let him bring it (her)" (Ibid.)

108. מַהוּ יְבִיאֶהָ. אֶלָּא מֵהָכָא אוֹלִיפְנָא רָזָא לִצְלוֹתָא. דְּבַר נָשׁ דְּדָחִיל לְמָארֵיהּ וּמְכַוֵּין לִבֵּיהּ וּרְעוּתֵיהּ בִּצְלוֹתָא, אַתְקִין תִּקּוּנָא דִּלְעֵילָא, כְּמָה דְּאוּקִימְנָא. בְּקַדְמֵיתָא בְּשִׁירִין וְתוּשְׁבְּחָן, דְּקָאָמְרִין מַלְאָכִין עִלָּאִין לְעֵילָא. וּבְהַהוּא סִדּוּרָא דְּתוּשְׁבְּחָן דְּקָא אָמְרֵי יִשְׂרָאֵל לְתַתָּא, אִיהִי קְשִׁיטַת גַּרְמָהָא, וְאִתְתַּקָּנַת בְּתִקּוּנָהָא. כְּאִתְּתָא דְּאִתְקַשְּׁטַת לְבַעְלָהּ.

108. HE ASKS: What is THE MEANING OF "let him bring her?" AND ANSWERS: here we learn the meaning of prayer. For when a man fears his Maker and devotes his heart and will to prayer, he forms a supernal arrangement, like we said. First by the songs and praises that the high angels say above; and in the series of praises that Yisrael say down below, MALCHUT adorns herself, and arranges herself like a woman adorning herself for her husband.

109. וּבְסִדּוּרָא דִּצְלוֹתָא, בְּהַהוּא תִּקּוּנָא דִּצְלוֹתָא דְּמִיּוּשָׁב, אַתְקִינוּ עוֹלְמְתָהָא וְכָל אִינּוּן דִּילָה. וּמִתְקַשְׁטָן כָּל אִינּוּן בַּהֲדָה, לְבָתַר דְּאִתְתָּקַן כֹּלָּא וְאִתְסְדָרוּ, כַּד מָטוּ לֶאֱמֶת וְיַצִּיב, כְּדֵין כֹּלָּא מִתְתַּקְנָא, אִיהִי וְעוֹלְמְתָהָא, עַד דְּמָטוּ לִגְאַל יִשְׂרָאֵל, כְּדֵין אִצְטְרִיךְ לְמֵיקָם כֹּלָּא עַל קִיוּמַיְיהוּ.

109. In the order of the prayer that is said sitting down, THAT IS, FROM THE BENEDICTION 'WHO FORMS LIGHT' UNTIL THE PRAYER OF AMIDAH, all those maids were prepared, THE SEVEN MAIDS OF MALCHUT, and all her retinue are adorned with her. After all was arranged and prepared, when reaching 'True and certain', then everything is ready, she and her maids, in reaching 'who has redeemed Yisrael'. Then everyone has to stand up.

110. בְּגִין דְּכַד בַּר נָשׁ מָטֵי לֶאֱמֶת וְיַצִּיב, וְכֹלָּא אִתְתָּקַן. עוֹלְמְתָהָא נַטְלֵי לָהּ, וְאִיהִי נְטִילַת גַּרְמָהּ לְגַבֵּי מַלְכָּא עִלָּאָה. כֵּיוָן דְּמָטוּ לִגְאַל יִשְׂרָאֵל, כְּדֵין מַלְכָּא קַדִּישָׁא עִלָּאָה נָטִיל בְּדַרְגּוֹי, וְנָפִיק לְקַבְּלָא לָהּ.

110. By the time a man reaches 'True and certain', everything is already established, the maids conduct MALCHUT, and she bears herself to the high King, ZEIR ANPIN. Once we reach 'who has redeemed Yisrael' the high Holy King travels with His grades, IN THE ORDER OF THE THREE COLUMNS, and comes out to receive her, MALCHUT.

111. וַאֲנָן, מִקַּמֵּי מַלְכָּא עִלָּאָה בָּעֵינָן לְקַיְימָא עַל קִיוּמָנָא, בְּאֵימָתָא בִּרְעָדָה. דְּהָא כְּדֵין אוֹשִׁיט יְמִינֵיהּ לְגַבָּהּ, וּלְבָתַר שְׂמָאלֵיהּ, דְּשַׁוֵּוי לָהּ תְּחוֹת רֵישָׁהּ, וּלְבָתַר אִתְחַבָּקוּ תַּרְוַויְיהוּ כַּחֲדָא בִּנְשִׁיקוּ. וְאִלֵּין אִינּוּן

תְּלַת קַדְמְיָתָא, וּבָעֵי בַּר נָשׁ לְשַׁוְּאָה לִבֵּיהּ וּרְעוּתֵיהּ, וּלְכַוְּונָא בְּכָל הָנֵי תִּקוּנִין וְסִדּוּרִין דִּצְלוֹתָא. פּוּמֵיהּ וְלִבֵּיהּ וּרְעוּתֵיהּ כַּחֲדָא.

111. And we have to stand up before the high Holy King in awe and trembling, for then He reaches His right hand to her, WHICH IS THE BENEDICTION OF 'THE SHIELD OF ABRAHAM' THE SECRET OF THE RIGHT COLUMN. Then He put His left hand under her head, ACCORDING TO THE SECRET OF "HIS LEFT HAND IS UNDER MY HEAD" (SHIR HASHIRIM 2:6), WHICH IS THE BENEDICTION OF 'YOU ARE ETERNALLY MIGHTY', WHICH IS THE LEFT COLUMN. They then embrace together in KISSES, IN THE BENEDICTION OF 'THE HOLY EL', WHICH IS THE CENTRAL COLUMN FOR FROM THERE ON IS THE SECRET OF THE KISS UNTIL THE LAST THREE BENEDICTIONS. These are the first three benedictions OF THE AMIDAH. A man should devote his heart and will, and meditate on all those arrangements and sequences of the prayer, with his mouth, heart and will together.

112. הַשְׁתָּא דְּמַלְכָּא עִלָּאָה וּמַטְרוֹנִיתָא אִינּוּן בְּחִבּוּרָא בְּחֶדְוָה בְּאִינּוּן נְשִׁיקִין. מַאן דְּאִצְטְרִיךְ לְמִשְׁאַל שְׁאֶלְתִּין, יִשְׁאַל. דְּהָא כְּדֵין שַׁעֲתָא דִּרְעוּתָא אִיהוּ. כֵּיוָן דְּשָׁאִיל בַּר נָשׁ שְׁאֶלְתּוֹי מִקַּמֵּי מַלְכָּא וּמַטְרוֹנִיתָא, כְּדֵין יַתְקִין גַּרְמֵיהּ בִּרְעוּתֵיהּ וְלִבֵּיהּ לִתְלָתָא אַחֲרָנִין, לְאִתְעֲרָא חֶדְוָה דִּטְמִירוּ, דְּהָא מֵאִלֵּין תְּלַת אִתְבְּרַכָא בִּדְבֵקוּתָא אַחֲרָא. וְיַתְקִין בַּר נָשׁ גַּרְמֵיהּ לְמֵיפַק מִקַּמַּיְיהוּ, וּלְאַנְחָא לוֹן בְּחֶדְוָה גְּנִיזָא דְּאִלֵּין תְּלַת. וְעַכַּ"ד, דְּיהֵא רְעוּתֵיהּ, דְּיִתְבָּרְכוּן תַּתָּאֵי, מֵאִינּוּן בִּרְכָּאן דְּחֶדְוָה טְמִירָא.

112. Now that the high King and Malchut are blissfully united in those kisses, whoever needs to ask for any request OR PETITIONS, may do so, because it is a time of goodwill. Since a man submits his requests before the King and Queen, NAMELY, IN THE MIDDLE TWELVE BENEDICTIONS, then he should prepare himself, in will and heart, to the last three BENEDICTIONS, to stir the secret bliss, because from these three BENEDICTIONS he is blessed by a different devotion, THE SECRET OF UNISON. And a man should prepare to leave them in this secret bliss in these three BENEDICTIONS, AS WAS EXPOUNDED AT LENGTH. Therefore he should

wish it, that the lower beings be blessed from those three benedictions of the secret bliss.

113. וּכְדֵין אִצְטְרִיךְ לְמִנְפַּל עַל אַנְפּוֹי, וּלְמִמְסַר נַפְשֵׁיה, בְּשַׁעֲתָא דְּאִיהִי נַקְטָא נַפְשִׁין רוּחִין. כְּדֵין אִיהִי שַׁעֲתָא לְמִמְסַר נַפְשֵׁיה בְּגוֹ אִינּוּן נַפְשִׁין דְּאִיהִי נַקְטָא, דְּהָא כְּדֵין צְרוֹרָא דְּחַיֵּי אִיהוּ כַּדְקָא יֵאוֹת.

113. Then he should prostrate himself and offer his Nefesh, at the time when MALCHUT takes hold of the Nefashot and Ruchot. For then is the time to offer one's Nefesh among all those Nefashot she takes, because then the bundle of life, WHICH IS MALCHUT, is as it should be.

114. מִלָּה דָּא שְׁמַעְנָא בְּרָזִין דְּבוּצִינָא קַדִּישָׁא, וְלָא אִתְיְיהִיב לִי רְשׁוּ לְגַלָּאָה, בַּר לְכוּ חֲסִידֵי עֶלְיוֹנִין. דְּאִי בְּהַהִיא שַׁעֲתָא דְּאִיהִי נַקְטָא נַפְשִׁין וְרוּחִין בִּרְעוּ דִּדְבֵיקוּתָא חֲדָא, אִיהוּ יְשַׁוֵּי לִבֵּיה וּרְעוּתֵיה לְדָא, וְיָהִיב נַפְשֵׁיה בִּדְבֵקוּתָא, בְּהַהוּא רְעוּתָא, לְאִכְלְלָא לָה בְּהַהוּא דְּבֵקוּתָא. אִי אִתְקַבְּלַת בְּהַהִיא שַׁעֲתָא בְּהַהוּא רְעוּתָא, דְּאִינּוּן נַפְשִׁין רוּחִין וְנִשְׁמָתִין דְּאִיהִי נַקְטָא. הַאי אִיהוּ בַּר נָשׁ דְּאִתְצְרִיר בִּצְרוֹרָא דְּחַיֵּי בְּהַאי עָלְמָא, וּבְעָלְמָא דְּאָתֵי.

114. This I heard among the secrets of the holy luminary, but I was not given permission to reveal it, except for you, lofty pious ones. If, when MALCHUT takes hold of HUMAN Nefashot and Ruchot, a man, with a single devoted wish, sets his heart and wish to surrender his Nefesh with devotion and wish of incorporating his Nefesh in such devotion; and if THE OFFERING OF HIS NEFESH is then acceptable, when the Nefashot, the Ruchot and the Neshamot that she holds are willing, this man is bundled in the bundle of life in this world and in the World to Come.

115. וְתוּ דְּבָעֵיָא לְאִתְכַּלְּלָא מִכָּל סִטְרִין, מַלְכָּא וּמַטְרוֹנִיתָא, מִלְעֵילָּא וּמִתַּתָּא, וּלְאִתְעַטְּרָא בְּנִשְׁמָתִין בְּכָל סִטְרִין. אִתְעַטְּרַת בְּנִשְׁמָתִין מִלְעֵילָּא, וְאִתְעַטְּרַת בְּנִשְׁמָתִין מִתַּתָּא. וְאִי בַּר נָשׁ יְכַוֵּין לִבֵּיה וּרְעוּתֵיה לְכָל דָּא, וְיִמְסֹר נַפְשֵׁיה מִתַּתָּא בִּדְבֵקוּתָא בִּרְעוּתָא כְּמָה דְּאִתְּמַר. כְּדֵין

קוּדְשָׁא בְּרִיךְ הוּא קָארֵי לֵיה שָׁלוֹם לְתַתָּא, כְּגַוְונָא דְּהַהוּא שָׁלוֹם דִּלְעֵילָא. הַהוּא דְּבָרִיךְ לָה לְמַטְרוֹנִיתָא וְאַכְלִיל לָה וְאַעֲטַר לָה בְּכָל עִטְרִין.

115. Also when the King and the Queen, TIFERET AND MALCHUT, need to be included on all sides, above and below, and be adorned with souls on all sides. She is adorned with souls from above and souls from below, NAMELY, FROM THOSE WHO SURRENDER HER THEIR SOULS. And when a man directs his heart and will to it, and gives her his soul from below, devotedly and willingly, as we said, then the Holy One, blessed be He, names him "peace" below, after that peace of above, WHICH IS YESOD THAT IS CALLED PEACE. That PEACE blesses the Queen and incorporates her and adorns her on all sides.

116. אוּף הָכִי, הַאי בַּר נָשׁ קוּדְשָׁא בְּרִיךְ הוּא קָרֵי לֵיה שָׁלוֹם לְתַתָּא, כד"א וַיִּקְרָא לוֹ יְיָ' שָׁלוֹם. וְכָל יוֹמוֹי הָכִי קָרָאן לֵיה לְעֵילָא, שָׁלוֹם. בְּגִין דְּאַכְלִיל וְאַעֲטַר לְמַטְרוֹנִיתָא לְתַתָּא, כְּגַוְונָא דְּהַהוּא שָׁלוֹם לְעֵילָא.

116. So the Holy One, blessed be He, names that man peace, as is written: "and Hashem called him peace" (Shoftim 6:24). And all his days he is thus called above 'peace', because he comprised and adorned the Queen from below, as did the upper peace, WHICH IS YESOD, AS WAS MENTIONED BEFORE.

117. וְכַד אִסְתַּלָּק הַהוּא בַּר נָשׁ מֵהַאי עָלְמָא, נִשְׁמָתֵיה סַלְקָא וּבַקְעָא בְּכָל אִינוּן רְקִיעִין, וְלֵית מַאן דְּיִמְחֵי בִּידָה. וְקוּדְשָׁא בְּרִיךְ הוּא קָרֵי לָה וְאָמַר יָבֹא שָׁלוֹם. וּשְׁכִינְתָּא אָמְרָה, יָנוּחוּ עַל מִשְׁכְּבוֹתָם וְגוֹ'. וְיִפְתְּחוּן לָה תְּלֵיסַר טוּרֵי דְּאֲפַרְסְמוֹנָא דַּכְיָא, וְלָא יְהֵא מַאן דְּיִמְחֵי בִּידָה. וְע"ד, זַכָּאָה אִיהוּ מַאן דְּיִשַׁוֵּי לִבֵּיה וּרְעוּתֵיה לְדָא. וְעַל דָּא כְּתִיב, כֹּל נְדִיב לִבּוֹ יְבִיאֶהָ אֵת תְּרוּמַת יְיָ' לְגַבֵּי מַלְכָּא עִלָּאָה, כְּמָה דְּאִתְּמַר.

117. And when that man passes away from this world, his soul goes up and cleaves all the firmaments, and no one can stop it. The Holy One, blessed be

-227-

He, calls it and says, "let peace enter" (Yeshayah 57:2) and the Shechinah says "them that rest in their graves" (Ibid.). Thirteen mountains of pure balsam trees are opened before the soul, and none can detain it. Therefore happy is he, who puts his heart and will into it. That is why it is written: "whoever is of a willing heart, let him bring it, an offering of Hashem," to the high King, NAMELY as I said.

118. אָרִים ר׳ אַבָּא קָלֵיהּ, וְאָמַר, וַוי ר׳ שִׁמְעוֹן, אַנְתְּ בַּחַיִּין, וַאֲנָא בָּכֵינָא עֲלָךְ. לָא עֲלָךְ בָּכֵינָא, אֶלָּא בָּכֵינָא עַל חַבְרַיָּיא, וּבְכֵינָא עַל עָלְמָא. רִבִּי שִׁמְעוֹן כְּבוּצִינָא דִשְׁרָגָא, דְּאַדְלִיק לְעֵילָא וְאַדְלִיק לְתַתָּא. וּבִנְהוֹרָא דְּאַדְלִיק לְתַתָּא, נְהִירִין כָּל בְּנֵי עָלְמָא, וַוי לְעָלְמָא, כַּד יִסְתָּלַּק נְהוֹרָא דִלְתַתָּא בִּנְהוֹרָא דִלְעֵילָא. מַאן יַנְהִיר נְהוֹרָא דְאוֹרַיְיתָא לְעָלְמָא. קָם ר׳ אַבָּא וְנָשִׁיק לר׳ חִיָּיא. א״ל מִלִּין אִלֵּין הֲווֹ תְּחוֹת יְדָךְ, וְעַ״ד קוּדְשָׁא בְּרִיךְ הוּא שַׁדְרַנִי עַד הָכָא, לְאִתְחַבְּרָא עִמְּכוֹן זַכָּאָה חוּלָקִי.

118. Rabbi Aba raised his voice and said, Woe, Rabbi Shimon, you are among the living, and I already weep for you. Not for you I weep, but for the friends, for the world I weep; THAT THEY WILL BE ORPHANED WHEN YOU PASS AWAY FROM THE WORLD. Rabbi Shimon is like the light of a candle that burns above and burns below. And with the light that he lit down below shine all the people of the world. Woe to the world when the terrestrial light will pass AND BE ABSORBED IN the celestial light . Who will illuminate the light of Torah for the world? Rabbi Aba stood and kissed Rabbi Chiya. He said to him, those thoughts were with you, therefore the Holy One, blessed be He, sent me here to join you, happy is my portion.

119. רִבִּי יוֹסֵי פָּתַח קְרָא אֲבַתְרֵיהּ וְאָמַר, וְכָל חֲכַם לֵב בָּכֶם יָבֹאוּ וְיַעֲשׂוּ וְגו׳, הַאי קְרָא אוּקְמוּהָ. אֲבָל תָּא חֲזֵי, בְּשַׁעֲתָא דְּאָמַר קוּדְשָׁא בְּרִיךְ הוּא לְמֹשֶׁה, הָבוּ לָכֶם אֲנָשִׁים חֲכָמִים וּנְבוֹנִים, אַשְׁגַּח בְּכָל יִשְׂרָאֵל, וְלָא אַשְׁכַּח נְבוֹנִים, הֲדָא הוּא דִכְתִיב, וָאֶקַּח אֶת רָאשֵׁי שִׁבְטֵיכֶם אֲנָשִׁים חֲכָמִים וִידוּעִים, וְאִלּוּ נְבוֹנִים לָא כְּתִיב. וְאִי תֵּימָא דְּנָבוֹן אִיהוּ דַּרְגָּא עִלָּאָה מֵחָכָם, הָכִי אִיהוּ וַדַּאי.

119. Afterwards, Rabbi Yosi opened the discussion with the following verse "And every wise hearted individual among you shall come and make..." (Shemot 35:5). We already explained this text but come and see, when the Holy One, blessed be He, said to Moses "Take wise men, and understanding" (Devarim 1:13), he searched throughout Yisrael but did not find men of understanding. This is why, "So I took the chief of your tribes, wise men, and known" (Ibid. 15), but 'understanding' is not mentioned. You might say that understanding is in a grade superior to wisdom, AND THAT IS WHY HE DID NOT FIND MEN OF UNDERSTANDING, and this of course is right, THAT UNDERSTANDING IS SUPERIOR TO WISDOM.

120. מַה בֵּין הַאי לְהַאי. חָכָם, הָא אוּקְמוּהָ, דַּאֲפִילוּ תַּלְמִיד הַמַּחְכִּים לְרַבֵּיהּ אִקְרֵי חָכָם. חָכָם, דְּיָדַע לְגַרְמֵיהּ כָּל מַה דְּאִצְטְרִיךְ. נָבוֹן כַּמָּה דַּרְגִּין אִית בֵּיהּ, דְּאִסְתָּכַּל בְּכֹלָּא, וְיָדַע בְּדִילֵיהּ וּבְאַחֲרָנִין. וְסִימָנָךְ, יוֹדֵעַ צַדִּיק נֶפֶשׁ בְּהֶמְתּוֹ. צַדִּיק מוֹשֵׁל יִרְאַת אֱלֹהִים. וְהָכָא חֲכַם לֵב דַּיְיקָא. בַּלֵב חָכָם, וְלָא בְּאַתְרָא אַחֲרָא, בְּגִין דְּקַיְּימָא בַּלֵב, וְנָבוֹן לְעֵילָא וְתַתָּא, אִסְתָּכַּל בְּדִילֵיהּ וּבְאַחֲרָנִין.

120. HE ASKS: What is the difference between them, BETWEEN A WISE MAN AND A MAN OF UNDERSTANDING? AND REPLIES: THAT we explained about a wise man, that even a pupil who imparts wisdom to his rabbi is considered wise. A wise man knows for himself what is ought to be done. A man of understanding has many grades in him, because he examines everything and knows for himself and for others. You may derive this from "A righteous man regards the life of his beast (Heb. behemah)" (Mishlei 12:10) FOR THE RIGHTEOUS, YESOD, IMPARTS TO MALCHUT, THAT IS THE SECRET OF YUD HEI VAV HEI OF THE NUMERICAL VALUE OF 52, WHICH IS THE NUMERICAL VALUE OF BEHEMAH. And also "righteous ruling in the fear of Elohim" (II Shmuel 23:3), AS THE RIGHTEOUS, YESOD, RULES AND FILLS MALCHUT, THAT IS CALLED 'FEAR OF ELOHIM', WITH PLENTY. And here, "wise hearted" is precise, MEANING THAT THE WISE MENTIONED HERE IS OF THE ASPECT IN MALCHUT, THAT IS CALLED WISE HEARTED. Man is wise in his heart, THAT IS MALCHUT and not elsewhere, because wisdom lies in the heart, MALCHUT, AND NOT ELSEWHERE. But a man of understanding exist both above and below, and observes himself and others.

11. The ascension of prayer

A Synopsis

Rabbi Yosi tells us about the external service of deeds that relies on the twelve outer limbs, and the internal service of prayer that relies on the twelve internal organs of the body. A man's prayer is considered a worship of the Ruach, and it has great power above. Rabbi Yosi goes on to tell of the rulers of the day and the rulers of the night, who are all different. Prayer ascends to them; if the man is righteous they kiss the prayer and it ascends even higher. We are told of many guardians, first of the four sides, and then of the guardians of the firmaments. Rabbi Yosi says that on the east the twelve letters of the Holy Name soar and ascend with the prayer. The prayers of those who pray broken-heartedly ascend to the south, while the prayers of those who pray for deliverance from enemies ascend to the north. After the prayers ascend to the four directions they are escorted up and through the firmaments into their gates. As the prayer reaches the seventh firmament it unites Zeir Anpin and Malchut, and the righteous man is blessed. Rabbi Yosi then turns to a discussion of the six precepts of the Torah, and describes their meaning in some detail. He says that these six precepts correspond to Chesed, Gvurah, Tiferet, Netzach, Hod and Yesod. We learn that there are thirteen more precepts that draw the thirteen attributes of mercy; thus the man who puts his heart and will into his prayers to perfect them every day is a happy man. Rabbi Yitzchak reminds us that those who worshipped the golden calf died, and Moses gathered the children of Yisrael together and gave them the laws of Shabbat.

121. פָּתַח וְאָמַר, וַיֹּאמֶר לִי עַבְדִּי אַתָּה וְגוֹ', הָכָא בִּצְלוֹתָא דְּבָעֵי בַּר נָשׁ לְצַלָּאָה קַמֵּיהּ דְּקוּדְשָׁא בְּרִיךְ הוּא, דְּאִיהִי פּוּלְחָנָא חֲדָא רַבָּא וְיַקִּירָא, מֵאִינוּן פּוּלְחָנִין דְּמָארֵיהּ. תָּא חֲזֵי, אִית פּוּלְחָנָא דְּקוּדְשָׁא בְּרִיךְ הוּא, דְּקַיְימָא בְּעוֹבָדָא, דְּאִיהוּ פּוּלְחָנָא דְּקַיְימָא בְּעוֹבָדָא דְגוּפָא, וְאִיהוּ פּוּלְחָנָא. וְאִית פּוּלְחָנָא דְּקוּדְשָׁא בְּרִיךְ הוּא, דְּאִיהוּ פּוּלְחָנָא פְּנִימָאָה יַתִּיר, דְּאִיהוּ עִקְרָא דְּכֹלָּא, קַיְימָא בְּהַהוּא פּוּלְחָנָא פְּנִימָאָה, דְּאִיהוּ עִקְרָא דְּכֹלָּא.

121. He opened with "and said to me, you are My servant..." (Yeshayah 49:3). Here THIS REFERS TO the prayer man should recite before the Holy One, blessed be He, which is a great and precious service among the

worships of his Master. Come and see, some worships to the Holy One, blessed be He, are based on deeds, that is, based on physical activity, NAMELY, PRECEPTS BASED ON ACTION; and that is considered a service. And there is worship of the Holy One, blessed be He, that is a more internal worship, which is the essence of all, it has to do with inner work, which is the essence of all, NAMELY, PRECEPTS THAT CONCERN SPEECH AND INTENTION.

122. בְּגוּפָא אִית תְּרֵיסָר שַׁיְיפִין, דְּקַיְימִין בְּעוֹבָדָא דְּגוּפָא, כְּמָה דְּאוֹקִימְנָא. וְאִינּוּן שַׁיְיפִין דְּגוּפָא, וּפוּלְחָנָא דְּקוּדְשָׁא בְּרִיךְ הוּא, דְּעוֹבָדָא קַיְּימָא בְּהוּ. בְּגִין דְּפוּלְחָנָא דְּקוּדְשָׁא בְּרִיךְ הוּא, בִּתְרֵין סִטְרִין, שַׁיְיפִין דְּגוּפָא לְבַר, וְאִית תְּרֵיסָר שַׁיְיפִין אַחֲרָנִין, פְּנִימָאִין לְגוֹ מִן גּוּפָא. וְאִינּוּן תִּקּוּנִין פְּנִימָאִין לְגוֹ מִן גּוּפָא, לְאִתְתַּקְּנָא בְּהוּ תִּקּוּנָא דְּרוּחָא, דְּאִיהוּ פוּלְחָנָא יַקִּירָא פְּנִימָאָה דְּקוּדְשָׁא בְּרִיךְ הוּא, כְּמָה דְּאוֹקִימְנָא גּוֹ רָזִין פְּנִימָאִין דְּקָאָמַר ר״ש, וְאִינּוּן רָזָא דְּחָכְמְתָא עִלָּאָה, וְאִתְיְדִיעוּ בֵּינֵי חַבְרַיָּא, זַכָּאָה חוּלָקֵהוֹן.

122. In the body there are twelve organs that relate to physical activity, as we said, WHICH ARE TWO ARMS AND TWO LEGS; THREE JOINTS IN EACH, AND THREE TIMES FOUR ARE TWELVE. These are the members of the body, and the worship of the Holy One, blessed be He, THROUGH action related PRECEPTS is based on them. For there are two ways to serve the Holy One, blessed be He: THE FIRST IS by the outer limbs, THE TWELVE JOINTS OF THE ARMS AND LEGS; THE SECOND TALKS OF the twelve internal organs inside the body, THE BRAIN, HEART, LIVER, MOUTH, TONGUE, THE FIVE LOBES OF THE LUNG AND TWO KIDNEYS. They are the internal fixtures inside the body, with which to establish the Ruach, which is the inner and precious worship of the Holy One, blessed be He. THESE PRECEPTS ARE BASED ON SPEECH, SUCH AS PRAYER, BENEDICTION AND THANKSGIVING, as we explained from the inner secrets that Rabbi Shimon told, and it is the secret of the supernal wisdom, that is known among the friends, happy is their portion.

123. צְלוֹתָא דְּבַר נָשׁ, אִיהוּ פּוּלְחָנָא דְּרוּחָא, וְאִיהוּ קַיְּימָא בְּרָזִין עִלָּאִין, וּב״נ לָא יַדְעִין, דְּהָא צְלוֹתָא דְּבַר נָשׁ בָּקְעַת אֲוִירִין, בָּקְעַת

רְקִיעִין, פַּתְחַת פִּתְחִין, וְסַלְקָא לְעֵילָא.

123. A man's prayer is considered the worship of the Ruach, WHICH IS OF THE SECOND KIND OF SERVICE MENTIONED ABOVE THAT CONCERNS SPEECH. It is based on supernal secrets, but men do not know that a man's prayer can cleave the ether and the firmaments, opens gates and ascends.

124. בְּשַׁעֲתָא דְּנָהִיר נְהוֹרָא, וְאִתְפְּרַשׁ נְהוֹרָא מִן חֲשׁוֹכָא, כְּדֵין כָּרוֹזָא אָזְלָא בְּכֻלְּהוּ רְקִיעִין, אִתְתַּקָּנוּ מָארֵי דְּפִתְחִין, מָארֵיהוֹן דְּהֵיכָלִין, כָּל חַד וְחַד עַל מַטְרֵיהּ. בְּגִין דְּאִינּוּן דְּשֻׁלְטָנֵיהוֹן בִּימָמָא, לָאו אִינּוּן דְּשֻׁלְטָנֵיהוֹן בְּלֵילְיָא. וְכַד עָאל לֵילְיָא, אִתְעַבָּרוּ שׁוּלְטָנִין דִּימָמָא, וְאִתְמְנוּן שֻׁלְטָנִין אַחֲרָנִין, דְּשָׁלִיטִין בְּלֵילְיָא, וְאִתְחַלְּפָן אִלֵּין בְּאִלֵּין.

124. And when the MORNING light breaks, and the light is separated from darkness, a proclamation sounds in all the firmaments: be ready, rulers of the gates, rulers of the chambers, each one in his post, for those who rule by day are not those who rule by night. And when night comes, the day rulers withdraw and other rulers are assigned to rule by night. And they interchange.

125. וְרָזָא דָּא, אֶת הַמָּאוֹר הַגָּדוֹל לְמֶמְשֶׁלֶת הַיּוֹם וְגוֹ'. וּמֶמְשֶׁלֶת הַיּוֹם וּמֶמְשֶׁלֶת הַלַּיְלָה, שׁוּלְטָנִין אִינּוּן דִּי מְמָנָן דִּי מְמָנָן בִּימָמָא, וְשׁוּלְטָנִין אִינּוּן דִּי מְמָנָן בְּלֵילְיָא. וְאִלֵּין אִקְרוּן מֶמְשֶׁלֶת הַיּוֹם. וְאִלֵּין אִקְרוּן מֶמְשֶׁלֶת הַלַּיְלָה.

125. This is the secret of "the greater light to rule by day..." (Beresheet 1:16). The day rulers and night rulers REFER TO those who are in charge by day and those who are in charge by night. The ones are considered the day rule and the others are considered the night rule.

126. כַּד עָאל לֵילְיָא, כָּרוֹזָא נָפְקָא, אִתְתַּקָּנוּ שׁוּלְטָנִין דְּלֵילְיָא, כָּל חַד וְחַד לְאַתְרֵיהּ. וְכַד נָהִיר יְמָמָא, כָּרוֹזָא נָפְקָא, אִתְתַּקָּנוּ שׁוּלְטָנִין דִּימָמָא, כָּל חַד וְחַד לְאַתְרֵיהּ. וְכַד כָּרוֹזָא אַכְרִיז, כְּדֵין כֻּלְּהוּ כָּל חַד וְחַד, אִתְפְּקַד עַל הַהוּא אֲתַר דְּאִתְחֲזֵי לֵיהּ. כְּדֵין שְׁכִינְתָּא קַדְמָא,

וְנַחְתָּא, וְיִשְׂרָאֵל עָאלִין לְבֵי כְּנִשְׁתָּא, לְשַׁבְּחָא לְמָארֵיהוֹן, פַּתְחִין
בְּשִׁירִין וְתוּשְׁבְּחָן.

126. And when night comes, a proclamation resounds, 'be prepared, rulers of the night, each one in his post. And when the day breaks the proclamation resounds, 'be prepared, rulers of the day, each one in his post'. And when the proclamation is heard, each one is assigned a place he is worthy of. Then the Shechinah goes forward and descends, and Yisrael go into the synagogue to praise their Master and start to sing and give thanks.

127. דְּבָעֵי לֵיהּ לב"נ, כֵּיוָן דְּאַתְקִין גַּרְמֵיהּ בְּפוּלְחָנָא דְּעוֹבָדָא, בְּתִקּוּנֵי
דְּמִצְוָה וּקְדוּשָׁה, לְיַחֲדָא לִבֵּיהּ בְּתִקּוּנָא דְּפוּלְחָנָא פְּנִימָאָה דְּמָארֵיהּ,
וּלְשַׁוָּאָה לִבֵּיהּ וּרְעוּתֵיהּ בְּהַהוּא פּוּלְחָנָא דְּאִינּוּן מִלִּין, דְּהָא מִלָּה
סַלְּקָא.

127. For it is incumbent upon a man to have prepared himself for the worship by deed, ᴛᴏ ᴡɪᴛ, ᴏꜰ ᴛʜᴇ ꜰɪʀꜱᴛ ᴋɪɴᴅ, with the implements of precepts and holiness, ᴛʜᴀᴛ ᴀʀᴇ ᴛʜᴇ ꜰʀɪɴɢᴇꜱ (HEʙ. *ᴛᴢɪᴛᴢɪᴛ*) ᴀɴᴅ ᴛᴇꜰɪʟɪɴ; ʜᴇ ꜱʜᴏᴜʟᴅ consecrate his heart to establish the inner work for his Master, ᴛʜᴀᴛ ɪꜱ, ᴛʜᴇ ꜱᴇᴄᴏɴᴅ ᴋɪɴᴅ, and put his heart and will to that work by those words ɪɴ ᴛʜᴇ ᴘʀᴀɪꜱᴇꜱ, because the speech goes ᴜᴘ.

128. וְאִינּוּן מְמָנָן דְּקַיְימִין בַּאֲוֵירָא, אִתְמְנּוּן לְד׳ סִטְרֵי עָלְמָא. לְסְטַר
מִזְרָח אִתְמַנָּא מְמָנָא חַד, דְּקַיְּימָא בַּאֲוֵירָא לְהַהוּא סִטְרָא, גְּזַרְדִּי"א
שְׁמֵיהּ, וְעִמֵּיהּ סַרְכִין מְמָנָן אַחֲרָנִין, דְּאִינּוּן מְחַכָּאן לְהַהִיא מִלָּה
דִּצְלוֹתָא, וְסַלְּקָא בַּאֲוֵירָא בְּהַהוּא סִטְרָא, וְנָטִיל לָהּ הַאי מְמָנָא.

128. And all those guards who stand in the air, are assigned over the four directions of the world. To the east is appointed one guardian who stands in the air and is called Gzardia. With him are other appointed ministers. They await that utterance of the prayer that rises in the air on that side, and that guardian takes it.

129. אִי הִיא מִלָּה כַּדְקָא יָאוּת, הוּא, וְכָל אִינּוּן סַרְכִין נַשְׁקִין לְהַהִיא

מִלָּה, וְסַלְקִין עִמָּה עַד הַהוּא אֲוִירָא דִּרְקִיעָא לְעֵילָא, דְּתַמָּן מִמָּנָן סָרְכִין אַחֲרָנִין. בְּשַׁעֲתָא דְּנַשְׁקֵי לְהַהִיא מִלָּה, פַּתְחֵי וְאָמְרֵי, זַכָּאִין אַתּוּן יִשְׂרָאֵל, דְּיַדְעִיתוּ לְאַעְטְרָא לְמָארֵיכוֹן בְּעִטְרִין קַדִּישִׁין זַכָּאָה אִיהוּ פּוּמָא, דְּמִלָּה דְּעִטְרָא דָּא נָפְקָא מִנֵּיהּ.

129. And if that speech is proper, all the ministers kiss that speech, and go up with it until they reach the air of that firmament, where there are other ministers. When they kiss that utterance, they open and say, happy are you, Yisrael, who can bedeck their Master with holy crowns. Happy is the mouth, from which that crowning speech came forth.

130. כְּדֵין פַּרְחִין אַתְוָון דְּקָיְימִין בַּאֲוִירָא, דְּבִשְׁמָא קַדִּישָׁא דִּתְרֵיסַר אַתְוָון, דְּהַהוּא שְׁמָא שַׁלִּיט בַּאֲוִירָא, וְהַאי אִיהוּ שְׁמָא, דַּהֲוָה טָאס בֵּיהּ אֵלִיָּהוּ, עַד דְּאִסְתַּלָּק לִשְׁמַיָּא. וְהַיְינוּ דְּקָאָמַר עוֹבַדְיָה לְאֵלִיָּהוּ, וְרוּחַ יְיָ' יִשָּׂאֲךָ. בְּגִין דְּבִשְׁמָא דָּא, הֲוָה אֵלִיָּהוּ טָאס בֵּיהּ בַּאֲוִירָא, וְהַאי אִיהוּ שְׁמָא דְּשַׁלִּיט בַּאֲוִירָא.

130. Then the twelve letters of the Holy Name that stand in the air soar, for that name has power over the air. And that is the name Elijah soared with until he went up to heaven. This is the meaning of what Ovadyah told Elijah, "the spirit of Hashem shall carry you" (Melachim I 18:12), for Elijah soared in the air by means of that name that rules the air.

131. וְאִינּוּן אַתְוָון פַּרְחִין וְסַלְקִין בְּהַהִיא מִלָּה, וְהַהוּא מְמָנָא דְּמַפְתְּחָן דַּאֲוִירָא בִּידֵיהּ, וְכָל אִינּוּן מְמָנָן אַחֲרָנִין, כֻּלְּהוּ סַלְקִין בֵּיהּ עַד רְקִיעָא, וְאִתְמְסַר בִּידָא דִּמְמָנָא אַחֲרָא, לְסַלְּקָא לְעֵילָא.

131. And these letters soar and ascend with that particular word, and that guard who has the keys to the air, and all the other assigned chiefs all go with it up to the firmament, where another chief is assigned to carry it further up.

132. לִסְטַר דָּרוֹם, אִית מְמָנָא אַחֲרָא דְּשַׁלְטָא בַּאֲוִירָא לְהַהוּא סְטַר, וְכַמָּה מְמָנָן אַחֲרָנִין וְסַרְכִין עִמֵּיהּ. פְּסַגְנִיָ"ה שְׁמֵיהּ, וְלֵיהּ אִתְמַסְרָאן

מִפִּתְחָן דַּאֲוִירָא לְהַהוּא סְטַר. וְכָל אִינּוּן מָארֵי דְעָקוּ, דְּצַלָּאן צְלוֹתָא
לְמָארֵיהוֹן מִגּוֹ עַקְתָּא, מִגּוֹ תְּבִירוּ דְלִבָּא, אִי הַהִיא מִלָּה כַּדְקָא יֵאוֹת,
סַלְקָא לַאֲוִירָא בְּהַהוּא סִטְרָא, וְנָטִיל לָהּ הַאי מְמָנָא, וְנָשִׁיק לָהּ כַּד
נָשִׁיק לָהּ, פָּתַח וְאָמַר, קוּדְשָׁא בְּרִיךְ הוּא יָחוֹס עֲלָךְ, וּבְגִינָךְ יִתְמְלֵי
רַחֲמִין.

132. To the south, CHESED, there is another chieftain who rules the air on that side, and some chiefs and ministers together with him. His name is Pesagniyah. He has the keys to the air on that side, and those who are laden with troubles, and pray brokenheartedly to their Master from the midst of their troubles with a broken heart - if their utterance is worthy, it ascends into the air of that side. There the chieftain receives and kisses it. When he kisses it, he says: may the Holy One, blessed be He, have mercy upon you and be filled with compassion for you.

133. סַלְקִין עִמָּהּ כָּל אִינּוּן מְמָנָן קַדִּישִׁין, וְכָל אִינּוּן סַרְכִין דְּהַהוּא
סִטְרָא. וּפָרְחִין אַתְוָון דִּשְׁמָא קַדִּישָׁא, דְּאִינּוּן ד' אַתְוָון, דְּמִתְעַטְּרִין
וְשַׁלְטִין בְּהַהוּא סִטְרָא דַּאֲוִירָא, וְסַלְקִין בְּהַהוּא סִטְרָא דַּאֲוִירָא, עַד
רְקִיעָא, עַד הַהוּא מְמָנָא דִּרְקִיעָא דְּשַׁלִּיט בְּהַהוּא סִטְרָא.

133. All the holy ministers and all the chieftains on that side go up with it. For on that side, the letters soar of the Holy Name EHEYEH, OF THE TWELVE-LETTERED NAME, THAT IS, FOUR LETTERS ON EACH SIDE AS MENTIONED. The ministers, who rule over this side of the air, go on that side, up to the SOUTHERN firmament, WHICH IS CHESED, NAMELY, THE SIXTH FIRMAMENT, AS WE EXPOUNDED AT LENGTH, up to the chief of the firmament who governs that SOUTH side. FOR ON THE SOUTHERN FIRMAMENT THERE IS ALREADY ANOTHER MINISTER BY THE NAME OF ANFI'EL.

134. לְסְטַר צָפוֹן, אִית מְמָנָא אַחֲרָא, וְעִמֵּיהּ כַּמָּה סַרְכִין מְמָנָן
דְּשַׁלְטִין בַּאֲוִירָא, וְהַהוּא מְמָנָא פְּתַחְיָ"ה שְׁמֵיהּ, וְהַאי אִתְמַנָּא בַּאֲוִירָא
לְהַהוּא סִטְרָא, וְכָל אִינּוּן דִּמְצַלָּאן צְלוֹתִין עַל בַּעֲלֵי דְבָבוּ דְּעָקִין לוֹן,

וְכַד מִלָּה דְּהַהִיא צְלוֹתָא סַלְקָא לַאֲוֵירָא בְּהַהוּא סִטְרָא, אִי זַכָּאָה הוּא, נָטִיל לָהּ הַאי מְמָנָא, וְנָשִׁיק לָהּ.

134. On the northern side, WHICH IS GVURAH, there is another chief WHO RULES THE AIR, and with him some appointed ministers who rule the air; this chief is called Petachiyah and he is in charge over the air on that side. And the utterance of all those who pray for deliverance from enemies who distress them, ascends into the air of that side; if that individual is righteous, the chief accepts and kisses it.

135. כְּדֵין אִתְּעַר רוּחָא חֲדָא דְּנָפְקָא מִגּוֹ תְּהוֹמָא בְּסִטְרָא דְּצָפוֹן, וְהַהוּא רוּחָא קָארֵי בְּכָל אִינּוּן אֲוֵירִין, וְנַטְלֵי כֻּלְּהוּ הַהִיא מִלָּה, וְסַלְקִין לָהּ עַד רְקִיעָא וְנַשְׁקִין לָהּ. פָּתְחֵי וְאַמְרֵי, מָרָךְ יִרְמֵי שַׂנְאָךְ לְקַמָּךְ.

135. Then one Ruach is roused and emerges from the abyss on the northern side, and that spirit calls out to all the airs, and they all take that utterance, raise it to the NORTHERN firmament, WHICH IS THE FIFTH FIRMAMENT, and kiss it. They open and say 'may your Master cast your enemy from before you'.

136. וְאָזְלָא וְסַלְקָא וּבַקְעָא אֲוֵירִין עַד דְּסַלְקִין עִמָּהּ לְגַבֵּי רְקִיעָא קַדְמָאָה סַלְקָא צְלוֹתָא, וּמָטָאת לְגַבֵּי חַד מְמָנָא, דְּאִתְמָנָא לְסְטַר מַעֲרָב, וְתַמָּן קַיְימִין תִּשְׁעָה פִּתְחִין, וּבְהוּ קַיְימִין כַּמָּה סַרְכִין, וְכַמָּה מְמָנָן, וְעָלַיְיהוּ מְמָנָא חַד דִּי שְׁמֵיהּ זְבוּלִי״אֵל.

136. HERE STARTS THE SEQUENCE OF THE ASCENSION OF THE PRAYER. THE PRAYER ascends higher and higher and cleaves airs, until it is escorted into the first firmament of Malchut of Asiyah. The prayer ascends and reaches the chief that is appointed over the west side, WHICH IS MALCHUT, where there are nine gates , in which several chieftains are stationed, whose superior is called Zevuli'el.

137. וְדָא אִיהוּ דְּבָעֵי לְשַׁמְּשָׁא בְּהַאי רְקִיעָא בִּימָמָא, וְלָא אִתְיְהִיב לֵיהּ רְשׁוּ, עַד דְּסָלִיק נְהוֹרָא דְּסִיהֲרָא, וּכְדֵין אַפִּיק כָּל אִינּוּן חֵילִין,

וְכָל אִינּוּן מְמָנָן. וְכַד נָהִיר יְמָמָא, עָאלִין כֻּלְּהוּ בְּפִתְחָא חֲדָא, דְּאִינּוּן
ט׳ פְּתְחִין, דְּאִיהוּ פִּתְחָא עִלָּאָה עַל כֻּלְּהוּ. וְכַד צְלוֹתָא סַלְקָא, עָאלַת
בְּהַהוּא פִּתְחָא, וְכֻלְּהוּ סַרְכִין, וְכֻלְּהוּ מְמָנָן, נָפְקִין מֵהַהוּא פִּתְחָא.
וַעֲלֵיהוֹן זְבוּלִיאֵ״ל, הַהוּא רַב מְמָנָא, וְנַפְקֵי כֻּלְּהוּ וְנַשְׁקֵי לָהּ, וּמַטְאָן
עִמָּהּ עַד רְקִיעָא תְּנְיָינָא.

137. And he wants to govern this firmament by day, but was not given permission, until the moonlight shines, NAMELY, BY NIGHT. He then takes out his armies and all the chieftains. When daylight breaks they all ascend through one of the nine gates, which is the most superior. And when the prayer enters that HIGHEST gate, all the ministers and chieftains go out of that gate, with Zevuli'el the superior chief over them. THAT IS, THERE IS NO OTHER CHIEF THERE BUT THE SAID ZEVULI'EL WHO IS APPOINTED OVER THE AIR AND ALSO OVER THAT SUPERIOR GATE, and they all go out and kiss it and come with it to the second firmament.

138. וְכַד סַלְקָא צְלוֹתָא עַד הַהוּא רְקִיעָא, אִתְפְּתָחוּ תְּרֵיסַר תַּרְעִין
דְּהַהוּא רְקִיעָא. וּבְהַהוּא תַּרְעָא דִּתְרֵיסַר, קָאֵים מְמָנָא חַד, דִּשְׁמֵיהּ
עֲנָ״אֵל, וְהַאי מְמָנָא עַל כַּמָה חַיָּילִין, עַל כַּמָה מַשְׁרְיָין, וְכַד צְלוֹתָא
סַלְקָא, קָאֵים הַאי מְמָנָא וְכָרִיז עַל כָּל אִינּוּן פִּתְחִין וְאָמַר, פִּתְחוּ
שְׁעָרִים וְגו׳, וְכֻלְּהוּ תַּרְעִין פְּתִיחִין, וְעָאלַת צְלוֹתָא בְּכָל אִינּוּן פִּתְחִין.

138. And when the prayer rises to that firmament, YESOD, its twelve gates are opened, and in the twelfth gate stands a chief by the name of Ana'el. He is in charge over some hosts and legions, and when the prayer arises, this chief stands and proclaims concerning those gates "open the gates" (Yeshayah 26:2) and all the gates are opened, and the prayer enter all the gates.

139. כְּדֵין, אִתְּעַר חַד מְמָנָא סָבָא דְּיוֹמִין, דְּקָאֵים לְסְטַר דָּרוֹם, דִּשְׁמֵיהּ
עֲזַרְיָא״ל סָבָא, וְלִזְמְנִין אִתְקְרֵי מַחֲנִיאֵ״ל, בְּגִין דְּאִתְמַנָּא עַל שִׁתִּין
רִבּוֹא מַשְׁרְיָין, וְכֻלְּהוּ מָארֵי דְּגַדְפִין, מָארֵי דְּמַשְׁרְיָין, מַלְיָין עַיְינִין.
וּלְגַבַּיְיהוּ קַיְימִין אִינּוּן מַשְׁרְיָין מָארֵיהוֹן דְּאוּדְנִין. וְאִקְרוּן אוּדְנִין, בְּגִין

דְּאִינוּן צַיְיתִין, כָּל אִינוּן דִּמְצַלָּאן צְלוֹתְהוֹן בִּלְחִישׁוּ, בִּרְעוּתָא דְלִבָּא, דְּלָא אִשְׁתְּמַע הַהוּא צְלוֹתָא לְאַחֲרָא. הַאי צְלוֹתָא סַלְקָא, וְצַיְיתִין לָה כָּל אִינוּן דְּאִקְרוּן מָארֵי דְּאוּדְנִין.

139. Then an ancient chief is aroused, who stands to the south, by the name of Azri'el Saba, who is sometimes called Machni'el , since he is chief over six hundred thousand camps (Heb. *machanot*), all of them winged; camps of eyed ones. Next to them are camps of the eared ones, that are called 'ears', since they listen to all those who whisper their prayers,in silence, with devotion, that prayer is not heard by anyone else. That prayer rises and is heard by all those who are called 'the eared ones'.

140. וְאִי הַהִיא צְלוֹתָא אִשְׁתְּמַע לְאוּדְנִין דְּבַר נָשׁ, לֵית מַאן דְּצָיֵית לָה לְעֵילָא, וְלָא צַיְיתִין לָה אַחֲרָנִין, בַּר מַאן דְּשָׁמַע בְּקַדְמֵיתָא, בְּג"כ בָּעֵי לְאִסְתַּמְּרָא דְּלָא יִשְׁמְעוּן לְהַהִיא צְלוֹתָא בְּנֵי נָשָׁא. וְתוּ, דְּמִלָּה דִּצְלוֹתָא אִתְאַחֲדָא בְּעָלְמָא עִלָּאָה, וּמִלָּה דְּעָלְמָא עִלָּאָה, לָא אִצְטְרִיךְ לְמִשְׁמַע.

140. And if that prayer is overheard by another man, no one will accept it above, and it is never received once it was first heard by someone, THAT IS, PEOPLE OTHER THAN THE MAN WHO OVERHEARD IT. This is why we ought to be careful, lest that prayer is overheard by people. Another reason is that the words of the prayer are united in the supernal world, ZEIR ANPIN, and an utterance of the supernal world ought not to be heard.

141. כְּגַוְונָא דָא, מַאן דְּקָרֵי בְּסִפְרָא דְּאוֹרַיְיתָא, חַד קָרֵי, וְחַד לִשְׁתּוֹק, וְאִי תְּרֵי קָרָאן בְּאוֹרַיְיתָא, גַּרְעֵי מְהֵימְנוּתָא דִּלְעֵילָא, בְּגִין דְּחַד קָלָא וְדִבּוּר כֹּלָא חַד כְּדֵין תְּרֵין קָלִין וּתְרֵין דִּבּוּרִין, אִיהוּ גְּרִיעוּתָא דִּמְהֵימְנוּתָא. אֶלָּא דְּיֶהֱא קָלָא וְדִבּוּר חַד כְּמָה דְּאִצְטְרִיךְ, בְּגִין דְּיֶהֱא הַהוּא קָלָא וְהַהוּא דִּבּוּר חַד.

141. In the same manner, when reading the Torah, one reads aloud and the other one is silent. If two read the Torah, they lessen the Faith of above, since one voice and utterance are all one, but two voices and two utterances

cause lack and blemish to the Faith, WHICH IS MALCHUT. Thus, there should only be one voice and one utterance, so that that one voice, ZEIR ANPIN WHICH IS CALLED VOICE, and the one utterance, MALCHUT THAT IS CALLED UTTERANCE, will be one.

142. וְהַהוּא מְמָנָא, שְׁמֵיהּ עַזְרִי״אֵל סָבָא. כַּד הַהִיא צְלוֹתָא סַלְקָא בִּלְחִישׁוּ, כָּל אִינּוּן שִׁתִּין רִבּוֹא מַשְׁרְיָין, וְכָל אִינּוּן מָארֵי דְּעַיְינִין, וְכָל אִינּוּן מָארֵי דְּאוּדְנִין, כֻּלְּהוּ נַפְקֵי וְנַשְׁקֵי לְהַהִיא מִלָּה דִּצְלוֹתָא דְּסַלְקָא. הֲדָא הוּא דִכְתִיב, עֵינֵי יְיָ׳ אֶל צַדִּיקִים וְאָזְנָיו אֶל שַׁוְעָתָם. עֵינֵי יְיָ׳ אֶל צַדִּיקִים, אִלֵּין מָארֵי דְּעַיְינִין דִּלְתַתָּא, בְּגִין דְּאִית מָארֵי דְּעַיְינִין לְעֵילָּא. וְאָזְנָיו אֶל שַׁוְעָתָם, אִלֵּין מָארֵיהוֹן דְּאוּדְנִין.

142. And that minister's name is Azri'el Saba. When the prayer rises secretly, all those 600,000 camps and all those eared and eyed beings, all come out and kiss that word of the mounting prayer, as written, "The eyes of Hashem are towards the righteous, and His ears are open to their cry" (Tehilim 34:16). "The eyes of Hashem are towards the righteous" refers to the eyed ones from below, NAMELY, THOSE SAID ANGELS IN THE FIRMAMENT OF YESOD OF ASIYAH, since there are eyed ones above. Therefore it is written: "The eyes of Hashem are towards the righteous, and His ears are open to their cry" refers to the eared ones.

143. רְקִיעָא תְּלִיתָאָה, הַהִיא צְלוֹתָא סַלְקָא וּמָטֵי לְהַהוּא רְקִיעָא, וְתַמָּן הַהוּא מְמָנָא דְּאִקְרֵי גְּדַרְיָ״ה, וְעִמֵּיהּ כַּמָּה סַרְכִין וְכַמָּה מְמָנָן. וְאִיהוּ מְשַׁמֵּשׁ ג׳ זִמְנִין בְּיוֹמָא, לָקֳבֵל חַד שַׁרְבִיטָא דִּזְהֲרָא דְּנָפִיק, סָלִיק וְנָחִית וְלָא קַיְימָא בְּאֲתָר חַד, וְהַאי אִיהוּ שַׁרְבִיטָא דְּנָטִיל ג׳ זִמְנִין וְאִתְגְּנִיז. וְכַד צְלוֹתָא סַלְקָא, נָחִית הַהוּא שַׁרְבִיטָא, וְסָגִיד קַמֵּי הַהוּא צְלוֹתָא, וְאִקְרֵי הַאי רְקִיעָא, רְקִיעָא דְּשַׁרְבִיטָא.

143. The third firmament IS NETZACH AND HOD OF ASIYAH. The prayer mounts and reaches that firmament, where there is a minister by the name of Gedariah, accompanied by some ministers and chieftains. He ministers three times a day before a scepter of light that comes out, goes up and down, and is never still in one place. This is the scepter, which travels three times and

then is concealed. When the prayer ascends, the scepter descends and bows before this prayer. The THIRD firmament, NETZACH AND HOD OF ASIYAH, is called the firmament of the scepter, NAMED AFTER THE SCEPTER THAT IS ACTIVE IN IT.

144. וְכַד סַלְקָא הַהִיא צְלוֹתָא, הַהוּא מְמָנָא בָּתַר דְּסָגִיד, בָּטַשׁ, בְּהַהוּא שַׁרְבִיטָא בְּטִינָרָא, תַּקִיפָא דִּזְהִיר, דְּאִיהוּ קָאִים בְּאֶמְצָעִיתָא דְּהַהוּא רְקִיעָא, וְנַפְקוּ מִגּוֹ הַהוּא טִינָרָא, תְּלַת מְאָה וְשַׁבְעִין וְחָמֵשׁ חַיָּילִין דְּאִינּוּן גְּנִיזִין תַּמָּן מִן יוֹמָא דְּאוֹרַיְיתָא נַחְתַּת לְאַרְעָא, בְּגִין דְּאִתְתַּקְפוּ לְסַרְבָא דְּלָא תֵּחוֹת לְאַרְעָא, וְאַנְזִיף בְּהוּ קוּדְשָׁא בְּרִיךְ הוּא, וְעָאלוּ גּוֹ הַהוּא טִינָרָא. וְלָא נָפְקִין בַּר הַהוּא זִמְנָא דִּצְלוֹתָא סַלְקָא, פַּתְחֵי וְאַמְרֵי יְיָ' אֲדוֹנֵינוּ מָה אַדִּיר שִׁמְךָ וְגוֹ'. דָּא הִיא צְלוֹתָא, דְּסַלְקָא עַל כָּל אִינּוּן רְקִיעִין. כְּדֵין סַגְדִּין לְגַבָּהּ.

144. And when that prayer rises, that minister, after bowing TOWARDS THE PRAYER, strikes with that scepter a strong luminous rock, placed in the middle of that firmament, and 375 troops come out of it that were concealed there from the day the Torah come down to the earth. And since they insisted on refusing AND WITHHOLDING the Torah from descending, to the earth, the Holy One, blessed be He, rebuked them and they entered into that rock. And they do not leave THAT PLACE except when prayer goes up. Then they open and say, "Hashem our Master, how majestic is Your name in all the earth..." (Tehilim 8:2). This is the prayer, WHICH IS CALLED MAJESTIC, SINCE it mounts over all those firmaments and then they bow before it.

145. מִכָּאן וּלְהָלְאָה, צְלוֹתָא מִתְעַטְּרָא בְּעִטְּרִין עִלָּאִין, וְסַלְקָא לְגוֹ רְקִיעָא רְבִיעָאָה, וּכְדֵין שִׁמְשָׁא נָפִיק בְּדַרְגּוֹי, וְשַׁמְשִׁי"אֵל רַב מְמָנָא נָפִיק, וּתְלַת מְאָה וְשִׁתִּין וְחָמֵשׁ מַשִׁרְיָין סַלְקִין עִמֵּיהּ, לְגוֹ הַהוּא רְקִיעָא, וְאִקְרוּן יְמוֹת הַחַמָּה, וְכֻלְּהוּ מְעַטְּרָן לְהַהִיא צְלוֹתָא, בְּעִטְּרִין דְּבוּסְמִין דְּגִנְתָּא דְּעֵדֶן.

145. From now on the prayer is adorned with supernal crowns and ascends into the forth firmaments, WHICH IS TIFERET. Then the sun, WHICH IS TIFERET, comes out with its grades, and Shamshi'el (from Heb. *shemesh* lit.

'sun') the superior chief comes out and ascends into that firmament together with 365 camps, that are called the solar days, SINCE THEY ARE GRADES THAT COME FROM THE SUN, WHICH IS TIFERET. And they all adorn the prayer with perfumed crowns from the Garden of Eden.

146. וְתַמָּן אִתְעַכְּבַת צְלוֹתָא, עַד דְּכָלְהוּ מַשִׁרְיָין סַלְקִין עִמָּה לְגוֹ הַהוּא רְקִיעָא חֲמִישָׁאָה, וְתַמָּן אִיהוּ מְמָנָא חַד גַּדְרִי״אֵל שְׁמֵיה, וְהוּא מָארֵי קְרָבִין דִּשְׁאַר עַמִּין. וְכַד צְלוֹתָא סַלְקָא, כְּדֵין אִזְדַּעְזָע הוּא, וְכָל מַשִׁרְיָין דִּילֵיה, וְאִתְבַּר חֵילַיְיהוּ, וְנַפְקִי וְסַגְדֵּי, וּמְעַטְּרִין לְהַהִיא צְלוֹתָא.

146. There the prayer stays some time until all the troops ascend with it into the fifth firmament, WHICH IS GVURAH. The minister Gadri'el is there, who is in charge over wars waged by the other nations. FOR GVURAH IS THE SECRET OF THE LEFT COLUMN, TO WHICH THE NATIONS ARE ATTACHED. And when the prayer goes up, he and all his troops shudder, and their might is enfeebled. They go out and bow, and adorn that prayer.

147. וְסַלְקִין עִמָּה עַד דְּמָטוּ לְגַבֵּי רְקִיעָא שְׁתִיתָאָה, וּכְדֵין נָפְקִין כַּמָּה חַיָּילִין, וְכַמָּה מַשִׁרְיָין, וּמְקַבְּלִין לְהַהוּא צְלוֹתָא, וְסַלְקִין בַּהֲדָה, עַד דְּמָטוּ לְשַׁבְעִין תַּרְעִין, דְּתַמָּן קָאִים חַד מְמָנָא, דִּי שְׁמֵיה עַנְפִּי״אֵל, רַב מְמָנָא. וְאִיהוּ מְעַטֵּר לְהַהִיא צְלוֹתָא, בְּשַׁבְעִין עִטְרִין.

147. They mount with it until they reach the sixth firmament, CHESED, when some hosts and legions come out and receive that prayer until they arrive at seventy gates, WHICH ARE THE SEVEN SFIROT – CHESED, GVURAH, TIFERET, NETZACH, HOD, YESOD AND MALCHUT, EACH INCLUDING TEN. FOR CHESED INCLUDES IN IT ALL THE SEVEN LOWER SFIROT. There stands a chief by the name of Anfi'el, who is the supreme chief, who adorns the prayer with seventy crowns.

148. וְכֵיוָן דְּמִתְעַטְּרָא צְלוֹתָא בְּכָל הָנֵי עִטְרִין, כְּדֵין מִתְחַבְּרָן כָּל אִינוּן

חַיָּילִין דְּכֻלְּהוּ רְקִיעִין, וְסַלְּקִין לְהַהִיא צְלוֹתָא דְּמִתְעַטְּרָא בְּכָל עִטְרִין,
לְגַבֵּי רְקִיעָא שְׁבִיעָאָה. וּכְדֵין עָאלַת צְלוֹתָא, וְסַנְדַּלְפְ״ן רַב יַקִּירָא
עִלָּאָה דְּכָל מַפְתְּחָן דְּמָארֵיהּ בִּידֵיהּ, אָעִיל לְהַהוּא צְלוֹתָא, לְגוֹ שִׁבְעָה
הֵיכָלִין.

148. And after the prayer is bedecked with all those crowns, the soldiers from all firmaments, WHO ACCOMPANIED THE PRAYER UP TO HERE, FROM ONE FIRMAMENT TO ANOTHER, jointly raise the prayer to the seventh firmament, BINAH, WHICH INCLUDES THE FIRST THREE SFIROT. Then the prayer enters THAT PLACE, and Sandalphon, the precious, supreme minister, who has all his Master's keys in his hands, ushers the prayer into seven chambers OF YETZIRAH. (THE CHAMBERS THAT WERE ALREADY PRINTED IN BERESHEET 2 ARE MISSING HERE).

149. שִׁבְעָה הֵיכָלִין אִלֵּין, אִינּוּן הֵיכָלִין דְּמַלְכָּא, וְהַאי צְלוֹתָא כַּד
מִתְעַטְּרָא בְּכָל הָנֵי עִטְרִין, כַּד עָאלַת, מְחַבֵּר לוֹן כַּחֲדָא, לְאִתְעַטְּרָא
לְעֵילָּא לְמֶהֱוֵי כֹּלָּא חַד כַּדְקָא יֵאוֹת. וּשְׁמָא דְּקוּדְשָׁא בְּרִיךְ הוּא,
מִתְעַטְּרָא בְּכָל עִטְרִין, עֵילָּא וְתַתָּא, לְמֶהֱוֵי חַד, וּכְדֵין בְּרָכוֹת לְרֹאשׁ
צַדִּיק כְּתִיב.

149. These seven chambers are the King's chambers, VIZ. THE SEVEN CHAMBERS OF MALCHUT OF ATZILUT WHERE THE KING, ZEIR ANPIN, IS UNITED. And when this prayer, adorned with all those crowns, goes up there, it unites ZEIR ANPIN AND MALCHUT together and crowns them from above. Thus everything becomes one, as is befitting, and the name of the Holy One, blessed be He, MALCHUT, is decorated on all sides, above and below and becomes one WITH ZEIR ANPIN. Then "blessings are upon the head of the righteous" (Mishlei 10:6), FOR YESOD, THAT IS CALLED RIGHTEOUS, BESTOWS BLESSINGS ON MALCHUT .

150. זַכָּאָה חוּלָקֵיהּ דְּבַר נָשׁ, דְּיָדַע לְסַדְּרָא צְלוֹתֵיהּ כַּדְקָא יֵאוֹת.
בְּהַאי צְלוֹתָא דְּמִתְעַטְּרָא בֵּיהּ קוּדְשָׁא בְּרִיךְ הוּא, אִיהוּ מְחַכֶּה עַד
דְּיִסְתַּיְּימוּן כָּל צְלוֹתְהוֹן דְּיִשְׂרָאֵל, וּכְדֵין כֹּלָּא אִיהוּ בִּשְׁלִימוּ כַּדְקָא
יֵאוֹת, עֵילָּא וְתַתָּא. עַד הָכָא מִלִּין דִּצְלוֹתָא, לְמִנְדַּע רָזִין עִלָּאִין, מִכָּאן

וּלְהַלְאָה אִית פְּקוּדֵי אוֹרַיְיתָא, דְּאִינּוּן קַיְימִין בְּמִלָה, כְּמָה דְּקַיְימִין בְּעוֹבָדָא.

150. Happy is the portion of the person, who knows how to arrange his prayer properly, for when it is AS IT OUGHT TO BE the Holy One, blessed be He, bedecks Himself with it, while waiting for all the prayers of Yisrael to be completed AND INCLUDED IN THE WHOLE PRAYER. Then all is properly complete above and below. So far were discussed the matters of prayer, to know the lofty secrets IN IT. From now on, there are precepts of the Torah that are based on speech, just as there are OTHERS that are based on actions.

151. וְאִינּוּן שִׁית פְּקוּדִין, וְקַיְימִין אוּף הָכָא בִּצְלוֹתָא. חַד, לְיִרְאָה אֶת הַשֵּׁם הַנִּכְבָּד וְהַנּוֹרָא. תִּנְיָינָא, לְאַהֲבָה אוֹתוֹ. תְּלִיתָאָה, לְבָרְכוֹ. רְבִיעָאָה, לְיַחֲדוֹ. חֲמִישָׁאָה, לְבָרֵךְ כַּהֲנָא יַת עַמָּא. שְׁתִיתָאָה, לְמִסוֹר נִשְׁמָתֵיה לֵיה. וְאִלֵּין שִׁית פְּקוּדִין דְּקַיְימִין בִּצְלוֹתָא דְּמִלָה, בַּר אִינּוּן פְּקוּדִין דְּקַיְימִין בְּעוֹבָדָא, כְּגַוְונָא דְּצִיצִית וּתְפִלִין.

151. There are six precepts, that are observed during the prayer: 1) "that you may fear this glorious and fearful name" (Devarim 28:58). 2) "to love Him (Devarim 10:12). 3) to bless Him. 4) to profess His unity. 5) that the priest would bless the people. 6) to surrender the soul to Him. These are the six precepts that apply to prayer, BASED ON speech, excepting those that are based on action, like the fringes (Heb. *Tzitzit*) and Tefilin.

152. לְיִרְאָה אֶת הַשֵּׁם, פְּקוּדָא דָּא קַיְימָא בְּאִלֵּין תּוּשְׁבְּחָן דְּקָאָמַר דָּוִד מַלְכָּא, וּבְאִינּוּן קָרְבָּנִין דְּאוֹרַיְיתָא, דְּתַמָּן בָּעֵי בַּר נָשׁ לְדַחֲלָא מִקַּמֵּי מָארֵיה, בְּגִין דְּאִינּוּן שִׁירִין קַיְימִין בְּהַהוּא אֲתָר דְּאִקְרֵי יִרְאָה. וְכָל אִינּוּן הַלְלוּיָה, דְּאִינּוּן רָזָא דְּיִרְאָה דְּקוּדְשָׁא בְּרִיךְ הוּא. וּבָעֵי בַּר נָשׁ לְשַׁוָּאָה רְעוּתֵיה בְּאִינּוּן שִׁירִין בְּיִרְאָה, וְאוֹקְמוּהָ חַבְרַיָּיא כָּל אִינּוּן רָזִין דְּשִׁירִין וְתוּשְׁבְּחָן, וְכָל אִינּוּן רָזִין דְּהַלְלוּיָה.

152. HE EXPLAINS THESE SIX PRECEPTS: 1) this precept applies to the poems of King David, and the sacrifices mentioned in the Torah, for there a

man should indicate fear of his Master, since these particular chants are in a place called fear, THAT IS MALCHUT. And all these Haleluyas THAT ARE WRITTEN, allude to the secret of the fear of the Holy One, blessed be He, WHICH IS MALCHUT. Therefore a person should be attentive to those chants with awe. Already the friends explained all the secret of the chants and praises, and all the secrets of Haleluyah.

153. כֵּיוָן דְּמָטֵי ב"נ לִישְׁתַּבַּח, יְשַׁוֵּי רְעוּתֵיהּ לְבָרְכָא לֵיהּ לְקוּדְשָׁא בְּרִיךְ הוּא , כְּגוֹן יוֹצֵר אוֹר, יוֹצֵר הַמְּאוֹרוֹת. לְאַהֲבָה אוֹתוֹ, כַּד מָטֵי לְאַהֲבַת עוֹלָם, וְאָהַבְתָּ אֶת יְיָ' אֱלֹהֶיךָ, דְּדָא אִיהוּ רָזָא דִּרְחִימוּ דְּקוּדְשָׁא בְּרִיךְ הוּא, וְהָא אוּקְמוּהָ. לְיַחֲדָא לֵיהּ, שְׁמַע יִשְׂרָאֵל יְיָ' אֱלֹהֵינוּ יְיָ' אֶחָד, דְּהָכָא קַיְימָא רָזָא דְּיִחוּדָא דְּקוּדְשָׁא בְּרִיךְ הוּא, לְיַחֲדָא שְׁמֵיהּ בִּרְעוּתָא דְּלִבָּא כַּדְקָא חֲזֵי. וּמִתַּמָּן וּלְהָלְאָה אַדְכָּרוּתָא דִיצִיאַת מִצְרַיִם, דְּאִיהוּ פְּקוּדָא לְאַדְכְּרָא יְצִיאַת מִצְרַיִם דִּכְתִיב וְזָכַרְתָּ כִּי עֶבֶד הָיִיתָ בְּאֶרֶץ מִצְרָיִם.

153. 2) Upon reaching "praised be," one should concentrate on the benedictions before the Holy One, blessed be He, such as "blessed are You...who forms light... blessed are You, Hashem, creator of the luminaries." 3) "to love Him": upon reaching "eternal love" followed by "and you shall love Hashem your Elohim," which is the secret of the love of the Holy One, blessed be He. 4) to profess His unity: NAMELY, "Hear, O Yisrael, Hashem our Elohim Hashem is One" (Devarim 6:4), for here is the secret of the unifying of the Holy One, blessed be He, and we ought to declare His unity with a willing heart as is fit. From there on is the remembrance of the exodus from Egypt. It is a precept to mention the emergence from Egypt, as is written: "but you shall remember that you were a bondsman in the land of Egypt" (Devarim 5:15).

154. לְבָרְכָא כַּהֲנָא יַת עַמָּא, בְּגִין לְאַכְלְלָא יִשְׂרָאֵל כַּחֲדָא, בְּשַׁעֲתָא דְּנַטְלִין בִּרְכָאן לְעֵילָא, דְּהָא בְּהַהִיא שַׁעֲתָא נַטְלָא כְּנֶסֶת יִשְׂרָאֵל בִּרְכָאן, וְשַׁעֲתָא דִּרְעוּתָא הוּא, לְמִסוֹר נַפְשֵׁיהּ לְגַבֵּיהּ, וּלְמֵיהַב לֵיהּ נִשְׁמָתָא בִּרְעוּתָא דְּלִבָּא, כַּד נַפְלִין עַל אַנְפִּין, וְאָמְרִין אֵלֶיךָ יְיָ' נַפְשִׁי אֶשָּׂא, דִּיכַוֵּין לִבֵּיהּ וּרְעוּתֵיהּ לְגַבֵּיהּ, לְמִמְסַר לֵיהּ נַפְשָׁא בִּרְעוּתָא

שְׁלִים. וְאִלֵּין אִינוּן שִׁית פִּקּוּדִין דְּקַיְּימִין בִּצְלוֹתָא, דְּסַלְּקִין לְגַבֵּי שִׁית מֵאָה פִּקּוּדִין דְּאוֹרַיְיתָא.

154. 5) That the priest would bless the people, in order to unite Yisrael together while they receive blessings from above, for at that time, the Congregation of Yisrael, MALCHUT, receives blessings. 6) And it is a time of goodwill to surrender one's soul to Him with a willing heart, when one prostrates and says, "To You, Hashem, do I lift up my soul" (Tehilim 25:1), when one should direct his heart and will to surrender his soul with complete devotion. These are the six precepts pertaining to prayer that correspond to the six hundred precepts of the Torah.

155. וְאִי תֵּימָא תְּלֵיסָר אַחֲרָנִין יַתִּיר. אִינוּן קַיְּימִין לְאַמְשָׁכָא תְּלֵיסָר מְכִילָן דְּרַחֲמֵי, דְּכֹלָּא כְּלִילָן בְּהוּ. שִׁית פִּקּוּדִין אִלֵּין, דִּצְלוֹתָא מִתְעַטְּרָא בְּהוּ.

155. You may argue there are thirteen more precepts in the Torah, FOR THERE ARE SIX HUNDRED AND THIRTEEN PRECEPTS, AND WHY SAY THAT SIX PRECEPTS ARE EQUIVALENT TO SIX HUNDRED. HE REPLIES: the purpose OF THE THIRTEEN PRECEPTS is to draw the all encompassing thirteen attributes of Mercy. NAMELY, THE THIRTEEN ATTRIBUTES OF MERCY THAT WE SAY, CORRESPOND TO THEM, and the prayer adorns itself with the six precepts, TO WIT, CORRESPONDING TO CHESED, GVURAH, TIFERET, NETZACH, HOD AND YESOD, THAT THE PRAYER, WHICH IS THE SECRET OF MALCHUT, RECEIVES FROM ZEIR ANPIN.

156. זַכָּאָה חוּלָקֵיהּ, מַאן דְּיְשַׁוֵּי לִבֵּיהּ וּרְעוּתֵיהּ לְדָא, וּלְאַשְׁלְמָא לוֹן בְּכָל יוֹמָא. וּבְאִלֵּין תַּלְיָין אַחֲרָנִין סַגִּיאִין. אֲבָל כַּד מָטֵי בַּר נָשׁ לְאַתְרִין אִלֵּין, אִצְטְרִיךְ לֵיהּ לְכַוְּונָא לִבֵּיהּ וּרְעוּתֵיהּ, לְאַשְׁלְמָא הַהוּא פִּקּוּדָא דְּקַיְּימָא בְּהַהוּא מִלָּה. וּכְדֵין אַכְרִיזוּ עָלֵיהּ וְאַמְרֵי, וַיֹּאמֶר לִי עַבְדִּי אַתָּה יִשְׂרָאֵל אֲשֶׁר בְּךָ אֶתְפָּאָר. אָתָא ר' אַבָּא וּנְשָׁקֵיהּ.

156. Happy is the portion of he who puts his heart and will to it to perfect them every day. And upon them depend many other things. However, when a man reaches these passages, he should concentrate his heart and will to

complete that precept that is connected to that particular word; then the proclamation resounds "and He said to me, you are My servant, Yisrael, in whom I will be glorified" (Yeshayah 49:3). Rabbi Aba approached and kissed him.

157. פָּתַח ר' יִצְחָק אֲבַתְרֵיהּ וְאָמַר, וַיַּקְהֵל מֹשֶׁה אֶת כָּל עֲדַת בְּנֵי יִשְׂרָאֵל וְגוֹ'. אֲמַאי כָּנֵישׁ לוֹן. בְּגִין לְמִמְסַר לוֹן שַׁבָּת כְּמִלְּקַדְמִין, דְּהָא בְּקַדְמֵיתָא עַד לָא עֲבְדוּ בְּנֵי יִשְׂרָאֵל יַת עֶגְלָא, מָסַר לוֹן אֶת הַשַּׁבָּת. וְדָא אִיהוּ דְּלָא נַטְרוּ אִינּוּן עֵרֶב רַב. כֵּיוָן דְּשַׁמְעוּ בֵּינִי וּבֵין בְּנֵי יִשְׂרָאֵל, אָמְרוּ וַאֲנָן מִלָּה דָּא אִתְמְנַע מִינָן, מִיַּד וַיִּקָּהֵל הָעָם עַל אַהֲרֹן וְגוֹ', וְאִתְמְשְׁכוּ סַגִּיאִין אֲבַתְרַיְיהוּ. לְבָתַר דְּמִיתוּ אִינּוּן דְּמִיתוּ, כָּנֵישׁ מֹשֶׁה לִבְנֵי יִשְׂרָאֵל בִּלְחוֹדַיְיהוּ, וְיָהַב לוֹן שַׁבָּת כְּמִלְּקַדְמִין, הֲדָא הוּא דִכְתִּיב שֵׁשֶׁת יָמִים תֵּעָשֶׂה מְלָאכָה וְגוֹ'.

157. Rabbi Yitzchak then opened after him, and said, "and Moses gathered all the Congregation of the children of Yisrael..." HE ASKS why he gathered them, AND REPLIES: In order to give them the laws of Shabbat as before. For before Yisrael created the golden calf, He gave them the Shabbat. And this is what the mixed multitude did not keep. When they heard the verse "between Me and the children of Yisrael" (Shemot 31:17), they said: but from us this is withheld! Quickly "the people gathered themselves together against Aaron" (Shemot 32:1) IN ORDER TO MAKE THE CALF, and many followed them. And after those WHO WORSHIPPED THE CALF died, Moses gathered the Congregation of Yisrael alone, and gave them the laws of Shabbat as before, as is written: "six days shall work be done..." (Shemot 35:2).

12. A fire on Shabbat eve

A Synopsis

Rabbi Yitzchak says there is a very high secret why "You shall kindle no fire throughout your habitations on the Shabbat day," and talks about the shining star that comes from the north and strikes another seventy stars, until all seventy become one and the star expands into a blazing flame that extends across a thousand mountains. We are told that the storm wind that Elijah saw is that star that swallowed up the others. It is called a storm wind because it disturbs everything above and below, and it came from the north, since "out of the north the evil shall break forth." We read of the "great cloud," the cloud of darkness that hides the light. The "fire flaring up" refers to the fire of judgment, "and a brightness was about it"; this means that although it is from the side of defilement a man should not treat it with contempt because there is a brightness about it. Rabbi Hamnuna Saba (the elder) disagrees, saying that it should indeed be treated with contempt because inside it is "the form of Chashmal," that can be translated as 'beasts of fire muttering'. But now we hear from Rabbi Shimon the secret mystery of how these meanings are symbolized in the circumcision of the foreskin, that allows the light to be revealed. Rabbi Hamnuna Saba (the elder) says that the snake seduced Eve with the brightness of that star that was spoken of earlier. Finally, then, we are told why people must not kindle another fire from those that are hidden.

158. לֹא תְבַעֲרוּ אֵשׁ בְּכָל מוֹשְׁבֹתֵיכֶם, הָכָא אִית רָזָא דְרָזִין, לְאִינּוּן דְּיָדְעֵי חָכְמְתָא עִלָּאָה, רָזָא דְשַׁבָּת הָא אוּקְמוּהָ חַבְרַיָּיא. אֲבָל רָזָא דָא, אִתְמְסַר לְחַכִּימֵי עֶלְיוֹנִין, דְּהָא שַׁבָּת רָזָא עִלָּאָה הוּא.

158. "You shall kindle no fire throughout your habitations" (Shemot 35:3). Here there are most high mysteries revealed to those in possession of supernal wisdom. The friends have already expounded on the secret of Shabbat, yet this mystery was given to the wisest men, for it is a very high secret.

159. ת"ח בְּשַׁעֲתָא דְיוֹמָא שְׁתִיתָאָה מָטָא זִמְנָא דְעֶרֶב, כְּדֵין, כֹּכָבָא חַד מִסִּטְרָא דְצָפוֹן נָהִיר, וְעִמֵּיהּ שַׁבְעִין כֹּכְבִין אַחֲרָנִין, וְהַהוּא כֹּכָבָא בָּטַשׁ בְּאִינּוּן כֹּכְבִין אַחֲרָנִין, וְאִתְכְּלִילוּ כֻּלְּהוּ בְּהַהוּא כֹּכָבָא, וְאִתְעֲבֵיד

חַד כְּלָלָא דְּשַׁבְעִין. וְהַהוּא כֹּכָבָא אִתְפָּשַׁט, וְאִתְעֲבֵיד כְּמָדוּרָא חֲדָא, לְהִיטָא בְּכָל סִטְרִין. כְּדֵין אִתְפָּשַׁט הַהוּא מָדוּרָא סַחֲרָנַיְיהוּ דְּאֶלֶף טוּרִין, וְקַיְימָא כְּחַד חוּטָא דְּסָחֲרָא.

159. Come and see, on Friday, when evening sets, a shining star comes from the north and with it seventy other stars; the star smites these SEVENTY stars, which become incorporated in that star and WITHIN IT all seventy become one. That star then expands and turns into a blazing flame on all sides. This flame is extended across a thousand mountains, and stands UPON THEM like a thread encircling THEM.

160. וְהַאי מָדוּרָא דְּאֶשָּׁא, מָשִׁיךְ לְגַבֵּיהּ גְּווֹנִין אַחֲרָנִין דִּלְגוֹ מִנֵּיהּ. גְּווֹן קַדְמָאָה יְרוֹקָא. כֵּיוָן דְּקַיְימָא הַאי גְּווֹנָא, סַלְקָא הַהוּא מָדוּרָא דְּאֶשָּׁא, וְדָלִיג לְעֵילָא עַל הַהוּא גְּווֹן יְרוֹקָא, וְעָאל לְגוֹ מִנֵּיהּ, וְשָׁדֵי לְהַהוּא גְּווֹן יְרוֹקָא לְבַר, וְקַיְימָא יְרוֹקָא לְבַר, וְהַהוּא מָדוּרָא דְּאֶשָּׁא דְּכֹכָבָא כְּלִילָא לְגוֹ.

160. And this flaming mass draws to it other colors that are inside it UNDERNEATH ITS OWN COLOR. The first color is green, WHICH IS THE LIGHT OF THE CENTRAL COLUMN. When this color is established that flame of fire jumps upon this green color and enters inside it and throws the green color out. The green color stays out, and the flame of fire of that star INCLUDED OF SEVENTY STARS IS inside.

161. לְבָתַר, אַמְשִׁיךְ אֲבַתְרֵיהּ גְּווֹן אַחֲרָא תִּנְיָינָא חִוָּורָא, וְהַהוּא חִוָּורָא עָאל לְגוֹ, כֵּיוָן דְּקַיְימָא הַאי גְּווֹן, סַלְקָא הַהוּא מָדוּרָא דְּאֶשָּׁא דְּהַהוּא כֹּכָבָא, וְשָׁדֵי לְהַהוּא חִוָּורָא לְבַר, וְעָאל אִיהוּ לְגוֹ. וְכֵן כָּל אִינּוּן גְּווֹנִין, עַד דְּשַׁדֵי לוֹן לְבַר, וְעַיֵּיל אִיהוּ לְגוֹ, וְקָרִיב לְגַבֵּי הַהִיא נְקוּדָה טְמִירָא, לְמֵיטַל נְהוֹרָא.

161. Afterwards it draws to it a second color, white, THE LIGHT OF THE RIGHT COLUMN. This white color shone inside, but after that color is established, the flame of fire of the star rose, expelling the white color, and

entering inside. The same procedure transpired with all the other colors. It threw them out, went inside and approached the hidden point, to receive light.

162. פָּתַח וְאָמַר, וָאֵרֶא וְהִנֵּה רוּחַ סְעָרָה בָּאָה מִן הַצָּפוֹן וְגוֹ'. יְחֶזְקֵאל חָמָא לְהַאי חֵיזוּ, בְּתִקּוּנָא דְּלָא קַיְּימָא, בַּר בְּשַׁעֲתָא דְּשַׁלִּיט הַהוּא כֹּכָבָא כִּדְקָאֲמָרָן, אֲבָל הַאי קְרָא אוּקְמוּהָ. וְהִנֵּה רוּחַ סְעָרָה, אוּקְמוּהָ, דַּהֲוָה אָתֵי לְמִכְבַּשׁ כָּל עָלְמָא, לְקַמֵּיהּ דִּנְבוּכַדְנֶצַר חַיָּיבָא. אֲבָל רוּחַ סְעָרָה דָּא, אִיהוּ הַהוּא כֹּכָבָא דְּקָאֲמָרָן, דְּבָלַע שַׁבְעִין כֹּכָבִין אַחֲרָנִין, וְדָא אִיהוּ רוּחַ סְעָרָה דְּחָמָא אֵלִיָּהוּ, מְפָרֵק הָרִים וּמְשַׁבֵּר סְלָעִים, וְדָא דְּקַיְּימָא תָּדִיר קֳדָם כֹּלָּא, לְמֵיטַר הַהוּא דִּלְגוֹ, כִּקְלִיפָה לְמוֹחָא.

162. He opened and said, "and I looked, and, behold, a storm wind came out of the north..." (Yechezkel 1:4). Yechezkel saw that vision in a pattern that appears only when that star rules, as we said, FOR IT DOES NOT ALWAYS RULE BUT IS HIDDEN. We explained that "and behold, a storm wind," refers to the wind that comes to conquer the world for Nebuchadnezzar. Yet the storm wind is that star we mentioned that swallowed seventy other stars. This is the storm wind Elijah had seen, OF WHICH IS SAID "rending the mountains and breaking up the rocks" (I Melachim 19:11), FOR THERE IS NO FORCE THAT COULD WITHSTAND IT. It is that which always stands against all THE KLIPOT ON THE OUTSIDE to protect what is inside, like a shell protects the fruit.

163. וְאַמַּאי אִקְרֵי סְעָרָה. דְּסָעִיר כֹּלָּא, עֵילָא וְתַתָּא. בָּאָה מִן הַצָּפוֹן, דְּהָא מִן הַהוּא סִטְרָא קָא אַתְיָא, וְסִימָנָךְ, מִצָּפוֹן תִּפָּתַח הָרָעָה, דְּהָא כַּמָּה סִטְרִין אַחֲרָנִין אִתְאַחֲדָן בְּהַהוּא רוּחַ סְעָרָה, וּבְג"כ נָפְקָא מִן הַצָּפוֹן.

163. Why is it called a storm? because it storms against everything above and below, AND NOTHING CAN STAND IN ITS WAY. It "came out of the north," for this is the side it came from. We can tell this from the verse "out of the north the evil shall break forth" (Yirmeyah 1:14). For many other aspects besides the north hold on to that storm wind. Therefore THE SCRIPTURE SAYS ABOUT THEM, that it comes out from the north.

164. עֲנָן, בְּגִין דְּאִיהִי סוּסְפִּיתָא דְּדַהֲבָא. וּמִסִּטְרָא דְּצָפוֹן אִתְאַחֲדָא דָּא. וְהַאי אִיהִי נְקוּדָה אֶמְצָעִיתָא, דְּקַיְּימָא בְּחוּרְבָּא. וּבְגִין דְּיָדַע לְמִפְתֵּי, שַׁלִּיט בְּגוֹ נְקוּדָה דְּיִשׁוּבָא, וְכָל מִלִּין דְּיִשׁוּבָא. בַּר אַרְעָא דְיִשְׂרָאֵל, כַּד שָׁרָאן יִשְׂרָאֵל בְּגַוָּה, אִיהוּ לָא שַׁלְטָא עֲלַיְיהוּ, וּלְבָתַר דְּחָבוּ יִשְׂרָאֵל שַׁלְטָא עַל אַרְעָא קַדִּישָׁא, בְּגִין דִּכְתִיב הֵשִׁיב אָחוֹר יְמִינוֹ מִפְּנֵי אוֹיֵב.

164. THE SECOND KLIPAH MENTIONED IN EZEKIEL IS CALLED 'A GREAT CLOUD'. IT IS CALLED a cloud because it is the dross of gold. This dross clings to the northern side, NAMELY, TO THE LEFT COLUMN, and is the central point, which abides in deserted places. Once it learned how to seduce EVE, it controls the central point of the inhabited world and everything that pertains to it, save the land of Yisrael. When Yisrael dwelt in it, it had no power over it, but later when Yisrael sinned, it took control over the holy land too. That is shown in the verse "He has drawn back His right hand from before the enemy" (Eichah 2:3).

165. עֲנָן גָּדוֹל דָּא, אִיהוּ עֲנָנָא דְּחַשׁוֹכָא, דְּאַחֲשִׁיךְ כָּל עָלְמָא. תָּא חֲזֵי, מַה בֵּין עֲנָנָא לַעֲנָנָא. הַהוּא עֲנָנָא דִּכְתִיב וַעֲנַן יְיָ׳ עֲלֵיהֶם יוֹמָם. וַעֲנָנְךָ עוֹמֵד עֲלֵיהֶם. הַאי אִיהוּ עֲנָנָא דְּנָהִיר וְזָהִיר, וְכָל נְהוֹרִין אִתְחֲזוֹן גּוֹ הַהוּא עֲנָנָא. אֲבָל עֲנָנָא דָּא, עֲנָנָא חָשׁוּךְ, דְּלָא נָהִיר כְּלָל, אֲבָל מָנַע כָּל נְהוֹרִין, דְּלָא יַכְלִין לְאִתְחֲזָאָה קַמֵּיהּ.

165. HE ASKS why it is called a great cloud, AND ANSWERS: For it is a cloud of darkness that darkened the whole world. Come and see, there are different clouds. Of that cloud, it is written: "and the cloud of Hashem was upon them by day" (Bemidbar 10:34), and "that your cloud stands over them" (Bemidbar 14:14). That cloud is shining and luminous and all lights are seen within that cloud. But this cloud OF THE KLIPOT is a cloud of darkness that sheds no light, but prevents all the lights from being seen through it.

166. גָּדוֹל, אֲמַאי אִקְרֵי גָּדוֹל, וְהָא זְעֵיר אִיהוּ. אֶלָּא גָּדוֹל אִיהוּ, כֵּיוָן

דְּשַׁלִּיט. ד״א גָּדוֹל, הַהוּא חֲשׁוֹכָא גָּדוֹל, כֵּיוָן דְּכַסֵּי כָּל נְהוֹרִין וְלָא אִתְחֲזוּן קַמֵּיה, וְאִיהוּ גָּדוֹל עַל כָּל עוֹבָדִין דְּעָלְמָא.

166. HE ASKS: IT IS CALLED GREAT. YET IF IT IS DARK why call it great, if it is small? HE ANSWERS: it is indeed great, because it has power. Also IT IS CALLED great, since the darkness in it is great, and it covers all the lights, so that they are not seen because of it. And it is greater than anything done in the world.

167. וְאֵשׁ מִתְלַקַּחַת, דְּהָא אֶשָּׁא דְּדִינָא קַשְׁיָא, לָא אַעֲדֵי מִנֵּיה לְעָלְמִין. וְנֹגַהּ לוֹ סָבִיב, אע״ג דְּכָל הַאי קַיְּימָא בֵּיה, נֹגַהּ לוֹ סָבִיב. מֵהָכָא אוֹלִיפְנָא, דְּאַף עַל גַּב דְּלֵית סִטְרָא דָּא, אֶלָּא סִטְרָא דִמְסָאֲבוּ, נֹגַהּ לוֹ סָבִיב, וְלָא אִצְטְרִיךְ לֵיה לְבַר נָשׁ, לְדַחְיָיא לֵיה לְבַר. מ״ט. בְּגִין דְּנֹגַהּ לוֹ סָבִיב, סִטְרָא דִקְדוּשָׁה דִמְהֵימְנוּתָא אִית לֵיה, וְלָא אִצְטְרִיךְ לְאַנְהָגָא בֵּיה קַלָנָא. וְע״ד אִצְטְרִיךְ לְמֵיהַב לֵיה חוּלָקָא, בְּסִטְרָא דִקְדוּשָׁא דִמְהֵימְנוּתָא.

167. "And a fire flaring up" (Yechezkel 1:4) alludes to the fire of rigorous Judgment that never leaves it. MEANING THAT THE KLIPAH ITSELF IS NOT FIRE - RIGOROUS JUDGMENT - BUT THE FIRE THAT CAME FROM BELOW FROM THE STORM WIND. IT CATCHES THE FIRE AND NEVER LEAVES IT. "And a brightness was about it" (Ibid.), INDICATES THAT even though all this is in THE KLIPAH OF A FIRE FLARING UP, NEVERTHELESS, "a brightness was about it." Hence we learn that though this is but the side of defilement, there is a brightness about it, that there is brightness and the illumination of holiness around it. Therefore a man should not cast it out. The reason is that since "a brightness was about it," it has part in the holy side of Faith, and one should not treat it with contempt. Therefore it should be given a part in the holy side of Faith.

168. רַב הַמְנוּנָא סָבָא, הָכִי אָמַר, וְכִי נֹגַהּ לוֹ סָבִיב, וְאִצְטְרִיךְ לְאַנְהָגָא בֵּיה קַלָנָא, הַאי נֹגַהּ לוֹ, לְגוֹ אִיהוּ, וְלָא קַיְּימָא לְבַר. וּבְגִין דְּקַיְּימָא הַהוּא נֹגַהּ לוֹ מִגּוֹ, כְּתִיב וּמִתּוֹכָהּ כְּעֵין הַחַשְׁמַל מִתּוֹךְ הָאֵשׁ. מִתּוֹכָהּ

דְּמַאן. מִתּוֹכָה דְּהַהוּא נֹגַהּ. כְּעֵין הַחַשְׁמַל: חָשׁ, מָל, הָא אוּקְמוּהָ, חֵיוָון דְּאֶשָׁא מְמַלְּלָא.

168. Rabbi Hamnuna Saba said that, THIS WAS WRITTEN AS A QUESTION, 'is there a brightness about it?' Therefore it should be treated with contempt, because there is brightness only inside it, not outside AND AROUND THE FIRE FLARING UP. And since that brightness is inside, it is written: "and out of the midst of it, as it were the color of electrum (Heb. *chashmal*)" (Yechezkel 1:4). In the midst of what – of that brightness. The color of Chashmal consists of the letters of chash mal, namely, muttering fiery living creatures (Heb. *chayot esh memalelot*).

169. אֲבָל מִבּוּצִינָא קַדִּישָׁא שְׁמַעֲנָא עָלָהּ רָזָא דְּרָזִין. כַּד עָרְלָה שַׁרְיָ עַל קַיָּימָא קַדִּישָׁא לְסָאֲבָא מַקְדְּשָׁא, כְּדֵין הַהוּא מַקְדְּשָׁא, אִתְעַכָּב מִלְּגַלָּאָה רָזָא דְּאָת קַיָּימָא, מִגּוֹ עָרְלָה. וְכַד הַאי נֹגַהּ עָאל לְגוֹ, וְאַפְרִישׁ בֵּין עָרְלָה, וּבֵין מַקְדְּשָׁא, כְּדֵין אִקְרֵי חַשְׁמַל חָשׁ וְאִתְגַּלְּיָא. מָל, מַהוּ מָל. כד"א מָל יְהוֹשֻׁעַ. רָזָא דְּאָת קַיָּימָא, אִתְעַכָּב מִלְּאִתְגַּלָּאָה מִגּוֹ עָרְלָה.

169. But from the holy luminary we heard the most secret mysteries concerning the subject. When the foreskin rests on the member of the holy covenant and defiles the temple, WHICH IS THE GLANS PENIS, THE SECRET OF MALCHUT, then that temple is prevented from exposing the secret of the sign of the covenant inside the foreskin. And when that brightness enters and separates the foreskin from the temple, it is called Chashmal, WHICH MEANS it hastens (Heb. *chash*) to be revealed. BUT, HE ASKS, THERE IS ALSO 'Mal' IN CHASHMAL. What is 'Mal'? HE ANSWERS: it is written, "Joshua circumcised (Heb. *mal*)" (Yehoshua 5:4), WHICH ALLUDES TO the secret sign of the covenant (circumcision) that was detained from revealing its light by the foreskin. BUT NOW, SINCE HE ALREADY CIRCUMCISED (HEB. *MAL*), THE LIGHT IS REVEALED. AND THE MEANING OF CHASHMAL IS THAT HE HASTENED (HEB. *CHASH*) TO EXPOSE, SINCE HE ALREADY CIRCUMCISED (HEB. *MAL*) THE FORESKIN.

170. וְאִית רָזָא אַחֲרָא, דְּהָא נְהוֹרָא דִּילֵיהּ, אִתְחֲזֵי וְלָא אִתְחֲזֵי, וְכַד

אִתְגַּלְיָא חַשְׁמַל אִתְעֲבָר נְהוֹרֵיהּ. אֲבָל רָזָא קַדְמָאָה, אִיהוּ בְּרָזָא דִּקְרָא כְּדְקָא יֵאוֹת, וְכֹלָּא שַׁפִּיר אִיהוּ, וְיֵאוּת הוּא.

170. Another secret states, that the light OF THE KLIPOT was both visible and invisible, WHICH MEANS THAT THERE WAS STILL IN THEM A TINY RAY THAT MAY BE SEEN ONCE, but when Chashmal was revealed, their light was gone COMPLETELY. But the first secret THAT WE SAID, is well embedded in the written verse while this secret cannot fit properly in the writing. Nonetheless, All is well and correct, FOR BOTH ARE TRUE.

171. בְּהַאי נֹגַהּ, מְפַתֵּי לְאִתְּתָא, לְנַטְלָא נְהוֹרָא. וְע"ד כְּתִיב, וְחָלָק מִשֶּׁמֶן חִכָּהּ, שַׁוֵּי הַהוּא נְהוֹרָא לְקַבְלֵיהּ דִּבְּרִית. וּבְגִינֵי כַּךְ מְפַתֵּי לֵיהּ, וְנַטְלָא נְהוֹרֵיהּ. וְדָא אִיהוּ פִּתּוּיָא דִּמְפַתֵּי לְאִתְּתָא, דִּכְתִיב נֹפֶת תִּטֹּפְנָה שִׂפְתֵי זָרָה וְגוֹ'.

171. With this brightness, THE SNAKE seduced the woman EVE to receive light. That is the meaning of "and her mouth is smoother than oil" (Mishlei 5:3), for it put light against the covenant. That is why it seduced her and she took its light. This is the temptation with which it tempted the woman, as written "for the lips of a strange woman drip honey..." (Ibid.).

172. ת"ח, בְּיוֹמָא שְׁתִיתָאָה כַּד מָטָא זִמְנָא דְּעֶרֶב, דְּלִיג לְגוֹ, הַהוּא מְדוּרָה דְּאֶשָּׁא, וְסַלְקָא לְעֵילָּא לְאַעֲלָא גּוֹ גַּוְונִין. כְּדֵין מִתְתַּקְּנִין יִשְׂרָאֵל לְתַתָּא, וּמְסַדְּרִין סְעוּדָתִין, וּמַתְקְנִין פָּתוֹרִין, כָּל חַד וְחַד פָּתוֹרֵיהּ. כְּדֵין חַד שַׁלְהוֹבָא נָפִיק וּבָטַשׁ בְּהַהוּא מְדוּרָה, כֵּיוָן דְּבָטַשׁ בֵּיהּ, מִתְגַּלְגְּלָן הַהוּא שַׁלְהוֹבָא, וְהַהוּא מְדוּרָה וְעָאלִין בְּנוּקְבָּא דִּתְהוֹמָא רַבָּא, וְאִתְטַמְּרָן וְיָתְבַת תַּמָּן.

172. Come and see, on Friday, WHICH IS YESOD, when evening sets, AT ITS CONCLUSION, the burning flame, THE STORM WIND, leaps inside to enter within the colors. Then Yisrael make ready below, fix the meals and set the tables, each his own table. A flame of fire then comes out and strikes the burning flame, AND JOINS IT. Once it struck and they joined, the flame of

fire and that flame roll TOGETHER, and enter a hollow in a great abyss, where they sit concealed.

173. וְהַהוּא שַׁלְהוֹבָא אִיהוּ מִסְטְרָא דִּימִינָא, וּבְגִין דְּהוּא מִסְטְרָא דִּימִינָא, אַעְבַּר לְהַהוּא מְדוּרָה, וְאָעִיל לֵיהּ לְנוּקְבָּא דִּתְהוֹמָא רַבָּא, וְיָתִיב תַּמָּן עַד דְּנָפִיק שַׁבַּתָּא. כֵּיוָן דְּנָפַק שַׁבַּתָּא, אִצְטְרִיךְ לְהוּ לְעַמָּא דְיִשְׂרָאֵל לְבָרְכָא עַל אֶשָּׁא, וְנַפְקָא הַהוּא שַׁלְהוֹבָא, בְּבִרְכְתָא דִּלְתַתָּא, וְשָׁלִיט עַל הַהוּא מְדוּרָה כָּל הַהוּא לֵילְיָא, וְאִתְכַּפְיָא הַהוּא מְדוּרָה.

173. And that flame of fire is from the right. Since it is from the right side, it canceled THE JUDGMENTS OF that fire and put it into the cavern in the great abyss. There it sits IN THE GREAT ABYSS, until Shabbat is concluded. When Shabbat is concluded, Yisrael must say the benediction over fire. By that benediction from below, the flame of fire comes out and has power over that flame all that night AFTER SHABBAT. And this flame is subdued, FOR ITS POWER IS CONCEALED.

174. תָּא חֲזֵי, כֵּיוָן דְּעָאל שַׁבַּתָּא, וְאִתְטְמַּר הַהוּא מְדוּרָה, כָּל אֶשִּׁין דְּאֶשָּׁא קַשְׁיָא אִתְטְמָרוּ וְאִתְכַּפְיָין, וַאֲפִילוּ אֶשָּׁא דְּגֵיהִנָּם, וְחַיָּיבִין דְּגֵיהִנָּם, אִית לוֹן נַיְיחָא. וְכֹלָּא תַּתָּא וְעֵילָּא אִית לְהוּ נַיְיחָא. כַּד נָפַק שַׁבַּתָּא, וּמְבָרְכִין יִשְׂרָאֵל עַל נוּרָא, כְּדֵין נָפְקִין כָּל אֶשִּׁין דְּמִתְטַמְרָן, כָּל חַד וְחַד לְאַתְרֵיהּ. וּבְגִין דְּלָא לְאִתְעָרָא אֶשָּׁא אַחֲרָא, כְּתִיב לֹא תְבַעֲרוּ אֵשׁ בְּכֹל מוֹשְׁבֹתֵיכֶם בְּיוֹם הַשַּׁבָּת, וְהָא אוּקְמוּהָ, אֶשָּׁא דְּמַדְבְּחָא אֲמַאי.

174. Come and see, when Shabbat enters and that flame was hidden IN THE GREAT ABYSS, all the flames of the harmful fire are hidden and subdued, FOR THE FLAME, WHICH IS A STORM WIND, IS THE ROOT OF ALL THE STRICT JUDGMENTS. And even the fire of Gehenom rests, and all the evil therein have respite, and all, above and below have rest. And at the end of Shabbat, when Yisrael recite the benediction over fire, all the hidden flames come out and return each to its place. In order not to kindle another flame OF THOSE THAT ARE HIDDEN, it is written: "You shall kindle no fire

throughout your habitations on the Shabbat day" (Shemot 35:3). And it was already explained why the fire on the altar is allowed ON SHABBAT.

13. What is Shabbat

A Synopsis

Rabbi Hamnuna Saba (the elder) says that when Shabbat enters, the crier proclaims throughout all the firmaments, 'be prepared, O Chariots; be prepared, O legions, before your Master.' After this a spirit, the light of Chesed, comes from the south and is called 'the precious garment of Shabbat.' It enfolds all the armies of the right side. Then the person whose table is properly set is happy because his table is perfected in the palace, Malchut. When Shabbat arrives everyone must wash themselves so that the holy supernal spirit can rest on them. Rabbi Hamnuna Saba (the elder) tells us about the other six days, the work days. Then he says the word Shabbat is derived from 'shavat' in "because in it he rested (shavat)," but it also refers to the three patriarchs joined with Malchut. In the high Shabbat, every point is the most important part of the eye.

175. אֶלָּא כַּד עָאל שַׁבְּתָא, כָּרוֹזָא קָרֵי בְּכוּלְהוּ רְקִיעִין, אִתְתְּקָנוּ רְתִיכִין, אִתְתְּקָנוּ מַשְׁרְיָין, לְקַדְמוּת מָארֵיכוֹן. כְּדֵין נָפִיק חַד רוּחָא מִסִּטְרָא דְדָרוֹם, וְהַהוּא רוּחָא אִתְפְּרַשׁ עַל כָּל אִינוּן חֵילִין וּמַשְׁרְיָין דְּלִסְטַר יְמִינָא, וְאִתְלַבְּשָׁן בֵּיהּ, וְהַהוּא רוּחָא אִקְרֵי לְבוּשָׁא דִּיקָר דְּשַׁבְּתָא. כְּדֵין פָּתוֹרֵי דְּהַאי עָלְמָא, מִתְתַּקְּנָן בְּחַד הֵיכָלָא. זַכָּאָה חוּלְקֵיהּ דְּהַהוּא בַּר נָשׁ, דְּסִדּוּרָא דְּפָתוֹרֵיהּ אִתְחֲזֵי תַּמָּן כַּדְקָא יָאוּת, וְקַיְּימָא כֹּלָּא מִתְתַּקְּנָא, בְּלָא כִּסּוּפָא, אֵינָשׁ כְּפוּם חֵילֵיהּ.

175. When Shabbat enters, the crier proclaims throughout all the firmaments 'be prepared, O Chariots; be prepared, O legions, before your Master'. Then a spirit comes from the south, WHICH IS THE LIGHT OF CHESED. That spirit expands over all those armies and legions of the right side, and they wrap themselves in it. That spirit is called 'the precious garment of Shabbat'. Then the tables people set in this world are placed in one chamber, WHICH IS MALCHUT. Happy is the portion of the person, whose set table is considered well prepared, and everything is arranged without shame, each man according to his means.

176. כַּד עָאל שַׁבְּתָא, אִצְטְרִיכוּ אִינוּן עַמָּא קַדִּישָׁא לְאַסְחָאָה גַרְמַיְיהוּ מִשְּׁמוּשָׁא דְחוֹל, מַאי טַעֲמָא. בְּגִין דִּבְחוֹל, רוּחָא אַחֲרָא אַזְלָא וְשַׁטְיָא

וְשַׁרְיָא עַל עַמָּא. וְכַד בָּעֵי בַּר נָשׁ לְנָפְקָא מִן הַהוּא רוּחָא, וּלְאַעֲלָא בְּרוּחָא אַחֲרָא קַדִּישָׁא עִלָּאָה, בָּעֵי לְאַסְחָאָה גַּרְמֵיהּ, לְמִשְׁרֵי עֲלֵיהּ הַהוּא רוּחָא עִלָּאָה קַדִּישָׁא.

176. When Shabbat comes in, the holy nation has to wash themselves from the work week's habits. What is the sense? During the work week, a different spirit roams and hovers about the people, and when a person wishes to be released from that spirit and come into the influence of another, holy and Supernal Spirit, he should wash himself, so that that holy Supernal Spirit shall rest upon him.

177. ת"ח רָזָא עִלָּאָה דְּמִלָּה, כָּל אִינּוּן שִׁית יוֹמִין, אִתְאַחֲדָן בְּרָזָא דְּחַד נְקוּדָה קַדִּישָׁא, וְכֻלְּהוּ יוֹמִין אִתְאַחֲדָן בֵּיהּ. וְאִית יוֹמִין אַחֲרָנִין, דְּקַיְימִין לְבַר בְּסִטְרָא אַחֲרָא. וְאִית יוֹמִין אַחֲרָנִין, דְּקַיְימִין לְגוֹ מֵעֲגוּלָא קַדִּישָׁא, וְאִתְאַחֲדָן בִּנְקוּדָה קַדִּישָׁא.

177. Come and see the lofty meaning of the matter. All these six days, CHESED, GVURAH, TIFERET, NETZACH, HOD AND YESOD OF ZEIR ANPIN are united within the secret of a certain holy point, MALCHUT, and all the days become one with it. There are other days that stand outside on the Other Side, namely, CHESED, GVURAH, TIFERET, NETZACH, HOD AND YESOD OF THE KLIPOT and there are days which are CHESED, GVURAH, TIFERET, NETZACH, HOD AND YESOD OF MALCHUT that stand inside the holy circle, united within the holy point, MALCHUT OF MALCHUT.

178. וְיִשְׂרָאֵל קַדִּישִׁין, וְכָל אִינּוּן דְּמִתְעַסְּקִין בִּקְדוּשָׁה, כָּל יוֹמִין דְּשַׁבַּתָּא, אִתְאַחֲדָן כָּל אִינּוּן שִׁית יוֹמִין, בְּאִינּוּן שִׁית יוֹמִין דִּלְגוֹ דְּאִתְאַחֲדָן בְּהַהִיא נְקוּדָה, אִתְאַחֲדָן בְּהַאי, בְּגִין לְנַטְרָא לוֹן. וְכָל אִינּוּן שִׁית יוֹמִין דְּשַׁבַּתָּא, הַהִיא נְקוּדָה טְמִירָא אִיהִי. כֵּיוָן דְּעָאל שַׁבַּתָּא, כְּדֵין סַלְקָא הַהִיא נְקוּדָה, וְאִתְעַטְּרָא וְאִתְאַחֲדָא לְעֵילָּא, וְכֻלְּהוּ טְמִירִין בְּגַוָּהּ.

178. And holy Yisrael and all those who work in holiness all the days of Shabbat, THEIR six days are joined with the six inner days which are

CHESED, GVURAH, TIFERET, NETZACH, HOD AND YESOD OF MALCHUT that are united within the point of MALCHUT OF MALCHUT to guard and keep it. And all the six days of that Shabbat pertain to that hidden point. And when Shabbat commences, the point, MALCHUT OF MALCHUT, ascends and is crowned and united above, and they are all hidden in it.

179. ת״ח, אִית יָמִים וְאִית יָמִים. יְמֵי חוֹל, כְּמָה דְּאִתְּמַר, וְאִלֵּין קַיְימִין לְבַר לְעַמִּין. יְמֵי הַשַּׁבָּת, דְּאִינּוּן יְמֵי הַשָּׁבוּעַ, קַיְימִין לְיִשְׂרָאֵל. וְכַד סַלְקָא הַאי נְקוּדָה, כֹּלָּא אִתְגְּנִיז, וְאִיהִי סַלְקָא, כֵּיוָן דְּאִיהִי סַלְקָא, אִקְרֵי שַׁבָּת.

179. Come and see, there are days and there are days. THERE ARE workdays, as we learned, that are outside for the nations CHESED, GVURAH, TIFERET, NETZACH, HOD AND YESOD OF THE OTHER SIDE. The days of Shabbat, the six weekdays, exist for Yisrael CHESED, GVURAH, TIFERET, NETZACH, HOD AND YESOD OF MALCHUT. When this point ascends, everything is concealed THE SIX SFIROT IN IT and it goes up. Once it ascends, it is called Shabbat.

180. מַהוּ שַׁבָּת. אִי תֵּימָא בְּגִין שְׁבִיתָה, דִּכְתִּיב כִּי בוֹ שָׁבַת, יָאוֹת הוּא. אֲבָל רָזָא דְּמִלָּה, כֵּיוָן דְּסַלְקָא הַאי נְקוּדָה, וּנְהוֹרָא נָהִיר, כְּדֵין מִתְעַטְּרָא אִיהִי בַּאֲבָהָן, כֵּיוָן דְּמִתְעַטְּרָא אִיהִי בַּאֲבָהָן, כְּדֵין אִתְחַבְּרַת וְאִתְאַחֲדַת בְּהוּ, לְמֶהֱוֵי חַד, וְאִקְרֵי כֹּלָּא שַׁבָּת. שַׁבָּת: ש׳ בַּת. שׁ׳ הָא אוּקְמוּהָ, רָזָא דִּתְלַת אֲבָהָן, דְּמִתְאַחֲדָן בְּבַת יְחִידָה, וְאִיהִי מִתְעַטְּרָא בְּהוּ, וְאִינּוּן בְּעָלְמָא דְּאָתֵי. וְכֹלָּא אִיהוּ חַד. וְדָא אִיהוּ ש׳ בַּת, לְמֶהֱוֵי כֹּלָּא חַד.

180. HE ASKS: what is Shabbat, NAMELY, WHY IS IT CALLED BY THE NAME SHABBAT? You may say it is due to rest from work, as written, "because in it He rested (Heb. *shavat*)" (Beresheet 2:3), and this is correct. But the secret of the matter is that since that point ascended and its light is shining, it adorns itself with the patriarchs, CHESED, GVURAH AND TIFERET OF ZEIR ANPIN. When it does so, it is joined and united with them and together everything is called Shabbat. THAT IS TO SAY, THE PATRIARCHS TOGETHER WITH MALCHUT ARE CALLED SHABBAT. The

word 'Shabbat IS COMPOSED OF THESE LETTERS Shin and the segment Bat. It has been explained that Shin refers to the three patriarchs who are united in the only daughter (Heb. *bat*) WHICH IS MALCHUT. FOR THE THREE BARS OF THE HEBREW LETTER SHIN ALLUDE TO THE THREE PATRIARCHS, CHESED, GVURAH AND TIFERET. And she, WHO IS CALLED DAUGHTER is crowned with them; and THE PATRIARCHS are crowned in the World to Come, WHICH IS BINAH, and all is one. And Shabbat indicates that all are one.

181. וְאִי תֵּימָא, שַׁבָּת הַגָּדוֹל, וְאִיהוּ לְעֵילָא, אֲמַאי אִקְרֵי שַׁבָּת. אֶלָּא וַדַּאי הָכִי הוּא. וְרָזָא דְּמִלָּה, בְּכָל אֲתַר נְקוּדָה דְּאִיהִי עִקָּרָא דְּכָל עֵינָא, אִקְרֵי בַּת. כד"א, שָׁמְרֵנִי כְּאִישׁוֹן בַּת עָיִן, בְּגִין דְּאִיהִי עִקָּרָא דְּכָל עֵינָא, אִקְרֵי בַּת.

181. You may say that the Great Shabbat, WHICH IS BINAH THAT IS ALSO CALLED SHABBAT, is high up WHERE CHOCHMAH IS HIDDEN AND NOT REVEALED. Why is it called Shabbat? HE ANSWERS: assuredly it is so CALLED SHABBAT, and the secret thereof is that the point is always the essence of the eye, THAT IS, IT HAS CHOCHMAH IN IT, WHICH IS CALLED EYES. It is named pupil (Heb. *bat*), as is written: "keep me as the apple (Heb. *bat*) of the eye" (Tehilim 17:8).

182. עָלְמָא דְּאָתֵי, אִיהוּ הֵיכָלָא לְהַהִיא נְקוּדָה עִלָּאָה, וְכַד אִיהִי קַיְּימָא, וְנַטְלָא בְּגַדְפָהָא לַאֲבָהָן, לְאִתְעַטְּרָא לְעֵילָא אִקְרֵי כֻּלָּא שַׁבָּת. וְכַד אֲבָהָן מִתְעַטְּרָן לְעֵילָא, בְּגוֹ נְקוּדָה עִלָּאָה, אִקְרֵי שַׁבָּת. נְקוּדָה תַּתָּאָה כַּד מִתְעַטְּרָא בַּאֲבָהָן אִקְרֵי שַׁבָּת.

182. The World to Come, BINAH, is a chamber to that supernal point, NAMELY TO SUPERNAL CHOCHMAH. And when it rises and takes the patriarchs in its wings to bedeck them above, they all are called Shabbat, in a way that the patriarchs, adorned above in the supernal point, are called Shabbat. And when the point below, MALCHUT, is adorned by the patriarchs, it is called Shabbat.

14. The additional soul

A Synopsis

We are told that Malchut is the lowest point, and when it emerges on Shabbat night it expands along with its lights and spreads its wings over the world to protect it. Then another spirit of Neshamah is added to each person, and joy replaces sorrow and wrath. Ruach descends, washes itself in perfumes from the Garden of Eden, and rests upon the holy nation. Sixty Chariots descend with it when it goes down to the Garden of Eden. The Ruach is the secret of Shabbat that dwells below, and since it joins in the pleasures and delights of Yisrael on that day, it should be given pleasure in food and drink. During the other six days it is gladdened by the supernal spirit of the Ancient of Ancients, and on the Shabbat it takes pleasure from the body in the meal of faith. Rabbi Shimon explains that every Nefesh of Yisrael is adorned on Shabbat by the crown of the Ruach that dwells inside them. When Shabbat leaves and the Ruach goes up, the Nefesh feels sorrow for what it lost. We read of the reason for performing marital duties on Shabbat nights; Rabbi Shimon explains the difference between intercourse on that night and intercourse the rest of the week and in the daytime – on this night a holy superior Ruach descends into the holy children.

183. הַאי נְקוּדָה תַּתָּאָה כַּד סַלְקָא וְאִתְחֲזִיַת, וְאִתְקַשִּׁיטַת. כְּדֵין כָּל חֶדְוָה אִשְׁתְּכַח לְעֵילָא וְתַתָּא, וְעָלְמִין כֻּלְּהוּ בְּחֶדְוָה. וּבְהַאי לֵילְיָא, הַאי נְקוּדָה אִתְפָּשַׁט נְהוֹרָאָה, וּפָרִישׂ גַּדְפוֹי עַל עָלְמָא, וְכָל שִׁלְטוֹנִין אַחֲרָנִין מִתְעַבְרָן, וּנְטִירוּ אִשְׁתְּכַח עַל עָלְמָא.

183. The lower point, MALCHUT, when it emerges to become seen, NAMELY WHEN IT RECEIVES CHOCHMAH CALLED SIGHT, and is decorated WITH SUPERNAL MOCHIN, there is bliss above and below and all the worlds are in joy. At SHABBAT night, the point expands along with its lights, and spreads its wings over the world. Then all other rulers are removed, and the world is protected.

184. וּכְדֵין אִתּוֹסָף רוּחַ נִשְׁמָתָא בְּיִשְׂרָאֵל, עַל כָּל חַד וְחַד, וּבְהַהִיא נִשְׁמָתָא יְתֵירָא, נַשְׁיָין כָּל עִצְבָא וְחֵימָתָא, וְלָא אִשְׁתְּכַח בַּר חֶדְוָה, לְעֵילָא וְתַתָּא. הַהוּא רוּחָא דְּנָחִית וְאִתּוֹסָף בִּבְנֵי עָלְמָא, כַּד נָחִית,

אִתְסְחֵי בְּבוּסְמִין דְּגִנְתָּא דְעֵדֶן, וְנָחִית וְשָׁרָא עַל עַמָּא קַדִּישָׁא, זַכָּאִין אִינּוּן, כַּד הַאי רוּחָא אִתְּעַר.

184. Then a Ruach of the Soul is added to Yisrael, to each and every one. With this additional soul all sorrow and wrath are forgotten, and above and below there is only joy. That Ruach that went down as an addition to the world's inhabitants, when it comes down, washes itself with perfumes of the Garden of Eden, and descends to rest upon the holy nation. Happy are they when that Ruach is aroused.

185. בְּהַהִיא שַׁעֲתָא דְּהַהוּא רוּחָא נָחִית נַחְתִּין עִמָּה לְגוֹ גִּנְתָּא דְעֵדֶן, שִׁתִּין רְתִיכִין, מִתְעַטְרִין לְשִׁית סִטְרִין. וְכַד מָטֵי לְגִנְתָּא דְעֵדֶן, כְּדֵין כָּל אִינּוּן רוּחִין וְנִשְׁמָתִין דְּגִנְתָּא דְעֵדֶן, כֻּלְּהוּ מִתְעַטְּרֵי בְּהַהוּא רוּחָא. כְּרוֹזֵי קָרֵי וְאָמַר, זַכָּאִין אַתּוּן יִשְׂרָאֵל, עַמָּא קַדִּישָׁא, דִּרְעוּתָא דְּמָארֵיכוֹן אִתְּעַר לְגַבַּיְיכוּ.

185. When the Ruach descends, sixty Chariots decorate the six directions, descend with it to the Garden of Eden. THE SIX ENDS ARE THE SIX SFIROT, CHESED, GVURAH, TIFERET, NETZACH, HOD AND YESOD, EACH CONSISTING OF TEN, AMOUNTING TO SIXTY IN ALL. When the Ruach arrives in the Garden of Eden, then all these spirits and souls in the Garden of Eden, are bedecked with it. The crier calls and announces: happy are Yisrael, a holy nation, for the good will of your Master is awakened toward you.

186. רָזָא דְּרָזִין לְיַדְעֵי חָכְמְתָא, זַכָּאִין אִינּוּן כַּד הַאי רוּחָא אִתְּעַר. הַאי רוּחָא אִיהוּ אִתְפַּשְּׁטוּתָא דְּהַאי נְקוּדָה, וְנָפְקָא מִינָּהּ, וְאִתְפַּשְּׁטָא בְּעָלְמָא, וְהַהוּא הֲוֵי רָזָא דְּשַׁבָּת, דְּשַׁרְיָא לְתַתָּא, וְעַל דָּא כְּתִיב בֵּיהּ שְׁמִירָה, וְשָׁמְרוּ בְנֵי יִשְׂרָאֵל אֶת הַשַּׁבָּת, וְהָא אוּקְמוּהָ, שַׁבָּת לָא כְּתִיב, אֶלָּא אֶת הַשַּׁבָּת, לְאַסְגָּאָה הַהוּא רוּחָא דְּשָׁרֵי עַל כֹּלָּא, וְאִצְטְרִיךְ לְנַטְרָא לֵיהּ, הוֹאִיל וְקַיְּימָא עִמֵּיהּ דְּבַר נָשׁ, וְעַל דָּא כְּתִיב, כָּל שׁוֹמֵר שַׁבָּת מֵחַלְּלוֹ.

186. The most guarded mystery is for those familiar in wisdom. Happy are

they when that Ruach is aroused. That Ruach is the expansion of the point, MALCHUT. It comes from it and spreads throughout the world. And that RUACH is the secret of Shabbat that dwells below. Therefore it is written regarding it that it should be kept: "Wherefore the children of Yisrael shall keep the Shabbat" (Shemot 31:16). It has been explained that it does not say "Shabbat," but "the Shabbat," alluding to that additional Ruach that dwells in everything and should be kept, since it stays with man. Therefore it is written: "that keeps the Shabbat and does not profane it" (Yeshayah 56:2).

187. בְּהַאי רָזָא אִית רָזָא אַחֲרָא. הַאי רוּחָא, אִתְהֲנֵי בְּהַאי יוֹמָא, מֵהֲנָאוֹתָן דְּיִשְׂרָאֵל, וּמֵעִנּוּגָא דִּלְהוֹן, וּבג"ד, בָּעֵי לְמֵיהַב לֵיהּ עִנּוּגָא, בְּמֵיכְלָא וּבְמִשְׁתְּיָא, תְּלַת זִמְנִין, בִּתְלַת סְעוּדָתִין, דִּתְלַת דַּרְגֵּי מְהֵימְנוּתָא, כְּמָה דְּאוּקְמוּהָ. וְהַאי נָטִיל חֶדְוָה וְעִנּוּגָא, בְּאִינּוּן סְעוּדָתֵי דְּיִשְׂרָאֵל. זַכָּאָה חוּלְקֵיהּ, מַאן דְּאַהֲנֵי לֵיהּ, וּמְעַנֵּג לֵיהּ, בְּהַאי יוֹמָא.

187. Within that secret there is another one. That Ruach partakes on this day in the pleasures and delights of Yisrael. It therefore should be given pleasure in food and drink three times in the three meals of the three grades of the Faith, as was explained. And that RUACH receives gladness and pleasure from these meals of Yisrael. Happy is he who gladdens and delights it on that day.

188. הַאי רוּחָא, אִתְהֲנֵי כָּל שִׁיתָא יוֹמִין, מֵרוּחָא עִלָּאָה דְּעַתִּיקָא דְּכָל עַתִּיקִין. וּבְיוֹמָא דְּשַׁבַּתָּא, כֵּיוָן דְּנָחִית, וְאִתְסְחֵי בְּגִנְתָּא דְּעֵדֶן בְּלֵילְיָא, אִתְעַנָּג מֵעִנּוּגָא דְּגוּפָא, בִּסְעוּדָתֵי דִּמְהֵימְנוּתָא, וְאִתְעַטָּר הַאי רוּחָא מֵעֵילָּא וְתַתָּא, וְאִתְרְוֵי בְּכָל סִטְרִין, בְּעִטְרָא דִּלְעֵילָּא וְתַתָּא.

188. That Ruach enjoys during the six days the Supernal Spirit of the most Ancient. On Shabbat day, after descending and washing in the Garden of Eden during the night, it takes pleasure in the physical pleasure at the meal of Faith, and is adorned above and below. It is situated on all sides, VIZ. IN CHOCHMAH AND CHASSADIM, on the higher crown, CHASSADIM, and the lower crown, CHOCHMAH.

189. וְהוֹאִיל וְקַיְימָא עִמֵּיהּ דְּבַר נָשׁ, אִצְטְרִיךְ לֵיהּ לְנַטְרָא לֵיהּ. וְע"ד

כְּתִיב וְשָׁמְרוּ בְנֵי יִשְׂרָאֵל. אֶת הַשַּׁבָּת, שַׁבָּת דָּא, הוּא הַהִיא נְקוּדָה
תַּתָּאָה. אֶת הַשַּׁבָּת, דָּא הוּא הַאי רוּחָא, אִתְפַּשְׁטוּתָא דְּהַהִיא נְקוּדָה.
הַהוּא אִתְפַּשְׁטוּתָא, כַּד אִתּוֹסָף קְדוּשָׁן וּבִרְכָּאן מִלְּעֵילָא, עַל הַהִיא
נְקוּדָה, אִתְנְהִיר כֹּלָּא, וְאִתְעֲבִיד רוּחָא נְהִירָא בְּכָל סִטְרִין, אִתְפְּלַג
לְעֵילָא וְנָהִיר. וְאִתְפְּלַג לְתַתָּא וְנָהִיר. וְדָא הוּא דִּכְתִיב בֵּינִי וּבֵין בְּנֵי
יִשְׂרָאֵל חוּלָק אַחֲסָנָא אִית לָן כַּחֲדָא.

189. Since it is with man, it should be properly kept. Therefore it is written: "Wherefore the children of Yisrael shall keep the Shabbat." Shabbat is the lower point, MALCHUT. "The Shabbat" refers to that Ruach which is the expansion of that point. This expansion, when holiness was added to that point, and blessings from above, everything became illuminated, and THE EXPANSION turned into a Ruach luminous on all sides. HALF OF IT divides and turns up and shines, and HALF OF IT divides and turns down and shines. This is the meaning of "between Me and the children of Yisrael" (Shemot 31:16), FOR THE RUACH WAS DIVIDED BETWEEN HIM AND YISRAEL, and together we share a portions and heritage.

190. חוּלָקָא דִּלְעֵילָא, אִתְעַטָּר בְּהַאי יוֹמָא, מֵעֲנוּגָא עִלָּאָה קַדִּישָׁא,
וְאִתְהֲנֵי מִזִּיוָא עִלָּאָה דְּעַתִּיקָא דְּכָל עַתִּיקִין. חוּלָקָא תַּתָּאָה, אִתְעַטָּר
בְּהַאי יוֹמָא, מֵעֲנוּגָא דִּלְתַתָּא, דְּאִתְהֲנֵי בְּהֲנֵי סְעוּדָתֵי. וְע״ד, בָּעֵי
לְעַנְּגָא לֵיהּ, בְּמֵיכְלָא וּבְמִשְׁתְּיָא בִּלְבוּשֵׁי יְקָר, וּבְחֶדְוָה דְּכֹלָּא.

190. The upper portion is adorned on that day by the higher, holy pleasure and enjoys the supernal glow of the most Ancient, WHICH IS KETER. The lower portion is adorned on that day with the lower pleasure, by enjoying the meals PREPARED BY YISRAEL; therefore one should delight it with food and drink, with respectable attire, and much joy.

191. וְכַד מִתְעַטְּרָא הַאי חוּלָקָא לְתַתָּא, וְאִתְנְטִיר כְּמָה דְּאִצְטְרִיךְ,
סַלְקָא לְעֵילָא, וְאִתְחַבְּרָא בְּהַהוּא חוּלָקָא אַחֲרָא. וְהַאי נְקוּדָה נָטִיל
כֹּלָּא מֵעֵילָא וְתַתָּא, וְאִתְכְּלִילָא מִכָּל סִטְרִין. וּבְגִין דְּמִתְעַטְּרָא בְּשַׁבָּת,
מֵעֵילָא וּמַתַּתָּא, כָּל שְׁאָר יוֹמִין יָהִיב חֵילָא לְכֹלָּא, וְאִתְיְיהִיב לֵיהּ

שׁוּלְטָנוּ מֵעֵילָא וּמִתַּתָּא. וּבְרָזִין דְּסִפְרָא דִּשְׁלֹמֹה מַלְכָּא, אִשְׁתְּכַח רָזָא דָא, וְאוּקְמוּהָ בּוּצִינָא קַדִּישָׁא, זַכָּאָה חוּלָקֵיהוֹן דְּיִשְׂרָאֵל.

191. When the lower portion is adorned and kept as it ought, it rises up high and joins the other, HIGHER portion. And that point, MALCHUT, receives everything FROM THE RUACH, from the upper PORTION and the lower PART, and is incorporated on all sides. And since it is adorned by Shabbat from above and from below, all the rest of the days, WHICH ARE CHESED, GVURAH, TIFERET, NETZACH, HOD AND YESOD give power to everything, and MALCHUT is given dominion above and below. And among the secrets of the book of King Solomon is this secret, which the holy luminary, RABBI SHIMON, explained. Happy is the portion of Yisrael.

192. כְּתִיב וַיִּנָּפַשׁ, וְאוּקְמוּהָ וַוי נֶפֶשׁ דְּאָבְדַת וְשַׁפִּיר אִיהוּ. אֲבָל אִי הָכִי וַוי גּוּפָא אִצְטְרִיךְ לְמֵימַר, דְּמִנֵּיהּ אָבְדַת נֶפֶשׁ. אֲבָל רָזָא דְמִלָּה, בְּבַר נָשׁ אִית נֶפֶשׁ, דְּנַטְלָא וּמָשִׁיךְ לְגַבֵּיהּ לְהַאי רוּחָא מֵעֶרֶב שַׁבָּת. וְהַהוּא רוּחָא שַׁרְיָא בְּגַוֵּוהּ דְּהַהִיא נֶפֶשׁ, וְדַיְירָא בָּהּ כָּל יוֹמָא דְשַׁבַּתָּא. וּכְדֵין, הַהוּא נֶפֶשׁ, יְתֵירָה בִּרְבוּיָא וְתוֹעַלְתָּא יַתִּיר מִמַּה דַּהֲוָה.

192. It is written: "and He rested (Heb. *vayinafash*)" (Shemot 31:17), which is explained as, woe for the loss of the Nefesh. This is correct, but if this is so, it should have been said, woe to the body for losing the Nefesh, YET IN 'VAYINAFASH' ONLY THE NEFESH IS INDICATED. HE REPLIES: the secret of the matter is that in each person there is a Nefesh, which draws to itself and receives THAT SAID Ruach from Shabbat eve. And that Ruach dwells and rests in the Nefesh throughout the Shabbat day. Then the Nefesh is in a state of more greatness and more benefited than it used to be.

193. וְעַל דָּא תָּנֵינָן, כָּל נַפְשָׁאן דְּיִשְׂרָאֵל מִתְעַטְּרָן בְּיוֹמָא דְּשַׁבַּתָּא, וְעִטְרָא דִלְהוֹן, דְּשַׁרְיָא הַאי רוּחָא בְּגַוַּויְיהוּ. כֵּיוָן דְּנָפַק שַׁבַּתָּא, וְהַהוּא רוּחָא סַלְקָא לְעֵילָא, כְּדֵין וַוי לְנֶפֶשׁ, דְּאָבְדַת מַה דְּאָבְדַת. אָבְדַת הַהוּא עִטְרָא עִלָּאָה, וְהַהוּא חֵילָא קַדִּישָׁא דַּהֲוָה בָּהּ, וְדָא הוּא וַיִּנָּפַשׁ, וַוי נֶפֶשׁ, דְּאָבְדַת מַה דְּאָבְדַת.

193. Therefore we learned that every Nefesh of Yisrael is adorned on the day of Shabbat, and their crown is that SAID Ruach, which dwells inside them. When Shabbat leaves and the Ruach goes up, woe to the Nefesh for losing that which it lost, THAT IS, that superior crown and that holy power that it had. And that is the meaning of "vayinafash," woe (Heb. *vay*) to the Nefesh, for losing what it lost.

194. עוֹנָתָן דְּחַכִּימִין, דְּיַדְעֵי רָזִין עָלָּאִין, מְלֵילְיָא דְּשַׁבַּתָּא לְלֵילְיָא דְּשַׁבַּתָּא, וְאוֹקְמוּהַ. אֲבָל מִלָּה דָּא שָׁאִילְנָא לְבוּצִינָא קַדִּישָׁא, דְּהָא חֲזֵינָן דְּהַאי כִּתְרָא תַּתָּאָה, נָקְטָא מַה דְּנָקְטָא בִּימָמָא, וּבְלֵילְיָא יָהִיב מְזוֹנָא לְכָל חֵילֵיהּ, כְּמָה דְּאוֹקְמוּהַ, דִּכְתִּיב וַתָּקָם בְּעוֹד לַיְלָה וַתִּתֵּן טֶרֶף לְבֵיתָהּ וְחֹק לְנַעֲרוֹתֶיהָ. נָקְטָא בִּימָמָא, וְיָהֲבָא בְּלֵילְיָא. וְהַשְׁתָּא אֲמַר מַר דְּזִוּוּגָא אִשְׁתְּכַח בְּהַאי לֵילְיָא.

194. The wise who are initiated in the high secrets, perform their marital duty on Shabbat nights, as was explained. However, this subject I asked the holy luminary, for we see that the lower crown, MALCHUT, receives what she receives FROM ZEIR ANPIN THROUGH COUPLING by day, and at night gives nourishment to all her armies as stated in the verse "She rises also while it is yet night, and gives food to her household, and a portion to her maidens" (Mishlei 31:15). She receives THROUGH INTERCOURSE by day, and by night she gives, SO THERE IS NO INTERCOURSE AT NIGHT. Yet now you say, Master, that there is union on that night OF SHABBAT.

195. אָמַר, וַדַּאי זִוּוּגָא אִשְׁתְּכַח בְּלֵילְיָא דָּא. מ"ט. בְּגִין דְּהַאי לֵילְיָא, אַפְרִישַׁת נִשְׁמָתִין לְכָל אִינּוּן חַכִּימִין, דְּיַדְעִין רָזִין דְּחָכְמְתָא. וְחִבּוּרָא, וְזִוּוּגָא, לָא אִשְׁתְּכַח בְּיוֹמָא אַחֲרָא בְּכָל חֶדְוָה, בְּלָא עִרְבּוּבְיָא אַחֲרָא, כְּגוֹן דָּא. בְּגִין דְּאִינּוּן נִשְׁמָתִין דְּפָלִיגַת, פְּלִיגַת לוֹן בְּחַכִּימִין, בְּצַדִּיקִים, בַּחֲסִידֵי כַּדְקָא יָאוֹת. וּבְכָל לֵילְיָא וְלֵילְיָא, זִוּוּגָא אִשְׁתְּכַח וַדַּאי. אֵימָתַי בְּפַלְגוּת לֵילְיָא. וְהָא אוֹקִימְנָא. אֲבָל לָא בְּכָל סִטְרִין כְּהַאי זִוּוּגָא.

195. He said, but of course there is union on that night. The reason is that that night OF SHABBAT, WHICH IS MALCHUT, distributes souls to those wise men who are versed in the secret of wisdom. And there is no union on

any other day that is completely joyful and without a mixture FROM THE OTHER SIDE, like on that NIGHT, since these souls that she distributes, she distributes them to the wise, the righteous and the pious, as fit. Similarly, a union surely occurs every night BETWEEN ZEIR ANPIN AND MALCHUT, at midnight, as was already explained, but it is not COMPLETE on all sides like that union OF SHABBAT NIGHT.

196. וּבְגִין דָּא, חַכִּימִין דְּיַדְעִין רָזִין, בַּעְיָין לְסַדְרָא שִׁמּוּשָׁא דִּלְהוֹן, בְּהַאי לֵילְיָא. מַאי טַעֲמָא. בְּגִין דְּכָל יוֹמֵי דְּשַׁבְּתָא, אִית לוֹן רוּחָא אַחֲרָא דְּשַׁרְיָא עַל עָלְמָא, וּבְהַאי לֵילְיָא אִית לוֹן רוּחָא אַחֲרָא קַדִּישָׁא עִלָּאָה, דְּנַחְתָּא לִבְנֵי קַדִּישִׁין, וְהַהוּא רוּחָא נָשִׁיב מֵעַתִּיקָא דְּכָל עַתִּיקִין, וְנַחְתָּא לְגוֹ נְקוּדָה תַּתָּאָה, לְמֵיהַב בָּהּ נַיְיחָא לְכֹלָּא, וְדָא אִתְפְּלִיג לְכָל סִטְרִין, לְעֵילָא וְתַתָּא, כְּמָה דְּאַתְּ אָמַר בֵּינִי וּבֵין בְּנֵי יִשְׂרָאֵל.

196. For that reason, the wise men who know these secrets, should organize and perform their conjugal duties on that night. Why? because on all the days of the week, we have a different Ruach dwelling in the world. On this night we have another holy, superior Ruach that descends to the holy children. This Ruach blows from the most Ancient, KETER, and goes down to the lower point, to bring therein rest for all. This Spirit is divided on all sides, above and below, as was said "between Me and the children of Yisrael" (Shemot 31:16).

197. וְכַד אִינּוּן חַכִּימִין, יַתְבִין בְּהַהוּא רוּחָא קַדִּישָׁא, רוּחָא עִלָּאָה, בָּעָאן לְשַׁמְּשָׁא עַרְסַיְיהוּ, דְּהַאי רוּחָא אַמְשִׁיךְ אֲבַתְרֵיהּ לְתַתָּא, כָּל אִינּוּן נִשְׁמָתִין קַדִּישִׁין, וְיָרְתִין קַדִּישֵׁי עֶלְיוֹנִין, בְּהַאי רוּחָא, נִשְׁמָתִין קַדִּישִׁין לִבְנֵיהוֹן כַּדְקָא יֵאוֹת.

197. When these wise man dwell with that holy Ruach, the supernal Ruach, they should perform their marital duty, for that Ruach draws down with it all the holy souls. And lofty saints inherit from it holy souls for their children, as fit.

15. The safe-keeping on Shabbat

A Synopsis

When the spirit of Ruach rests upon the world it protects all Yisrael from harm, from evil spirits and prosecutors. Rabbi Shimon says that on the eve of the fourth day one should be careful of the Other Side, for curses and maledictions exist when the moon is not full; therefore a man should not go out alone. On Shabbat eve the evil ones disperse to a hole in the ground, but a person should still be careful in case they see him on their way to the hole or in case he is harmed by the mere sight of them. Still, there is protection, because when Shabbat enters, everyone from Yisrael is given an additional Neshamah. The tabernacle of peace, Binah, is also spread over the people to protect them. When the people come to pray in the synagogue the higher and lower worlds are happy together; this day is the day of the soul.

198. כֵּיוָן דְּהַאי רוּחָא שָׁרָא עַל עָלְמָא, כָּל רוּחִין בִּישִׁין, וְכָל מְקַטְרְגִין בִּישִׁין, אִסְתָּלָקוּ מֵעָלְמָא וְלָא בָּעֵינָן לְצַלָּאָה עַל נְטוּרָא, בְּגִין דְּיִשְׂרָאֵל אִינוּן נְטִירִין בְּהַהוּא רוּחָא, וְסֻכַּת שָׁלוֹם פְּרִיסַת גַּדְפָהָא עֲלַיְיהוּ, וְאִינּוּן נְטִירִין מִכֹּלָא.

198. When this spirit rests on the world, all the evil spirits and prosecutors are gone from the world, and we do not need to pray for protection. For Yisrael are kept protected by that spirit, and the tabernacle of peace, MALCHUT, spreads its wings over them, and keeps them safe from all harm.

199. וְאִי תֵּימָא, הָא תָּנֵינָן, דְּלָא יִפּוֹק בַּר נָשׁ יְחִידַאי, לָא בְּלֵילְיָא רְבִיעָאָה דְּשַׁבַּתָּא, וְלָא בְּלֵילְיָא דְּשַׁבַּתָּא, וּבַעֵי בַּר נָשׁ לְאִסְתַּמְרָא. וְהָא אַמְרָן, דִּבְלֵילְיָא דְּשַׁבַּתָּא נְטִירִין בְּנֵי נָשָׁא מִכָּל מְקַטְרְגִין דְּעַלְמָא, וְלָא בָּעֵינָן לְצַלָּאָה עַל נְטוּרָא.

199. You may say: we learned that a man should not walk solitary on the eve of the fourth day of the week and on Shabbat eve, and that a man should be careful. We, on the other hand, said that on Shabbat eve all people are kept from prosecution, and we do not have to pray for safety.

200. תָּא חֲזֵי, הָכִי הוּא וַדַּאי, לֵילְיָא רְבִיעָאָה דְּשַׁבַּתָּא, בָּעֵינָן

לְאִסְתַּמְּרָא מִנַּיְיהוּ, מ"ט. בְּגִין דִּכְתִיב יְהִי מְאֹרֹת, מְאֶרֶת כְּתִיב חָסֵר, וְהָא אוּקְמוּהָ, דִּבְגִין דְּהִיא חֲסֵרָה, כַּמָּה חֲבִילֵי טְהִירִין אִתְכְּלִילָן בְּהַאי מְאֹרֹת. לְוָוטִין וּמְאֹרֹת אִינּוּן בְּגְרִיעוּתָא דְּסִיהֲרָא, וְכֻלְּהוּ שַׁלִיטִין בְּהַהוּא לֵילְיָא.

200. HE ANSWERS: Come and see, it is certainly so that on the eve of the fourth day of the week, one should be careful OF THE OTHER SIDE. The reason is in the verse "let there be lights (Heb. *me'orot*)" (Beresheet 1:14). Me'orot is spelled without Vav, WHICH INDICATES THAT THE MOON WAS WANING. And since the moon, MALCHUT, is waning, some troops of spirits were included in these curses (Heb. *me'erot*) for there are curses and maledictions when the moon is not full, which all have power on that night; THEREFORE A MAN SHOULD NOT GO OUT ON HIS OWN.

201. בְּלֵילְיָא דְּשַׁבְּתָא, כֵּיוָן דְּכֻלְּהוּ מִתְבַּדְּרָן לְאַעֲלָא בְּנוּקְבָּא דְּעַפְרָא, דְּלָא יַכְלִין לְשַׁלְטָאָה, בָּעֵי בַּר נָשׁ יְחִידָאי, לְאִסְתַּמְּרָא. וְתוּ, אַף עַל גַּב דְּלָא יַכְלִין לְשַׁלְטָאָה, אִתְחַזְיָין לְזִמְנִין, וּבַר נָשׁ יְחִידָאי בָּעֵי לְאִסְתַּמְּרָא.

201. On Shabbat eve, all demons disperse to enter a hole in the ground SO they would not be able to have power and cause harm. WE LEARN FROM IT THAT BEFORE THEY GO INTO THE HOLE THEY DO HAVE POWER TO HARM. THEREFORE, a man should be careful not to go out alone, FOR THEY COULD HARM HIM ON THEIR WAY TO THE HOLE IN THE GROUND. Also, even though they have no power, they could sometimes be seen, and man should guard himself FROM SEEING THEM, FOR HE COULD BE HARMED BY THE SIGHT.

202. מִלָּה דָּא הָכִי תָּנֵינָן, וְאִי הָכִי גְּרִיעוּתָא דְּנְטוּרָא אִיהוּ. אֲבָל בְּשַׁבְּתָא נְטִירוּ אִשְׁתְּכַח לְעַמָּא קַדִּישָׁא, וְקוּדְשָׁא בְּרִיךְ הוּא כַּד עָאל שַׁבְּתָא, מְעַטֵּר לְכָל חַד וְחַד מִיִּשְׂרָאֵל, וּבָעֵי דְּיִנְטְרוּן לֵיהּ לְהַאי עִטְרָא קַדִּישָׁא, דְּאִתְעַטְּרוּ בֵּיהּ, וְאַף עַל גַּב דְּאִינּוּן לָא אִשְׁתְּכָחוּ בְּיִשׁוּבָא, לְזִמְנִין לְבַר נָשׁ יְחִידָאי אִתְחַזוּן, וְאִתְרַע מַזָּלֵיהּ. וְאִצְטְרִיךְ לֵיהּ לְבַר

נָשׁ, לְאִתְעַטְּרָא בְּעִטְרָא קַדִּישָׁא, וּלְנַטְרָא לֵיהּ.

202. HE MENTIONS THE MEANING HE LEARNED CONCERNING THE MATTER, SAYING THAT this is the way he learned it IN THE FOLLOWING WORDS. HE ASKS: If it is so, THAT A MAN SHOULD NOT GO OUT ALONE ON SHABBAT EVE, then the protection is inadequate. HE ANSWERS: still there is protection on Shabbat for the holy nation, and when Shabbat commences, the Holy One, blessed be He, bedecks everyone from Yisrael WITH AN ADDITIONAL SOUL. They should keep the holy crown they were adorned with. And though they, THE DEMONS, are not in inhabited places, they nevertheless appear before lone persons and diminish their good fortune. A person should be adorned with the holy crown and guard it.

203. סוֹף סוֹף, נְטִירוּ אִשְׁתְּכַח בְּהַהוּא לֵילְיָא לְעַמָּא קַדִּישָׁא, הוֹאִיל וְסֻכַּת שָׁלוֹם פְּרִיסָא עַל עַמָּא, דְּהָא תָּנֵינָן, בְּכָל אֲתָר דְּסֻכַּת שָׁלוֹם אִשְׁתְּכַח, סִטְרָא אַחֲרָא לָא אִשְׁתְּכַח תַּמָּן. וְעַ"ד נְטוּרָא אִיהוּ וּנְטוּרָא שְׁכִיחַ.

203. And last, there is keeping for the holy nation, since the tabernacle of peace, BINAH, is spread over the people. For we learned that wherever the tabernacle of peace is present, the Other Side is not. Therefore the tabernacle is considered to be protection, and there is protection available.

204. יוֹמָא דְּשַׁבַּתָּא, חֶדְוָה אִיהוּ לְכֹלָּא, וְכֹלָּא אִתְנְטַר לְעֵילָּא וְתַתָּא. וּנְקוּדָה תַּתָּאָה נַהֲרָא לְסַלְּקָא לְעֵילָּא, בִּשְׁפִירוּ דְּעִטְרִין שַׁבְעִין חוּלָקִין יַתִּיר, וְסָבָא דְּכָל סָבִין אִתְּעַר.

204. Shabbat day is joy for all, and everything is protected above and below. And the lower point, MALCHUT, shines in rising higher with the beauty of seventy crowns, THAT ARE the additional parts FROM SHABBAT EVE. And the eldest of the old, KETER is awakened TO GIVE AFFLUENCE TO IT.

205. כְּדֵין כַּד סָלִיק נְהוֹרָא, עַמָּא קַדִּישָׁא מְקַדְּמֵי לְבֵי כְּנִשְׁתָּא בִּלְבוּשׁ יְקָר בְּחֶדְוָה, מִתְעַטְּרָן בְּעִטְרָא קַדִּישָׁא דִּלְעֵילָּא, בְּהַהוּא רוּחָא דְּקַיְּימָא

עֲלַיְיהוּ לְתַתָּא, מְשַׁבְּחָן בְּשִׁירִין וְתוּשְׁבְּחָן, וְסַלְּקִין תּוּשְׁבְּחָן לְעֵילָא, וְעֶלָּאִין וְתַתָּאִין כֻּלְּהוּ בְּחֶדְוָה, וּמִתְעַטְּרָן כֻּלְּהוּ כַּחֲדָא. פַּתְחֵי עִלָּאֵי וְאַמְרֵי, זַכָּאִין אַתּוּן עַמָּא קַדִּישָׁא בְּאַרְעָא, דְּמָארֵיכוֹן אִתְעַטָּר עֲלַיְיכוּ, וְכָל חֵילִין קַדִּישִׁין, מִתְעַטְּרִין בְּגִינֵיכוֹן.

205. When dawn rises, the holy nation hasten to come to the synagogue gladly, dressed in their best attire, and bedeck themselves with that holy, high crown from above, and with that spirit, THE ADDITIONAL SOUL, which awaits them below. They sing with praises and hymns, and the hymns go up. The higher and the lower beings are all glad, adorned together. The higher beings begin by saying 'happy are you, a holy nation upon the earth, for your Master is bedecked through you, and all the holy armies are crowned for your sake.'

206. הַאי יוֹמָא, יוֹמָא דְּנִשְׁמָתִין אִיהוּ, וְלָאו יוֹמָא דְגוּפָא, בְּגִין דְּשֻׁלְטָנוּ דִּצְרוֹרָא דְנִשְׁמָתִין אִיהוּ, וְקַיְימָן עִלָּאִין וְתַתָּאִין כֻּלְּהוּ בְּזִוּוּגָא חֲדָא, בְּעִטְרָא דְרוּחָא יְתֵירָא עִלָּאָה קַדִּישָׁא.

206. This day is the day of the soul, not of the body, because it is in the power of the bundle of souls, BINAH. The higher and lowers beings are all in unison, with the crown of the additional, holy, supernal Ruach.

16. The Shabbat prayer

A Synopsis

We learn that the Shabbat prayer consists of three prayers that correspond to three Shabbats (Binah, Zeir Anpin and Malchut) that are all really one. Anyone in the synagogue must occupy himself solely with praises, prayers and study of the Torah. Shabbat is the day of the souls. We are told of many things – of the praise to another grade, of the secret of the luminous light, of the hymn to the World to Come, and of the mystery of the 22 sacred letters in the prayer, "El, blessed, great in knowledge…" When the praise reaches the holy throne Malchut it waits there until all Yisrael recite the high Kedusha of the Musaf; then Malchut rises to Ima, Binah and Zeir Anpin rises to Aba. With the passage, "Moses rejoiced in the gift of his portion…," the Written Law, Tiferet up high, becomes connected to the lower Torah, the Oral Law, Malchut.

207. צְלוֹתָא דְּשַׁבְּתָא, דְּעַמָּא קַדִּישָׁא, תְּלַת צְלוֹתִין אִשְׁתְּכָחוּ בְּהַאי יוֹמָא, לָקֳבֵל תְּלַת שַׁבְּתֵי, וְאוּקְמוּהָ, וְכֻלְּהוּ חַד. כֵּיוָן דְּעָאלוּ עַמָּא קַדִּישָׁא לְבֵי כְּנִישְׁתָּא, אָסִיר לְאִשְׁתַּדְּלָא אֲפִילוּ בְּצוֹרֶךְ בֵּי כְּנִישְׁתָּא, אֶלָּא בְּמִלֵּי תוּשְׁבְּחָן וּצְלוֹתָא, וְאוֹרַיְיתָא, וְכַדְקָא חֲזֵי לוֹן.

207. The Shabbat prayer of the holy people consists of three prayers, which correspond to three Shabbatot (Heb. plural), BINAH, ZEIR ANPIN AND MALCHUT THAT RULE TOGETHER, as was explained. And all of them are one. Once the holy nation comes to the synagogue, they are not allowed to concern themselves even with the needs of the synagogue, but with words of praise, prayers and Torah study, as they ought.

208. וּמַאן דְּאִשְׁתְּדַּל בְּמִלִּין אַחֲרָנִין, וּבְמִלִּין דְּעָלְמָא, דָּא אִיהוּ בַּר נָשׁ דְּקָא מְחַלֵּל שַׁבְּתָא, לֵית לֵיהּ חוּלָקָא בְּעַמָּא דְּיִשְׂרָאֵל. תְּרֵין מַלְאָכִין מְמָנָן עַל דָּא, בְּיוֹמָא דְּשַׁבְּתָא, וְאִינּוּן שַׁוּוֹ יְדֵיהוֹן עַל רֵישֵׁיהּ, וְאַמְרֵי, וַוי לִפְלַנְיָא, דְּלֵית לֵיהּ חוּלָקָא בְּקוּדְשָׁא בְּרִיךְ הוּא. וְעַ"ד, בָּעֵי לְאִשְׁתַּדְּלָא בִּצְלוֹתָא וּבְשִׁירִין וּבְתוּשְׁבְּחָן דְּמָארֵיהוֹן, וּלְאִשְׁתַּדְּלָא בְּאוֹרַיְיתָא.

208. And whoever is occupied with other things and with worldly matters, desecrates the Shabbat, and has no portion in the people of Yisrael. Two angels are appointed to that task on Shabbat. They put their hands on his head and say: Woe to so and so, who has no portion in the Holy One, blessed be He. Therefore they should strive to pray, sing and praise their Master, and study the Torah.

209. הַאי יוֹמָא, אִיהוּ יוֹמָא דְּנִשְׁמָתִין, דְּאִתְעַטְּרָא הַהוּא צְרוֹרָא דְּנִשְׁמָתִין. בְּג״כ מְשַׁבְּחֵי בְּתוּשְׁבְּחָן תֻּשְׁבַּחְתָּא דְּנַשְׁמָתָא, וְהַיְינוּ נִשְׁמַת כָּל חַי תְּבָרֵךְ אֶת שִׁמְךָ יְיָ' אֱלֹהֵינוּ וְרוּחַ כָּל בָּשָׂר וְכוּ'. וְלֵית תֻּשְׁבַּחְתָּא אֶלָּא בְּסִטְרָא דְּנִשְׁמָתָא וְרוּחָא, וְהַאי יוֹמָא, קַיְימָא בְּרוּחָא וְנִשְׁמָתָא, וְלָאו דְּגוּפָא.

209. Shabbat is the day of the souls, for with it the bundle of souls, BINAH, is decorated. To that purpose the praise of the souls is sung 'The soul of every living being shall bless Your name, Hashem our Elohim, and the spirit of all flesh...(Heb. *nishmat*)'. Praises refer solely to the side of the Ruach and Neshamah. This day too pertains to the Ruach and Neshamah and not to the body.

210. תֻּשְׁבַּחְתָּא דְּדַרְגָּא אַחֲרָא עִלָּאָה, רָזָא דְּיוֹמָא, שִׁמְשָׁא קַדִּישָׁא דְּאִיהוּ נְהוֹרָא דִּימָמָא, הַיְינוּ יוֹצֵר אוֹר. רָזָא דִּנְהוֹרָא דְּנָהִיר, דְּמִנֵּיהּ אִתְזָנָן וְנָהֲרִין כָּל אִינּוּן חַיָּילִין, רְתִיכִין, וְכֹכְבַיָּא וּמַזָּלֵי, וְכָל אִינּוּן דְּשַׁלְטִין עַל עָלְמָא.

210. The song of another high grade, the secret of the day and the holy sun, ZEIR ANPIN, which is daylight, is THE BENEDICTION 'who forms light'. That is the secret of the luminous light, from which all the armies and Chariots, stars and constellations, and all those who rule the world, take their sustenance and light.

211. תֻּשְׁבַּחְתָּא דְּעָלְמָא דְּאָתֵי בְּיוֹמָא דָּא, הַיְינוּ אֵל אָדוֹן. וְתוּשְׁבַּחְתָּא דָּא, אִיהוּ בְּרָזָא דְּעֶשְׂרִין וּתְרֵין אַתְוָון עִלָּאִין קַדִּישִׁין, דְּמִתְעַטְּרָן בַּאֲבָהָן וּבִרְתִיכָא עִלָּאָה קַדִּישָׁא.

211. The hymn to the World to Come, BINAH, on that day is 'El, the Master over all works'. It is based on the meaning of the twenty two sacred high and holy letters that crown themselves with the patriarchs, CHESED, GVURAH AND TIFERET, and with the holy supernal Chariot, BINAH.

212. אַתְוָון זְעִירִין, אִינּוּן עֶשְׂרִין וּתְרֵין אַתְוָון, דְּאִינּוּן בְּעָלְמָא תַּתָּאָה, דְּאִינּוּן אֵל בָּרוּךְ גְּדוֹל דֵּעָה וְכוּ', וְלָא אִית בֵּין תֵּיבָה לַתֵּיבָה, רְוָוחָא אַחֲרָא, אֶלָּא אָת רְשִׁימָא בְּכָל תֵּיבָה וְתֵיבָה. וּבְעָלְמָא עִלָּאָה, אִית רְוָוחָא, וְסִטְרִין קַדִּישִׁין, בֵּין אָת לְאָת. וְדָא אִיהוּ, תּוּשְׁבַּחְתָּא עַל תּוּשְׁבַּחְתָּא, דְּאַתְוָון עִלָּאִין דְּיוֹמָא שְׁבִיעָאָה, קָא מְשַׁבַּח וְאָמַר לְמַלְכָּא עִלָּאָה יוֹצֵר בְּרֵאשִׁית.

212. The small letters, the twenty two letters of the lower world, MALCHUT, are in the prayer "El, blessed, great in knowledge..." The letters appear in each successive word in alphabetical order, and nothing breaks the sequence in between. NAMELY, THE INITIALS FOLLOW THE ALPHABETICAL ORDER. In the upper world, BINAH, EACH SEQUENTIAL ALPHABET LETTER BEGINS A PHRASE OF A FEW WORDS. Thus there is space and holy places between the letters. This is the highest praise, formed by the supernal letters of the seventh day, BINAH. It praises and proclaims before the high King 'who formed the world at the beginning', WHICH IS CHOCHMAH, THE SUPERNAL POINT.

213. כַּד תּוּשְׁבַּחְתָּא דָא סַלְקָא לְעֵילָא, שִׁתִּין רְתִיכִין עִלָּאִין דְּקָאֲמָרָן, מִזְדַּמְּנִין וְנַטְלֵי לְהַאי תּוּשְׁבַּחְתָּא מֵעַמָּא קַדִּישָׁא, וְסַלְקֵי לָהּ לְאִתְעַטְּרָא בָּהּ, בְּכַמָּה רְתִיכִין עִלָּאִין, דִּי מְמָנָן, וְכָל אִינּוּן צַדִּיקַיָּיא דִּבְגִנְתָּא דְעֵדֶן, כֻּלְּהוּ מִתְעַטְּרָן בְּתוּשְׁבַּחְתָּא דָא, וְכָל אִינּוּן רְתִיכִין, וְכָל אִינּוּן נִשְׁמָתִין דְּצַדִּיקַיָּיא, כֻּלְּהוּ סַלְקִין בְּתוּשְׁבַּחְתָּא דָא, עַד רָזָא דְכוּרְסְיָיא.

213. When this praise, "El, the Master over all works," rises, the sixty high Chariots we mentioned IN THE GARDEN OF EDEN, unite to take it from the holy nation, and elevate it to adorn some high Chariots, for the chiefs and all the righteous in the Garden of Eden. They all bedeck themselves with this praise, and all the Chariots and the souls of the righteous mount with that praise up to the secret of the throne, MALCHUT.

214. כַּד מָטָא לְכוּרְסְיָיא קַדִּישָׁא, תּוּשְׁבַּחְתָּא דָּא דְכָל יִשְׂרָאֵל, קַיְימָא תַּמָּן, עַד זִמְנָא דְּקָאמְרֵי קְדוּשָׁה עִלָּאָה דְּמוּסָף. וּכְדֵין סְלוּקָא דִּלְתַתָּא לְעֵילָא, לְאִתְאַחֲדָא כֹּלָּא לְעֵילָא לְעֵילָא, לְמֶהֱוֵי כֹּלָּא חַד. דָּא אִיהִי תּוּשְׁבַּחְתָּא, דְּסַלְקָא עַל כֻּלְּהוּ תּוּשְׁבְּחָן.

214. When the praise THAT WAS SUNG by all Yisrael reaches the holy throne, MALCHUT, it waits there until YISRAEL recite the high Kedusha (lit. 'sanctification') of the Musaf (lit. 'the additional prayer'), NAMELY 'THEY SHALL CROWN YOU'. Then THOSE below may rise up, VIZ. MALCHUT, THE THRONE, RISES TO IMA – BINAH, AND ZEIR ANPIN RISES TO ABA, WHICH IS THE SECRET OF THE SUPERNAL POINT. In that way everything is united high up and becomes one. THUS, THE PRAISE "EL, THE MASTER..." WHICH ALREADY ASCENDED WITH MALCHUT TO BINAH, BINAH RECITES IT TO THE SUPERNAL KING, WHO IS CHOCHMAH. This praise is superior to all praises.

215. מִכָּאן וּלְהָלְאָה, סִדּוּרָא דִּצְלוֹתָא דִּשְׁאָר יוֹמֵי, עַד יִשְׂמַח מֹשֶׁה וְכוּ', חֶדְוָותָא דְּדַרְגָּא עִלָּאָה, עִקָּרָא דַּאֲבָהָן, דְּחַדֵּי בְּהַהוּא עַדְבָא דִּילֵיהּ, כַּד סָלִיק כּוּרְסְיָיא לְגַבֵּיהּ, וְנָטִיל לָהּ, וּמִתְחַבְּרָאן כַּחֲדָא. וְדָא אִיהוּ חֶדְוָה דְּאוֹרַיְיתָא עִלָּאָה דִּלְעֵילָא, תּוֹרָה שֶׁבִּכְתָב. דְּחַדֵּי בְּאוֹרַיְיתָא דִּלְתַתָּא, תּוֹרָה שֶׁבְּעַל פֶּה, וְאִתְחַבְּרוּ דָּא בְּדָא.

215. Hereafter, the prayer continues as on the rest of the days, until the passage 'Moses rejoiced in the gift of his portion...' that is the rejoicing of the higher grade, TIFERET THAT IS CALLED MOSES, AND THE SECRET OF JACOB the most valuable patriarch, THE COLUMN THAT RECONCILES AND UNITES CHESED AND GVURAH THAT ARE CALLED ABRAHAM AND ISAAC. He is happy in his portion, MALCHUT, because the throne THAT IS MALCHUT goes up to him. He takes it and they are fused into one. This is the joy of the Torah, which is the Written Law, TIFERET, that rejoices in the lower Torah, the Oral Law, MALCHUT, and they unite with each other.

216. כֵּיוָן דְּאִתְחַבְּרוּ כַּחֲדָא, בָּעֵי ב"ן לְאַכְלְלָא בְּהַהוּא חֶדְוָה לְעַמָּא קַדִּישָׁא, יִשְׂמְחוּ בְמַלְכוּתְךָ שׁוֹמְרֵי שַׁבָּת וְכוּ', או"א רְצֵה נָא בִמְנוּחָתֵנוּ.

216. Once they are united, we should include the holy nation in that rejoicing, by SAYING "May they rejoice in Your kingdom, those who observe the Shabbat...our Elohim and Elohim of our fathers, accept our rest."

17. The secret of the Torah scroll

A Synopsis

In this section we are reminded that we have already been told why the Torah scroll is read on Shabbat, and that the mysteries of all the small details of the text were given to Moses on Mount Sinai. The question is asked why then the scroll is lacking all those mysteries of verse division, tonal accents and Massoretic readings. We are told that the bare letters of the Written Law, Tiferet, are brought into the Oral Law, Malchut, and cause her to conceive the accents and Massoretic readings. He explains why on the Shabbat seven people read the Torah in public, yet on festivals only five people read and on Yom Kippur six people are called up. We read about the throne chair that is made into the reader's desk; when the Torah scroll is put there the people should concentrate as though they were standing below Mount Sinai to receive the Torah. We learn about the prayer that should be prayed, and that only one person is allowed to read, as though Elohim were reading to the people below. The reader should perfect his reading, and never read into the portion of the next Shabbat. 53 Chariots are assigned to the service of the Torah, each one to a portion of a certain Shabbat. The Chariot raises the reading before God; then the portion, the throne and Zeir Anpin all become one.

217. רָזָא דְּס״ת בְּיוֹמָא דָּא, הָא אוּקְמוּהָ תָּנֵינָן כְּתִיב, וַיִּקְרְאוּ בַסֵּפֶר תּוֹרַת הָאֱלֹהִים מְפוֹרָשׁ וְשׂוֹם שֶׂכֶל וַיָּבִינוּ בַּמִּקְרָא וְהָא אוּקְמוּהָ רָזָא, דְּאִינּוּן פְּסוּקֵי טַעֲמֵי, וּמַסּוֹרֶת, וְכָל אִינּוּן דִּיּוּקִין, וְרָזִין עִלָּאִין, כֹּלָּא אִתְמְסַר לְמֹשֶׁה מִסִּינַי. אִי בְּכָל הָנֵי דִּיּוּקִין אִתְמְסַר אוֹרַיְיתָא לְמֹשֶׁה, סֵפֶר תּוֹרָה דְּאִיהוּ בְּכָל אִינּוּן קְדוּשָׁאן, אֲמַאי אִיהוּ חָסֵר, מִכָּל הָנֵי תִּקּוּנִין, וְרָזִין, דְּאִתְמְסָרוּ לֵיהּ לְמֹשֶׁה בְּאוֹרַיְיתָא.

217. The reason of reading the Torah scroll on that day was already expounded. We learned that "So they read in the book, in the Torah scroll of Elohim distinctly, and gave the sense, and caused them to understand the reading" (Nechemyah 8:8). We also explained that the mysteries of the verse divisions, the tonal accents, the Massoretic readings and all the small details, together with the supernal secrets, were given to Moses on Mount Sinai. HE ASKS: If the Torah was given to Moses together with all these details, and the Torah scroll given with these sanctities, why then is it

lacking all those corrections and mysteries that were given to Moses inside the Torah?

218. אֶלָּא רָזָא דָא, כַּד כּוּרְסְיָיא קַדִּישָׁא מִתְעַטְּרָא, וְאִתְכְּלִילַת בַּתּוֹרָה שֶׁבִּכְתָב, כָּל אִינּוּן דִּיּוּקְנִין, וְכָל אִינּוּן טַעֲמִין וּמַסוֹרוֹת, כֻּלְּהוּ עָאלִין בִּגְנִיזוּ, וְאִתְרְשִׁימוּ בְּגוֹ כּוּרְסְיָיא קַדִּישָׁא, וְאִינּוּן דִּיּוּקְנִין, דְּאָעִיל אוֹרַיְיתָא דִּבִכְתָב, בְּאוֹרַיְיתָא דִּבְעַל פֶּה, וּבְהוּ אִתְעַבְּרַת, כְּאִתְּתָא דְּאִתְעַבְּרַת מִן דְּכוּרָא, וְאִשְׁתָּאֲרוּ אַתְווֹן עִלָּאִין לְחוֹדַיְיהוּ בִּקְדוּשָׁיְיהוּ כַּדְקָא חֲזֵי. וּלְאִתְחֲזָאָה בְּבֵי כְּנִישְׁתָּא, דְּהָא אִתְבָּרְכַת וְאִתְעַטְּרַת כּוּרְסְיָיא מֵרָזָא דְּתוֹרָה שֶׁבִּכְתָב, וְתַמָּן אָעִיל כָּל אִינּוּן דִּיּוּקְנִין, וְאִיהִי אִתְקַדְּשַׁת מִנֵּיהּ, בָּעֵי לְאִתְחֲזָאָה בְּאַתְווֹן לְחוֹדַיְיהוּ כַּדְקָא יָאוֹת.

218. HE ANSWERS: The secret of the matter is that when the holy throne, MALCHUT, is decorated by and incorporated in the Written Law, TIFERET, then all those punctuation marks, tonal accents and Massoretic points are impressed upon the holy throne FROM TIFERET and concealed therein. On the other hand the shapes (letters) of the Written Law, TIFERET, are brought into the Oral Law, MALCHUT, and cause her to conceive, as a woman conceiving from the male. So the high letters IN THE WRITTEN LAW remain alone in their sanctity as should be, WITHOUT ADDITIONAL SIGNS and are thus shown in synagogue. For the throne, MALCHUT, is blessed and adorned by the secret of the Written Law, and in it, IN MALCHUT, are put all those shapes, WHICH ARE ACCENTS AND MASSORETIC READINGS AS MENTIONED so it is sanctified by the Written Law. The bare letters alone ought to be seen.

219. וּכְדֵין, כֹּלָּא אִתְקַדָּשׁ בִּקְדוּשָׁה עִלָּאָה כַּדְקָא חֲזֵי, כ"ש וְכ"ש בְּהַאי יוֹמָא. בְּהַאי יוֹמָא בָּעֵי לְסַלְּקָא שִׁבְעָה גוּבְרִין, לָקֳבֵל שִׁבְעָה קָלִין, דְּאִינּוּן רָזָא דְּאוֹרַיְיתָא. וּבְזִמְנִין וּבְמוֹעֲדִין חָמֵשׁ, גוֹ רָזָא דָא. בְּיוֹמָא דְּכִפּוּרֵי שִׁית. גוֹ רָזָא עִלָּאָה דָא.

219. Then everything is sanctified with most high sanctity as fit, most certainly and especially on this day, SHABBAT. On this day seven people are called up to publicly read the Torah. They correspond to seven voices,

CHESED, GVURAH, TIFERET, NETZACH, HOD, YESOD AND MALCHUT OF ZEIR ANPIN, which are the inner mystery of the Torah, ZEIR ANPIN. On festivals, only five people are called up in accordance with this principle, BECAUSE THE SEVEN SFIROT ARE PRINCIPALLY FIVE, CHESED, GVURAH, TIFERET, NETZACH AND HOD; YESOD IS THEIR INCLUSION FROM THE GIVING PART AND MALCHUT INCLUDES THEM ON THE RECEIVING PART. On Yom Kippur (Day of Atonement) six people are called up, according to this higher mystery, VIZ. THE SIX SFIROT OF ZEIR ANPIN: CHESED, GVURAH, TIFERET, NETZACH, HOD AND YESOD OF ZEIR ANPIN.

220. וְכֹלָּא רָזָא חֲדָא. חָמֵשׁ, דְּאִינּוּן חָמֵשׁ דַּרְגִּין לְתַתָּא, מִדַּרְגָּא דְּאוֹר קַדְמָאָה לְתַתָּא, וְאִינּוּן רָזָא דְּאוֹרַיְיתָא. שִׁית, דְּאִינּוּן שִׁית סִטְרִין וְכֹלָּא רָזָא חֲדָא. שֶׁבַע אִינּוּן שֶׁבַע קַלִין. וְכֻלְּהוּ רָזָא חֲדָא, אִלֵּין וְאִלֵּין.

220. All these rules HE EXPLAINS, come from the same principle. The five people CALLED UP ON HOLIDAYS, correspond to the five grades CHESED, GVURAH, TIFERET, NETZACH AND HOD, that are beneath the grade of the ancient light, BINAH AND THE FIRST THREE SFIROT, below IN ZEIR ANPIN. They are the secret of the Torah, FOR ZEIR ANPIN IS CALLED TORAH. The six people ON YOM KIPPUR correspond to the six directions, THAT IS, THE FIVE SFIROT AND YESOD THAT INCLUDES THEM. All comes from the same mystery. FOR THERE IS NO ADDITION TO THE PRINCIPAL FIVE SFIROT. The seven PEOPLE CALLED UP ON SHABBAT CORRESPOND TO the seven voices, FOR MALCHUT INCLUDEDS THEM TOO. All these combinations stem from the one secret, NAMELY THAT THEY ALLUDE TO THE SFIROT OF ZEIR ANPIN.

221. בְּר״ח אִתּוֹסָף חַד עַל תְּלָתָא, בְּגִין שִׁמְשָׁא, דְּנָהִיר בְּהַהוּא זִמְנָא, לְסִיהֲרָא, וְאִתּוֹסַף נְהוֹרָא עַל סִיהֲרָא, וְהַיְינוּ רָזָא דְּמוּסָף. בְּסֵפֶר תּוֹרָה, בָּעֵי לְשַׁתְּמַע חַד קָלָא וְדִבּוּר.

221. On the day of the new month, one person is added, WHO CORRESPONDS TO MALCHUT, to the three readers ON WEEKDAYS, THAT ALLUDE TO CHESED, GVURAH AND TIFERET OF ZEIR ANPIN, because at that time the sun, ZEIR ANPIN, shines upon the moon, MALCHUT. This is the secret of the Musaf (lit. 'additional prayer') OF THE NEW MONTH THAT

SIGNIFIES THE SAID ADDITION. Upon reading the Torah only one voice and speech ought to be heard.

222. סִדּוּרָא לְסַדְּרָא עַמָּא קַדִּישָׁא בְּיוֹמָא דָא, וּבִשְׁאַר יוֹמִין דְּסֵפֶר תּוֹרָה בָּעֵי לְסַדְּרָא וּלְתַקְּנָא תִּקּוּנָא, בְּחַד כֻּרְסְיָיא דְּאַקְרֵי תֵּיבָה, וְהַהוּא כֻּרְסְיָיא דְּלֶהֱוֵי בְּשִׁית דַּרְגִּין, לְסַלְקָא בְּהוֹ וְלָא יַתִּיר, דִּכְתִיב וְשֵׁשׁ מַעֲלוֹת לַכִּסֵּא. וְדַרְגָּא חַד לְעֵילָא, לְשַׁוָּאָה עָלֵיהּ סֵפֶר תּוֹרָה, וּלְאַחֲזָאָה לֵיהּ לְכֹלָּא.

222. The holy nation should fix and prepare on that day, as well as other days WHEN the Torah scroll IS READ, a throne to become a reader's desk. That throne must have six steps, THE SIX SFIROT OF MALCHUT, leading to it and no more, as is written: "and there were six steps to the throne" (II Divrei Hayamim 9:18), WHICH ALLUDES TO MALCHUT. And there is also one step above, THAT REFERS TO CHOCHMAH OF MALCHUT – THE READER'S DESK, to put on it the Torah scroll and show it to everyone. BECAUSE THE READER'S DESK, THE SECRET OF CHOCHMAH OF MALCHUT, ENABLES THE TORAH SCROLL TO BE SEEN, THAT IS THE SECRET OF ZEIR ANPIN. FOR SIGHT IS AVALIABLE ONLY IN MALCHUT.

223. כַּד סָלִיק ס״ת לְתַמָּן, כְּדֵין בָּעָאן כָּל עַמָּא לְסַדְּרָא גַּרְמַיְיהוּ לְתַתָּא, בְּאֵימָתָא בִּדְחִילוּ בִּרְתֵת בְּזִיעַ, וּלְכַוְּונָא לִבַּיְיהוּ, כְּמָה דְּהַשְׁתָּא קַיְימִין עַל טוּרָא דְּסִינַי לְקַבְּלָא אוֹרַיְיתָא, וְיֵהוֹן צַיְיתִין וְיִרְכוּן אוּדְנַיְיהוּ. וְלֵית רְשׁוּ לְעַמָּא לְמִפְתַּח פּוּמֵיהוֹן, אֲפִילוּ בְּמִלֵּי דְּאוֹרַיְיתָא, וְכָל שֶׁכֵּן בְּמִלָּה אַחֲרָא, אֶלָּא כֻּלְּהוּ בְּאֵימָתָא, כְּמַאן דְּלֵית לֵיהּ פּוּמָא וְהָא אוּקְמוּהָ, דִּכְתִיב וּכְפִתְחוֹ עָמְדוּ כָל הָעָם. וְאָזְנֵי כָל הָעָם אֶל סֵפֶר הַתּוֹרָה.

223. When the Torah scroll is put there, the whole people should make themselves ready down below, with awe and fear, quaking and trembling, and to meditate in their heart, as if there were standing now beneath Mount Sinai to receive the Torah. They should listen and lend their ears. For the people are not permitted to open their mouths even to discuss the Torah, not to mention other matters. But they are all in awe, as one who is speechless.

And we already explained it in relation to the words: "and when he opened it, all the people stood up" (Nechemyah 8:5), and "and the ears of all the people were attentive to the book of the Torah" (Ibid. 3).

224. אר״ש, כַּד מַפְּקִין ס״ת בְּצִבּוּרָא, לְמִקְרֵא בֵּיה, מִתְפַּתְּחָן תַּרְעֵי שְׁמַיָּא דְרַחֲמִין, וּמְעוֹרְרִין אֶת הָאַהֲבָה לְעֵילָא, וְאִבְעֵי לֵיה לְבַר נָשׁ לְמֵימַר הָכִי.

224. Rabbi Shimon said that when the Torah scroll is brought out to be read in public, the heavenly gates of Mercy open and stir the love of above. Then one should thus pray:

225. בְּרִיךְ שְׁמֵיה דְּמָארֵי עָלְמָא, בְּרִיךְ כִּתְרָךְ וְאַתְרָךְ, יְהֵא רְעוּתָךְ עִם עַמָּךְ יִשְׂרָאֵל לְעָלַם, וּפוּרְקַן יְמִינָךְ, אַחֲזֵי לְעַמָּךְ בְּבֵית מַקְדְּשָׁךְ, וּלְאַמְטוֹיֵי לָנָא מִטּוּב נְהוֹרָךְ, וּלְקַבְּלָא צְלוֹתָנָא בְּרַחֲמִין. יְהֵא רַעֲוָא קֳדָמָךְ, דְּתוֹרִיךְ לָן חַיִּים בְּטִיבוּ, וְלֶהֱוֵי אֲנָא פְּקִידָא בְּגוֹ צַדִּיקַיָּא, לְמִרְחַם עָלַי, וּלְמִנְטַר יָתִי, וְיַת כָּל דִּילִי, וְדִי לְעַמָּךְ יִשְׂרָאֵל. אַתְּ הוּא זָן לְכֹלָּא, וּמְפַרְנֵס לְכֹלָּא, אַתְּ הוּא שַׁלִּיט עַל כֹּלָּא, אַתְּ הוּא דְּשַׁלִּיט עַל מַלְכַיָּא, וּמַלְכוּתָא דִּילָךְ הוּא. אֲנָא עַבְדָּא דְקוּדְשָׁא בְּרִיךְ הוּא, דְּסָגִידְנָא קַמֵּיה, וּמִקַּמֵּי דִּיקַר אוֹרַיְיתֵיה, בְּכָל עִידָן וְעִידָן. לָא עַל אֱינָשׁ רָחִיצְנָא, וְלָא עַל בַּר אֱלֹהִין סָמִיכְנָא, אֶלָּא בֵּאלָהָא דִשְׁמַיָּא, דְּהוּא אֱלָהָא קְשׁוֹט, וְאוֹרַיְיתֵיה קְשׁוֹט, וּנְבִיאוֹהִי קְשׁוֹט, וּמַסְגֵּי לְמֶעְבַּד טַבְוָון וּקְשׁוֹט. בֵּיה אֲנָא רָחִיץ, וְלִשְׁמֵיה קַדִּישָׁא יַקִּירָא אֲנָא אֵימַר תּוּשְׁבְּחָן. יְהֵא רַעֲוָא קֳדָמָךְ, דְּתִפְתַּח לִבָּאי בְּאוֹרַיְיתָךְ וְתֵיהַב לִי בְּנִין דִּכְרִין דְּעָבְדִין רְעוּתָךְ. וְתַשְׁלִים מִשְׁאֲלִין דְּלִבָּאי, וְלִבָּא דְכָל עַמָּךְ יִשְׂרָאֵל לְטָב וּלְחַיִּין וְלִשְׁלָם אָמֵן.

225. Blessed be the name of the Master of the universe, blessed be Your crown and Your place. May Your good will be with Your people Yisrael for ever, and the redemption of Your right hand be shown to Your people in Your Temple. May You bestow on us the bounty of Your light, and accept our prayers in mercy. May it please You, that You shall lengthen our lives

in goodness, and that I, Your servant, shall be remembered among the righteous, so as to have mercy upon me and safeguard me and all that is mine, and that of Your people Yisrael. You are that giver of nourishment and sustenance for all. You rule over all. You rule over kings, and the kingdom is Yours. I am the servant of the Holy One, blessed be He; before Him I bow, and before the majesty of His Torah at all times. Not upon man do I put my trust, nor upon angels do I rely, but only upon Elohim in heaven, that is the Elohim of truth, and Whose Torah is truth, and Whose prophets are true; that acts with much kindness and truth. In Him do I put my trust, and to His holy and precious name do I sing praises. May it beYour will to open my heart to Your Torah, and to grant me male children to do Your wish; and may You fill the proper requests of my heart, and the heart of all Your people Yisrael for good and life and peace. Amen.

226. וְאָסִיר לְמִקְרֵי בְּסִפְרָא דְאוֹרַיְיתָא, בַּר חַד בִּלְחוֹדוֹי, וְכֹלָּא צַיְיתִין וְשַׁתְקִין, בְּגִין דְּיִשְׁמְעוּן מִלִּין מִפּוּמֵיהּ, כְּאִילוּ קַבִּילוּ לָהּ הַהִיא שַׁעֲתָא מִטּוּרָא דְסִינַי. וּמַאן דְּקָרֵי בְּאוֹרַיְיתָא, לֶהֱוֵי חַד קָאֵים עֲלֵיהּ, וְשָׁתִיק. דְּלָא יִשְׁתְּמַע בַּר דִּבּוּר חַד בִּלְחוֹדוֹי, לָא תְּרֵין דִּבּוּרִין, לְשׁוֹן קֹדֶשׁ חַד, וְחַד הוּא, וְלָא תְּרֵין דִּבּוּרִין, וְאִי תְּרֵין מִשְׁתַּכְּחִין בס"ת, גְּרִיעוּתָא דְּרָזָא דִמְהֵימְנוּתָא אִיהוּ וּגְרִיעוּתָא דִּיקָרָא דְּאוֹרַיְיתָא אִשְׁתְּכַח בס"ת, וּבָעֵי חַד קָלָא. מְתַרְגֵּם חַד. וְרָזָא דָּא קְלִיפָה וּמוֹחָא.

226. Only one person is allowed to read the Torah, and everyone else are to listen in silence, to hear the words of his mouth, as if they were now receiving it on Mount Sinai. There should be one person standing next to the reader, VIZ. THAT WAS CALLED UP TO THE READING. And he must be silent so that only one speech is heard and not two. THERE SHOULD BE ONE WHO READS IN the holy tongue, not two, because if two read the Torah, it would diminish the secret of the Faith, and the majesty of the Torah is reduced. It is essential to have only one voice. THERE ALSO SHOULD BE one translator, in the secret of the shell and the fruit. BECAUSE THE TRANSLATOR IS CONSIDERED THE SHELL, AND THE READER IN THE HOLY TONGUE ALLUDES TO THE FRUIT. THERE IS NO FRUIT WITHOUT A SHELL.

227. כֹּלָּא שַׁתְקִין, וְחַד קָארֵי, דִּכְתִיב וַיְדַבֵּר אֱלֹהִים אֵת כָּל הַדְּבָרִים

הָאֵלֶּה לֵאמֹר אִיהוּ לְעֵילָא, וְכָל עַמָּא לְתַתָּא, דִּכְתִּיב וַיִּתְיַצְבוּ בְּתַחְתִּית הָהָר. וּכְתִיב וּמֹשֶׁה עָלָה אֶל הָאֱלֹהִים.

227. All are silent and one reads, as is written: "And Elohim spoke all these words, saying" (Shemot 20:1). He is above ON THE TOP OF THE MOUNTAIN, and the people are below, as is written: "they took their positions at the base of the Mountain" (Shemot 19:17), and "And Moses went up to Elohim" (Ibid. 3). FOR THERE WAS ONE READER, AND ONE CALLED UP TO THE READING, ON THE TOP OF THE MOUNTAIN; AND ALL THE PEOPLE AT THE BASE OF THE MOUNTAIN LISTENED IN SILENCE. SO SHOULD IT BE WITH THE TORAH SCROLL.

228. וְהַהוּא דְּקָאֲרֵי בְּאוֹרַיְיתָא, יְשַׁוֵּי לְבֵּיהּ וּרְעוּתֵיהּ לְאִינּוּן מִלִּין, וְכִי אִיהוּ שְׁלִיחָא דְּמָארֵיהּ, בְּסִדּוּרָא דְּהַנֵּי מִלִּין, לְמִשְׁמַע לְכָל עַמָּא, דְּהָא אִיהוּ קָאִים כְּדוּגְמָא עֵלָּאָה. בְּגִין כַּךְ, מַאן דְּסָלִיק לְמִקְרֵי בְּאוֹרַיְיתָא, יְסַדֵּר אִינּוּן מִלִּין בְּקַדְמֵיתָא בְּבֵיתֵיהּ, וְאִי לָאו, לָא יִקְרֵי בְּאוֹרַיְיתָא, מְנָלָן מֵהַהוּא דִּבּוּר, עַד דְּלָא יָשְׁמַע אוֹרַיְיתָא לְעַמָּא קַדִּישָׁא מַה כְּתִיב, אָז רָאָה וַיְסַפְּרָהּ הֵכִינָהּ וְגַם חֲקָרָהּ, וּלְבָתַר, וַיֹּאמֶר לָאָדָם הֵן יִרְאַת יְיָ' הִיא חָכְמָה וְגוֹ'.

228. The reader of the Torah should concentrate in his heart and will, upon that he reads, and realize he is the messenger of his Master in the orderly uttering of the verses before the whole people, for he is the likeness of the high one, LIKE THE HOLY ONE, BLESSED BE HE, AT THE GIVING OF THE LAW. For that reason he who is summoned to read the Torah, should rehearse first at his home. And if he did not REHEARSE, he must not read. Whence do we know that? From what THE HOLY ONE, BLESSED BE HE, said, before He uttered aloud the Torah to the holy people, as is written: "then He saw it, and related to: He established it, and searched it out" (Iyov 28:27), and then "to man He said, Behold, the fear of Hashem, that is wisdom..." (Ibid. 28). FOR BEFORE RECITING IT TO MAN, HE PREPARED AND RELATED TO HIMSELF EACH AND EVERY UTTERANCE. SO IT BEHOOVES EVERY READER TO DO.

229. אָסִיר לֵיהּ לְמַאן דְּקָאֲרֵי בְּאוֹרַיְיתָא לְמִפְסַק פַּרְשְׁתָא, אוֹ אֲפִילּוּ

מִלָּה חֲדָא, אֶלָּא בַּאֲתָר דְּפָסַק מֹשֶׁה פַּרְשְׁתָּא לְעַמָּא קַדִּישָׁא, יַפְסִיק. וְלָא יַפְסִיק מִלִּין דְּפַרְשְׁתָּא דְּשַׁבְּתָּא דָּא, בְּפַרְשְׁתָּא דְּשַׁבְּתָּא אַחֲרָא.

229. The reader must not break the reading of the Portion of the Law, not even by one word, save at the places Moses indicated to the holy people. Also he must not read into the next portion of the following Shabbat.

230. רָזָא דָא, בְּשַׁעֲתָא דְּאִיפְסִיקוּ פַּרְשְׁיָין, כָּל חַד וְחַד אִתְעַטְּרָא וְקַיְימָא קַמֵּי קוּדְשָׁא בְּרִיךְ הוּא. כֵּיוָן דְּאַשְׁלִימוּ לְמִפְסַק הָנֵי פַּרְשְׁיָין דְּכָל שַׁתָּא, אִתְעַטְּרוּ קַמֵּיהּ קוּדְשָׁא בְּרִיךְ הוּא, וְאַמְרֵי אֲנָא מִשַּׁבַּת פְּלוֹנִי, וַאֲנָא מִשַּׁבָּת פְּלוֹנִי.

230. The secret thereof is that when all the portions are read, as divided, each and every one is adorned with a crown and stands before the Holy One, blessed be He. When all the divided portions of the year are completely read, they all come adorned before the Holy One, blessed be He, and say: I am of this Shabbat, I am of that Shabbat.

231. בְּהַהִיא שַׁעֲתָא, קָרָא לְיוֹפִיאֵ"ל רַב מְמָנָא, וּלְחַמְשִׁין וּתְלַת רְתִיכִין קַדִּישִׁין דִּתְחוֹת יְדֵיהּ, דְּאִתְמָנוּן בְּשִׁמּוּשָׁא דְּאוֹרַיְיתָא, וְכָל רְתִיכָא וּרְתִיכָא מָנֵי לֵיהּ, לְהַאי רְתִיכָא עַל פַּרְשְׁתָּא פְּלַנְיָא, דִּבְשַׁבַּת פְּלוֹנִי. וּרְתִיכָא פְּלוֹנִי, עַל פַּרְשְׁתָּא פְּלַנְיָא, דְּשַׁבָּת פְּלוֹנִי. וְכָל חַד וְחַד, מְשַׁמְּשָׁא לְאוֹרַיְיתָא, דְּהַהוּא שַׁבָּת דִּילֵיהּ. וְאָסִיר לָן לְעָרְבָא אִלֵּין בְּאִלֵּין, וְלָא לְאַעֲלָא רְתִיכָא בִּרְתִיכָא דְּחַבְרֵיהּ, אֲפִילוּ כְּמְלָא נִימָא. וַאֲפִילוּ בְּחַד תֵּיבָה, אוֹ אֲפִילוּ בְּאָת חַד, אֶלָּא כָּל חַד וְחַד, כְּמָה דְּפָסִיק לוֹן קוּדְשָׁא בְּרִיךְ הוּא , וּכְמָה דְּמָנֵי לוֹן בְּאִינּוּן פַּרְשְׁיָין, כָּל חַד וְחַד עַל מַטְרֵיהּ.

231. At that time, the Holy One, blessed be He, calls Yofi'el, the supreme chief, and the fifty three Chariots under his command, CORRESPONDING TO THE FIFTY THREE PORTIONS OF THE TORAH. The Chariots were assigned to the service of the Torah, each Chariot to a certain portion of a certain

Shabbat. Each one of them is at the service of its own weekly portion of the Torah, and we must not disarrange them and cause the Chariots to touch each other, even by a hairbreadth, or by one word, or even by one letter. Each portion ought to be as the Holy One, blessed be He, decreed, NAMELY IN THE SAME WAY THEY WERE ADORNED BEFORE HIM, and THE CHARIOTS SHOULD BE as appointed over the apportioned passages, each to its post.

232. וְעַל דָּא, כַּד מִתְעַטְּרָא פַּרְשְׁתָּא דָא, סַלְקָן אִינּוּן מִלִּין דְּהַהִיא פַּרְשְׁתָּא, דְּאִשְׁתְּלִים בְּצִבּוּרָא, וְנָטִיל לוֹן הַהוּא רְתִיכָא, דִּמְמָנָא בְּהַהִיא פַּרְשְׁתָּא, וְסָלִיק לוֹן קָמֵי קוּדְשָׁא בְּרִיךְ הוּא, וְאַלֵּין מִלִּין מַמָּשׁ, קַיְימִין קַמֵּיהּ וְאַמְרִין, אֲנָא פַּרְשְׁתָּא פְּלָנְיָא, דְּאַשְׁלִימוּ לִי צִבּוּרָא פְּלוֹנִי, הָכִי וְהָכִי.

232. With the crowning of each portion, its words go up after the completion of the public reading, and are received by the Chariot in charge of that portion. That Chariot raises them before the Holy One, blessed be He, and these actual words stands before Him, and say 'I come of a certain portion that was read this way and that, in such and such a congregation', TO SHOW WHETHER THEY WERE READ CORRECTLY OR INCORRECTLY.

233. אִי אִשְׁתְּלִים כַּדְקָא חֲזֵי לֵיהּ, סַלְקִין אִינּוּן מִלִּין, וּמִתְעַטְּרָן עַל כּוּרְסְיָיא קַדִּישָׁא, וְהַהוּא רְתִיכָא מְשַׁמְּשָׁא קַמֵּיהּ, כָּל רְתִיכָא וּרְתִיכָא, פַּרְשְׁתָּא דְּכָל שַׁבְּתָא וְשַׁבְּתָא, וְכֻלְּהוּ מִתְעַטְּרָן בְּגוֹ כּוּרְסְיָיא קַדִּישָׁא, וּבְהוּ אִיהִי סַלְקָא לְאִתְיַחֲדָא לְעֵילָּא לְעֵילָּא, וְאִתְעֲבֵיד כֹּלָּא כְּלָלָא חֲדָא. בְּגִין כָּךְ, זַכָּאָה חוּלָקֵיהּ מַאן דְּאַשְׁלִים פַּרְשְׁתָּא דְּכָל שַׁבְּתָא וְשַׁבְּתָא, כַּדְקָא יָאוּת, כְּמָה דְּאַפְסִיקוּ לְעֵילָּא.

233. If the complete portion was properly read, its words mount and adorn the holy throne, WHICH IS MALCHUT, and a Chariot is assigned to serve it. Each Chariot is assigned to serve the portion of each Shabbat, MEANING TO ITS OWN PORTION. And all are decorated within the holy throne, which rises with them to be united above, WITH ZEIR ANPIN, so that all, THE PORTION, THE THRONE AND ZEIR ANPIN, become one. For that reason

happy is the portion of him, who completes the reading of the weekly portion in a proper manner, according to the division fixed above.

234. תְּרֵי זִמְנֵי, קָרֵינָן בס״ת בְּשַׁבְּתָא, בַּמִּנְחָה, בְּשַׁעֲתָא דְּדִינָא תַּלְיָא, לְעֵידָן עֶרֶב. צְרִיכִין לְאַכְלְלָא שְׂמָאלָא בִּימִינָא, דְּהָא אוֹרַיְיתָא מִתְּרֵין סִטְרִין אִתְיְיהִיבַת, דִּכְתִּיב מִימִינוֹ אֵשׁ דָּת לָמוֹ, יְמִינָא וּשְׂמָאלָא. בַּג״כ סֵפֶר תּוֹרָה בַּמִּנְחָה דִּי בַּעֲשָׂרָה פְּסוּקִין, אוֹ יַתִּיר, אֲבָל לָא שְׁלִימוּ דְּפַרְשָׁתָא, דְּהָא שְׁלִימוּ דְּפַרְשָׁתָא לָא הֲוֵי, אֶלָּא בִּימִינָא, וִימִינָא תַּלְיָיא עַד שַׁעֲתָא דְּמִנְחָה, וְהָא אוּקְמוּהָ.

234. The Torah is read twice on Shabbat, IN THE MORNING, AND at dusk (Minchah), when Judgment hangs over the world ON WEEKDAYS, before sunset. We should combine left and right, as the Torah was given from both sides, as is written: "from His right hand went a fiery law for them" (Devarim 33:2). FOR THE TORAH IS FIRE, WHICH ALLUDES TO THE LEFT, TOGETHER WITH HIS RIGHT HAND, NAMELY right and left. THEREFORE IT IS READ IN THE MORNING, WHICH ALLUDES TO THE RIGHT, AND AT DUSK, WHICH ALLUDES TO THE LEFT. For that reason ten verses or more are read in the Book of the Law at Minchah, but not a whole portion, because a whole portion exists only in the right, and the right prevails only before the time of Minchah, BUT AT MINCHAH IS THE LEFT. And this was already explained.

235. בַּשֵּׁנִי בְּשַׁבְּתָא, וּבַחֲמִישִׁי בְּשַׁבְּתָא, בְּגִין דְּקָא נַחְתִּין דַּרְגִּין לְתַתָּא, דְּאִינּוּן כְּלָלָא דְּאוֹרַיְיתָא. וְאִי תֵּימָא, הָא נְבִיאִין מִתְפָּרְשָׁן לְתַתָּא. אֶלָּא הָכִי הוּא וַדַּאי, אֲבָל הָנֵי דִלְתַתָּא, כֻּלְּהוּ כְּלָלָא דְּאוֹרַיְיתָא, וְכָל חַד וְחַד כְּלִיל לְכָל חַד וְחַד.

235. On the second and on the fifth days of the week we read the Torah, because the grades descend. FOR ON WEEKDAYS JACOB AND RACHEL TAKE THE DUTY OF THE GREAT MALE AND FEMALE, which are the whole of the Torah, WHOM THEY CLOTHE FROM THE CHEST DOWNWARD OF ZEIR ANPIN, JACOB CORRESPONDING TO THE TORAH LIKE ZEIR ANPIN. You may say that only the prophets extend downward, FOR JACOB

CLOTHES ONLY NETZACH, HOD AND YESOD OF ZEIR ANPIN, THE GRADES OF THE PROPHETS, BUT NOT OF THE TORAH, WHICH IS THE ASPECT OF CHESED, GVURAH AND TIFERET. THEREFORE WHY READ THE TORAH? HE REPLIES: assuredly this is so, THAT JACOB CLOTHES ONLY NETZACH, HOD AND YESOD OF ZEIR ANPIN, but all of those who are below, THE NINE SFIROT OF JACOB, the Torah is comprised of them all. TO WIT, THE WHOLE OF JACOB CORRESPONDS TO CHESED, GVURAH AND TIFERET, WHICH ARE THE TORAH, LIKE ZEIR ANPIN. And each of these three Sfirot is comprised of the other, AND SINCE THEY CONSIST OF ONE ANOTHER, EACH HAS IN IT CHESED, GVURAH AND TIFERET.

236. וְרָזָא דְמִלָּה, אִלֵּין דַּרְגִּין עִלָּאִין, אִינּוּן אִקְרוּן פַּרְשְׁתָּא חֲדָא, וּלְבָתַר נָפְקִין מִנַּיְיהוּ תֵּשַׁע דַּרְגִּין, דְּאִתְאַחֲדָן כַּחֲדָא, וּבְגִין כַּךְ תִּשְׁעָה גּוּבְרִין, תְּלַת בְּשַׁבְּתָא בַּמִּנְחָה, וּתְלַת בְּיוֹמָא תִּנְיָינָא, וּתְלַת בְּיוֹמָא חֲמִשָׁאָה, הָא תִּשְׁעָה.

236. The secret of the matter is that these upper grades, THE SEVEN SFIROT OF ZEIR ANPIN are called one portion, NAMELY THE WEEKLY PORTION. From them emanate nine grades bound together, THE NINE SFIROT OF JACOB. This is why nine people are called to read the Torah; three on Shabbat's Minchah, CORRESPONDING TO CHOCHMAH, BINAH AND DA'AT OF JACOB, three on Monday, CORRESPONDING TO CHESED, GVURAH AND TIFERET OF JACOB, and three on Thursday, CORRESPONDING TO NETZACH, HOD AND YESOD OF JACOB. Altogether there are nine people. IT WAS ALREADY EXPLAINED THAT THE NINE SFIROT ARE INCLUDED THE ONE WITHIN THE OTHER, AND THUS EACH HAS CHESED, GVURAH AND TIFERET THAT ARE THE TORAH, EVEN NETZACH, HOD AND YESOD.

237. וּבְסִפְרָא דְּרַב יֵיבָא סָבָא, בַּמִּנְחָה בְּשַׁבְּתָא, הָא אִתְּעַר רָזָא דִשְׂמָאלָא, וּנְקוּדָה תַּתָּאָה, בְּהַהוּא סִטְרָא דִשְׂמָאלָא, מְקַבְּלָא רָזָא דְאוֹרַיְיתָא, כְּדֵין בְּהַהִיא שַׁעֲתָא, נַטְלָא מִסִּטְרָא דִשְׂמָאלָא, וּמִדִּילֵיהּ קָרֵינָן.

237. It is written in the book of Rav Yeba Saba (the elder) that, on Minchah of Shabbat, the mystery of the left is awakened, and the lower point,

MALCHUT, receives from the left side the mystery of the Torah. At that time MALCHUT is going from the left, from which side we read THE TORAH. THAT IS TO SAY, THAT THOUGH MALCHUT HERSELF IS NOT CONSIDERED THE WRITTEN LAW, YET SINCE SHE RECEIVES THE ASPECT OF THE WRITTEN LAW FROM THE LEFT SIDE OF ZEIR ANPIN, WE READ THE TORAH.

238. דְּהָא אִיהִי קַיְימָא בְּרָזָא דְּתֵשַׁע, וְקַרֵינָן תֵּשַׁע, וְאִינוּן שִׁית דְּחוֹל, וּתְלַת בְּשַׁעֲתָא דְּאִתְּעַר שְׂמָאלָא בְּשַׁבְּתָא, וּלְאִתְכַּלְלָא כֹּלָא כַּחֲדָא. וְאִיהִי מִתְעַטְּרָא בְּהוּ, בִּתְלַת סִטְרִין, כְּגַוְונָא דִּתְלַת סִטְרִין עִלָּאִין, דְּאִינוּן כְּלָלָא דְּפַרְשְׁתָּא דְּשַׁבְּתָּא. זַכָּאָה חוּלָקֵיהּ מַאן דְּזָכֵי לִיקָרָא דְּשַׁבְּתָא, זַכָּאָה אִיהוּ בִּתְרֵין עָלְמִין, בְּעָלְמָא דֵין, וּבְעָלְמָא דְאָתֵי.

238. For MALCHUT is based on the secret of the nine SFIROT, and therefore we call up nine PEOPLE, THAT IS, six PEOPLE – CHESED, GVURAH, TIFERET, NETZACH, HOD AND YESOD OF MALCHUT – on weekdays, MONDAY AND THURSDAY, and three PEOPLE, THAT ARE HER FIRST THREE SFIROT, when the left awakens on Shabbat, AT MINCHAH OF SHABBAT; and we unite them into one. MALCHUT adorns herself with them on three sides, RIGHT, LEFT, AND CENTRAL, like the upper three sides, CHESED, GVURAH AND TIFERET, that are included in the weekly portion, THAT WE READ IN THE MORNING. Happy is the portion of whoever is worthy of the preciousness of Shabbat, he is happy on both worlds, this world and the World to Come.

18. The secrets of Shabbat

A Synopsis

The passage begins with "let no man go out of his place on the seventh day," saying that it is a profanation of the Shabbat to work with one's hands or to walk more than 2,000 cubits out of the city limits. Now we hear that it is good to draw out the Shabbat as long as possible. At the end of it the wicked are turned back to Sheol and the demons torture them again in Gehenom. We are told that it is wrong to fast on the Shabbat because it is a day for pleasure and rejoicing; recompense for this error can only be made by fasting on the first day of the week. We learn now of the significance of the 32 paths in Chochmah, the three grades of holy apples and the seventy words in the Testimony of Faith and the Kidush. We read a discussion of the prayers in the morning, the daytime, the evening and the night, and of their different results.

239. כְּתִיב אַל יֵצֵא אִישׁ מִמְּקוֹמוֹ בַּיּוֹם הַשְּׁבִיעִי מַהוּ מִמְּקוֹמוֹ. תָּנֵינָן, מִמְּקוֹמוֹ מֵהַהוּא אֲתַר דְּאִתְחֲזֵי לְמֵהַךְ. וְרָזָא דְּמִלָּה, דִּכְתִיב בָּרוּךְ כְּבוֹד יְיָ' מִמְּקוֹמוֹ. וְדָא אִיהוּ מָקוֹם, וְדָא אִיהוּ רָזָא דִּכְתִיב כִּי הַמָּקוֹם אֲשֶׁר אַתָּה עוֹמֵד עָלָיו. אֲתַר יְדִיעָא אִיהוּ לְעֵילָא, וְקָרֵינָן לֵיהּ מָקוֹם, דְּאִשְׁתְּמוֹדַע בֵּיהּ יְקָרָא עִלָּאָה דִּלְעֵילָא. וּבְג״כ, אַזְהָרוּתָא לְב״נ דְּהָא מִתְעַטְּרָא בְּעִטְרָא קַדִּישָׁא דִּלְעֵילָא, דְּלָא יִפּוֹק מִינֵּיהּ דְּאִי יִפּוֹק מִנֵּיהּ, קָא מְחַלֵּל שַׁבְּתָא. בִּידוֹי, בַּעֲבִידְתָּא. כְּמָה דְּאוֹקִימְנָא. בְּרַגְלוֹי, לְמֵהַךְ לְבַר מִתְּרֵי אַלְפִין אַמִּין, כָּל אִלֵּין חֲלוּלָא דְּשַׁבְּתָא אִיהוּ.

239. It is written: "let no man go out of his place on the seventh day" (Shemot 16:30). HE ASKS: What is his place, AND ANSWERS: We learned that 'from his place' MEANS from within the place it is fit to walk in. THAT IS OUT OF MORE THAN TWO THOUSANDS CUBITS OUTSIDE THE CITY LIMITS. The secret of this matter is written in the verses, "blessed be the glory of Hashem from His place" (Yechezkel 3:12), which refers to a specified place, and "for the place on which you stand" (Shemot 3:5). For there is a known place above, MALCHUT, by the name of 'place', in which the high glory of above is made known, WHICH IS MALCHUT. Therefore a man who is adorned with the holy crown of above is warned, not to leave the place, for if he does, that is profanation of the Shabbat. NEITHER should

he work with his hands, NOR walk with his feet over two thousand cubits out of city limits, for all these are profanation of the Shabbat.

240. אַל יֵצֵא אִישׁ מִמְּקוֹמוֹ, דָּא אִיהוּ אֲתָר יְקָרָא דִּקְדוּשָׁה דָּא, דְּהָא מִנֵּיהּ לְבַר, אֲתָר דֶּאֱלֹהִים אֲחֵרִים אִיהוּ. בָּרוּךְ כְּבוֹד יְיָ' מִמְּקוֹמוֹ. כְּבוֹד יְיָ' דִּלְעֵילָא. מִמְּקוֹמוֹ, דָּא כְּבוֹד דִּלְתַתָּא וְדָא אִיהוּ רָזָא דַּעֲטָרָא דְּשַׁבְּתָא, בְּג"כ אַל יֵצֵא אִישׁ מִמְּקוֹמוֹ, בְּרִיךְ הוּא לְעָלַם וּלְעָלְמֵי עָלְמִין.

240. "let no man go out of his place" refers to the holy place of glory, WHICH IS MALCHUT; for beyond it, lies the place of other Elohim. "Blessed be the glory of Hashem from His place": 'the glory of Hashem' is the glory above, BINAH; His place' is the lower glory, MALCHUT. This is the secret of the crown of Shabbat, and therefore "let no man go out of his place." Blessed be He for ever and ever.

241. כְּתִיב הִנֵּה מָקוֹם אִתִּי, מָקוֹם אִתִּי, וַדַּאי דָּא אִיהוּ מָקוֹם טָמִיר וְגָנִיז, דְּלָא אִתְיְידַע כְּלַל. מַשְׁמַע דִּכְתִיב אִתִּי, אֲתָר דְּלָא אִתְגַּלְיָא, וְקַיְימָא טְמִירָא, וְדָא אִיהוּ אֲתָר עִלָּאָה לְעֵילָא לְעֵילָא, הֵיכָלָא עִלָּאָה טָמִיר וְגָנִיז. אֲבָל דָּא, אִיהוּ אֲתָר לְתַתָּא כִּדְקָאמְרָן. וְדָא אִיהוּ מָקוֹם דְּאִתְפְּרַשׁ לְעֵילָא, וְאִתְפְּרַשׁ לְתַתָּא, וּבְג"כ אַל יֵצֵא אִישׁ מִמְּקוֹמוֹ בְּיוֹם הַשְּׁבִיעִי.

241. It is written, "There is a place by me" (Shemot 33:21). The 'place by me' assuredly refers to a hidden and concealed place that is utterly unknown, BINAH. 'by me' INDICATES that this place which is not revealed and remains hidden, is the most high place, viz. the supernal hidden and concealed chamber, SUPERNAL BINAH. But this PLACE HERE is the lower place, MALCHUT, as we said. This place is extended above IN BINAH, and below IN MALCHUT. Therefore "let no man go out of his place on the seventh day."

242. וּמַדֹּתֶם מִחוּץ לָעִיר אֶת פְּאַת קֵדְמָה אַלְפַּיִם בָּאַמָּה וְגוֹ', הָא אוֹקְמוּהָ בְּאִינּוּן רָזִין עִלָּאִין. אֲבָל אַלְפַּיִם בָּאַמָּה, דִּירָתָה תְּרֵין סִטְרִין

לְכָל סְטָר, וְאִיהִי מִתְעַטְּרָא תָּדִיר בִּתְרֵין סִטְרִין, בֵּין לְעֵילָא בֵּין לְתַתָּא. וְסִימָנָךְ שְׁכִינָה לָא שַׁרְיָא לְבַר מִתְּחוּמָא דְּאִתְחֲזֵי לָהּ.

242. It is written: "And you shall measure from outside the city limits on the east side two thousand cubits..." (Bemidbar 35:5). We already expounded on these high secrets. But two thousand cubits ARE MEASURED BECAUSE MALCHUT, THAT IS CALLED 'CITY', inherited two sides, RIGHT AND LEFT. FOR CHOCHMAH CLOTHED IN CHASSADIM AND CHASSADIM CLOTHED IN CHOCHMAH AMOUNT TO TWO THOUSANDS, BECAUSE THE SFIROT OF CHOCHMAH ARE BY THE THOUSANDS. AND MALCHUT is always adorned on both sides both above and below. You can tell that from the Shechinah that does not hover outside the boundary proper to Her, WHICH IS OUTSIDE THE TWO COLUMNS.

243. כַּד נָפַק שַׁבְּתָא, צְרִיכִין יִשְׂרָאֵל דִּלְתַתָּא, לְאַעְכָּבָא, דְּהָא יוֹמָא רַבָּא עִלָּאָה אִיהוּ. וּבְהַאי יוֹמָא, אוּשְׁפִּיזָא רַבָּא וְיַקִּירָא, קָא שַׁרְיָא עֲלֵיהּ, בְּגִין כָּךְ בָּעֵי לְאִתְעַכְּבָא, לְאִתְחֲזָאָה דְּלָא דַּחֲקִין בְּאוּשְׁפִּיזָא קַדִּישָׁא. כְּדֵין פַּתְחֵי יִשְׂרָאֵל וְאַמְרֵי, וְהוּא רַחוּם יְכַפֵּר עָוֹן וְגו', דְּתִקּוּנָא שַׁפִּירָא אִיהוּ בְּהַאי לֵילְיָא, כֵּיוָן דְּדִינָא אִתְהַדָּר לְאַתְרֵיהּ, מַה דְּלָא אִתְחֲזֵי כַּד עָיֵיל שַׁבְּתָא, דְּדִינָא אִסְתַּלָּק, וְלָא אִשְׁתְּכַח.

243. When Shabbat withdraws, it behooves Yisrael below to delay it, THAT IS, TO TAKE FROM THE WEEK DAYS AND ADD TO THE HOLY, because this is a great and high day, and on that day a great and precious visitor stays with it, THE ADDITIONAL SOUL. For that reason one should detain the guest and show that there is no hurry to press the holy guest BY ESCORTING HIM OUT. Then Yisrael commence with the hymn "And He being merciful, will forgive iniquity..." which is fit to be said on that night, since Judgment returns to its place, not like on Shabbat eve, when Judgment is gone and is not present.

244. בְּשַׁעֲתָא דְּפַתְחֵי יִשְׂרָאֵל וַיְהִי נֹעַם, וּקְדוּשְׁתָּא דְּסִדְרָא, כָּל אִינּוּן חַיָּיבִין דְּגֵיהִנָּם, פַּתְחִין וְאַמְרֵי, זַכָּאִין אַתּוּן יִשְׂרָאֵל עַמָּא קַדִּישָׁא, זַכָּאִין אַתּוּן צַדִּיקַיָּיא, דְּנַטְרֵי פִּקּוּדֵי אוֹרַיְיתָא. וַוי לוֹן לְחַיָּיבַיָּא, דְּלָא

זָכוּ לְמֵיטַר אוֹרַיְיתָא, כְּדֵין דוּמ"ה קַדִים, וְכָרוֹזָא אִתְּעַר וְאָמַר, יָשׁוּבוּ
רְשָׁעִים לִשְׁאוֹלָה כָּל גּוֹיִם שְׁכֵחֵי אֱלֹהִים. וְכָל אַלֵּין חֲבִילֵי טְהִירִין,
טַרְדִין לוֹן בְּגֵיהִנָּם, וְלֵית מַאן דִּמְרַחֵם עֲלֵיהוֹן. זַכָּאִין אִינוּן כָּל נַטְרֵי
שַׁבַּתָּא בְּהַאי עָלְמָא, וְקָא מְעַנְּגֵי לְהַהוּא עֹנֶג דְּשַׁרְיָא מִלְּעֵילָא,
כִּדְקָאַמְרָן.

244. While Yisrael start TO RECITE the prayer "and let the pleasantness" and the holy prayer, NAMELY "AND YOU ARE HOLY…" all the wicked in Gehenom open and say 'happy are you, holy nation of Yisrael, and you righteous, that keep the precepts of the Torah. Woe to the evil who were not worthy of observing the Torah'. Then Dumah makes haste, and a crier resounds: "the wicked shall be turned back to Sheol, all the nations that forget Elohim" (Tehilim 9:18). Then all those troops of demons torture them in Gehenom, and no one has pity for them. Happy are those who observe Shabbat in this world, and please the delight that hovers above, NAMELY, THE SUPERNAL SPIRIT, as mentioned.

245. הַאי מַאן דְּשָׁרֵי בְּתַעֲנִיתָא בְּשַׁבַּתָּא, תְּרֵי מִתְּעָרֵי עָלֵיהּ קַמֵּי
מַלְכָּא קַדִּישָׁא. חַד, הַהוּא רוּחָא עִלָּאָה קַדִּישָׁא דְּאִצְטְרִיךְ לְאִתְעַנְּגָא,
וְלָא אִתְעַנָּג. וְחַד, הַהוּא מְמָנָא דְּקַיְּימָא עַל מַאן דְּשָׁרֵי בְּתַעֲנִיתָא,
וְסַנְגַּרְיָ"ה שְׁמֵיהּ. וְסַלְקִין קַמֵּי מַלְכָּא קַדִּישָׁא, וּמִתְּעָרֵי עָלֵיהּ.

245. Whoever fasts on Shabbat, two are stirred against him before the Holy One, blessed be He. One is the holy Supernal Spirit, that should have been pleased but was not. The other is a chief in charge of those who fast, by the name of Sangaryah. They rise to discuss him before the Holy King.

246. וְהַהוּא רוּחָא אִסְתַּלָּק גָּרִיעַ מֵהַהוּא אִתְהֲנוּתָא דִּלְתַתָּא. וְכַד הַאי
רוּחָא לָא אִשְׁתְּלִים לְתַתָּא, רוּחָא אַחֲרָא דִּלְעֵילָא לָא אִשְׁתְּלִים. כֵּיוָן
דְּלָא אִשְׁתְּלִים לְתַתָּא וּלְעֵילָא, כְּדֵין אִתְחֲזֵי הַהוּא ב"ן לְאִתְלַטְיָא,
וּלְאִתְעַנְשָׁא. אֶלָּא כֵּיוָן דְּאִשְׁתְּלִים זִמְנָא אַחֲרָא, וְהַהוּא מְמָנָא
דְּאִתְמַנָּא עַל עִנּוּיָא וְתַעֲנִיתָא, אִשְׁתְּלִים גּוֹ אִינוּן מְמָנָן אַחֲרָנִין,
בְּעֹנוּגָא דִּלְעֵילָא, קוֹרְעִין לֵיהּ כָּל גְּזַר דִּינָא, דְּאִתְגְּזַר מֵאִינוּן שַׁבְעִין

שְׁנִין עִלָּאִין.

246. The spirit was gone since there was lack OF PLEASURE and delight, down below, and when that spirit is not perfected below, another upper spirit is not perfected. Since there is no perfection above and below, this man deserves to be cursed and punished. But if there was perfection at a different time, BY THAT SAME MAN, and the chief in charge of fasting is perfected among other chiefs in the upper pleasure, the verdict is remitted, that was sentenced by seventy high years, CHESED, GVURAH, TIFERET, NETZACH, HOD, YESOD AND MALCHUT.

247. לְמַלְכָּא דְּחַדֵי בְּהִלּוּלָא דִּילֵיהּ, וְכָל בְּנֵי נָשָׁא חַדָּאן עִמֵּיהּ, חָמָא חַד בַּר נָשׁ יָהִיב בְּקוֹלָר, פָּקִיד עֲלוֹי, וְשַׁרְיִיוּהוּ. בְּגִין דְּיִשְׁתַּכְחוּן כֹּלָּא בְּחֶדְוָה.

247. In the same manner, a king, rejoicing in his banquet with all the people rejoicing about him, when he saw a man sitting chained, he ordered that he would be set free, so that all shall be in gladness.

248. וּלְבָתַר, מִתְהַדְּרִין אִלֵּין מְמָנָן דְּעָנְשִׁין לִבְנֵי נָשָׁא, וְאִתְפָּרְעִין מִנֵּיהּ דְּב"נ, עַל דְּאִשְׁתְּכַח בְּגִינֵיהּ גְּרִיעוּתָא עֵילָא וְתַתָּא. מַאי תַּקַנְתֵּיהּ. לֵיתִיב תַּעֲנִיתָא עַל תַּעֲנִיתָא. מַאי טַעֲמָא. דָּא בָּטִיל עֲנוּגָא דְּשַׁבְּתָא, יְבַטֵּל עֲנוּגָא דְּחוֹל.

248. Afterwards, the same officers return who punish the men, and exact their due from the man that was the cause of diminution above and below, FOR HE DID NOT HAVE PLEASURE ON SHABBAT. How can he amend: by fasting on another day against his fast ON SHABBAT. What is the sense? For he who stopped pleasure on Shabbat, shall stop FOR THAT REASON pleasure on a weekday.

249. וְאִי אִיהוּ מְבַטֵּל עֲנוּגָא דְּשַׁבְּתָא, וְקָא מִתְעַנַּג בַּחוֹל, דָּמֵי כְּמַאן דְּחָשַׁב לְמִלָּה אַחֲרָא, יַתִּיר מִמָּה דְּחָשִׁיב לֵיהּ לְקוּדְשָׁא בְּרִיךְ הוּא. רוּחָא עִלָּאָה, קַדִּישָׁא דְּקוּדְשִׁין דְּשַׁרְיָא עֲלֵיהּ, לָא עָנִיג, וּבָטִיל לֵיהּ

מִנֵּיהּ. רוּחָא אַחֲרָא דְּחוֹל, דְּשַׁרְיָא לְבָתַר עַל עָלְמָא, חָשִׁיב וְקָא מְעַנְּגָא
לֵיהּ. כְּדֵין מְהַדְּרִין וּמִתְפָּרְעִין מִנֵּיהּ, בְּהַאי עָלְמָא, וּבְעָלְמָא דְּאָתֵי.

249. And if he stops pleasure on Shabbat but has pleasure on a weekday, he is considered as if he values other things more than the Holy One, blessed be He. For he did not give pleasure to the Supernal Spirit, the Holy of Holies, that rested on him, and neglected it; but to another weekday spirit that will remain afterwards in the world he pays attention and gives it pleasure. They then return to exact punishment in this world and in the World to Come.

250. בְּגִין כָּךְ, אִצְטְרִיךְ תַּעֲנִיתָא אַחֲרִינָא, בְּיוֹמָא קַדְמָאָה דְּחוֹל,
בְּזִמְנָא דְּשַׁרְיָא עַל עָלְמָא הַהוּא רוּחָא דְּחוֹל. וּבְהַאי אִית לֵיהּ אַסְוָותָא,
כֵּיוָן דְּלָא חָשִׁיב לְרוּחָא דְּחוֹל. וְסִימָנִיךְ וְהֵשִׁיב אֶת הַגְּזֵלָה אֲשֶׁר גָּזָל
וְגוֹ'. גַּזְלָן, לָא חָשִׁיב לְקוּדְשָׁא בְּרִיךְ הוּא, לָא חָשִׁיב לִבְנֵי נָשָׁא, בְּגִין
כָּךְ לֵית לֵיהּ עוֹנְשָׁא כְּגַנָּב גַּנָּב, דְּחָשִׁיב לִבְנֵי נָשָׁא, יַתִּיר מִקוּדְשָׁא בְּרִיךְ
הוּא, אִית לֵיהּ עוֹנְשָׁא בְּהַאי עָלְמָא, וּבְעָלְמָא דְּאָתֵי. זַכָּאָה אִיהוּ, מַאן
דְּאִשְׁתְּלִים לְתַתָּא, לְהַהוּא עוֹנֶג עִלָּאָה כַּדְקָא חֲזֵי.

250. To correct it he should fast on the first day of the week, when a weekday spirit abides in the world. By that he may make good his offense, by not considering the weekday spirit MORE THAN THE SHABBAT SPIRIT. It is learned from the verse "he shall restore that which he took violently away..." (Vayikra 5:23). A robber has no consideration either for the Holy One, blessed be He, or for people, therefore his punishment is not as great as that of a thief, who has consideration for people more than for the Holy One, blessed be He. He is punished in this world and in the World to Come. Happy is he who properly perfects down below the high delight.

251 יוֹמָא דָא, מִתְעַטְּרָא בְּשַׁבְעִין עִטְרִין, וּשְׁמָא עִלָּאָה קַדִּישָׁא,
אִשְׁתְּלִים בְּכָל סִטְרִין, וְאִתְנְהִירוּ כֻּלְהוּ דַרְגִּין, וְכֹלָּא בְּחֶדְוָה דְּבִרְכָּאן,
וּבְקְדוּשָׁה עַל קְדוּשָׁה, וְתוֹסֶפֶת דִּקְדוּשָׁה.

251. That day is bedecked with seventy crowns, FOR IT IS THE SEVENTH

DAY IN WHICH THE SEVEN SFIROT CHESED, GVURAH, TIFERET, NETZACH, HOD, YESOD AND MALCHUT WERE PERFECTED AND DECORATED, EACH CONTAINING TEN, ALTOGETHER THERE ARE SEVENTY CROWNS. And the highly Holy Name, BINAH, is perfected on all sides, FROM THE THREE COLUMNS, WHICH ARE THE SECRET OF THE PATRIARCHS, and all the grades shine all in the gladness of the benedictions, with sanctity upon sanctity, and the additional sanctity (Heb. *Kedusha* of *Musaf*). THE BENEDICTIONS COME FROM BINAH AND THE SANCTIFICATIONS FROM CHOCHMAH.

252. קְדוּשָׁה דְּמַעֲלֵי שַׁבְּתָא, דָּא אִיהִי קְדוּשָׁה דְּשַׁבָּת בְּרֵאשִׁית. דְּהָא אִתְקַדַּשׁ מִתְּלָתִין וּתְרֵין שְׁבִילִין, וּתְלַת דַּרְגִּין דְּתַפּוּחִין קַדִּישִׁין. וּבָעֵינָן לְאַדְכְּרָא עַל הַאי קְדוּשָׁה, כְּלָלָא דְּעוֹבָדָא דִּבְרֵאשִׁית, וְנַיְיחָא בְּרָזָא דִּתְלָתִין וּתְרֵין שְׁבִילִין, וּתְלַת דַּרְגִּין דְּאִתְכְּלִילָן בְּהוּ, רָזָא דְּסַהֲדוּתָא דְּעוֹבָדָא דִּבְרֵאשִׁית, דְּהַיְינוּ וַיְכֻלּוּ הַשָּׁמַיִם וְהָאָרֶץ וְכָל צְבָאָם וְגוֹ'. וַיְכַל אֱלֹהִים, דְּאִית בְּסַהֲדוּתָא דָּא, תְּלָתִין וַחֲמֵשׁ תֵּיבִין. תְּלָתִין וּתְרֵין שְׁבִילִין, וּתְלַת דַּרְגִּין דְּתַפּוּחִין קַדִּישִׁין.

252. The sanctity of the commencement of Shabbat, MALCHUT, is the same sanctity of Shabbat of Creation, WHICH IS IN THE SECRET OF BINAH, THE SECRET OF 32 TIMES ELOHIM IS MENTIONED IN THE ACTS OF CREATION, SANCTIFIED BY THE 32 PATHS OF CHOCHMAH. ALSO MALCHUT was sanctified by the 32 paths OF CHOCHMAH and the three grades of holy apple trees. THE APPLES REPRESENT THE PRINCIPLE OF THE THREE COLUMNS THAT CORRESPOND TO THE THREE COLORS OF THE APPLE: WHITE, RED AND GREEN THAT DRAW CHOCHMAH THAT IS THE SECRET OF SANCTITY. THEREFORE THEY ARE CONSIDERED HOLY APPLES, AND MALCHUT THAT RECEIVES THEM IS CALLED A FIELD OF HOLY APPLE TREES. And the entire act of creation and the rest ON THE SEVENTH DAY must be mentioned in this sanctification according to the principle of the 32 paths of Chochmah and the three grades OF APPLE TREES incorporated in them, that is the secret of the testimony regarding the acts of Creation, namely, "Thus the heavens and the earth were finished, and all their host. And by the seventh day Elohim ended..." (Beresheet 2:1-2). This testimony contains 35 words IN CORRESPONDENCE WITH the 32 paths and three grades of the holy apples.

253. תְּלַת דַּרְגִּין, דְּאִינוּן: שְׁבִיעִי. שְׁבִיעִי. שְׁבִיעִי. וְאִית בֵּיהּ רָזָא
דְּעָלְמָא עִלָּאָה, וְרָזָא דְּעָלְמָא תַּתָּאָה, וְרָזָא דְּכָל מְהֵימְנוּתָא. תְּלַת
זִמְנִין אֱלֹהִים, חַד, עָלְמָא תַּתָּאָה. וְחַד, פַּחַד יִצְחָק. וְחַד, עָלְמָא עִלָּאָה
קַדִּישָׁא, קֹדֶשׁ קוּדְשִׁין. בָּעֵי ב"נ לְמִסְהַד סַהֲדוּתָא דָּא, בְּחֶדְוָה,
בִּרְעוּתָא דְּלִבָּא, לְאַסְהֲדָא קַמֵּי מָארֵיהּ דִּמְהֵימְנוּתָא. וְכָל מַאן דְּיַסְהִיד
דָּא, וְיִשַׁוֵּי לִבֵּיהּ וּרְעוּתֵיהּ לְדָא, מְכַפֵּר עַל כָּל חוֹבוֹי.

253. The three grades that are the three times 'seventh' IN "THUS THE HEAVENS…WERE FINISHED," contain the mystery of the upper world, BINAH, THAT IS CALLED 'SEVENTH' FROM BELOW UP, STARTING FROM YESOD; and the secret of the lower world, MALCHUT THAT IS CALLED 'SEVENTH', WHEN YOU COUNT FROM CHESED; and the secret of all the Faith, WHICH IS THE CROWN OF YESOD OF ZEIR ANPIN, THAT IS CONSIDERED AS MALCHUT OF ZEIR ANPIN AND NAMED 'SEVENTH'. IN THE TEXT "THUS THE HEAVENS…WERE FINISHED" the word Elohim is mentioned three times. One stands for the lower world, MALCHUT BY THE NAME OF ELOHIM, another one stands for the "fear of Isaac," THAT IS GVURAH OF ZEIR ANPIN AND IS CALLED ELOHIM, and one stands for the holy upper world, the Holy of Holies, THAT IS BINAH BY THE NAME OF ELOHIM. A man should give this testimony gladly and willingly, and to testify before the Master of the Faith. And whoever gives this testimony and puts his heart and mind to it, his sins are thereby atoned.

254. בָּא"י אמ"ה אק"ב וְרָצָה בָנוּ וְכוּ', הַאי קִידּוּשָׁא אִיהוּ בְּחַד
מַתְקְלָא, לָקֳבֵל סַהֲדוּתָא דִּמְהֵימְנוּתָא, וְאִינוּן תְּלָתִין וַחֲמֵשׁ תֵּיבִין
אַחֲרָנִין, כְּמָה דְּאִית בְּוַיְכֻלּוּ. כֹּלָּא סַלְקִין לְשַׁבְעִין תֵּיבִין, לְאִתְעַטְּרָא
בְּהוּ שַׁבָּת, דְּמַעֲלֵי שַׁבְּתָא. זַכָּאָה חוּלָקֵיהּ דְּבַר נָשׁ, דִּיְכַוֵּון רְעוּתֵיהּ
לְמִלִּין אִלֵּין, לִיקָרָא דְּמָארֵיהּ.

254. The kiddush (lit. 'sanctification') of the day – "Blessed are You, Hashem our Elohim, King of the universe, who has sanctified us by His commandments and has taken pleasure in us…" – is the kiddush that balances the testimony of Faith "THUS THE HEAVENS…WERE FINISHED," and likewise it contains thirty five other words, as in "thus the heavens…"

TOGETHER there are seventy words, with which to adorn Shabbat in its beginning, NAMELY MALCHUT. Happy is the portion of whoever meditates upon these things to the glory of his Master.

255. קִידוּשָׁא דְּיוֹמָא, הָא אוּקְמוּהָ בּוֹרֵא פְּרִי הַגֶּפֶן, וְלָא יַתִּיר. דְּהָא יוֹמָא קָאִים לְקַדְּשָׁא לֵיה, מַה דְּלֵית הָכִי בְּלֵילְיָא, דְּאֲנָן צְרִיכִין לְקַדְּשָׁא לֵיה, בְּהָנֵי מִלִּין, כְּמָה דְּאוֹקִימְנָא. וְלָא אִתְקַדָּשׁ הַאי לֵילְיָא, אֶלָּא בְּעַמָּא קַדִּישָׁא לְתַתָּא, כַּד שַׁרְיָא עֲלַיְיהוּ הַהוּא רוּחָא עִלָּאָה. וַאֲנָן בָּעֵינָן לְקַדְּשָׁא לֵיה בִּרְעוּתָא דְּלִבָּא, לְכַוְּונָא דַּעְתָּא לְהַאי.

255. The kiddush in the morning consists, as we said, of the blessing over the cup of wine, and no more, because the day, ZEIR ANPIN, sanctifies MALCHUT, WHICH IS THE SECRET OF THE CUP OF WINE. FOR BY DAY, MALE AND FEMALE ASCEND TO ABA AND IMA, THE SECRET OF HOLINESS, AND ARE SANCTIFIED THROUGH THEM. But at night, we should sanctify MALCHUT by the recital we mentioned, THE SEVENTY WORDS. The night, MALCHUT is sanctified only by the holy nation down below, at the time when the higher spirit, THE ADDITIONAL SOUL, rests upon them. And we should sanctify it with a willing heart and meditate upon it.

256. וְיוֹמָא אִיהוּ קָא מְקַדְּשָׁא לֵיה. וְיִשְׂרָאֵל מְקַדְּשֵׁי בִּצְלוֹתִין וּבָעוּתִין, וּמִתְקַדְּשִׁין בִּקְדוּשָׁתֵיה, בְּהַאי יוֹמָא. זַכָּאִין יִשְׂרָאֵל, עַמָּא קַדִּישָׁא, דְּאַחֲסִינוּ יוֹמָא דָּא, אַחֲסָנַת יְרוּתָא לְעָלְמִין.

256. And the day, SHABBAT, THE PRINCIPLE OF ZEIR ANPIN THAT ASCENDED TO THE SUPERNAL ABA AND IMA AND BECAME SANCTIFIED LIKE THEM, IT sanctifies MALCHUT THAT IS CALLED CUP, NOT WE. and Yisrael sanctify by prayers and supplications, AS THROUGH THE PRAYERS OF THE MORNING, THE MUSAF PRAYER AND THE REPETITION OF THE AMIDAH BY THE CANTOR, WE RAISE MALE AND FEMALE TO ABA AND IMA, AND THEY NEED NO KIDUSH TO SANCTIFY THEM FURTHER, for they are sanctified by the sanctity OF ZEIR ANPIN IN ABA AND IMA on that day. Happy are Yisrael, the holy nation, that inherited this day as an everlasting heritage.

19. The luminaries of fire

A Synopsis

We are told that at the end of Shabbat permission is given to the lower chiefs to govern the world, and a man must now separate the holy from the secular. At this time he must say the blessing over the light of fire. This fire is not the everyday fire but Shabbat's fire that comes from the fire of above drawn down to the altar, Malchut. When this fire is blessed by the benediction all the other fires are given permission to illuminate. Four Chariots appear (Michael, Gabriel, Uriel and Raphael), each in charge of a legion of angels that are shining with that blessed fire; they are called the lights of the fire. We are told of the fingers of the right hand, how they allude to the lights of the fire, how they are raised to demonstrate the supernal sanctity of the upper grades that rule over all, and how they are bent to point at the lower grades, the Chariots. At the end of Shabbat, Malchut lets out the luminaries of fire as if they were created anew at that moment, and they are assigned their place to rule. The higher grades are called the luminaries of light, that rule by day and shine by the supreme light, Binah.

257. לְבָתַר דְּנָפִיק שַׁבַּתָא, בָּעֵי בַּר נָשׁ לְאַפְרָשָׁא, בֵּין קֹדֶשׁ לְחוֹל. אֲמַאי. דְּהָא אִתְיְהִיב רְשׁוּ לִמְמָנָן דִּלְתַתָּא לְשַׁלְטָאָה עַל עָלְמָא, וּבְכָל עוֹבָדִין דְּעָלְמָא, לְאַחֲזָאָה יִחוּדָא, בְּאֲתַר קַדִּישָׁא, בִּקְדוּשָׁה עִלָּאָה, וּלְאַפְרָשָׁא לְתַתָּא מִיִּחוּדָא עִלָּאָה, וּלְבָרְכָא עַל נְהוֹרָא דְּאֶשָּׁא.

257. At the end of Shabbat, it behooves a man to separate the holy from the secular. Why? The reason is that permission is now given to the lower chiefs to govern the world, and all its matters. ONE HAS to demonstrate the unity in a holy place in supernal holiness, THAT IS SHABBAT, separate the lower beings from the supernal unity, and say the blessing over the light of fire.

258. בְּגִין דְּכָל אֶשִּׁין אַחֲרָנִין, אִתְטַמְרוּ וְאִתְגְּנִיזוּ בְּיוֹמָא דְּשַׁבַּתָּא, בַּר אֶשָּׁא חַד דִּקְדוּשָׁה עִלָּאָה, דְּאִתְגַּלְיָא וְאִתְכְּלִילָא בִּקְדוּשָׁא דְּשַׁבַּתָּא. וְכַד הַאי אֶשָּׁא אִתְגַּלְיָיא, כָּל אֶשִּׁין אַחֲרָנִין אִתְטַמְרוּ, וְאִתְגְּנִיזוּ קַמֵּיהּ. וְהַאי אֶשָּׁא, אִיהִי דַּעֲקֵידָה דְּיִצְחָק, דְּאִתְלְהָטַת עַל גַּבֵּי מַדְבְּחָא. בְּגִין

כָּךְ, בָּעֵי לְבָרְכָא עַל נְהוֹרָא דְּאֶשָּׁא. וְהַאי אֶשָּׁא, לָא בָּעֵי אֶשָּׁא דְחוֹל, אֶלָּא אֶשָּׁא דְשַׁבָּת, וְהַאי אֶשָּׁא, אִיהוּ אֶשָּׁא דְּנָפִיק מֵהַהוּא אֶשָּׁא דִלְעֵילָא.

258. For all other fires are hidden and concealed on Shabbat, except the one fire of supernal holiness that is revealed and included in the holiness of Shabbat, WHICH IS MALCHUT CLOTHING BINAH. And when this fire is revealed, all other fires are hidden and concealed before it. And that is the fire of the Binding of Isaac, THE CENTRAL COLUMN THAT TIES AND BINDS THE LEFT COLUMN, CALLED ISAAC, SO IT WOULD SPREAD ITS LIGHT ONLY FROM BELOW UPWARD, IN ORDER TO BE INCLUDED IN THE RIGHT. It burns on the altar ON SHABBAT. FOR THE ALTAR FIRE THAT BURNS ALSO ON SHABBAT IS DRAWN FROM THE CENTRAL COLUMN TO MALCHUT THAT IS NAMED ALTAR. For that reason we should say the blessing over the luminary of the fire AT THE END OF SHABBAT. This fire is not the everyday fire but Shabbat's fire that comes from the fire of above, FOR IT IS DRAWN FROM THE CENTRAL COLUMN TO THE ALTAR, WHICH IS MALCHUT.

259. וְדָא אִיהוּ אֶשָּׁא דְּסָבִיל אֶשָּׁא. וְכֵיוָן דְּהַאי אֶשָּׁא דְּנָפִיק מֵאֶשָּׁא דִלְעֵילָא אִתְבָּרְכָא בְּבִרְכָה דִּנְהוֹרָא, כְּדֵין כָּל שְׁאַר אֶשִׁין אַחֲרָנִין נָפְקִין, וְאִתְמַנָּן בְּדוּכְתַּיְיהוּ, וְאִתְיְיהִיב לוֹן רְשׁוּתָא לְאַנְהָרָא.

259. This is the fire that sustains fire, VIZ. THE FIRE WITHIN MALCHUT. And when that fire which emanates from the upper fire, FROM THE CENTRAL COLUMN, is blessed by the blessing over light, all the other fires go out and are assigned to their places, NAMELY, they are given permission to illuminate.

260. בְּהַהִיא שַׁעֲתָא דְּקָא מְבָרְכִין עַל אֶשָּׁא, אִזְדַּמְנָן אַרְבַּע רְתִיכִין, אַרְבַּע מַשְׁרְיָין לְתַתָּא, לְאַנְהָרָא מֵהַהוּא אֶשָּׁא מְבָרְכָא, וְאִינּוּן אִקְרוּן מְאוֹרֵי הָאֵשׁ. בְּגִין כָּךְ, בָּעֵינָן לְאַכְפְּיָא ד' אֶצְבְּעָאן דִּידָא דִּימִינָא, וּלְאַנְהָרָא לוֹן מִגּוֹ הַהוּא נְהוֹרָא דִּשְׁרָגָא דְמִתְבָּרְכָא.

260. When we recite the blessing over fire, appear four Chariots, four lower legions, MICHAEL, GABRIEL, URIEL AND RAPHAEL, EACH IN CHARGE

OVER A LEGION OF ANGELS, which are shining with that fire OF MALCHUT that was blessed. They are called the luminaries of fire, BECAUSE THEIR ILLUMINATION IS COMING FROM THE FIRE OF MALCHUT THAT WAS BLESSED, and therefore we should bend the four fingers of the right hand, so the light of the blest candle would shine upon them.

261. וְאִינּוּן אֶצְבְּעָאן, רֶמֶז לְאִינּוּן מְאוֹרֵי הָאֵשׁ, דְּנָהִירֵי וְשַׁלְטֵי מֵהַהוּא נְהוֹרָא דִּשְׁרָגָא דְּמִתְבָּרְכָא. וּבְגִין דְּאִינּוּן דַּרְגִּין לְתַתָּא, כַּד אַחֲזֵי בַּר נָשׁ אֶצְבְּעָאן קַמֵּי הַהוּא נְהוֹרָא דִּשְׁרָגָא, בָּעֵי לְאַכְפְּיָיא לוֹן קַמֵּיהּ, בְּגִין דְּהַהוּא נְהוֹרָא שַׁלְטָא עֲלַיְיהוּ, וְאִינּוּן נָהֲרִין מִנֵּיהּ.

261. These fingers allude to the luminaries of fire, NAMELY, THE SAID FOUR CHARIOTS, which shine and rule from within the light of the blest candle. And since they are lower grades, a person, when showing his fingers in front of the light of the candle, should bend them before it, since this light rules over them and they shine with its light.

262. בִּשְׁאָר בִּרְכָאן בָּעֵינָן לְזַקְפָּא לוֹן לְאֶצְבְּעָאן, בְּגִין לְאַחֲזָאה קְדוּשָׁה עִלָּאה, דְּדַרְגִּין עִלָּאִין, דְּשַׁלְטִין עַל כֹּלָּא, דִּשְׁמָא קַדִּישָׁא אִתְעֲטַר בְּהוּ וְאִתְקַדַּשׁ בְּהוּ, וְאִתְבָּרְכָן כֻּלְּהוּ דַּרְגִּין כַּחֲדָא, וְנָהֲרִין מִגּוֹ בּוּצִינָא עִלָּאה דְּכֹלָּא, וּבְג"כ בָּעֵינָן לְזַקְפָּא לוֹן לְעֵילָּא. וְהָכָא בָּעֵינָן לְאַכְפְּיָיא אֶצְבְּעָאן קַמֵּי שְׁרָגָּא, בְּגִין לְאַחֲזָאה דַּרְגִּין דִּלְתַתָּא, דְּנָהֲרִין מִגּוֹ בּוּצִינָא דִּלְעֵילָּא, וּמֵהָכָא שַׁלְטִין וְנָהֲרִין מִנָּהּ, וְאִינּוּן מְאוֹרֵי הָאֵשׁ.

262. When reciting other blessings, THAT ARE PRIESTLY BENEDICTION, one should raise the fingers, to demonstrate the supernal sanctity of the upper grades that rule over all, THE SECRET OF THE GRADES IN THE RIGHT OF ZEIR ANPIN THAT DRAW THEIR HOLINESS FROM SUPERNAL ABA AND IMA, THE SECRET OF HOLINESS. For the Holy Name, MALCHUT, is crowned and sanctified by them; thus all the grades together are blessed and shine from within the highest luminary, THE FIRST THREE SFIROT OF BINAH, THE ROOT TO ALL THE CHASSADIM. For that reason one should raise one's fingers. But in this blessing, we must bend our fingers before the candle, to point at the lower grades, THE FOUR SAID CHARIOTS, that shine

from within the upper luminary, WHICH IS MALCHUT, for thence they rule and shine forth; these are the luminary of fire.

263. בְּכָל יוֹמָא אֲנָן מְבָרְכֵינָן מְאוֹרֵי אוֹר, דְּאִינוּן נְהוֹרִין עִלָּאִין, דְּקַיְימָן בְּהַהוּא אוֹר קַדְמָאָה, וְאִתְבָּרְכָן כֻּלְּהוּ דַרְגִּין, וְנָהֲרִין כֻּלְּהוּ כַּחֲדָא, מִגּוֹ בּוּצִינָא עִלָּאָה. וְהָנֵי אִקְרוּן מְאוֹרֵי הָאֵשׁ. וּבְגִינֵי רָזָא דָא, מְבָרְכִין בּוֹרֵא מְאוֹרֵי הָאֵשׁ.

263. Every day we say the blessing over the luminaries of light, "WHO CREATES LIGHT," "WHO CREATES THE LUMINARIES," that refer to the supernal lights which dwell in that primordial light, WHICH IS CHESED. Then all the grades are blessed and shine forth together by the supreme luminary, BINAH. BUT these IN HERE are called the luminaries of fire. For that secret reason do we bless 'who creates the lights of fire'.

264. וְאִי תֵּימָא, אֲמַאי בּוֹרֵא, וְלָא אָמְרוּ מֵאִיר מְאוֹרֵי הָאֵשׁ. הוֹאִיל וְקָא נַהֲרִין מֵהַהוּא אֵשׁ, מֵהַהוּא בּוּצִינָא מְבָרְכָא. אֶלָּא כֵּיוָן דְּעָאל שַׁבַּתָּא, כָּל אִינוּן דַּרְגִּין דִּלְתַתָּא, וְכָל אִינוּן דְּנָהֲרִין וְשַׁלְטִין, כֻּלְּהוּ עָאלִין וְאִתְכְּלִילוּ בְּהַאי שְׁרָגָא, וְאִתְטַמָּרוּ וְאִתְגְּנִיזוּ, וְאִתְנְטָרוּ בֵּיהּ, וְלָא יִתְחֲזוּן בֵּיהּ, אֶלָּא הַהוּא נְקוּדָה בִּלְחוֹדָהָא, וְכֻלְּהוּ אִתְטַמָּרוּ בְּגַוּוֹהּ, כָּל יוֹמָא דְשַׁבַּתָּא.

264. And one may ask why say, 'who creates the luminaries of light' and not 'who lights'? AND HE ANSWERS: because the luminaries shine by that fire of the blessed luminary, WHICH IS THE FIRE DRAWN TO IT FROM THE CENTRAL COLUMN. However, with the commencement of Shabbat, all the lower grades, THE SAID FOUR CHARIOTS, and all those which shine and rule BY THE LIGHT OF THAT FIRE, enter and become included in that candle, MALCHUT, and are kept hidden and concealed in it; they are there invisible save that point alone, MALCHUT. All of them are hidden and stored in it the whole of Shabbat day.

265. כֵּיוָן דְּנָפַק שַׁבַּתָּא, אַפִּיק לוֹן לְכָל חַד וְחַד, כְּאִילּוּ הַהִיא שַׁעֲתָא אִתְבְּרִיאוּ, וְנָפְקוּ כֻּלְּהוּ וְאִתְבְּרִיאוּ כְּמִלְּקַדְמִין, וְאִתְמְנִיאוּ עַל דוּכְתַּיְיהוּ

לְשַׁלְטָאָה כְּדֵין אִתְבָּרְכָא הַאי שְׁרָגָּא, וְאִתְכַּפְיָין קַמֵּיהּ, לְאַנְהָרָא. כֵּיוָן
דְּנָהֲרִין, כְּדֵין אִתְמְנוּן כָּל חַד וְחַד עַל דּוּכְתֵּיהּ.

265. At the end of Shabbat, MALCHUT lets out those LUMINARIES OF FIRE, each and every one, as if they were created anew at that moment. They all come out and are created as in the beginning, and are assigned to their place to rule. The candle is then blessed and they bow before it and shine. THIS IS THE MEANING OF BENDING THE FINGERS. Now that they shine, they are appointed each to its place.

266. כְּגַוְונָא דָא, אִינוּן דַּרְגִּין עִלָּאִין, דְּאִקְרוּן מְאוֹרֵי אוֹר, שַׁלְטִין
בִּימָמָא, וְנָהֲרִין מִגּוֹ בּוֹצִינָא עִלָּאָה. בְּשַׁעֲתָא דְּרָמַשׁ לֵילְיָא, הַהוּא
בּוֹצִינָא עִלָּאָה כָּנִישׁ לוֹן, וְאָעִיל לוֹן בְּגַוֵּויהּ, עַד דְּנָהִיר יְמָמָא. כֵּיוָן
דִּמְבָרְכִין יִשְׂרָאֵל עַל נְהוֹרָא בִּימָמָא, כְּדֵין אַפִּיק לוֹן בִּשְׁלִימוּ דִּנְהוֹרָא.
וְעַ״ד מְבָרְכִין יוֹצֵר הַמְּאוֹרוֹת, וְלָא אַמְרֵי בּוֹרֵא, וְהָכָא בּוֹרֵא מְאוֹרֵי
הָאֵשׁ. בְּגִין דְּאִינוּן דַּרְגִּין לְתַתָּא.

266. In the same manner, the higher grades are called the luminaries of light. They rule by day and shine by the supreme luminary, BINAH. As night falls, the supreme luminary gathers them and absorbs them within itself, until daybreak. When Yisrael bless over the daylight, it lets them out fully radiant. Therefore we bless Hashem "who forms luminaries" and not "who creates," THOUGH THEY ARE RENEWED EVERY MORNING; But here AT THE END OF SHABBAT, we use the verb 'to create' AND THE REASON IS that it refers to the lower grades.

267. וְכֹלָּא אִיהוּ רָזָא דְּאֶצְבְּעָאן, בְּהוּ רָמִיז דַּרְגִּין עִלָּאִין, וְדַרְגִּין
תַּתָּאִין. דַּרְגִּין עִלָּאִין אִשְׁתְּמוֹדְעָאן, בִּזְקִיפוּ דְּאֶצְבְּעָאן לְעֵילָּא. וּבְזְקִיפוּ
דְּאֶצְבְּעָאן, אִתְבָּרְכָן דַּרְגִּין עִלָּאִין, וְדַרְגִּין תַּתָּאִין כַּחֲדָא. וּבְמִאִיכוּ
דְּאֶצְבְּעָאן, אִתְבָּרְכָן לְאַנְהָרָא דַּרְגִּין תַּתָּאִין לְחוֹדַיְיהוּ.

267. And all is symbolized by the fingers, in which we find allusion to the higher grades, THE LUMINARIES OF LIGHT, and the lower grades, THE LUMINARIES OF FIRE. The higher grades are recognized by the raising of

the finger, THAT SHOWS THE LIGHT SPREADING FROM THE FIRST THREE SFIROT FROM ABOVE DOWNWARD. By the raising of the fingers, the upper and lower grades are blessed together. By lowering the fingers, WHICH ALLUDES TO THE SIX DIRECTIONS THAT DO NOT SHINE BUT FROM BELOW UPWARD, only the lower grades, MALCHUT AND THE CHARIOTS DRAWN FROM IT, are blessed so they may shine.

20. The fingernails

A Synopsis

We learn that the fingernails are the secret of the luminaries of fire while the inner parts of the fingers are the secret of the luminaries of light. This is why the fingernails should be exposed to the candle when the blessing over the candle is said, but the inner fingers must not face that light. The nails should be exposed to draw Chochmah from that candle. Now we are told that we should smell perfumes at the end of Shabbat because the additional Neshamah and the Ruach leave man, leaving the Nefesh naked. The meaning of "and he smelt the smell of his garments" is explained, referring to the garments of Adam that were given to him by God before he sinned. The fingernails are a remnant, and must not be grown, and must not be thrown away, because they emanate from the back and are of filth.

268. וְרָזָא דָא, טוּפְרֵי דַאֲחוֹרֵי אֶצְבְּעָאן. וְאֶצְבְּעָאן לְחוּדַיְיהוּ לְגוֹ. טוּפְרֵי דַאֲחוֹרֵי אֶצְבְּעָאן, אִינּוּן אַנְפִּין אַחֲרָנִין, דְּאִצְטְרִיכוּ לְאַנְהָרָא מִגּוֹ הַהוּא שְׁרָגָא, וְאִינּוּן אַנְפִּין דְּאִקְרוּן אֲחוֹרַיִים. אֶצְבְּעָאן לְגוֹ בְּלָא טוּפְרִין, אִלֵּין אִינּוּן אַנְפִּין פְּנִימָאן אִתְכַּסְיָין. וְרָזָא דָא, וְרָאִיתָ אֶת אֲחוֹרָי. אִלֵּין אֲחוֹרֵי, אֶצְבְּעָאן, לַאֲחוֹרָא בְּטוּפְרֵיהוֹן. וּפָנַי לֹא יֵרָאוּ, אִלֵּין אֶצְבְּעָאן לְגוֹ, בְּלָא טוּפְרִין, דְּאִינּוּן אַנְפִּין פְּנִימָאִין.

268. This is the secret meaning of the fingernails at the back of the fingers, WHICH IS THE SECRET OF THE LUMINARIES OF FIRE, and the fingers themselves on the inside OF THE HAND, THE SECRET OF THE LUMINARIES OF LIGHT. HE EXPLAINS THAT the fingernails at the back of the fingers are considered 'outer (Heb. *acherim*) countenance', that need to shine from within the candle, MALCHUT, which face is named "achoraim (lit. 'hind-parts')." The fingers inside THE HAND, without the nails, are the 'inner (Heb. *pnimiyim*) countenance' that is covered, BECAUSE THERE IS NO SIGHT, CHOCHMAH, IN THEM. This is the secret of the verse, "and you shall see My back (Heb. *achorai*)" (Shemot 33:23). For 'My back' ALLUDES TO the nails at the back of the fingers. "but My face (Heb. *panai*) shall not be seen" (Ibid.) refers to the fingers on the inside OF THE HAND, the part without nails, the 'inner countenance'.

269. וְכַד מְבָרְכִינָן עַל שְׁרָגָא, בָּעֵי לְאַחֲזָאָה אֲחוֹרֵי אֶצְבְּעָאן בְּטוּפְרִין, לְאִתְנַהֲרָא מִגּוֹ הַהוּא שְׁרָגָא, וּפְנִימָאֵי דְּאֶצְבְּעָאן, לָא אִצְטְרִיכוּ לְאַחֲזָאָה לוֹן לְאִתְנַהֲרָא מִגּוֹ הַהוּא שְׁרָגָא, דְּהָא אִינּוּן לָא נַהֲרִין, אֶלָּא מִגּוֹ שְׁרָגָא עִלָּאָה דִּלְעֵילָּא לְעֵילָּא, דְּאִיהִי טְמִירָא וּגְנִיזָא דְּלָא אִתְגַּלְּיָיא כְּלָל. וְאִינּוּן לָא נַהֲרִין מִגּוֹ שְׁרָגָא דְּאִתְגַּלְּיָא כְּלָל, בְּגִין כַּךְ בָּעֵי לְאַחֲזָאָה אֲחוֹרֵי אֶצְבְּעָאן בְּטוּפְרִין. וּפְנִימָאֵי דְּאֶצְבְּעָאן, לָא בָּעֵי לְאַחֲזָאָה קַמֵּי הַאי שְׁרָגָא. טְמִירִין אִינּוּן, וּבִטְמִירוּ אִתְנַהֲרִין. פְּנִימָאִין אִינּוּן, וּמִפְּנִימָאִין אִתְנַהֲרָן. עִלָּאִין אִינּוּן, וּמֵעֵלָּאָה אִתְנַהֲרָן. זַכָּאִין אִינּוּן יִשְׂרָאֵל, בְּעָלְמָא דֵּין, וּבְעָלְמָא דְּאָתֵי.

269. When we say the blessing over the candle, we should expose the nails at the back of the fingers, WHICH ALLUDES TO THE FOUR CHARIOTS, to be illumined by that candle, WHICH REFERS TO MALCHUT. But the inner side of the fingers must not be exposed to the light of the candle to shine by it, MALCHUT, because they do not shine save by the supernal, most high candle, CHOCHMAH OF ZEIR ANPIN, which is covered and concealed, AND ITS CHOCHMAH is not revealed at all. They do not shine from the uncovered candle, MALCHUT IN WHICH CHOCHMAH IS REVEALED. Therefore the nails at the back of the fingers should be exposed, TO DRAW CHOCHMAH FROM THAT CANDLE, MALCHUT. But the inner side of the fingers must not be seen by that candle, because it is hidden and shines secretly, AND DOES NOT RECEIVE CHOCHMAH FROM THAT CANDLE. For it pertains to the inner part and shines from the inner side, it is supernal and therefore illumines from the supernal luminaries. Happy are Yisrael in this world and in the World to Come.

270. וּבָעֵי לְאָרְחָא בְּבוּסְמִין, כַּד נָפִיק שַׁבַּתָּא, עַל דְּאִסְתַּלָּק הַהוּא רוּחָא, וְנַפְשָׁא דְּבַר נָשׁ אִשְׁתְּאָרַת בְּעַרְטוּלָא, בְּגִין הַהוּא סְלִיקוּ, דְּאִסְתַּלָּק רוּחָא מִנֵּיהּ וְהָא אוּקְמוּהָ.

270. It behooves us at the end of Shabbat to smell spices, because that Ruach leaves MAN, THE ADDITIONAL SOUL OF SHABBAT, and the Nefesh of man is left naked, because the Ruach left it. We already expounded on the subject.

271. כְּתִיב וַיָּרַח אֶת רֵיחַ בְּגָדָיו וַיְבָרְכֵהוּ וְגוֹ'. הַאי קְרָא אוּקְמוּהָ

וְאִתְּמַר, אֲבָל ת"ח, רֵיחָא אִיהוּ קְיוּמָא דְּנַפְשָׁא, בְּגִין דְּאִיהוּ מִלָּה דְּאָעִיל לְנַפְשָׁא, וְלָא לְגוּפָא. ת"ח, כְּתִיב וַיָּרַח אֶת רֵיחַ בְּגָדָיו, הָא אוּקְמוּהָ, אִינוּן לְבוּשֵׁי דְּאָדָם קַדְמָאָה הֲווֹ, דְּיָהַב לֵיהּ קוּדְשָׁא בְּרִיךְ הוּא לְאַלְבָּשָׁא לוֹן.

271. It is written: "and he smelt the smell of his garments" (Beresheet 27:27). This was already explained, and we learned it. But come and see, the smell is sustenance to the Nefesh, because it enters the Nefesh and not the body. Come and see, the verse "and he smelt the smell of his garments," refers, as explained, to the garments of Adam, that were given to him by the Holy One, blessed be He, to wear.

272. בְּגִין דְּהָא כַּד חָב אָדָם, אִתְעֲדֵי מִנֵּיהּ הַהוּא לְבוּשָׁא יַקִּירָא, דְּאִתְלָבַּשׁ בֵּיהּ בְּקַדְמֵיתָא, כַּד אָעִיל לֵיהּ בְּגִנְתָּא דְּעֵדֶן. וּלְבָתַר דְּחָב, אַלְבִּישׁ לֵיהּ בִּלְבוּשָׁא אַחֲרָא, לְבוּשָׁא קַדְמָאָה, דְּאִתְלָבַּשׁ בֵּיהּ אָדָם בְּגִנְתָּא דְּעֵדֶן, אִיהוּ הֲוָה מֵאִינוּן רְתִיכִין, דְּאִקְרוּן אֲחוֹרַיִים, וְאִינוּן לְבוּשִׁין דְּאִקְרוּן לְבוּשֵׁי טוּפְרָא.

272. When Adam sinned, that precious garment he received when the Holy One, blessed be He, placed him in the Garden of Eden, was stripped from him, and he was given another garment. The original garment he put on first in the Garden of Eden was of the Chariots that are called hind-parts, which are the garments by the name garments of nails.

273. וְכַד הֲוָה בְּגִנְתָּא דְּעֵדֶן, כָּל אִינוּן רְתִיכִין, וְכָל אִינוּן מַשִׁרְיָין קַדִּישִׁין, כֻּלְּהוּ סַחֲרִין לֵיהּ לְאָדָם, וְאִתְנְטִיר מִכֹּלָּא, וְלָא הֲוָה יָכִיל מִלָּה בִּישָׁא לְאִתְקָרְבָא בַּהֲדֵיהּ. כֵּיוָן דְּחָב, וְאִתְעֲדוּ מִנֵּיהּ אִינוּן לְבוּשִׁין, דָּחִיל מְמַלִּין בִּישִׁין, וְרוּחִין בִּישִׁין, וְאִסְתַּלְּקוּ מִנֵּיהּ אִינוּן מַשִׁרְיָין קַדִּישִׁין, וְלָא אִשְׁתְּאָרוּ בֵּיהּ, אֶלָּא אִינוּן רָאשֵׁי טוּפְרֵי דְּאֶצְבְּעָאן, דְּסַחֲרִין לוֹן לְטוּפְרִין סַחֲרָנוּ דְּזוּהֲמָא אַחֲרָא.

273. When Adam was in the Garden of Eden, all those Chariots and holy legions surrounded him, and thus he was completely protected, and nothing

evil could approach him. Once he sinned and those nail-garments were stripped of him, he started to fear evil things and evil spirits, and the holy legions THAT SURROUNDED AND PROTECTED HIM left. From those garments nothing remained but the nails at the tip of the fingers, surrounded by the filth of the Other SIDE.

274. וּבְגִין כַּךְ, לָא לִיבְעֵי לֵיהּ לְבַר נָשׁ לְרַבָּאָה אִינּוּן טוּפְרִין דְּזוּהֲמָא, דְּהָא כְּמָה דְּאַסְגִּיאוּ, הָכִי נָמֵי אַסְגֵּי עֲלֵיהּ קַסְטוּרָא, וְיִדְאַג בְּכָל יוֹמָא, וּבָעֵי לְסַפְּרָא לוֹן, וְלָא יִרְמֵי לוֹן, דְּלָא יַעֲבִיד קָלָנָא בְּהַהוּא אֲתָר, דְּיָכִיל הַהוּא בַּר נָשׁ לְאִתְּזְקָא. וְכֹלָּא כְּגַוְונָא עִלָּאָה. דְּהָא לְכֻלְּהוּ אֲחוֹרַיִים, סַחֲרָא סִטְרָא אַחֲרָא, וְלָא אִצְטְרִיךְ לֵיהּ בַּאֲתָר דְּעָלְמָא.

274. For that reason we must not grow our fingernails, for there is filth in them, and as they grow, so grows in relation to it the power of Judgment, FROM THE POWER OF THE KLIPOT THAT NOURISHES FROM THE PART OF THE NAILS THAT OUTGROWS THE FLESH. One should see to it daily, to cut the nails, but not throw them, so as not to show contempt for the place, FOR THEY EMANATE FROM A HIGH PLACE AS MENTIONED, because a man might be harmed by it. All that follows a higher pattern, because the Other Side is around all THE hinder VESSELS ABOVE. IN THE SAME MANNER, THE NAILS ARE SURROUNDED BY FILTH, BECAUSE THEY EMANATE FROM THE BACK, AS MENTIONED. And they should not exist in the place of the world, NAMELY IN INHABITED PLACES.

21. Smelling the myrtle branches

A Synopsis

We are told that after Adam sinned, God made him other garments from the leaves of the Garden's trees, that were lights. These garments were made of the earthly Garden of the World of Asiyah. Adam's garments emanated the fragrance of that higher Garden; the Nefesh and Ruach of Isaac were composed by that smell. This is why we should smell fragrance at the end of Shabbat to let the soul be calmed; the best odor is myrtle, for the sustenance of the holy place from which the souls emanate is called myrtle. Thus the Nefesh, Malchut, is sustained.

275. לְבָתַר עֲבַד לֵיהּ לְאָדָם, לְבוּשִׁין אַחֲרָנִין, מִטַרְפֵּי אִילָנִין דְּגִנְתָּא דְּעֵדֶן דְּאַרְעָא. דְּהָא בְּקַדְמֵיתָא הֲוֹו לְבוּשִׁין, מֵאִינוּן אֲחוֹרַיִים דְּגִנְתָּא דִּלְעֵילָּא, וְהַשְׁתָּא מִגִּנְתָּא דְּאַרְעָא, וְנַפְקֵי מִגִּנְתָּא. וְאִינוּן לְבוּשִׁין הֲוֹו סַלְקִין רֵיחִין וּבוּסְמִין דְּגִנְתָּא, דְּנַפְשָׁא מִתְיַישְׁבָא בְּהוּ, וְחַדֵי בְּהוּ. הה"ד וַיָּרַח אֶת רֵיחַ בְּגָדָיו וַיְבָרֲכֵהוּ, דְּהָא אִתְיַישְׁבָא נַפְשֵׁיהּ וְרוּחֵיהּ דְּיִצְחָק בְּהַהוּא רֵיחָא.

275. Afterwards, the Holy One, blessed be He, made for Adam other garments from the leaves of the trees in the Garden of Eden. IT IS WRITTEN: "DID HASHEM ELOHIM MAKE COATS OF SKIN (HEB. OR, AYIN RESH)" (BERESHEET 3:21). HOWEVER, RABBI MEIR'S TORAH SCROLL HAD IT AS COATS OF LIGHT (HEB. OR, ALEPH RESH), FOR THEY WERE INDEED MADE OF LEAVES OF THE TREES IN THE GARDEN OF EDEN, THAT WERE LIGHTS. The reason for that is that at first his garments were made from the back of the higher garden, MALCHUT OF ATZILUT, but now AFTER THE SIN his garments were made of the earthly garden, OF THE WORLD OF ASIYAH, and came from the garden. The original garments were emanating smells and perfumes of the garden, by which the Nefesh is calmed and gladdened. This is the meaning of the verse "and he smelt the smell of his garments," for the Nefesh and Ruach of Isaac were composed by that smell.

276. בג"ד כַּד נָפַק שַׁבְּתָא, בָּעֵי לְאָרְחָא בְּבוּסְמִין, לְאִתְיַישְׁבָא נַפְשֵׁיהּ בְּהַהוּא רֵיחָא, עַל הַהוּא רֵיחָא עִלָּאָה קַדִּישָׁא דְּאִסְתַּלָּק מִינָהּ. וְהַהוּא רֵיחָא מְעַלְּיָא דְּבוּסְמִין אִיהוּ הֲדַס. דְּהָא קִיּוּמָא דַּאֲתָר קַדִּישָׁא

דְּנִשְׁמָתִין נָפְקִין מִנֵּיהּ, הֲדַס אִיהוּ. וְדָא אִיהוּ קִיּוּמָא דְּנַפְשָׁא, כְּגַוְונָא דִּלְעֵילָּא, לְאִתְקַיְּימָא מֵהַהוּא עַרְטוּלָא דְּאִשְׁתְּאָרַת.

276. For that reason, at the conclusion of Shabbat, we should smell spices, to let the Nefesh be calmed by the fragrance, instead of the high and holy fragrance that left it. And the most worthy odor is that of the myrtle, for the sustenance of the holy place, NAMELY, MALCHUT, from which the souls emanate, is the myrtle. It also gives sustenance to the Nefesh of man, as well as the high one, so it may be maintained when it is left naked, AFTER THE DEPARTURE OF THE ADDITIONAL SOUL OF SHABBAT

277. כַּד נָפַק שַׁבַּתָּא, אִתְלַבַּשׁ אָדָם, בְּאִינּוּן לְבוּשִׁין דְּגִנְתָּא דְעֵדֶן דְּאַרְעָא, דְּסַלְּקִין רֵיחִין וּבוּסְמִין, לְקַיְּימָא נַפְשֵׁיהּ, עַל הַהוּא רוּחָא קַדִּישָׁא עִלָּאָה יַקִּירָא דְּאִסְתַּלָּק מִנֵּיהּ. וַהֲדַס אִיהוּ קִיּוּמָא דְּנַפְשָׁא וַדַּאי. כְּגַוְונָא עִלָּאָה, דְּאִתְקַיְּימָא קִיּוּמָא דְּנַפְשָׁא.

277. At the conclusion of Shabbat, Adam wore the garments of the MENTIONED earthly Garden of Eden, that emanate fragrance and perfumes, in which to sustain his Nefesh, INSTEAD OF the holy supernal and precious Ruach, THE SECRET OF THE SUPERNAL SPLENDOR OF ATZILUT, that departed from him. And the myrtle gives certain sustenance to the Nefesh, as well as to the high one, and thus the Nefesh, MALCHUT, is sustained, AS MENTIONED ABOVE.

22. The Supernal Spirit

A Synopsis

Rabbi Yitzchak says that the additional Neshamah gladly descends on man on the Shabbat to gladden his Nefesh. As man is given pleasure, which is the spirit, and gives it pleasure, so will he have enjoyment in the World to Come. Rabbi Aba is happy with this explanation. He says that he saw today the three high luminaries that shine upon this world and the World to Come, and they are the three rabbis, Rabbi Chiya, Rabbi Yosi and Rabbi Yitzchak. He says all these utterances will go up before the holy throne and be taken by the chief minister Metatron who will turn them into crowns for his master. As the sun has set, the four rabbis go to a village and sleep, then arise at midnight to study the Torah. Rabbi Aba says this is the time when God and all the righteous in the Garden of Eden listen to the voice of the righteous on earth.

278. הַהוּא רוּחָא עִלָּאָה דְּנָחִית עָלֵיהּ דְּבַר נָשׁ בְּחֶדוּ, וְחַדֵּי לְנַפְשֵׁיהּ, כְּדֵין קַיְּימָא נַפְשָׁא דְּבַר נָשׁ, כְּגַוְונָא דְּעָלְמָא דְּאָתֵי, דְּזַמִּין לְאִתְהֲנָאָה מִנֵּיהּ, כְּמָה דְּבַר נָשׁ, אַהֲנֵי לְהַאי רוּחָא בְּעָלְמָא דָּא. הָכִי הַהוּא רוּחָא אַהֲנֵי לֵיהּ לְבַר נָשׁ, לְעָלְמָא דְּאָתֵי, דִּכְתִּיב אָז תִּתְעַנַּג עַל יְיָ' וְגוֹ'. וּכְתִיב וְהִשְׂבִּיעַ בְּצַחְצָחוֹת נַפְשֶׁךָ. כְּמָה דְּבַר נָשׁ, רַוֵּי לְהַהוּא עֲנוּגָא, וְאַהֲנֵי לֵיהּ, הָכִי נָמֵי אִיהוּ רַוֵּי לֵיהּ לְעָלְמָא דְּאָתֵי. כְּדֵין כַּד בַּר נָשׁ זָכֵי, וְאַשְׁלִים שְׁלִימוּ דִּיקָרָא דְּשַׁבְּתָא כִּדְקָאָמְרָן, קוּדְשָׁא בְּרִיךְ הוּא קָארֵי עָלֵיהּ וְאָמַר, וַיֹּאמֶר לִי עַבְדִּי אָתָּה יִשְׂרָאֵל אֲשֶׁר בְּךָ אֶתְפָּאָר.

278. The high spirit, THE ADDITIONAL SOUL, gladly descends upon man ON SHABBAT, to gladdens his Nefesh. Then the Nefesh of man is transcended, so to speak, into the World to Come, in which it is to find pleasure in the future FROM THE SPIRIT. As man gives pleasure to the spirit in this world, so does the spirit give pleasure to man in the World to Come. As is written: "then shall you delight yourself in Hashem..." (Yeshayah 58:14), and "and satisfy your soul in drought" (Ibid. 11). As man is given pleasure, WHICH IS THE SPIRIT, and gives it pleasure, so will he have enjoyment in the World to Come. Then when a man is worthy of and accomplishes the precious wholeness of Shabbat, as we said, the Holy One, blessed be He, says to him "You are My servant, Yisrael, in whom I will be glorified" (Yeshayah 49:3).

279. קָם רִבִּי אַבָּא, וּשְׁאַר חַבְרַיָּיא, וְנַשְׁקוּ רֵישֵׁיה. בָּכוּ וְאָמְרוּ, זַכָּאָה חוּלָקָנָא דְּאָרְחָא דָּא זַמִּין קוּדְשָׁא בְּרִיךְ הוּא לְקַבְּלָן. אָמַר ר׳ אַבָּא, לִי זַמִּין קוּדְשָׁא בְּרִיךְ הוּא אָרְחָא דָּא, בְּגִין לְאִתְחַבְּרָא עִמְּכוֹן. זַכָּאָה אִיהוּ חוּלָקִי, דְּזָכֵינָא לְאָרְחָא דָּא.

279. Rabbi Aba and the rest of the friends stood up, and they kissed his head, OF RABBI YITZCHAK. They wept and said 'happy is our portion, that the Holy One, blessed be He, led us into this way'. And Rabbi Aba said 'the Holy One, blessed be He, led me into this way so I may be with you. Happy is my portion, to be worthy to be in this way'.

280. אָמַר לְהוּ, אֵימָא לְכוּ מַה דַּחֲמֵינָא, יוֹמָא דָּא נָפַקְנָא לְאָרְחָא, וַחֲמֵינָא נְהוֹרָא חֲדָא, וְאִתְפְּלָג לִתְלַת נְהוֹרִין, וְאַזְלוּ קָמָאי, וְאִתְטַמָּרוּ. וְאָמֵינָא וַדַּאי שְׁכִינְתָּא חֲמֵינָא, זַכָּאָה חוּלָקִי. וְהַשְׁתָּא אִינּוּן תְּלַת נְהוֹרִין דַּחֲמֵינָא, אַתּוּן אִינּוּן, וַדַּאי אַתּוּן נְהוֹרִין, וּבוֹצִינִין עִלָּאִין, לְאַנְהֲרָא בְּעָלְמָא דֵּין וּבְעָלְמָא דְּאָתֵי.

280. He said to them, I will repeat to you what I saw today when I went on the way. I saw one light divided into three lights. They went ahead of me and then were hidden. I said, 'assuredly I have seen the Shechinah, happy is my portion'. And the three lights I have seen, are you, THAT IS, RABBI CHIYA, RABBI YOSI AND RABBI YITZCHAK. You are the lights and high luminaries that shine upon this world and the World to Come.

281. אָמַר רִבִּי אַבָּא עַד הָכִי לָא יְדַעְנָא, דְּכָל אִלֵּין מַרְגְּלָן סְתִימִין הֲווֹ תְּחוֹת יְדַיְיכוּ, כֵּיוָן דַּחֲמֵינָא, דְּהָא בִּרְעוּתָא דְּפִקּוּדָא דְּמָארֵיכוֹן אִתְאַמְרוּ מִלִּין אִלֵּין, יְדַעְנָא, דְּכֻלְּהוּ מִלִּין סַלְּקִין יוֹמָא דָּא, לְגוֹ כּוּרְסְיָּיא עִלָּאָה, וְנָטִיל לוֹן הַהוּא מָארֵי דְּאַנְפִּין, וְעָבֵיד מִנַּיְיהוּ עָטְרִין לְמָארֵיה. וְיוֹמָא דָּא מִתְעַטְּרִין שִׁתִּין רְתִיכִין קַדִּישִׁין, לִיקָרָא דְּכֻרְסְיָּיא, בְּאִלֵּין מִלִּין דְּאִתְאַמְרוּ הָכָא, יוֹמָא דָּא.

281. Rabbi Aba said, until now I did not know that all these hidden jewels were in your possession. Since I saw that these words were said by the

instructed will of your Master, I know that all these utterances go up on this day before the high throne, WHICH IS BINAH, and are taken by the chief minister, METATRON, who turns them into crowns for his Master. This day is crowned by sixty holy Chariots, CORRESPONDING TO CHESED, GVURAH, TIFERET, NETZACH, HOD AND YESOD, to honor the throne, BINAH, by these words that were said in this day.

282. אַדְהָכִי זָקַף עֵינוֹי, וְחָמָא דְּאַעֲרַב שִׁמְשָׁא. אָמַר ר' אַבָּא, נְהַךְ לְגַבֵּי הַאי כְּפַר, דְּאִיהוּ קָרִיב לְגַבָּן בְּמַדְבְּרָא. אָזְלוּ וּבֵיתוּ תַּמָּן. בְּפַלְגוּת לֵילְיָא, קָם ר' אַבָּא וּשְׁאַר חַבְרַיָּיא, לְאִשְׁתַּדְּלָא בְּאוֹרַיְיתָא, אָמַר רִבִּי אַבָּא, מִכָּאן וּלְהָלְאָה נֵימָא מִלִּין לְאִתְעַטְּרָא בְּהוּ צַדִּיקַיָּא דְּבְגִנְתָּא דְּעֵדֶן, דְּהַשְׁתָּא אִיהוּ זִמְנָא, דְּקוּדְשָׁא בְּרִיךְ הוּא וְכָל צַדִּיקַיָּא דְּבְגִנְתָּא דְּעֵדֶן, צַיְיתִין לְקָלֵיהוֹן דְּצַדִּיקַיָּא דִּי בְּאַרְעָא.

282. While he was speaking, he lifted his eyes and saw that the sun set. Rabbi Aba said, let us go into that village in the desert, that is close to us. They went and slept there. By midnight, Rabbi Aba and the rest of the friends woke up to study Torah. Rabbi Aba said, from now on we shall say words with which to crown the righteous in the Garden of Eden, for now is the time when the Holy One, blessed be He, and all the righteous in the Garden of Eden listen to the voice of the righteous on earth.

23. The firmaments of Asiyah

A Synopsis

Rabbi Aba opens with a discussion of "The heavens are the heavens of Hashem, but He has given the earth to the children of man," asking why it says, "The heavens are the heavens." Rabbi Shimon says that there are heavens down below in the world of Asiyah, and earth beneath it, and there are heavens above in the world of Atzilut, and earth beneath this heaven. Everything that exists above exists below.

The heavens below are like ten curtains, the ten Sfirot, that God made together with the legions of angels in them in order to rule over the lower world. The tenth firmament is the principal one, of Keter. The ninth firmament is Chochmah that rules over all the lower ones. Rabbi Shimon goes on to explain the relationship of the firmaments to one another. Rabbi Aba asks if no firmament rules over the land of Yisrael, how can it still have rain and dew? Rabbi Shimon explains that God rules over it directly. We then hear of the portals within each firmament, and how the authority of the chiefs lie between those portals.

283. פָּתַח רִבִּי אַבָּא וְאָמַר, כְּתִיב הַשָּׁמַיִם שָׁמַיִם לַיְיָ' וְהָאָרֶץ נָתַן לִבְנֵי אָדָם הַאי קְרָא אִית לְאִסְתַּכְּלָא בֵּיה, וְהָכִי אִצְטְרִיךְ לְמֵימַר הַשָּׁמַיִם לַיְיָ', וְהָאָרֶץ נָתַן לִבְנֵי אָדָם. מַאי הַשָּׁמַיִם שָׁמַיִם. אֶלָּא הָכָא אִית לְאִסְתַּכְּלָא, בְּגִין דְּאִית שָׁמַיִם, וְאִית שָׁמַיִם. שָׁמַיִם לְתַתָּא, וְאֶרֶץ לְתַתָּא מִנַּיְיהוּ. שָׁמַיִם לְעֵילָּא, וְאֶרֶץ לְתַתָּא מִנַּיְיהוּ. וְכָל דַּרְגִּין עִלָּאִין וְתַתָּאִין, כֻּלְּהוּ כְּגַוְונָא דָא, אִלֵּין בְּאִלֵּין.

283. Rabbi Aba opened the discussion with the verse, "The heavens are the heavens of Hashem, but He has given the earth to the children of men" (Tehilim 115:16). We should look carefully into this verse, for it should have been said "the heavens are to Hashem, but He has given the earth to the children of men." Why say "the heavens are the heavens." HE ANSWERS: we should note that there are heavens and heavens; there are heavens down below, IN THE WORLD OF ASIYAH, and earth beneath it, and there are heavens above, IN THE WORLD OF ATZILUT, and earth beneath this heaven. And all the higher and lower grades ARE DRAWN in the same fashion one from the other. AND EVERYTHING THAT EXISTS ABOVE, ALSO EXISTS BELOW. THEY RESEMBLE EACH OTHER AS THE SEAL RESEMBLES

THE INSIGNIA, AND ALL THAT IS IN THE SEAL IS ALSO IN THE INSIGNIA. EACH ONE DOWN BELOW RECEIVES FROM ITS COUNTERPART ABOVE.

284. שָׁמַיִם לְתַתָּא, אִינּוּן עֶשֶׂר יְרִיעוֹת, כד"א נוֹטֶה שָׁמַיִם כַּיְרִיעָה. וְקוּדְשָׁא בְּרִיךְ הוּא עֲבַד לוֹן, וּמַשִׁרְיָין דִּי בְּגַוַּוייהוּ, לְאַנְהָגָא אַרְעָא תַּתָּאָה. תְּשִׁיעָאָה אַנְהִיג לְתַתָּאֵי, דְּסַחֲרָן כְּקוּפְטְרָא דְּקַרְלְהוּ. עֲשִׂירָאָה, אִיהוּ עִקָּרָא.

284. The heavens below, IN THE WORLD OF ASIYAH, are like ten curtains, THAT IS, TEN SFIROT, as written in the verse, "who stretches out the heavens like a curtain" (Tehilim 104:2). The Holy One, blessed be He, made them together with the legions OF ANGELS in them, in order to rule over the lower world OF ASIYAH. The ninth FIRMAMENT, CHOCHMAH rules over the lower beings and circles them like a string of precious stones, THAT CIRCLES THE NECK, WHICH MEANS THAT NOTHING IS MADE IN THE LOWER WORLD SAVE BY HIM. THIS IS THE INNER MEANING OF THE VERSE "IN WISDOM HAVE YOU MADE THEM ALL" (IBID. 24). The tenth FIRMAMENT is the principal FIRMAMENT, SINCE IT IS THE SFIRAH OF KETER, THE ROOT AND SOURCE TO ALL THE OTHER NINE SFIROT.

285. וּבְכֻלְּהוּ מַשִׁירְיָין מְמָנָן עַד שְׁבִיעָאָה. מִשְּׁבִיעָאָה וּלְהָלְאָה, אִית נְהוֹרָא דְּאִתְפָּשַׁט לְתַתָּא, מִגּוֹ כּוּרְסְיָיא עִלָּאָה, וְנָהִיר לַעֲשִׂירָאָה. וַעֲשִׂירָאָה, מֵהַהוּא נְהִירוּ דְּנָקְטָא, יָהִיב לִתְשִׁיעָאָה, וְאִיהוּ לִתְמִינָאָה וּלְתַתָּא.

285. In all THE FIRMAMENTS there are assigned camps, up to the seventh firmament, WHICH IS CHESED. BUT IN THE FIRST THREE FIRMAMENTS THERE ARE NO APPOINTEES. From the seventh FIRMAMENT upwards, IN THE FIRST THREE SFIROT, KETER, CHOCHMAH AND BINAH, a light emanates down from the high throne, WHICH IS MALCHUT OF ATZILUT, and illumines the tenth FIRMAMENT, WHICH IS KETER OF ASIYAH, and the tenth FIRMAMENT gives the light it received to the ninth FIRMAMENT, WHICH IS CHOCHMAH. THE NINTH FIRMAMENT ILLUMINES the eighth FIRMAMENT, WHICH IS BINAH and downward.

286. הַאי תְּמִינָאָה, כַּד אִתְפַּקְדוּן חֵילֵי דְּכוֹכְבַיָּא, וְאַפִּיק לוֹן, הַהוּא

נְהִירוּ, קַיְּימָא וְיָהִיב חֵילֵיהּ לְכָל חַד וְחַד, לְאִתְמַנָּאָה בְּהַהוּא אֲתָר דְּאִצְטְרִיךְ. דִּכְתִּיב הַמּוֹצִיא בְּמִסְפָּר צְבָאָם וְגוֹ', מֵרֹב אוֹנִים, דָּא אִיהוּ זֹהֲרָא דִּלְעֵילָּא, דְּאִקְרֵי רוֹב אוֹנִים.

286. In the eighth FIRMAMENT THERE ARE STARS, and when the hosts of stars are enumerated, and it brings them out, that same light IT RECEIVED FROM THE FIRMAMENT OF CHOCHMAH, gives from its strength to each and every one so it may be assigned in its own place as needed. This is written in, "that brings out their host by number...because of the greatness of his might" (Yeshayah 40:26). The greatness of his might is the supernal radiant splendor, IT RECEIVED FROM THE FIRMAMENT OF CHOCHMAH, which is called 'greatness of might'.

287. וּבְכָל רְקִיעָא וּרְקִיעָא, אִית מְמָנָא, וְאִתְפְּקַד עַל עָלְמָא, וְעַל אַרְעָא, לְאַנְהָגָא כֹּלָּא. בַּר אַרְעָא דְּיִשְׂרָאֵל, דְּלָא אַנְהִיג לָהּ רְקִיעָא, וְלָא חֵילָא אַחֲרָא, אֶלָּא קוּדְשָׁא בְּרִיךְ הוּא בִּלְחוֹדוֹי, וְהָא אוּקְמוּהָ. וְאִי תֵּימָא הֵיךְ שַׁרְיָא לְמַגָּנָא רְקִיעָא עַל אַרְעָא דְּיִשְׂרָאֵל, וְהָא מִטְרָא וְטַלָּא מֵרְקִיעָא נָחִית עָלָהּ, כִּשְׁאַר כָּל אַרְעָא אַחֲרָא.

287. In each firmament there is a chief assigned to a world and a land, to rule over all of them, except over the land of Yisrael. No firmament rules over it, nor other force, but the Holy One, blessed be He, alone. This was already explained. But, one may ask, how is there a firmament over the land of Yisrael without effect, and still there is rain and dew over it like any other land?

288. אֶלָּא, בְּכָל רְקִיעָא וּרְקִיעָא אִית מְמָנָן שַׁלְטִין עַל עָלְמָא, וְהַהוּא מְמָנָא דְּשַׁלְטָא עַל הַהוּא רְקִיעָא, יָהִיב מֵחֵילָא דְּאִית לֵיהּ לְהַהוּא רְקִיעָא, וְהַהוּא רְקִיעָא נָקִיט מֵהַהוּא מְמָנָא, וְיָהִיב לְתַתָּא לְאַרְעָא. וְהַהוּא מְמָנָא לָא נָקִיט, אֶלָּא מִתַּמְצִית דִּלְעֵילָּא. אֲבָל אַרְעָא קַדִּישָׁא, לָא שַׁלִּיט עַל הַהוּא רְקִיעָא דַּעֲלֵיהּ מְמָנָא אַחֲרָא, וְלָא חֵילָא אַחֲרָא, אֶלָּא קוּדְשָׁא בְּרִיךְ הוּא בִּלְחוֹדוֹי וְאִיהוּ פָּקִיד לְאַרְעָא קַדִּישָׁא בְּהַהוּא רְקִיעָא.

288. HE REPLIES THAT in each firmament there are assigned chiefs who rule the world, and the chief who rules over a certain firmament, gives it from his strength, and the firmament receives it and transmits it to the land. That chief gets but the remnant of that light above, FOR THE PEOPLES OF THE WORLD ARE SUSTAINED BY THE REMNANT ALONE. But the Holy Land is not under the rule of any firmament and other assigned chief, nor any other force but under the Holy One, blessed be He, alone. And He rules over the Holy Land from the firmament above it.

289. בְּכָל רְקִיעָא וּרְקִיעָא, אִית פִּתְחִין יְדִיעָן, וְשׁוּלְטָנוּ דְּכָל מְמָנָן, מִפִּתְחָא לְפִתְחָא רְשִׁימָא, וּמֵהַהוּא פִּתְחָא וּלְהַלָּן, לָא שַׁלְטָא אֲפִילּוּ כִּמְלֹא נִימָא, וְלָא עָאל דָּא, בִּתְחוּמָא דְּפִתְחָא דְּחַבְרֵיה, בַּר כַּד אִתְיְהִיב לֵיה רְשׁוּ, לְשַׁלְטָאָה חַד עַל חַבְרֵיה. כְּדֵין, שַׁלְטִין מַלְכִּין דִּי בְּאַרְעָא, חַד עַל חַבְרֵיה.

289. In each firmament there are several designated portals, and the authority of each chief lies between two portals. He has no authority outside his area, even by a hairbreadth, except when he is given permission to rule over his fellow-chief. Then the kings on earth also rule one over another. NAMELY, THE KINGS OF THE LANDS DESIGNATED UNDER THESE FIRMAMENTS AND CHIEFS.

290. בְּאֶמְצָעִיתָא דְּכֻלְּהוּ רְקִיעִין, אִית פִּתְחָא חֲדָא, דְּאִקְרֵי גְּבִילוֹ"ן, וּתְחוֹת הַאי פִּתְחָא, אִית שַׁבְעִין פִּתְחִין אַחֲרָנִין לְתַתָּא, וְשַׁבְעִין מְמָנִין נַטְרִין, מֵרָחִיק תְּרֵי אַלְפִין אַמִּין, דְּלָא קָרְבִין לְגַבֵּיה. וּמֵהַהוּא פִּתְחָא אָרְחָא סָלִיק לְעֵילָא לְעֵילָא, עַד דִּי מָטָא לְגוֹ כּוּרְסַיָּיא עִלָּאָה, וּמֵהַהוּא פִּתְחָא לְכָל סִטְרִין דִּרְקִיעָא, עַד תַּרְעָא דְּפִתְחָא דְּאִקְרֵי מַגְדּוֹ"ן, דְּתַמָּן אִיהוּ סִיּוּמָא דִּרְקִיעָא דִּתְחוּמָא דְּאַרְעָא דְּיִשְׂרָאֵל.

290. In the middle of the firmaments, ABOVE THE LAND OF YISRAEL, WHICH IS IN THE MIDDLE OF THE WORLD, there is an opening by the name of Gevilon. Under that portal there are seventy other portals, and seventy chiefs guard them from two thousand cubits away, IN THE SECRET OF SHABBAT LIMIT, FROM THE OPENING GEVILON, which they do not approach. From this opening a way mounts higher and higher until it

reaches the supernal throne, WHICH IS MALCHUT, and from this opening ITS AUTHORITY IS SPREAD over to all the quarters of the firmament up to the opening called Magdon, where the firmament over the land of Yisrael ends.

291. וְכָל אִינּוּן ע׳ פִּתְחִין, דִּרְשִׁימִין גּוֹ הַהוּא פִּתְחָא דְּאִקְרֵי גְבִילוֹ״ן, כֻּלְּהוּ רְשִׁימִין בְּכוּרְסְיָּיא קַדִּישָׁא, וְכֻלְּהוּ קָרִינָן לוֹן שַׁעֲרֵי צֶדֶק, דְּלָא שַׁלִּיט אַחֲרָא עָלַיְיהוּ. וְקוּדְשָׁא בְּרִיךְ הוּא פָּקִיד לְאַרְעָא דְּיִשְׂרָאֵל בְּהַהוּא רְקִיעָא, מִפִּתְחָא לְפִתְחָא, בִּפְקִידוּ כְּמָה דְּאִצְטְרִיךְ. וּמִתַּמְצִיתָא דְּהַהוּא פְּקִידָא, נַטְלִין אִינּוּן שַׁבְעִין מְמָנָן, וְיָהֲבִין לְכֻלְּהוּ מְמָנָן אַחֲרָנִין.

291. All the seventy doors marked in that opening called Gevilon, are engraved on the holy throne, and are named "gates of righteousness," AFTER MALCHUT WHICH IS CALLED RIGHTEOUSNESS, for no other rules over them. And the Holy One, blessed be He, rules over the land of Yisrael in that firmament from one opening to another, THAT IS FROM THE OPENING CALLED GEVILON TO THE OPENING CALLED MAGDON. From His worthy authority, NAMELY FROM THE FULL NEEDED INFLUENCE, the remnant is given to the SAID seventy chiefs, who transmit it to all the other chiefs THAT RULE OVER THE PEOPLES OF THE WORLD.

24. The firmaments over the Garden of Eden

A Synopsis

Rabbi Shimon tells us of the firmament that stands upon the earthly Garden of Eden. When God made it, he brought fire and water from the Throne of Glory (the World of Binah) and put them together to form our firmament. He added to this other fire and water from the holy high heaven, which then made the firmament expand. We are told of that expansion, and the movement of the letters that illuminate, and of the Chariots. We read of the garments that the souls are worthy of wearing; in these garments the good deeds are recorded, and the angels clothe the souls of the righteous with them in the Garden. We are told however that in those days immediately following death, the soul is punished before it enters the Garden of Eden. We hear that the 22 letters are engraved upon the firmament; they distill dew on all those who study the Torah. Rabbi Shimon says that the lower garments of the earthly Garden of Eden are connected with deeds and the higher garments are connected with the intention and the will of the spirit in the heart. Now he tells us that we cannot know the source of the river that flows out of Eden because if this place were disclosed and revealed down below, then that place of the higher holy Eden would have to be disclosed and known also. Therefore this Eden is not revealed even to the souls in the Garden of Eden. Rabbi Shimon explains the meaning of the name Elohim, and then he says that when the soul leaves the darkness of this world it longs to see the light of the upper world, like one thirsting for water. In the river that flows out of Eden sit all the souls clad in their precious garments, without which they would not be able to bear the lights; now they slake their thirst in the brightness. The souls of the righteous ascend by way of the pillar in the middle of the Garden through the door of the firmament of the Garden of Eden. The souls go out and listen to the sweet voice that comes of the firmament's revolving. Later they receive the illumination of Chochmah; from the joy and gladness caused by what they see, they go up and down, come near and retreat. Rabbi Shimon turns to, "And over the heads of the living creatures there was the likeness of a firmament, like the color of the terrible ice, stretched out over their heads above." He speaks about the firmament above and the firmament below. When souls ascend they bathe in the river of fire and are washed in it, not consumed but purified. We learn of Behinom, that place of purification in Gehenom. We learn that God brings out the sun after the purification and heals the broken soul: this is the meaning of, "But to you who fear my name the sun of righteousness shall

arise with healing in its wings." Rabbi Shimon tells us that at every new moon and Shabbat the souls in the lower Garden of Eden hover about the world and see the bodies of the wicked being punished, and they watch the sick and suffering. Then they go back to the Garden of Eden and tell these things to Messiah, who cries for the wicked. Messiah enters the temple of the sick that exists in the Garden of Eden and calls upon him all the diseases, pains and agonies of Yisrael. But for him, no man would ever have been able to bear the sufferings of Yisrael for the punishments of the Torah. Rabbi Shimon says that Rabbi Elazar also used to take sufferings upon himself for the sake of Yisrael. For now, Messiah detains the illnesses and agonies until a man passes away from the world and receives punishment. Finally, Rabbi Shimon says those who observe the precepts of the Torah are happy, because when the point down below wants to be delighted in the Garden of Eden by the souls of the righteous, it is like a mother, happy and delighted with her sons.

292. בְּגִנְתָּא דְּעֵדֶן דִּלְתַתָּא, רְקִיעָא דְקַיְּימָא עָלֵיהּ, אִית בֵּיהּ רָזִין עִלָּאִין. כַּד עֲבַד קוּדְשָׁא בְּרִיךְ הוּא רְקִיעָא אַיְיתֵי אֵשׁ וּמַיִם, מִגּוֹ כּוּרְסֵי יְקָרֵיהּ, וְשִׁתֵּף לוֹן כַּחֲדָא, וְעָבַד מִנְּהוֹן רְקִיעָא לְתַתָּא, וְאִתְפָּשְׁטוּ עַד דִּמְטוּ לְהַהוּא אֲתָר דְּגִנְתָּא דְּעֵדֶן, וְיָתְבוּ. מַה עֲבַד קוּדְשָׁא בְּרִיךְ הוּא. נָטַל מִשְּׁמַיִם עִלָּאִין קַדִּישִׁין, אֵשׁ וּמַיִם אַחֲרָנִין דְּמִשְׁתַּכְּחִין וְלָא מִשְׁתַּכְּחִין, דְּאִתְגַּלְיָין וְלָא אִתְגַּלְיָין, וּמֵאִינוּן אֵשׁ וּמַיִם, דְּאִתְנְטָלוּ מִשְּׁמַיִם עִלָּאִין, עֲבַד מִנַּיְיהוּ מְתִיחוּ דִּרְקִיעָא, וּמָתַח לֵיהּ עַל הַאי גִּנְתָּא דִּלְתַתָּא, וּמִתְחַבֵּר גּוֹ רְקִיעָא אַחֲרָא.

292. Upon the lower, EARTHLY, Garden of Eden there stands a firmament, in which are contained high mysteries. When the Holy One, blessed be He, made the firmament, He brought fire and water from the Throne of Glory, WHICH IS THE WORLD OF BRIYAH, and put them together to form the lower firmament, OF OUR EARTH. They expanded until they reached that place, the Garden of Eden, and settled, THAT IS, EXPANDED NO MORE. What did the Holy One, blessed be He, do? He took from the holy high heaven, CHOCHMAH AND BINAH OF ZEIR ANPIN, CALLED HEAVEN OF ATZILUT, other fire and water, that both exist and do not exist, both disclosed and not disclosed. From these fire and water taken from the high heaven, He caused the firmament to expand, and stretched them over the

lower Garden of Eden. That firmament, WHICH IS DA'AT, is united with the other firmament, OF OUR EARTH, WHICH IS TIFERET.

293. אַרְבַּע גְּווֹנִין, בְּהַהוּא מְתִיחוּ דִּרְקִיעָא דְּעַל גִּנְתָּא, חִיוָּר וְסוּמָק יָרוֹק וְאוּכָם. לְגַבֵּי הָנֵי גְּווֹנִין, אִית אַרְבַּע פִּתְחִין, לְתַתָּא מֵהַהוּא מְתִיחוּ דִּרְקִיעָא. וְאִינוּן פְּתִחִין לְאַרְבַּע סִטְרִין דִּרְקִיעָא דְּעַל גַּבֵּי גִנְתָּא. מֵאִינוּן אֵשׁ וּמַיִם, דְּאִתְעֲבֵיד מִנְּהוֹן הַהוּא רְקִיעָא. מִתְפַּתְּחִין בְּאַרְבַּע פִּתְחִין, אַרְבַּע נְהוֹרִין.

293. In the expansion of that firmament upon the garden, four colors are displayed: white, red, green and black. THEY ARE THE THREE COLUMNS, RIGHT, LEFT AND CENTRAL, WHITE, RED AND GREEN; AND BLACK WHICH IS MALCHUT THAT RECEIVES FROM THESE THREE COLUMNS. In these colors there are four openings underneath the expansion of the firmament. They open to the four sides of the firmament above the garden. FOR SOUTH AND NORTH ARE CHESED AND GVURAH, AND EAST AND WEST ARE TIFERET AND MALCHUT. From the fire and water from which the firmament was made, THE MENTIONED CHOCHMAH AND BINAH OF ZEIR ANPIN, four lights come through these four doors.

294. לְסְטַר יְמִינָא בְּהַהוּא פִּתְחָא, מִגּוֹ מְתִיחוּ דְּסְטַר מַיָּא, נַהֲרִין תְּרֵין נְהוֹרִין, בְּאִינוּן תְּרֵין פִּתְחִין, בְּפִתְחָא הַיְמִינָא, וּבְפִתְחָא דְּאִיהוּ לָקֳבֵל אַנְפִּין.

294. On the opening to the right from the expansion of the water aspect OF THE FIRMAMENT, THAT IS MADE OF FIRE AND WATER, NAMELY FROM THE LIGHT OF CHASSADIM, two lights shine through the two doors: through the right opening, IN THE SOUTH WHICH IS CHESED, and through the frontal opening, THAT IS, IN THE EAST WHICH IS TIFERET. BECAUSE EAST AND WEST ARE CALLED FRONT AND BACK. AND THE LIGHT OF CHASSADIM ALSO ILLUMINES IN TIFERET AS WE ALREADY KNOW.

295. גּוֹ נְהוֹרָא דְּנָהִיר לִסְטַר יְמִינָא, אִתְרְשִׁים אָת חַד, נָהִיר וּבָלִיט, וְנָצִיץ בְּנְצִיצוּ, מִגּוֹ הַהוּא נְהוֹרָא, וְאִיהוּ אָת מ', וְקַיְּימָא בְּאֶמְצָעִיתָא

דְּהַהוּא נְהוֹרָא דִּפְתִחָא. אָת דָּא, סַלְקָא וְנַחְתָּא, וְלָא קָאִים בְּאֲתָר חַד. הַהוּא נְהוֹרָא, נָטִיל לְהַהוּא אָת וְאַפִּיק לָהּ, בג"כ לָא קַיְּימָא בְּאֲתָר חַד.

295. Within the light that illumines to the right, one letter engraved, stands out and glitters from inside the light. It is the letter Mem, THE FIRST LETTER OF 'MICHAEL', which stands in the middle of that light at that opening. This letter goes up and down, and does not stand still. That light ON THE RIGHT SIDE takes that letter out, therefore it does not stand still. THIS IS THE MYSTERY OF "AND THE LIVING CREATURES RAN AND RETURNED" (YECHEZKEL 1:14), FOR THEY DO NOT STAND STILL.

296. גּוֹ נְהוֹרָא דְּנָהִיר בְּסִטְרָא דְּאִיהוּ לְקָבֵל אַנְפִּין, אִתְרְשִׁים אָת חַד, דְּנָהִיר וּבָלִיט וְנָצִיץ בְּנְצִיצוּ גּוֹ הַהוּא נְהוֹרָא, וְאִיהִי אָת ר', וּלְזִמְנִין אִתְחֲזֵי ב' וְקַיְּימָא בְּאֶמְצָעִיתָא דְּהַהוּא נְהוֹרָא דִּפְתִחָא. וְסַלְקָא וְנַחְתָּא, לְזִמְנִין אִתְגַּלְיָא, וּלְזִמְנִין לָא אִתְגַּלְיָא, וְלָא קַיְּימָא בְּאֲתָר חַד. אִלֵּין תְּרֵין אַתְוָון קַיְּימִין, וְכַד נִשְׁמָתָא דְּצַדִּיקַיָּא עָאלַת בְּגִנְתָּא דְּעֵדֶן, אִלֵּין תְּרֵין אַתְוָון נַפְקִין מִגּוֹ הַהוּא נְהוֹרָא, וְקַיְּימִין עַל הַהִיא נִשְׁמָתָא, וְסַלְקֵי וְנַחְתֵּי.

296. Within the light that illumines the side opposite the front, THAT IS EAST WHICH IS TIFERET, one letter is engraved, shining and standing out and glitters from inside the light. It is the letter Resh, WHICH IS THE FIRST LETTER OF THE ANGEL RAPHAEL. Sometimes the letter Bet is seen, THE FIRST LETTER THE ANGEL BOEL. It stands in the center of that light in the opening, going up and down. Sometimes it is seen and sometimes not. And it does not stand still, IN ACCORDANCE WITH THE MYSTERY OF "AND THE LIVING CREATURES RAN AND RETURNED." These two letters stand IN THE CENTER OF THE LIGHT IN THE TWO OPENINGS, and when the souls of the righteous come to Garden of Eden, these two letters step out of the light, and stand by that soul, and go up and down, IN ACCORDANCE WITH THE MYSTERY OF "AND THE LIVING CREATURES RAN AND RETURNED." AND WHAT IS SAID HERE THAT THE EAST IS CALLED RAPHAEL IS IN OPPOSITION TO SOME EXPLANATIONS IN WHICH URIEL IS THE EAST.

297. כְּדֵין, מֵאִינּוּן תְּרֵין פִּתְחִין, מְקַדְּמֵי וְנַחְתֵּי מֵעֵילָּא, תְּרֵין רְתִיכִין.

רְתִיכָא חֲדָא עִלָּאָה, דְּאִיהִי רְתִיכָא דְּמִיכָאֵל, רַב סְגָנִין. רְתִיכָא
תִּנְיָינָא, דְּאִיהִי רְתִיכָא מֵהַהוּא רַב מְמָנָא, דְּאִקְרֵי בּוֹאֵ"ל. וְדָא אִיהוּ
שִׁמְשָׁא יַקִּירָא דְּאִקְרֵי רְפָאֵ"ל. וְאִינּוּן נַחְתִּין וְקַיְימִין עַל נִשְׁמָתָא,
אַמְרִין לָהּ שָׁלוֹם בּוֹאֶךְ. יָבֹא שָׁלוֹם יָבֹא שָׁלוֹם. כְּדֵין אִינּוּן תְּרֵין אַתְוָון,
סַלְּקִין וְקַיְימִין בְּאַתְרַיְיהוּ, וְאִתְגְּנִיזוּ גּוֹ הַהוּא נְהוֹרָא, דְּאִינּוּן פִּתְחִין.

297. From the two doors, two Chariots then hasten to come down. One supernal Chariot is the Chariot of Michael, the great prince, and the second Chariot is of the superior chief Boel, who is the important minister called Raphael. They go down and stand by the soul and tell it, 'come in peace, it "shall enter in peace" (Yeshayah 57:2), enter in peace'. The two letters then mount, stand in their places and are concealed within the light of the doors.

298. תְּרֵין פִּתְחִין אַחֲרָנִין, תְּרֵין נְהוֹרִין אַחֲרָנִין קָא מְלַהֲטִין, מִנְּהִירוּ
דְּאֶשָּׁא, בְּאִינּוּן פִּתְחִין חַד לִסְטַר שְׂמָאלָא, וְחַד לַאֲחוֹרָא. תְּרֵין אַתְוָון
אַחֲרָנִין, מְלַהֲטִין בְּאִינּוּן נְהוֹרִין, וּנְצִיצִין בְּגַוַּוייְהוּ, אָת חַד ג', וְאָת חַד
נ', וְכַד אַתְוָון קַדְמָאֵי מִתְהַדְּרָן לְאַתְרַיְיהוּ, אִלֵּין תְּרֵין אַחֲרָנִין נְצוֹצִין,
סַלְּקִין וְנַחְתִּין, נָפְקִין מֵאִינּוּן נְהוֹרִין, וְקַיְימִין עַל נִשְׁמָתָא.

298. Through the other two openings shine two other lights, glowing from the light of the fire in the openings, one to the left side and one to the rear. Two other letters burn within the lights and glitter therein. One is the letter Gimel and one letter is Nun, WHICH ARE THE FIRST LETTERS OF THE ANGEL GABRIEL AND THE ANGEL NURIEL. And when the first two letters return to their place, these two letters glitter and go up and down, leave the lights IN THE OPENINGS and stand by the soul.

299. כְּדֵין נַחְתִּין תְּרֵין רְתִיכִין, מֵאִינּוּן תְּרֵין פִּתְחִין. רְתִיכָא חֲדָא אִיהוּ
רְתִיכָא דְּגַבְרִיאֵל, רַב מְמָנָא וְיַקִּירָא. רְתִיכָא תִּנְיָינָא, אִיהִי רְתִיכָא
אַחֲרָא קַדִּישָׁא דְּנוּרִיאֵ"ל רַב מְמָנָא, וְנַחְתִּין מֵאִינּוּן פִּתְחִין, וְקַיְימִין עַל
נִשְׁמָתָא, וְאַתְוָון מִתְהַדְּרָן לְאַתְרַיְיהוּ.

299. Two Chariots then descend from the two openings. One is the Chariot

of Gabriel, a high delegate and honorable chief. The second is another holy Chariot of the high superior Nuriel. They descend from the doors and stand by the soul. And the letters Gimel and Nun go back to their places.

300. בְּדֵין, אִלֵּין תְּרֵין רְתִיכִין, עָאלִין לְגוֹ הֵיכְלָא חֲדָא טְמִירָא דְּגִנְתָּא, דְּאִקְרֵי אֲהֲלוֹ"ת, וְתַמָּן תְּרֵיסָר זִינֵי בּוּסְמִין גְּנִיזִין, דִּכְתִיב נֵרְדְּ וְכַרְכֹּם קָנֶה וְקִנָּמוֹן וְגוֹ'. וְאִינּוּן תְּרֵיסָר זִינֵי דְּבוּסְמִין דִּלְתַתָּא.

300. The two Chariots then ascend into a hidden chamber called 'Ohalot' (lit. 'tents'), where there are twelve kinds of concealed sweet spices, as is written: "Nard and saffron, calamus and cinnamon, with all trees of frankincense..." (Shir Hashirim 4:14). These are ALSO the twelve kinds of spices of the lower GARDEN OF EDEN.

301. וְתַמָּן כָּל אִינּוּן לְבוּשִׁין דְּנִשְׁמָתִין, דְּאִתְחֲזוּן לְאִתְלַבְּשָׁא בְּהוּ, כָּל חַד וְחַד, כַּדְקָא חֲזֵי. בְּהַהוּא לְבוּשָׁא, אִתְרְשִׁימוּ כָּל אִינּוּן עוֹבָדִין טָבִין, דְּעָבַד בְּהַאי עָלְמָא. וְכֻלְּהוּ רְשִׁימִין בֵּיהּ, וּמַכְרִיזֵי הַאי אִיהוּ לְבוּשָׁא דִּפְלָנְיָא, וְנַטְלִין לְהַהוּא לְבוּשָׁא וְאִתְלַבְּשַׁת בֵּיהּ הַהִיא נִשְׁמְתָא דְּצַדִּיקַיָּא דִּבְגִנְתָּא, כְּגַוְונָא דְּדִיּוּקְנָא דְּהַאי עָלְמָא.

301. There you may also find the garments, the souls are worthy of wearing, each according to the soul's worth. In that garment, the good deeds are recorded, which he did in this world. All are written and proclaim, 'this is the garment of so-and-so'. AND THE ANGELS take the garments and clothe the souls of the righteous in the garden, in the likeness of the form of this world.

302. וְהָנֵי מִילֵּי, מִתְּלָתִין יוֹמִין וְאֵילָךְ, דְּהָא כָּל תְּלָתִין יוֹמִין, לֵית לָךְ נִשְׁמְתָא דְּלָא תְּקַבֵּל עוֹנְשָׁא, עַד לָא תֵּיעוּל לְגִנְתָּא דְּעֵדֶן. כֵּיוָן דְּקַבִּילַת עוֹנְשָׁא, עָאלַת לְגִנְתָּא דְּעֵדֶן, כְּמָה דְּאוּקְמוּהָ. לְבָתַר דְּאִתְלַבְּנַת, אִתְלַבְּשַׁת כֵּיוָן דְּאִתְלַבְּשַׁת בְּהַאי לְבוּשָׁא, יַהֲבִין לָהּ אֲתָר כְּמָה דְּאִתְחֲזֵי לָהּ. כְּדֵין, כָּל אִינּוּן אַתְוָון, נַחְתִּין, וְסַלְּקִין אִינּוּן רְתִיכִין.

302. This takes place only at the thirtieth day and afterwards. For in the thirty days AFTER DEATH, there is no soul that is not punished before entering the Garden of Eden. Once it is punished, it enters the Garden of Eden, as explained. And after it was blanched, NAMELY, AFTER PURIFICATION OF THE FILTH OF THIS WORLD BY PUNISHMENT, it wears THE SAID GARMENT. Once it wore the garment, it is given place according to its worth. Then, AFTER THE SOUL RECEIVES ITS PLACE, all the letters MEM, RESH, GIMEL, NUN, WHICH ARE THE INITIALS OF THE MENTIONED ANGELS, go down, and the Chariots OF THOSE FOUR ANGELS MENTIONED go back up to their places. FOR AFTER THE ANGELS COME BACK, AN IMPRESSION OF THEIR ILLUMINATION MUST REMAIN. THIS IS THE SECRET OF FOUR THE LETTERS MEM, RESH, GIMEL, NUN.

303. הַהוּא רְקִיעָא אֲהָדַר תְּרֵין זִמְנִין בְּכָל יוֹמָא, בְּהַהוּא נְטִילוּ דְּהַאי רְקִיעָ אַחֲרָא, דְּמִתְדַּבַּק בֵּיהּ. וְהַאי רְקִיעָא לָא נָפִיק לְבַר מִגִּנְתָּא. רְקִיעָא דָא, מְרֻקְמָא בְּכָל זִינֵי גַּוְונִין.

303. That firmament revolves twice a day by the journey of another firmament that is attached to it. And that firmament does not go out of the Garden OF EDEN, FOR IT ONLY HOVERS ABOVE THE GARDEN EXCLUSIVELY; this firmament is embroidered with many colors, TO WIT, WHITE, RED, GREEN AND BLACK, WHICH ARE CHESED, GVURAH, TIFERET AND MALCHUT.

304. תְּרֵין וְעֶשְׂרִין אַתְוָון רְשִׁימִין מְחַקְּקָן, בְּהַהוּא רְקִיעָא, כָּל אָת וְאָת, נָטִיף טַלָּא, מִטַּלָּא דִּלְעֵילָּא עַל גִּנְתָּא. וּמֵהַהוּא טַלָּא דְּאַתְוָון אִתְסַחְיָין אִינּוּן נִשְׁמָתִין, וּמִתַּסְיָין, בָּתַר דְּטָבְלוּ בִּנְהַר דִּינוּר לְאִתְדַּכָּאָה. וְטַלָּא לָא נָחִית, אֶלָּא מִגּוֹ אַתְוָון דִּרְשִׁימִין וּמְחַקְּקָן בְּהַהוּא רְקִיעָא, בְּגִין דְּאִינּוּן אַתְוָון כְּלָלָא דְּאוֹרַיְיתָא. וְהַהוּא רְקִיעָא רָזָא דְּאוֹרַיְיתָא, דְּהָא מֵאֵשׁ וּמַיִם דְּאוֹרַיְיתָא אִתְעֲבִיד.

304. The twenty two letters are impressed and engraved upon that firmament, ABOVE THE GARDEN OF EDEN, each letter distilling dew, from the higher dew, over the Garden. By that dew, WHICH IS ILLUMINATION OF CHASSADIM, the souls are bathed and healed, after immersing themselves in

the river of fire for purification. The dew comes down only from within the letters that are impressed and engraved upon that particular firmament, because these letter are the entirety of the Torah, FOR THEY ARE DRAWN FROM ZEIR ANPIN OF ATZILUT, named Torah because it was made from the fire and water of the Torah, THAT IS, FROM THE FIRE AND WATER OF ZEIR ANPIN OF ATZILUT.

305. וְע"ד אִינּוּן נַגְדִּין טַלָּא, עַל כָּל אִינּוּן דְּאִשְׁתַּדְּלוּ בְּאוֹרַיְיתָא לִשְׁמָהּ בְּהַאי עָלְמָא. וְאִלֵּין מִלִּין רְשִׁימִין בְּגִנְתָּא דְּעֵדֶן, וְסַלְּקִין עַד הַהוּא רְקִיעָא וְנַטְלִין מֵאִינּוּן אַתְוָון הַהוּא טַלָּא, לְאַתְזָנָא הַהִיא נִשְׁמָתָא. הֲדָא הוּא דִכְתִיב, יַעֲרֹף כַּמָּטָר לִקְחִי תִּזַּל כַּטַּל אִמְרָתִי.

305. Therefore they distill dew on all those that are occupied in the Torah for its sake in this world. For these words that are engraved in the Garden of Eden, go up to the firmament ABOVE THE GARDEN OF EDEN and take from those TWENTY TWO letters THAT ABIDE THERE, dew to nourish the soul. This is the meaning of "my doctrine shall drop as the rain, my speech shall distill as the dew" (Devarim 32:2)

306. בְּאֶמְצָעִיתָא דְּהַאי רְקִיעָא, קַיְּימָא פִּתְחָא חֲדָא, לָקֳבֵל פִּתְחָא דְּהֵיכְלָא דִּלְעֵילָא, דְּבְהַהוּא פִּתְחָא, פַּרְחִין נִשְׁמָתִין מִגִּנְתָּא דִּלְתַתָּא לְעֵילָא, בְּחַד עַמּוּדָא דְּנָעִיץ בְּגִנְתָּא, עַד הַהוּא פִּתְחָא.

306. In the middle of that firmament, there is an opening, facing the opening of the supernal chamber, IN YETZIRAH, through which the souls soar from the lower Garden of Eden upward by means of a pillar that is stuck in the EARTH OF Garden of Eden AND REACHES that opening.

307. גּוֹ הַהוּא רְקִיעָא בְּהַהוּא פִּתְחָא דְּאִיהוּ בְּאֶמְצָעִיתָא דִּרְקִיעָא דְּבְגִנְתָּא, עָאלִין בְּגַוֵּהּ תְּלַת גַּוְונִין דִּנְהוֹרָא כְּלִילָן כַּחֲדָא, וְנָהֲרָן לְגַוְונִין דְּהַהוּא עַמּוּדָא. וּכְדֵין עַמּוּדָא דָּא, נָצִיץ וְאִתְלְהִיט בְּכַמָּה גַּוְונִין דְּמִתְלַהֲטָן. בְּכָל שַׁעֲתָא, נַהֲרִין צַדִּיקַיָּא, מֵהַהוּא זִיוָא עִלָּאָה. אֲבָל בְּכָל שַׁבָּתָא וְשַׁבָּתָא, וּבְכָל רֵישׁ יַרְחָא, אִתְגַּלְיָיא שְׁכִינְתָּא, יַתִּיר

מִשְׁאָר זִמְנֵי בְּהַאי רְקִיעָא, וְאַתְיָין כֻּלְּהוּ צַדִּיקַיָּא, וְסַגְדִּין לְגַבֵּיהּ.

307. Into that firmament, within that opening in the middle of the firmament above the garden, three colors of light enter, mixed together. They ARE CHOCHMAH, BINAH, DA'AT, WHICH shine upon the colors of that pillar, WHICH GOES UP THERE. Then the pillar glitters and glows by the glowing colors. AND THE RIGHTEOUS, WHO ASCENDED BY WAY OF THAT PILLAR INTO THE FIRMAMENT, RECEIVE THE LIGHTS THROUGH THAT PILLAR. The righteous glow at any time from that high effulgence; THAT GOES ON, CONSTANTLY, but on Shabbat and the beginning of the month more than on other times because the Shechinah is then noticeably revealed in that firmament, and all the righteous come to bow before Her.

308. זַכָּאָה חוּלָקֵיהּ, מַאן דְּזָכֵי לְהָנֵי לְבוּשֵׁי דְּקָאֲמָרָן, דְּמִתְלַבְּשָׁן בְּהוּ צַדִּיקַיָּא בְּגִנְתָּא דְּעֵדֶן. אִלֵּין מֵעוֹבָדִין טָבִין, דְּעָבֵיד בַּר נָשׁ, בְּהַאי עָלְמָא, בְּפִקּוּדֵי אוֹרַיְיתָא. וּבְהוֹן קַיְּימָא נִשְׁמְתָא בְּגִנְתָּא דְעֵדֶן לְתַתָּא, וְאִתְלַבְּשַׁת בְּהָנֵי לְבוּשִׁין יַקִּירִין.

308. Happy is the portion of whoever is worthy of the said garments. These garments are made from the good deeds one did in this world by the precepts of the Torah, THE COMMANDMENTS CONNECTED TO ACTION, and through them the soul stands in the lower Garden of Eden wrapped in these precious garments.

309. כַּד סַלְקָא נִשְׁמְתָא בְּהַהוּא פִּתְחָא דִּרְקִיעָא לְעֵילָא, אִזְדַּמְּנָן לָהּ לְבוּשִׁין אַחֲרָנִין יַקִּירִין עִלָּאִין, דְּאִינוּן מֵרְעוּתָא וְכַוָּונָה דְּלִבָּא בְּאוֹרַיְיתָא וּבִצְלוֹתָא, דְּכַד סַלְקָא הַהוּא רְעוּתָא לְעֵילָא, מִתְעַטַּר בָּהּ מַאן דְּמִתְעַטְּרָא, וְאִשְׁתְּאַר חוּלָקָא לְהַהוּא בַּר נָשׁ, וְאִתְעֲבֵד מִנֵּיהּ לְבוּשִׁין דִּנְהוֹרָא, לְאִתְלַבְּשָׁא בְּהוּ נִשְׁמְתָא. לְסַלְקָא לְעֵילָא. וְאַף עַל גַּב דְּאוּקְמוּהָ, דְּאִינוּן לְבוּשִׁין בְּעוֹבָדִין תַּלְיָין. אִלֵּין לָא תַּלְיָין אֶלָּא בִּרְעוּתָא דְּרוּחָא, כְּמָה דְּאִתְּמַר, לְקַיְּימָא גּוֹ מַלְאָכִין רוּחִין קַדִּישִׁין וְדָא אִיהוּ בְּרִירוּ דְּמִלָּה. וּבוּצִינָא קַדִּישָׁא, אוֹלִיף הָכִי מֵאֵלִיָּהוּ, לְבוּשִׁין דִּלְתַתָּא בְּגִנְתָּא דְּאַרְעָא בְּעוֹבָדִין. לְבוּשִׁין דִּלְעֵילָא, בִּרְעוּתָא וְכַוָּונָא

דְּרוּחָא בְּלִבָּא.

309. When the soul ascends through the door of the higher firmament, other lofty and precious garments are presented before it, MADE BY PRECEPTS CONNECTED WITH wish and intention of the heart, study and prayer. For when that wish goes up, it is used as a crown, and part of it remains for that person, and is made into garments of light for the soul to wear when it ascends. And though it was said that the garments OF THE SOUL IN THE LOWER GARDEN OF EDEN depend on deeds, AS WAS MENTIONED BEFORE, nevertheless, those THAT GO UP TO THE HIGH FIRMAMENT depend on the wish of the spirit alone, as we said, to be among the angels, who are holy spirits. This is the clarification of the matter, and the holy luminary, RABBI SHIMON, learned it so from Elijah, that the lower garments of the earthly Garden of Eden ARE CONNECTED with deeds and the higher garments ARE CONNECTED with the intention and the wish of the spirit that is in the heart.

310. וְנָהָר יוֹצֵא מֵעֵדֶן לְהַשְׁקוֹת אֶת הַגָּן וְגו', הָא אוּקְמוּהָ, אֲבָל בְּהַאי גִּנְתָּא דִלְתַתָּא, נָהָר יוֹצֵא מֵעֵדֶן וַדַּאי. וְאִצְטְרִיךְ לְמִנְדַּע, הַאי נָהָר דְּנָפִיק בְּגִנְתָּא דִלְתַתָּא, בְּאָן אֲתַר עִקָּרָא וְשָׁרְשָׁא דִּילֵיהּ. בְּאָן אֲתַר, בְּעֵדֶן. עֵדֶן דָּא רָזָא עִלָּאָה אִיהוּ, וְלָא אִתְיְיהִיב רְשׁוּ לְשַׁלְטָאָה בֵּיהּ עֵינָא דְּסֻכְלְתָנוּ. וְרָזָא דְּמִלָּה אַלְמָלֵי אֲתַר דָּא אִתְמְסַר לְתַתָּא לְאִתְגַּלְּאָה, אֲתַר דְּעֵדֶן עִלָּאָה קַדִּישָׁא, אִתְמְסַר אוּף הָכִי לְמִנְדַּע. אֶלָּא בְּגִין טְמִירוּ דִּיקָרָא דְּעֵדֶן עִלָּאָה קַדִּישָׁא, אִתְטְמַר וְאִתְגְּנִיז עֵדֶן תַּתָּאָה, דְּהַהוּא נָהָר נָגִיד וְנָפִיק מִנֵּיהּ. וְע"ד לָא אִתְמְסַר לְאִתְגַּלְּאָה, אֲפִילוּ לְאִינּוּן נִשְׁמָתִין דִּבְגִנְתָּא דְּעֵדֶן.

310. It is written: "and a river went out of Eden to water the garden..." (Beresheet 2:10). This verse was explained. But assuredly a river flows out of Eden (lit. 'pleasure') of the Garden below, THE LOWER GARDEN OF EDEN. One should know that river that is flowing out of the lower Garden, its whereabouts and source. HE ANSWERS: THERE IS NO QUESTION about its location BECAUSE it is in Eden, SAME AS THE RIVER WHICH FLOWS OUT OF EDEN OF ATZILUT, WHICH IS CHOCHMAH OF ATZILUT. But Eden is a very high mystery and permission was not given for the mind's eye to

have power over it. The secret of the matter is that if this place, NAMELY, EDEN, WHICH IS CHOCHMAH IN THE FIRMAMENTS OF THE LOWER GARDEN OF EDEN, were disclosed and revealed down below; then that place of the higher holy Eden WOULD HAVE TO be disclosed and known. But in order to keep the secrecy of the honor of the higher holy Eden, WHICH IS CHOCHMAH OF ATZILUT, WHICH MUST NOT BE REVEALED, the lower Eden too is hidden and concealed, WHICH IS CHOCHMAH IN THE FIRMAMENTS OF THE LOWER GARDEN OF EDEN, out of which the river in the Garden of Eden emanates. Therefore this Eden is not revealed even to the souls in the Garden of Eden.

311. כְּמָה דְּהַאי נָהָר אִתְפְּרַשׁ וְנָפִיק מִגּוֹ עֵדֶן, לְאַשְׁקָאָה לְגִנְתָּא דִּלְעֵילָא, הָכִי נָמֵי מִגּוֹ הַהוּא פִּתְחָא דְּאֶמְצָעִיתָא נָפִיק חַד נְהוֹרָא, דְּאִתְפְּרַשׁ לְד' סִטְרִין, בְּד' פִּתְחִין דְּקָאָמְרָן. אֲתָר דְּקַיְימִין אִינוּן אַתְוָון רְשִׁימָן. וְהַהוּא נְהוֹרָא דְּאִתְפְּרַשׁ לְאַרְבַּע נְהוֹרִין, בְּד' אַתְוָון דְּנִיצוֹצִין, נָפִיק מֵעֵדֶן, אֲתָר דְּזָהֲרָא נְקוּדָה לְעֵילָא.

311. As this river, BINAH, TIFERET AND MALCHUT, departs and flows out of Eden, WHICH IS CHOCHMAH AT THE TOP OF ARICH ANPIN, to water the upper garden, MALCHUT OF ATZILUT; a light comes out of the center door OF THE GARDEN'S FIRMAMENTS, divided between the four openings in the four directions, where the letters MEM, GIMEL, RESH, NUN, are written. This light, divided into four lights and four glittering letters, goes out of Eden, where the upper point shines, WHICH REFERS TO CHOCHMAH, THE ASPECT OF THE HIGHEST POINT, OF THE FIRMAMENTS OF THE EARTHLY GARDEN OF EDEN.

312. וְהַהוּא נְקוּדָה אִתְנְהִיר, וְאִתְעֲבֵיד עֵדֶן לְאַנְהָרָא. וְלָא אִית מַאן דְּשַׁלִּיט לְמֶחֱמֵי וּלְמִנְדַּע לְהַאי נְקוּדָה, בַּר הַהוּא נְהִירוּ דְּאִתְפָּשַׁט מִנֵּיהּ, דְּסַגְדִּין לְקַמֵּיהּ אִינוּן צַדִּיקַיָּא דִּבְגִנְתָּא דְּעֵדֶן, כְּמָה דְּאִתְּמַר. וְהַאי נְקוּדָה תַּתָּאָה, אִיהִי גִּנְתָּא לְגַבֵּי עֵדֶן עִלָּאָה, אֲתָר דְּלָא אִתְיְיהִיב לְמִנְדַּע וּלְאִסְתַּכְּלָא.

312. That UPPER point shines and causes Eden to shine. No one is able to see and comprehend that point, only the light spreading from it BY WAY OF

THE DOOR IN THE MIDDLE OF THE SAID FIRMAMENTS. The righteous in the Garden of Eden bow before the light, as we learned. And this lower point, MALCHUT WITHIN THE GARDEN OF EDEN, is the garden to the supernal Eden, THE UPPER POINT, CHOCHMAH, where it is not possible to know and behold.

313. עַל כָּל דָּא כְּתִיב, עַיִן לֹא רָאָתָה אֱלֹהִים זוּלָתְךָ. שְׁמָא דָּא אִתְפְּרַשׁ, אֱלֹהִים זוּלָתְךָ, דָּא נְקוּדָה תַּתָּאָה קַדִּישָׁא, דְּאִיהוּ יָדַע הַאי עֵדֶן דִּלְתַתָּא, דְּטָמִיר בְּגִנְתָּא, וְלֵית אַחֲרָא מַאן דְּיָדַע לֵיהּ. אֱלֹהִים זוּלָתְךָ, דָּא עֵדֶן עִלָּאָה עַל כֹּלָּא, דְּאִיהוּ רָזָא דְּעָלְמָא דְּאָתֵי, דְּאִיהוּ יָדַע לִנְקוּדָה תַּתָּאָה, בְּחַד צַדִּיק דְּנָפִיק מִנֵּיהּ, נָהָר דְּרַוֵּי לֵיהּ, וְלֵית מַאן דְּיָדַע לֵיהּ בַּר אִיהוּ, דִּכְתִיב אֱלֹהִים זוּלָתְךָ, דְּאִיהוּ אָחִיד לְעֵילָא לְעֵילָא עַד אֵין סוֹף.

313. This is referred to in the verse "no eye has ever seen that Elohim, beside You" (Yeshayah 64:3). This name, ELOHIM, is explained: A) 'Elohim, beside You' is the lower holy point, MALCHUT OF ATZILUT NAMED ELOHIM, that knows the lower Eden IN THE EARTHLY GARDEN OF EDEN, hidden in the garden, which is known by none other, SAVE MALCHUT OF ATZILUT. B) 'Elohim, besides You' is the uppermost Eden, above all, the secret of the World to Come, THAT IS CHOCHMAH OF ATZILUT NAMED UPPER EDEN, WHEN REVEALED IN BINAH OF ATZILUT BY THE NAME 'THE WORLD TO COME', CALLED ELOHIM. It knows the lower point MALCHUT OF ATZILUT, by means of a certain righteous that flows out of it – the river which waters it, NAMELY, THE RIVER THAT FLOWS OUT OF EDEN, WHICH IS YESOD, CALLED RIGHTEOUS. No one else knows it besides Him, as is written: 'Elohim, beside You', that is connected above up to the Endless Light.

314. וְהַאי נָהָר דְּנָפִיק מֵעֵדֶן לְתַתָּא, רָזָא אִיהוּ לְחַכִּימִין, בְּרָזָא דִּכְתִיב, וְהִשְׂבִּיעַ בְּצַחְצָחוֹת נַפְשֶׁךָ. וּמִלָּה דָּא אִתְפְּרַשׁ לְעֵילָא וְתַתָּא. נִשְׁמָתָא דְּנָפְקָא מֵהַאי עָלְמָא דְּחָשׁוֹכָא, אִיהִי תָּאִיבַת לְמֶחֱמֵי בִּנְהִירוּ דְּעָלְמָא עִלָּאָה, כְּהַאי בַּר נָשׁ דְּתָאִיב לְמִשְׁתֵּי בִּתְאִיבוּ לְמַיָּא, הָכִי כָּל חַד וְחַד, אִיהוּ צַחְצָחוֹת, כְּמָה דְּאַתְּ אָמַר, צָחֵה צָמָא, מֵאִינוּן

צָחוֹת דִּנְהוֹרִין דְּגִנְתָּא וּרְקִיעָא וְהֵיכָלִין דְּגִנְתָּא.

314. This river, flowing out of Eden of the lower GARDEN OF Eden, is a mystery enclosed to the wise, based on the secret meaning of the verse "and satisfy your soul in drought (Heb. *tzach'tzachot*)" (Yeshayah 58:11). This explanation applies both above and below. When the soul leaves the darkness of this world, it longs to see the light of the upper world, like a man in his thirst desiring to drink water. Thus each one is thirsty as it says, "dried up (Heb. *tzicheh*) with thirst" (Yeshayah 5:13), SIMILARLY 'TZACH'TZACHOT' MEANS 'THIRSTY FOR LIGHTS'. SINCE it thirsts for the brightness (Heb. *tzachut*) of the lights of the garden, the firmaments and the chambers in the Garden.

315. וְהַהוּא נָהָר דְּנָפִיק מֵעֵדֶן, כָּל אִינּוּן נִשְׁמָתִין בִּלְבוּשֵׁי יְקַר, יַתְבִין עַל הַהוּא נָהָר, וְאִלְמָלֵא הַהוּא לְבוּשָׁא, לָא יַכְלִין לְמִסְבַּל. וּכְדֵין מִתְיַישְׁבָן, וְרַוְּוין בְּאִינּוּן צָחוֹת, וְיָכְלֵי לְמִסְבַּל. וְהַהוּא נָהָר אִיהוּ תִּקּוּנָא דְּנִשְׁמָתִין, לְאַתְיַישְׁבָא, וּלְאִתְזְנָא וּלְאִתְהֲנָאָה, מֵאִינּוּן צָחוֹת וְנִשְׁמָתִין אִתְתַּקָּנָן עַל הַהוּא נָהָר, וּמִתְיַישְׁבָן בֵּיה.

315. In the river that flows out of Eden sit all the souls clad in precious garments. Without the garments, they would not be able to bear THE LIGHTS. Now they sit and slack their thirst within the brightness, for they are able to stand it. This river amends the souls so they would be able to be sustained by and enjoy the brightness. The souls are amended by it and settled by it.

316. הַהוּא נָהָר עִלָּאָה דִּלְעֵילָּא, אַפִּיק נִשְׁמָתִין, וּפַרְחִין מִנֵּיהּ, לְגוֹ גִנְתָּא, דְּהַאי נָהָר דִּלְתַתָּא בְּגִנְתָּא דְּאַרְעָא, אַתְקִין נִשְׁמָתִין, לְאִתְתַּקְנָא לְאִתְיַישְׁבָא, בְּאִינּוּן צָחוֹת. כְּגַוְּונָא דָּא בְּהַאי עָלְמָא לְבַר, בְּרֵיחָא דְּמַיָּא מִתְיַישְׁבָא נַפְשָׁא לְאִתְנַהֲרָא, דְּהָא מֵעִיקָּרָא כְּגַוְּונָא דָּא נָפְקָא. וּבְגִין דְּמִתַּתְקְנִין נִשְׁמָתִין עַל הַהוּא נָהָר דְּנָגִיד וְנָפִיק מֵעֵדֶן, יַכְלִין לְאִתְיַישְׁבָא בְּאִינּוּן צָחוֹת עִלָּאִין, וּלְסַלְּקָא לְעֵילָּא. בְּהַהוּא פִּתְחָא דְּאֶמְצָעִיתָא דִּרְקִיעָא וְחַד עַמּוּדָא דְּקָאִים בְּאֶמְצָעוּת גִּנְתָּא דְּקָאֲמָרָן.

316. As the high river, YESOD OF ZEIR ANPIN, lets out souls and they soar from it into the garden, MALCHUT OF ATZILUT, SO does the lower river in the terrestrial garden prepare the souls so they would be amended and settle within the brightness, like in this exterior world, where the souls are settled and shine within the smell of water. For at first they came out this way, AS WAS ALREADY SAID. And since the souls are prepared in the river that flows out of Eden, they are able to be settled in the upper brightness, and ascend higher by way of the door in the middle of the firmament and the pillar that stands in the middle of the garden, as was explained. THUS IS EXPLAINED THE VERSE "AND SATISFY...TZACHTZACHOT (LIT. 'DRAUGHT', ALSO 'BRIGHTNESS')," ABOVE AND BELOW. THE BRIGHTNESS ABOVE WAS NOW EXPLAINED. THE BRIGHTNESS BELOW ARE THE LIGHTS OF THE GARDEN, THE FIRMAMENTS AND THE CHAMBERS AS WAS SAID. BOTH ARE FORMED BY THE RIVER THAT FLOWS OUT OF EDEN.

317. בְּהַהוּא עַמוּדָא סַלְּקִין לְעֵילָא, גּוֹ הַהוּא פִּתְחָא דִּרְקִיעָא, וּבֵיהּ סַחֲרָנֵיהּ, אִית בֵּיהּ עָנָן וְעָשָׁן וְנֹגַהּ. וְאע״ג דְּאוּקְמוּהַ לְהַאי קְרָא, אֲבָל עָנָן וְעָשָׁן אִלֵּין מִלְּבַר, וְנֹגַהּ מִלְּגוֹ. וְדָא אִיהוּ לְחַפְיָיא עַל אִינוּן דְּסַלְּקִין לְעֵילָא, דְּלָא יִתְחַזוּן מִקַּמֵּי אִינוּן דְּיַתְבִין לְתַתָּא.

317. THE SOULS OF THE RIGHTEOUS ascend by way of the pillar IN THE MIDDLE OF THE GARDEN, through the door of the firmament OF THE GARDEN OF EDEN. Around the pillar there are "a cloud and smoke...and the shining" (Yeshayah 4:5). THIS IS THE SECRET OF THE VERSE "AND HASHEM WILL CREATE UPON EVERY DWELLING PLACE OF MOUNT ZION, AND UPON HER ASSEMBLIES, A CLOUD AND SMOKE BY DAY, AND THE SHINING..." And though this verse was already explained, yet the cloud and smoke WERE outside and the shining light inside, in order to cover those who mount, so they would not be seen by those who stay below.

318. וְהָא הָכָא רָזָא דְּרָזִין, כַּד הַאי נְקוּדָה בָּעָא לְאִתְתַּקְּנָא בְּתִקּוּנוֹי, וּלְאִתְקַשְּׁטָא, בְּשַׁבָּתֵי וּבְזִמְנֵי וּבְחַגֵּי, מְשַׁדֵּר אַרְבַּע אַנְפִּין דְּנֶשֶׁר, וְקַיְימִין עַל הֵיכָלָא דְּאִקְרֵי דְּרוֹר, וְהַיְינוּ מָר דְּרוֹר. וּבְגִין דָּא בְּשַׁתָּא דְּיוֹבְלָא, בָּעֵינָן לְאַכְרְזָא דְּרוֹר, כד״א וּקְרָאתֶם דְּרוֹר. וְאִינוּן אַרְבַּע אַנְפִּין יַהֲבִין קָלָא, וְלֵית מַאן דְּיִשְׁמַע לֵיהּ, בַּר אִינוּן נִשְׁמָתִין דְּאִתְחַזוּן

לְסַלְּקָא, וְאִינּוּן מִתְכַּנְּשִׁין תַּמָּן, וְנַטְלֵי לוֹן אִלֵּין ד' אַנְפִּין, וְאַעֲלִין לוֹן
לְגוֹ, בְּהַהוּא עַמּוּדָא דְקָיְּימָא בְּאֶמְצָעִיתָא.

318. This is a secret mystery. When the point, THE GARDEN WHICH IS
MALCHUT OF BINAH OF THE EARTH OF ASIYAH, CALLED POINT, wanted
to be properly fixed, and be adorned on Shabbat and the festivals and
holidays; THE HOLY ONE, BLESSED BE HE, sent it the four faces of the
eagle. They stand upon the temple called Dror, OF "pure (Heb. *dror*) myrrh"
(Shemot 30:23). For that reason, at the time of Jubilee, we should proclaim
freedom, as says the verse "and proclaim liberty (Heb. *dror*)...TO ALL ITS
INHABITANTS" (Vayikra 25:10). These four aspects utter a sound, NAMELY,
THEY PROCLAIM FREEDOM TO ALL THE INHABITANTS OF THE GARDEN,
and no one hears it save the souls worthy of ascending. And they gather
there, IN THE TEMPLE OF FREEDOM, and are taken by the four aspects and
put inside the pillar that stands in the middle OF THE GARDEN.

319. וּבְהַהִיא שַׁעֲתָא סַלְקָא הַהוּא עַמּוּדָא, עֲנָנָא וְאֶשָּׁא וּתְנָנָא, וְנֹגַהּ
מִלְּגוֹ. וְאִלֵּין תְּרֵין אִקְרוּן, מְכוֹן הַר צִיּוֹן וּמִקְרָאֶיהָ. מְכוֹן הַר צִיּוֹן, דָּא
אִיהוּ תִּקּוּנָא דִלְעֵילָּא, כַּד נְקוּדָה תַּתָּאָה מִתְקַשְּׁטָא, וְאִינּוּן מִקְרָאֶיהָ
דְּהַהִיא נְקוּדָה לְאִתְקַשְּׁטָא.

319. At that time the pillar raises cloud, fire, smoke and bright light from
within. These two, THE ILLUMINATION OF FREEDOM AND THE SOULS, are
called "dwelling place of Mount Zion, and...her assemblies," OF WHICH IT
IS WRITTEN: "AND HASHEM WILL CREATE UPON EVERY DWELLING
PLACE OF MOUNT ZION, AND UPON HER ASSEMBLIES, A CLOUD AND
SMOKE BY DAY, AND THE SHINING OF A FLAMING FIRE BY NIGHT"
(YESHAYAH 4:5). For the dwelling place of Mount Zion is the higher
amendment, when the lower point is adorned, TO WIT, IT IS THE
ILLUMINATION OF FREEDOM BY THE FOUR FACES OF THE EAGLE OF
ABOVE. And they, THE SOULS, are called by that point to be adorned.
MEANING, THESE SOULS THAT HEARD THE LIBERATION CALL, ARE
CONSIDERED HER INVITED GUESTS CALLED TO HER.

320. כֵּיוָן דְּסַלְּקִין אִלֵּין נִשְׁמָתִין עַד הַהוּא פִּתְחָא דִרְקִיעָא, כְּדֵין,
הַהוּא רְקִיעָא סָחֲרָא סַחֲרָנֵי דְּגִנְתָּא, תְּלַת זִמְנִין. וּמִקָּל נְעִימוּ דְּסָחֲרָא

הַהוּא רְקִיעָא, נָפְקִין כָּל אִינּוּן נִשְׁמָתִין וְשַׁמְעִין הַהוּא נְעִימוּ דְּהַהוּא
רְקִיעָא, וְחָמָאן הַהוּא עַמּוּדָא, דְּסַלְּקָא אֶשָּׁא וַעֲנָנָא וּתְנָנָא וְנֹגַהּ
דְּלָהִיט, וְסַגְדִין כֻּלְּהוּ. כְּדֵין נִשְׁמָתִין סַלְּקִין בְּהַהוּא פִּתְחָא, עַד דְּסַלְּקִין
לְגוֹ עִגּוּלָא, דְּסַחֲרָא בְּהַהִיא נְקוּדָה. כְּדֵין חָמָאן מַה דְּחָמָאן. וּמִגּוֹ
נְהִירוּ וְחֶדְוָותָא מֵהַהוּא דְּחָמָאן, סַלְּקִין וְנַחְתִּין קַרְבִין וְרַחֲקִין.

320. When the souls mount and arrive at the opening of that firmament, then that firmament revolves three times around the garden. From the sweet voice that comes of the firmament's revolving, the souls in the door of the firmament go out and listen to the sweetness of the firmament and see the pillar THROUGH WHICH THEY ASCENDED, that emits fire, cloud, smoke and a bright light. They all bow LOWERING THEIR HEAD, they then ascend through that opening, until they reach the circle that goes round that point, NAMELY, INTO THE FIRMAMENT THAT REVOLVES AROUND THE GARDEN CALLED POINT, WHICH IS THE SECRET OF CHOCHMAH. Then they see what they see, TO WIT, THEY RECEIVE THE ILLUMINATION OF CHOCHMAH BY THE NAME OF SIGHT. From the joy and gladness caused by what they see, they go up and down, come near and retreat, IN THE SECRET OF "RAN AND RETURNED" (YECHEZKEL 1:14).

321. וְאִיהִי תָּאִיבָא לְגַבַּיְיהוּ, וּמִתְקַשְּׁטָא בִּנְהִירוּ. כְּדֵין אַלְבִּישׁ קִנְאָה
חַד צַדִּיק עִלָּאָה, וְאִסְתָּכַּל בִּנְהוֹרָא וּשְׁפִירוּ דְּהַאי נְקוּדָה, וּבְתִקּוּנָהָא,
וְאָחִיד בָּהּ, וְסָלִיק לָהּ לְגַבֵּיהּ, וְנָהִיר נְהוֹרָא בִּנְהוֹרָא, וַהֲווֹ חַד. כָּל
חֵילָא דִשְׁמַיָּיא פַּתְחֵי בְּהַהִיא שַׁעֲתָא וְאָמְרֵי, זַכָּאִין אַתּוּן צַדִּיקַיָּיא,
נַטְרֵי אוֹרַיְיתָא, זַכָּאִין אִינּוּן דְּמִשְׁתַּדְּלִין בְּאוֹרַיְיתָא, דְּהָא חֶדְוָותָא
דְּמָארֵיכוֹן הֲוֵי בְּכוּ, דְּהָא עֲטָרָא דְּמָארֵיכוֹן, מִתְעַטֵּר בְּכוֹן.

321. CHOCHMAH, THE SECRET OF THE SUPERNAL POINT, desires them and decorates them with its light. MEANING, THE SOULS THAT ROSE TO IT BECOME WITHIN IT AS MAYIN NUKVIN (LIT. 'FEMALE WATERS'). Then one supernal Righteous is clad with jealousy, YESOD OF THE WORLD OF YETZIRAH, regards the light and beauty of that point and its establishments, seizes it and brings it up to him TO YETZIRAH, and light shines into light. TO WIT, THE LIGHT OF CHASSADIM IN YESOD SHINES INTO THE LIGHT

OF CHOCHMAH WITHIN THE POINT and they become one. NAMELY, THEY UNITE. All the legions of heaven open and say at that time 'happy are the righteous, who observe the Torah, happy are you to be occupied in the Torah, for the joy of your Master is in you, who adorn the crown of your Master, FOR THEY BROUGHT ABOUT THAT UNITY.

322. כְּדֵין כֵּיוָן דְּנַהֲרִין נְהוֹרִין בִּנְהוֹרָא, תְּרֵין נְהוֹרִין מִתְחַבְּרָן כַּחֲדָא, וְנַהֲרִין. לְבָתַר אִינּוּן גַּוְונִין נַחְתִּין, וְאִסְתַּכְּלָן לְאִשְׁתַּעְשְׁעָא בְּאִינּוּן נִשְׁמָתִין דְּצַדִּיקַיָּיא, וּמְתַקְּנֵי לוֹן לְעַטְרָא לְעֵילָא. וְעַל דָּא אִתְּמַר, עַיִן לֹא רָאָתָה אֱלֹקִים זוּלָתְךָ יַעֲשֶׂה לִמְחַכֵּה לוֹ.

322. When light shines into light, NAMELY, THE LIGHT OF CHASSADIM INTO THE LIGHT OF CHOCHMAH, the two lights become one and illumine. Then the colors, THE LIGHTS OF THE UNITY, go down and observe so as to take pleasure in the righteous, THAT ASCENDED AS FEMALE WATERS, AS MENTIONED, and prepare them to be adorned above. Concerning this the verse says "no eye has ever seen that Elohim, beside You, will do such a thing for him who waits for him" (Yeshayah 64:3).

323. פָּתַח ר"ש וְאָמַר, כְּתִיב וּדְמוּת עַל רָאשֵׁי הַחַיָּה רָקִיעַ כְּעֵין הַקֶּרַח הַנּוֹרָא נָטוּי עַל רָאשֵׁיהֶם מִלְמָעְלָה. הַאי קְרָא אוּקְמוּהָ, אֲבָל אִית רָקִיעַ וְאִית רָקִיעַ, רָקִיעַ דִּלְתַתָּא אִיהוּ קַיְּימָא עַל גַּבֵּי ד' חֵיוָון. וּמִתַּמָּן אִתְפָּשַׁט וְשָׁארֵי דְּיוּקְנָא דְּחַד נוּקְבָּא, דַּאֲחוֹרֵי דְּכוּרָא, וְדָא אִיהוּ רָזָא דִּכְתִיב, וְרָאִיתָ אֶת אֲחוֹרָי. כד"א, אָחוֹר וָקֶדֶם צַרְתָּנִי. וּכְתִיב וַיִּקַּח אַחַת מִצַּלְעוֹתָיו.

323. Rabbi Shimon opened the discussion and said, it is written: "And over the heads of the living creatures there was the likeness of a firmament, like the color of the terrible ice, stretched out over their heads above" (Yechezkel 1:22). This scripture was already explained, but there is firmament and firmament. The firmament below stands upon four living creatures, THE FOUR LIVING CREATURES WITHIN MALCHUT, THE SECRET OF MICHAEL, GABRIEL, RAPHAEL AND NURIEL. Thence this firmament extends and takes a female form, MALCHUT, at the back of the male, ZEIR ANPIN. This is the recondite meaning in the verse "and you shall see My

back" (Shemot 33:23), MEANING THAT MALCHUT IS AT THE BACK OF ZEIR
ANPIN, as is written: "You have formed me behind and before" (Tehilim
139:5), WHICH ALLUDES TO ZEIR ANPIN IN FRONT AND MALCHUT IN THE
BACK. It is similarly written: "and He took one of his ribs" (Beresheet 2:21),
ALLUDING TO ZEIR ANPIN AND MALCHUT, THAT WERE DOUBLED-FACED,
FRONT AND BACK, AND THEN WERE SAWED, WHICH THE SAID VERSE
ALLUDES TO.

324. רָקִיעַ דִּלְעֵילָּא אִיהוּ קַיְימָא עַל גַּבֵּי חֵיוָון עִלָּאִין, וּמִתַּמָּן אִתְפְּשַׁט
וְשָׁארֵי דִּיּוּקְנָא דְּחַד דְּכוּרָא, דְּאִיהוּ רָזָא עִלָּאָה. וְהָנֵי תְּרֵין רְקִיעִין, חַד
אִקְרֵי קְצֵה הַשָּׁמַיִם. וְחַד אִקְרֵי מִקְצֵה הַשָּׁמַיִם. דִּכְתִיב וּלְמִקְצֵה
הַשָּׁמַיִם וְעַד קְצֵה הַשָּׁמָיִם. רֵאשֵׁי הַחַיָּה דִּלְתַתָּא אִינוּן אַרְבַּע חֵיוָון,
דְּאִינוּן נְהוֹרִין עִלָּאִין, עַל אִינוּן אַרְבַּע אַתְוָון רְשִׁימִין, דִּי בְּגוֹ אִינוּן
אַרְבַּע פִּתְחִין, דִּבְגִנְתָּא דְּעֵדֶן.

324. The firmament above rests upon the supernal living creatures,
CHESED, GVURAH AND TIFERET OF ZEIR ANPIN. Thence, FROM THAT
FIRMAMENT, extends and prevails a male form, which is a higher secret
ABOVE THE FEMALE. THIS REFERS TO ZEIR ANPIN. These two firmaments
are called, the one, 'end of the heaven' and the other 'from the end of the
heaven', as is written: "from the end of the heaven to the end of the
heaven" (Devarim 4:32). The heads of the lower living creatures IN MALCHUT, refer
to the four living creatures, which are supernal lights upon the four letters
engraved on the four doors in the Garden of Eden. AND THESE FOUR
LIVING CREATURES ARE THE SECRET OF THE AFOREMENTIONED ANGELS.

325. וְאַף עַ"ג דְּאָמְרָן עֵדֶן דִּלְתַתָּא בְּאַרְעָא, הָכִי הוּא וַדַּאי. אֲבָל כֹּלָּא
רָזָא עִלָּאָה אִיהוּ, כְּמָה דְּאִתְּמַר דְּהַאי נְקוּדָה דְּקָאָמְרָן, כְּמָה דְּאִית לָהּ
חוּלָקָא לְעֵילָּא, הָכִי נָמֵי אִית לָהּ חוּלָקָא לְתַתָּא בְּאַרְעָא. וְהַאי גִּנְתָּא
לְתַתָּא, אִיהוּ חוּלָקָא דְּהַהִיא נְקוּדָה לְאִשְׁתַּעְשְׁעָא בְּרוּחֵי דְּצַדִּיקַיָּיא
בְּאַרְעָא, וְאִתְהֲנֵי בְּכָל סִטְרִין לְעֵילָּא וְתַתָּא. לְעֵילָּא בְּצַדִּיק. לְתַתָּא
בְּהַהוּא אִיבָּא דְּצַדִּיק, וְלָא אִשְׁתְּכַח שַׁעֲשׁוּעָא עֵילָּא וְתַתָּא אֶלָּא
בְּצַדִּיק. וְהַאי גִּנְתָּא אִיהוּ, מֵהַהִיא נְקוּדָה דְּאִקְרֵי עֵדֶן.

325. And though we said that the lower Eden is on earth, AND THE GARDEN RECEIVES FROM THE LOWER EDEN, YOU SAY THAT THE GARDEN RECEIVES FROM THE FOUR LIVING CREATURES. HE ANSWERS: everything is a very high mystery, as we learned. For the said point, MALCHUT OF ATZILUT, as it has a part above, IN ATZILUT, so it has a part below on earth, NAMELY, AS IT IS THE TENTH PART OF ATZILUT, SO IT IS THE TENTH PART OF EARTH, THAT IS, THE GARDEN. The lower garden is part of the point ON EARTH, and is delighted by the spirits of the righteous on earth, taking pleasure on every side, above and below. Above it enjoys the Righteous, YESOD OF ZEIR ANPIN, and below the fruit of the Righteous, THE SOULS OF RIGHTEOUS PEOPLE BORN OF YESOD OF ZEIR ANPIN. The sole delight above or below caused TO MALCHUT, is by the Righteous. FOR ITS FRUIT IS ALSO CONSIDERED AS THE RIGHTEOUS AS IT IS. AND THEREFORE AS THE UPPER MALCHUT RIDES THE FOUR LIVING CREATURES, SO THE LOWER MALCHUT, THE GARDEN, RECEIVES FROM THE FOUR LIVING CREATURES AS SAID. And the garden is DRAWN from that point called Eden, THAT IS, ALSO LIKE MALCHUT ABOVE. FOR SHE IS DISCERNED AS THE LOWER CHOCHMAH DUE TO HER BEING DRAWN FROM THE HIGHER EDEN, SO TOO, THE GARDEN, THAT IS LOWER MALCHUT IS DRAWN FROM THE LOWER EDEN, IN A WAY THAT IT RECEIVES FROM BOTH. HOWEVER, THE FOUR LIVING CREATURES ARE FROM MALCHUT HERSELF, WHILE EDEN IS THE HIGHER LIGHT DRAWN TO MALCHUT, ABOVE, AND BELOW.

326. אִינּוּן רָאשֵׁי הַחַיָּה, אִלֵּין אַרְבַּע רֵישֵׁי אַנְפִּין. חַד אַרְיֵה, דִּכְתִיב וּפְנֵי אַרְיֵה אֶל הַיָּמִין. וְחַד שׁוֹר, דִּכְתִיב וּפְנֵי שׁוֹר מֵהַשְׂמֹאל. וְחַד נֶשֶׁר, דִּכְתִיב וּפְנֵי נֶשֶׁר לְאַרְבַּעְתָּן. אָדָם כְּלָלָא דְּכֹלָּא, דִּכְתִיב וּדְמוּת פְּנֵיהֶם פְּנֵי אָדָם. וְאִלֵּין אַרְבַּע רֵישֵׁי חֵיוָון דְּנַטְלִין לָהּ לְכוּרְסְיָיא קַדִּישָׁא, וּמִגּוֹ מְטוּלָא דִּילְהוֹן זָעִין. וּמֵהַהוּא זִיעָא דְּמָטוּלָא דִּילְהוֹן, אִתְעֲבֵיד הַהוּא נָהָר דִּי נוּר. דִּכְתִיב, נְהַר דִּי נוּר נָגֵד וְנָפֵק מִן קָדָמוֹהִי אֶלֶף אַלְפִין יְשַׁמְשׁוּנֵהּ.

326. The heads of the living creature are the four faces. One is a lion, as said "the face of a lion on the right side" (Yechezkel 1:10), WHICH IS CHESED, NAMELY, MICHAEL. One is an ox, as is written: "the face of an ox on the left side," WHICH IS GVURAH, NAMELY, GABRIEL. One is an eagle, as is

written: "they four also had the face of an eagle," WHICH IS TIFERET, NAMELY RAPHAEL. Man embraces them all, as said "and the likeness of their faces was that of a man" (Ibid.), WHICH IS MALCHUT RECEIVING FROM THEM ALL, NAMELY NURIEL. FROM ANOTHER POINT OF VIEW, MICHAEL IS OF THE RIGHT, LION; GABRIEL OF THE LEFT, OX; URIEL IN THE MIDDLE, TIFERET; RAPHAEL IS THE FACE OF A MAN. These are the four heads of the living creatures that carry the holy throne, MALCHUT, and perspire because of the burden. The sweat because of the load they carry becomes the river Di Nur (lit. 'of fire'), as is written: "A fiery stream issued and came forth from before him; a thousand thousands served him" (Daniel 7:10)

327. וְנִשְׁמָתִין כַּד סַלְקִין, אִתְסַחְיָין בְּהַהוּא נָהָר דִּי נוּר, וְסַלְקִין לְקוּרְבָּנָא וְלָא אִתּוֹקְדָן, אֶלָּא אִתְסַחְיָין. תָּא חֲזֵי מִסַּלָמַנְדְּרָא, דְּעַבְדִין מְנָּה לְבוּשָׁא. וּמִגּוֹ דְּאִיהִי מְנוּרָא, לָא אִתְסַחְיָיא הַהוּא לְבוּשָׁא, אֶלָּא בְּנוּרָא, אֶשָּׁא אָכִיל זוּהֲמָא דְּבֵיהּ, וְאִתְסַחֵי הַהוּא לְבוּשָׁא. הָכִי נָמֵי נִשְׁמָתָא דִּי נוּר דְּאִתְנְטִילַת מִגּוֹ כּוּרְסַיָּיא קַדִּישָׁא. דִּכְתִיב בָּהּ כָּרְסְיֵהּ שְׁבִיבִין דִּי נוּר. בְּזִמְנָא דְּבַעְיָיא לְאִתְסַחְיָיא מֵהַהוּא זוּהֲמָא דְּבָהּ, אִתְעַבְּרַת בְּנוּרָא וְאִתְסַחְיָיא. וְנוּרָא אַכְלָא כָּל הַהוּא זוּהֲמָא דִּי בְּנִשְׁמְתָא. וְנִשְׁמְתָא אִתְסַחְיָיא וְאִתְלַבְּנַת.

327. When the souls ascend, they bathe in the river of fire and are offered as sacrifice, not consumed but washed. Come and look at the salamander that is born of fire. A garment is made of it, that is washed only by fire. The fire eats away the filth and the garment is washed. So is the soul, made by the fire taken from the holy throne, MALCHUT, concerning which the verse says, "his throne was fiery flames" (Ibid. 9). When it is time for the soul to be washed from the filth, it passes through fire and is washed, the fire consuming all uncleanness and the soul cleansed and blanched.

328. וְאִי תֵּימָא אִי הָכִי עוֹנְשָׁא לֵית לָהּ לְנִשְׁמָתָא בְּהַאי. תָּא חֲזֵי, וַוי לְנִשְׁמָתָא דְּסַבְלַת אֶשָּׁא נוּכְרָאָה, וְאע"ג דְּאִיהִי אִתְלַבְּנָא. אֲבָל כַּד זוּהֲמָא אִיהוּ סַגִּי עֲלָה, וַוי לְנִשְׁמָתָא דְּסַבְלַת הַהוּא עוֹנְשָׁא, בְּגִין דְּהַהוּא זוּהֲמָא בִּתְרֵי זִמְנֵי אִתְלַבְּנַת בְּנוּרָא.

328. And if you say that the soul undergoes no penance that way, FOR IT IS

ONLY WASHED, come and see, woe to the soul that endures a strange fire, though it is purified by it. But when there is much pollution then woe to the soul that undergoes such punishment, for the filth is twice blanched.

329. זִמְנָא קַדְמָאָה כֵּיוָן דְּקַבִּילַת עוֹנְשָׁא בְּגוּפָא, אַזְלָא נִשְׁמָתָא, וְנַטְלֵי לָהּ, וְאַעֲלִין לָהּ בְּגוֹ אֲתָר חַד דְּאִקְרֵי בֶּן הִנֹּם, וַאֲמַאי אִקְרֵי בֶּן הִנֹּם. אֶלָּא אֲתָר חַד אִיהוּ בְּגֵיהִנָּם, דְּתַמָּן אִתְצְרִיפוּ נִשְׁמָתִין, בְּצֵרוּפָא, לְאִתְלַבְּנָא עַד לָא עָאלִין בְּגִנְתָּא דְּעֵדֶן. תְּרֵין מַלְאָכִין שְׁלִיחָן זְמִינִין בְּגִנְתָּא דְּעֵדֶן, וְקַיְימִין לְתַרְעָא, וְצַוְוחִין לְגַבֵּי אִינּוּן מְמָנָן דְּבְהַהוּא אֲתָר דְּגֵיהִנָּם, בְּגִין לְקַבְּלָא הַהִיא נִשְׁמָתָא.

329. After the first time the body received punishment, the soul is taken and put in a place called Ben-hinom. Why is it so called? because there is one place in Gehenom where the souls are cleansed by being burned in a melting pot before entering the Garden of Eden. Two appointed messengers stand ready at the gate of the Garden of Eden and cry to the chieftains in charge over that place in Gehenom to receive that soul.

330. וְהַהִיא נִשְׁמָתָא עַד לָא אִתְלַבְּנַת בְּנוּרָא, אִינּוּן שְׁלִיחָן צַוְוחִין לְגַבַּיְיהוּ, וְאַמְרֵי הִנֹּם. וּבְזִמְנָא דְּהִיא אִתְלַבְּנַת, אִינּוּן מְמָנָן נָפְקִין עִמָּהּ מֵהַהוּא אֲתָר, וְזַמִּינֵי לָהּ לְגַבֵּי פִּתְחָא דְּגִנְתָּא דְּעֵדֶן, דְּתַמָּן אִינּוּן שְׁלִיחָן וְאַמְרֵי לוֹן הִנֹּם. הָא אִינּוּן נִשְׁמָתִין דְּהָא אִתְלַבְּנוּ, כְּדֵין אַעֲלִין לְהַהִיא נִשְׁמָתָא בְּגִנְתָּא דְּעֵדֶן.

330. That soul, before it is bleached by fire, the messengers cry TO THE CHIEFTAINS and say, 'here they are (Heb. *hinam*)'. And while it is cleansed, the chieftains go out with it from that place and put it at the entrance of the Garden of Eden, where the same messengers STAND. THE CHIEFTAINS say TO THE MESSENGERS, 'here they are', NAMELY, here are the purified souls. Then the soul is put in the Garden of Eden. FOR THAT REASON THAT PLACE IN GEHENOM IS CALLED BEN-HINOM.

331. וְכַמָּה אִיהִי תְּבִירָא מִגּוֹ הַהוּא תְּבִירוּ דְּאִתְלַבְּנוּתָא דְּגֵיהִנָּם.

דְּהַהוּא תְּבִירוּ דְּאֶשָּׁא תַּתָּאָה. וְאע״ג דְּנָחִית מִלְּעֵילָא, אֲבָל כֵּיוָן דְּמָטָא
לְאַרְעָא לְתַתָּא, אִיהוּ אֶשָּׁא דְּלָא דָּקִיק, וְנִשְׁמָתָא אִתְעֲנָשָׁא בֵּיהּ,
וְאִתְבָּרַת. כְּדֵין קוּדְשָׁא בְּרִיךְ הוּא אַפִּיק שִׁמְשָׁא דְּנָהִיר מֵאִינּוּן אַרְבַּע
פִּתְחִין דְּנָהֲרִין בִּרְקִיעָא דְּעַל גִּנְתָּא, וּמָטָא לְהַהִיא נִשְׁמָתָא וְאִתְּסִיאַת.
הה״ד וְזָרְחָה לָכֶם יִרְאֵי שְׁמִי שֶׁמֶשׁ צְדָקָה וּמַרְפֵּא בִּכְנָפֶיהָ.

331. How broken IS THE SOUL from the breaking of the purification in Gehenom, because it was broken by lowly fire. And though it descended from above, FROM THE RIVER OF FIRE, yet when it reaches the earth below, the fire there is not fine, and the soul is punished by it and is broken. Then the Holy One, blessed be He, brings out the sun, NAMELY, THE SUPERNAL LIGHT, which illumines the four openings that shine upon the firmament above the Garden of Eden. It reaches the soul and heals it. This is written in, "But to you who fear My name the sun of righteousness shall arise with healing in its wings" (Malachi 3:20).

332. זִמְנָא תִּנְיָינָא, לְבָתַר דְּיָתְבָא בְּגִנְתָּא דְּעֵדֶן דִּלְתַתָּא, כָּל הַהוּא
זִמְנָא דְּיָתְבָא וְעַד כְּעַן לָא אִתְפְּרָשַׁת מֵאִינּוּן מִלִּין דְּחֵיזוּ דְּהַאי עָלְמָא
מִכֹּל וָכֹל. וְכַד סַלְקִין לָהּ לְעֵילָא, אִצְטְרִיךְ לְאִתְפְּרָשָׁא, מִכֹּל חֵיזוּ וּמִכֹּל
מִלִּין דִּלְתַתָּא. וְאַעְבְּרוּ לָהּ בְּהַהוּא נְהַר דִּי נוּר, כְּדֵין נִשְׁמָתָא אִתְלַבְּנַת
בֵּיהּ מִכֹּל וָכֹל. וְנָפְקַת וְאִתְחֲזִיאַת קַמֵּי מָארֵי דְּעָלְמָא בְּרִירָא מִכֹּל
סִטְרִין. כֵּיוָן דְּאִסְתַּכְּלַת בְּהַהוּא נְהוֹרָא אִתְּסִיאַת וְאִשְׁתְּלִימַת מִכֹּלָּא.
וּכְדֵין קַיְימִין אִינּוּן נִשְׁמָתִין בִּלְבוּשִׁין, מִתְעַטְּרִין קַמֵּי מָארֵיהוֹן. זַכָּאָה
חוּלָקֵיהוֹן דְּצַדִּיקַיָּיא בְּעָלְמָא דֵּין וּבְעָלְמָא דְּאָתֵי.

332. The second time, THE SOUL IS PURIFIED BY FIRE after sitting in the lower Garden of Eden for some time, because it has not yet separated itself entirely from all worldly matters. And when it is brought up, TO THE UPPER GARDEN OF EDEN, it must part completely from every worldly sight and matter. For that reason it is immersed in the river of fire, where the soul is thoroughly blanched. Then it comes out to be seen before the Master of the universe, clear on all sides. Having looked at that light, it is completely healed. Then these souls stand clad and adorned before their Master. Happy is the portion of the righteous in this world and in the next.

333. וְאִינּוּן נִשְׁמָתִין דִּבְגִנְּתָּא דְּעֵדֶן דִּלְתַתָּא, שַׁטָאן בְּכָל רֵישֵׁי יַרְחֵי וְשַׁבַּתֵּי, וְסַלְקִין עַד הַהוּא אֲתָר דְּאִקְרֵי חוֹמוֹת יְרוּשָׁלַם. דְּתַמָּן כַּמָה מְמָנָן וּרְתִיכִין דְּנַטְרֵי אִינּוּן חוֹמוֹת. דִּכְתִּיב, עַל חוֹמוֹתַיִךְ יְרוּשָׁלַם הִפְקַדְתִּי שׁוֹמְרִים. וְסַלְקִין עַד הַהוּא אֲתָר, וְלָא עָאלִין לְגוֹ, עַד דְּאִתְלַבְּנָן. וְתַמָּן סַגְדִין, וְחַדָּאן מֵהַהוּא נְהִירוּ, וְתַיְיבִין לְגוֹ גִּנְתָּא.

333. The souls in the lower Garden of Eden roam at every new moon and Shabbat, and rise to the place called 'the walls of Jerusalem', THE OUTSKIRTS OF MALCHUT OF ATZILUT, where some chieftains and Chariots guard the walls, as is written: "I have set watchmen upon your walls, O Jerusalem" (Yeshayah 62:6). They rise to that place but do not enter inside MALCHUT before they are cleansed. There they bow and rejoice in the light, and return into the LOWER Garden OF EDEN.

334. נָפְקִין מִתַּמָּן וְשָׁטָאן בְּעָלְמָא, וְחָמָאן בְּאִינּוּן גּוּפִין דְּחַיָּיבַיָּא, בְּהַהוּא עוֹנְשָׁא דִּילְהוֹן, דִּכְתִּיב, וְיָצְאוּ וְרָאוּ בְּפִגְרֵי הָאֲנָשִׁים הַפּוֹשְׁעִים בִּי כִּי תוֹלַעְתָּם לֹא תָמוּת וְאִשָּׁם לֹא תִכְבֶּה וְהָיוּ דֵרָאוֹן לְכָל בָּשָׂר. מַאי לְכָל בָּשָׂר. לְאִינּוּן שְׁאָר גּוּפִין דִּבְסַחֲרָנַיְיהוּ, וְהָא אוּקְמוּהָ. וּלְבָתַר מְשַׁטְטֵי וּמִסְתַּכְּלָן בְּאִינּוּן מָארֵיהוֹן דְּכְאֵבִין, וּבְנֵי מַרְעִין, וְאִינּוּן דְּסַבְלִין עַל יִחוּדָא דְּמָארֵיהוֹן, וְתָבִין וְאָמְרִין לֵיהּ לִמְשִׁיחָא.

334. They leave GARDEN OF EDEN, and hover about the world and see the bodies of the wicked being punished, as is written: "and they shall go forth, and look upon the carcasses of the men that have rebelled against Me, for their worm shall not die, neither shall their fire be quenched; and they shall be an abhorrence to all flesh" (Yeshayah, 66:24). 'All flesh' refers to the bodies around them, as already explained. Then they roam and watch the sick and suffering, and those who suffer for the unification the Holy Name. They go back TO THE GARDEN OF EDEN and tell that to the Messiah, WHO IS IN THE GARDEN OF EDEN.

335. בְּשַׁעֲתָא דְּאָמְרִין לֵיהּ לִמְשִׁיחָא צַעֲרָא דְיִשְׂרָאֵל בְּגָלוּתְהוֹן, וְאִינּוּן חַיָּיבַיָּא דִּי בְּהוֹן, דְּלָא מִסְתַּכְּלֵי לְמִנְדַּע לְמָארֵיהוֹן, אָרִים קָלָא וּבְכֵי, עַל אִינּוּן חַיָּיבִין דִּבְהוּ. הה"ד, וְהוּא מְחוֹלָל מִפְּשָׁעֵינוּ מְדוּכָּא

מֵעֲוֹנוֹתֵינוּ תַּיְיבִין אִינּוּן נִשְׁמָתִין וְקַיְימִין בְּאַתְרַיְיהוּ.

335. When they tell the Messiah about the sorrow of Yisrael in exile, and about the wicked ones among them, who do not care to know their Master; he raises his voice in crying for the wicked among them, as is written: "But he was shuddered because of our transgressions, heart broken because of out iniquities" (Yeshayah 53:5). The souls return and remain in their places.

336. בְּגִנְתָּא דְּעֵדֶן אִית הֵיכְלָא חֲדָא, דְּאִקְרֵי הֵיכְלָא דִּבְנֵי מַרְעִין. כְּדֵין מָשִׁיחַ עָאל בְּהַהוּא הֵיכְלָא, וְקָרֵי לְכָל מַרְעִין וְכָל כְּאֵבִין, כָּל יְסוּרֵיהוֹן דְּיִשְׂרָאֵל, דְּיֵיתוּן עָלֵיהּ, וְכֻלְּהוּ אַתְיָין עָלֵיהּ. וְאִלְמָלֵא דְּאִיהוּ אָקִיל מֵעֲלַיְיהוּ דְּיִשְׂרָאֵל, וְנָטִיל עָלֵיהּ, לָא הֲוֵי בַּר נָשׁ דְּיָכִיל לְמִסְבַּל יְסוּרֵיהוֹן דְּיִשְׂרָאֵל, עַל עוֹנְשֵׁי דְּאוֹרַיְיתָא. הה"ד אָכֵן חֳלָיֵינוּ הוּא נָשָׂא וְגו'. כְּגַוְונָא דָּא רִבִּי אֶלְעָזָר בְּאַרְעָא.

336. In the Garden of Eden there is one temple called the temple of the sick. The Messiah enters that temple, and calls upon all the diseases, the pains and agonies of Yisrael to descend upon him. And they all descend upon him. But for him, who eases them off Yisrael and takes them upon himself, no man would have been able to bear the sufferings of Yisrael for the punishments of the Torah. This is the meaning of "he has borne our sicknesses..." (Ibid. 4). In the same manner, Rabbi Elazar on earth, USED TO TAKE SUFFERINGS UPON HIMSELF FOR THE SAKE OF YISRAEL.

337. בְּגִין דְּלֵית חוּשְׁבָּנָא, לְאִינּוּן יִסּוּרִין דְּקַיְימִין עָלֵיהּ דְּב"נ בְּכָל יוֹמָא, עַל עוֹנְשֵׁי דְּאוֹרַיְיתָא, וְכֻלְּהוּ נַחְתּוּ לְעָלְמָא, בְּשַׁעֲתָא דְּאִתְיְהִיבַת אוֹרַיְיתָא. וְכַד הֲווֹ יִשְׂרָאֵל בְּאַרְעָא קַדִּישָׁא, בְּאִינּוּן פּוּלְחָנִין וְקָרְבָּנִין דַּהֲווֹ עַבְדֵי, הֲווֹ מְסַלְּקִין כָּל אִינּוּן מַרְעִין וְיִסּוּרִין מֵעָלְמָא. הַשְׁתָּא מָשִׁיחַ מְסַלֵּק לוֹן מִבְּנֵי עָלְמָא, עַד דְּנָפִיק בַּר נָשׁ מֵהַאי עָלְמָא, וּמְקַבֵּל עוֹנְשֵׁיהּ, כְּמָה דְּאִתְּמַר. כַּד אִינּוּן חוֹבִין יַתִּיר דְּעַיְילִין לוֹן לְגוֹ בְּגוֹ גֵּיהִנָּם, בְּאִינּוּן מְדוֹרִין תַּתָּאִין אַחֲרָנִין, וּמְקַבְּלִין עוֹנְשָׁא סַגִּי מִסַּגִיאוּת זוּהֲמָא דִּי בְּנִשְׁמָתָא, כְּדֵין אַדְלִיקוּ נוּרָא יַתִּיר, לְמֵיכַל הַהוּא זוּהֲמָא.

337. The sufferings, daily in wait for man for the punishments of the Torah, are innumerable; and they all descended into the world when the Torah was given. When Yisrael dwelt in the Holy Land, they averted those illnesses and agonies by way of sacrifices. Now, the Messiah removes them from the world, until a man passes away from the world and receives punishment, and as we learned. When the sins are many, the person is put in Gehenom, in the lower sections, where he receives heavy punishment because of the pollution in the soul. Then more fire is kindled to consume that filth.

338. זַכָּאִין אִינוּן דְּנַטְרֵי פִּקּוּדֵי אוֹרַיְיתָא. הַהִיא נְקוּדָה קַדִּישָׁא, דְּאִיהִי בַּעְיָא לְאִשְׁתַּעְשְׁעָא לְעֵילָּא וּלְתַתָּא בְּרוּחֵיהוֹן דְּצַדִּיקַיָּיא, כְּמָה דְּאִתְּמַר. כַּד הַהִיא נְקוּדָה בָּעָא לְאִשְׁתַּעְשְׁעָא לְתַתָּא בְּרוּחֵיהוֹן דְּצַדִּיקַיָּיא, כְּאִמָּא דְּחַדָאת עַל בְּנָהָא, וְאִשְׁתַּעְשְׁעָא בְּהוֹן, ה"ן בְּפַלְגוּת לֵילְיָא אִיהִי נַחְתָּא וְאִשְׁתַּעְשְׁעָא בְּהוּ.

338. Happy are those who observe the precepts of the Torah. Because the holy point, MALCHUT, wants to be delighted above IN ITS PLACE, and below, IN THE GARDEN OF EDEN, with the spirits of the righteous, as we learned. And when the point down below wants to be delighted IN THE GARDEN OF EDEN by the souls of the righteous, it is like a mother, happy and delighted with her children. So at midnight it descends INTO THE GARDEN OF EDEN, and is delighted by them.

25. The firmament above Malchut

A Synopsis

Rabbi Shimon speaks now about the higher firmament above Malchut that is embroidered with holy colors, that are Chesed, Gvurah, Tiferet and Malchut. In this firmament the 22 letters are written and adorned with crowns that are an aspect of Binah. Rabbi Shimon tells us of Yud Hei Vav Hei, of the 32 paths of wisdom, and of the additional Vav to make Vav Yud Hei Vav Hei, which then alludes to male and female. He tells of the lights, the colors, the Chariots and armies that are sustained by the holy dew that is the eternal flame of judgment. We learn of the firmaments of the Other Side, shining with worldly matters, and other firmaments above; all colors come from the eighth firmament, Binah. God is called by name, and this is significant because a name means perception; what we do not perceive we can not call by name. Therefore from here upward no wise man can by use of his intelligence know or grasp any but a slight illumination. When one worships his Master in prayer, will and intention he connects his will as a fire to coal, and unites the lower and higher firmaments. Rabbi Shimon tells us that the secret of secrets where all thoughts and wills are kept is in the secret of the Endless Light, that should be meditated on every day. At night the souls of the righteous return up to their source. The chieftains who are appointed over these souls sacrifice them as fragrant sacrifice to their Master. Then Malchut gives the souls birth as before; this is the secret of "they are new every morning."

339. רָקִיעַ דְּקָאמְרָן דְּקַיְימָא עַל גִּנְתָּא, אִיהִי קַיְימָא עַל ד' רֵישֵׁי חֵיוָון, וְאִינּוּן ד' אַתְוָון דְּקָאמְרָן, אִינּוּן רָזָא דְּד' חֵיוָן. וְהַאי רְקִיעָא קַיְימָא עָלַיְיהוּ, כְּמָה דְּאִתְּמַר. רְקִיעַ דְּהַהִיא נְקוּדָה, קַיְימָא לְעֵילָּא, עַל אִינּוּן ד' חֵיוָון עִלָּאִין דְּקָאמְרָן, וְהַהוּא רְקִיעָא אִיהוּ אִתְרְקַם בְּגַוְונִין קַדִּישִׁין.

339. The firmament above the garden stands upon the four heads of the living creatures, that are the four letters MEM, RESH, GIMEL AND NUN, said to be the mystery of the living creatures, MICHAEL, GABRIEL, RAPHAEL AND NURIEL. And that firmament stands upon them as said. The firmament of the point, THE FIRMAMENT ABOVE MALCHUT, stands upon high four living creatures as said. THEY ARE SUPERIOR COMPARED TO THOSE OF THE LOWER GARDEN OF EDEN. That firmament ABOVE

MALCHUT OF ATZILUT is embroidered with holy colors. AS THERE ARE
FOUR COLORS IN THE FIRMAMENT ABOVE THE LOWER GARDEN, SO IS
THE UPPER FIRMAMENT ABOVE MALCHUT EMBROIDERED WITH COLORS.
'THE ZOHAR' EXPLAINS TO US THAT ALL THAT WAS SAID CONCERNING
THE FIRMAMENT OVER THE LOWER GARDEN OF EDEN, ALSO APPLIES
FOR THE UPPER FIRMAMENT ABOVE MALCHUT OF ATZILUT.

340. בְּהַאי רָקִיעַ אִסְתַּכְּלָן אַרְבַּע חֵיוָון, וְכָל אִינּוּן חַיָּילִין לְתַתָּא. כַּד
הַאי רָקִיעַ אַנְהִיר בִּגְוָונוֹי וְנָצִיץ, כְּדֵין יַדְעִין כָּל אִינּוּן רְתִיכִין, וְכָל
אִינּוּן חַיָּילִין וּמַשִׁירְיָין, דְּהָא טַרְפָּא דִּילְהוֹן אִזְדַּמַּן. רְקִיעָא דָא
מְרֻקְמָא בְּכָל גַּוְונִין קַדִּישִׁין, בֵּיהּ קַיְימִין אַרְבַּע פִּתְחִין רְשִׁימִין, בְּאַרְבַּע
אַתְוָון מְנַצְצָן.

340. The four living creatures and all the armies below observe at the
firmament ABOVE THE UPPER MALCHUT, to see when it is shining and
glittering in its colors. THE FOUR MENTIONED COLORS, CHESED,
GVURAH, TIFERET AND MALCHUT WITHIN THE FIRMAMENT ITSELF,
SHINE THROUGH THE PORTALS. The Chariots and all the armies and
legions know then that there is food to be had, FOR THEY RECEIVE IT
THROUGH THE PORTALS. This firmament is embroidered with holy colors,
THE FOUR LIGHTS OF CHESED, GVURAH, TIFERET AND MALCHUT.
Therein are four doors, THROUGH EACH SHINES ONE COLOR. AND THE
LIGHTS are impressed upon four glittering letters.

341. פִּתְחָא חֲדָא רְשִׁימָא לִסְטַר מִזְרָח, וּבֵיהּ קַיְימָא בְּהַהוּא פִּתְחָא אָת
חַד, וְהַהוּא אָת אִיהוּ א', וְדָא נָצִיץ וְסָלִיק וְנָחִית בְּהַאי פִּתְחָא. פִּתְחָא
דָא נָהִיר וְנָצִיץ מִנְּצִיצוּ עִלָּאָה. וְהַאי אָת נָצִיץ וּבָלִיט בְּגַוֵּיהּ, וְאִיהִי
נַחְתָּא וְסַלְקָא, וְאִתְרְשִׁים בְּהַהוּא פִּתְחָא.

341. One portal is to the east, TIFERET. One letter stands in it, SAME AS IN
THE FIRMAMENT ABOVE THE GARDEN, ONLY THERE STANDS THE LETTER
RESH, THE FIRST LETTER OF RAPHAEL, AND HERE STANDS ALEPH, THE
FIRST LETTER OF THE NAME ADONAI. This letter glitters and goes up and
down inside the portal. This portal is shining and scintillating from the
supernal glittering, THAT IS FROM ONE OF THE COLORS OF CHESED,

GVURAH, TIFERET AND MALCHUT, THE LIGHTS WITHIN THE FIRMAMENT ITSELF. The letter ALEPH glitters and stands out in it, going up and down, and gets marked in that opening.

342. פִּתְחָא תִּנְיָינָא, רְשִׁימָא לְסְטַר צָפוֹן, וּבֵיהּ קַיְימָא אָת חַד, וְאִיהִי אָת ד'. וְדָא קַיְימָא וְנָצְצָא, סַלְקָא וְנַחְתָּא, וְלָהֲטָא בְּהַהוּא פִּתְחָא. לִזְמְנִין נָצִיץ בִּנְצִיצוּ, וּלְזִמְנִין אִתְטְמַר הַהוּא נְהוֹרָא, וְלָא נָהִיר. וְעַל דָּא, אָת דָּא לָא קַיְימָא בְּקִיוּמָא תָּדִיר, וְאָת דָּא אִתְרְשִׁים בְּהַהוּא פִּתְחָא.

342. The second portal is inscribed in the northern side, GVURAH. In it stands one letter, the letter Dalet OF THE NAME ADONAI. It stands glittering, going up and down and glowing in that portal TO THE NORTH. Sometimes it glitters sparklingly and sometimes it is concealed and therefore does not shine. Therefore this letter is not stable in its presence. This letter is stamped upon that door.

343. פִּתְחָא תְּלִיתָאָה, אִיהוּ פִּתְחָא דְּקַיְימָא לְסְטַר מַעֲרָב, וּבֵיהּ קַיְימָא אָת חַד, דְּאִתְרְשִׁים וְאִתְנְהִיר בְּהַהוּא פִּתְחָא. וְדָא אִיהוּ אָת נ', וְהַאי אָת נָצִיץ בִּנְצִיצוּ בְּהַהוּא פִּתְחָא.

343. The third door is to the west, MALCHUT. In it stands one letter stamped upon the door and shines there. This is the letter Nun OF THE NAME ADONAI. This letters glitters sparkingly in that portal.

344. פִּתְחָא רְבִיעָאָה, דָּא אִיהוּ פִּתְחָא דְּקַיְימָא לְסְטַר דָּרוֹם, וּבֵיהּ קַיְימָא רְשִׁימוּ דְּחַד נְקוּדָה תַּתָּאָה זְעֵירָא, דְּאִתְחֲזֵי וְלָא אִתְחֲזֵי, וְדָא אִיהִי אָת י', וְאִלֵּין אַרְבַּע אַתְוָון לְאַרְבַּע סִטְרִין, נָצְצִין בְּהַהוּא רָקִיע, בְּאִינּוּן פִּתְחִין.

344. The fourth door is to the south, CHESED. In it stands the impression of a lower small point, visible yet invisible. This is the letter Yud OF THE NAME ADONAI. These four letters OF ADONAI (ALEPH-DALET-NUN-YUD) GLITTER to the four sides of the firmament, in the FOUR doors AT ITS ENDS.

345. בְּהַאי רָקִיעַ רְשִׁימִין אַתְוָון אַחֲרָנִין, בְּכִתְרִין עַל רֵישַׁיְיהוּ. וְאִינוּן עֶשְׂרִין וּתְרֵין אַתְוָון, מִתְעַטְרָן בְּכִתְרִין. רְקִיעָא דָא נָטִיל וְסָחֲרָא עַל גַּבֵּי חֵיוָון, בִּרְשִׁימוּ דְּאַתְוָון, רָזָא דְּחוּשְׁבַּן דִּיחוּדָא, בְּרָזָא דְּצֵרוּפָא חֲדָא וְאִינוּן: א״ט ב״ח ג״ז ד״ו.

345. In this firmament, other letters are written, with crowns on their heads. These are the twenty two letters adorned with crowns. THE TWENTY TWO LETTERS ARE THE MYSTERY OF ZEIR ANPIN INCLUDED IN THIS FIRMAMENT OF MALCHUT. THE CROWNS ABOVE THEIR HEADS ARE AN ASPECT OF BINAH, WHICH IS KETER OF ZEIR ANPIN. FOR THE ROOT OF EACH LETTER, NAMED CROWN, COMES FROM BINAH. This firmament moves and revolves over the living creatures, upon which the letters are marked, based on the reckoning of the unity, the secret of one ALPHABETICAL combination, that are: Aleph-Tet, Bet-Chet, Gimel-Zayin, Dalet-Vav.

346. אִלֵּין אַתְוָון סָחֲרָן בְּהַהוּא רָקִיעַ, בְּרָזָא דְּאַתְוָון אַחֲרָנִין, עִלָּאִין קַדִּישִׁין סְתִימִין. וְאִינוּן אַתְוָון אַחֲרָנִין סְתִימִין, סָחֲרִין לְהַהוּא רָקִיעַ, וּכְדֵין אִתְחֲזְיָין אִלֵּין אַתְוָון בְּגִלְגּוּלָא, דְּאִינוּן א״ט ב״ח, וּרְשִׁימִין בְּהַאי רְקִיעָא.

346. These letters, ALEPH-TET, BET-CHET, GIMEL-ZAYIN, DALET-VAV, go round this firmament based on the secret of other high, holy and undisclosed letters, THAT COME FROM BINAH. And those other undisclosed letters revolve round that firmament, and are then seen when turned into the letters mentioned before – Aleph-Tet, Bet-Chet, GIMEL-ZAYIN, DALET-VAV and are stamped upon this firmament.

347 בְּשַׁעֲתָא דְּאִתְנְהִיר הַאי רְקִיעָא, אִתְנַהֲרָן בֵּיהּ אַרְבַּע רָזִין דִּשְׁמָהָן קַדִּישִׁין, וְאִינוּן צֵרוּפָא בְּצֵרוּפִין דִּתְלָתִין וּתְרֵין שְׁבִילִין. כְּדֵין נָחִית טַלָּא מֵהַאי רְקִיעָא, בְּאִינוּן אַתְוָון דְּרָזָא דִּשְׁמָא קַדִּישָׁא, וְאִתְזָנוּ כָּל אִינוּן רְתִיכִין, וְכָל אִינוּן חַיָּילִין וּמַשִׁירְיָין קַדִּישִׁין, וְנַטְלֵי כֻּלְּהוּ בְּחֶדְוָה.

347. When this firmament shines, four secrets are luminous in it, THE FOUR LETTERS YUD HEI VAV HEI, of the Holy Names in combinations. THESE ARE THE TWELVE COMBINATIONS OF THE YUD HEI VAV HEI of the thirty two paths. NAMELY, IT ILLUMINATES THIRTY TWO PATHS OF WISDOM UPON THE TWELVE NAMES. Then dew, THE HOLY ABUNDANCE, descends from this firmament by these letters in the mystery of the Holy Name, THAT IS, WITH THE TWELVE COMBINATIONS OF YUD HEI VAV HEI. And all the holy Chariots, armies and legions are sustained and gladly receive it.

348. בְּשַׁעֲתָא דְּדִינָא תַּלְיָיא, אִלֵּין אַתְוָון אִתְטַמָּרוּ, וְאִתְגְּנִיזוּ ד' גּוֹ ד', וְאִינוּן ט"ח ז"ו. בְּשַׁעֲתָא דְּאִלֵּין אִתְגְּנִיזוּ וְאִתְטַמָּרוּ, כְּדֵין קָלָא דְּסִטְר צָפוֹן אִתְּעַר, וְיָדְעֵי דְּדִינָא שַׁרְיָיא עַל עָלְמָא. וּבְהַאי רְקִיעָא אִתְרְשִׁים גַּוְונָא חֲדָא, דְּכָלִיל כָּל גַּוְונִין.

348. When Judgment impends upon the world, the letters hide and are concealed inside the four LETTERS, NAMELY ALEPH, BET, GIMEL, DALET WHICH ARE THE ROOTS, hide and disappear, and these, Tet, Chet, Zayin Vav are left, NAMELY, THE BRANCHES WITHOUT THE ROOTS. Once ALEPH, BET, GIMEL, DALET are concealed and hide, a voice resounds in the north side, WHERE JUDGMENTS LIE, and makes it known that Judgment impends upon the world. In this firmament, one color is imprinted, that includes all other colors. THIS IS MALCHUT RECEIVING FROM THE THREE COLUMNS, WHICH SYMBOLIZE THE THREE COLORS.

349. כַּד נָטִיל הַאי רְקִיעָא מִסִּטְרָא דְּמִזְרָח, אִינוּן אַרְבַּע רֵישִׁין דְּקָאמְרָן, בְּאַרְבַּע אַתְוָון, נַטְלִין כֻּלְּהוּ בְּמַטְלָנִין, וְסַלְקֵי בִּסְלִיקוּ לְעֵילָּא. וְכַד אִינוּן נַטְלִין וְסַלְקִין לְעֵילָּא, אִסְתַּלְּקַת מַאן דְּאִסְתַּלְּקַת. וְאַתְוָון אִתְהַדָּרוּ וְאִתְחֲזִיִּין בִּשְׁלִימוּ, בְּרָזָא קַדְמָאָה, א"ט ב"ח ג"ז ד"ו, וְאִתְרְקַם הַהוּא רְקִיעָא, כְּדֵין אִתְנְהִיר בִּנְהִירוּ.

349. When the firmament on the east side, THE CENTRAL COLUMN, travels; the four heads, THE FOUR ROOTS, which allude to the four letters, ALEPH, BET, GIMEL AND DALET, all travel and ascend, THAT IS, THEY DISAPPEAR. And when they disappear, something disappears, TO WIT, THE ILLUMINATION OF CHOCHMAH DOES SINCE THE ROOTS OF ALEPH-TET, BET-CHET,

GIMEL-ZAYIN, DALET-VAV GO UP. AFTERWARDS, the letters ALEPH, BET, GIMEL AND DALET reappear WITHIN THE BRANCHES whole like in the first combination Aleph-Tet, Bet-Chet, Gimel-Zayin, Dalet-Vav. They are woven into the firmament and it illuminates with the light OF CHOCHMAH.

350. וְכַד הַאי רְקִיעָא אִתְנְהִיר כְּמִלְּקַדְמִין, בְּאִלֵּין אַתְוָון, כּוּלְּהוּ אִתְהַדְרוּ וְשָׁאֲגֵי לְמִטְרַף טַרְפָּא וּמְזוֹנָא. כֵּיוָן דְּאִינּוּן שָׁאֲגֵי וְסַלְּקִין קָלָא, הַהוּא קָלָא אִשְׁתְּמַע לְעֵילָא לְעֵילָא, וּכְדֵין נַטְלָא בִּרְכָאן וְקִדּוּשָׁן, מַאן דְּנַטְלָא.

350. When the firmament shines upon the letters as before, UPON THE LETTERS, ALEPH-TET, BET-CHET...everyone roars again and seeks food. Once they roar and cry aloud, it is heard above, and those WHO ARE WORTHY come to collect blessings and holy things.

351. סָחֲרָן אַתְוָון וּמִתְגַּלְגְּלָן, וְסָחֲרָן הַהוּא רְקִיעָא, וְקָיְימָן אִינּוּן אַתְוָון לִסְטַר דָּרוֹם. כֵּיוָן דְּקָיְימִין אִינּוּן אַתְוָון לִסְטַר דָּרוֹם, סַלְּקִין וְנָצְצָן בִּנְצִיצוּ וְלַהֲטִין. כְּדֵין בְּאֶמְצָעִיתָא דְּהַהוּא רְקִיעָא, רְשִׁימוּ חַד אִתְרְשִׁים, וְהַהוּא רְשִׁימוּ אִיהוּ אָת חַד, וְאִיהוּ י'. כֵּיוָן דְּאַת דָּא אִתְרְשִׁים וְאִתְחֲזְיָיא, כְּדֵין לָהֲטִין אֲבַתְרֵיהּ, תְּלַת אַתְוָון אַחֲרָנִין, וְאִינּוּן הו"ה.

351. The letters ALEPH-TET, BET-CHET...turn around and revolve ROUND THE THREE COLUMNS. They go round the firmament ABOVE MALCHUT and come to stand on the southern side. They mount glittering and sparkling in the glow. Then in the middle of that firmament an impression is stamped. This impression is comprised of one letter Yud. Once it is written down and seen, the other three letters, Hei Vav Hei start to glow AND THE NAME YUD HEI VAV HEI IS ILLUMINATING.

352. אִלֵּין אַתְוָון מְנַצְצָן בְּאֶמְצָעוּ דְּהַאי רְקִיעָא, סַלְּקִין וְנַחְתִּין, מְלַהֲטִין בִּתְרֵיסַר לַהֲטִין. כְּדֵין לְבָתַר דְּאִלֵּין תְּרֵיסַר זִמְנִין מְלַהֲטָן, נַחְתָּא מַאן דְּנַחְתָּא, וְאִתְכְּלִילַת בְּאִינּוּן אַתְוָון, וְאִתְעַטְּרַת בְּהוּ, וְלָא

אִתְיָידָעַת. כְּדֵין, כֻּלְּהוּ חַיָּילִין, וְכָלְהוּ מַשִׁירְיָין, בְּחֶידוּ. וְסַלְּקִין שִׁירִין
וְתוּשְׁבְּחָן.

352. These letters, YUD HEI VAV HEI, glitter in the middle of the firmament, go up and down and burn, glowing with twelve glitters, NAMELY, WITH THE TWELVE PERMUTATIONS OF THE HOLY NAME. After they burn and glow twelve times, something descends, THE ILLUMINATION OF CHOCHMAH. It is absorbed in the letters OF THE TWELVE PERMUTATIONS OF THE HOLY NAME YUD HEI VAV HEI, crowned by them and becomes unknown. Then all the troops and camps rejoice and utter songs and hymns.

353. רְקִיעָא דָא נָטְלָא תִּנְיָינוּת, וְסַחֲרָא וּמִתְגַּלְגְּלָא, וְאִינּוּן אַתְוָון
קַדְמָאֵי דְּקָאמָרַן, דְּאִינּוּן א״ט ב״ח, כֻּלְּהוּ אִתְכְּלִילוּ בְּאִינּוּן אַתְוָון
עִלָּאִין, רָזָא דִּשְׁמָא קַדִּישָׁא דְּקָאמָרַן, וְסַחֲרָן הַהוּא רְקִיעָא, וְקַיְימִין
אִינּוּן אַתְוָון דַּהֲווֹ בְּאֶמְצָעִיתָא רָזָא דִּשְׁמָא קַדִּישָׁא, כֻּלְּהוּ אִתְרְשִׁימוּ
לְסְטַר צָפוֹן, וְאִתְרְשִׁימוּ וְלָא אִתְרְשִׁימוּ. לֵית מַאן דְּיִסְתָּכַּל בְּהַהוּא
סְטְרָא, כֻּלְּהוּ אִתְחַפְיָין, וְאָמְרֵי בְּקָל נְעִימוּ בָּרוּךְ כְּבוֹד יְיָ' מִמְּקוֹמוֹ.
אִתְחַפְיָין מִסְּטְרָא דְּצָפוֹן וְאָמְרִין דָּא אִתְחַפְיָין מִכָּל סְטְרִין וְאַמְרִין דָּא.

353. The firmament travels a second time, revolves and turns round THE THREE COLUMNS. And the first letters, mentioned above, Aleph-Tet, Bet-Chet...are all included within the supernal letters that are in the mystery of Holy Name, YUD HEI VAV HEI as we said. They turn round the firmament, and the letters, YUD HEI VAV HEI, the secret of the Holy Name, which were standing in its midst, were imprinted on the northern, LEFT side. Imprinted and not imprinted, because no one looks at that side, NAMELY, TO DRAW CHOCHMAH WHICH IS THE SECRET OF SIGHT. All are wrapped BY CHOCHMAH and say in a pleasant voice, "Blessed be the glory of Hashem from His place" (Yechezkel 3:12). They wrap themselves in the northern side, WHICH IS THE SECRET OF THE LEFT COLUMN, and say it. Then they are wrapped on all sides and say it, NAMELY, "BLESSED BE THE GLORY OF HASHEM FROM HIS PLACE." THE REASON IS THAT THE NORTH SIDE COMPRISES ALL THE THREE SIDES. THE SENSE IS THAT CHOCHMAH IS REVEALED ONLY WITHIN MALCHUT THAT RECEIVES FROM THE THREE

COLUMNS, AND NOT WITHIN THE THREE COLUMNS THEMSELVES.

354. רְקִיעָא דָא סָחֲרָא כְּמִלְּקַדְמִין, וְאִתְגַּלְגְּלָא מִסִּטְרָא לְסִטְרָא. כְּדֵין קָל נְעִימוּ דִּמְשִׁירְיָין סַגִּיאִין בְּסִטְרָא דָא, וְקָל נְעִימוּ דִּמְשִׁירְיָין סַגִּיאִין בְּסִטְרָא דָא, וְכֵן לְד' סִטְרִין. בְּהַהִיא שַׁעֲתָא הַהוּא רְקִיעָא אִתְנְהִיר בִּנְהִירוּ אַחֲרָא, יַתִּיר מִכְּמָה דַּהֲוָה, וְקַיְּימָא בִּנְהִירוּ בִּגְוָון אַחֲרָא, כְּלִילָא בְּכָל גְּוָונִין.

354. AFTER EXPLAINING THE ACTIONS DONE IN THE FIRMAMENT ON ITS THREE SIDES, EAST, SOUTH AND NORTH, WHICH ARE THE THREE COLUMNS; HE NOW EXPLAINS THE ACTIONS DONE ON THE WEST SIDE OF THE FIRMAMENT, WHICH IS MALCHUT THAT RECEIVES FROM ALL THE SIDES TOGETHER. HE SAYS, this firmament revolves as before and sways from side to side, TO ALL FOUR SIDES, UNTIL IT REACHES WEST, WHICH IS MALCHUT. Then a pleasant voice of many troops OF ANGELS arises from this side, and a pleasant voice of many troops on that side, and so on all sides, EAST, SOUTH, NORTH AND WEST. At that time the firmament illuminates with another, greater light than it used to ILLUMINATE IN THE THREE SIDES, FOR IN IT THE LIGHT OF CHOCHMAH IS REVEALED, WHICH IS REVEALED ONLY IN MALCHUT. It illuminates, displaying another color, that comprises all colors. FOR MALCHUT COMPRISES THE THREE COLORS IN THE THREE COLUMNS.

355. וְאִלֵּין אַתְוָון דְּקָאמְרָן, סַלְּקִין לְעֵילָא בְּהַהוּא רְקִיעָא, וּמְקַבְּלִין לְאָת חַד דְּאִיהִי עִלָּאָה, דְּקָא מִתְחַבְּרָא בִּשְׁמָא דָא, דְּאִלֵּין אַתְוָון. בְּגִין דְּאע"ג דְּאִלֵּין אַתְוָון דִּשְׁמָא קַדִּישָׁא, הַאי אִיהוּ שְׁמָא דְּאִתְכְּלִיל לְתַתָּא, בְּגִין דְּרָזָא דָא אִתְכְּלִיל לְעֵילָא, וְאִתְכְּלִיל לְתַתָּא, וְכַד אִתְכְּלִיל לְתַתָּא, אִלֵּין אַתְוָון סַלְּקִין לְקַבְּלָה לְאָת חַד דְּהָא מֵהַהוּא אָת אִתְזְנוּ אִלֵּין אַתְוָון לְתַתָּא, וְהַהוּא אָת אִיהוּ ו'. וְנָחִית וְאִתְחַבְּרוּ אִלֵּין אַתְוָון. בְּהַהוּא אָת, וּכְדֵין כֻּלְּהוּ בְּעִטּוּרָא חֲדָא, וְאִתְעֲבֵיד שְׁמָא שְׁלִים.

355. These letters we mentioned, YUD HEI VAV HEI, mount up to that firmament, NAMELY, TO ZEIR ANPIN, where they receive one supernal letter

FROM IT, which unites with the name of those letters YUD HEI VAV HEI. For though these letters are of the Holy Name, YUD HEI VAV HEI, NEVERTHELESS this name is included below, THAT IS, IN THE FIRMAMENT OF MALCHUT. For the secret of that name is included above IN ZEIR ANPIN and below IN MALCHUT. And when it is included below IN MALCHUT, the letters OF YUD HEI VAV HEI go up to receive one letter FROM ZEIR ANPIN, for the letters YUD HEI VAV HEI below, IN MALCHUT, are sustained by that letter. It is the letter Vav, which descends INTO MALCHUT, where the letters, YUD HEI VAV HEI, are united with it, NAMELY 'VAV YUD HEI VAV HEI', IN WHICH THE FIRST VAV INDICATES ZEIR ANPIN CONNECTED WITH THE HOLY NAME WITHIN MALCHUT, BASED ON THE PRINCIPLE OF 'HE AND HIS COURTHOUSE'. Then they become one crown and one complete name is formed.

356. לְתַתָּא, שְׁמָא שְׁלִים וְלָא שְׁלִים. שְׁמָא שְׁלִים בַּחֲמֵשׁ אַתְוָון אִיהוּ, וַיְדֹנַ״ד. רָזָא דְּכַר וְנוּקְבָא בִּרְמִיזוּ. שְׁמָא שְׁלִים בְּתֵשַׁע אַתְוָון, אִינּוּן יְדֹנַ״ד אֱלֹהִים. דָּא אִיהוּ שְׁמָא שְׁלִים מִכֹּלָּא. שְׁמָא אַחֲרָא אִיהוּ בִּרְמִיזוּ, וְאִיהוּ בְּחָמֵשׁ כְּדְקָאָמְרָן. אֲבָל דָּא אִיהוּ שְׁלִים בְּכֹלָּא.

356. THE HOLY NAME YUD HEI VAV HEI below is complete yet incomplete. IT IS COMPLETE IN ITSELF, AND INCOMPLETE, BEING INCLUDED IN THE ASPECT OF MALCHUT. A whole name includes five letters, VAV YUD HEI VAV HEI, IN WHICH THE VAV FROM ZEIR ANPIN, UNITED WITH YUD HEI VAV HEI, ALLUDES TO ZEIR ANPIN AND ITS COURTHOUSE, MALCHUT. This is the secret which alludes to male and female, FOR THE VAV ALLUDES TO MALE, AND YUD HEI VAV HEI ALLUDES TO FEMALE. THE ENTIRE whole name INDICATING COMPLETENESS consists of nine letters, that are Yud Hei Vav Hei, Elohim, WHEREBY YUD HEI VAV HEI, ALLUDES TO MALE AND Elohim TO FEMALE. Together the name is completely whole. The other name, Vav YUD HEI VAV HEI, is an allusion, FOR THE VAV REFERS TO MALE, and contains five letters as said. But this NAME OF NINE LETTERS YUD HEI VAV HEI, ELOHIM is entirely complete.

357. כֵּיוָן דְּמִתְחַבְּרָן אִלֵּין אַתְוָון, הַהוּא רְקִיעָא אַנְהִיר בִּתְלָתִין וּתְרֵין נְהוֹרִין, כְּדֵין כֹּלָּא אִיהוּ בְּחֶדְוָוה, כֹּלָּא קָאִים בְּרָזָא חֲדָא עֵילָּא וְתַתָּא. כָּל אִינּוּן רְתִיכִין, וְכָל אִינּוּן מַשִׁירְיָין, כֻּלְּהוּ קַיְימִין בְּרָזָא דִּשְׁלִימוּ.

וְכָל דַּרְגִּין מְתַקְּנָן עַל אַתְרַיְיהוּ, כָּל חַד וְחַד כַּדְקָא יֵאוֹת.

357. When the letters are united, NAMELY, VAV-HEI-VAV-YUD-HEI, the firmament illuminates with thirty two lights, TO WIT, THE THIRTY TWO PATHS OF CHOCHMAH. Then all is filled with joy, and is one mystery, above and below. All the Chariots and the troops are in the secret of completeness, and all the grades are established in their place, each as it ought.

358. בְּהַאי רְקִיעָא קָאֵים לִסְטַר צָפוֹן, חַד שַׁלְהוֹבָא נָהִיר, דְּלָא שָׁכִיךְ תָּדִיר, וְאִיהוּ רָשִׁים בְּאַתְוָון אַחֲרָנִין, לִימִין, וְאִינּוּן עֶשֶׂר שְׁמָהָן, וְסַלְקִין לְשַׁבְעִין שְׁמָהָן, וְכֻלְּהוּ רְשִׁימִין בְּהַאי רְקִיעָא, וְנַהֲרִין כֻּלְּהוּ כַּחֲדָא.

358. In the firmament OF MALCHUT, to the north, WHERE CHOCHMAH IS LUMINOUS WITHIN MALCHUT, there is one flame that shines forever. TO WIT, THE JUDGEMENT VERDICT WHERE CHOCHMAH IS REVEALED. THIS JUDGMENT IS NAMED 'FLAME'. Other letters are imprinted to its right, the ten names turned into seventy names. THEY DERIVE FROM THE SEVENTY TWO NAMES OF THE HOLY NAME OF 72 (AYIN BET) LETTERS, AS WAS SAID, THAT THEY ARE THE SECRET OF SEVENTY MEMBERS OF THE SANHEDRIN AND THE TWO WITNESSES. All are engraved upon this firmament and illuminate together.

359. מֵהַאי רְקִיעָא, נַטְלִין כָּל אִינּוּן רְקִיעִין דִּלְתַתָּא, דִּלְסְטַר קְדוּשָׁה, עַד דְּמָטוּ לְאִינּוּן רְקִיעִין אַחֲרָנִין דִּלְסְטַר אַחֲרָא, וְאִלֵּין אִקְרוּן יְרִיעוֹת עִזִּים, כְּד"א וַיַּעַשׂ יְרִיעֹת עִזִּים לְאֹהֶל עַל הַמִּשְׁכָּן.

359. From this firmament travel all the lower firmaments on the side of holiness, until they reach the other firmaments of the Other Side, called "curtains of goats' hair," as is written: "And he made curtains of goats' hair for the tent over the tabernacle" (Shemot 36:14).

360. בְּגִין דְּאִית יְרִיעוֹת וְאִית יְרִיעוֹת, יְרִיעוֹת הַמִּשְׁכָּן, אִינּוּן יְרִיעוֹת דְּאִקְרוּן רְקִיעֵי חִיוָון דְּמַשְׁכְּנָא קַדִּישָׁא. יְרִיעוֹת עִזִּים. אִינּוּן רְקִיעִין אַחֲרָנִין דְּסִטְרָא אַחֲרָא. אִלֵּין רְקִיעִין בְּרָזָא דִּרְתִּיכִין דְּרוּחִין קַדִּישִׁין.

וְאִלֵּין רְקִיעִין דִּלְבַר, דְּקַיְימִין בְּמִלִּין דְּעָלְמָא, וְאִינּוּן סִטְרִין דְּתִיּוּבְתִּין, וְעוֹבָדִין דְּגוּפָא. וְאִלֵּין חַפְיָין עַל אִינּוּן רְקִיעִין דִּלְגוֹ, כִּקְלִיפָה עַל מוֹחָא. רְקִיעִין דִּלְגוֹ אִינּוּן הַהוּא קְלִישׁוּ, דְּקַיְימָא עַל מוֹחָא, וְאִלֵּין אִקְרוּן שָׁמַיִם לַיְיָ'. לִשְׁמָא חֲדָא דָּא דִּלְתַתָּא.

360. There are curtains and curtains. The curtains of the tabernacle are called the firmaments of the living creatures of the holy tabernacle. The curtains of goats' hair are other firmaments of the Other Side. These firmaments OF THE TABERNACLE are based on the secret of the Chariots of the holy spirits, and those firmaments outside, THE CURTAINS OF GOATS' HAIR, shine with worldly matters, and are considered aspects of repentance and bodily worship BY PEOPLE. And they cover the firmaments inside as a shell covers the fruit. The firmaments inside are like a thin SKIN MEMBRANE around the brain, and called "the heavens of Hashem," NAMELY, the one name YUD HEI VAV HEI, down below IN MALCHUT.

361. רְקִיעִין אַחֲרָנִין לְעֵילָא, וְאִינּוּן רְקִיעִין פְּנִימָאִין, דְּאִקְרוּן רְקִיעֵי הַחַיּוֹת, דְּאִינּוּן רָזָא דִּשְׁמָא קַדִּישָׁא, בְּרָזָא דְּחֵיוָון רַבְרְבָן עִלָּאִין, וְאִלֵּין אִינּוּן רָזִין דְּאַתְוָון עִלָּאִין, בְּרָזֵי דְּאוֹרַיְיתָא, כְּלָלָא דְּעֶשְׂרִין וּתְרֵין אַתְוָון, מְחַקְּקָן רְשִׁימִין, דְּנַפְקֵי מִגּוֹ רְקִיעָא עִלָּאָה תְּמִינָאָה. דְּאִיהוּ רְקִיעַ דְּעַל גַּבֵּי חֵיוָון עִלָּאִין, וְהַאי אִיהוּ דְּלֵית לֵיהּ חֵיזוּ. הַאי אִיהוּ טָמִיר וְגָנִיז, לֵית בֵּיהּ גָּוֶון.

361. There are other firmaments above: the inner firmaments OF ZEIR ANPIN, named the firmaments of the living creatures. They are the secret of the Holy Name, YUD HEI VAV HEI, according to the mystery of the large upper living creatures, CHESED, GVURAH, TIFERET AND MALCHUT FROM THE CHEST UPWARD OF ZEIR ANPIN. They are the secret of the high letters of the mysteries of the Torah, NAMELY, the whole of the twenty two letters engraved and impressed, coming from the eighth firmament, BINAH, above the high living creatures, CHESED, GVURAH, TIFERET AND MALCHUT OF ZEIR ANPIN. This FIRMAMENT has no visibility, concealed and hidden without hues.

362. כָּל גַּוְונִין מִנֵּיהּ נַפְקֵי. בֵּיהּ לֵית גָּוֶון, לָא אִתְחֲזֵי, וְלָא אִתְגַּלְיָיא,

הַאי אִיהוּ דְּאַפִּיק כָּל נְהוֹרִין. בֵּיהּ לָא אִתְחֲזֵי, לָא נְהִירוּ, וְלָא חָשׁוֹךְ, וְלָא גַּוְוּן כְּלָל, בַּר נִשְׁמָתִין דְּצַדִּיקַיָּיא, דְּחָמָאן מִגּוֹ רְקִיעָא תַּתָּאָה, כְּמִבָּתַר כּוֹתְלָא, נְהִירוּ דְּאַפִּיק וְנָהִיר הַאי רְקִיעָא עִלָּאָה, וְהַהוּא נְהִירוּ דְּלָא פָּסַק, לֵית מַאן דְּיָדַע לֵיהּ, לֵית מַאן דְּקָאִים בֵּיהּ.

362. All the colors are coming from THE EIGHTH FIRMAMENT, BINAH. In ITSELF, there are no colors, it is neither seen nor appears. This is the meaning of it letting out all luminaries, FOR ALL MOCHIN OF THE THREE COLUMNS OF BINAH COME OUT, but in ITSELF no light is seen, nor darkness, nor any other color, except for the souls of the righteous, who watch from the lower firmament OF MALCHUT, as if from behind a wall, the light sent to shine by the upper firmament, BINAH. And no one is able to know or bear that light OF BINAH which never stops.

363. מִתְּחוֹת דָּא, כָּל אִינוּן רְקִיעִין אִתְכְּלִילוּ בִּשְׁמָא דָּא אִקְרֵי שָׁמַיִם וְאִלֵּין אִקְרוּן הַשָּׁמַיִם אִינוּן דִּשְׁמָא עִלָּאָה אִקְרֵי בְּהוֹן, אִינוּן דִּשְׁמָא קַדִּישָׁא אִתְעֲטָר בְּהוֹן. וְעַ"ד כְּתִיב, הַשָּׁמַיִם שָׁמַיִם לַיְיָ', לְהַהוּא גְּנִיזוּ דִּרְקִיעָא עִלָּאָה, דְּקָאִים עָלַיְיהוּ.

363. Underneath THE FIRMAMENT OF BINAH, all the firmaments were designed to completeness by that name and are thus called 'heavens'. Of those called IN THE SCRIPTURE 'the heavens', some bear the Supernal Name YUD HEI VAV HEI OF ZEIR ANPIN, and with some, the Holy Name, MALCHUT, is adorned, FOR THE FIRMAMENTS OF MALCHUT RECEIVE FROM THE FIRMAMENTS OF ZEIR ANPIN. Therefore it is written: "the heaven are the heavens of Hashem" (Tehilim 115:16), that is, they are concealed in the supernal firmament, BINAH, that is situated over them.

364. עַד הָכָא רֶמֶז לִשְׁמָא קַדִּישָׁא, דְּקוּדְשָׁא בְּרִיךְ הוּא אִקְרֵי בִּשְׁמָהָן. מִכָּאן וּלְהָלְאָה, לֵית חַכִּים בְּסָכְלְתָנוּ, דְּיָכִיל לְמִנְדַּע וּלְאִתְדַּבְּקָא כְּלָל. בַּר נְהִירוּ חַד זְעֵיר בְּלָא קִיּוּמָא, לְאִתְיַישְׁבָא בֵּיהּ. זַכָּאָה חוּלָקֵיהּ מַאן דְּעָאל וְנָפַק, וְיָדַע לְאִסְתַּכְּלָא בְּרָזִין דְּמָארֵיהּ, וּלְאִתְדַּבְּקָא בֵּיהּ.

364. Up to THE FIRMAMENT OF BINAH, the Holy Name, YUD HEI VAV

HEI. is alluded to, IN THE VERSE "THE HEAVENS ARE THE HEAVENS TO YUD HEI VAV HEI." For the Holy One, blessed be He, BINAH, is called by names, AND A NAME MEANS PERCEPTION, FOR WHAT WE DO NOT PERCEIVE, WE DO NOT CALL BY NAME. From now upward, HIGHER THAN BINAH, no wise man can, by use of intelligence, know and grasp anything but one slight illumination, that is not enough to grasp fully. Happy is the portion of whoever comes in and goes out and knows how to behold the mysteries of his Master, and be devoted to Him.

365. בְּרָזִין אִלֵּין יָכִיל בַּר נָשׁ לְאִתְדַּבְּקָא בְּמָארֵיהּ, לְמִנְדַּע שְׁלִימוּ דְּחָכְמָה בְּרָזָא עִלָּאָה, כַּד פָּלַח לְמָארֵיהּ בִּצְלוֹתָא, בִּרְעוּתָא, בְּכַוֵּון לִבָּא, אַדְבַּק רְעוּתֵיהּ כְּנוּרָא בְּגַחַלְתָּא, לְיַיחֲדָא אִינוּן רְקִיעִין תַּתָּאִין דְּסִטְרָא דִקְדוּשָׁה, לְאַעְטְרָא לוֹן בִּשְׁמָא חֲדָא תַּתָּאָה. וּמִתַּמָּן וּלְהָלְאָה לְיַיחֲדָא אִינוּן רְקִיעִין עִלָּאִין פְּנִימָאִין, לְמֶהֱוֵי כֻּלְּהוּ חַד, בְּהַהוּא רְקִיעָא עִלָּאָה דְּקַיְּימָא עֲלַיְיהוּ.

365. By these mysteries a man can be devoted to his Master and know the wholeness of wisdom in the high secret. While he worships his Master in prayer, will and intention of the heart, he connects his will as a fire to coal, to unite these lower firmaments of the holy side, FROM MALCHUT, and bedeck them with a lower name, YUD HEI VAV HEI IN THE FIRMAMENTS OF MALCHUT, and from there on, to unite the inner and high FIRMAMENTS OF ZEIR ANPIN, so they would all become one in the supernal firmament OF BINAH, that is situated over them.

366. וּבְעוֹד דְּפוּמֵיהּ וְשִׂפְוָותֵיהּ מְרַחֲשָׁן, לִבֵּיהּ יְכַוֵּון, וּרְעוּתֵיהּ יִסְתַּלַּק לְעֵילָא לְעֵילָא, לְיַיחֲדָא כֹּלָּא בְּרָזָא דְּרָזִין, דְּתַמָּן תְּקִיעוּ דְּכָל רְעוּתִין וּמַחֲשָׁבִין בְּרָזָא דְּקַיְּימָא בְּאֵין סוֹף, וּלְכַוְּונָא בְּהַאי בְּכָל צְלוֹתָא וּצְלוֹתָא, בְּכָל יוֹמָא וְיוֹמָא לְאַעְטְרָא כָּל יוֹמוֹי, בְּרָזָא דְּיוֹמִין עִלָּאִין בְּפוּלְחָנֵיהּ.

366. While his mouth and lips are moving, he should concentrate his heart, and his will should soar higher and higher, to unite all in the secret of secrets, where all wills and thoughts are kept. This place is in the secret of

the Endless Light. One must meditate upon it in each prayer everyday, to adorn his days in the secret of the high days, CHESED, GVURAH, TIFERET, NETZACH, HOD, YESOD AND MALCHUT, in his worship.

367. בְּלֵילְיָא יְשַׁוֵּי רְעוּתֵיהּ, דְּהָא אִתְפְּטַר מֵעָלְמָא דָּא, וְנִשְׁמָתֵיהּ נָפְקַת מִנֵּיהּ, וְיַהֲדַר לָהּ לְמָארֵי דְּכֹלָּא, בְּגִין דְּכָל לֵילְיָא וְלֵילְיָא, הַהִיא נְקוּדָה קַיְּימָא, לְאַכְלָלָא בְּגַוָּוהּ אִינּוּן נִשְׁמָתִין דְּצַדִּיקַיָּיא.

367. At night he should pay attention that he is about to pass away and his soul leaves to return to the Master of all. For every night, the point MALCHUT absorbs the souls of the righteous. THAT IS, THE SOULS OF THE RIGHTEOUS MOUNT TO MALCHUT EVERY NIGHT BY MEANS OF MAYIN NUKVIN.

368. רָזָא דְּרָזִין לְמִנְדַּע לְאִינּוּן חַכִּימֵי לִבָּא. רְקִיעָא דָּא תַּתָּאָה, בְּרָזָא דְּהַהִיא נְקוּדָה קַיְּימָא, כְּמָה דְּאָמְרָן. הַהוּא רְקִיעָא אִיהוּ כָּלִיל מֵעֵילָּא וּמִתַּתָּא, וִיסוֹדָא דִּילֵיהּ לְתַתָּא כְּהַאי שְׁרַגָּא דְּסַלְקָא נְהוֹרָא אוּכְמָא, לְאִתְאַחֲדָא בִּנְהוֹרָא חִוָּורָא, וִיסוֹדָא דִּילָהּ אִיהוּ לְתַתָּא, בְּהַהִיא פְּתִילָה בְּמִשְׁחָא. אוּף הָכִי לְתַתָּא, הַהִיא נְקוּדָה. בִּימָמָא אִתְכְּלִילַת מִלְּעֵילָּא, וּבְלֵילְיָא אִתְכְּלִילַת מִתַּתָּא, בְּאִינּוּן נִשְׁמָתִין דְּצַדִּיקַיָּיא.

368. The mystery of mysteries is to be known by the wise of heart. The lower firmament is established by the secret of the point MALCHUT, as we said. This firmament consists of high and low, and its base down below is like a candle emitting black light, to be united with white light, OVER THE BLACK LIGHT, THAT IS, FROM ABOVE. Its base is below, in the wick of oil. So is that point, MALCHUT, BASED below. During the day it is united above, WITH ZEIR ANPIN, at night it is united below with the souls of the righteous.

369. וְכָל מִלִּין דְּעָלְמָא, אָהַדְרוּ כֻּלְּהוּ, לְעִקָּרָא וִיסוֹדָא וְשָׁרְשָׁא, דְּנָפְקוּ מִנֵּיהּ. וְכַמָּה לֵילְוָון זִמְנִין לְנַטְלָא כָּל חַד וְחַד מַה דְּאִתְחֲזֵי לֵיהּ. כד"א אַף לֵילוֹת יִסְּרוּנִי כִלְיוֹתָי. נַפְשָׁא אַזְלַת וְשָׁטַאת, וְתָבַת לְהַהוּא עִקָּרָא

דְּאִתְחֲזֵי לָהּ. גּוּפָא קָאִים שָׁכִיךְ כְּאַבְנָא, וְאַהְדָר לְהַהוּא אֲתָר דְּאִתְחֲזֵי
לֵיהּ, לְמִשְׁרֵי עֲלוֹי, וּבְגִין כַּךְ תָּב גּוּפָא לְסִטְרֵיהּ, וְנַפְשָׁא לְסִטְרָהּ.

369. All that is in the world go back to their source and root from which the came, and for a few nights each of them is going to take what it deserves. This is written in, "my kidneys also admonish me in the night" (Tehilim 16:7). FOR EVERYTHING GOES BACK TO ITS SOURCE, and the soul hovers back to its root, that fits it, ABOVE. And the body stays quiet as a stone and goes back to the place fit to hover above it, TO WIT, THE OTHER SIDE THAT WILL PREVAIL OVER IT AFTER DEATH. For that reason the body returns to its side, and the soul to its side.

370. גּוּפָא שָׁרֵי עֲלוֹי רָזָא דְּסִטְרָא אַחֲרָא, וּבְגִין כַּךְ אִסְתְּאָבוּ יְדוֹי, וּבָעֵי
לְאַסְחָאָה לוֹן. כְּמָה דְּאוּקִימְנָא, דְּהָא בְּלֵילְיָא כֹּלָּא תָּב לְאַתְרֵיהּ,
וְנִשְׁמָתְהוֹן דְּצַדִּיקַיָּיא סַלְקִין וְאִתְהַדְרָן לְאַתְרַיְיהוּ, וְאִתְעַטְרַת בְּהוּ מַה
דְּאִתְעַטְרַת, וְאִתְכְּלִילַת מִכָּל סִטְרִין, כְּדֵין סַלְקָא יְקָרָא דְּקוּדְשָׁא בְּרִיךְ
הוּא וְאִתְעַטָּר מִכֹּלָּא.

370. After the body returns TO ITS SIDE, the secret of the Other Side prevails upon it, and therefore the hands are defiled and should be washed, as we explained that at night everything returns to there its place, ITS ROOT. The souls of the righteous mount and return to their source, THEIR ROOT WHICH IS MALCHUT OUT OF WHICH THEY WERE BORN. And the one who wishes to, NAMELY, MALCHUT, is bedecked with crowns, whole on all sides, ABOVE AND BELOW. Then the glory of the Holy One, blessed be He, rises to be adorned by all.

371. בְּלֵילְיָא שַׁלְטָאן מְמָנָן דְּאִתְפְּקָדוּ עַל אִינּוּן נִשְׁמָתִין דְּצַדִּיקַיָּיא,
לְסַלְקָא לוֹן לְעֵילָּא, וּלְקָרְבָא לוֹן קָרְבָּן נַיְיחָא לְגַבֵּי מָארֵיהוֹן. הַהוּא
מְמָנָא דְּאִתְפְּקַד עַל כָּל אִינּוּן מַשִׁירְיָין, סוֹרִיָ"א שְׁמֵיהּ רַב מְמָנָא. כֵּיוָן
דְּנִשְׁמָתָא סַלְקָא בְּכָל אִינּוּן רְקִיעִין, כְּדֵין מְקָרְבִין לָהּ לְגַבֵּיהּ, וְאָרַח בָּהּ
כְּמָה דְּאַתְּ אָמַר, וַהֲרִיחוֹ בְּיִרְאַת יְיָ'. כְּמָה דְּזַמִּין מַלְכָּא מְשִׁיחָא
לְמֶעְבַּד בְּעָלְמָא, וְעַל יְדֵיהּ אַעֲבְרוּ כֻּלְּהוּ בְּפִקְדוֹנָא עַל יְדֵיהּ, לְאַתְקַרְבָא
לְהָלְאָה.

371. The chieftains appointed over the souls of the righteous rule at night. They elevate them, and sacrifice them as fragrant sacrifice to their Master. The chief appointed over these legions is called Suriya, a supreme chief. Once the soul mounts through all these firmaments, it is brought before him, SURIYA, and he smells it, same as in the verse "and he will inhale the scent of the fear of Hashem" (Yeshayah 11:13). Namely, as will the King Messiah do in the world of the future, SO DOES CHIEF SURIYA, and the souls pass before him, under his charge, to further approach MALCHUT.

372. וְכֻלְּהוּ נִשְׁמָתִין כַּד אִתְקְרִיבוּ לְהַהוּא אֲתָר דְּאִתְקְרִיבוּ, וְאִתְחַזְיָן תַּמָּן, דָּא אִיהוּ רָזָא, כֻּלְּהוּ נִשְׁמָתִין אִתְכְּלִילוּ בְּהַהִיא נְקוּדָה, וְנַטְלָא לוֹן זִמְנָא חֲדָא, כְּמַאן דְּבָלַע בְּלִיעוּ דְּמִלָּה, וְאִתְעַבְּרָא כְּאִתְּתָא דְּמִתְעַבְּרָא. רָזָא דָּא לְמָארֵי מְדִין. כַּד הַאי נְקוּדָה אִתְעַבְּרַת, כְּאִתְּתָא דְּמִתְעַבְּרָא, אִתְהֲנֵי מֵהַהִיא הֲנָאוּתָא, דְּאִתְכְּלִילַת נִשְׁמָתָא מֵהַאי עָלְמָא, בְּאִינוּן עוֹבָדִין, וּבְהַהִיא אוֹרַיְיתָא דְּאִשְׁתַּדַּלַת בָּהּ בִּימָמָא. וְנַטְלָא הַהוּא רְעוּ דְּהַאי עָלְמָא, וּבֵיהּ אִתְהֲנֵי בְּחֶדְוָה, וְאִתְכְּלִילַת מִכָּל סִטְרִין.

372. All souls approaching that place, NAMELY MALCHUT, are seen there. This is a secret: THEN all the souls are contained within that point, MALCHUT, and it takes them at once, as if swallowing them, and conceives like a woman. This secret is for the scholars engrossed in the law, when this point conceives as a woman in conception. It has pleasure having the soul of this world included in it, together with its deeds and study of the Torah during that day. It takes that will of this world and gladly rejoices in it, becoming whole on all sides, ABOVE AND BELOW.

373. לְבָתַר אַפִּיקַת לוֹן לְבַר, וְאוֹלִידַת לוֹן כְּמִלְּקַדְמִין, וְנִשְׁמָתָא אִיהִי חַדְתָּא הַשְׁתָּא כְּמִלְּקַדְמִין, וְרָזָא דָּא חֲדָשִׁים לַבְּקָרִים. חֲדָשִׁים וַדַּאי כְּמָה דְאִתְּמַר. מַה טַּעַם אִינוּן חֲדָשִׁים. בְּגִין רָזָא דִּכְתִיב, רַבָּה אֱמוּנָתֶךָ. רַבָּה וַדַּאי, דְּיָכְלָא לְאַכְלְלָא לוֹן, וּלְאַעֲלָא לוֹן לְגַוַּוהּ, וְאַפִּיקַת לוֹן וְאִינוּן חַדְתִּין. וְעַל דָּא נַקְטָא אַחֳרָנִין מִלְעֵילָא בִּימָמָא. זַכָּאִין אִינוּן צַדִּיקַיָּיא בְּעָלְמָא דֵין, וּבְעָלְמָא דְּאָתֵי.

373. Then MALCHUT lets them out, and gives them birth as before. FOR THE SOULS ARE THE OFFSPRING OF MALCHUT, and the soul is now new as in its birth. This is the secret of "they are new every morning..." (Eichah 3:23), THAT ALLUDES TO THE SOULS, which are certainly new EVERY MORNING. What is the sense of their being new? It is in the secret at the end of the verse "great is Your faithfulness" (Ibid.). FOR MALCHUT IS NAMED FAITH AND it is indeed great and can contain THE SOULS, let them in and bring them out when they are new. Therefore it receives others from above, during the day. Happy are the righteous in this world and the World to Come.

374. אַדְהָכִי נָהַר יְמָמָא, אָמַר רִבִּי אַבָּא, נְקוּם וּנְהַךְ, וְנוֹדֶה לְרִבּוֹן עָלְמָא. קָמוּ וְאָזְלוּ, וְצַלוּ, וּלְבָתַר אָהַדְרוּ חַבְרַיָּיא לְגַבֵּיהּ, אָמְרוּ לֵיהּ, מַאן דְּשָׁרֵי, לְסַיֵּים שְׁבָחָא. זַכָּאָה חוּלָקָנָא בְּאוֹרְחָא דָא, דְּכָל הַאי זָכִינָא לְאַעֲטְרָא לֵיהּ לְקוּדְשָׁא ב"ה, בְּרָזִין דְּחָכְמְתָא.

374. In the meantime, the daylight broke. Rabbi Aba said 'let us rise and go to thank the Master of the universe.' So they prayed. Afterwards the friends came back TO RABBI ABA and said to him 'whoever started, let him finish praising'. Happy is our portion on the way, that we so deserved to adorn the Holy One, blessed be He, with the secrets of wisdom.

26. "And Betzalel made the ark"

A Synopsis

Rabbi Aba tells us that the ark symbolizes Malchut, and the Written Torah symbolizes Zeir Anpin, so the ark is a mystery in which the Written Torah is put. Rabbi Aba discusses the meaning of the number of boards in the ark. He also says that there is the ark of the Malchut of holiness and the ark of the Malchut of the Other Side. This leads into a discussion of, "All these things did the king Aravna give to the king," and the conquest of Jerusalem by David. Seeing the slaughter during that conquest, Hashem told the angel of destruction to stop.

Through an examination of the letters in the name Aravna and the word 'aron' (ark) and the name Adam, Rabbi Aba ascertains that the holy side is called the ark (aron) of the covenant. He says it is fit for the body, i.e. that the image form of man should be put into it. Therefore when the righteous die they are put in a coffin (aron); this alludes to the union of Zeir Anpin and the Ark of the covenant. Because they do not pertain to the body of Adam, there are no created bodies to the Other Side.

375. פָּתַח רִבִּי אַבָּא וְאָמַר, וַיַּעַשׂ בְּצַלְאֵל אֶת הָאָרוֹן עֲצֵי שִׁטִּים וְגוֹ'. הָכָא, אע"ג דְּכָל רָזִין דְּמַשְׁכְּנָא הָא אוּקְמוּהָ חַבְרַיָּיא בְּאִדְרָא קַדִּישָׁא. הָכָא אִית לְאִסְתַּכְּלָא, דְּהָא רָזָא דָא מִתְעַטְּרָא בְּכַמָּה רָזִין, לְמֵילַף חָכְמְתָא. אָרוֹן דָּא אִיהוּ רָזָא לְמִיעַל תּוֹרָה שֶׁבִּכְתָב. וְאִתְגְּנִיז בֵּיהּ בְּשִׁית לוּחִין מִסַחֲרִין, וְדָא אִקְרֵי אָרוֹן. כַּד סָחֲרָן אִינּוּן שִׁית לְמֶהֱוֵי כַּחֲדָא, כְּדֵין אִיהוּ גוּפָא חַד לְאַעֲלָא בֵּיהּ רָזָא דְּאוֹרַיְיתָא, בְּשִׁית סִטְרִין.

375. Rabbi Aba opened the discussion and said "and Betzalel made the ark of Acacia wood..." (Shemot 37:1). Though the friends explained all the secret of the tabernacle at the holy assembly, nevertheless we should look in here, for this secret is adorned with several mysteries as to impart wisdom. This ark is a mystery in which the Written Torah is put. FOR THE ARK SYMBOLIZES MALCHUT AND THE WRITTEN TORAH SYMBOLIZES ZEIR ANPIN. The Torah is concealed within its six boards round it, FOR THE ARK IS MADE OF SIX BOARDS ROUND IT, FOUR BOARDS AROUND THE SIDES, ONE ABOVE AND ONE BELOW; ALTOGETHER THERE ARE SIX. This is called an ark. When the six boards, THE SECRET OF CHESED, GVURAH,

TIFERET, NETZACH, HOD AND YESOD OF MALCHUT, become one, they turn into a vessel in which the secret of the Torah can be put, which is composed of six endings, CHESED, GVURAH, TIFERET, NETZACH, HOD AND YESOD, NAMELY, ZEIR ANPIN.

376. וְאִינּוּן לוּחִין, אִינּוּן חָמֵשׁ, וְעָאלִין בֵּיה חָמֵשׁ סְפָרִים, וְאִינּוּן חָמֵשׁ אִינּוּן שִׁית, בְּחַד דַּרְגָּא דְּאָעִיל בָּה בִּגְנִיזוּ, דְּאִקְרֵי רָזָא דְכֹלָּא, וְהַאי אִיהוּ רָזָא דִּבְרִית. כַּד עָאל דָּא, גּוֹ אִינּוּן חָמֵשׁ לוּחִין, כְּדֵין קַיְּימָא אֲרוֹנָא וְאוֹרַיְיתָא, בְּרָזָא דְּתִשְׁעַ דַּרְגִּין, דְּאִינּוּן תְּרֵין שְׁמָהָן, יְהֹוָ"ה אֱלֹהִי"ם. וּלְבָתַר קַיְּימָא לוּחָא חֲדָא, רָזָא לְמֵיעַל תּוֹרָה שֶׁבִּכְתָב. וְאִתְגְּנִיז בֵּיהּ בְּשִׁית לוּחִין מְסַחֲרִין, וְדָא אִקְרֵי כֹּלָּא, וְכֻלְּהוּ קַיְּימֵי בִּגְנִיזוּ.

376. But there are five boards TO THIS ARK, FOUR ON THE SIDES AND ONE BELOW, CORRESPONDING TO CHESED, GVURAH, TIFERET, NETZACH AND HOD. FOR THE BOARD ON TOP IS THE SECRET OF THE COVERING OF THE ARK, AND IS NOT OF THE ARK PROPER. Five books are put in it, THE FIVE BOOKS OF THE TORAH, CORRESPONDING TO CHESED, GVURAH, TIFERET, NETZACH AND HOD OF ZEIR ANPIN. These five boards become six, together with one grade, that comes in secretly, called the secret of all, and is the secret of the covenant. BEING YESOD, AND CONCEALED, THERE IS NO BOARD CORRESPONDING TO IT IN THE ARK. When it enters within those five boards, the ark and the Torah are established in the secret of the nine grades, the two names Yud Hei Vav Hei, Elohim, WHICH CONSIST OF NINE LETTERS. Then there is one board, a high secret, THE COVERING, that covers all. THIS IS THE SECRET OF THE FIRMAMENT THAT GOES ROUND AND ABOVE ALL, THE EIGHTH FIRMAMENT, BINAH. Hence, SINCE THE COVERING OF THE ARK IS ABOVE THEM ALL, they are concealed, THAT IS, INVISIBLE.

377. הָכָא אִית לָן לְאִסְתַּכְּלָא, וּלְמִנְדַּע רָזִין דַּאֲרוֹנָא, אִית אָרוֹן וְאִית אָרוֹן, דָּא לָקֳבֵל דָּא. פָּתַח וְאָמַר, הַכֹּל נָתַן אֲרַוְנָה הַמֶּלֶךְ לַמֶּלֶךְ וְגוֹ'. וְכִי אֲרַוְנָה מֶלֶךְ הֲוָה וְאע"ג דְּחַבְרַיָּיא אוּקְמוּהָ, אֶלָּא דָוִד, דִּכְתִיב בֵּיהּ כָּל מַכֵּה יְבוּסִי וְיִגַּע בַּצִּנּוֹר וְגוֹ' וְאִיהוּ נָטַל וְתָפִיס לִירוּשְׁלַם, וּמִדִּידֵיהּ

הֲוָה, אַמַּאי קָנָה בְּכַסְפָּא. וְאִי תֵּימָא אע״ג דַּהֲוַות יְרוּשְׁלַם דִּידֵיהּ
דְּדָוִד, הַהוּא אֲתָר אַחֲסַנְתֵּיהּ דַּאֲרוֹנָה הֲוָה, כְּמָה דַּהֲוָה בְּנָבוֹת
הַיִּזְרְעֵאלִי, דְּאע״ג דְּשַׁלִּיט אַחְאָב, וַהֲוָה מַלְכָּא, אִצְטְרִיךְ לְמִתְבַּע
לְנָבוֹת הַהוּא כֶּרֶם, אוֹף הָכִי דָּוִד.

377. Here we should look and know the secret of the ark. For there is ark and ark, TO WIT, MALCHUT OF HOLINESS, AND MALCHUT OF THE OTHER SIDE, one against the other. He opened and said "All these things did the king Aravna give to the king..." (II Shmuel 24:23). HE ASKS: But was Aravna a king? Though the friends explained it, yet David, upon whom was written: "Whoever smites the Yevusite, and gets up to the aqueduct" (II Shmuel 5:8), took hold of and conquered Jerusalem, WHERE HIS TEMPLE LIES; why did he pay Aravna for the place? You may say that though Jerusalem was David's, NEVERTHELESS it was a heritage of Aravna AND THEREFORE HAD TO BE BOUGHT, as in the case of Navot the Jesreelite. Although Achav was ruler and king, he had to obtain his permission for the vineyard. So did David.

378. אֶלָּא וַדַּאי אֲרוֹנָה מַלְכָּא הֲוָה, וְהַהוּא אֲתָר בִּרְשׁוּתֵיהּ הֲוָה, וַהֲוָה
שַׁלִּיט עֲלוֹי, וְכַד מָטָא זִמְנָא לְנָפְקָא מִתְּחוֹת יְדֵיהּ, לָא נָפִיק אֶלָּא
בְּסַגִּיאוּת דָּמָא וְקָטוֹלָא בְּיִשְׂרָאֵל. לְבָתַר קָאִים הַהוּא מַלְאָכָא מְחַבְּלָא
עַל הַהוּא אֲתָר, וְתַמָּן כַּד הֲוָה קָטִיל, וְקָאִים בְּהַהוּא אֲתָר, לָא הֲוָה
יָכִיל, וְתָשַׁשׁ חֵילֵיהּ.

378. HE ANSWERS: Assuredly Aravna was a king, and that place was under his authority and possession. When the time arrived for the place to be free of his rule, it did not happen, save by much bloodshed and killing among Yisrael, THAT IS, THROUGH WAR. Later, the angel of destruction stood upon that place in order to kill, but could not for his strength failed him.

379. וְהַהוּא אֲתָר, אֲתָר דְּאִתְעֲקַד בֵּיהּ יִצְחָק הֲוָה, דְּתַמָּן בָּנָה אַבְרָהָם
מַדְבְּחָא, וְעָקַד לֵיהּ לְיִצְחָק בְּרֵיהּ. כֵּיוָן דְּחָמָא קוּדְשָׁא בְּרִיךְ הוּא הַהוּא
אֲתָר, אִתְמְלֵי רַחֲמִין, הה״ד, רָאָה יְיָ' וַיִּנָּחֵם וְגוֹ'. מַהוּ רָאָה יְיָ'. חָמָא
עֲקֵידַת יִצְחָק בְּהַהוּא אֲתָר, וְתָב וְרִיחַם עֲלַיְיהוּ מִיַּד.

-361-

379. This was the place where Isaac was bound, where Abraham built the altar to sacrifice his son Isaac. When the Holy One, blessed be He, saw that place, He was filled with pity, as is written: "Hashem beheld, and He relented..." (I Divrei Hayamim 21:15). What did Hashem behold? The binding of Isaac, immediately He felt compassion towards them.

‏380. וַיֹּאמֶר לַמַּלְאָךְ הַמַּשְׁחִית רַב עַתָּה וְגוֹ'. מַהוּ רַב. הָא אוּקְמוּהָ, טוֹל הָרַב. אֶלָּא הָכִי הוּא, כְּתִיב הָכָא רַב, וּכְתִיב הָתָם, רַב לָכֶם שֶׁבֶת בָּהָר הַזֶּה. אוֹף הָכִי נָמֵי רַב, רַב לָךְ לְמֶהֱוֵי הַאי אֲתָר תְּחוֹת יְדָךְ, שְׁנִין סַגִּיאִין הֲוָה תְּחוֹת יְדָךְ, מִכָּאן וּלְהָלְאָה רַב, אַהֲדַר אַתְרָא לְמָארֵיהּ. וְעכ"ד בְּמוֹתָא וּמָמוֹנָא נָפַק מִתְּחוֹת יְדֵיהּ.

380. And He said to the angel of destruction "it is enough (Heb. *rav*)" (Ibid.). What is the meaning of 'rav'? It was explained as 'take the greater one' (Heb. *rav*). But here the meaning of 'enough' is as in "you have dwelt long enough in this mountain" (Devarim 1:6) 'Enough' here means that the place was in your possession for many years, and from now on it is enough. Return the place to its owners. Despite that, it could only be taken from him through sacrifice of lives and money.

‏381. אֲמַאי אִקְרֵי אֲרַוְנָה. אֶלָּא כְּתִיב אֲרַוְנָה וּכְתִיב אָרְנָן. בְּעוֹד דְּהַהוּא אֲתָר הֲוָה תְּחוֹת יְדֵיהּ, אִקְרֵי אֲרַוְנָה אֲרוֹן דְּסִטְרָא אַחֲרָא. וְעַל דְּאִתּוֹסְפוּ בֵּיהּ אַתְוָון יַתִּיר, הָכִי אִצְטְרִיךְ לְאִתּוֹסְפָא לְהַהוּא רַע עַיִן, רָזָא דְּסִטְרָא אַחֲרָא, וְהַהוּא תּוֹסֶפֶת אִיהוּ גְּרִיעוּתָא לְגַבֵּיהּ.

381. HE ASKS: Why is he called Aravna? AND REPLIES: there is the name 'Aravna' and 'Ornan' (I Divrei Hayamim 21:15). THE REASON IS THAT while the place was still in his possession, it was called 'Aravna (from Heb. *aron* lit. 'ark'), alluding to the ark of the Other Side, THEIR MALCHUT. And as there are letters added, ARVANA INSTEAD OF ARON, so there is an addition to the evil-eyed, which is the secret of the Other Side, for to him an addition is considered diminution.

‏383. בְּסְטַר קְדוּשָׁה גַּרְעִין לֵיהּ אַתְוָון, וְאִתּוֹסָף קְדוּשָׁתֵיהּ. וְדָא רָזָא דִּכְתִיב, עַל שְׁנֵי עָשָׂר בָּקָר. גָּרַע מֵ"ם דְּלָא כְּתִיב שְׁנַיִם, אֶלָּא שְׁנֵי.

-362-

וּלְסִטְרָא אַחֲרָא יַהֲבִין לֵיהּ תּוֹסֶפֶת אַתְוָון, דִּכְתִּיב וַיַּעַשׂ יְרִיעוֹת עִזִּים
לְאֹהֶל עַל הַמִּשְׁכָּן עַשְׁתֵּי עֶשְׂרֵה יְרִיעוֹת, תּוֹסֶפֶת אַתְוָון וְאִיהוּ
גְרִיעוּתָא. וּבְסִטְרָא דִּקְדוּשָׁה, שְׁנֵי עָשָׂר וְלָא יַתִּיר. וְהָכָא עַשְׁתֵּי עֶשְׂרֵה.
וְכֹלָּא אִיהוּ גְּרִיעוּ לְגַבֵּיהּ, וְהָכִי אִצְטְרִיךְ לְהַהוּא רַע עַיִן, לְאַשְׁלְמָא
עֵינֵיהּ וְאִיהוּ בִּגְרִיעוּ.

382. On the side of holiness, once letters are deducted, holiness is accumulated. This is the secret of the verse "twelve (Heb. *shnei asar*) oxen" (I Melachim 7:25) in which one letter is missing, Shnei instead of Sheneim. The Other Side, though, is given additional letters, as is written: "and he made curtains of goats' hair for the tent over the tabernacle" (Shemot 36:14). In 'twelve curtains' there is an additional letter, Ayin, to Shtei Esrei. This implies diminution, FOR ASHTEI IMPLIES ONE SHORT OF SHTEI ESREI. On the holy side IT IS WRITTEN: Shnei Asar, WITHOUT MEM, and no more, and here it is written Asthtei Esrei, WITH AN ADDITIONAL AYIN (LIT. 'EYE'), to imply diminution. So deserves the evil eyed, that wishes to fill his eyes, that is, his (eye) Ayin, and is thus lessened, IN THE SECRET OF 'MORE IS LESS'.

383. ת"ח, סִטְרָא דִּקְדוּשָׁה אִקְרֵי אֲרוֹן הַבְּרִית. וְהַהוּא אֲרוֹן הַבְּרִית,
אִתְחֲזֵי לְגוּפָא לְמֵיעַל בֵּיהּ דִּיּוּקְנָא דְּאָדָם. וְעַל רָזָא דָּא, אִינּוּן חֲסִידֵי
קַדִּישִׁין, כַּד הֲווֹ מִפְטְרֵי מֵהַאי עָלְמָא, הֲווֹ אַעֲלִין לוֹן בְּאָרוֹן. דְּהָא
סִטְרָא אַחֲרָא לָא מִתְתַּקַּן בְּגוּפָא, וְלָאו אִיהִי בִּכְלָלָא דְּגוּפָא דְּאָדָם.
וּבְגִין דָּא לָא אִתְבְּרוּן גּוּפַיָּיא לְהַהוּא סִטְרָא אַחֲרָא, בְּגִין דְּלָאו אִינּוּן
בִּכְלָלָא דְּגוּפָא דְּאָדָם.

383. Come and see, the holy side is called the ark (Heb. *aron*) of the covenant, ALLUDING TO MALCHUT OF HOLINESS. That ark of the covenant, MALCHUT CONNECTED TO THE COVENANT – YESOD, is fit for the body, ZEIR ANPIN, that is, that the human (Heb. *adam*) form should be put in it, NAMELY, YUD HEI VAV HEI, FULLY SPELLED WITH ALEPH'S HAS THE SAME NUMERICAL VALUE AS ADAM. In accordance with this mystery, when the holy pious pass away, they are put in a coffin (Heb. *aron*), AN ALLUSION TO THE UNION OF ZEIR ANPIN AND THE ARK OF COVENANT. For the Other

Side cannot be established within a body, and has no part in one, IN ZEIR ANPIN. For that reason no bodies were created to the Other Side, for they are not part of the human body .

27. He should not be put in a coffin

A Synopsis

Rabbi Aba opens by telling us that Joseph was put into a coffin in Egypt. He deserved to be put in a coffin because he kept the holy covenant intact, and only the righteous are accorded that privilege. If a man impaired the covenant in the past and now also desecrates his coffin, he is sentenced and put into Gehenom, never to leave. Rabbi Aba says this is true only of those who did not repent enough to wipe out their misdeeds. If someone sinned and did not repent, he may not see the face of the Shechinah. Rabbi Aba explains that it was Betzalel who made the ark instead of those wise men who made the tabernacle because he was of a grade that symbolizes the holy covenant.

384. בְּיוֹסֵף מַה כְּתִיב, וַיִּישֶׂם בָּאָרוֹן תְּרֵין יוֹדִין אֲמַאי. אֶלָּא דְּאִתְחַבָּר בְּרִית בִּבְרִית. רָזָא דִלְתַתָּא בְּרָזָא דִּלְעֵילָא. וְעָאל בַּאֲרוֹנָא. מַאי טַעֲמָא. בְּגִין דְּנָטַר בְּרִית קַדִּישָׁא, וְאִתְקַיָּים בֵּיהּ. לְהָכִי אִתְחֲזֵי לְאַעֲלָה בַּאֲרוֹנָא, וְכֹלָּא כַּדְקָא חֲזֵי.

384. It is written concerning Joseph, "and he was put (Heb. *vayisem*) in a coffin (Heb. *aron*)" (Beresheet 50:26). HE ASKS: Why IS VAYISEM SPELLED with two Yuds? HE ANSWERS: It shows the connection between one covenant and another covenant, FOR YUD ALLUDES TO THE COVENANT, NAMELY, TO YESOD; AND THE TWO WRITTEN YUDS, CORRESPONDING TO THE TWO COVENANTS, one in the secret of the lower COVENANT, and the other in the secret of the upper COVENANT, THE ARK (HEB. *ARON*) OF THE COVENANT. Then he was placed in a coffin (Heb. *aron*). Why so? because he observed the holy covenant, which was established through him. Therefore he deserved to be put in a coffin. And everything is proper.

385. בָּכָה ר' אַבָּא וְאָמַר, וַוי לִבְנֵי עָלְמָא, דְּלָא יַדְעֵי לְהַהוּא כְּסוּפָא. וַוי לְהַהוּא עוֹנְשָׁא, דְּכָל מַאן דְּבָעֵי עָאל בַּאֲרוֹנָא. בְּגִין דְּלָא אִצְטְרִיךְ לְמֵיעַל בַּאֲרוֹנָא, בַּר צַדִּיק, דְּיָדַע בְּנַפְשֵׁיהּ, וְאִשְׁתְּמוֹדַע בְּגַרְמֵיהּ, דְּלָא חָטָא בְּהַהוּא בְּרִית, אֶת קַיָּימָא קַדִּישָׁא, מֵעוּלְמוֹי, וְקָא נָטִיר לֵיהּ

כְּדְקָא יָאוּת. וְאִי לָאו, לָא אִצְטְרִיךְ לֵיהּ לְמֵיעַל בַּאֲרוֹנָא, וּלְמִפְגַּם אֲרוֹנָא.

385. Rabbi Aba wept and said, woe to people who are unaware of that disgrace, and woe to the punishment exacted from all those who wish to be put in a coffin, AFTER THEIR DEATH. For only the righteous may be put in a coffin, who knows himself and sees that he did not offend the covenant, the sign of the holy covenant, during his lifetime, and kept it as he should. And if this is not so, he must not be put in a coffin (Heb. *aron*) AFTER HIS DEATH and impair the ark (Heb. *aron*). FOR THE IMPAIRMENT REACHES THE ARK OF THE COVENANT.

386. רָזָא אִצְטְרִיךְ לְאִתְחַבְּרָא בְּאָת קַיָּימָא קַדִּישָׁא דְּאִיהוּ רָזָא דְּאִתְחֲזֵי לֵיהּ, וְלָא לְאַחֲרָא. דְּהָא אֲרוֹן לָא אִתְחַבַּר אֶלָּא בְּצַדִּיק, דְּנָטִיר אֶת קַיָּימָא קַדִּישָׁא. וּמַאן דְּפָגִים בְּרִית וְעָאל בַּאֲרוֹנָא, וַוי לֵיהּ, דְּפָגַם לֵיהּ בְּחַיּוֹי. וַוי לֵיהּ דְּפָגִים לֵיהּ בְּמִיתָתֵיהּ. וַוי לֵיהּ מֵהַהוּא עוֹנְשָׁא. וַוי לֵיהּ דְּפָגִים אָת וְאָרוֹן קַיָּימָא קַדִּישָׁא. וַוי לֵיהּ לְהַהוּא כְּסוּפָא, דְּנָקְמִין מִנֵּיהּ נַקְמַת עָלְמִין, נוּקְמָא דְּעָלְמָא דָּא, וְנוּקְמָא דְּהַהוּא פְּגִימוּ. וְרָזָא דָּא כְּתִיב כִּי לֹא יָנוּחַ שֵׁבֶט הָרֶשַׁע עַל גּוֹרָל הַצַּדִּיקִים.

386. The inner meaning of this is that A MAN has to be connected with the sign of the holy covenant, the secret that is fit for him, WHICH ALLUDES TO YESOD OF ZEIR ANPIN, and not for the other, THE OTHER SIDE. For the ark (or coffin), ALLUDING TO MALCHUT, is united only with the righteous who keeps the sigh of the holy covenant. And whoever impairs the member of the covenant and is nevertheless put in a coffin, woe to him, for impairing it in his life, woe to him for impairing it in his death. Woe to him who receives this punishment, for impairing the sign of the covenant, and the holy ark of the covenant. Woe to the disgrace, for which there will be forever upon him the revenge of this world and of that impairment. This is the secret of the verse "for the scepter of wickedness shall not rest upon the share allotted to the righteous" (Tehilim 125:3).

387. בְּשַׁעֲתָא דְּדַיְינִין לֵיהּ בְּהַהוּא עָלְמָא, מִסְתַּכְּלָן בְּעוֹבָדוֹי, אִי הֲוָה

פְּגִים רָזָא דִּבְרִית קַדִּישָׁא דְּחָתִים בְּבִשְׂרֵיהּ. וְהַשְׁתָּא פָּגִים אֲרוֹנָא דִּילֵיהּ
בְּהַאי. הַאי לֵית לֵיהּ חוּלָקָא בְּצַדִּיקַיָּיא. מִסְתַּכְּלָן בֵּיהּ, וְדַיְינִין לֵיהּ,
וּמַפְּקֵי לֵיהּ לְבַר מִכְּלָלָא דְּאָדָם. כֵּיוָן דְּאַפְּקֵי לֵיהּ מִכְּלָלָא דְּאָדָם, אַפְּקֵי
לֵיהּ מִכְּלָלָא דְּכֻלְּהוּ אַחֲרָנִין, דְּאִתְעַתְּדוּ לְחַיֵּי עָלְמָא, וְיָהֲבֵי לֵיהּ
לְהַהוּא סִטְרָא דְּלָא אִתְכְּלִיל בְּרָזָא דְּגוּפָא דְּאָדָם. כֵּיוָן דְּאִתְמְסַר
לְהַהוּא סִטְרָא, וַוי לֵיהּ, דְּאַעֲלִין לֵיהּ בְּגֵיהִנָּם, וְלָא נָפִיק מִנֵּיהּ לְעָלְמִין.
עַ״ד כְּתִיב וְיָצְאוּ וְרָאוּ בְּפִגְרֵי הָאֲנָשִׁים הַפֹּשְׁעִים בִּי וְגוֹ'. אִינוּן
דְּאִשְׁתָּארוּ מִכְּלָלָא דְּאָדָם.

387. When a man is judged in that world, his deeds are examined. If he used to impair the secret of the holy covenant stamped in his flesh, and now he also desecrates his coffin, he is not of the righteous. They look at him and sentence him to be excluded from the community of mankind, and from those who were given eternal life. He is given to that side, which has no part in the secret of man, NAMELY, THE OTHER SIDE, AS MENTIONED. When he is delivered to that side, woe to him, for he is put in Gehenom, never to leave. Upon this says the verse "and they shall go forth, and look upon the carcasses of the men that have rebelled against Me'..." (Yeshayah 66:24). These stay apart from mankind, THAT IS, THEY WERE LEFT OUT OF HUMANITY.

388. וְהָנֵי מִלֵּי כַּד לָא עָבֵד תְּיוּבְתָּא שְׁלֵימָתָא. תְּיוּבְתָּא דְּאִיהִי
אִתְחַזְיָיא לְחַפְיָיא עַל כָּל עוֹבָדוֹי. וְעַכ״ד טַב לֵיהּ דְּלָא יֵעוּל בַּאֲרוֹנָא,
דְּהָא כָּל זִמְנָא דְּגוּפָא קַיָּים, נִשְׁמָתָא אִתְדָּנַת, וְלָא עָאלַת לְאַתְרָהּ. בַּר
אִינוּן חֲסִידֵי עֶלְיוֹנִין קַדִּישִׁין, דְּאִתְחֲזוֹן לְסַלְּקָא בְּגוּפַיְיהוּ, זַכָּאָה
חוּלָקֵיהוֹן בְּעָלְמָא דֵין וּבְעָלְמָא דְּאָתֵי.

388. That is true only for those who did not repent completely, enough to wipe their misdeeds. It is nevertheless better for them not to be put in a coffin, for as long as the body exists, the soul is judged and does not go to its place, save the high righteous worthy of ascending in their bodies. Happy is their portion in this world and in the World to Come.

389. בְּגִין דְּלֵית חוֹבָא דְּקַשְׁיָא קַמֵּיהּ קוּדְשָׁא בְּרִיךְ הוּא, כְּהַאי מַאן

דִּמְשַׁקֵּר וּפָגִים לְהַאי אָת קַיָּימָא קַדִּישָׁא. וְדָא לָא חָמֵי אַנְפֵּי שְׁכִינְתָּא, עַל חוֹבָא דָּא כְּתִיב וַיְהִי עֵר בְּכוֹר יְהוּדָה רַע בְּעֵינֵי יְיָ'. וּכְתִיב לֹא יְגוּרְךָ רָע.

389. For there is not a graver offense before the Holy One, blessed be He, than that of lying and impairing the holy sign of the covenant. That person may not see the face of the Shechinah, if he thus sins, as is written: "And Er, Judah's firstborn, was wicked in the sight of Hashem" (Beresheet 38:7) and also "nor shall evil dwell with You" (Tehilim 5:5), FOR THIS OFFENSE IS CALLED 'EVIL'.

390. מַה כְּתִיב הָכָא, וַיַּעַשׂ בְּצַלְאֵל אֶת הָאָרוֹן. וְכִי אֲמַאי לָא עָבְדוּ אִינּוּן חַכִּימִין, דְּעָבְדוּ מַשְׁכְּנָא, יַת אֲרוֹנָא. אֶלָּא בְּצַלְאֵל, סִיּוּמָא דְּגוּפָא דְּאִיהוּ רָזָא דִּבְרִית קַדִּישָׁא, וְנָטַר לֵיהּ, וְאִיהוּ קָאִים בְּעַדְבָּא דְּחוּלָקֵיהּ. אִיהוּ אִשְׁתְּדַּל בְּעוֹבָדָא דִּילֵיהּ, וְלָא אַחֲרָא. אָתוּ כֻּלְּהוּ חַבְרַיָּיא, וְנָשְׁקוּ לֵיהּ.

390. It is written: "and Betzalel made the ark" (Shemot 37:1). HE ASKS: Why did not the wise men who made the tabernacle proceed to build the ark? HE REPLIES THAT Betzalel was of the grade of the ending part of the body, which symbolizes the holy covenant, and kept it. Therefore he deserves the part allotted to him, THE ARK HE MADE, NAMELY, MALCHUT. He strove in what he did, and not another. All the friends came and kissed Rabbi Aba.

28. "The path of just men is like gleam of sunlight"

A Synopsis

Rabbi Shimon opens with, "but the path of just men is like the gleam of sunlight, that shines ever more brightly until the height of noonday." He says that "the path" is the way of truth. Another explanation draws a distinction between "the path" and 'the way', maintaining that "the path" is the word that describes the way of the righteous, who have opened it for the first time; also, the Shechinah now goes into that place that has been opened. Rabbi Shimon moves to, "And Joshua the son of Nun was full of the spirit of wisdom, for Moses had laid his hands upon him...," comparing Moses to the sun and Joshua to the moon. When the moon is full it is in completeness and is called Yud Hei Vav Hei.

391. כַּד מָטוּ לְגַבֵּי דְּרִבִּי שִׁמְעוֹן, וְסַדְרוּ מִלִּין אִלֵּין קַמֵּיה, כָּל מַה דְּאִתְּמַר בְּהַהוּא אוֹרְחָא. פָּתַח וְאָמַר, וְאוֹרַח צַדִּיקִים כְּאוֹר נֹגַהּ הוֹלֵךְ וָאוֹר עַד נְכוֹן הַיּוֹם. הַאי קְרָא אִתְּמַר. אֲבָל הַאי קְרָא אִית לְאִסְתַּכְּלָא בֵּיה, וְאוֹרַח צַדִּיקִים, הַהוּא אוֹרְחָא דְּצַדִּיקַיָּיא אָזְלוּ בֵּיה, אִיהוּ אֹרַח קְשׁוֹט. אוֹרְחָא דְּקוּדְשָׁא בְּרִיךְ הוּא אִתְרְעֵי בֵּיה. אוֹרְחָא דְּאִיהוּ אָזִיל קַמַּיְיהוּ, וְכָל אִינּוּן רְתִיכִין, אַתְיָין לְמִשְׁמַע מִלִּין דְּאִינּוּן מְמַלְּלָן וְאָמְרֵי בְּפוּמַיְיהוּ. כְּאוֹר נֹגַהּ: דְּנָהִיר וְאָזִיל, וְלָא אִתְחֲשָׁךְ כְּלָל, כְּאוֹרַח דְּאִינּוּן חַיָּיבַיָּא, דְּאוֹרַח דִּילְהוֹן אִתְחֲשָׁךְ תָּדִיר, כד"א דֶּרֶךְ רְשָׁעִים כָּאֲפֵלָה וְגוֹ'.

391. When they came to Rabbi Shimon, they repeated before him what was said on that way. He opened and said "but the path of just men is like the gleam of sunlight, that shines ever more brightly until the height of noonday" (Mishlei 4:18). This verse was already explained. Nevertheless, we should look at it. "The path of just men," NAMELY, THE PATH, in which the righteous walk, is the way of truth, preferred by the Holy One, blessed be He, a way in which the Holy One, blessed be He, goes before them, and all the Chariots come to hear the words of their mouths. "The gleam" that shines forth is not darkened as in the way of the wicked, whose way is always dark, as is written: "the way of the wicked is like darkness..." (Ibid. 19).

392. ד"א וְאוֹרַח צַדִּיקִים. מַה בֵּין אוֹרַח לְדֶרֶךְ, הָא אוּקְמוּהָ. אֲבָל אוֹרַח הוּא, דְּהַשְׁתָּא אִתְפְּתַח וְאִתְגַּלְיָיא, וְאִתְעֲבֵיד בְּהַהוּא אֲתַר אוֹרַח,

דְּלָא כְּתִישׁוּ בֵּיהּ רַגְלִין מִקַּדְמַת דְּנָא. דֶּרֶךְ: כד"א כְּדוֹרֵךְ בְּגַת, דְּכַתְשִׁין בֵּיהּ רַגְלִין כָּל מַאן דְּבָעֵי.

392. There is another explanation concerning "the path of the just men." The difference between a way and a path was already explained. But a path means a certain place, in which a path was just now opened, discovered and formed, where no feet have yet trodden. A way is "that treads in the winepress" (Yeshayah 63: 2), anybody who wishes can tread it.

393. וְע"ד לְצַדִּיקַיָּיא קָארֵי אֹרַח, דְּאִינּוּן הֲווֹ קַדְמָאֵי לְמִפְתַּח הַהוּא אֲתָר. וְלָא עַל אֲתָר אִיהוּ אֶלָּא אע"ג דְּאַחֲרָנִין בְּנֵי עָלְמָא אָזְלֵי בְּהַהוּא אֲתָר, הַשְׁתָּא דְּאַזְלִין בֵּיהּ צַדִּיקַיָּיא, אִיהוּ אֲתָר חַדְתָּא, דְּהַשְׁתָּא חַדְתָּא אִיהוּ הַהוּא אֲתָר כְּמָה דְּלָא אָזִיל בֵּיהּ בַּר נָשׁ אַחֲרָא לְעָלְמִין. בְּגִין דְּצַדִּיקַיָּיא עַבְדִין חַדְתָּא לְכָל הַהוּא אֲתָר, בְּכַמָּה מִלִּין עִלָּאִין דְּקוּדְשָׁא בְּרִיךְ הוּא אִתְרְעֵי בְּהוֹן.

393. Therefore for the righteous, A WAY IS called a path, for they were the first to uncover it. And not of the place IS IT SAID THAT IT WAS OPENED, for though other people walk in this particular place, nevertheless now when righteous walk it, it is new, AS IF NEWLY OPENED, and not trodden by anyone else before. This is so because the righteous renew that entire place with many NEW holy expositions, with which the Holy One, blessed be He, is pleased.

394. וְתוּ, דִּשְׁכִינְתָּא אַזְלָא בְּהַהוּא אֲתָר, מַה דְּלָא הֲוַות מִקַּדְמַת דְּנָא. ובג"כ אֹרַח צַדִּיקִים אִקְרֵי, בְּגִין דְּאִתְאֲרַח בֵּיהּ אוּשְׁפִּיזָא עִלָּאָה קַדִּישָׁא. דֶּרֶךְ: אִיהוּ פָּתוּחַ לְכֹלָּא, וְכַתְשִׁין בֵּיהּ כָּל מַאן דְּבָעֵי, אֲפִילוּ אִינּוּן חַיָּיבִין. דֶּרֶךְ, רָזָא דָּא, הַנּוֹתֵן בַּיָּם דָּרֶךְ, בְּגִין דְּדָרִיךְ בֵּיהּ סִטְרָא אַחֲרָא, דְּלָא אִצְטְרִיךְ, וְשַׁלִּיט לְסַאֲבָא מַשְׁכְּנָא. וְע"ד, צַדִּיקַיָּיא בִּלְחוֹדַיְיהוּ, קַיְימֵי וְשַׁלְטֵי בְּהַהוּא אֲתָר דְּאִקְרֵי אוֹרַח. כְּמָה דְּאוֹקִימְנָא דֶּרֶךְ פָּתוּחַ לְכֹלָּא, לְהַאי סִטְרָא וּלְהַאי סִטְרָא.

394. Furthermore, the Shechinah now goes into that place, a thing which did not happen before. Therefore it is called "the path (Heb. *orach*) of just

men," for a holy and high visitor (Heb. *ore'ach*) came to visit, NAMELY THE SHECHINAH. A way is opened for all, and whoever wants to, can tread it, even the wicked. A way is in the mystery of the verse "who makes a way in the sea" (Yeshayah 43:16), FOR IN THE SEA THE WAY IS NOT SAFE, since the Other Side treads in it, and though uninvited, rules it and defiles the tabernacle. Therefore the righteous alone exist in and rule the specified place called path, as I explained. For a way is open and available to all, to this and that side, TO HOLINESS AND DEFILEMENT.

395. וְאַתּוּן קַדִּישֵׁי עֶלְיוֹנִין, אוֹרַח קַדִּישָׁא עִלָּאָה אִזְדָּמַן לְגַבַּיְיכוּ, וְאָרְחַתּוּן בֵּיהּ וּמִלִּין מְעַלְיָין עִלָּאִין אִתְסָדְרוּ קָמֵי עַתִּיק יוֹמִין. זַכָּאָה חוּלָקֵיכוֹן.

395. And you, holy saints, a high and holy path was presented before you, and you were its guests; supernal and excellent matters were expounded before the Ancient One (Heb. *Atik Yomin*). Happy is your portion.

396. פָּתַח ר"ש וְאָמַר, וִיהוֹשֻׁעַ בֶּן נוּן מָלֵא רוּחַ חָכְמָה כִּי סָמַךְ מֹשֶׁה וְגוֹ', בְּכַמָּה אֲתָר תָּנֵינָן, דְּמֹשֶׁה אַנְפּוֹי כְּאַנְפֵּי שִׁמְשָׁא, וִיהוֹשֻׁעַ כְּאַנְפֵּי סִיהֲרָא. דְּלֵית נְהוֹרָא לְסִיהֲרָא, אֶלָּא נְהוֹרָא דְּשִׁמְשָׁא כַּד נָהַר לְסִיהֲרָא, וְסִיהֲרָא מִגּוֹ שִׁמְשָׁא אִתְמַלְיָיא. וְכַד אִתְמַלְיָיא, כְּדֵין קַיְימָא בְּאַשְׁלְמוּתָא.

396. Rabbi Shimon opened the discussion and said "And Joshua the son of Nun was full of the spirit of wisdom, for Moses had laid his hands upon him..." (Devarim 34:9). We learned a few time that the face of Moses was like that of the sun, WHICH IS ZEIR ANPIN, and that of Joshua was like the face of the moon, WHICH IS MALCHUT, for the moon does not have light save the light of the sun, ZEIR ANPIN, that shines upon the moon, MALCHUT. The moon grows full from the sun. When it is full, it is whole.

397. אִשְׁתְּלִימוּתָא דְּסִיהֲרָא, מַאן אִיהוּ. רָזָא דְּכֹלָּא, דְּאִקְרֵי דְּמוּת בְּרָזָא דִּשְׁמָא עִלָּאָה יְיָ'. דְּהָא בִּשְׁמָא דָּא לָא קָאִים, בַּר בְּזִמְנָא דְּקַיְימָא בְּאַשְׁלְמוּתָא. דְּהָא כַּמָּה שְׁמָהָן אִינּוּן דְּאַחֲסִינָא, וְאִתְקְרֵי בְּהוּ כָּךְ כְּפוּם

שַׁעֲתָא דְּקַיְימָא בֵּיה, הָכִי אִקְרֵי בְּהַהוּא שְׁמָא מַמָּשׁ. וְכַד קַיְימָא בְּרָזָא
דְּאַשְׁלָמוּתָא וְאִשְׁתְּלִימַת מִכָּל סִטְרִין, כְּדֵין אִקְרֵי יְדֹוָ״ד אַשְׁלְמוּתָא
דִּילָהּ, כְּאַשְׁלָמוּתָא דִּלְעֵילָא. דְּיָרְתָא בְּרַתָּא לְאִמָּהּ.

397. HE ASKS: What is the fullness of the moon, AND ANSWERS: the
mystery of all this is that the image, THE SECRET OF MALCHUT, is named
after the secret of the upper Name, Yud Hei Vav Hei. It does not bear that
name, YUD HEI VAV HEI save in its fullness. For many are the names it
inherited, and bears according to its state. And when it is in the state of the
secret of fullness, whole on all sides, it is called Yud, Hei, Vav, Hei, for its
completeness resembles the completeness of above, THAT IS, ZEIR ANPIN
CALLED YUD HEI VAV HEI. THEREFORE MALCHUT TOO IS CALLED YUD
HEI VAV HEI for the daughter inherited her mother. THAT SHE RECEIVED
ALL THE MOCHIN FROM IMA, THAT IS BINAH, THROUGH ZEIR ANPIN.

29. "The fifteenth day of this seventh month"

A Synopsis

Rabbi Shimon explains the mystery of the fifteenth day of the month, talking about the fullness of the moon and saying that Joshua is full of the spirit of wisdom because of his designation 'son of Nun'. We learn that a spirit, Ruach, issued from the expansion of the higher firmament, and it formed a temple below, Malchut in its fullness. Joshua is "full of the spirit of wisdom" because "Moses laid his hands upon him." Moses is considered to be the face of the sun and Joshua the face of the moon. Rabbi Shimon tells the rabbis that each of them is also filled with the spirit of wisdom because God has laid his hands upon them.

398. וְהַיְינוּ בַּחֲמֵיסָר יוֹמִין, דִּכְתִיב בַּחֲמִשָּׁה עָשָׂר יוֹם לַחֹדֶשׁ הַשְּׁבִיעִי הַזֶּה. וּכְתִיב אַךְ בֶּעָשׂוֹר לַחֹדֶשׁ הַשְּׁבִיעִי. וְכֹלָּא רָזָא חֲדָא, כַּד קַיְימָא עָלְמָא דְּאָתֵי בְּרָזָא דְּכָל עֶשֶׂר אֲמִירָן, עַל הַאי חֹדֶשׁ, אִקְרֵי בֶּעָשׂוֹר. וְכַד אִתְרְשִׁימַת סִיהֲרָא בְּאַשְׁלְמוּתָא חֲדָא בֵּינַיְיהוּ, אִקְרֵי בַּחֲמִשָּׁה עָשָׂר, דְּהָא ה' אִתְחַבְּרַת וְאִתְחַקְקַת בֵּינַיְיהוּ.

398. MALCHUT IS NAMED YUD HEI VAV HEI ON the fifteenth day, as is written: "The fifteenth day of this seventh month" (Vayikra 23:34), and: "on the tenth of this seventh month" (Ibid. 27). All has the same meaning: when the World to Come, BINAH, composed of the secret of the ten utterances, ITS TEN SFIROT, rests upon this month, MALCHUT, it is called 'the tenth'. And when the moon is impressed between THE TEN SFIROT OF BINAH, for one wholeness, MALCHUT is called 'the fifteenth', since Hei (= 5), WHICH IS MALCHUT, was joined and engraved among THE TEN SFIROT OF BINAH.

399. וְרָזָא דָּא י"ה ו"ה וְכַד קַיְימָא בִּשְׁמָא דָּא, כְּדֵין אִתְחַבָּר בָּהּ, וְאִיהִי אִתּוֹסְפָא אִיהִי, בְּרָזָא דְּאָת ה' כְּמִלְּקַדְמִין. חֲדָא, לְאִתְחַקְּקָא וּלְאִתְחַבְּרָא בְּרָזָא דִּלְעֵילָּא. וַחֲדָא לְמֵיהַב מְזוֹנָא לְתַתָּא. וּכְדֵין קַיְימָא סִיהֲרָא בְּאַשְׁלְמוּתָא לְכָל סְטְרִין, עֵילָּא וְתַתָּא, בְּרָזָא דִּשְׁמָא דָּא, לְמֶהֱוֵי כֹּלָּא רָזָא חֲדָא, וּשְׁלִימוּ חַד.

399. This is the secret reason, why MALCHUT IS CALLED Yud Hei Vav Hei. When it is called by that name, YUD HEI VAV HEI, it is connected to the LAST Hei OF YUD HEI VAV HEI, and added to BECOME A PART OF the secret of the last Hei OF YUD HEI VAV HEI, as before. THEN IT IS PART OF THE SECRET OF THE WHOLE NAME YUD HEI VAV HEI AND IS ITS LAST HEI, so it is a) engraved and united with the secret of above. IN THIS SENSE MALCHUT TAKES ALL THE NAME YUD HEI VAV HEI. b) to give sustenance below. IN THIS SENSE IT IS UNITED WITH THE LAST HEI OF YUD HEI VAV HEI. Then the moon is whole on all sides, above and below in the secret of the name YUD HEI VAV HEI so everything becomes one secret and one wholeness.

400. יְהוֹשֻׁעַ דָּא אִיהוּ רָזָא דְּאַשְׁלָמוּתָא דְּסִיהֲרָא, בְּאִלֵּין אַתְוָון בֶּן נוּ"ן, נוּ"ן וַדַּאי דְּהָא נוּן רָזָא דְּסִיהֲרָא אִיהִי. מָלֵא בְּרָזָא דְּאַשְׁלָמוּתָא דִּשְׁמָא קַדִּישָׁא, כְּדֵין אִיהוּ מָלֵא רוּחַ חָכְמָה וַדַּאי.

400. Joshua is the secret of making the moon complete by the letters 'son of Nun'. Assuredly it is Nun (= 50), THAT IS, BASED ON THE SECRET OF THE FIFTY GATES, SAME AS BINAH, for Nun is the mystery of the moon when it is full by means of the fullness of the Holy Name YUD HEI VAV HEI. Then he is "full of the spirit of wisdom (lit. 'Chochmah')" (Devarim 34:9), TO WIT, IS IN THE SECRET OF THE SIX ENDS OF CHOCHMAH CALLED SPIRIT.

401. בְּגִין דִּנְקוּדָה עִלָּאָה דְּאִיהִי י', אִתְפַּשֵּׁט וְאַפִּיק רוּחַ, וְהַהוּא רוּחַ עָבִיד הֵיכָלָא. וְהַהוּא רוּחַ אִתְפַּשֵּׁט, וְאִתְעָבֵיד שִׁית סִטְרִין. הַהוּא רוּחַ אִתְפַּשֵּׁט, בְּרָזָא דְּכָל אִלֵּין. וְאַמְלֵי וְעָבֵיד הֵיכָלָא לְתַתָּא, וְאִתְמְלֵי כֹּלָּא, וְאִתְעָבֵיד רָזָא דִּשְׁמָא קַדִּישָׁא, בְּאַשְׁלָמוּתָא חֲדָא.

401. When the upper point, Yud OF YUD HEI VAV HEI, NAMELY CHOCHMAH, expanded, it issued a spirit, TO WIT, THE SIX ENDS OF CHOCHMAH. This spirit formed a chamber, BINAH, from which it spread and became six ends, THAT IS, ZEIR ANPIN. The spirit was spread through all these, THAT IS, AS THE SIX ENDS OF CHOCHMAH AND BINAH and filled and formed a lower chamber, MALCHUT IN ITS FULLNESS. So everything was filled and became, WITHIN MALCHUT, the secret of the Holy Name YUD HEI VAV HEI, as one whole.

402. וּבג"ד יְהוֹשֻׁעַ מָלֵא רוּחַ חָכְמָה, בְּגִין כִּי סָמַךְ מֹשֶׁה אֶת יָדָיו עָלָיו,
דְּאִיהוּ אָרִיק בִּרְכָאן עָלֵיהּ, וְאִתְמְלֵי בֵּירָא מִנֵּיהּ. וְאַתּוּן קַדִּישֵׁי
עֶלְיוֹנִין, כָּל חַד מִנַּיְיכוּ אִתְמְלֵי רוּחַ חָכְמָה, וְקַיְּימָא בְּאַשְׁלְמוּתָא,
בְּרָזִין דְּחָכְמְתָא. בְּגִין דְּקוּדְשָׁא בְּרִיךְ הוּא הוּא אִתְרְעֵי בְּכוּ, וְאַסְמִיךְ
יְדוֹי עֲלַיְיכוּ. זַכָּאָה חוּלָקִי דְּעֵינַי חָמוּ דָּא, וְחָמוּ שְׁלִימוּ דְרוּחַ חָכְמְתָא
בְּכוּ.

402. For this reason Joshua is "full of the spirit of wisdom," because "Moses laid his hands upon him" (Ibid.). For Moses, CONSIDERED TO BE THE FACE OF THE SUN, WHICH IS ZEIR ANPIN, poured out his blessings upon him, and the well was filled from it, MALCHUT, THAT IS, JOSHUA, WHO IS THE FACE OF THE MOON, WAS FILLED BY ZEIR ANPIN, AS SAID. And you, exalted saints, each one of you is filled with the spirit of wisdom, and is full of the mysteries of wisdom, since the Holy One, blessed be He, takes pleasure in you and has laid His hands upon you. Happy is my portion that my eyes beheld it, and beheld the spirit of wisdom in its wholeness.

30. Whoever eats without a prayer

A Synopsis

Rabbi Shimon opens with "You shall not eat with the blood, neither shall you practice divination nor soothsaying." He says that whoever eats without praying for his blood is the same as someone who practices divination and soothsaying. We learn that during the nights the souls go up, and since man is sustained by the power that permeates the blood he tastes death, for the power of the blood is not strong enough to receive the power of the Neshamah. Therefore when a man awakens he is not pure; the Other Side has power over a place vacant of soul. Even after a person washes himself with water, the Nefesh rules him, not the Neshamah. But when he prays, the power of the Neshamah is strengthened and the man is properly perfected with the Nefesh below and the Neshamah above. Finally, Rabbi Shimon explains how a man who eats before praying is considered a diviner and a soothsayer.

403. פָּתַח וְאָמַר, כְּתִיב לֹא תֹאכְלוּ עַל הַדָּם לֹא תְנַחֲשׁוּ וְלֹא תְעוֹנֵנוּ. הַאי קְרָא אוּקְמוּהָ, וְרָזָא דְמִלָּה, הַאי מַאן דְּאָכִיל בְּלָא צְלוֹתָא, דִּיצַלֵּי עַל דָּמֵיהּ, שָׁקִיל אִיהוּ כִּמְנַחֵשׁ וּמְעוֹנֵן.

403. He opened the discourse with the verse, "You shall not eat anything with the blood, neither shall you use enchantment nor soothsaying" (Vayikra 19:26). This was explained, but its secret is this: whoever eats without praying for his blood, is considered as if he practices divination and soothsaying.

404. בְּגִין דִּבְלֵילְיָא נִשְׁמְתָא סַלְקַת לְמֶחֱמֵי בְּרָזָא דִּיקָרָא עִלָּאָה, כָּל חַד וְחַד כְּמָה דְּאִתְחֲזֵי לֵיהּ. וְאִשְׁתְּאַר בְּהַהוּא חֵילָא דְּאִתְפְּשַׁט גּוֹ דָמָא, לְאִתְקַיְּימָא גוּפָא. וְעַל דָּא טָעִים טַעֲמָא דְמוֹתָא, וְהַהוּא חֵילָא לָא מִתְעַתְּדָא לְאִתְעָרָא גּוֹ הַהוּא חֵילָא דְּנִשְׁמְתָא, וּלְקַבְּלָא לֵיהּ. וְכַד אִתְעָר בַּר נָשׁ, לָאו אִיהוּ דְּכִי. וְהָא אוּקִימְנָא, דְּסִטְרָא אַחֲרָא שַׁלִּיט, עַל אֲתָר דְּקַיְּימָא בְּלָא נִשְׁמְתָא.

404. For at night the soul mounts and gazes upon the mystery of the supernal glory, each according to its merits. Man is sustained by the power that permeates the blood and preserves the body. Therefore he tastes death,

for the strength OF THE BLOOD is not able to awaken to the power of the soul and receive it. For that reason, when man awakens FROM SLEEP he is not pure. We already explained that the Other Side has power over a place vacant of soul.

405. כֵּיוָן דְּאִתְדָּכֵי בְּמַיָּא, וְאע״ג דְּאִשְׁתַּדַּל בַּר נָשׁ בְּאוֹרַיְיתָא, הַהִיא נִשְׁמְתָא לָא אִתְקַיְּימַת בְּאַתְרָה, וְלָא שַׁלְטָא בֵּיהּ בב״נ, בַּר חֵילָא דְּדָמָא בִּלְחוֹדוֹי, דְּאִקְרֵי נֶפֶשׁ, הַהִיא דְּאִתְפַּשְּׁטָא בִּדְמָא תָּדִיר, וְהָא אוֹקִימְנָא. וְכַד יְצַלֵּי ב״נ צְלוֹתָא דְּפוּלְחָנָא דְּמָארֵיהּ, כְּדֵין מִתְיַישְׁבָא חֵילָא דִּדְמָא בְּאַתְרֵיהּ, וְאִתְגַּבַּר חֵילָא דְּנִשְׁמְתָא, וְאִתְיַישְׁבָא עַל הַהוּא אֲתָר. וּכְדֵין בַּר נָשׁ אִשְׁתְּלִים קַמֵּי מָארֵיהּ, כְּמָה דְּאִצְטְרִיךְ, נֶפֶשׁ לְתַתָּא, וְרָזָא דְּמִלָּה דְּנִשְׁמְתָא לְעֵילָא.

405. After washing himself with water, though he is occupied in the Torah, the Neshamah is not kept in its place nor rules man, only the power of the blood alone does, which is called Nefesh. The Nefesh always permeates the blood, as we already explained. And when a man prays, worshipping his Master, then the power of the blood resumes its place, and the power of the Neshamah is strengthened, so it settles in that place IN THE BODY. Then a man is properly perfected before his Master, the Nefesh below and, the inner matter, the Neshamah, above.

406. וְע״ד, מַאן דְּצַלֵּי צְלוֹתָא עַד לָא יֵיכוּל, קָאִים גַּרְמֵיהּ כְּמָה דְּאִצְטְרִיךְ, וְסַלְקָא נִשְׁמְתָא עַל אֲתָר מוֹתְבָהּ כְּמָה דְּאִצְטְרִיךְ, וְאִי אָכִיל עַד לָא צַלֵּי צְלוֹתֵיהּ לְאִתְיַישְׁבָא דְּמָא עַל אַתְרֵיהּ, הָא אִיהוּ כִּמְנַחֵשׁ וּמְעוֹנֵן. בְּגִין דְּהָא אִיהוּ אָרְחֵיהּ דִּמְנַחֵשׁ, לְסַלְּקָא לִסְטַר אַחֲרָא, וּלְמָאֲכָא סִטְרָא דִּקְדוּשָׁה.

406. Therefore, whoever prays before eating, is considered to be in a good position. The Neshamah mounts to settle in its place as ought. But if he eats before praying, causing the blood to settle in its place, he is considered a diviner and a soothsayer. WHY? Because it is the way of the diviner to elevate the Other Side and humiliate the holy side.

407. אֲמַאי אִקְרֵי בַּר נָשׁ הַהוּא דְּאִשְׁתַּדַּל בְּהַהוּא סִטְרָא מְנַחֵשׁ. עַל

דְּאִשְׁתָּדַּל בְּהַהוּא נָחָשׁ, לְאַתְקְפָא חֵילֵיהּ וּלְאִתְגַּבְּרָא. וְדָא אִיהוּ כְּמַאן דְּפָלַח לֶאלֹהִים אֲחֵרִים. וְכֵן הַאי פָּלַח לְהַהוּא חֵילָא דְּדָמָא, וְלָא פָּלַח לֵיהּ לְקוּדְשָׁא בְּרִיךְ הוּא , לְאַתְקְפָא סִטְרָא דְּנִשְׁמָתָא, סִטְרָא דִּקְדוּשָׁה.

407. HE ASKS: Why is a man who tried to please that side, NAMELY, WHO ATE BEFORE PRAYING, CALLED an enchanter (Heb.*menachesh*)? HE REPLIES: IT IS SO since he worked hard for that serpent (Heb. *nachash*) OF THE KLIPOT, to raise its power and strength. It is like one worshipping other Elohim, serving the power of the blood, not the Holy One, blessed be He, by strengthening the side of the Neshamah, the holy side.

408. מְעוֹנֵן, דְּאִשְׁתָּדַּל בְּחוֹבָא, וְלָא אִשְׁתָּדַּל בִּזְכוּ. וְאִי תֵּימָא הָא קַיְּימָא נ' בְּאֶמְצָעִיתָא. הָכִי הוּא וַדַּאי, דְּהָא לָא יַכְלִין לְשַׁלְטָאָה בְּהַהוּא סִטְרָא אַחֲרָא, עַד דְּאִתְעָרְבֵי בֵּיהּ עֵרוּבָא דְּסְטַר קְדוּשָׁה, כְּחוּטָא חַד דָּקִיק. מַאן דְּבָעֵי לְקַיְּימָא שִׁקְרָא, יְעָרֵב בָּהּ מִלָּה דִּקְשׁוֹט, בְּגִין דְּיִתְקַיֵּים הַהוּא שִׁקְרָא. וְעַל דָּא עָוֹן מִלָּה דְּשֶׁקֶר הוּא, וּבְגִין לְקַיְּימָא לֵיהּ, עָאלִין בָּהּ מִלָּה דִּקְשׁוֹט, וְדָא אִיהוּ נ', בְּדָא מְקַיְּימֵי לְהַהוּא שֶׁקֶר. וּמַאן דְּלָא צַלֵּי צְלוֹתָא לְקַמֵּי קוּדְשָׁא בְּרִיךְ הוּא, עַד לָא יֵיכוּל עַל דָּמֵיהּ, כִּמְנַחֵשׁ וּמְעוֹנֵן.

408. HE ASKS: WHY A MAN WHO EATS BEFORE PRAYING IS CALLED a diviner, AND ANSWERS: BECAUSE he worked towards sins and did not place his effort for merits, FOR THE HEBREW WORD SOOTHSAYER – (HEB. ME'ONEN), IS DERIVED FROM THE LETTERS OF THE WORD 'SIN' (HEB. AVON). And if you say that there is an extra Nun in the middle OF THE WORD ME'ONEN, AND THEREFORE IT SHOULD HAVE BEEN SAID 'MA'ON' WITHOUT THE EXTRA NUN IN THE MIDDLE, THEN HE EXPLAINS THAT it is assuredly so, for we cannot have power over the Other Side, only when we mix in it a little from the holy side, as a thin thread. Whoever wishes for a lie to endure, should mix some truth in it, so the lie will prevail. Therefore, a sin is a lie and in order to keep it intact, some truth is added. This is the meaning of Nun IN THE MIDDLE OF THE WORD 'ME'ONEN', to keep the lie. THEREFORE he who does not pray for his blood (for himself) before the Holy One, blessed be He, before eating, is considered a diviner and soothsayer.

31. The four corrections of prayer

A Synopsis

Rabbi Shimon says that in a prayer, man's body and Nefesh are corrected and become whole. Prayer consists of four kinds of rectifications. The first is of the self, for a man should mend himself with precepts and holiness and sacrifices and offerings that will purify him. The second is of this world, to bless God for each deed in creation; this sustains the world. The third is the rectification of the higher world together with all its armies and camps. The fourth rectification is that of the prayer of Amidah, fixing the secret of the Holy Name or the wholly perfected name.

409. צְלוֹתָא דְּבַר נָשׁ, כְּמָה דְּאָמַרְתּוּן אַתּוּן קַדִּישֵׁי עֶלְיוֹנִין, זַכָּאָה חוּלָקֵיכוֹן, דְּהָא בִּצְלוֹתָא מִתַתְּקָן גּוּפֵיהּ וְנַפְשֵׁיהּ דְּבַר נָשׁ, וְאִתְעֲבֵיד שָׁלִים. צְלוֹתָא אִיהִי תִּקּוּנִין מְתַתְּקָנָן דְּמִתְתַּקְנָן כַּחֲדָא, וְאִינוּן אַרְבַּע. תִּקּוּנָא קַדְמָאָה, תִּקּוּנָא דְּגַרְמֵיהּ, לְאַשְׁתַּלְמָא. תִּקּוּנָא תִּנְיָינָא, תִּקּוּנָא דְּהַאי עָלְמָא. תִּקּוּנָא תְּלִיתָאָה, תִּקּוּנָא דְּעָלְמָא לְעֵילָא, בְּכָל אִינוּן חֵילֵי שְׁמַיָא. תִּקּוּנָא רְבִיעָאָה, תִּקּוּנָא דִּשְׁמָא קַדִּישָׁא, בְּרָזָא דִּרְתִיכִין קַדִּישִׁין, וּבְרָזָא דְּעָלְמִין כֻּלְּהוּ, עֵילָא וְתַתָּא בְּתִקּוּנָא כַּדְקָא יָאוּת.

409. The prayer of man is as you described it, exalted saints, happy is your portion. Through prayer, man's body and Nefesh are mended and become whole. Prayer consists of corrections carried out together, four CORRRECTIONS in all. The first correction is mending oneself so one may become whole. The second is correcting this world. The third is to correct the heavenly armies. The fourth is the correction of the Holy Name by means of the holy Chariots and of all the worlds, properly corrected above and below.

410. תִּקּוּנָא קַדְמָאָה תִּקּוּנָא דְּגַרְמֵיהּ, בְּגִין דְּאִצְטְרִיךְ לְאַתְקָנָא גַּרְמֵיהּ, בְּמִצְוָה וּקְדוּשָׁה, וּלְאִתְתַּקְנָא בְּקָרְבְּנִין וְעָלָוֶון לְאִתְדַּכָּאָה. תִּקּוּנָא תִּנְיָינָא, בְּתִקּוּנָא דְּקִיּוּמָא דְּהַאי עָלְמָא, בְּעוֹבָדָא דִּבְרֵאשִׁית, לְבָרְכָא לְקוּדְשָׁא בְּרִיךְ הוּא, עַל כָּל עוֹבָדָא וְעוֹבָדָא, בְּאִינוּן הַלְלוּיָה, הַלְלוּהוּ כָּל כֹּכְבֵי אוֹר הַלְלוּהוּ שְׁמֵי הַשָּׁמַיִם וְגוֹ' לְקַיְּימָא קִיּוּמָא דְּהַאי עָלְמָא.

וְעַל דָּא בְּבָרוּךְ שֶׁאָמַר, בָּרוּךְ, בָּרוּךְ עַל כֹּלָא.

410. HE EXPOUNDED UPON WHAT HE SAID, the first work I MENTIONED IS the correction of the self, for a man should correct himself with precepts and holiness, and with sacrifices and burnt offerings that will purify him. THE FRINGES (HEB. *TZITZIT*) ARE WHAT IS MEANT BY PRECEPT, AND TEFILIN ARE WHAT IS MEANT BY HOLINESS; BY SAYING THE PRAYER OF SACRIFICES AND BURNT OFFERINGS HE IS CORRECTED AS IF HE OFFERED THEM. The second correction is of this world, NAMELY, regarding the work of Creation to bless the Holy One, blessed be He, for every action, by saying "praise Him, all you stars of light, praise Him, heavens of heavens..." (Tehilim 148:3-4). IT IS SAID to sustain this world. Therefore we say 'Blessed be He who said', for 'blessed' MEANS blessed for everything.

411. תִּקּוּנָא תְּלִיתָאָה, דְּאִיהוּ תִּקּוּנָא לְעָלְמָא לְעֵילָא, בְּכָל אִינּוּן חַיָּילֵי חַיָּילִין וּמַשִׁרְיָין. יוֹצֵר מְשָׁרְתִים וַאֲשֶׁר מְשָׁרְתָיו וְגו', וְהָאוֹפַנִּים וְחַיּוֹת הַקֹּדֶשׁ. תִּקּוּנָא רְבִיעָאָה, תִּקּוּנָא דִּצְלוֹתָא, בְּתִקּוּנָא דְּרָזָא דִשְׁמָא קַדִּישָׁא כְּדְקָא אָמַרְתּוּן, זַכָּאָה חוּלָקֵיכוֹן. וְהָכָא רָזָא דְתִקּוּנָא דִשְׁמָא שְׁלִים. זַכָּאָה חוּלָקֵי עִמְּכוֹן בְּהַאי עָלְמָא וּבְעָלְמָא דְאָתֵי.

411. The third correction is on amending the higher world together with all its armies and camps, IS THE PRAISE 'Creator of ministering angels, all of Whose ministering angels...and the ofanim and the holy living creatures'. The fourth is the correction of the Amidah prayer, establishing the secret of the Holy Name, as you said, happy is your portion. And here is the secret of correcting the entire Name. Happy is my portion with you in this world and in the World to Come.

32. "fear your Elohim"

A Synopsis

Rabbi Shimon opens with, "You shall fear Hashem your Elohim; Him shall you serve," and, "but you shall fear your Elohim (lit. 'from your Elohim')." He says that 'from your Elohim' means from that place that is connected to and surrounds the inner brain from inside. We read that this is the Shechinah named Elohim, and there is a fire around it. There are three kinds of fire. The first receives fire gladly, and they love each other. In the second the brightness, the Shechinah, is seen; this fire gladly dwells within the first one. The third fire surrounds that brightness, and in it lies the fear of judgment. On the left side is the fear of punishment, but this must be joined with love that is drawn from the right. Rabbi Shimon says that we should not be afraid of strange deities. After this he talks about love, saying that He who worships with love joins the high place above, the holiness of the World to Come that is Binah and the right side that is Chesed of Zeir Anpin. Nothing has power over the level of fear but love.

412. פִּקּוּדֵי אוֹרַיְיתָא דְּאָמַרְתּוּן בִּצְלוֹתָא וַדַּאי הָכִי הוּא. פָּתַח וְאָמַר, כְּתִיב אֶת יְיָ׳ אֱלֹהֶיךָ תִּירָא אוֹתוֹ תַעֲבוֹד. וּכְתִיב, וְיָרֵאתָ מֵאֱלֹהֶיךָ. הַאי קְרָא אִית לְמֵימַר הָכִי, וְיָרֵאתָ אֱלֹהֶיךָ, בְּגִין דְּהָא כְּתִיב אֶת יְיָ׳ אֱלֹהֶיךָ תִּירָא מֵאֱלֹהֶיךָ. אֶלָּא רָזָא אִיהוּ, מֵאֱלֹהֶיךָ וַדַּאי, מֵהַהוּא אֲתָר דְּאִתְחַבָּר וְסָחֲרָא לְמוֹחָא דִּלְגוֹ, וְדָא אִיהוּ מֵאֱלֹהֶיךָ, דְּחִילוּ דָּא לְמִדְחַל לֵיהּ, דְּהָא תַּמָּן שַׁרְיָיא דִּינָא, וְאִיהוּ דִּינָא דְּאִשְׁתְּאִיב מִגּוֹ דִּינָא דִּלְעֵילָּא, בְּהַאי אֲתָר.

412. The precepts of the Torah you spoke of in relation to prayer, are assuredly so. He opened with the words: "You shall fear Hashem your Elohim; Him shall you serve" (Devarim 10:20) and "but shall fear your Elohim (lit. 'be afraid of your Elohim')" (Vayikra 19:14). The second verse should have been read "your Elohim," for it is written: "fear Hashem your Elohim" AND NOT "OF HASHEM YOUR ELOHIM." What is meant by "of your Elohim?" HE ANSWERS: The secret meaning is that "of your Elohim" surely refers to that place that is connected to and surrounds the inner fruit from inside. IT IS THE SHECHINAH NAMED ELOHIM, AND THE FIRE AROUND IT IS THE MYSTERY OF THE FIRE SURROUNDING THE

BRIGHTNESS, FROM WHICH JUDGMENT IS DRAWN UPON THE WICKED AS WILL BE EXPOUNDED LATER. This is what is meant by "of your Elohim," THAT IS, THE SURROUNDING FIRE. He should be feared, for Judgment prevails there, drawn from the higher Judgment in that place.

413. תְּלַת גְּווֹנֵי אֶשָּׁא הָכָא. אֶשָּׁא קַדְמָאָה, אִיהוּ אֶשָּׁא דְּקַבִּיל אֶשָּׁא בְּחֵידוּ, וְחַדָּאן דָּא בְּדָא בִּרְחִימוּ. אֶשָּׁא תִּנְיָינָא, אִיהוּ אֶשָּׁא דִּכְתִּיב בֵּיהּ וְנֹגַהּ לָאֵשׁ דְּאִתְחֲזֵי בֵּיהּ נֹגַהּ. וְדָא אִיהוּ אֶשָּׁא, דְּקַיְימָא גּוֹ אֶשָּׁא פְּנִימָאָה בְּחֵידוּ, כְּמָה דְּאִתְּמַר. אֶשָּׁא תְּלִיתָאָה, אִיהוּ אֶשָּׁא דְּסַחֲרָא לְהַהוּא נֹגַהּ. וּבְהַאי אֶשָּׁא שַׁאֲרֵי דְּחִילוּ דְּדִינָא, לְאַלְקָאָה חַיָּיבַיָּא.

413. There are three kinds of fire here. The first is the fire which receives fire gladly, and they are glad, and love each other. Upon the second fire it is written: "and there was a glowing brightness to the fire" (Yechezkel 1:13), for the brightness, WHICH IS THE SHECHINAH, is seen in it. This fire gladly dwells within the inner fire, as said, NAMELY, THE FIRST FIRE. The third fire surrounds that glowing brightness, and in it lies the fear of judgment that smites the wicked.

414. וְאַף עַ"ג דִּתְנֵינָן, דְּאַרְבְּעָה גְּווֹנֵי אֶשָּׁא נִינְהוּ, וְאִינּוּן אַרְבַּע דְּאִינּוּן חַד. אֲבָל הָכָא בְּהַהוּא אֶשָּׁא דְּקָאָמְרָן, שַׁאֲרֵי דְּחִילוּ דְּדִינָא, וְעַל דָּא כְּתִיב, וְיָרֵאתָ מֵאֱלֹהֶיךָ, מֵהַהוּא עוֹנָשָׁא דִּילֵיהּ.

414. And though we learned that there are four colors to fire, NAMELY, WHITE, RED, GREEN AND BLACK; and these four are one, EACH CONSISTS OF THESE FOUR COLORS, WHICH ARE CHESED, GVURAH, TIFERET AND MALCHUT; nevertheless this DOES NOT APPLY TO the fire mentioned before, WE ARE ONLY REFERRING TO THE AREA which is where lies the fear of judgment. THEREFORE WE PARTICULARLY EXPOUNDED AS REQUIRED UPON THREE FIRES ONLY AND NO MORE. About this speaks the verse "And you shall be afraid of your Elohim," MEANING, of His punishment. THIS IS WHY IT IS WRITTEN "OF YOUR ELOHIM."

415. וּבְהַהוּא יִרְאָה בָּעֵי לְשַׁוָּואָה רְעוּתֵיהּ, בִּדְחִילוּ וּרְחִימוּ כַּחֲדָא, לְמִדְחַל בְּהַאי סִטְרָא, וּלְמִרְחַם בְּהַאי סִטְרָא. וּבְאִינּוּן גַּוְונִין דְּקָאָמְרָן,

וְהַהוּא דְחִילוּ לֶהֱוֵי לְמִדְחַל מֵעוֹנָשָׁא. דְּמַאן דְּעָבַר עַל פִּקוּדֵי אוֹרַיְיתָא,
אִתְעֲנַשׁ בְּהַהוּא סִטְרָא דְּכַד שָׁארֵי הַהוּא סִטְרָא לְאַלְקָאָה, לָא שָׁכִיךְ
עַד דְּשָׁצֵי לֵיהּ מֵהַאי עָלְמָא, וּמֵעָלְמָא דְּאָתֵי. וּבְג״כ בָּעֵי לְמִדְחַל מֵהַאי
אֶשָׁא, דִּדְחִילוּ שַׁרְיָיא בֵּיהּ.

415. One should concentrate with love and fear together, to fear on one side, DRAWN FROM THE LEFT, and love on another side, DRAWN FROM THE RIGHT, with the said aspects, FOR MALCHUT TOO HAS THE FOUR ASPECTS: CHESED, GVURAH, TIFERET AND MALCHUT. That fear would be fear of punishment, THE LOWER FEAR, for whoever transgresses the precepts of the Torah is punished by the LEFT side. And once this side starts to strike, it never ceases until it exterminates him from this world and the World to Come. Therefore one should fear that fire, for there is fear within it.

416. וּמִנֵּיהּ אִתְפָּשַׁט אֶשָׁא לְבַר דִּדְחַלָּא אָחֳרָא, וְעַל דָּא כְּתִיב, לֹא
תִירָאוּ אֶת אֱלֹהֵי הָאֱמוֹרִי, דְּאָסִיר לְמִדְחַל מִנֵּיהּ. וְהַאי אֶשָׁא דִּדְחִילוּ
דְּקָאמְרָן, אִיהוּ קֹדֶשׁ וְאִשְׁתְּתַּף בִּקְדוּשָׁה, וְהַאי אִיהוּ דְּסַחֲרָא לְהַהוּא
נֹגַהּ דְּקָאמְרָן. וְהַהִיא אֶשָׁא אָחֳרָא דִּלְבַר, אִיהוּ דְּאִתְחַבַּר בְּהַאי
לְזִמְנִין. וּלְזִמְנִין אִתְעֲבָר מִנֵּיהּ, וְלָא אִתְחַבָּר בַּהֲדֵיהּ. וְכַד גְּרִים
דְּאִתְחַבָּר בְּהַאי, כְּדֵין הוּא אֶשָׁא דְּחָשׁוּךְ, וְאַחְשִׁיךְ וְכַסֵּי נְהִירוּ דְּאִלֵּין
אַחֳרָנִין. וְסִימָנִיךְ וְאֵשׁ מִתְלַקַּחַת, וְלָא דְּקַיְּימָא תָּדִיר, וְהָא אִתְּמַר.

416. From THE THIRD FIRE a fire is spread outwards to strange Elohim. Upon this says the verse "you shall not fear the Elohim of the Emorites" (Shoftim 6:10), because one must not be afraid of them. This fire of fear we mentioned, NAMELY, THE THIRD FIRE, is holy and takes part in holiness. It is that which surrounds the brightness. But the other fire outside is sometimes connected TO THIS FIRE OF FEAR, and sometimes separates from it and disconnects. And when SINS cause the fire outside to be joined with the fire OF FEAR, then the fire becomes dark, darkens and covers the other lights WITHIN THE BRIGHTNESS. This may be derived from the expression "a fire flaring up" (Yechezkel 1:4), for it is not ALWAYS burning, as was already explained.

417. לְבָתַר אַהֲבָה, כְּמָה דְּאוּקְמוּהָ דְּאַהֲבָה שַׁרְיָיא לְבָתַר יִרְאָה. וְרָזָא

דְּמִלָּה, כֵּיוָן דְּשָׁארֵי יִרְאָה עַל רֵישֵׁיהּ דְּבַר נָשׁ, אִתְּעַר לְבָתַר אַהֲבָה, דְּאִיהוּ יְמִינָא. דְּמַאן דְּפָלַח מִגּוֹ אַהֲבָה, אִתְדַּבַּק בַּאֲתַר עִלָּאָה לְעֵילָּא, וְאִתְדַּבַּק בִּקְדוּשָׁה דְּעָלְמָא דְּאָתֵי, בְּגִין דְּהָא סָלִיק לְאִתְעַטְּרָא וּלְאִתְדַּבְּקָא בִּסְטַר יְמִינָא.

417. After this there is love, as explained that love dwells after ATTAINING fear. The secret of the matter is that once fear dwells upon the head of man, WHICH IS FROM THE LEFT, love is awakened from the right, THAT IS, FROM CHESED OF ZEIR ANPIN. He who worships with love, cleaves the high place above, and joins the holiness of the World to Come, WHICH IS BINAH; for he rises and bedecks himself and joins the right side, WHICH IS CHESED OF ZEIR ANPIN, UPON WHICH DWELLS BINAH.

418. וְאִי תֵּימָא דְּפוּלְחָנָא דְּאִיהוּ מִסִּטְרָא דְּיִרְאָה לָאו אִיהוּ פּוּלְחָנָא. פּוּלְחָנָא יַקִּירָא אִיהוּ, אֲבָל לָא סָלִיק לְאִתְדַּבְּקָא לְעֵילָּא. וְכַד פָּלַח מֵאַהֲבָה, סָלִיק וְאִתְעַטַּר לְעֵילָּא, וְאִתְדַּבַּק בְּעָלְמָא דְּאָתֵי, וְדָא אִיהוּ בַּר נָשׁ דְּאִזְדְּמַן לְעָלְמָא דְּאָתֵי, זַכָּאָה חוּלְקֵיהּ דְּהָא שַׁלִּיט עַל אֲתַר דְּיִרְאָה, דְּהָא לֵית מַאן דְּשַׁלִּיט עַל דַּרְגָּא דְּיִרְאָה, אֶלָּא אַהֲבָה, רָזָא דִּימִינָא.

418. And if you say that worship out of fear is not considered worship, THIS IS NOT SO. For it is precious worship, though it does not rise to be joined above TO ZEIR ANPIN. And when one worships with love, one rises and bedecks oneself above and cleaves to the World to Come. This man is summoned to the World to Come. Happy is his portion, for he has power over the place of fear, and nothing has power over the level of fear but love, which is the mystery of the right, THE MYSTERY OF UNITY OF ZEIR ANPIN AND MALCHUT.

419. רָזָא דְּיִחוּדָא דְּאִצְטְרִיךְ לֵיהּ לְהַהוּא דְּאִתְחֲזֵי לְעָלְמָא דְּאָתֵי, לְיַחֲדָא שְׁמָא דְּקוּדְשָׁא בְּרִיךְ הוּא, וּלְיַיחֲדָא שַׁיְיפִין וְדַרְגִּין עִלָּאִין וְתַתָּאִין, לְאַכְלְלָא כֹּלְּהוּ, וּלְאַעֲלָאָה בַּאֲתַר דְּאִצְטְרִיךְ לְקַשְּׁרָא קִשְׁרָא. וְדָא אִיהוּ רָזָא דִּכְתִיב, שְׁמַע יִשְׂרָאֵל יְיָ׳ אֱלֹהֵינוּ יְיָ׳ אֶחָד.

419. The person, worthy of the World to Come, should avow the unity of the name of the Holy One, blessed be He, and connect the organs, MALE AND FEMALE, to the higher grades, ABA AND IMA, the high with the low, and to unite them all and put them in their proper place, IN THE BLESSED ENDLESS LIGHT, and tie knots. This is the secret of "Hear O Yisrael, Hashem our Elohim, Hashem is one" (Devarim 6:4).

33. The secret of Sh'ma

A Synopsis

We hear from Rabbi Shimon that 'name' (Shem) is included in 'hear' (Sh'ma). All is considered one, for Zeir Anpin and Malchut alluded to in the Sh'ma are united to be one with Yisrael Saba. The heart wishes to cleave to infinity where the supernal tabernacle shall be joined with the lower tabernacle. Rabbi Shimon speaks about the letters in Yud Hei Vav Hei and Yud Hei Yud Hei. We read that the purpose of the word 'one' is to strengthen the desire to bind all together and raise our will in fear and love up to infinity. 'One' is the secret of above, below and the four directions of the world.

420. וְרָזָא דִשְׁמַע, שֵׁם דְּסָלִיק לְע׳ שְׁמָהָן, וְדָא כְּלָלָא חֲדָא. יִשְׂרָאֵל: יִשְׂרָאֵל סָבָא, בְּגִין דְּאִית זוּטָא, דִּכְתִיב נַעַר יִשְׂרָאֵל וָאֹהֲבֵהוּ. וְדָא אִיהוּ יִשְׂרָאֵל סָבָא, רָזָא חֲדָא בִּכְלָלָא חֲדָא. שְׁמַע יִשְׂרָאֵל, הָכָא אִתְכְּלִילַת אִתְּתָא בְּבַעְלָהּ.

420. The secret meaning of the word sh'ma (lit. 'hear') is a name (Heb. *shem*), WHICH IS MALCHUT, amounting to Ayin (= 70) names, WHICH IS THE NAME OF SEVENTY TWO NAMES (AYIN BET= 72) OF THE UPPER CHARIOT, THAT IS, CHESED, GVURAH, TIFERET AND MALCHUT OF ZEIR ANPIN ABOVE THE CHEST. Everything is one whole, THAT IS, MALCHUT CALLED NAME IS INCLUDED WITHIN ZEIR ANPIN ABOVE THE CHEST, WHICH IS THE SECRET OF LARGE AYIN. 'Yisrael' refers to Yisrael – Saba, THE SIX ENDS OF BINAH. For there is also Small Yisrael, WHICH IS ZEIR ANPIN, as is written: "when Yisrael was a child, then I loved him" (Hoshea 11:1); BUT HERE it is Yisrael – Saba, one mystery into one whole, FOR ZEIR ANPIN AND MALCHUT ALLUDED TO IN THE 'SH'MA', ARE ONE WITH YISRAEL – SABA, FOR THEY RISE UP AND BECOME ONE WITH HIM. 'Sh'ma Yisrael' (lit. 'Hear, O Yisrael') INDICATES THAT here, IN YISRAEL – SABA, wife is united with her husband, THAT IS, MALCHUT WITH ZEIR ANPIN.

421 וּלְבָתַר דְּאִתְכְּלִילוּ דָּא בְּדָא בִּכְלָלָא חֲדָא, כְּדֵין אִצְטְרִיכוּ לְיַיחֲדָא שַׁיְיפִין, וּלְחַבְּרָא תְּרֵין מַשְׁכְּנִין כַּחֲדָא, בְּכֻלְהוּ שַׁיְיפִין, בִּרְעוּ דְלִבָּא,

לְאִסְתַּלְּקָא בִּדְבֵקוּתָא דְּאֵין סוֹף, לְאִתְדַּבְּקָא כֹּלָּא תַּמָּן, לְמֶהֱוֵי רְעוּתָא חֲדָא עִלָּאֵי וְתַתָּאֵי.

421. After ZEIR ANPIN AND MALCHUT were included the one within the other into one IN YISRAEL – SABA, then all the organs should be joined together, THE SIX ENDS OF ZEIR ANPIN AND MALCHUT, to unite two tabernacles together in all the organs, THE SUPERNAL DWELLING IS THE SECRET OF YUD-HEI, AND THE LOWER DWELLING IS THE SECRET OF VAV-HEI, with the heart wishing to rise to cleave with the Endless Light, where all, the upper and lower, will cleave and become one will.

422. וְרָזָא דָּא יְהֱוֵה, כד"א יִהְיֶה יְיָ' אֶחָד, בְּרָזָא דְּיִהְיֶה. י', לְיַחֲדָא וּלְאִתְדַּבְּקָא בה', דְּאִיהוּ הֵיכָלָא פְּנִימָאָה, לְאֲתַר גְּנִיזוּ דְּהַאי נְקוּדָה עִלָּאָה, דְּאִיהִי י'. וְדָא אִיהוּ רָזָא יְדֹוָ"ד אֱלֹהֵינוּ. אִלֵּין תְּרֵין שְׁמָהָן דְּאִינּוּן י"ה.

422. This is the inner meaning of 'Yud Hei Yud Hei', as is said "and Hashem will be (Heb. *yihyeh, Yud Hei Yud Hei*) one" (Zecharyah 14:9), NAMELY, ONE in the secret of Yud Hei Yud Hei: Yud OF YUD HEI YUD HEI, THE SECRET OF CHOCHMAH, is to be united and attached to the Hei OF YUD HEI YUD HEI, which is an inner chamber, BINAH, the place where the supernal point is concealed, which is Yud, CHOCHMAH. This is the secret of Yud Hei Vav Hei our Elohim. These two names are Yud Hei, CHOCHMAH AND BINAH, HASHEM BEING CHOCHMAH AND OUR ELOHIM BEING BINAH.

423. וּלְאַכְלְלָא כָּל שַׁיְיפִין בְּהַהוּא אֲתַר דְּנַפְקוּ מִנֵּיהּ, דְּאִיהוּ הֵיכָלָא פְּנִימָאָה, לְאֲתָבָא מִלִּין לְאַתְרֵיהוֹן, לְעִקָּרָא וִיסוֹדָא וְשָׁרְשָׁא דִּילְהוֹן, עַד הַהוּא אֲתַר דְּשָׁרְשָׁא דִּבְרִית.

423. Also all the body parts are put together, THE SIX ENDS OF ZEIR ANPIN AND MALCHUT, where they came from, in the inner chamber, BINAH, AS WAS SAID; and everything returns to its place, to its essence and root, up to where the root of the covenant is, THAT IS, ABA.

423. וּלְבָתַר אִינּוּן תְּרֵין אַתְוָון אַחֲרָנִין לְיַחֲדָא וּלְאִתְדַּבְּקָא י׳ בְּה׳. י׳ אִיהוּ רָזָא דִּבְרִית קַדִּישָׁא. וְהַאי ה׳ אִיהוּ הֵיכְלָא, אֲתָר גְּנִיזוּ דְּהַאי רָזָא דִּבְרִית קַדִּישָׁא דְּאִיהוּ י׳. וְאע״ג דְּאוֹקִימְנָא דְּאִיהוּ ו׳ תִּנְיָינָא. אֲבָל י׳, רָזָא דִּילֵיהּ לְיַחֲדָא לוֹן כַּחֲדָא.

424. Then the other two letters OF YUD HEI YUD HEI are combined and attached together, the Yud with the Hei. The Yud is the inner meaning of the holy covenant, TO WIT, YESOD OF ZEIR ANPIN. And the Hei is a temple, and a place to conceal the holy covenant, the Yud. NAMELY, MALCHUT IS A TEMPLE TO YESOD, AS BINAH IS A TEMPLE TO CHOCHMAH AS SAID. And though we explained that Yesod is the second Vav OF THE LETTER VAV FULLY SPELLED (VAV VAV), THE FIRST VAV BEING TIFERET AND THE SECOND BEING YESOD, WHY THEN IS IT SAID HERE TO BE YUD? HE ANSWERS: the implication of Yud is uniting them into one, THAT IS, WHEN IN THE SECRET OF UNITY WITH MALCHUT, YESOD IS CALLED YUD.

425. אֶחָד, לְיַחֲדָא מִתַּמָּן וּלְעֵילָא, כֹּלָּא כַּחֲדָא, וּלְסַלְּקָא רְעוּתָא לְאִתְקַשְּׁרָא כֹּלָּא בְּקִשּׁוּרָא חַד. לְסַלְּקָא רְעוּתֵיהּ בִּדְחִילוּ וּרְחִימוּ לְעֵילָא לְעֵילָא עַד אֵין סוֹף וְלָא יִשְׁתְּבַק רְעוּתָא מִכָּל אִינּוּן דַּרְגִּין וְשַׁיְיפִין, אֶלָּא בְּכֻלְּהוּ יִסְתְּלַּק רְעוּתֵיהּ לְאַדְבְּקָא לוֹן, וּלְמֶהֱוֵי כֹּלָּא קִשּׁוּרָא חֲדָא בְּאֵין סוֹף.

425. THE PURPOSE OF THE WORD One is to cause unity from there upward, THAT IS, FROM MALCHUT UPWARD, to awaken the desire to bind all together and awaken our wish with awe and love up to the Endless Light. This desire TO GO UP TO THE ENDLESS LIGHT will not be lacking in these grades and body parts, but will appear in them all, NOTHING SHALL BE WITHOUT IT, to attach them, so that all will be one unity bound together in the Endless Light.

426. וְדָא הוּא יִחוּדָא דְּרַב הַמְנוּנָא סָבָא, דְּאוֹלִיף מֵאָבוֹי, וַאֲבוֹי מֵרַבֵּיהּ, עַד פּוּמָא דְּאֵלִיָּהוּ, וְשַׁפִּיר אִיהוּ, וְיִחוּדָא בְּתִקּוּנָא. וְאע״ג דְּאֲנָן אוֹקִימְנָא לְהַאי בְּכַמָּה רָזִין, כֻּלְּהוּ רָזִין סַלְּקִין לְחַד. אֲבָל רָזָא דָא

אַשְׁכַּחְנָא בְּסִפְרֵיהּ, וְשַׁפִּיר אִיהוּ, וְיִחוּדָא בְּתִקּוּנָא. וְהָא אֲנָן בְּיִחוּדָא
דְּרָזָא אַחֲרָא אִתְּעֲרְנָא מִלִּין, וְאִיהוּ שַׁפִּיר, וְיִחוּדָא כַּדְקָא חֲזֵי וְהָכִי
הוּא. אֲבָל יִחוּדָא דָא, יִחוּדָא בְּתִקּוּנָא, וְדָא אִיהוּ יִחוּדָא דְּרַב הַמְנוּנָא
סָבָא.

426. This is the avowal of unity of Rav Hamnuna Saba (the elder), who learned it from his father, and his father from his Rabbi, and so on up to the mouth of Elijah. This avowal is very well and by reparation. And though we explained this avowal by many secrets, OTHER WAYS, all the secrets amount to one. But this I found in his book and it is well for it is an avowal of unity by amendment. We expounded upon another secret elsewhere, which is well and proper as it should be. But this avowal is by amendment, the avowal of Rav Hamnuna Saba (the elder).

427. וְתוּ הֲוָה אָמַר, מַאן דִּרְעוּתֵיהּ לְאַכְלְלָא כָּל רָזִין דְּיִחוּדָא בְּמִלָּה
דְּאֶחָד שַׁפִּיר טְפֵי. וּלְהָכִי אֲנָן מַאֲרִיכִין בְּאֶחָד, לְסַלְקָא רְעוּתֵיהּ מֵעֵילָא
לְתַתָּא, וּמִתַּתָּא לְעֵילָא, לְמֶהֱוֵי כֹּלָּא חַד. אֲבָל בְּרָזָא דָא יְהֹוָ"ה, סִימָנָא
אִיהוּ לְהַאי.

427. He also says that whoever wishes to unite all the secrets of the avowal of unity within the word One, this is better. Therefore we lengthen the pronunciation of 'one' to awaken the desire to draw from above downward and to raise from below upward, so all will be one. This is the secret of Yud Hei Yud Hei, that alludes to this, AS WE SAID.

428. וְהָא דְּתָנֵינָן אֶחָד רָזָא עֵילָא וְתַתָּא, וְאַרְבַּע סִטְרִין דְּעָלְמָא, הָכִי
אִיהוּ. לְיַחֲדָא עֵילָא וְתַתָּא כְּמָה דְּאִתְּמַר וְאַרְבַּע סִטְרִין דְּעָלְמָא, אִלֵּין
אִינּוּן רָזָא רְתִיכָא עִלָּאָה, לְאִתְכַּלְּלָא כֹּלָּא כַּחֲדָא, בְּקִשְׁרָא חֲדָא,
בְּיִחוּדָא חֲדָא עַד אֵין סוֹף, כְּמָה דְּאוֹקִימְנָא.

428. We learned THAT WITHIN THE WORD One is the secret of above, below and the four directions of the world. It is so, and we need to unite the higher and the lower as we said, THEY BEING ABA AND IMA AND MALE AND FEMALE. The four directions of the world are the secret of the supernal

Chariot, CHESED, GVURAH, TIFERET AND MALCHUT OF ZEIR ANPIN ABOVE THE CHEST, and we should put them all together in one bond, one unity, all the way to the Endless Light, as we explained.

34. Mentioning the exodus from Egypt

A Synopsis

Rabbi Shimon tells us that the upper and lower worlds could not be joined while the Shechinah was in exile. He speaks of the freedom of Malchut now united with Zeir Anpin. During the exile of the children of Yisrael the Shechinah always remained with them, but when she left the exile she asked God to redeem her four times (against the four exiles) so she would be free; she was thus redeemed four times by the Exodus. Therefore the four redemptions are repeated in the prayers, before and after "You have been the help of our fathers," to make them fortified and lasting. Lastly, Rabbi Shimon mentions the initiated who behold the holiness of their Master, saying that the mystery of surrendering the soul to one's Master is very important.

429. רָזָא לְאַדְכְּרָא יְצִיאַת מִצְרַיִם לְבָתַר. בְּגִין דַּהֲוַות שְׁכִינְתָּא בְּגָלוּתָא, וּבְזִמְנָא דְּאִיהִי בְּגָלוּתָא, לָאו אִיהוּ חִבּוּרָא, לְאִתְחַבְּרָא דָּא בְּדָא עָלְמָא תַּתָּאָה בְּעָלְמָא עִלָּאָה, וּלְאַחֲזָאָה חֵירוּ דְּהַהִיא גְּאוּלָה, דַּהֲוַות בְּכַמָּה אָתִין, בְּכַמָּה נִסִּין דְּעָבַד קוּדְשָׁא בְּרִיךְ הוּא. וְאִצְטְרִיךְ הַהוּא פּוּרְקָנָא לְאִתְדַּכְּרָא, וּלְאִתְחֲזָאָה דְּאַף עַל גַּב דַּהֲוַות בְּגָלוּתָא, הַשְׁתָּא חֵירוּ אִית לָהּ, מִיּוֹמָא דְּאִינּוּן קִשְׁרִין בְּמִצְרַיִם אִשְׁתְּרִיאוּ, אִינּוּן אָתִין וְנִסִּין אִתְעֲבִידוּ.

429. After THE MEDITATION OF SH'MA, there is a mystery of mentioning the Exodus from Egypt, since the Shechinah was in exile, and when She is in exile, there is no joining together the upper world, ZEIR ANPIN, and the lower world, MALCHUT. THEREFORE ONE NEEDS to demonstrate the freedom of that redemption FROM EGYPT carried out by several signs and miracles performed by the Holy One, blessed be He. This redemption ought to be mentioned and beheld, for though it occurred in exile, now it is free, since the day the bonds of Egypt were thrown open and several miracles were performed.

430. וְאִצְטְרִיךְ לְאַחֲזָאָה חֵירוּ דִּילָהּ, בְּגִין דְּאִתְחַבְּרָא בְּבַעֲלָהּ וּבְגִין לְאַסְמְכָא גְּאוּלָה לִתְפִלָּה, לְמֶהֱוֵי כֹּלָּא חַד בְּלָא פֵּרוּדָא, וְלָא לְאַחֲזָאָה תֵּרוּכִין, וְסִימָנִיךְ וְאִשָּׁה גְּרוּשָׁה מֵאִישָׁהּ לֹא יִקָּחוּ.

430. One ought to point at freedom OF MALCHUT, because she is united with her husband, ZEIR ANPIN; and also in order to bring nearer the uttering of the word redemption, YESOD, to the Amidah prayer, THE SECRET OF MALCHUT, so all will become one without separation or divorce, MEANING THAT MALCHUT IS DIVORCED IN EXILE FROM HER HUSBAND, ZEIR ANPIN. This is implied by "neither shall they take a woman put away from her husband" (Vayikra 21:7).

431. וְאִי תֵּימָא, וְהָא בְּגָלוּתָא אִיהִי, וְהָא אִתְתָּרְכַת, לָאו הָכִי, אֶלָּא וַדַּאי בְּגָלוּתָא אִיהִי, לְדַיְּירָא עִמְּהוֹן דְּיִשְׂרָאֵל, וּלְאַגָּנָא עֲלַיְיהוּ, אֲבָל לָא אִתְתָּרְכַת. וְהָא שְׁכִינְתָּא לָא אִתְחֲזֵי בְּבַיִת רִאשׁוֹן וּבְבַיִת שֵׁנִי. עַד דְּלָא גָּלוּ יִשְׂרָאֵל סַלְקָא לְעֵילָא, וּלְבָתַר אִיהִי שַׁוִּיאַת מָדוֹרָה עִמְּהוֹן. אֲבָל תֵּרוּכִין לָא הֲוַות לְעָלְמִין.

431. And you may say that she is in exile, and divorced FROM HER HUSBAND, ZEIR ANPIN. This is not so. She is in exile to dwell with Yisrael, FOR WHEREVER YISRAEL WERE EXILED, THE SHECHINAH IS WITH THEM, to protect them, but not put away BY ZEIR ANPIN. The Shechinah was not seen during the first Temple or the second Temple, WHEN YISRAEL SINNED, THEREFORE IT WAS NOT CONSIDERED AN EXILE, NOR SEPARATION. Before Yisrael went in exile, IF THEY SINNED, the Shechinah went up, and afterwards, WHEN THEY WENT IN EXILE, SHE DID NOT MOUNT UP, BUT Her abode was with Yisrael. But never was there separation.

432. וּבג״ד בָּעֵי לְאַחֲזָאָה פּוּרְקָנָא, דְּאִית בָּהּ אַרְבַּע גְּאוּלוֹת. וְרָזָא הָכָא, בְּשַׁעֲתָא דְּנָפְקָא שְׁכִינְתָּא מִגָּלוּתָא דְּמִצְרַיִם, תַּבְעַת מְקוּדְשָׁא בְּרִיךְ הוּא, דְּיִפְרוֹק לָהּ הַשְׁתָּא ד׳ זִמְנִין, דְּאִינּוּן ד׳ גְּאוּלוֹת, לָקֳבֵל אַרְבַּע גָּלְיוֹת. בְּגִין דְּתֶהֱא בַּת חוֹרִין, וְלָא תֶּהֱא מִתְתַּרְכָא. וּבְהַהִיא שַׁעֲתָא קַיְּימָא וְאִתְפָּרְקַת אַרְבַּע גְּאוּלוֹת, בְּהַהִיא יְצִיאַת מִצְרַיִם. וְהַשְׁתָּא דְּאִצְטְרִיכַת בְּתִקּוּנָהָא לְאִתְחַבְּרָא בְּבַעְלָהּ, אִצְטְרִיךְ לְאַחֲזָאָה הַהִיא גְּאוּלַת מִצְרַיִם, דְּאִית בָּהּ אַרְבַּע גְּאוּלוֹת.

432. For that reason we must display redemption, which enfolds four redemptions. The secret thereof is that when the Shechinah left the exile in Egypt, She asked the Holy One, blessed be He, to redeem Her four times, four redemptions, against the four exiles, so She would be free and no longer put away. THEREFORE at the time OF THE REDEMPTION FROM EGYPT, She was redeemed four redemptions, by the Exodus. TO WIT, WHEN RECEIVING MOCHIN OF THE EXODUS FROM EGYPT, THE SHECHINAH WAS REDEEMED FROM ALL FOUR KINGDOMS, THAT IS, FROM ALL THE EXILES UP TO THE COMING OF THE MESSIAH, IN A WAY THAT SHE WOULD NO LONGER BE CONSIDERED AS SEPARATED FROM HER HUSBAND ZEIR ANPIN. And now that the Shechinah needs to be prepared to be united with Her husband ZEIR ANPIN, we have to display that redemption from Egypt, that enfolds four redemptions. AND WITH THE AWAKENING OF MOCHIN OF THE EXODUS FROM EGYPT, SHE IS PREPARED TO BE UNITED WITH HER HUSBAND, BECAUSE THERE IS FREEDOM FROM ALL THE FOUR KINGDOMS.

433. וְעַל דָּא אִית לְאַדְכְּרָא בְּהַהִיא גְּאוּלָה, ד' זִמְנִין אֱמֶת. אֱמֶת. אֱמֶת. אֱמֶת. עַד עֶזְרַת אֲבוֹתֵינוּ. דְּדָא הוּא עֶזְרָה וְסָמֶךְ לְיִשְׂרָאֵל כֻּלְּהוּ. וּמִתַּמָּן וּלְהָלְאָה אַרְבַּע זִמְנִין אַחֲרָנִין, אֱמֶת, אֱמֶת, אֱמֶת, אֱמֶת. לְמֶהֱוֵי אַרְבַּע גְּאוּלוֹת אִלֵּין בְּקִיּוּמָא תַּקִּיף, בְּחוֹתָמָא תַּקִּיף דְּגוּשְׁפַּנְקָא דְּמַלְכָּא. ד' גְּאוּלוֹת כְּפוּלִין בְּקִיּוּמָא.

433. Therefore we mention that redemption four times: true, true, true, true, until the passage "You have been the help of our fathers," AGAINST THE FOUR REDEMPTIONS, for they are help and support for all Yisrael. And from "THE HELP OF OUR FATHERS" there are four more 'true', REPEATED, so the four redemptions would be fortified and lasting, sealed by the signet of the King. Therefore the four redemptions are repeated.

434. וְכֻלְּהוּ בְּהַהִיא יְצִיאַת מִצְרַיִם, דְּאִילּוּ לָא אִשְׁתְּכָחוּ אִינוּן ד' גְּאוּלוֹת בְּהַהִיא יְצִיאַת מִצְרַיִם, כָּל זִמְנָא דִּלְהֱוֵי גָּלוּתָא, לָא אִתְחַבְּרַת בְּתִקּוּנָהָא לְאִתְיַיחֲדָא שְׁמָא קַדִּישָׁא. וְעַ״ד אִית לְאַדְכְּרָא גְּאוּלָה דְּמִצְרַיִם תָּדִיר, בְּכָל קִדּוּשִׁין דְּקוּדְשָׁא בְּרִיךְ הוּא, בְּרִיךְ שְׁמֵיהּ לְעָלַם וּלְעָלְמֵי עָלְמַיָּיא.

434. All FOUR REDEMPTIONS concern the Exodus from Egypt, because were there not four redemptions in that exodus from Egypt, She would not be able to unite, together in her decorations WITH ZEIR ANPIN, whenever there is an exile, for the unification of the Holy Name. Therefore one should mention the redemption from Egypt always, in every sanctification (Heb. *kedusha*) of the Holy One, blessed be He. Blessed be His name for ever and ever.

435. רָזָא דִּקְדוּשָׁה הָא אוֹקִימְנָא, דְּהָא בִּקְדוּשָׁה מִתְקַדְּשֵׁי כֹּלָא, עֵילָא וְתַתָּא, וְכָל דַּרְגִּין, וְכָל רְתִיכִין עִלָּאִין וְתַתָּאִין, כֻּלְּהוּ מִתְקַדְּשֵׁי בִּקְדוּשָׁתָא דָּא. וּבִקְדוּשָׁה דָּא, אוֹקִימְנָא רָזִין עִלָּאִין, לְאִינּוּן מָארֵי רָזִין דְּמִסְתַּכְּלִין בִּקְדוּשָׁה דְּמָארֵיהוֹן, זַכָּאָה חוּלָקֵיהוֹן.

435. This is the mystery of sanctification, THAT IS, HOLY HOLY HOLY, THAT WE SAY. We explained that during sanctification, everything is sanctified above and below, THE ANGELS AND YISRAEL, and all the grades and the Chariots, upper and lower. We already explained its high mysteries to the initiated who behold the holiness of their Master, happy is their portion.

436. רָזָא לְמִמְסַר נַפְשָׁא לְמָארֵיה, שַׁפִּיר אִיהוּ, דְּקָא אֲמַרְתּוּן חַבְרַיָּיא, זַכָּאָה חוּלָקֵיכוֹן, וְזַכָּאִין עֵינֵי דְּחָמוּ כָּךְ, דְּזָכֵינָא בְּחַיֵּי, דְּמִתְעָרִין מִלִּין קַדִּישִׁין אִלֵּין בְּהַאי עָלְמָא, וְכֻלְּהוּ כְּתִיבֵי לְעֵילָא קַמֵּי מַלְכָּא קַדִּישָׁא.

436. The mystery of surrendering the soul to one's Master, that you expounded upon is very well. Friends, happy is your portion, and happy are my eyes to behold, while still alive, holy matters awakened in this world, written above before the Holy King.

35. "Then they who feared Hashem spoke to one another"

A Synopsis

Rabbi Shimon opens with: "Then they who feared Hashem spoke to one another and Hashem hearkened, and heard it: and a book of remembrance was written before him for those who feared Hashem, and took heed of His name." He tells us that this means that the holy Chariots and armies spoke with one another before God. And when these holy words rise up, the Holy King delights in them and they mount to His head and become a crown. We read that "they who feared Hashem" above means when they repent with love they stand before God. "They who feared Hashem" below means that afterwards they go down to earth, but even then their words retain their shape above. All the words that the righteous on earth bedeck themselves with stay standing before God in the same shape of wickedness turned into merit. And afterwards they are written in the book of remembrance before Him, so they would exist before Him always.

"Took heed of His name" means that those who value the importance of the Torah fix the wisdom of their Master's name in their hearts.

437. פָּתַח וְאָמַר אָז נִדְבְּרוּ יִרְאֵי יְיָ' אִישׁ אֶל רֵעֵהוּ וַיַּקְשֵׁב יְיָ' וַיִּשְׁמָע וַיִּכָּתֵב סֵפֶר זִכָּרוֹן לְפָנָיו לְיִרְאֵי יְיָ' וּלְחוֹשְׁבֵי שְׁמוֹ. הַאי קְרָא אִית לְאִסְתַּכְּלָא בֵּיה, אָז נִדְבְּרוּ, אָז דִּבְּרוּ מִבָּעֵי לֵיה, מַאי נִדְבְּרוּ. אֶלָּא נִדְבְּרוּ לְעֵילָא, מִכָּל אִינוּן רְתִיכִין קַדִּישִׁין, וְכָל אִינוּן חַיָּילִין קַדִּישִׁין.

437. He opened and said "Then they who feared Hashem spoke to one another and Hashem hearkened, and heard it: and a book of remembrance was written before Him for those who feared Hashem, and took heed of His name" (Malachi 3:16). We should examine this verse. It is written: "spoke to one another," but should have merely been written 'spoke'. Why is it so? HE ANSWERS: the holy Chariots and armies spoke with one another BEFORE THE HOLY ONE, BLESSED BE HE.

438. בְּגִין דְּאִינוּן מִלִּין קַדִּישִׁין, סַלְקִין לְעֵילָא, וְכַמָּה אִינוּן דִּמְקַדְּמֵי וְנַטְלִין לוֹן קַמֵּי מַלְכָּא קַדִּישָׁא, וּמִתְעַטְּרָן בְּכַמָּה עִטְרִין, בְּאִינוּן נְהוֹרִין עִלָּאִין, וְכֻלְּהוּ נִדְבְּרוּ מִקַּמֵּי מַלְכָּא עִלָּאָה. מַאן חָמֵי חֶדְוָון, מַאן חָמֵי תּוּשְׁבְּחָן, דְּסַלְקִין בְּכָל אִינוּן רְקִיעִין, כַּד סַלְקִין מִלִּין אִלֵּין, וּמַלְכָּא

קַדִּישָׁא מִסְתַּכַּל בְּהוּ, וְאִתְעַטַּר בְּהוּ, וְאִינּוּן סַלְּקִין וְיָתְבִין עַל חֵיקֵיהּ,
וּמִשְׁתַּעְשַׁע בְּהוּ, מִתַּמָּן סַלְּקִין עַל רֵישֵׁיהּ, וַהֲווֹ עֲטָרָה. וְעַ"ד אָמְרָה
אוֹרַיְיתָא, וָאֶהְיֶה שַׁעֲשׁוּעִים יוֹם יוֹם. וְהָיִיתִי לָא כְּתִיב, אֶלָּא וָאֶהְיֶה,
בְּכָל זְמַן, וּבְכָל עִידָן, דְּמִלִּין עִלָּאִין סַלְּקִין קַמֵּיהּ.

438. Since these holy words THEY SPOKE mount up, some hasten to carry them before the Holy King, and they are adorned with crowns of supernal light and speak about it with one another before the supernal King. Who has seen joys, and who has seen praises mounting through all the firmaments! And when these words rise, the Holy King looks at them and adorns Himself with them. They come up to sit in His lap, and He delights in them. From there, HIS BOSOM, they mount to His head and become a crown. Upon this the Torah said "and I will be daily His delight" (Mishlei 8:30). It is not written "I was," but "I will be," IN THE FUTURE TENSE, namely, anytime and whenever the supernal words mount before Him.

439. תְּרֵי זִמְנֵי כְּתִיב יִרְאֵי יְיָ', יִרְאֵי יְיָ'. אֶלָּא יִרְאֵי יְיָ' לְעֵילָּא, יִרְאֵי יְיָ'
לְתַתָּא. יִרְאֵי יְיָ' קַיְימִין לְתַתָּא, וְאִינּוּן מִלִּין קַיְימִין בְּדִיּוּקְנֵיהוֹן
לְעֵילָּא. וְרָזָא דָּא אַשְׁכַּחְנָא בְּסִפְרָא דַּחֲנוֹךְ, דְּכָל מִלִּין דְּצַדִּיקַיָּיא דִּי
בְּאַרְעָא, אִינּוּן מִתְעַטְּרָן, וְקַיְימָן קַמֵּי מַלְכָּא, וּמִשְׁתַּעְשַׁע בְּהוּ קוּדְשָׁא
בְּרִיךְ הוּא. וּלְבָתַר אִינּוּן נַחְתֵּי, וְקַיְימִין קַמֵּיהּ בְּדִיּוּקְנָא דְּהַהוּא צַדִּיק
דְּקָאָמַר לוֹן, וְאִשְׁתַּעְשַׁע קוּדְשָׁא בְּרִיךְ הוּא בְּהַהוּא דִּיּוּקְנָא. וּלְבָתַר
אִכְתִּיבוּ בְּסֵפֶר זִכָּרוֹן לְפָנָיו, לְקַיְּימָא קַמֵּיהּ בְּקִיּוּמָא תָּדִיר.

439. "They who feared Hashem" is written twice, NAMELY, "THEN THEY WHO FEARED HASHEM...AND A BOOK OF REMEMBRANCE WAS WRITTEN BEFORE HIM FOR THEM WHO FEARED HASHEM..." THE MEANING IS "they who fear Hashem" above, MEANS, WHEN THEY REPENT WITH LOVE, THEY STAND ABOVE BEFORE THE HOLY ONE, BLESSED BE HE. "They who fear Hashem" below MEANS THAT AFTERWARDS THEY GO DOWN TO THEIR PLACE ON EARTH. AND EVEN WHEN they who fear Hashem are already below, IN THEIR PLACE, those words retain their shape above. I found this secret in the book of Enoch, that all the words, that the righteous on earth bedeck themselves with, stand before the King. NAMELY, WHEN

THEY REPENT WITH LOVE, THEY ARE ADORNED WITH THEIR WICKEDNESS WHICH TURNED INTO MERIT AS SAID; they stand on their own above before the King, and the Holy One, blessed be He, is delighted by them. After that THE RIGHTEOUS descend AND THE WORDS STAY standing before Him in the same shape OF WICKEDNESS TURNED INTO MERIT, as the righteous uttered them. The Holy One, blessed be He, is delighted in that image. And afterwards they are written in the book of remembrance before Him, so they would exist before Him always.

440. וְלָחוֹשְׁבֵי שְׁמוֹ, מַאי וּלְחוֹשְׁבֵי שְׁמוֹ. הָא אוּקְמוּהָ, כָּל אִינוּן דִּמְחַשְׁבֵי מִלִּין דְּאוֹרַיְיתָא, לְאַדְבְּקָא לְמָארֵיהוֹן בְּרָזָא דִשְׁמָא קַדִּישָׁא, בְּגִין לְמִנְדַּע לֵיהּ, וּלְאִתְתַּקְּנָא חָכְמָה דִשְׁמֵיהּ בְּלִבַּיְיהוּ, דִּכְתִיב וּלְחוֹשְׁבֵי שְׁמוֹ, דְּהוּא רָזָא דִשְׁמָא קַדִּישָׁא.

440. HE ASKS: What is the meaning of "took heed of His name?" HE ANSWERS: It was already explained that those, who heed and value the words of Torah, cleave to their Master in the secret of the Holy Name, to know Him, so the wisdom of His name will be fixed upon their heart. OF THEM it is written, who "took heed of His name," for this is the secret of the Holy Name.

36. "And above the firmament"

A Synopsis

We hear the meaning of: "And above the firmament that was over their heads was the likeness of a throne, in appearance like a sapphire stone." The firmament refers to the lower firmament for no one can behold the one above. "A throne" refers to the throne below; had it said 'the throne' it would have meant the supernal throne, and this is impossible because the supernal throne cannot be seen; it is concealed and undisclosed. In "the likeness as the appearance of a man," "the appearance" includes all the forms of the utterances of wisdom. The secrets of Chochmah go up and stand in the likeness of man. Rabbi Shimon tells the rabbis that he can see the secret of man is impressed upon them all, and that the righteous are destined to be seen by all. He admonishes Rabbi Yosi for thinking of worldly matters, and Rabbi Yosi comes back to the words of the Torah, so his image is complete.

441. כְּתִיב וּמִמַּעַל לָרָקִיעַ אֲשֶׁר עַל רֹאשָׁם כְּמַרְאֵה אֶבֶן סַפִּיר דְּמוּת כִּסֵּא, הַאי קְרָא הָא אוּקְמוּהָ. אֲבָל וּמִמַּעַל לָרָקִיעַ, בְּהַהוּא רָקִיעַ לְתַתָּא, כְּמָה דְּאָמַרְתּוּן חַבְרַיָּיא, זַכָּאָה חוּלָקִי, וְזַכָּאָה חוּלָקֵיכוֹן. דְּהָא בִּרְקִיעָא דִּלְעֵילָּא, לֵית מַאן דְּאִסְתַּכַּל בֵּיהּ. וּמִלְעֵילָּא מִנֵּיהּ קַיְימָא הַהוּא אֶבֶן סַפִּיר, דְּהָא אִתְעֲרָנָא בֵּיהּ בְּרָזָא דְּהַהוּא מַרְגָּלִית טָבָא יַקִּירָא, כְּמָה דְּאוֹקִימְנָא.

441. It is written: "And above the firmament that was over their heads was the likeness of a throne, in appearance like a sapphire stone" (Yechezkel 1:26). This verse was already explained. Yet "above the firmament" refers to the lower firmament, BENEATH MALCHUT, as you, friends, have explained. FOR THEY MENTIONED IT IN THE NAME OF RABBI SHIMON, happy is my portion and happy is your portion. For nobody can behold the upper firmament, BINAH. BUT IT IS WRITTEN ABOUT THE FIRMAMENT BELOW WITHIN MALCHUT "AND YOU SHALL SEE MY BACK" (SHEMOT 33:23), and above THIS FIRMAMENT that sapphire stone is located, which we said IS MALCHUT, based on the inference of its being a good and precious pearl, as I explained.

442. דְּמוּת כִּסֵּא, וְלָא כְּתִיב דְּמוּת הַכִּסֵּא. בְּגִין דְּאִית כִּסֵּא, וְאִית

כָּסֵא. הַכִּסֵּא: עִלָּאָה טְמִירָא גְּנִיזָא דְּלָא אִתְגַּלְיָיא, וְלֵית מַאן דְּקַיְימָא
בֵּיהּ לְמִנְדַּע וּלְאִסְתַּכְּלָא. וְעַ"ד כְּתִיב כִּסֵּא סְתָמָא, דָּא כִּסֵּא דִּלְתַתָּא.

442. It is written: "the likeness of a throne" and not "the likeness of the throne," for there is throne and throne. "The throne" is supernal, concealed and undisclosed, that is, not revealed, and no one can bear look at it and know it, BEING BINAH. Therefore it is simply written: 'a throne' WITHOUT THE DEFINITE ARTICLE, for it is the lower throne, NAMELY, MALCHUT.

443. דְּמוּת כְּמַרְאֵה אָדָם, כֵּיוָן דְּאָמַר דְּמוּת, אֲמַאי כְּמַרְאֵה, דְּהָא סַגִּי
לֵיהּ דְּמוּת אָדָם. אֶלָּא דְּמוּת אָדָם, דָּא אִיהוּ רָזָא עִלָּאָה, בְּהַהוּא כָּבוֹד
עִלָּאָה, דִּיוּקְנָא דְּאָדָם. אֲבָל הָא דְּאִתּוֹסָף כְּמַרְאֵה, לְאַכְלְלָא אִינּוּן
דִּיוּקְנִין דְּמִלִּין דְּחָכְמְתָא, וְאִינּוּן רָזִין דְּחָכְמְתָא דְּסַלְקָן וּמִתְעַטְּרָן
לְעֵילָּא, וּלְבָתַר קַיְימִין בְּדִיוּקְנָא דְּאָדָם בְּהַהוּא דִּיוּקְנָא דְּצַדִּיקַיָּיא
דְּמְעַטְּרִין לוֹן, וּבְכֻלְּהוּ אִשְׁתַּעְשַׁע קוּדְשָׁא בְּרִיךְ הוּא בְּעִטְרוֹי.

443. "the likeness as the appearance of a man" (Yechezkel 1:26): HE ASKS: Since it was said "likeness," why add 'as the appearance'. Would not it suffice to say "the likeness of a man?" HE ANSWERS: "the likeness of man" represents the high secret of the high glory, THAT IS ZEIR ANPIN, IN YUD HEI VAV HEI FULLY SPELLED WITH ALEPH'S WHICH EQUALS THE NUMERICAL VALUE OF ADAM. This is the likeness of man SITTING ON THE THRONE WHICH IS MALCHUT; and the addition, "the appearance," includes all the forms of the words of wisdom CALLED SIGHT OR APPEARANCE, FOR CHOCHMAH IS SO CALLED. They are the secrets of Chochmah that go up and adorn themselves above, IN ZEIR ANPIN, and then assume the likeness of man, NAMELY, that form with which the righteous are bedecked. And in all these the Holy One, blessed be He, is delighted in His crowns.

444. וְאַתּוּן חַבְרַיָּיא, הָא קוּדְשָׁא בְּרִיךְ הוּא אִשְׁתַּעְשַׁע הַשְׁתָּא, בְּאִינּוּן
מִלִּין דְּקָא אֲמָרִיתוּ, מִתְעַטְּרָן בְּהַהוּא אוֹרְחָא. וְהָא קַיְימְתּוּן קַמֵּי
מָארֵיכוֹן בְּדִיוּקְנַיְיכוּ קַדִּישִׁין, דְּהָא אֲנָא בְּשַׁעְתָּא דַּחֲמֵינָא לְכוּ,
וְאִסְתַּכְּלָנָא בְּדִיוּקְנַיְיכוּ, חֲמֵינָא בְּכוּ דְּאַתּוּן רְשִׁימִין בְּרָזָא דְּאָדָם,

וְיָדַעְנָא דְּהָא דְּיוּקְנָא דִּילְכוֹן אִתְעַתְּדָא לְעֵילָא. וְהָכִי אִזְדַּמְּנָן צַדִּיקַיָּיא לְזִמְנָא דְּאָתֵי, לְאִשְׁתְּמוֹדְעָא לְעֵינַיְיהוּ דְּכֹלָּא, וּלְאַחֲזָאָה פַּרְצוּפָא קַדִּישָׁא לְקַמֵּי כָּל עָלְמָא, הה"ד כָּל רוֹאֵיהֶם יַכִּירוּם כִּי הֵם זֶרַע בֵּרַךְ יְיָ'.

444. And you, friends, the Holy One, blessed be He, is delighted even now with the words you said, and they are crowned on that way. And you have established THE LIKENESS OF A MAN before your Master by your holy forms, for when I beheld you and regarded your shapes, I saw that you were marked with the secret of man, and I knew that your shape is invited above. And so the righteous are destined to be recognized by everyone and display the sacred form of their countenances before the whole world. This is the meaning of the verse "All that see them shall acknowledge them, that they are the seed which Hashem has blessed" (Yeshayah 61:9).

445. אַדְהָכִי חָמָא לְרִבִּי יוֹסֵי, דַּהֲוָה מְהַרְהֵר בְּמִלֵּי דְּעָלְמָא. אָמַר לֵיהּ, יוֹסֵי קוּם אַשְׁלִים דְּיוּקְנָךְ, דְּאַתְּ חַד חָסֵר בָּךְ. קָם רִבִּי יוֹסֵי וְחַדֵּי בְּמִלִּין דְּאוֹרַיְיתָא, וְקָם קַמֵּיהּ, אִסְתְּכַּל בֵּיהּ ר"שׁ, א"ל, ר' יוֹסֵי, הַשְׁתָּא אַנְתְּ שְׁלִים קַמֵּי עַתִּיק יוֹמִין, וְדִיּוּקְנָךְ שְׁלִים.

445. While he was speaking he saw Rabbi Yosi contemplating worldly matters. He told him 'Yosi, stand and complete your image, for one letter is missing in you'. FOR SINCE HE WAS CONTEMPLATING WORLDLY THINGS, HE CALLED HIM YOSI AND NOT RABBI YOSI. Rabbi Yosi arose and rejoiced in words of Torah and stood before him. Rabbi Shimon looked upon him and said 'Rabbi Yosi, now you are whole before the Ancient One (Heb. *Atik Yomin*), and your image is whole.

37. "And they made the Head plate"

A Synopsis

Rabbi Shimon opens with: "And they made the plate (tzitz) of the holy crown of pure gold..." 'Tzitz' means 'to peek' and that is because the plate is to be looked at, for the plate reflects immediately the level of righteousness of the person looking at it. In the plate the letters of the Holy Name were engraved; when a righteous person stood before it the light would come from the plate and shine upon his face. The priest would notice this only the first time but not later. The reflection is because the mirror shines on him from above as an indication that God wants him. If a person stands before that plate and his face never shows the holy reflective light, the priest knows that he is an evildoer.

446. פָּתַח וְאָמַר, וַיַּעַשׂ אֶת צִיץ נֵזֶר הַקֹּדֶשׁ זָהָב טָהוֹר וְגוֹ'. אֲמַאי אִקְרֵי צִיץ. אִסְתַּכְּלוּתָא לְאִסְתַּכְּלָא בֵּיהּ. וּבְגִין דַּהֲוָה קַיְּימָא עַל אִסְתַּכְּלוּתָא דְּבַר נָשׁ, אִקְרֵי צִיץ. וְכָל מַאן דְּאִסְתָּכַּל בֵּיהּ בְּהַהוּא צִיץ אִשְׁתְּמוֹדְעָא בֵּיהּ.

446. He opened and said "And they made the Head plate (Heb. *tzitz*) of the holy crown of pure gold..." (Shemot 39:30). HE ASKS: Why is it called 'Tzitz' (lit. 'to peep')? AND ANSWERS: IT IS meant to be looked at. And since it is there for men to see, it is called 'tzitz'. And whoever glances at that glint, it is reflected at once on him WHETHER HE IS RIGHTEOUS OR NOT.

447. בַּצִּיץ הֲווֹ אַתְוָון דִּשְׁמָא קַדִּישָׁא גְּלִיפָן בְּגִלּוּפָא, וּמְחַקְקָן בֵּיהּ. וְאִי זַכָּאָה הֲוָה הַהוּא דְּקַיְימָא קַמֵּיהּ, אִינּוּן אַתְוָון דִּמְחַקְּקָן בֵּיהּ גּוֹ דַּהֲבָא, הֲווֹ בַּלְטִין מִתַּתָּא לְעֵילָּא, וְסַלְקִין מֵהַהוּא גְּלִיפוּ בִּנְהִירוּ, וַהֲווֹ נָהֲרִין בְּאַנְפִּין דְּהַהוּא בַּר נָשׁ.

447. HE EXPLAINS HIS WORDS. In the Head plate were the letters of the Holy Name, ornamentally engraved in it. If a righteous man stands before it, the letters engraved in gold would shine in relief and their lights would go from below upward protruding from the engraving, and shine in the face of that person.

448. נָצִיץ נְצִיצוּ בֵּיהּ, וְלָא נֹצְצִין. בְּשַׁעֲתָא קַדְמֵיתָא דְּאִסְתַּכַּל כַּהֲנָא בֵּיהּ, הֲוָה חָמֵי נְהִירוּ דְּאַתְוָון כֻּלְּהוּ בְּאַנְפִּין. וְכַד הֲוָה מִסְתַּכְּלָא לְעַיְינָא בֵּיהּ, לָא הֲוָה חָמֵי מִדֵּי, אֶלָּא נְהִירוּ דְּאַנְפּוֹי דְּנָהִיר, כְּאִילּוּ נִיצוֹצָא דְּדַהֲבָא הֲוָה נָצִיץ בֵּיהּ, בַּר דְּכַהֲנָא הֲוָה יָדַע חֵיזוּ דְּאִסְתַּכְּלוּתָא קַדְמָאָה, דַּהֲוָה חָמֵי לְפוּם שַׁעֲתָא, דְּהָא רְעוּתָא דְּקוּדְשָׁא בְּ"ה הֲוָה בֵּיהּ בְּהַהוּא בַּ"נ, וְיָדַע דְּאִיהוּ זַמִּין לְעָלְמָא דְּאָתֵי, בְּגִין דְּחֵיזוּ דָּא נָהֲרִין עֲלֵיהּ מִלְּעֵילָּא, וְקוּדְשָׁא בְּרִיךְ הוּא הֲוָה אִתְרָעֵי בֵּיהּ. וְכַד מִסְתַּכְּלִין בֵּיהּ לָא חָמָאן מִדֵּי, בְּגִין דְּחֵיזוּ דִּלְעֵילָּא לָא אִתְגַּלְיָיא אֶלָּא לְפוּם שַׁעֲתָא.

448. AT ONE TIME, the sparkling would shine in him, and AT ONE TIME it would not. HE EXPLAINS, when the priest looked first at the person, he saw the illuminations of all the letters on his face. But when he looked closely, he would see nothing but the light of his face, TO THE EXTENT of the sparkling coming from gold, shining on him, AND NO MORE. Only the priest understood what he saw at first glance, which he saw for a while, AND THE SAME WITH EVERYONE ELSE. IT IS because the Holy One, blessed be He, favors that man, WHO REGARDS THE HEAD PLATE, and knows that he is destined for the World to Come, as the sight THAT ILLUMINATED WITH THE LETTERS OF THE HEAD PLATE, shines on him from above, to say that the Holy One, blessed be He, is pleased with him. But when they look at him closely, later, TO EXAMINE HIM they would see nothing, since the upper mirror is seen in him only for a while.

449. וְאִי קַיְימָא בַּ"נ קַמֵּי הַהוּא צִיץ, וְאַנְפּוֹי לָא אִתְחֲזְיָין לְפוּם שַׁעֲתָא, חֵיזוּ קַדִּישָׁא. הֲוָה יָדַע כַּהֲנָא דְּהָא אִיהוּ תַּקִּיף מִצְחָא, וּבָעֵי לְכַפְּרָא עֲלֵיהּ, וּלְמִבְעֵי עֲלוֹי רַחֲמִין.

449. And if a person stands before that Head plate and his face does not show, NOT EVEN for a short time, the holy reflective sight, then the priest knows that he is brazen, and in need of atonement and mercy.

38. "let your eyes be on the field that they reap"

A Synopsis

Rabbi Yehuda reads the title verse from the book of Ruth. We are told that Boaz the judge of Yisrael saw Ruth's humility since she looked only in front of her, and he praised her eyes. He saw that she brought prosperity, for the more she gleaned, the more there was to glean in that field. Boaz saw that the Holy Spirit was upon her, and her eyes gave blessings. Now we are told of another explanation, where Boaz saw that many kings and rulers were destined to issue from her; the kings are like eyes because the eyes lead the body. Now we hear that 'the field' being reaped is Zion and Jerusalem, for the eyes that will issue from her shall rule in that field where the Torah is received. "And when you are thirsty" means that if you desire to be attached to a man and raise a seed you should "go to the vessels" who are the righteous, the vessels of Hashem – only God makes use of these vessels.

450. וַיַּעַשׂ אֶת צִיץ נֵזֶר הַקֹּדֶשׁ. ר' יְהוּדָה פָּתַח קָרָא בְּרוּת, עֵינַיִךְ בַּשָּׂדֶה אֲשֶׁר יִקְצֹרוּן וְגוֹ'. הַאי קְרָא אִית לְאִסְתַּכְּלָא בֵּיהּ, אֲמַאי אִצְטְרִיךְ הָכָא לְמִכְתַּב. א"ל ר' יִצְחָק, אִי הָכִי כַּמָּה קְרָאִין אִינּוּן בְּאוֹרַיְיתָא דְּאִתְחֲזִיאוּ דְּלָא אִצְטְרִיכוּ לְמִכְתַּב, וְחָמֵינָן דְּכֻלְּהוּ רָזִין עִלָּאִין. א"ר יְהוּדָה, הַאי קְרָא מַאן דְּחָמֵי וְלָא אִסְתָּכַּל בֵּיהּ, כְּמָה דְּלָא טָעִים תַּבְשִׁילָא דָּמֵי.

450. "And they made the Head plate (Heb. *tzitz*) of the holy crown" (Shemot 39:30). Rabbi Yehuda opened the discussion and read from the scroll of Ruth, "let your eyes be on the field that they reap..." (Rut 2:9). We have to examine the relevance of this verse here. Rabbi Yitzchak said to him, in the same way, there are many verses in the Torah that seem as if they do not need to be written, yet we see high secrets in them all. Rabbi Yehuda said that whoever looks at the verse but not closely, is like someone who never tasted a dish.

451. אֶלָּא רָזָא הָכָא, וּבְרוּחַ קוּדְשָׁא אִתְּמַר, בְּגִין דְּחָמָא בֹּעַז דַּיָּינָא דְּיִשְׂרָאֵל, עֲנָוְוַתְנוּתָא דְּהַהִיא צַדֶּקֶת, דְּלָא מְסַלְּקָא עֵינָא לְמֶחֱמֵי בַּאֲתָר אַחֲרָא, אֶלָּא לְקַמָּה. וְחָמָאת כָּל מַה דְּחָמָאת, בְּעֵינָא טָבָא, וְתוּקְפָּא

דְּמִצְחָא לָא הֲוָה בָּה, שְׁבַח עֵינָהָא.

451. HE ANSWERS: there is a mystery, which was written under the inspiration of the Holy Spirit. For Boaz, the judge of Yisrael, saw the humility of this righteous woman, who did not lift up her eyes to look elsewhere but in front of her, and he saw that whatever she beheld, she did so with a benevolent eye, and there was no impudence in her. He then praised her eyes.

452. בְּגִין דְּאִית עַיְינִין דִּבְגִינַיְיהוֹן לָא שַׁלְטָא בִּרְכְתָא בְּהַהוּא אֲתָר, וְאִיהוּ עֵינָא טָבָא חָמָא בָּה, דְּכָל מַה דְּאִסְתַּכְּלַת הֲוָה בְּעֵינָא טָבָא. וְתוּ, דְּחָמָא, דַּהֲוָה אַצְלַח בִּידָהָא, כָּל מַה דַּהֲוַות לַקְטָא, אִתּוֹסַף בְּחַקְלָא. וּבֹעַז אִסְתַּכַּל דְּרוּחָא קַדִּישָׁא שַׁרְיָיא עֲלָה, כְּדֵין פָּתַח וְאָמַר, עֵינַיִךְ בַּשָּׂדֶה אֲשֶׁר יִקְצֹרוּן וְגוֹ'. אִי תֵּימָא בְּגִין אִינוּן לַקְטִין כָּל אִינּוּן אַחְרָנִין, הֵיךְ אָמַר דְּתֵהַךְ אֲבַתְרַיְיהוּ, לָא אִצְטְרִיךְ לְמִכְתַּב אֶלָּא וְלָקְטְתְּ אַחֲרֵיהֶן, מַאי וְהָלַכְתְּ אַחֲרֵיהֶן, אֶלָּא בְּגִין עֵינָהָא קָאמַר. עֵינָהָא דַּהֲווֹ גַּרְמִין בִּרְכָּאן סַגִּיאִין, וְעַ"ד, וְהָלַכְתְּ אַחֲרֵיהֶן, בָּתַר עֵינַיִךְ. כָּל שְׁאָר בְּנֵי עָלְמָא לֵית לְהוּ רְשׁוּ לְמֵיהַךְ בָּתַר עֵינוֹי. וְאַנְתְּ לְבָתַר עֵינַיִךְ, דְּעֵינַיִךְ גַּרְמִין בִּרְכָּאן סַגִּיאִין.

452. For some eyes cause that there will be no blessing upon that place. AND BOAZ saw a benevolent eye in her, and also that she brings prosperity, for the more she gleaned, the more was to be gleaned in the field. And Boaz saw that the Holy Spirit was upon her. Then he said "let your eyes be on the field that they reap, and go after them." And if you say that it is for the other gleaners THAT HE TOLD RUTH "ON THE FIELD THAT THEY REAP, AND GO AFTER THEM"; THEREFORE why did he tell her to go after them and not to glean after them? What is the meaning of 'go after them'? He said that about her eyes, that brought many blessings, and therefore "go after them," after your eyes. No one in the world has permission to follow their eyes, but you SHALL GO after your eyes for they bestow many blessings.

453. ד"א עֵינַיִךְ בַּשָּׂדֶה אֲשֶׁר יִקְצֹרוּן. בֹּעַז חָמָא בְּרוּחַ קוּדְשָׁא, דִּזְמִינִין

לְנָפְקָא מִינָהּ מַלְכִין עִלָּאִין שַׁלִּיטִין דְּאִינּוּן עַיְינִין דְּכֹלָּא. כְּמָה דַּהֲוֵות
תָּמָר, דִּכְתִיב בָּהּ, וַתֵּשֶׁב בְּפֶתַח עֵינַיִם. אִתְיַישְּׁבַת בְּפִתְחָא דְּנָפְקִין
מִינָהּ מַלְכִין שַׁלִּיטִין עִלָּאִין, דְּאִקְרוּן עַיְינִין, כד"א אִם מֵעֵינֵי הָעֵדָה.
כְּמָה דְּכָל שַׁיְיפֵי גּוּפָא לָא אַזְלִין אֶלָּא בָּתַר עַיְינִין, וְעַיְינִין אִינּוּן
מְנַהֲגִין לְכָל גּוּפָא. אוּף הָכִי מַלְכִין וְסַנְהֶדְרִין, וְכָל אִינּוּן שַׁלִּיטִין, כֹּלָּא
אַזְלִין אֲבַתְרַיְיהוּ וּבְגִין כַּךְ אָמַר לָהּ עֵינַיִךְ אִלֵּין מַלְכִין וְשַׁלִּיטִין,
דִּזְמִינִין לְמֵיפַק מִינָהּ.

453. Another explanation concerning "let your eyes be on the field that they reap." Boaz looked at the Holy Spirit and saw that many high kings and rulers are destined to issue from her, and they are the eyes of all. She is like Tamar who "sat by the entrance of Einayim (lit. 'eyes')" (Beresheet 38:14), for she sat at the opening and through her issued high kings and rulers, called eyes. It is written: "through the eyes of the congregation" (Bemidbar 15:24), for as the members of the body follow the eyes alone and the eyes lead the body; so are kings and the Sanhedrin and all the rulers, everybody follows them. This is why he mentioned "your eyes," which are those kings and rulers destined to issue from her.

454. בַּשָּׂדֶה. מַאן שָׂדֶה. דָּא צִיּוֹן וִירוּשָׁלַם, דִּכְתִיב צִיּוֹן שָׂדֶה תֵחָרֵשׁ.
וּכְתִיב כְּרֵיחַ שָׂדֶה אֲשֶׁר בֵּרֲכוֹ יְיָ', דָּא יְרוּשָׁלַם. וְע"ד כְּתִיב עֵינַיִךְ
בַּשָּׂדֶה, דְּאִינּוּן עַיְינִין דִּילָהּ, דִּזְמִינִין לְמֵיפַק מִינָהּ, לָא יְהוֹן שַׁלִּיטִין
אֶלָּא בַּשָּׂדֶה. אֲשֶׁר יִקְצֹרוּן, דְּהָא מֵהַהוּא שָׂדֶה, הֲווֹ נַקְטִין כָּל בְּנֵי
עָלְמָא, תּוֹרָה, וּנְהוֹרָא דְּנָהִיר, דִּכְתִיב כִּי מִצִּיּוֹן תֵּצֵא תוֹרָה.

454. HE ASKS: It is written "in the field," what is a field? HE ANSWERS: it is Zion and Jerusalem, as is written: "Zion...be ploughed like a field" (Michah 3:12), and "as the smell of a field which Hashem had blessed" (Beresheet 27:27), which is Jerusalem. Therefore it is written: "let your eyes be on the field," for the eyes that will issue from her shall rule no place save the field. "that they reap": for from that field all the people receive Torah and shining light, as is written: "for out of Zion shall go forth Torah" (Yeshayah 2:3).

455. וְהָלַכְתְּ אַחֲרֵיהֶן, בְּאִלֵּין עוֹבָדִין דְּכַשְׁרָן, דַּאֲנָא חֲמֵינָא בָּךְ. הֲלֹא

צִוִּיתִי אֶת הַנְּעָרִים וְגו'. כְּמַשְׁמָעוֹ דִּילֵיהּ, בְּגִין דְּאִתְּתָא דַּעְתָּא קַלָּה. וְצָמִית, לִישָׁנָא דִּנְקִיּוּת נָקֵט, וְצָמִית, דְּאִי תִּיאוּבְתָּךְ לְאַדְבְּקָא בְּבַר נָשׁ לְקַיְּימָא זַרְעָא בְּעָלְמָא, וְהָלַכְתְּ אֶל הַכֵּלִים, אַלֵּין אִינּוּן צַדִּיקַיָּיא, דְּאִקְרוּן כְּלֵי יְיָ', דִּכְתִיב הִבָּרוּ נֹשְׂאֵי כְּלֵי יְיָ'. דִּזְמִינִין צַדִּיקַיָּיא לְאַיְיתָאָה לוֹן כָּל עָלְמָא, דּוֹרוֹנָא לְמַלְכָּא מְשִׁיחָא, וְאִינּוּן כְּלֵי יְיָ', מָאנִין דְּקוּדְשָׁא בְּרִיךְ הוּא אִתְהֲנֵי בְּהוּ, אַלֵּין אִינּוּן מָאנִין תְּבִירִין, תְּבִירִין אִינּוּן בְּהַאי עָלְמָא, בְּגִין לְקַיְּימָא אוֹרַיְיתָא. וְשִׁמוּשָׁא דְּקוּדְשָׁא בְּרִיךְ הוּא אִשְׁתְּמַּשׁ בְּהוּ, לָא אִשְׁתַּמַּשׁ אֶלָּא מִגּוֹ הָנֵי כֵּלִים. וְכַד תִּתְדְּבַק בְּהוּ וְשָׁתִית וְגו'.

455. "And you shall follow them": with the good deeds I see in you. "Have I not charged the young men that they shall not touch you?" (Rut 2:9), is to be understood AT FACE VALUE, for a woman's mind is easily swayed. THEREFORE HE WARNED THE YOUNG MEN NOT TO TOUCH HER. "And when you are thirsty" (Ibid.) is clean language, ITS MEANING IS that if you desire to be attached to a man and raise a seed, "go to the vessels" (Ibid.), to the righteous called the vessels of Hashem, as is written: "be clean, you that bear the vessels of Hashem" (Yeshayah 52:11). For the righteous are destined to be brought by the whole world as a gift to the King Messiah. These are the vessels the Holy One, blessed be He, takes delight in. They are broken vessels in this world for the sake of observing the Torah. And the Holy One, blessed be He, is waited upon only by them. And when you are attached to them, "drink..."

39. "and his heart was merry"

A Synopsis

We learn from Rabbi Yosi that "and his heart was merry" as written in "and Boaz ate and drank and his heart was merry" means that he said the benediction over his food; 'heart' refers to Malchut. Since food is of below, God cannot take satisfaction from it unless it is prayed over. But on the Shabbat the food itself and the pleasure of eating are included above and below. This is the secret of "For all things come of thee, and of your own have we given you." Whoever blesses God has to do it joyously with a benevolent eye. The four Chariots, in charge of the four directions of Malchut and the troops of angels, are nourished by that benediction after a meal. Now Rabbi Yosi explains, "for he gives of his bread to the poor," saying that a man with a benevolent eye gives to the poor out of his own blessing and joy. The other part of this meaning is that he gives to the place that needs sustenance from all sides, that is Malchut who has nothing by itself; in this sense Malchut is poor. From here Rabbi Yosi moves to discuss, "he went to lie down at the end of the heap," and "your belly is like a heap of wheat." Whoever says the benediction with joy ascends after death to the holy temples of Malchut called 'heap'. From each precept of the Master high secrets and high lights and radiances are suspended. Those who do not observe these precepts are impudent; when they looked upon the golden plate with the engraved letters of the Holy Name their hearts were broken so that they would feel shame and they would surrender before their Master.

456. רִבִּי יוֹסֵי פָּתַח וְאָמַר, וַיֹּאכַל בֹּעַז וַיֵּשְׁתְּ וַיִּיטַב לִבּוֹ. מַהוּ וַיִּיטַב לִבּוֹ. דְּבָרִיךְ עַל מְזוֹנֵיהּ, וְאוּקְמוּהָ. וְדָא הוּא רָזָא, דְּמַאן דִּמְבָרֵךְ עַל מְזוֹנֵיהּ, דָּא אוֹטִיב לְלִבֵּיהּ, וּמַאן אִיהוּ כְּמָה דִכְתִיב לְךָ אָמַר לִבִּי. וּכְתִיב צוּר לְבָבִי וְגוֹ'.

456. Rabbi Yosi opened the discussion with the verse "and Boaz ate and drank and his heart was merry" (Rut 3:7). What does it mean, "and his heart was merry?" It means that he said the blessing over his food. And it was explained that its meaning is that whoever says the blessing after the meal, he makes merry his heart. Who is such a one? He is alluded to in "to you my heart has said" (Tehilim 27:8), and "the firm strength of my heart" (Tehilim 73:26), REFERING TO MALCHUT CALLED HEART.

457. וּבְגִין דְּבִרְכַּת מְזוֹנָא חֲבִיבָא קַמֵּי קוּדְשָׁא בְּרִיךְ הוּא, כָּל מַאן דְּבָרֵיךְ עַל שַׂבְעָא, אוֹטִיב וְחַדֵּי לַאֲתָר אַחֲרָא, וְסִימָנָךְ סְעוּדָתֵי דְּשַׁבָּת, דְּאֲתָר אַחֲרָא אִתְהֲנֵי מֵהַהִיא בְּרָכָה דְּשַׂבְעָא וְחֶדְוָה. וְהָכָא אִתְהֲנֵי מֵהַהוּא בְּרָכָה דְּשַׂבְעָא דְּהַהוּא צַדִּיק בֹּעַז וְדָא וַיִּיטַב לִבּוֹ.

457. And since the blessing after the meal pleases the Holy One, blessed be He, whoever blesses when satisfied, does good and joy to another place, VIZ. MALCHUT, as shown by the meals of Shabbat. For that other place, MALCHUT, enjoys the blessing and the joy of satiation. Here MALCHUT takes pleasure in the blessing of satisfaction of Boaz the righteous. This is the meaning of "and his heart was merry."

458. מ"ט. בְּגִין דִּמְזוֹנָא אִיהוּ קָשֶׁה קַמֵּי קוּדְשָׁא בְּרִיךְ הוּא הַהוּא אֲתָר, וְכֵיוָן דְּבַר נָשׁ אָכִיל וְשָׁתֵי, וְקָא מְבָרֵךְ. הַהִיא בִּרְכָתָא סַלְקָא, וְאִתְהֲנֵי מֵאִינּוּן מִלִּין דְּשַׂבְעָא דְּסַלְקִין, וְאִשְׁתְּכַח דְּאִתְהֲנֵי מִמְּזוֹנָא מִתַּתָּא וּמִלְעֵילָא.

458. What is the reason, MALCHUT ENJOYS THE BLESSING AFTER THE MEAL? A man's food is troublesome to the Holy One, blessed be He, being of that place, THAT IS, MALCHUT. When he eats and drinks and says the blessing OVER FOOD, the blessing rises, and MALCHUT enjoys the rising words said by the satisfied man. So MAN enjoys the food below and MALCHUT above.

459. וְדָא אִיהוּ רָזָא דְּבֵין חַבְרַיָּיא. רָזָא בְּחוֹל לָא אִתְהֲנֵי הַהוּא אֲתָר, אֶלָּא מֵאִינּוּן מִלִּין דְּסַלְקִין מִגּוֹ שַׂבְעָא, וְכֻלְּהוּ מִלִּין מִתְעַטְּרָן וְרַוְיוֹן וְשַׂבְעִין בְּחֶידוּ, וְהַהוּא אֲתָר אִתְהֲנֵי מִנַּיְיהוּ. בְּשַׁבָּת אִיהוּ רָזָא אָחֳרָא, בִּמְזוֹנָא מַמָּשׁ, וּבְהַהוּא חֶדְוָה דִּמְזוֹנָא דְּמִצְוָה דְּשַׁבָּת, וּבְכֹלָּא אִשְׁתְּכַח כְּלִילָא מֵעֵילָא וְתַתָּא. וְרָזָא דָּא כִּי מִמְּךָ הַכֹּל וּמִיָּדְךָ נָתְנוּ לָךְ. וַדַּאי בַּהֲנָאוּתֵיהּ דָּא, וּבְהַהוּא חֶדְוָה דִּמְזוֹנָא דְּמִצְוָה דְּשַׁבָּת, כְּמָה דְּאוּקְמוּהָ.

459. This is a mystery among the friends. The mystery is that on weekdays, that place derives enjoyment only from the words coming from satiation,

NAMELY, FROM THE BLESSING AFTER THE MEAL. And all the words are crowned, satiated and satisfied with joy, and that place takes pleasure in them. On Shabbat it is another principle. MALCHUT ENJOYS the actual food and the pleasure in the food consumed to fulfill the Shabbat precept. AND THE FOOD ITSELF is totally included high and low. This is the secret of "for all things come of You, and of Your own have we given You" (I Divrei Hayamim 29:14). Assuredly MALCHUT PARTAKES OF this enjoyment OF MAN and the joy in eating to fulfill the Shabbat precept as explained.

460. מַאן דִּמְבָרֵךְ לְקוּדְשָׁא בְּרִיךְ הוּא מִגּוֹ שַׂבְעָא, בָּעֵי לְכַוְּונָא לְבֵּיה, וּלְשַׁוָּואָה רְעוּתֵיה בְּחֶדְוָה, וְלָא יִשְׁתְּכַח עָצִיב, אֶלָּא דִּיבָרֵךְ בְּחֶדְוָה בְּרָזָא דָא, וּלְשַׁוָּואָה רְעוּתֵיה דְּהָא אִיהוּ יָהִיב הַשְׁתָּא לְאָחֳרָא בְּחֶדְוָה, בְּעֵינָא טָבָא, וּכְמָה דְּאִיהוּ מְבָרֵךְ בְּחֶדְוָה וּבְעֵינָא טָבָא. הָכִי יָהֲבִין לֵיה בְּחֶדְוָה וּבְעֵינָא טָבָא. וּבג״כ לָא יִשְׁתְּכַח עָצִיב כְּלָל, אֶלָּא בְּחֶדְוָה, וּבְמִלִּין דְּאוֹרַיְיתָא, וִישַׁוֵּוי לְבֵּיה וּרְעוּתֵיה לְמֵיהַב בְּרָכָה דָא, בְּרָזָא דְּאִצְטְרִיךְ.

460. Whoever blesses the Holy One, blessed be He, when he is full, should have intention in his heart, and gladness in his mind, and must not be sad. But he has to bless joyously according to this secret, and pay attention that now he gives to another, gladly and with a benevolent eye. And as he blesses gladly with a benevolent eye, so he will be given gladly with a benevolent eye, and therefore one will not be in sadness at all, but in gladness and with words of the Torah. And one should be careful to bless the proper place, NAMELY, MALCHUT.

461. רָזָא הָכָא, אַרְבַּע רְתִיכִין שַׁלִּיטִין, בְּד׳ סְטָרִין וּמַשִׁירְיָין, אִתְזָנוּ מֵהַהִיא בִּרְכָתָא דְּשַׂבְעָא, וּבְאִינּוּן מִלִּין דְּבָרוּךְ אַתָּה, אִתְהֲנֵי וְאִתְרַבֵּי וְאִתְעַטָּר בֵּיה. וּמַאן דִּמְבָרֵךְ אִצְטְרִיךְ רְעוּתָא בְּחֶדְוָה, וּבְעֵינָא טָבָא, וְעַ״ד כְּתִיב, טוֹב עַיִן הוּא יְבוֹרָךְ.

461. Here is a secret: the four Chariots, in charge of the four directions OF MALCHUT and the troops OF ANGELS, are nourished by that blessing over satiety. And the words "Blessed are You," IN THE BLESSING AFTER THE

MEAL, MALCHUT enjoys, grows and adorns herself with them. And he who blesses, should do it willingly, joyously and with a benign eye. Therefore it is written: "he that has a generous eye shall be blessed" (Mishlei 22:9).

462. וְהָכָא שָׁפִיל לְסֵיפֵיהּ דִּקְרָא, דִּכְתִיב כִּי נָתַן מִלַּחְמוֹ לַדָּל. דְּאִי לָא תֵּימָא הָכִי, הַאי קְרָא לָאו רֵישֵׁיהּ סֵיפֵיהּ, וְלָאו סֵיפֵיהּ רֵישֵׁיהּ. אֶלָּא טוֹב עַיִן, כְּמָה דְּאוֹקִימְנָא, הוּא יְבָרֵךְ וַדַּאי, בְּעֵינָא טָבָא בְּחֶדְוָה. וְלָאו אִיהוּ לְמַגְּנָא לְבָרְכָא בְּחֶדְוָה, דְּהָא מֵהַהוּא בִּרְכָתָא, וּמֵהַהוּא חֶידוּ נָתַן מִלַּחְמוֹ לַדָּל, אֲתָר דְּאִצְטְרִיךְ לְאִתְּזָנָא מִכָּל סִטְרִין. אֲתָר דְּלֵית לֵיהּ מִגַּרְמֵיהּ כְּלוּם. אֲתָר דְּאִתְהֲנֵי מִכָּל סִטְרִין וְאִתְכְּלִיל מִכָּל סִטְרִין. מִלִּין אִלֵּין לָא אִתְמְסָרוּ אֶלָּא לְחַכִּימִין דְּיַדְעִין רָזִין עִלָּאִין וְאוֹרְחִין דְּאוֹרַיְיתָא.

462. Here we ought to understand the verse ending thoroughly, for it goes on to say "for he gives of his bread to the poor" (Ibid.). You may disagree with it THAT THE BEGINNING OF THE VERSE SPEAKS OF THE BLESSING AFTER THE MEAL, AND has no connection to the end, and the end has no connection to the beginning. But a man of benevolent eye, as we said, assuredly blesses gladly with a benign eye, and not for no reason does he joyously bless, for from that blessing and joy, "he gives of his bread to the poor," namely, to the place which needs sustenance from all sides, RIGHT AND LEFT, a place that has nothing to itself, but enjoys on all sides, and is included on all sides. THIS IS MALCHUT, WHICH IS THEREFORE CALLED POOR, OF WHICH IS SAID "FOR HE GIVES OF HIS BREAD TO THE POOR." These words are told solely to the wise men who know the high mysteries and the ways of the Torah.

463. תָּא חֲזֵי, בְּעֹז טַב עֵינָא הֲוָה תּוּקְפָּא דְּמִצְחָא לָא הֲוָה בֵּיהּ לְעָלְמָא. מַה כְּתִיב, וַיָּבֹא לִשְׁכַּב בִּקְצֵה הָעֲרֵמָה, רָזָא דִּכְתִיב, בְּטֶנְךָ עֲרֵמַת חִטִּים. מֵהָכָא אוֹלִיפְנָא, כָּל מַאן דִּמְבָרֵךְ בִּרְכַּת מְזוֹנָא כַּדְקָא יֵאוֹת, בְּחֶדְוָה בִּרְעוּתָא דְּלִבָּא, כַּד סָלִיק מֵהַאי עָלְמָא, אֲתָר אִתְתַּקְּנָא לֵיהּ, גּוֹ רָזִין עִלָּאִין בְּהֵיכָלִין קַדִּישִׁין. זַכָּאָה אִיהוּ בַּר נָשׁ דְּנָטִיר פִּקּוּדֵי דְּמָארֵיהּ, וְיָדַע רָזָא דִּילְהוֹן, דְּלֵית לָךְ פִּקּוּדָא וּפִקּוּדָא בְּאוֹרַיְיתָא, דְּלָא

תַּלְיָין בֵּיה רָזִין עִלָּאִין, וּנְהוֹרִין וְזִיוִין עִלָּאִין, וּבְנֵי נָשָׁא לָא יָדְעֵי, וְלָא
מַשְׁגִּיחִין בִּיקָרָא דְּמָארֵיהוֹן. זַכָּאָה חוּלְקֵיהוֹן דְּצַדִּיקַיָּיא, אִינּוּן
דְּמִשְׁתַּדְלֵי בְּאוֹרַיְיתָא זַכָּאִין אִינּוּן בְּעָלְמָא דֵּין וּבְעָלְמָא דְּאָתֵי.

463. Come and see, Boaz had a benevolent eye. He was never impudent. It
is written: "he went to lie down at the end of the heap" (Rut 3:7). This is the
secret of "your belly is like a heap of wheat" (Shir Hashirim 7:3), ALLUDING
TO MALCHUT. MALCHUT IS FOUND EVEN AT THE END OF THE HEAP.
From this I learned that whoever says the blessing over food properly, with
joy, willingly, when he ascends from this world, a place is prepared for him
amidst the high secrets, in the Temples OF MALCHUT CALLED HEAP, TO
WHICH THE VERSE ALLUDES. "HE WENT TO LIE" AFTER PASSING FROM
THE WORLD "AT THE END OF THE HEAP," WHICH IS MALCHUT. Happy is
the man who observes the precepts of his Master, and knows their secret
meanings, for from each precept, many high secrets, and high lights and
radiance's are suspended. And people do not know nor care for the glory of
their Master. Happy is the portion of the righteous, those who are occupied
in the Torah. Happy are they in this world and the World to Come.

464. תָּא חֲזֵי דְּהָא אָמְרוּ, דְּכָל אִינּוּן תַּקִּיפֵי מִצְחָא, דְּלֵית לְהוּ כִּסּוּפָא,
לֵית לְהוֹן חוּלָקָא בְּעָלְמָא דֵּין וּבְעָלְמָא דְּאָתֵי. כָּל אִינּוּן תַּקִּיפֵי מִצְחָא
דַּהֲווֹ בְּהוּ בְּיִשְׂרָאֵל, כַּד הֲווֹ מִסְתַּכְּלָן בְּהַהוּא צִיץ, הֲווֹ מִתָּבְרָן לִבַּיְיהוּ,
וּמִסְתַּכְּלָן בְּעוֹבָדַיְיהוּ. בְּגִין דְּצִיץ עַל אָת הֲוָה קָאִים, וְכָל מַאן
דְּמִסְתַּכַּל בֵּיה, הֲוָה מַכְסִיף בְּעוֹבָדוֹי. וְעַ"ד צִיץ מְכַפְּרָא עַל אִינּוּן
תַּקִּיפֵי אַנְפִּין, תַּקִּיפֵי מִצְחָא.

464. Come and see, it is said that all the impudent without shame have no
portion in this world or in the World to Come. All the impudent in Yisrael,
when they looked upon the plate, their heart broke and they searched their
deeds. Since the plate was based on a letter, AS 'HOLY TO HASHEM' WAS
ENGRAVED ON IT and whoever looked at it, felt ashamed for what he has
done; thus the plate atoned for the impudent and shameless.

465. אַתְוָון דִּרְזָא דִּשְׁמָא קַדִּישָׁא דַּהֲווֹ גְּלִיפִין עַל צִיצָא, הֲווֹ נָהֲרִין
וּבָלְטִין וְנָצְצִין. כָּל מַאן דַּהֲוָה מִסְתַּכֵּל בְּהַהוּא נְצִיצוּ דְּאַתְוָון, אַנְפּוֹי

נַפְלִין מֵאֵימָתָא, וַהֲוָה אִתְבַּר לְבֵּיה, וּכְדֵין צִיצָא מְכַפְּרָא עֲלַיְיהוּ. כְּגַוְונָא דָא כֵּיוָן דְּאִיהוּ גָּרִים לְתַבְרָא לְבֵּיה, וּלְאִתְכַּנְעָא מִקַּמֵּי מָארֵיה.

465. The letters of the secret of the Holy Name engraved upon the plate shone with glittering emitting light. Whoever looked upon the radiance of the letters, his face would fall in terror, and his heart would break. Then the plate atones for them that way, for it caused their heart to break and them to surrender before their Master.

40. The incense

A Synopsis

In this passage Rabbi Yosi tells of the great power of incense to break evil inclinations, to banish sorcery, and to protect us from the Other Side. It is as miraculous as the golden plate. Furthermore, whoever reads and studies intently the section on the preparation of the incense is protected. When the smoke of the incense went up like a pillar the priest saw the letters of the Holy Name soaring in the air and going up like a pillar; afterwards many Chariots circled it on all sides. It creates unity above and below, atoning for sin and idolatry.

466. כְּגַוְונָא דָא קְטֹרֶת, כָּל מַאן דְּאָרַח בְּהַהוּא תְּנָנָא, כַּד סָלִיק הַהוּא
עַמּוּדָא מֵהַהוּא מַעֲלֵה עָשָׁן, הֲוָה מְבָרֵר לִבֵּיהּ, בִּבְרִירוּ לְמִפְלַח
לְמָארֵיהּ, וְאַעְבָּר מִנֵּיהּ זוּהֲמָא דְּיֵצֶר הָרָע, וְלָא הֲוָה לֵיהּ אֶלָּא לִבָּא
חֲדָא, לָקֳבֵל אֲבוּהּ דְּבִשְׁמַיָּא. בְּגִין דִּקְטֹרֶת, תְּבִירוּ דְּיֵצֶר הָרָע אִיהוּ
וַדַּאי בְּכָל סִטְרִין. וּכְמָה דְּצִיץ הֲוָה קָאִים עַל נִיסָּא, אוּף קְטֹרֶת. דְּלֵית
לָךְ מִלָּה בְּעָלְמָא, לְמִתְבַּר לֵיהּ לְסִטְרָא אַחֲרָא, בַּר קְטֹרֶת.

466. So is the incense. Whoever smelled the smoke coming from the pillar OF SMOKE rising from the smoke raiser, would cleanse his heart totally to worship his Master, and the filth of the Evil Inclination would pass from him. He would have only one heart towards his father in heaven. Since incense breaks the Evil Inclination on all sides; as the plate is miraculous, so is the incense, for nothing in the world breaks the Other Side except incense.

467. ת"ח מַה מַּה כְּתִיב, קַח אֶת הַמַּחְתָּא וְתֶן עָלֶיהָ אֵשׁ מֵעַל הַמִּזְבֵּחַ
וְשִׂים קְטֹרֶת. מ"ט. כִּי יָצָא הַקֶּצֶף מִלִּפְנֵי יְיָ', הֵחֵל הַנָּגֶף. דְּהָא לֵית
תְּבִירוּ לְהַהוּא סִטְרָא בַּר קְטֹרֶת. דְּלֵית לָךְ מִלָּה חֲבִיבָה קָמֵי קוּדְשָׁא
בְּרִיךְ הוּא , כִּקְטֹרֶת. וְקַיְּימָא לְבַטְּלָא חַרְשִׁין, וּמִלִּין בִּישִׁין מִבֵּיתָא.
רֵיחָא וַעֲשָׁנָא דִּקְטֹרֶת דְּעַבְדֵי בְּנֵי נָשָׁא, בְּהַהוּא עוֹבְדָא אִיהוּ מְבַטֵּל,
כ"ש קְטֹרֶת.

467. Come and look at the verse "take a censer, and put fire in it from off the altar, and put on incense" (Bemidbar 17:11). What is the sense? "for

wrath is gone out from Hashem: the plague has begun" (Ibid.). Nothing breaks that side except for incense, for nothing is more delightful before the Holy One, blessed be He, than incense. It can revoke sorcery, and evil things at home. The smell and smoke of manmade incense cancels SORCERY, when done for that specific purpose, and incense all the more.

468. מִלָּה דָא גְּזֵרָה קַיָּימָא קַמֵּי קוּדְשָׁא בְּרִיךְ הוּא, דְּכָל מַאן דְּאִסְתְּכַּל וְקָרֵי בְּכָל יוֹמָא עוֹבָדָא דִּקְטֹרֶת, יִשְׁתְּזִיב מִכָּל מִלִּין בִּישִׁין חַרְשִׁין דְּעָלְמָא. וּמִכָּל פְּגָעִין בִּישִׁין, וּמֵהִרְהוּרָא בִּישָׁא, וּמִדִּינָא בִּישָׁא, וּמִמּוֹתָנָא, וְלָא יִתְזַק כָּל הַהוּא יוֹמָא, דְּלָא יָכִיל סִטְרָא אַחֲרָא לְשַׁלְטָא עֲלֵיהּ, וְאִצְטְרִיךְ דִּיכַוֵּין בֵּיהּ.

468. It is a standing decree before the Holy One, blessed be He, that whoever looks at and reads every day the section of the preparation of incense, he is protected from all evil things and sorcery in the world, from mishaps and evil brooding, from bad punishment and death, and shall not come to harm on that day, for the Other Side may not have power over him. Only he must read it intently.

469. אר"ש, אִי בְּנֵי נָשָׁא הֲווֹ יַדְעֵי כַּמָּה עִלָּאָה אִיהוּ עוֹבָדָא דִּקְטֹרֶת קַמֵּי קוּדְשָׁא בְּרִיךְ הוּא , הֲווֹ נַטְלֵי כָּל מִלָּה וּמִלָּה מִנֵּיהּ, וַהֲווֹ סַלְקֵי לֵהּ עֲטָרָה עַל רֵישַׁיְיהוּ, כְּכִתְרָא דְּדַהֲבָא. וּמַאן דְּאִשְׁתַּדַּל בֵּיהּ, בָּעֵי לְאִסְתַּכְּלָא בְּעוֹבָדָא דִּקְטֹרֶת, וְאִי יְכַוֵּין בֵּיהּ בְּכָל יוֹמָא, אִית לֵיהּ חוּלָקָא בְּהַאי עָלְמָא, וּבְעָלְמָא דְּאָתֵי, וְיִסְתַּלַּק מוֹתָנָא מִנֵּיהּ, וּמֵעָלְמָא, וְיִשְׁתְּזִיב מִכָּל דִּינִין דְּהַאי עָלְמָא, מִסְטְרִין בִּישִׁין, וּמִדִּינָא דְּגֵיהִנָּם, וּמִדִּינָא דְּמַלְכוּ אַחֲרָא.

469. Rabbi Shimon said, if people would know how lofty is the section of the preparation of incense before the Holy One, blessed be He, they would take each word and raise it to be adorned as a golden crown upon their heads. Whoever studies well the section on the formulation of the incense, has to examine it closely. And if he concentrates on it every day, he has a portion in this world and in the World to Come. Death is banished from him and from the world, and he is protected from this world's ordinances, the ordeal of Gehenom, and the judgment of other kingdom (Heb. *malchut*).

470. בְּהַהוּא קְטֹרֶת כַּד הֲוָה סָלִיק תְּנָנָא בְּעַמּוּדָא, כַּהֲנָא הֲוָה חָמֵי אַתְוָון דְּרָזָא דִשְׁמָא קַדִּישָׁא, פַּרְחִין בַּאֲוִירָא, וְסַלְקֵי לְעֵילָא בְּהַהוּא עַמּוּדָא. לְבָתַר כַּמָה רְתִיכִין קַדִּישִׁין סָחֲרִין לֵיהּ מִכָּל סִטְרִין, עַד דְּסָלִיק בִּנְהִירוּ וְחֶדְוָה, וְחַדֵּי לְמַאן דְּחַדֵּי, וְקָשַׁר קִשְׁרִין לְעֵילָא וְתַתָּא לְיַחֲדָא כֹּלָּא, וְהָא אוֹקִימְנָא. וְדָא מְכַפֵּר עַל יֵצֶר הָרָע, וְעַל ע״ז, דְּאִיהוּ סִטְרָא אַחֲרָא. וְהָא אוֹקְמוּהָ.

470. In that incense, when the smoke went up like a pillar, the priest saw the letters of the Holy Name soaring in the air and going up like a pillar, and afterwards, many Chariots circled it on all sides, and it goes up shining and joyous, and gladdens those who are gladdened, and binds bonds, THAT IS, CREATES UNITY, above and below, so that everything becomes one. This has already been explained. This atones for the Evil Inclination and idolatry, which is the Other Side as clarified.

41. "And you shall make an altar for the burning of incense"

A Synopsis

Rabbi Yosi says there are two altars, an inner one for fragrant spice burnt incense and an outer one for burnt offering. The Other Side is bound and tied to the altar; when he saw the smoke of incense rising he fled, leaving the tabernacle purified. Wherever the section of the incense is said with dedication death has no sway, even as Aaron bound the angel of death so he could have no power nor could he pronounce judgment. A man can escape judgment if he says twice a day the passage of the incense ordinance; upon this passage the world exists, and also the World to Come. If it is not said, judgment and plagues hover over the land and it is ruled by other nations. Rabbi Yosi tells us that the section of the incense is dearer to God and more important than all prayers. Incense does more than prayer by creating unity and bringing light and removing filth from the world. The incense unites Zeir Anpin and Malchut. Malchut then becomes Hei; the Hei unites with Vav, that is Zeir Anpin; the Vav arises to be adorned by the first Hei, Binah; that Hei is glittering by the Yud that is Chochmah. Then all their will rises to infinity, and all of them become one; the Holy Name shines and adorns itself, all the worlds rejoice, candles burn brightly, and there is food and blessing for all the worlds.

471. פָּתַח וְאָמַר, וַיַּעַשׂ מִזְבֵּחַ מִקְטַר קְטֹרֶת וְגוֹ'. הַאי קְרָא אִית לְאִסְתַּכְּלָא בֵּיה, בְּגִין דִּתְרֵין מַדְבְּחִין הֲווֹ, מַדְבְּחָא דִּעֵלָּוֹן, וּמַדְבְּחָא דִקְטֹרֶת בּוּסְמִין, דָּא לְבַר, וְדָא לְגוֹ. הַאי מַדְבְּחָא דִקְטֹרֶת, דְּאִיהוּ פְּנִימָאָה, אֲמַאי אִקְרֵי מִזְבֵּחַ, וְהָא לָא דַּבְחִין בֵּיהּ דִּבְחִין, וּמִזְבֵּחַ ע"ד אִקְרֵי.

471. He opened and said "And you shall make an altar for the burning of incense" (Shemot 30:1). We should look carefully into this verse. For there are two altars, of fragrant spice burnt incense and of burnt offering, the former an inner and the latter an outer one. Why is it called an altar if no animals are sacrificed upon it, to give it the name of altar?

472. אֶלָּא בְּגִין דִּבְטִיל וְכָפִית לְכַמָּה סִטְרִין בִּישִׁין, וּבְגִין דְּהַהוּא סִטְרָא בִּישָׁא כְּפִית לָא יָכִיל לְשַׁלְטָאָה, וְלָא לְמֶהֱוֵי קַטֵּיגוֹרָא, וְע"ד אִקְרֵי מִזְבֵּחַ. כַּד הַהוּא סִטְרָא בִּישָׁא הֲוָה חָמֵי עֲשָׁנָא דִקְטֹרֶת דְּסָלִיק,

אִתְכַּפְיָיא וְעָרַק, וְלָא יָכִיל לְקָרְבָא כְּלַל לְמַשְׁכְּנָא. וּבְגִין דָּא אִתְדְּכֵי
וְלָא אִתְעֲרַב בְּהַהוּא חֶדְוָה דִּלְעֵילָּא, בַּר קוּדְשָׁא בְּרִיךְ הוּא בִּלְחוֹדוֹי,
וּבְגִין דְּחָבִיבָא כ"כ, לָא קָאִים הַהוּא מִזְבֵּחַ, אֶלָּא לְגוֹ. דְּהַאי אִיהוּ
מִזְבֵּחַ דְּבִרְכָּאן אִשְׁתְּכָחוּ בֵּיהּ, וְע"ד סָתִים מֵעֵינָא.

472. Since some evil beings were neutralized and bound, and the Other Side is bound, it cannot rule nor denounce. Therefore it is called an altar (Heb. *mizbeach*), FOR THE OTHER SIDE IS BOUND AND TIED TO IT LIKE A SACRIFICED ANIMAL (HEB. *ZEVACH*). And when the Other Side saw the smoke of incense rising, he surrendered and fled, and could not approach the tabernacle, so it was purified. And no one delighted in that high joy but the Holy One, blessed be He, alone. Since He is very fond of it, the altar stands inside, for there are blessings in such an altar, and therefore it is not exposed, THAT IS, IT STANDS INSIDE.

473. מַה כְּתִיב בְּאַהֲרֹן, וַיַּעֲמֹד בֵּין הַמֵּתִים וּבֵין הַחַיִּים וַתֵּעָצַר
הַמַּגֵּפָה, דְּכָפִית לֵיהּ לְמַלְאַךְ הַמָּוֶת, דְּלָא יָכִיל לְשַׁלְטָאָה כְּלַל, וְלָא
לְמֶעְבַּד דִּינָא. סִימָנָא דָּא אִתְמְסַר בִּידָנָא, דִּי בְּכָל אֲתָר דְּקָאמְרֵי
בְּכַוְונָה, וּרְעוּתָא דְּלִבָּא עוֹבָדָא דִּקְטֹרֶת, דְּלָא שַׁלְטָא מוֹתָנָא בְּהַהוּא
אֲתָר, וְלָא יִתְזַק, וְלָא יַכְלִין שְׁאַר עַמִּין לְשַׁלְטָאָה עַל הַהוּא אֲתָר.

473. It is written about Aaron, "And he stood between the dead and the living, and the plague was stayed" (Bemidbar 17:13). For he bound the Angel of Death, so he could not have power at all, nor carry out punishment. A sign was given to us, that wherever the section of the incense is said with intention and a willing heart, death has no sway over that place, nor can it harm. Also other nations have no power over that place.

474. ת"ח מַה כְּתִיב, מִזְבֵּחַ מִקְטַר קְטֹרֶת. כֵּיוָן דִּכְתִיב מִזְבֵּחַ, אֲמַאי
אִקְרֵי מִקְטַר קְטֹרֶת. אֶלָּא בְּגִין דְּנַטְלֵי מֵהַאי אֲתָר לְאַקְטְרָא, כְּמָה
דְּעָבַד אַהֲרֹן. תּוּ, מִזְבֵּחַ אִצְטְרִיךְ לְאַקְטְרָא לְקֻדְשָׁא לֵיהּ בְּהַהוּא קְטֹרֶת,
וְע"ד מִקְטַר קְטֹרֶת. תּוּ, מִקְטַר קְטֹרֶת, כְּתַרְגּוּמוֹ, לְאַקְטְרָא קְטֹרֶת, דְּהָא
אָסִיר לְאַקְטְרָא בַּאֲתָר אַחֲרָא קְטֹרֶת, בַּר מִמַּחְתָּה.

474. Come and look at the verse, "an altar for the burning of incense" (Shemot 30:1). HE ASKS: Why is it called an altar, if it is meant for burning incense? HE ANSWERS: this is because FIRE is taken from that place to burn incense, like Aaron did, AS IS WRITTEN: "TAKE A CENSER, AND PUT FIRE IN IT FROM OFF THE ALTAR" (BEMIDBAR 17:11). Moreover, since it is an altar, it must be sanctified by that incense, therefore it is for the burning of incense. ANOTHER SENSE is that 'the burning of incense' literally means that incense must be burnt only in a censer.

475. ת״ח, הַאי מַאן דְּדִינָא רָדִיף אֲבַתְרֵיהּ, אִצְטְרִיךְ לְהַאי קְטֹרֶת, וּלְאָתָבָא קַמֵּי מָארֵיהּ, דְּהָא סִיּוּעָא אִיהוּ לְאִסְתַּלְּקָא דִּינִין מִנֵּיהּ, וּבְהַאי וַדַּאי מִסְתַּלְּקִין מִנֵּיהּ, אִי הוּא רָגִיל בְּהַאי, לְאַדְכְּרָא תְּרֵין זְמְנִין בְּיוֹמָא, בְּצַפְרָא וּבְרַמְשָׁא, דִּכְתִּיב קְטֹרֶת סַמִּים בַּבֹּקֶר בַּבֹּקֶר וּכְתִיב בֵּין הָעַרְבַּיִם יַקְטִירֶנָּה. וְדָא אִיהוּ קִיּוּמָא דְּעָלְמָא תָּדִיר, דִּכְתִּיב קְטֹרֶת תָּמִיד לִפְנֵי יְיָ' לְדֹרֹתֵיכֶם וַדַּאי הוּא קִיּוּמָא דְּעָלְמָא לְתַתָּא, וְקִיּוּמָא דְּעָלְמָא לְעֵילָּא.

475. Come and see, whoever is pursued by Judgment, is in need of incense and must repent before his Master. For INCENSE helps Judgment to disappear from him. And assuredly Judgment leaves him, if he is wont to say twice a day, morning and evening, the passage of the incense, as is written: "sweet incense every morning... at evening, he shall burn incense upon it" (Shemot 30:7-8). Upon this the world perpetually exists, as is said, "a perpetual incense before Hashem throughout your generations" (Ibid. 8). Assuredly, this world is sustained by it and so is the World to Come.

476. בְּהַהוּא אֲתָר דְּלָא אִדְכַּר בְּכָל יוֹמָא עוֹבָדָא דִּקְטֹרֶת, דִּינִין דִּלְעֵילָּא שַׁרְיָין בֵּיהּ, וּמוֹתָנִין סַגִּיאוּ בֵּיהּ, וְעַמִּין אַחֲרָנִין שַׁלְטִין עֲלֵיהּ. בְּגִין דִּכְתִּיב, קְטֹרֶת תָּמִיד לִפְנֵי יְיָ'. תָּמִיד אִיהוּ קַיְימָא לִפְנֵי יְיָ', יַתִּיר מִכָּל פּוּלְחָנִין אַחֲרָנִין, חֲבִיבָא אִיהוּ עוֹבָדָא דִּקְטֹרֶת, דְּהוּא יַקִּיר וְחָבִיב קַמֵּי קוּדְשָׁא בְּרִיךְ הוּא, יַתִּיר מִכָּל פּוּלְחָנִין וּרְעוּתִין דְּעָלְמָא. וְאע״ג דִּצְלוֹתָא אִיהִי מְעַלְיָיא מִכֹּלָּא, עוֹבָדָא דִּקְטֹרֶת הוּא יַקִּיר וְחָבִיב קַמֵּי קוּדְשָׁא בְּרִיךְ הוּא.

476. Wherever the section of incense formulation is not daily mentioned, WHEN NOT RECITED, judgment and many plagues hover above this place, and it is ruled by other nations. Therefore it is written: "a perpetual incense before Hashem." It stands always before Hashem, more than other devotions. The section of the incense is more precious and delightful to the Holy One, blessed be He, than all worship and petitions. And though prayer is most valuable, the section of the incense formulation is MORE highly regarded and precious to the Holy One, blessed be He.

477. תָּא חֲזֵי, מַה בֵּין צְלוֹתָא לְעוֹבָדָא דִּקְטֹרֶת. צְלוֹתָא אַתְקִינוּ לָהּ בַּאֲתָר דְּקָרְבְּנִין, דַּהֲווֹ עַבְדֵי יִשְׂרָאֵל, וְכָל אִינּוּן קָרְבְּנִין דַּהֲווֹ עַבְדִין יִשְׂרָאֵל, לָאו אִינּוּן חֲשִׁיבִין כִּקְטֹרֶת. וְתוּ מַה בֵּין הַאי לְהַאי. אֶלָּא צְלוֹתָא אִיהוּ תִּקּוּנָא לְאַתְקְנָא מַה דְּאִצְטְרִיךְ, קְטֹרֶת עָבֵיד יַתִּיר, מְתַקֵּן וְקָשִׁיר קְשָׁרִין, וְעָבֵיד נְהִירוּ יַתִּיר מִכֹּלָּא. וּמַאן אִיהוּ דְּאַעֲבַר זוּהֲמָא וְאִידְכֵּי מַשְׁכְּנָא, וְכֹלָּא אִתְנְהִיר וְאִתְתָּקַן וְאִתְקְשַׁר כַּחֲדָא.

477. Come and see the difference between prayer and the section of incense. Prayer was composed instead of the sacrifices offered by Yisrael. But all those sacrifices are not as valuable as the incense. Also, the difference between them is that prayer perfects whatever needs perfection. Incense, on the other hand, does more by both perfecting and binding, THAT IS, CREATING UNITY, and brings more light than anything else, which removes filth and cleanses the tabernacle. And everything is shining, perfected and joined together.

478. וע"ד בָּעֵינָן לְאַקְדְּמָא עוֹבָדָא דִּקְטֹרֶת לִצְלוֹתָא, בְּכָל יוֹמָא וְיוֹמָא, לְאַעְבְּרָא זוּהֲמָא מֵעָלְמָא, דְּאִיהוּ תִּקּוּנָא דְּכֹלָּא, בְּכָל יוֹמָא וְיוֹמָא. כְּגַוְונָא דְּהַהוּא קָרְבָּנָא חֲבִיבָא דְּאִתְרְעֵי בֵּיהּ קוּדְשָׁא בְּרִיךְ הוּא.

478. Therefore the section of incense is recited before the prayer every day, to remove filth from the world; for it perfects everything on that day, like a desired sacrifice with which the Holy One, blessed be He, is pleased.

479. מַה כְּתִיב בְּמֹשֶׁה וַיֹּאמֶר יְיָ' אֶל מֹשֶׁה קַח לְךָ סַמִּים נָטָף וְגוֹ' אע"ג דְּאוֹקְמוּהָ, אֲבָל מַאי שְׁנָא בְּעוֹבָדָא דָּא יַתִּיר מִכָּל מַה דְּאָמַר לֵיהּ.

אֶלָּא קַח לְךָ, לַהֲנָאָתָךְ וּלְתוֹעַלְתָּךְ. בְּגִין דְּכַד אִתְּתָא אִתְדַּכְּאַת, הֲנָאוּתָא דְּבַעְלָהּ אִיהוּ. וְרָזָא דָּא קַח לְךָ סַמִּים, לְאַעְבְּרָא זוּהֲמָא, לְאִתְקַדְּשָׁא אִתְּתָא בְּבַעְלָהּ. זַכָּאָה חוּלָקֵיהּ דְּמֹשֶׁה.

479. It is written of Moses, "And Hashem said to Moses, take to you sweet spices, balm..." (Shemot 30:34). This was already explained. Nevertheless, why is it written here: "take to you" (Ibid.) that was not said elsewhere?" HE ANSWERS: "Take to you" MEANS for your pleasure and benefit. For it is as a purified wife bringing pleasure to her husband. FOR INCENSE PURIFIED THE TABERNACLE, WHICH IS MALCHUT, THE BRIDE OF MOSES, WHO WAS A CHARIOT OF ZEIR ANPIN. This is the inner meaning of "take to you sweet spices," to remove the filth, so that the wife, MALCHUT, is sanctified by her husband, ZEIR ANPIN. Blessed is the portion of Moses.

480. כְּגַוְונָא דָּא קַח לְךָ עֵגֶל בֶּן בָּקָר, דְּאִתְּמַר לְאַהֲרֹן. לְכַפְּרָא עַל חוֹבֵיהּ, עַל הַהוּא עֵגֶל דְּאִיהוּ גָּרִים לוֹן לְיִשְׂרָאֵל. וְעַ״ד כְּתִיב בְּמֹשֶׁה, קַח לְךָ, לַהֲנָאָתָךְ, וּלְתוֹעַלְתָּךְ.

480. In the same manner, it is written of Aaron, "take you a young calf" (Vayikra 9:2). THIS ALSO MEANS FOR YOUR PLEASURE AND BENEFIT, NAMELY, to atone for his sin of the golden calf that he brought upon Yisrael. Therefore it is written of Moses, "'take to you," NAMELY, for your pleasure and benefit.

481. קְטֹרֶת קָשִׁיר קְשִׁירוּ, נָהִיר נְהִירוּ וְאַעְבַּר זוּהֲמָא. וְד׳ אִתְעֲבִיד ה׳, ה׳ אִתְחַבַּר בּוֹ׳. ו׳ סָלִיק וְאִתְעַטַּר בָּהּ׳. ה׳ אִתְנְהִיר בִּי׳. וְכֹלָּא סָלִיק רְעוּתָא לְאֵין סוֹף. וַהֲוֵי כֹּלָּא קְשִׁירוּ חַד, וְאִתְעֲבִיד חַד קְשִׁירוּ, בְּרָזָא חֲדָא דְּאִיהוּ קִשְׁרָא עִלָּאָה דְּכֹלָּא.

481. The incense joins things together, TO WIT, IT UNIFIES, brings light and removes filth. The Dalet becomes Hei, FOR BEFORE UNITING WITH ZEIR ANPIN, MALCHUT IS DALET, FOR WITHOUT CHASSADIM SHE DOES NOT SHINE AND IS POOR (HEB. *DALA*). BUT WHEN ZEIR ANPIN UNITES WITH HER, CHOCHMAH IN HER IS CLOTHED BY CHASSADIM AND SHE SHINES

WITH ALL PERFECTION AND BECOMES HEI. THE INCENSE UNIFIES ZEIR
ANPIN WITH MALCHUT, CAUSING THE DALET TO BECOME HEI. BY THIS
the Hei is united with Vav, WHICH IS ZEIR ANPIN, and the Vav rises to be
adorned by THE FIRST Hei, WHICH IS BINAH, AND SO RECEIVES PLENTY
FOR MALCHUT. That Hei, BINAH, is glittering from the Yud, WHICH IS
CHOCHMAH, IN ORDER TO BESTOW ON ZEIR ANPIN. And their will rises
to the Endless Light, and all of them, NAMELY, CHOCHMAH, BINAH, ZEIR
ANPIN AND MALCHUT, THAT ARE YUD HEI VAV HEI become one, bound
together in the one high secret, which is the loftiest bond. AND ALL THIS IS
DONE BY THE INCENSE.

482. מִכָּאן וּלְהָלְאָה, כֵּיוָן דְּכֹלָּא אִתְקַשְׁרָא בְּהַאי קִשְׁרָא, אִתְעַטַּר כֹּלָּא
בְּרָזָא דְּאֵין סוֹף. וְרָזָא דִּשְׁמָא קַדִּישָׁא אִתְנְהִיר, וְאִתְעַטַּר בְּכָל סִטְרִין,
וְעָלְמִין כֻּלְּהוּ בְּחֶדְוָה. וְאִתְנְהִירוּ בּוּצִינִין וּמְזוֹנִין וּבִרְכָּאן אִשְׁתְּכָחוּ
בְּכָל עָלְמִין, וְכֹלָּא בְּרָזָא דִּקְטֹרֶת. וְאִי זוּהֲמָא לָא אִתְעַבָּר כֹּלָּא לָא לָא
אִתְעֲבֵיד. דְּכֹלָּא בְּהַאי תַּלְיָיא.

482. From now onward, since everything was thus knotted together, it is all
adorned according to the secret of the Endless Light, and the secret of the
Holy Name shines and adorns itself on all sides, all the worlds rejoice,
candles burn brightly, and there is sustenance and blessings for all the
worlds. Everything was BROUGHT by the secret of incense. For if the filth
had not been removed BY THE INCENSE, this would not have taken place,
for everything depend on it.

483. ת"ח, קְטֹרֶת אִיהוּ קַדְמָאָה תָּדִיר, קָדַם לְכֹלָּא. וּבג"כ עוֹבָדָא
דִּקְטֹרֶת אִצְטְרִיךְ לְאַקְדְּמָא לִצְלוֹתָא, לְשִׁירִין וְתוּשְׁבְּחָן. בְּגִין דְּכָל דָּא
לָא סַלְקָא, וְלָא אִתְתַּקַּן, וְלָא אִתְקַשַּׁר, עַד דְּאִתְעֲבָּר זוּהֲמָא, מַה כְּתִיב
וְכִפֶּר עַל הַקֹּדֶשׁ וְגוֹ' בְּקַדְמֵיתָא, וּלְבָתַר וּמִפִּשְׁעֵיהֶם לְכָל חַטֹּאתָם. וְעַל
דָּא בָּעֵינָן לְכַפְּרָא עַל קוּדְשָׁא, וּלְאַעְבְּרָא זוּהֲמָא, וּלְאִתְדַּכְּאָה קַדְשָׁא.
וּלְבָתַר שִׁירִין וְתוּשְׁבְּחָאן וּצְלוֹתִין, כֹּלָּא כִּדְקָאַמְרָן.

483. Come and see, the incense always comes first and precedes everything.
For this reason the section of the incense comes before prayer, hymns and

praises. For nothing rises, is perfected or connected, before filth is removed BY INCENSE. It is written: "and he shall make atonement for the holy place" first, and then "because of their transgressions in all their sins" (Vayikra 16:16). Therefore, one should atone for the holy place, and remove filth, and purify the holiness BY USE OF INCENSE, and then sing hymns and pray, as we already said.

484. זַכָּאִין אִינּוּן יִשְׂרָאֵל בְּעָלְמָא דֵּין, וּבְעָלְמָא דְּאָתֵי, דְּהָא אִינּוּן יַדְעִין לְתַקְּנָא תִּקּוּנָא דִּלְעֵילָא וְתַתָּא, כִּדְבָעֵינָן לְתַקְּנָא תִּקּוּנָא מִתַּתָּא לְעֵילָא עַד דְּאִתְקָשַׁר כֹּלָּא כַּחֲדָא, בְּקִשּׁוּרָא חַד, בְּהַהוּא קִשּׁוּרָא עִלָּאָה כַּד בָּעֵינָן לְתַקְּנָא בְּתִקּוּנָא דְּאַתְוָון רְשִׁימִין, דְּקוּדְשָׁא בְּרִיךְ הוּא אִתְקְרֵי בְּהוֹן.

484. Happy are Yisrael in this world and in the World to Come, for they know how to perfect above and below, as this perfection is ought to be done, from below upward, until everything is bound together into one supernal knot, THAT IS, THE INCENSE. It is done when improvement is necessary by perfecting the engraved letters which constitute the name of the Holy One, blessed be He, THAT IS, YUD HEI VAV HEI.

42. "in sorrow you shall bring forth children"

A Synopsis

Rabbi Elazar asks his father Rabbi Shimon how this title passage applies to the supernal woman, Malchut. Rabbi Shimon replies by referring to "as the hart pants after the water brooks," coming to the conclusion that the female (Malchut) pants after the water (the light of Chassidim), conceives from the male and is in labor because she is under judgment. He says that when she gives birth God prepares for her a big supernal serpent; it bites that place and she delivers. The meaning of, "I will greatly multiply the pain of your childbearing," is that she shudders daily and is saddened by the deeds of the world. The sorrow of the title verse is the secret of the serpent that saddens the face of the world. Rabbi Shimon says that Malchut was originally as big as Zeir Anpin but she diminished her light and rule and has no power herself but what Zeir Anpin gives her, exactly like the moon and the sun, and so he rules over her. We are told that the serpent, sorrow, is required because he opened a way through which the upper souls descend into the world, and if it weren't for that opening, no souls would dwell inside man at all. In "sin crouches at the door," the 'door' is the door of Malchut, whose purpose is to give birth; the serpent stands at the door. However, Rabbi Shimon tells us, any souls that descend into holy bodies do not have the serpent present at their entrance because their gates are not closed, as they are drawn from the Right Column. But for everyone else the serpent rules over the body and Malchut rules over the soul, both being wrapped around one another. Lastly, we hear that when the serpent delivers before his time he dies at delivery, as written in, "He will destroy death forever," and "The dead men of your people shall live, my dead body shall arise."

485. ר"ש וְר' אֶלְעָזָר בְּרֵיהּ, הֲווֹ יַתְבֵי לֵילְיָא חַד, וְלָעָאן בְּאוֹרַיְיתָא. אָ"ר אֶלְעָזָר לְר"ש אֲבוֹי. הָא כְּתִיב וְאֶל הָאִשָּׁה אָמַר הַרְבָּה אַרְבֶּה עִצְבוֹנֵךְ וְהֵרוֹנֵךְ בְּעֶצֶב תֵּלְדִי בָנִים וְאֶל אִישֵׁךְ תְּשׁוּקָתֵךְ וְגוֹ'. וְאוֹלִיפְנָא דְּדָא אִיהוּ רָזָא עִלָּאָה. תֵּינַח לְתַתָּא, אֲבָל אִיהוּ כְּגַוְונָא דִּלְעֵילָא, מַאי אִיכָּא לְמֵימַר.

485. Rabbi Shimon and his son Rabbi Elazar were sitting one night and studying the Torah. Rabbi Elazar said to Rabbi Shimon his father, it is written: "To the woman He said, I will greatly multiply the pain of your

childbearing. In sorrow you shall bring forth children; and yet your desire shall be to your husband..." (Beresheet 3:16). We learned that this high secret, TAHT IS, WHICH APPLIES ALSO TO MALCHUT ABOVE, IS true below FOR THE PHYSICAL WOMAN. But if this is the reflection of above, TO WIT, THE SUPERNAL WOMAN, MALCHUT, WAS TOLD "IN SORROW YOU SHALL BRING FORTH CHILDREN," what then is the meaning of all this?

486. פָּתַח ר״ש וְאָמַר, כְּאַיָּל תַּעֲרֹג עַל אֲפִיקֵי מָיִם וְגוֹ'. הַאי קְרָא אוּקְמוּהָ. אֲבָל חַיָּה חֲדָא אִית בְּעָלְמָא, וְאִיהִי שַׁלְטָא בְּשׁוּלְטָנָא עַל אֶלֶף מַפְתְּחָן בְּכָל יוֹמָא. וְאִיהִי נוּקְבָא וְתִיאוֹבְתָּא דִּילָה תָּדִיר עַל אֲפִיקֵי מַיִם לְמִשְׁתֵּי וּלְאִתְרַוָּאָה מִצְחוּתָא, דִּכְתִיב כְּאַיָּל תַּעֲרֹג עַל אֲפִיקֵי מָיִם.

486. Rabbi Shimon opened the discussion and said, "as the hart longs for the water brooks" (Tehilim 42:2). This verse was already explained, yet there is a living creature in the world, WHICH IS MALCHUT; it has in its charge a thousand keys every day, NAMELY, THE ILLUMINATION OF CHOCHMAH CALLED THOUSAND. This animal is female, and is always desirous of the water brooks, THAT IS, OF CHASSADIM OF ZEIR ANPIN, IN WHICH CHOCHMAH CLOTHES ITSELF, to drink and quench her thirst. FOR CHOCHMAH IN HER CANNOT ILLUMINATE WITHOUT CHASSADIM AND THEREFORE IT IS DARK AND ATHIRST FOR THE LIGHT OF CHASSADIM CALLED WATER, as is written: "as the hart longs for the water brooks."

487. הָכָא אִית לְאִסְתַּכְּלָא. בְּקַדְמֵיתָא כְּתִיב כְּאַיָּל, וְלָא כְּתִיב כְּאַיֶּלֶת, וּלְבָתַר תַּעֲרֹג, וְלָא כְּתִיב יַעֲרוֹג. אֲבָל רָזָא דָּא, דְּכַר וְנוּקְבָא תַּרְוַויְיהוּ כַּחֲדָא דְּלָא לְאַפְרְשָׁא לוֹן, וְחַד אִיהוּ, דְּלָא אִצְטְרִיךְ לְסַלְּקָא דָּא מִן דָּא, אֶלָּא תַּרְוַויְיהוּ כַּחֲדָא. וְהַאי נוּקְבָא, תַּעֲרֹג עַל אֲפִיקֵי מַיִם, וְאִיהִי מִתְעַבְּרָא מִן דְּכוּרָא, וְקָשֵׁי עָלָהּ דְּהָא עַל דִּינָא קַיְימָא.

487. Here we should look closely. In the beginning it is written 'hart', WHICH IS MASCULINE, and not THE FEMININE 'doe'. Later it is written 'longs' IN THE FEMININE FORM. The secret thereof is that male and female are together and must not be separated, nor mentioned the one without the

other, only together. The female longs for the water brooks, conceives from the male, and is in labor because he is under judgment.

488. וְכַד אוֹלִידַת קוּדְשָׁא בְּרִיךְ הוּא זַמִּין לָהּ חַד חִוְיָא עִלָּאָה רַבְרְבָא, וְאָתֵי וְנָשִׁיךְ לְגַבֵּי הַהוּא אֲתַר, וְאוֹלִידַת. וְרָזָא דָא הַרְבָּה אַרְבֶּה עִצְבוֹנֵךְ וְהֵרֹנֵךְ, בְּגִין דְּאִיהִי מִתְחַלְחֲלָא בְּכָל יוֹמָא, וּבְעַצִּיבוּ עַל עוֹבָדִין דְּעָלְמָא. בְּעֶצֶב תֵּלְדִי בָנִים. בְּעֶצֶב, דָּא רָזָא דְּחִוְיָא, דְּעָצִיב אַנְפֵּיהוֹן דְּעָלְמָא.

488. When she gives birth, the Holy One, blessed be He, prepares for her a big supernal serpent. It bites that place and she delivers. This is the meaning of "I will greatly multiply the pain of your childbearing" (Beresheet 3:16), because she shudders daily, and is saddened by the deeds of the world. "In sorrow you shall bring forth children" (Ibid.): this sorrow is the secret of the serpent which saddens the face of the people, FOR IT BROUGHT DEATH TO THEM BY THE TEMPTATION OF THE TREE OF KNOWLEDGE OF GOOD AND EVIL, AND SHE NEEDS HIM TO OPEN THE OPENING SO SHE CAN DELIVER.

489. וְאֶל אִישֵׁךְ תְּשׁוּקָתֵךְ, כד"א תַּעֲרוֹג עַל אֲפִיקֵי מַיִם. וְהוּא יִמְשָׁל בָּךְ, הָא אוֹקִימְנָא רָזָא, דְּאִיהוּ שַׁלִּיט עֲלָהּ. וְכָל דָּא לָמָּה. בְּגִין דְּאָמְרָה סִיהֲרָא, כְּמָה דִּתְנֵינָן. וּבְג"כ אַזְעִירַת נְהוֹרָאָה, וְאַזְעִירַת שׁוּלְטָנָהָא, וְלֵית לָהּ רְשׁוּ מִגַּרְמָהּ, בַּר כַּד יָהֲבִין לָהּ חֵילָא.

489. "And yet your desire shall be to your husband" (Ibid.) is connected to "longs for the water brooks" (Tehilim 42:2). SHE IS DESIROUS OF ZEIR ANPIN THAT WILL FILL HER WITH ABUNDANCE OF CHASSADIM SO SHE WILL QUENCH HER THIRST. "and he shall rule over you" (Beresheet 3:16) refers to the meaning that he, ZEIR ANPIN, rules over her, MALCHUT. And all this is BECAUSE IN THE BEGINNING SHE WAS AS BIG AS ZEIR ANPIN, AND HE DID NOT RULE OVER HER, and since the moon said, as we learned, THAT SHE IS MALCHUT, WHO SAID THAT IT IS NOT POSSIBLE FOR TWO KINGS TO RULE UNDER ONE CROWN, SHE WAS TOLD TO DIMINISH HERSELF. For that reason she diminished her light, and her rule, and has no power of her own but what power ZEIR ANPIN gives her. AND SO HE RULES OVER HER, AS IS SAID, "AND HE SHALL RULE OVER YOU."

490. בְּעֶצֶב תֵּלְדִי בָנִים, כְּמָה דְּאוֹקִימְנָא. וְאִי תֵּימָא אֲמַאי אִצְטְרִיךְ חִוְיָא לְדָא. אֶלָּא דָא פָּתַח אוֹרְחָא לְנַחְתָּא כָּל אִינּוּן נִשְׁמָתִין דְּעָלְמָא. דְּאִלְמָלֵא לָא פָּתַח אוֹרְחִין לְנַחְתָּא לְתַתָּא, לָא יִשְׁרֵי בְּגַוֵּיהּ דְּבַר נָשׁ, מַה כְּתִיב לַפֶּתַח חַטָּאת רֹבֵץ. מַאי לַפֶּתַח. לְהַהוּא פֶּתַח דְּאִתְעַתְּדָא לְאוֹלְדָא, לְאַפָּקָא נִשְׁמָתִין לְעָלְמָא, אִיהוּ קָאֵים לְגַבֵּי הַהוּא פֶּתַח.

490. "In sorrow you shall bring forth children" is explained THAT SORROW IS THE INNER MEANING OF THE SERPENT. And if you say, why do we need this serpent. HE ANSWERS: he opened a way through which the souls descend into the world, and but for that opening through which the souls can descend, no SOULS would dwell inside man. It is written: "sin crouches at the door" (Beresheet 4:7). What is this door? It is the door OF MALCHUT, which purpose is to give birth, to deliver souls into the world. He, THE SERPENT, stands at the door.

491. וְכָל אִינּוּן נִשְׁמָתִין דְּאִצְטְרִיכוּ לְנַחְתָּא בְּגוּפִין קַדִּישִׁין, לָא קָאֵים אִיהוּ לְהַהוּא פֶּתַח, וְלֵית לֵיהּ רְשׁוּ בְּהַהִיא נִשְׁמָתָא. וְאִי לָאו, הָא חִוְיָא נָשִׁיךְ, וְאִסְתָּאַב הַהוּא אֲתָר, וְלָאו אִיהִי נִשְׁמָתָא דְּאִתְדַּכְיָיא וְהָכָא אִיהוּ רָזָא עִלָּאָה, בְּעֶצֶב תֵּלְדִי בָנִים. רָזָא דָּא, דָּא נָחָשׁ, דְּהָא עִמֵּיהּ אוֹלִידַת נִשְׁמָתִין, בְּגִין דְּדָא דְּדָא אִיהוּ עַל גּוּפָא, וְדָא עַל נִשְׁמָתָא, וְתַרְוַוייְהוּ דָּא בְּדָא. דָּא נָקִיט נִשְׁמָתָא, וְדָא נָקִיט גּוּפָא.

491. But all the souls that descend into holy bodies, NAMELY, THE SOULS DRAWN FROM THE RIGHT COLUMN, THE SERPENT is not present at the entrance. FOR THEN MALCHUT IS NOT OBLIGED TO DRAW CHOCHMAH FROM THE POWER OF THE LEFT COLUMN. HER GATES ARE NOT CLOSED SO THERE IS NO NEED FOR THE SERPENT TO OPEN THEM. The serpent has no dominion over that soul. Otherwise, the serpent bites, and that place is defiled, and such soul does not remain pure. OF THESE IT IS WRITTEN: "In sorrow you shall bring forth children," and the secret thereof is the serpent, with whom she bears souls, THAT IS, HE OPENS THE DOOR, AS WAS SAID. For the one, THE SERPENT, rules over the body, THE BODY BEING BORN OF THE DEFILEMENT OF THE SERPENT, and the other, MALCHUT, rules over the soul, AS SOULS ISSUE FORM HER. Both ARE CLOTHED with each other, one attached to the soul and one to the body.

492. וּזְמִינָא דָא חִוְיָא, לְאוֹלָדָא כָּל אִינּוּן גּוּפִין, עַד לָא יֵיתֵי זִמְנָא דִּילֵיהּ, הה"ד בְּטֶרֶם תָּחִיל יָלָדָה. זִמְנָא דְּחִוְיָא לְאוֹלָדָא בְּשֶׁבַע שְׁנִין, וְהָכָא בְּשִׁית, מַה דְּלָאו אִיהוּ זִמְנֵיהּ. וּבְהַהוּא זִמְנָא דְּאוֹלִיד לוֹן, מֵהַהוּא לֵידָה יָמוּת. דִּכְתִיב בִּלַּע הַמָּוֶת לָנֶצַח. וּכְתִיב יִחְיוּ מֵתֶיךָ נְבֵלָתִי יְקוּמוּן.

492. The serpent is destined to deliver all those bodies before his time is due. This is the meaning of the verse "before she travailed, she brought forth" (Yeshayah 66:7). Because though the serpent gives birth after seven years, here he bears after six years, that is, before his time. And when he bears at that time, he dies at delivery, as is written: "He will destroy death forever" (Yeshayah 25:8), and "The dead men of your people shall live, my dead body shall arise" (Yeshayah 26:19).

43. The resurrection of the dead

A Synopsis

Rabbi Shimon says at the time of the resurrection the dead will awaken in the holy land because Joseph kept the covenant on their behalf. Here Messiah is destined to be revealed. All the troops in the land of Galilee will return to their ancestors' piece of land and everyone will recognize one another. God will give each person his embroidered garment, and all will come and praise him in Jerusalem that shall then expand on all sides. Then God will rejoice with them. It is written: "Wake up and rejoice you who dwell lowly in the dust."

493. אר״ש, בְּהַהוּא זִמְנָא דְּיִתְעָרוּן מֵתֵי עָלְמָא, וְיִתְעַתְּדוּן בְּאַרְעָא קַדִּישָׁא, יְקוּמוּן חַיָּילִין חַיָּילִין, כֻּלְהוּ עַל אַרְעָא דְּגָלִיל, בְּגִין דְּתַמָּן זַמִּין מַלְכָּא מְשִׁיחָא לְאִתְגַּלָּאָה, בְּגִין דְּאִיהוּ חוּלָקֵיה דְּיוֹסֵף, וְתַמָּן אִתְבְּרוּ בְּקַדְמֵיתָא. וּמִתַּמָּן שָׁארוּ לְאִגְלָאָה מִכָּל אַתְרַיְיהוּ, וּלְאִתְבַּדְּרָא בֵּינֵי עֲמַמַיָּא, כד״א וְלֹא נֶחְלוּ עַל שֶׁבֶר יוֹסֵף.

493. Rabbi Shimon said, at that time when the dead of the world will arise and prepare themselves to go to the Holy Land, troops upon troops shall rise upon the land of the Galilee. For there King Messiah is destined to be revealed, as this is the portion of Joseph, and the place where they were first broken and whence they were exiled from their habitations to be dispersed among the nations as said "but they are not grieved for the ruin of Joseph" (Amos 6:6).

494. וַאֲמַאי יְקוּמוּן תַּמָּן, בְּגִין דְּאִיהוּ חוּלָקֵיה דְּהַהוּא דְּאִשְׁתְּוֵי בְּאֲרוֹנָא, דִּכְתִיב וַיִּישֶׂם בָּאָרוֹן בְּמִצְרָיִם, וּלְבָתַר אִתְקְבַר בְּאַרְעָא קַדִּישָׁא, דִּכְתִיב וְאֶת עַצְמוֹת יוֹסֵף אֲשֶׁר הֶעֱלוּ בְנֵי יִשְׂרָאֵל מִמִּצְרַיִם קָבְרוּ בִשְׁכֶם. וְדָא אִיהוּ דְּקָאִים בְּקִיּוּמָא דִּבְרִית, יַתִּיר מִכֹּלָּא.

494. Why shall THOSE WHO ARE ABOUT TO RESURRECT awaken there? Because it is the heritage of him who was put in the ark, as is written: "and he was put in a coffin (also: ark) in Egypt" (Beresheet 50:26). After that he

was buried in the Holy Land, as was written: "And the bones of Joseph, which the children of Yisrael brought up out of Egypt, they buried in Shchem" (Yehoshua 24:32). And he, JOSEPH, kept the covenant more than all THE TRIBES.

495. וּבְהַהוּא זִמְנָא דְּיִתְעָרוּן כֻּלְּהוּ חַיָּילִין חַיָּילִין, כֻּלְּהוּ יְהַכוּן דָּא לְחוּלַק אֲבָהַתְהוֹן, וְדָא לְחוּלַק אֲבָהַתְהוֹן, דִּכְתִיב וְשַׁבְתֶּם אִישׁ אֶל אֲחוּזָּתוֹ. וְיִשְׁתְּמוֹדְעוּן דָּא לְדָא. וְזַמִּין קוּדְשָׁא בְּרִיךְ הוּא לְאַלְבָּשָׁא לוֹן לְכָל חַד וְחַד לְבוּשֵׁי מְרֻקְמָן, וְיֵיתוּן כֻּלְּהוּ וִישַׁבְּחוּן לְמָארֵיהוֹן בִּירוּשְׁלֵם, וְיִתְחַבְּרוּן תַּמָּן אוּכְלוֹסִין אוּכְלוֹסִין, וִירוּשְׁלֵם יִתְמְשַׁךְ לְכָל סִטְרִין, יַתִּיר מִמַּה דְּאִתְמְשַׁךְ כַּד אִתְחַבָּרוּ תַּמָּן מִגָּלוּתָא.

495. At that time, when all the troops shall rise UPON THE LAND OF THE GALILEE, they shall all return each to his ancestors' inheritance as is written: "and you shall return every man to his possession" (Vayikra 25:10), and everybody will recognize each other. The Holy One, blessed be He, will give each and every one embroidered garments. And all will come and praise their Master in Jerusalem, where multitude will assemble, and Jerusalem shall extend on all sides, more than it expanded when they assembled when returned from the exile.

496. כֵּיוָן דְּיִתְחַבְּרוּן וִישַׁבְּחוּן לְמָארֵיהוֹן, קוּדְשָׁא בְּרִיךְ הוּא יֶחֱדֵי עִמְּהוֹן, הה"ד וּבָאוּ וְרִנְּנוּ בִמְרוֹם צִיּוֹן, וּלְבָתַר וְנָהֲרוּ אֶל טוּב יְיָ' וְגוֹ', כָּל חַד וְחַד לְחוּלָקֵיה, וְחוּלַק אֲבָהָתוֹי. וְאַחֲסַנְתְּהוֹן דְּיִשְׂרָאֵל תְּהֵא, עַד רָמָתָא דְרוֹמָא, וְתַמָּן יֵלְפוּן אוֹרַיְיתָא, וְהָא אוֹקִמוּהָ, וּכְתִיב הָקִיצוּ וְרַנְּנוּ שׁוֹכְנֵי עָפָר וְגוֹ'.

496. And when they gather and praise their Master, the Holy One, blessed be He, will rejoice with them, as said, "Therefore they shall come and sing in the height of Zion," and then "shall flow to the bounty of Hashem" (Yirmeyah 31:11). Each one shall return to his property and the property of his ancestors. And the heritage of Yisrael shall reach to the heights of Rome, where Torah will be studied, as was already explained. As written: "Wake up and rejoice you who dwell lowly in the dust" (Yeshayah 26:19).

בָּרוּךְ ה׳ לְעוֹלָם אָמֵן וְאָמֵן.

Blessed is Hashem for ever. Amen and Amen.

NOTES

NOTES

NOTES

NOTES

NOTES

NOTES

NOTES

NOTES

NOTES

NOTES

NOTES

NOTES

NOTES

NOTES